Manual Of Theology: In Two Parts, Christian Doctrine And Church Order

John Leadley Dagg

MANUAL OF THEOLOGY.

IN TWO PARTS.

FIRST PART . . . . CHRISTIAN DOCTRINE.

SECOND PART . . . CHURCH ORDER.

BY

JOHN L. DAGG, D. D.

LATE PRESIDENT OF MERCER UNIVERSITY, GA.

CHARLESTON, S. C.:

SOUTHERN BAPTIST PUBLICATION SOCIETY.

RICHMOND: VA. S. S. & PUBLICATION BOARD.

MACON: GA. B. B. & COLPORTEUR SOCIETY.

SELMA: ALA. B. B. & BOOK DEPOSITORY.

NEW ORLEANS B. B. DEPOSITORY.

1859.

C.

MANUAL OF THEOLOGY.

First Part.

A TREATISE ON

CHRISTIAN DOCTRINE.

BY

J. L. DAGG.

The doctrine which is according to godliness.—1 Tim. vi. 3

CHARLESTON, S. C.:

SOUTHERN BAPTIST PUBLICATION SOCIETY.

RICHMOND: VA. S. S. & PUBLICATION BOARD.
MACON: GA. B. B. & COLPORTEUR SOCIETY.
SELMA: ALA. B. B. & BOOK DEPOSITORY.
NEW ORLEANS B. B. DEPOSITORY.

1859.

PREFACE.

This volume is designed for the use of those who have not time and opportunity to study larger works on theology. In preparing it, my aim has been to present the system of Christian doctrine with plainness and brevity; and to demonstrate, at every point, its truth, and its tendency to sanctify the heart. Men who have inclination and talent for deep research, will prefer more elaborate discussions; but if the novice in religion shall be assisted in determining what is truth, and what the proper use to be made of it, the chief end for which I have written will have been attained.

In delineating divine truth, we may exhibit it in different aspects and relations. We may view it as coming forth from God, with supreme authority; or as a system revealed by Jesus Christ, all the parts of which beautifully harmonize with each other, and cluster around the doctrine of the cross, the central point of the system; or as entering the human heart by the agency of the Holy Spirit, and transforming it into the image of God. This last view I have labored to render prominent in these pages. The moral and religious principle in man needs a suitable influence for its development and perfection; and such influence this book finds in the truths here presented. The adaptedness of a doctrine to produce this effect, it regards

(iii)

as a proof of its truth and divine origin; and it accordingly deduces the articles of faith, to a great extent, from the inward exercises of piety. But this is not the only method relied on for demonstrating their truth. Other sources of religious knowledge have been examined, and especially the Bible in which the truth of God is directly made known. To this holy book, as the highest standard, the last appeal is always made; and the harmony of its decisions, with the deductions from our inward experience, is carefully observed for the confirmation of our faith. While the system has been viewed as emanating from God, and as operating on man, attention has not been directed exclusively to its origin, or its termination. The convergence of all its lines in the glorious centre, the cross of Christ, has not been overlooked. The reader will, I hope, find proof in these pages, that the doctrine of the cross is the doctrine according to godliness.

It has been no part of my design, to lead the humble inquirer into the thorny region of polemic theology. To avoid everything that has been a subject of controversy, was impossible; for every part of divine truth has been assailed. But it has been my plan to pursue our course of investigation, affected as little as possible by the strife of religious disputants, and to know no controversy, but with the unbelief of our own hearts. The questions which are most likely to perplex sincere inquirers have been examined; and, if they have not been thoroughly elucidated, and fully answered, I hope they have been so disposed of as to leave the mind at rest, peacefully reposing on truth clearly revealed, and patiently waiting for the light of eternity to dispel all remaining darkness.

In religion, men appear naturally fond of the difficult and the obscure; perhaps, because they there find escape from the disquieting light of clearly revealed truth. Even the novice, leaving the subjects that are plain, plunges into deep investigations, and abstruse reasonings, which the skilful theologian thinks it wiser to avoid. Hence arises a necessity of frequently reminding the inquirer, that there are subjects which extend far beyond the limits of his vision; and that, in laboring to explore them further than he is guided by revelation, he is in danger of mistaking hypothesis, and the deductions of fallacious reasoning for the truth of God. Hypothesis may be lawfully admitted for the removal of objections, if it be remembered that it is only hypothesis; and abstruse reasoning must be allowed, when it becomes needful to go into its labyrinth, for the purpose of extricating those who have lost themselves therein; but, for direct proof of all the articles of faith, this book relies on express declarations of God's word, or such deductions as are adapted to plain and practical minds.

Any one who may desire to see a history of religious opinions, will not find it in this work. Religion is an affair between every man and his God; and every man should seek to know the truth for himself, whatever may be the opinions of others respecting it. It has been my aim to lead the mind of the reader directly to the sources of religious knowledge, and incite him to investigate them for himself, without respect to human authority. He may learn, from the help which I am proffering him, what my views are, but I will here give him the caution, once for all, not to adopt any opinion which I may advance, farther than it is well sustained by the word of God. Had I wished him to fix his faith on human authority, I should have adduced quotations from writers of celebrity in support of my opinions; but I have chosen not to do so. It is my desire that the reader should see, in the doctrine here presented, so far as respects human authority, nothing but the mere opinion of a fallible worm; but that so far as it is sustained by the word of God, he should receive it as the truth of God.

This volume contains nothing respecting the externals of religion. The form of godliness is important as well as its power, and the doctrine respecting it is a component part of the Christian system; but I have been unable to include it in the present work.

If this humble attempt to benefit others should be unsuccessful, it has not been useless to myself. In the near prospect of eternity, I have found it good to examine again the foundation on which my faith rests. If the perusal of these pages give as much profit and pleasure to the reader, as the preparing of them has given to the writer, we may find reason in the future world to rejoice together, that Christian friends have called for this little service to the cause of the Redeemer.

CONTENTS.

BOOK FIRST.

STUDY OF RELIGIOUS TRUTH.

CHAPTER I.

BOOK SECOND.

DOCTRINE CONCERNING GOD.

INTRODUCTION.

(vii)

BOOK THIRD.

DOCTRINE CONCERNING THE WILL AND WORKS OF GOD.

INTRODUCTION.

CHAPTER I.

CHAPTER II.

CHAPTER III.

BOOK FOURTH.

DOCTRINE CONCERNING THE FALL AND PRESENT STATE OF MAN.

INTRODUCTION.

CHAPTER I.

CHAPTER II.

CHAPTER III.

BOOK FIFTH

DOCTRINE CONCERNING JESUS CHRIST.

INTRODUCTION.

CHAPTER I.

CHAPTER II.

CHAPTER III.

BOOK SIXTH.

DOCTRINE CONCERNING THE HOLY SPIRIT.

INTRODUCTION.

CHAPTER I.

CHAPTER II.

CHAPTER III.

BOOK SEVENTH.

DOCTRINE CONCERNING DIVINE GRACE.

INTRODUCTION.

CHAPTER I.

CHAPTER II.

CHAPTER III.

CHAPTER IV.

BOOK EIGHTH.

DOCTRINE CONCERNING THE FUTURE WORLD.

INTRODUCTION.

CHAPTER I.

CHAPTER II.

CHAPTER III.

CHAPTER IV.

CHAPTER V.

MANUAL OF THEOLOGY.

BOOK FIRST.

STUDY OF RELIGIOUS TRUTH.

CHAPTER I.

THE OBLIGATION.

THE study of religious truth ought to be undertaken and prosecuted from a sense of duty, and with a view to the improvement of the heart. When learned, it ought not to be laid on the shelf, as an object of speculation; but it should be deposited deep in the heart, where its sanctifying power ought to be felt. To study theology, for the purpose of gratifying curiosity, or preparing for a profession, is an abuse and profanation of what ought to be regarded as most holy. To learn things pertaining to God, merely for the sake of amusement, or secular advantage, or to gratify the mere love of knowledge, is to treat the Most High with contempt.

Our eternal interests are involved in the subject of religion, and we should study it with a view to these interests. A farmer should study agriculture, with a view to the increase of his crop; but if, instead of this he exhausts himself in inquiring how plants propagate their like, and how the different soils were originally produced, his grounds will be overrun with briers and thorns, and his barns will be empty. Equally unprofitable will be that study of religious doctrine which is directed to the mere purpose of speculation. It is as if the food necessary for the sustenance of the body, instead of being eaten and digested, were merely set out in such order as to gratify the sight. In this case, the body would certainly perish with hunger; and, with equal certainty will the soul famish if it feed not on divine truth.

When religious doctrine is regarded merely as an object of speculation, the mind is not content with the simple truth as it is in Jesus, but wanders after unprofitable questions, and becomes entangled in difficulties, from which it is unable to extricate itself. Hence arises the skepticism of many. Truth, which would sanctify and save the soul, they wilfully reject, because it will not gratify all their curiosity, and solve all their perplexities. They act as the husbandman would, who should reject the whole science of agriculture, and refuse to cultivate his grounds, because there are many mysteries in the growth of plants, which he cannot explain.

If we set out, in our search for religious truth, from a sense of duty, and with the purpose of making the best possible use of it, we may hope for success. The Lord will bless our efforts; for he has promised, "If any man will do his will, he shall know of the doctrine."[1] As we advance, we shall find out all that is necessary for any practical purpose; and the sense of duty, under which we proceed, will not drive us beyond this point.

The sense of religious obligation which moves us to seek the knowledge of the truth, though disregarded by a large part of mankind, belongs to the constitution of human nature. Man was originally designed for religion, as certainly as the eye was formed for the purpose of vision. It will be advantageous to consider well this fact, at the outset of our inquiries. We shall then feel that we are proceeding according to the best dictates of human nature.

The various parts of the world which we inhabit, are admirably adapted to each other. Many of these adaptations present themselves to our most careless observation; and, if we search for them with diligence, they multiply to our view beyond number. The seed falls to the ground from its parent stalk, like a grain of sand; but, unlike the sand, it contains in its minute dimensions, a wonderful provision for the production of a future plant. This provision, however, would prove unavailing, if it did not find a soil adapted to give nourishment to the young germ. Moisture is also needed: and the vapor, rising from a distant sea, is wafted to the

---

[1] John vii. 17.

place by the wind, and, condensed in the atmosphere, descends in the fertilizing shower. But all these adaptations are insufficient, if warmth is not supplied; and, to complete the process, the sun, at the distance of ninety-five millions of miles, sends forth his enlivening beams. Such complications of arrangements abound in all the works of nature.

The purposes which these adaptations accomplish, are often perfectly obvious. In plants and animals, they provide for the life of the individual and the continuance of the species. Plants are adapted to become food for animals; and plants and animals render important benefit to man. But man, too, has his adaptations; and, from a consideration of these, his proper place in the great system of the universe may be inferred.

Like other animals, man is so constituted, that provision is made for the continuance of his life, and of the race. Were there no higher indications in his constitution, he might eat and drink, like other animals; and the indulgence of his natural appetites and propensities might be the highest end of his being. But, for human beings so to brutalize themselves, is a manifest degradation of their nature. They possess endowments, which, as every one feels, fit them for far nobler purposes.

The high intellectual powers of man, call for appropriate exercise. His knowledge is not confined to objects near at hand, nor to such relations and properties of things as are immediately perceived by the senses; but his reason traces remote relations, and follows the chain of cause and effect through long successions. From the present moment he looks back through past history, and connects events in their proper order of dependence. By his knowledge of the past he is able to anticipate and prepare for the future. In the causes now existing, he can discover the effects which will be developed long hereafter. Such endowments agree well with the opinion that he is an immortal being, and that the present transitory life is preparatory to another which will never end; but they, by no means, accord with the supposition, that he dies as the brute. No one imagines that the ox, or the ass, is concerned with the question whether an immortality awaits him, for which it is important that he should prepare; but the idea of a future state has had a place in the human mind in all ages, and under all forms of religion. The bee and the ant provide for the approaching winter; and the winter, for which their instincts lead them to prepare, comes upon them. If the future life, which men have so generally looked for, which their minds are so fitted to expect, and for which many have labored to prepare, with unceasing care, should never be realized, the case would violate all analogy, and be discordant with the harmony of universal nature.

The human mind is fitted for continued progress in knowledge; and, therefore, for a state of immortality. This adaptation includes an insatiable desire of knowledge, and an ability to acquire it. The little chicken, not many hours after it has left the shell in which its feeble existence commenced, is able to select its food, to roam abroad in search of it, and to return to its mother's wing for protection. Man is born into the world, the most helpless of animals. Tedious weeks pass away before the development of his intellectual powers begins to appear. The progress is slow, and many months of gradual improvement pass, before he becomes equal in ability for self-preservation, to many other creatures that have lived a few hours. These animals, however, stop at a point beyond which, it may be said, they never go. The birds of the present age build their nests just as they were built five thousand years ago; and the admirable social arrangements found among bees and ants have undergone no improvement. But no point, no line, bounds the progress of the human mind. Though we are now familiar with the great improvements which have been made in arts and sciences, we contemplate them with admiration and astonishment; and we feel that a boundless career is open before the intellect of man, inviting the efforts which he finds himself internally prompted to make. But, as far as each individual of the race is concerned, the vast fields of knowledge open before him in vain, his power to explore them exists in vain, and the desire to explore burns in vain in his breast, if the present life, which flies as the weaver's shuttle, is the only opportunity granted, and if all his hopes and aspirations are to be forever buried in the grave.

The moral faculties with which man is endowed, adapt him to a state of subjection to moral government. Our minds are so constituted, that we are capable of perceiving a moral quality in actions, and of approving or disapproving them. A consciousness of having done what is right, affords us one of our highest pleasures; and the anguish of remorse for evil deeds, is as intolerable as any suffering of which the human heart is susceptible. Our conscience exercises a moral government within us, and rewards or punishes us for actions according to their moral character. Much of our happiness depends on the approbation of those with whom we associate. Hence, we find moral government without, as well as within; and at every point, in our relations to intelligent beings, we feel its restraints. Where are the bounds of this moral government? It must be as extensive as our relations to moral beings, and as lasting as our existence.

That men are immortal and under a moral government, by which their future state will be made happy or miserable, according to their conduct in the present life, are fundamental truths of religion. Man is a religious animal; because a persuasion of his immortality and an expectation of future retribution so readily find a place in his mind. No one imagines that such thoughts were ever entertained for a moment, by any one of the innumerable brute animals that have trodden the earth. But in the human race, such thoughts have been prevalent in all nations and ages; have mingled with the cogitations of the learned and the unlearned, the wise and the unwise; and have blended religion thoroughly with the history of mankind.

The considerations which have been presented, establish the claim of religious truth to our highest respect and most diligent investigation. He who disregards its claim acts contrary to his own nature, and degrades himself to the level of the beast that perishes. That men do so degrade themselves, is a fact which correct views of religious truth cannot overlook: "The ox knoweth his owner, and the ass his master's crib; but Israel doth not know, my people doth not consider."[1] It is a peculiar glory and excellence of the Christian revelation, that it is adapted to this fallen condition of mankind; and that it has power to effect a restoration. It is medicine for the sick, as well as food for the healthy. A healthy appetite calls for food; and the food, when received, administers needed nourishment; so that between the healthy stomach and the nutritious food, the adaptation is reciprocal. But in sickness the stomach loathes food, and rejects the medicine which is needed to effect a cure: yet the adaptation of the medicine to the

---

[1] Is. i. 3.

2

condition of the sick man still remains. Just so it is with respect to the gospel of Christ. Though rejected by men, it is "worthy of all acceptation," because it is a remedy, precisely adapted to our depraved state. Thousands of thousands have experienced its restoring power, and unite in recommending its efficacy to the multitudes who are unwilling to make trial of it.

In contemplating the truths of religion, we may view them in various aspects. We may consider them as proceeding from God; as demonstrated by abundant proof; as harmonizing with one another; and as tending to the glory of God. It is interesting and instructive to view them in immediate contact with the human heart, and, like the Spirit of God, brooding over the original chaos, bringing order out of confusion, and infusing light and life where darkness and death had previously reigned. In exerting this new-creating power, the divinity of Christian truth appears; and the demonstration of it is the more satisfactory, because practical, and leveled to the capacity of all.

As religious beings, let us seek to understand the truths of religion. As immortal beings, let us strive to make ourselves acquainted with the doctrine on which our everlasting happiness depends. And let us be careful that we do not merely receive it coldly into our understandings, but that its renewing power is ever operative in our hearts.

CHAPTER II.

SOURCES OF KNOWLEDGE.

WE find ourselves in a world where we have no continuing abode. Within us, and without us, we have proofs and admonitions that our chief interests lie in another world, and that our chief business in this is to prepare for the future state, into which we shall very soon enter. We need information respecting that unseen world and the right method of preparing for it, and no other knowledge can be so important to us as this. Can it be that we have no means of acquiring it? For our guidance in the things of this world, every necessary provision has been made. We possess eyes; and the world in which we are placed affords the light that is needed to render them useful in directing our steps. We possess understanding; and means of knowledge from without are presented, by which we may select the objects of our pursuit, and the best methods of gaining them. We may hence infer that some means of knowledge respecting our highest interests must exist. The sources from which this knowledge may be obtained, are the following:

1. *Our moral and religious feelings.*—Brute animals have instincts by which they are guided; and in man, also, instinctive propensities exist, adapted to his nature and the condition and circumstances of his being. Maternal affection is not confined to brutes as an instinct peculiar to them, but it is found in the highest degree in the human mother; and in her breast, mingles with moral and religious feelings peculiar to human nature and inseparable from it. The human mother feels the moral obligation to take care of her child, antecedent to all reasoning on the subject. When we determine what is right or wrong by a process of reasoning, we judge according to some law, or rule of right; but, in this case, the mother is a law to herself. She needs no teaching from without, to inform her that it is her duty to take care of her offspring. Sin may so debase human nature, that mothers may be without natural affection—and such mothers may evince no moral feeling; but, however it may be buried under our corruptions, the moral principle is an element of our nature. Because of it, even the heathen are a law unto themselves, and show the work of the law written in their hearts. The moral feeling which at first co-operates with the mother's instinctive affection to induce her to take care of her child, co-operates afterwards with her reason in devising the best method of promoting its good.

When it was to be determined which of two women was the mother of a living child claimed by both, the wisdom of Solomon decided, that the maternal relation existed where maternal affection existed. On the same principle we may, from our moral and religious feelings, infer our relation to moral government and to the Supreme Ruler. From this law, written in the heart, we might obtain much religious knowledge, if the fall of man had not obscured the writing.

2. *The moral and religious feelings of our fellow-men.*—We are formed for society, and are capable of benefiting each other in the things of this life, and of that which is to come. The judgments of others assist our judgments; and their moral and religious feelings may, in like manner, assist ours. In the approbation or disapprobation of mankind, we may find an important means of knowing what is right or wrong. Hence, it is a rule of duty to do those things which are "of good report."

If an ancient writing is transmitted to us in numerous copies, all of which are mutilated and greatly effaced, the probability of ascertaining what the original was is far greater, when we compare many copies with each other, than it would be, if we possessed one copy only. For the same reason, the moral and religious feeling of mankind generally, is a source of knowledge more to be relied on, than that which is opened for our examination in the moral nature of a single individual. A hardened transgressor's own conscience may fail to reprove him, when his crimes shock the moral sense of the whole community; and, from their disapprobation, he might learn the iniquity of his conduct, though all moral feeling were extinguished in his own breast.

In examining this second source of knowledge, we observe the common consent of mankind, that there is a God; that he ought to be worshipped; that there is a difference between virtue and vice; that a moral government exists, which is partly administered in this life by Divine Providence; that the soul of man is immortal; and that a future retribution awaits all men after death. These truths of religion appear in the history of mankind, through all the corruptions which have covered and obscured them.

3. *The course of Nature.* — Things are so arranged by the Creator and Ruler of the world, that some actions tend to promote, and others to destroy, the happiness of the individual and of society. By observing the tendency of actions, we may learn what to do and what to avoid. God has established the nature of things, and the voice of Nature is the voice of God. Conscience is God speaking within us, but, because of man's apostasy from God, it often delivers false oracles. Hence, we do well to turn our ear to the voice of God, speaking in universal Nature.

The tendency of vice to produce misery, is obvious to every one who observes the course of things around him. Drunkards and gamblers impoverish themselves, ruin their families, waste their health, and bring themselves to an untimely grave, not unfrequently by violent, and sometimes by suicidal hands. In ten thousand ways, crime of every species exhibits its pernicious tendency, and, in this arrangement of things, the moral government of God is clearly seen, and the conduct which he approves, is pointed out by the finger of his Providence. Enough of God's moral government appears in the present life, to demonstrate its existence; and the imperfection which is manifest in its present administration, furnishes satisfactory proof that it extends beyond the present life, and is perfected in the world to come.

The religious knowledge which may be obtained from the three sources which have been enumerated, constitutes what is called Natural Religion. Though insufficient to meet the wants of man in his fallen condition, it teaches the fundamental truths on which all religion is based, and leads to the higher source of knowledge by which we may become wise to salvation. This is

4. *Divine Revelation.*—Because all other means of knowledge are insufficient to bring men to holiness and happiness, God has been pleased, in pity to our race, to make known his will by special revelation. Besides his voice in conscience and in Nature, he utters his voice from heaven. This revelation was anciently made by prophets, who were commissioned to speak to men in his name, and afterwards by his Son from heaven. To us, in these latter days, he speaks in his written word, the Bible, which is the perfect source of religious knowledge, and the infallible standard of religious truth.

The Bible consists of two parts:—1. The Old Testament, or Hebrew Scriptures. This is the book very carefully preserved by the Jews throughout the world, and held sacred by them as a revelation from God. 2. The New Testament. This consists of various writings, which have been carefully preserved by the Christians of past ages, and are now regarded by them as a revelation from God, made through the immediate followers of Jesus Christ.

We shall here assume that the Bible is a revelation from God. If the reader has any doubt on this point, he may study, to advantage, any of the numerous works extant on the Evidences of Christianity; or, in the absence of more elaborate productions, he may read a small tract by the Author, entitled, The Origin and

Authority of the Bible. [This Tract has been introduced into the present work as an Appendix, pp. 26–42.]

Inspiration and transmission of the Scriptures.—The Bible, though a revelation from God, does not come immediately from him to us who read it, but is received through the medium of human agency. It is an important question, whether its truth and authority are impaired by passing through this medium. Human agency was employed in the first writing of the Scriptures, and afterwards in transmitting them, by means of copies and translations, to distant places, and succeeding generations.

The men who originally wrote the Holy Scriptures, performed the work under the influence of the Holy Spirit. Such was the extent of this influence, that the writing, when it came forth from their hands, was said to be given by inspiration of God. So Paul said, with special reference to the Old Testament: "All Scripture is given by inspiration of God, and is profitable . . . that the man of God may be perfect, thoroughly furnished unto all good works."[1] Though Moses and the prophets executed the writing, it is said to have been given by God, and the perfection attributed to it demonstrates that it had not suffered by the instrumentality which he had chosen to employ. Christ referred to the Hebrew Scriptures, as the word of God.[2] Paul represents what was spoken by the prophets, as spoken by God.[3] Peter attributes to the writings of Paul equal authority with that of the Old Testament Scriptures.[4] Paul also claims equal authority for what he spoke and wrote.[5] Christ promised to his apostles, after his departure, the gift of the Holy Spirit, and described the effect of his influence on them in these words: "It is not ye that speak, but the Spirit of your father which speaketh in you."[6] This gift of the Holy Spirit was poured out upon them on the day of Pentecost; and their possession of it was proved by their power to speak with tongues, and work miracles. From all this, we learn that what was spoken and written by inspiration, came with as high authority as if it had proceeded from God without the use of human instrumentality. When Peter said to the lame man, "In the name of Jesus Christ of Nazareth, rise up, and walk,"[7] the voice which spoke was Peter's, but the

---

[1] 2 Tim. iii. 16, 17. [2] Mark vii. 13.   [3] Heb. i. 1.   [4] 2 Peter iii. 16.
[5] 1 Cor. xiv. 37; 1 Thess. iii. 10.   [6] Matt. x. 20.   [7] Acts iii. 6.

power which restored the ankle bones, was God's. The words, though Peter's, were spoken under divine influence, or the divine power would not have accompanied them. So the gospel, received from the lips of the apostles, was received, "not as the word of men, but as it is in truth the word of God."[1] The men who spoke and wrote as they were moved by the Holy Ghost, were the instruments that God used to speak and write his word. Their peculiarities of thought, feeling, and style, had no more effect to prevent what they spoke and wrote from being the word of God, than their peculiarities of voice or of chirography.

The question, whether inspiration extended to the very words of revelation, as well as to the thoughts and reasonings, is answered by Paul: "We preach, not in the *words* which man's wisdom teacheth, but which the Holy Ghost teacheth."[2] The thoughts and reasonings in the minds of the inspired writers, were not a revelation to others until they were expressed in words; and if the Holy Spirit's influence ceased before expression was given to these thoughts and reasonings, he has not made a revelation to mankind. On this supposition, we cannot read the Bible as the word of God, but as the word of men; of good and honest men, it is true, but nevertheless of fallible men. The opinion that the expression is merely human, undermines the confidence with which the word of God deserves to be regarded; because we know not when, or how far, that expression may fail to convey the meaning of the Holy Spirit. It can no longer be said, that the Scriptures are "a more sure word of prophecy,"[3] that "they cannot be broken,"[4] and that the things *written* "are the commandments of the Lord."[5]

The doctrine of plenary inspiration, if properly understood, does not imply that the Holy Spirit employed the writer as an unconscious instrument. It maintains that his memory, and other mental powers, were employed in the execution of the work, as truly as his hand; but it insists that the latter was as certainly controlled by the unerring guide as the former. Nor does the doctrine imply, that the Holy Spirit is the original author of every word contained in the sacred volume. It records the speeches of Satan, and of the Orator Tertullus, and records them faithfully; but the Holy Spirit was not the author of these speeches.

---

[1] 1 Thess. ii. 13.   [2] 1 Cor. ii. 13.   [3] 2 Peter i. 19.
[4] John x. 35.   [5] 1 Cor. xiv. 37.

In 1 Cor. ch. 7, Paul distinguishes between what he delivered, as a commandment of the Lord, and what he spoke without such commandment. It may appear, at first view, that he disclaims inspiration with regard to the things of the last kind. But if it be admitted, that these things were matters of human advice without divine authority, it does not follow, that the writing which contains his advice, is uninspired. The inspired word which records the speeches of Satan and Tertullus, may record the prudent counsel of a wise apostle, even when that counsel does not come with the full sanction of divine authority. But, in giving this counsel, Paul says, " I think that I have the Spirit, of God," v. 40; and, if he thought that he gave it by the Spirit, it would be rash in us to think otherwise. We are not to understand the word " think," as implying doubt in Paul's mind, and we need have no doubt that the counsel which he gave, was by the wisdom from above.

Although the Scriptures were originally penned under the unerring guidance of the Holy Spirit, it does not follow, that a continued miracle has been wrought to preserve them from all error in transcribing. On the contrary, we know that manuscripts differ from each other; and where readings are various, but one of them can be correct. A miracle was needed in the original production of the Scriptures; and, accordingly, a miracle was wrought; but the preservation of the inspired word, in as much perfection as was necessary to answer the purpose for which it was given, did not require a miracle, and accordingly it was committed to the providence of God. Yet the providence which has preserved the divine oracles, has been special and remarkable. They were at first committed to the Jews, who exercised the utmost care in their preservation and correct transmission. After the Christian Scriptures were added, manuscript copies were greatly multiplied; many versions were prepared in other languages; innumerable quotations were made by the early fathers; and sects arose which, in their controversies with each other, appealed to the sacred writings, and guarded their purity with incessant vigilance. The consequence is, that, although the various readings found in the existing manuscripts, are numerous, we are able, in every case, to determine the correct reading, so far as is necessary for the establishment of our faith, or the direction of our practice in every important particular. So little, after all, do the copies differ from each other, that these minute differences, when viewed in contrast with their general agreement, render the fact of that agreement the more impressive, and may be said to serve practically, rather to increase, than impair our confidence in their general correctness. Their utmost deviations do not change the direction of the line of truth; and if they seem in some points to widen that line a very little, the path that lies between their widest boundaries, is too narrow to permit us to stray. As copies of the Holy Scriptures, though made by fallible hands, are sufficient for our guidance in the study of divine truth; so translations, though made with uninspired human skill, are sufficient for those who have not access to the inspired original. Unlearned men will not be held accountable for a degree of light beyond what is granted to them; and the benevolence of God in making revelation, has not endowed all with the gift of interpreting tongues. When this gift was miraculously bestowed in ancient times, it was for the edification of all: and now, when conferred in the ordinary course of providence, the purpose of conferring it is the same. God has seen it wiser and better to leave the members of Christ to feel the necessity of mutual sympathy and dependence, than to bestow every gift on every individual. He has bestowed the knowledge necessary for the translation of his word on a sufficient number of faithful men, to answer the purpose of his benevolence; and the least accurate of the translations with which the common people are favored, is full of divine truth, and able to make wise to salvation.

A full conviction that the Bible is the word of God, is necessary to give us confidence in its teachings, and respect for its decisions. With this conviction pervading the mind when we read the sacred pages, we realize that God is speaking to us, and when we feel the truth take hold of our hearts, we know that it is God with whom we have to do. When we study its precepts, all our powers bow to them, as the undoubted will of our sovereign Lord; and when we are cheered and sustained by its consolations, we receive them as blessings poured down from the eternal throne. Nature and science offer no light that can guide us in our search for immortal bliss; but God has given us the Bible, as a lamp to our feet, and a light to our path. Let us receive the gift with gratitude and commit ourselves to its guidance.

APPENDIX.

Origin and Authority of the Bible.

I. ORIGIN.

WE are rational beings; and, as such, the desire of knowledge is natural to us. In early childhood, as each new object of interest comes under our notice, we ask, who made it; and as we advance in years, the same inquisitiveness attends us, and prompts us to investigate the sources of knowledge which are ever opening before us. Brutes may look with indifference on the works of God, and tread under foot the productions of human ingenuity, without inquiry into their origin; but rational men cannot act thus without violence to the first principles of their nature. Among the objects which have occupied a large space in human thought, and which claim our consideration, the BIBLE stands conspicuous. Its antiquity; the veneration in which it has been held, and continues to be held, by a large part of mankind; and the influence which it has manifestly exerted on their conduct and happiness, are sufficient, if not to awaken higher emotions, at least to attract our curiosity, and excite a desire to know its origin and true character.

We are moral beings. The Bible comes to us as a rule of conduct. The claim which is set up for it is, that it is the highest standard of morals, admitting no appeal from its decisions. We are, therefore, under the strongest obligations to examine the foundation of this claim.

We are, if the Bible is true, immortal beings. Heathen philosophers have conjectured that man may be immortal; and infidels have professed to believe it; but, if we exclude the Bible, we have no means of certain knowledge on this point. Yet it is a matter of the utmost importance. If we are immortal, we have interests beyond the grave which infinitely transcend all our interests in the present life. What folly, then, it is, to reject the only source of information on this momentous subject! Besides, if we have such interests in a future world, we have no means of knowing how to secure them, except from the Bible. Shall we throw this book from us, and trust to vain conjecture, on questions in which our all is involved? it would be folly and madness.

Let us then inquire, whence came the Bible? Is it from heaven, or from men? If it is from men, is it the work of good men, or of bad men?

If bad men had been the authors of the Bible, they would have made it to their liking. If made to please them, it would please other men of like character. But it is not a book in which bad men delight. They hate it. Its precepts are too holy; its doctrines too pure; its denunciations against all manner of iniquity too terrible. It is not at all written according to the taste of such men. There are men who prize the Bible; who pore over its pages with delight; who have recourse to it in all their perplexities and sorrows; who seek its counsels to guide them, and its instructions to make them wise; who esteem its words more than gold, and feast on them as their sweetest food. But who are these men? They are those who detest all deceit and falsehood, and whom this very book has transformed, from men of iniquity and vice, to men of purity and holiness. It is impossible, therefore, that the Bible should be the work of bad men.

It remains that the Bible must be either from heaven or from good men. So pure a stream cannot proceed from a corrupt fountain. If it be from good men, they will not wilfully deceive us. Let us, then, look to the account which they have given of its origin: "All Scripture is given by inspiration of God."[1] "The things that I write unto you are the commandments of the Lord."[2] "And so we have the prophetic word more firm, to which ye do well to take heed, as to a lamp shining in a dark place, until the day dawn, and the morning star arise in your hearts; knowing this first, that no prophecy of Scripture is of private invention. For never, at any time, was prophecy brought by the will of man, but the holy men of God spake, being moved by the Holy Ghost."[3]

It may, perhaps, be objected to the use of these quotations, that we permit the Bible to speak for itself; but this is no unprecedented procedure. If a stranger were passing through our neighborhood, and we were desirous to know whence he came, it would not be unnatural to propose the inquiry to the man himself. If there were about him marks of honesty and simplicity of character, and if, after our most careful investigations, it should appear that

---

[1] 2 Tim. iii. 16. [2] 1 Cor. xiv. 37.
[3] 2 Peter i. 19, 20, 21; *Macknight's Translation.*

he has no evil design to accomplish, and no interest to promote by deceiving us, we should rely on the information we derive from him. Such a stranger is the Bible; and why may we not rely on its testimony concerning itself? Nay, it is not a stranger. Though claiming a heavenly origin, it has long dwelt on earth, and gone in and out among us, a familiar companion. We have been accustomed to hear its words; and have known them to be tried with every suspicion, and every scrutiny, and no falsehood has been detected. More, it has been among us as a teacher of truth and sincerity; and truth and sincerity have abounded just in proportion as its teachings have been heeded. Old men of deceit have shrunk from its probings, and trembled at its threatenings; and young men have been taught by it to put away all lying and hypocrisy. Can it be that the Bible itself is a deceiver and impostor? Impossible! It must be, what it claims to be, a book from heaven — the Book of God.

The truth that the Bible is from God, is not only testified by the inspired men who wrote it, but it is established by many other decisive proofs, some of which we shall proceed to consider.

The Divine origin of the Bible is proved by the CHARACTER OF THE REVELATION which it contains.

The *character of God*, as exhibited in the Bible, cannot be of human origin. We know what sort of gods men make; for they have multiplied them without number. They carve deities from blocks of wood and stone, and worship them with stupid adoration; but this is not the most debasing and abominable idolatry of which they are guilty. Their vain imaginations fashion gods more vile than these. The blocks of wood or stone may take the form of birds, four-footed beasts, and creeping things; but the deities which derive their origin from the imaginations of men have passions and propensities that are beastly, and even worse than beastly. Such are the objects which they worship with laborious and costly devotion. Let any man visit the temples of the heathen, observe their horrid ceremonies, and study the character of their gods; and then let him say whether these gods, and the God of the Bible, are from one common origin.

Some objectors may allege that the deities to which we have referred are those of uncivilized tribes. What then? Were the gods of the most civilized nations better than these? What were the divinities which were worshipped by the ancient Greeks and Romans, even by their sages and philosophers, whose talents and genius have been admired in every age? Jupiter, their Optimus Maximus, best and greatest, was a monster of crime; and Venus, Bacchus, Mercury, Mars, and the rest of their deities, were his fit companions. They were patrons and examples of vice. The infidel Rousseau has drawn their character correctly. "Cast your eyes over all the nations of the world, and all the histories of nations. Amid so many inhuman and absurd superstitions, amid that prodigious diversity of manners and characters, you will find every where the same principles and distinctions of moral good and evil. The paganism of the ancient world produced, indeed, abominable gods, who on earth would have been shunned or punished as monsters, and who offered as a picture of supreme happiness only crimes to commit and passions to satiate. But vice, armed with this sacred authority, descended in vain from the eternal abode; she found, in the heart of man, a moral instinct to repel her. The continence of Xenocrates was admired by those who celebrated the debaucheries of Jupiter — the chaste Lucretia adored the unchaste Venus—the most intrepid Roman sacrificed to Fear. He invoked the god who dethroned his father, and he died without a murmur by the hand of his own. The most contemptible divinities were served by the greatest men. The holy voice of Nature, stronger than that of the gods, made itself heard, and respected, and obeyed on earth, and seemed to banish as it were to the confinement of heaven, guilt, and the guilty."[1]

Go now to the Pantheon, and study the character and works of Rome's innumerable deities. After infidelity has acknowledged that they are monsters, more vicious than men, and sending forth a corrupting influence into human society, invite her to study the character of Jehovah, the God of the Bible, a Spirit, whose form cannot be represented; a Being whose eyes cannot behold iniquity, who is glorious in holiness, fearful in praises, and doing wonders; and who requires to be worshipped in the beauty of holiness. Let her stand with Moses in the cleft of the rock, and hear the Lord proclaim his name: "The LORD, the LORD God, merciful and gracious, long-suffering and abundant in goodness and truth, keeping

---

[1] Brown's Philosophy of the Human Mind, vol. iii. p. 138.

mercy for thousands, forgiving iniquity, and transgression, and
sin, and that will by no means clear the guilty."[1] Surely she
will bow her head with reverence, and confess, *this is the voice of
God.*

The account of the *life and character of Christ* given in the
gospels, is not a fiction of human invention. The introduction of
Christianity, its existence in the world, the persecutions which it
has encountered, its spread in spite of opposition, and the influence
which it has exerted on nations and governments, are all so inter-
woven with the history of the last eighteen hundred years, that all
history must be doubted, if these are fables. The evidence that
there were such men as Alexander and Julius Cæsar, is not so
abundant and indisputable as that Jesus Christ appeared at the
time and place stated in the gospels. The accounts of his life,
sufferings, and death, given by Matthew, Mark, Luke, and John,
come down to us with all the marks of authentic history. No
signs of fraud can be detected in the narratives. The admirable
simplicity of the writers, their ingenuousness in relating the faults
and weaknesses of their own characters, their artlessness in de-
picting the sublime virtues of their Master, and recording his
stupendous works, and the unimpassioned manner in which they
described the cruel treatment he received from his persecutors and
murderers; all these considerations place the truth of their narratives beyond question. Add to all this, that they had sufficient
means of knowing the truth of the facts which they have recorded;
that they attested the sincerity of their faith in them by enduring
tortures and death; and that those who received their testimony,
and transmitted it to us, testified their faith in it by like endurance.
No other facts in the history of the world have evidence so strong.
But if this evidence can be rejected, an insuperable difficulty still
remains. It is impossible to account for the existence of the gospels on any other supposition, than that they are what they profess to be, true delineations of a real character. The authors were
incapable of conceiving such a fiction. Even such men as Virgil
and Homer were incapable of such an effort. They could conceive
and describe such characters as Æneas and Ulysses, but not such
a character as Jesus Christ. Besides, the learning of the world

---

[1] Ex. xxxiv. 6, 7.

was arrayed against Christianity; and to the unlearned and humble fishermen of Galilee the task was assigned of recording the life and works of Jesus of Nazareth. That such men should have transmitted to succeeding ages a fiction such as this, is incredible —impossible. Another quotation from Rousseau will show the overpowering influence of these considerations on the mind of an infidel: "I will confess to you further, that the majesty of the Scripture strikes me with admiration, as the purity of the gospel hath its influence on my heart. Peruse the works of our philosophers, with all their pomp of diction—how mean—how contemptible — are they, compared with the Scripture! Is it possible, that a book at once so simple and sublime should be merely the work of man? Is it possible that the sacred personage whose history it contains should be himself a mere man? Do we find that he assumed the air of an enthusiast or ambitious sectary? What sweetness, what purity in his manner! What an affecting gracefulness in his delivery! What sublimity in his maxims! What profound wisdom in his discourses! What presence of mind! What subtilty. What truth in his replies! How great the command over his passions! Where is the man, where the philosopher, who could so live and die, without weakness and without ostentation? Shall we suppose the Evangelic History a mere fiction? Indeed, my friend, it bears not the marks of fiction. On the contrary, the history of Socrates, which nobody presumes to doubt, is not so well attested as that of Jesus Christ. The Jewish authors were incapable of the diction, and strangers to the morality contained in the gospels; the marks of whose truth are so striking and invincible, that the inventor would be a more astonishing character than the hero."[1]

If the gospels give a true account of Jesus Christ, he was a teacher from heaven; and both the doctrine which he taught, and the Scriptures, to which he often appealed as of divine authority, are from God.

The *method of salvation* revealed in the Bible is not a human device. The preaching of Christ crucified was to the Jews a stumbling-block, and to the Greeks foolishness, yet salvation by the Cross is the grand peculiarity of the gospel. Were Christianity

---

[1] Fuller's Works, vol. ii. p. 69.

a cunningly-devised fable, a doctrine so offensive to mankind would not have been made prominent in the scheme. To this day, men of proud intellect and corrupt heart reject the doctrine of salvation by the obedience and sufferings of another. To the humble and contrite, oppressed with a sense of sin, and seeking, from the borders of despair, some divine method of escape from the wrath to come, this doctrine is thrice welcome; but the humble and contrite are not the men to cheat the world with a forged system of religion.

The BLESSINGS which the Bible confers on mankind have their origin in infinite Benevolence.

Compare the condition of those nations where Paganism reigns, with that of the nations where the most corrupt forms of Christianity exist, and you will find the latter preferable. Institute another comparison between these, and the lands where a purer Christianity prevails, and where the Bible, instead of being withheld from the common people, is open to the reading of all, and you will perceive a far better state of human society, where the Sacred Volume is best known. Compare, again, in these most favored lands, the families where the Bible is least regarded, with those in which its doctrines are revered and its precepts obeyed, and you will be sensible that a heavenly influence pervades the latter. But even in such families as these, the individual members often differ widely from each other. Though they may all worship at the same altar, and read the same Bible, some have the word of truth on their lips only, while others treasure it up deep in their hearts, and find it sweeter to their taste than honey and the honeycomb. What elevation of character, what pure and unsullied bliss do the latter enjoy! Take, lastly, an individual of the last most favored class, and compare the different moments of his life—those in which the Bible is least regarded, with those in which he feasts on its truths and promises, and experiences joy unspeakable and full of glory, while he receives the divine word into his heart; and you will have a full view of the blessed influence which the Bible can impart. We know that the sun is a source of light and heat, because all is dark and cold when his beams are absent; and light and heat are found to increase in proportion as we draw nearer to him. Precisely so it is with the Bible. From Paganism, cold and dark, where the Bible is unknown, to the saint in his most rapturous devotions, when he has the sweetest foretaste of heaven which mortals on earth can enjoy; the light of truth which fills the understanding, and the warmth of love which glows in the heart, bear an exact proportion to the proximity of the Bible. If the sun, which enlightens the material world, is the work of a benevolent Creator, much more may we ascribe to the same benevolence the authorship of the Bible, the source of spiritual illumination.

Having compared the Bible to the sun, it may be a fit occasion to remark that both these lights have their darknesses — the Bible its obscurities, and the sun its spots. The Deist may cavil at the one, and the Atheist at the other; but the cavils of both are alike absurd and unavailing. Because there are spots in the sun, shall we conclude that God did not make it, or that it is not a blessing to mankind? Yet this conclusion would not be more irrational than to deny that God is the author of the Bible, or that the Bible is a blessing to the world, because there are obscurities found in its pages. Suppose it be admitted that the spots in the sun, and the obscurities in the Bible are imperfections, is God the author of nothing in which imperfections exist? If everything material, and everything human, be marked with imperfection, may not God nevertheless glorify himself by things material and human? The new Jerusalem has no need of a material sun to enlighten it, because the glory of God and the Lamb is the light thereof; but God has fixed the sun in the firmament to enlighten this world of matter; and the sun in the firmament, notwithstanding its spots, declares its Maker's glory. So God may make revelation of Himself to the pure intelligences of heaven in language free from human imperfection; but when He speaks to mortals on earth, He uses the language of mortals; and whatever may be the imperfection of the medium, this revelation of God displays his glory in the brightest light in which human eyes can behold it.

But are the spots in the sun and the obscurities in the Bible to be accounted imperfections? The light of the sun is pure and abundant; and, if it were deficient, the deficiency might be supplied, as well by enlarging the sun, as by removing its spots. It would, therefore, be as rational to complain that the sun is not larger, as to complain that there are spots in its disc. In like manner, the light of God's Word is pure, and sufficient to make men wise to salvation; and we might as well complain that the Bible is not larger, as that it contains obscurities. Besides, the

3

obscurities of the Bible may have a beneficial use. If, as some astronomers suppose, the solar spots are the body of the sun, seen through the partings of its luminous atmosphere, they can scarcely be deemed imperfections; much less can they be so regarded, if they are streams of gas rising in the sun's atmosphere, and diffusing itself to become fuel for the lamp of day. According to the latter hypothesis, the spots are as far from being imperfections, as are the clouds that sometimes darken our sky, but which are the rich sources of the earth's fertility, and the granaries of our bread. So, some of the obscurities of the Bible are the deep things of God, seen through the light of revelation — the inscrutable mystery of the divine nature appearing through the light with which He has clothed Himself. Other mysteries are, in process of time, dissipated; and, like clouds which burst, pour out a blessing. It was a mystery "that the Gentiles should be fellow-heirs and partakers of the promise of Christ by the gospel;" but in due time this mystery was explained, and the bursting cloud poured the richest blessing on all the Gentile world. The Old Testament dispensation was dark, abounding with shadows of good things to come; but since the Sun of Righteousness has arisen, the dark places have been illuminated, and are full of instruction. Prophecies have been delivered in obscure language; but their fulfilment has interpreted them. Some obscurities have given occasion to the infidel to charge the Bible with contradictions; but a careful examination of the inspired word has not only served to repel the charge by reconciling the apparent discrepancies, but it has added new proof that the Scriptures were written by undesigning and honest men, without any collusion; and that there is perfect harmony in their statements, even when apparently most discordant. Men of superior intellect may find a pleasant and profitable exercise of their powers in investigating those parts of the Bible which are less clear; while its plainest truths are adapted to men of least capacity, and are sufficient for their necessities. Here are waters in which "a lamb may wade," and in which "an elephant may swim." There is yet another use of Bible obscurities. When God gave a law to mankind, he did not give one which it was impossible to violate, but one which men, as free agents, might violate, and by violating bring ruin on their souls. So, when he gave a revelation to mankind, he did not give one which could not be caviled at, but one at which men might cavil, and, by caviling, bring wrath upon themselves. The obscurities of the Bible serve for this use; for the Bible itself declares, that it contains "some things hard to be understood, which they that are unlearned and unstable wrest unto their own destruction." Let those who choose rather to cavil at the obscurities of the Bible, than to walk in its light, read this declaration, and fear and tremble.

The revelations contained in the Bible have the attestation of MIRACLES. It is a plain dictate of common sense, that Almighty God, who created and governs the world, may direct its movements as He chooses. He appointed the laws of Nature, and He may suspend these laws whenever He pleases, and turn the course of things out of the ordinary channel. It is equally clear, that none but the Author of Nature can effect such changes. It follows, therefore, that miracles, if wrought in attestation of a revelation professing to be from Heaven, stamp upon it the seal of Omnipotence. Persons who saw such miracles wrought, reasoned well when they said: "We know that thou art a teacher come from God; for no man can do these miracles that thou doest, except God be with him."

Though miracles furnished, to those who saw them with their own eyes, a more impressive evidence than to us who see them through the light of history, yet the argument founded on them is perfectly conclusive, even at the present time. That Moses and the prophets, Christ and his apostles, performed works truly miraculous, is as well attested as any ancient fact whatever. The character of the works attributed to them, their number, the circumstances in which they were performed, the absence of everything indicating fraud or imposture, the sufferings by which the witnesses demonstrated their sincerity, the credence which their testimony obtained rapidly and extensively, and in the face of bitter persecution, and the absence of all counter testimony; all these considerations compel the belief that miracles were wrought, and if wrought, the revelation which they attest must be from God. The evidence, though it may be less impressive, is not less decisive than it would have been if we had personally witnessed the miracles.

We are not wholly indebted for the evidence of miracles, to the light of history. It does not need historical proof to satisfy our minds that the pyramids of Egypt were built by human labor and skill. We are as well satisfied of this, as if we had seen them rise under the hands of the workmen. We know that they are the work of man, because they resemble, in kind, other works of man. But he who gazes on these stupendous structures, may turn his eyes to the great globe beneath them, and feel equally well assured that it is not the work of man. So, in contemplating a system of heathen mythology or philosophy, we may be convinced that it is of human origin, because it bears the marks of man's workmanship; but in contemplating the Bible, and the religion which it has introduced into the world, we may be as well assured that the origin of these is superhuman. A system so destitute of everything which could recommend it to the carnal mind, and claiming to be attested "with signs and wonders, and with divers miracles," could not, in the absence of such miracles, obtain, according to the ordinary course of things, easy and extensive credence among mankind, and become firmly established in their confidence. The propagation, in such circumstances, must itself have been miraculous. It is of no importance to the present argument, whether the miracle was wrought before the eyes of him who received the doctrine, or on his mind, to incline him to receive it. In either case, there was a miracle, an interposition of Divine Power, and such an interposition demonstrated that the doctrine was from God.

The PROPHECIES which the Bible contains, must have proceeded from infallible foreknowledge. This is proved by their exact fulfilment.

Daniel prophesied to Nebuchadnezzar, the proud head of the Babylonian empire, then in its glory and strength, that this empire would give place to three others which were to arise after it.[1] This succession of empires, the Babylonian, the Medo-Persian, the Grecian, and the Roman, is more fully described afterward in the prophecies of Daniel, together with a series of events extending down to the present time.[2] More than a century before the time of Daniel, the prophet Isaiah predicted[3] the taking of Babylon by the Persians, who were, at the time of the prediction, a feeble and obscure nation. He foretold the very name of the Persian leader, and the manner of his entrance into the city, through gates which, by a special ordering of Providence, were carelessly left open by

---

[1] Dan. ii. 39, 45.   [2] Ch. vii. 12.   [3] Is. xxi. 9; xlv. 1, 3.

the Babylonians in their drunken festivity. Other prophets foretold the destruction and final desolation of Babylon,[1] and of Nineveh;[2] the overthrow of ancient Tyre by Nebuchadnezzar,[3] and afterward of insular Tyre by Alexander,[4] and the decline and present state of Egypt,[5] once the proudest of nations. All these predictions were made when the events predicted were so improbable, that they could not be foreknown by any human sagacity; yet history, and the reports of travellers, attest their exact accomplishment. Many other examples of fulfilled prophecy might readily be cited.

The prophecies concerning the Jews are remarkable, and we refer to them with the more satisfaction, because the reader has probably, to some extent, personal knowledge of the facts predicted. These people are scattered through our nation, and through most of the nations on earth. Their synagogues, in which they meet to worship the God of their fathers, are found in all our principal cities. The Scriptures of the Old Testament are regularly read in their public worship, and are regarded with religious veneration, as their sacred book, received from God by their ancient prophets, and handed down to them from their forefathers. This book minutely describes,[6] in the language of prediction, the sufferings which they have undergone; their wonderful preservation as a distinct people, notwithstanding these sufferings, and their dispersed condition among all nations. Other ancient tribes, when scattered, have been lost in the general mass of mankind; but these people, after centuries of dispersion and persecution, still remain distinct, and stand forth to the world as witnesses of the wonderful fulfilment of the predictions respecting them, uttered by their ancient prophets.

The sacred writings of the Jews not only contain predictions of the dispersion, sufferings, and wonderful preservation of this people, but also furnish explanation of these extraordinary events. The book describes a covenant between this nation and the God whom they worship, and its records show that they have repeatedly violated this covenant, and suffered the threatened penalty. The whole history of the nation illustrates the dealings of God with

---

[1] Jer. li. [2] Nahum i, iii. [3] Ezek. xxvi. 7, 11.
[4] Ibid. xxvii. 32. [5] Ibid. xxix. [6] Lev. xxvi; Deut. xxvii. xxx.

them, in accordance with the stipulations of this covenant. Once before, as a punishment of their unfaithfulness, they were driven from their land into captivity for seventy years, yet they were preserved and brought back. The prophetic declarations of their sacred volume explain that their present dispersion and sufferings are, in like manner, in consequence of their crimes, and that their preservation is in prospect of another restoration. Their condition, therefore, resembles that of a malefactor nailed to the cross, with his accusation written over his head; a fit punishment for the nation that crucified the Lord of glory. They hold in their hands the book which specifies their crimes and predicts their sufferings, and they furnish, in their persons, the spectacle of these predictions fulfilled. They not only claim that their book is divine, but they are the proof of its divinity.

The Jews may be made witnesses for the New Testament also, which they reject, and for Christianity, which they hate. What crime so great, has extended their dispersion and sufferings through the long period of eighteen centuries? The New Testament gives the only satisfactory answer to this inquiry, and it answers in perfect accordance with their own Scriptures. They have rejected and crucified their King, their long-expected Messiah, whom their prophets had foretold. It was predicted that he would appear before the tribe of Judah should become extinct, or should cease to maintain a distinct government of its own;[1] before the second temple should be destroyed;[2] and in 490 years from the decree of Cyrus to rebuild Jerusalem.[3] At this time Jesus Christ appeared, claiming to be their Messiah, and furnishing most abundant proofs that he came from God; yet, as their prophets had foretold, they rejected him,[4] and united with Gentile rulers to destroy him.[5] Their own Scriptures, and their confessed hatred of Jesus Christ, fully make out the crime for which they suffer, and these unite with the known fact of their sufferings to demonstrate the Messiahship of Jesus and the divine origin of Christianity.

The New Testament contains various predictions[6] which have been exactly fulfilled concerning the destruction of Jerusalem; the calamities of the Jews; their dispersion and their preservation;

---

[1] Gen. xlix. 10. [2] Haggai ii. 7, 9. [3] Dan. ix. 24–27. [4] Is. liii. 3.
[5] Ps. ii. 1, 2. [6] Matt. xxiv; Mark xiii; Luke xxi.

also concerning the persecutions of Christianity; its spread through the world, and the Papal Apostasy.[1] Besides these, it contains predictions, yet not accomplished, of the conversion of the Gentiles, the restoration of the Jews, and the millennial state of the Church. When these shall have been fulfilled, the prophetical evidence now constantly accumulating will be complete.

In concluding this brief inqiry into the origin of the Bible, we may admire and adore the wonderful providence of God, which has made his enemies the preservers and witnesses of his revelation. The Jews, who killed the prophets and crucified the Son of God himself, have preserved and transmitted the Scriptures of the Old Testament, and are now witnesses to the world of its divine origin, and the truth of its prophecies. The Roman Catholic Church, the great Antichrist, or man of sin, drunk with the blood of the saints, has transmitted to us the Scriptures of the New Testament, and now gives, in the same two-fold manner, its testimony to this part of the Sacred Volume. Even the infidel scoffer is made an unconscious witness. In its pages, his very scoffs are predicted, and his corrupt heart, from which, rather than from sober judgment, these scoffs proceed, is portrayed with an accuracy and skill which bespeak the Author divine, the Searcher of hearts. The word which "is quick and powerful, and sharper than any two-edged sword, piercing even to the dividing asunder of soul and spirit, and of the joints and marrow, and is a discerner of the thoughts and intents of the heart," must be "the word of God." Even the reluctant tongue of the infidel, as in the case of Rousseau, is sometimes constrained to utter its testimony aloud; and at other times, when danger comes or death threatens, his alarm and terror divulge the truth, that his rock is not as our rock, himself being judge. Unhappy infidel! Is there a God? Hast thou an immortal soul? Until thou canst, with unfaltering hardihood, answer, No to both these inquiries, do not cast away from thee the Bible, the Book of God, the Light of immortality.

II. AUTHORITY.

THOUGH the Bible was written by inspired men, they are to be regarded merely as the instruments chosen, fitted, and employed

---

[1] 2 Thess. ii. 3–12; 1 John ii. 18; 1 Tim. iv. 1–3.

by God, for the production of this work. God himself is the author of the Bible. When we read its sacred pages, we should realize that God speaks to us, and when we suffer it to lie neglected, we should remember that we are refusing to listen to God, when he proffers to instruct us on subjects of infinite moment.

The Bible contains the *testimony* of God, and is therefore a Rule of *Faith*. The declarations of an honest man ought to be believed, much more ought those which are made by the God of truth; "if we receive the witness of men, the witness of God is greater." To reject the testimony of God, is to make him a liar. To call a fellow-man a liar, is to offer an insult of the grossest character. This insult we offer to the great God, when we refuse to receive his testimony, given to us in his holy Word.

The Bible contains the *precepts* of God, and is therefore a Rule of *Duty*. We are bound to obey the commands of parents and civil rulers, but God has a higher claim on our obedience. He is our Father in heaven, and the Supreme Lawgiver of the universe. Against this high authority we rebel, when we refuse to obey the precepts of the Bible.

The Bible contains the *promises* of God, and is therefore a Rule of *Hope*. It determines, not only what we are to believe and to do, but also what we are to expect. It presents, as the foundation of our hope, the promise and the oath of God, two immutable things, in which it is impossible for God to lie. We look to him as the rewarder of those that diligently seek him, and all our confidence respecting the nature and extent of this reward, and the certainty of our obtaining it, is founded on the sure word of prophecy, the Bible.

Whether, as a rule of faith, of duty, or of hope, the authority of the Bible is *supreme*. We may rely on the testimony of men, but they sometimes deceive us. We may regulate our conduct by the command of those who are over us, or by the dictates of our own conscience, but rulers may command what is wrong, and conscience is not infallible. We may cherish hopes founded on human promises, or the natural tendencies of things, but human promises are often delusive, and the promises of Nature are buds which, however beautiful and fragrant, are often blasted before they produce fruit. God never deceives. "The grass withereth, and the flower thereof falleth away, but the word of the Lord endureth forever." When the Bible speaks, all else may be silent, and its decisions leave no room for doubt and admit no appeal.

The authority of the Bible is *independent*. It was not conferred on it by the inspired men who wrote it; nor does it derive any from the persons who have transmitted it to us. The purest church on earth cannot invest it with authority; much less can the corrupt Church of Rome. The inspired writers referred the authority of what they wrote to God; and here it must rest. The transcribers of the manuscripts, who have been the agents of Providence in preserving and transmitting the Sacred Volume to us, and the printers and bookbinders by whose labors this volume is so widely circulated, have conferred no authority on it, and it has received as little from the Church of Rome as from these. It possesses authority simply because it is the word of God.

The authority of the Bible is *immediate*. Its address is directly from God, and directly to the mind and heart of every individual reader. We have no mediator but Christ, and no infallible interpreter but the Holy Spirit. We may derive assistance from men in understanding the Bible, but they have no right to understand it for us. We should employ our own minds in the study of God's Word, and allow no human interpreter to intervene between God and our own conscience. We should say, each one for himself, " Speak, Lord, for thy servant heareth."

What a precious gift is the Bible! Who will not prize it? Who will not bind it to his heart? We stand on the narrow isthmus of life, between two oceans, the boundless past and the boundless future. The records of eternity past are beyond our reach, but the Ancient of Days has opened them, and has revealed to us in the Bible whatever it is necessary that we should know. The vanishing present is all important to us, because on it depends our everlasting all, but who will instruct us how to use the swiftly passing moments as we ought? The only wise God has condescended to speak to us in the Bible, and to teach us how to order our steps in life's short way, so as to insure life eternal. The future world is just before us. For myself, I realize that I am standing on the shore of the boundless ocean, with but an inch of crumbling sand remaining. I hear the shrieks of the dying infidel at my side, to whose view all is covered with impenetrable darkness. He, too, has come to the brink, and would gladly refuse to proceed, but he cannot. Perplexed, terrified, shuddering, he plunges in and sinks, he knows not whither. How precious, at this trying moment, is the Book of God! How cheering this Light from heaven! Before it I see the shades retiring. The Bible lifts its torch—nay, not a feeble torch, such as reason may raise, to shine on the darkness and render it visible; the Bible sheds the light of the noonday sun on the vast prospect before me, and enables me, tranquil and joyful, to launch into eternity with the full assurance of hope. Mortals, hastening to the retributions of eternity, be wise; receive the revelation from heaven presented to you in the Bible; attend diligently to its instructions, and reverence its authority, as the word of the final Judge before whom you will soon appear.

BOOK SECOND.

DOCTRINE CONCERNING GOD.

INTRODUCTION.

DUTY OF LOVE TO GOD.

"Thou shalt love the Lord thy God with all thine heart, and with all thy soul, and with all thy might."[1] In this manner the Bible commands the chief of all duties. No reasons are assigned for the requirement. No proof is adduced that God exists, or that he possesses such perfections as entitle him to the supreme love of his creatures. Jehovah steps forth before the subjects of his government, and issues his command. He waits for no formal introduction. He lifts up his voice with majesty. Without promise, and without threat, he proclaims his law, and leaves his subjects to their responsibility.

From the manner of this announcement, we may derive instruction. It is not necessary that we should enter into a formal demonstration that God exists, or a formal investigation of his attributes, before we begin the duty of loving him. We already know enough of him for this; and to postpone the performance of the duty until we have completed our investigations, is to commence them with unsanctified hearts, and in rebellion against God. From the dawn of our being we have had demonstrations of God's existence and character, blazing around us like the light of noonday. The heavens and the earth have declared his glory; his ministers and people have proclaimed his name; he is not to us an unknown God, except so far as our minds are wilfully blind to the displays of his glory. If, therefore, we withhold the affections of our hearts, we can have no excuse in the plea that more evidence is

---

[1] Deut. vi. 5.

(43)

needed. And with hearts so alienated from God at the outset, all our religious inquiries are likely to be unprofitable. What probability is there that further proof will produce its proper impression and effect on our minds, if that which is already in our possession is unheeded or abused? If, from what we already know of God, we admire and love him, we shall desire to know more of him, and shall prosecute the study with profit and delight; but, if we have already shut him out of our hearts, all our intellectual investigations respecting him may be expected to leave us in spiritual blindness.

The duty required corresponds, in character, to the religion, of which it is an essential part. Heathen gods could not claim the supreme love of their worshippers; and heathen minds had no idea of a religion founded on supreme love to their deities. To some extent, they were objects of fear; and much that appertained to their supposed character and history, served for amusement, or to interest the imagination; but the conduct attributed to them was often such as even heathen virtue disapproved. Hence, they could not be objects of supreme love; and no one claimed it for them. The requirement of supreme love demonstrates the religion of the Bible to be from the true God; and when we begin our religious investigations with the admission of this obligation, and the full recognition of it in our hearts, we may be assured that we are proceeding in the right way.

The simplicity of the requirement is admirable. No explanation of the duty is needed. Forms of worship may be numerous and various, and questions may arise as to the forms which will be most acceptable. Many outward duties of morality are often determined with much difficulty. Perplexing questions arise as to the nature of repentance and faith, and the uninformed need instruction respecting them. But no one needs to be told what love is; the humblest mind can understand the requirement, and may feel pleasure in the consciousness of rendering obedience to it; and the learned philosopher stands in the presence of this precept as a little child, and feels its power binding every faculty that he possesses. This simple principle pervades all religion, and binds all intelligences, small and great, to God, the centre of the great system. Between it and the power of gravitation in the natural world, which binds atoms and masses, pebbles and vast planets, a beautiful analogy may be traced.

The comprehensiveness of the precept is not less admirable. From it rises the precept, Love thy neighbor as thyself; and on these two all the law rests. We love our neighbors because they are God's creatures, and the subjects of his government, and because he has commanded us. We love God supremely, because he is the greatest and best of beings; and we love other beings, according to the importance of each in the universal system of being. One principle pervades both precepts, as one principle of gravitation binds the earth to the sun, and the parts of the earth to each other. This law binds angels to the throne of God, and to each other; and binds men and angels together, as fellow-subjects of the same sovereign. The decalogue is this law expanded, and adapted to the condition and relations of mankind. Love is not only the fulfilling of the law, but it is also the essence of gospel morality. All Christian obedience springs from it; and, without it, no form of obedience is acceptable to God. He who loves God supremely, cannot be guilty of that unbelief which makes God a liar, and he cannot reflect on the sins which he has committed against God, without sincere penitence.

We must not overlook the tendency of this precept to produce universal good. Every one knows how much the order and happiness found in human society, depend on love. If all kind affections were banished from the hearts of men, earth would be converted at once into a pandemonium. What love is left on earth renders it tolerable, and the love which reigns in heaven makes it a place of bliss. Perfect obedience to the great law of love is sufficient to render all creatures happy. It opens, within the breast, a perennial source of enjoyment; and it meets, from without, the smile and blessing of an approving God.

Though the religion of love is clearly taught in the book of God only, yet, when we have learned it there, we can discover its agreement with natural religion. It will be useful to observe how the moral tendencies of our nature accord, on this point, with the teachings of revelation.

The wickedness of man has been a subject of complaint in all ages. The ancient heathen complained of the degeneracy of their times, and talked of a golden age, long passed, in which virtue

prevailed. In modern heathen nations, together with the depravity that prevails, some sense of that depravity exists; and everywhere the necessity or desirableness of a more virtuous state of
society is admitted. In Christian lands, the very infidels, who
scoff at all religion with one breath, will, with the next, satirize the
wickedness of mankind. It is the united judgment of every nation,
and every age, that the practice of men falls below their own standard of virtue. It is, therefore, necessary, in order to acquire the
best notions of virtue that nature can give us, to turn away from
the practice of men to those moral sentiments implanted in the
human breast, which condemn this practice, and urge to higher
virtue.

It is well known that men judge the actions of others with more
severity than their own. Our appetites and passions interfere with
the decisions of conscience, wnen our own conduct is the subject
of examination. Hence, the general moral sense of mankind is a
better standard of virtue than the individual conscience. In looking to the judgment of others, with a view to determine the morality of our actions, the judgment of those is especially to be regarded who are to be benefited or injured by our deeds. Hence,
natural religion approves the rule — Do unto others as you would,
in like circumstances, that they should do unto you.

When the vice of others interferes with our happiness, we are
then most keenly sensible of its existence and atrocity. However
vague our notions of virtue may be, we always conceive of it as
tending to promote the happiness of others. Yet it is not every
tendency to promote happiness which we conceive to be virtuous.
The food that we eat, and the couch on which we lie, tend to promote our happiness; yet we do not ascribe virtue to these inanimate things. Virtue belongs only to rational and moral agents;
and the promotion of happiness must be intentional to be accounted
virtuous. There is still another limitation. Men sometimes confer
benefits on others, with the expectation of receiving greater benefits
in return. Where the motive for the action is merely the benefit
expected in return, the common judgment of mankind refuses to
characterize the deed as virtuous. To constitute virtue, there must
be an intentional promotion of happiness in others; and this intention must be disinterested. Natural religion does not deny that a
higher standard of morality may exist; but it holds that disinte-

rested benevolence is virtue, and it determines the morality of actions by the disinterested benevolence which they exhibit.

Some have maintained that self-love is the first principle of virtue, its central affection, which, spreading first to those most nearly related to us, extends gradually to others more remote, and widens at length into universal benevolence. This system of morality is self-contradictory. While it claims to aim at universal happiness, it makes it the duty of each individual to aim, not at this public good, but at his own private benefit. Whenever the interest of another comes in conflict with his own, it is made his duty to aim at the latter, and to promote that of his neighbor only so far as it may conduce to his own. It is true, that the advocates of this system bring in reason as a restraining influence, and suppose that it will so regulate the exercise of self-love as to result in the general good. According to this system, if we, in aiming at our own happiness, practise fraud and falsehood with a view to promote it, and find ourselves defeated in the attainment of our object, we may charge our failure, not on the virtuous principle by which it is assumed that we have been moved, but on the failure of our reason to restrain and regulate it so as to attain its end. If it be said, that conscience will not permit us to be happy in the practise of fraud and falsehood, and that self-love, aware of this, avoids those practices so inconsistent with our internal peace, it is clearly admitted that conscience is a higher principle of our nature, to the decisions of which our self-love is compelled to yield.

As virtue aims at the general good, it must favour the means necessary for the attainment of this end. Civil government and laws, enacted and executed in wisdom and justice, are highly conducive to the general welfare, and these receive the approbation and support of the virtuous. Were an individual of our race, by a happy exception to the general rule, born with a virtuous bias of the mind, instead of the selfish propensity natural to mankind; and were this virtuous bias fostered and developed in his education, he would be found seeking the good of all. His first benefits conferred, would be on those nearest to him; but his disinterested benevolence would not stop here. As his acquaintance extended into the ramifications of society, his desire and labour for the general good would extend with it, and civil government, wholesome laws, and every institution tending to public benefit, would receive his cordial approbation and support; and every wise and righteous governor, and every subordinate individual, aiming at the public good, would be an object of his favour. If we suppose the knowledge of this individual to increase, and his virtuous principles to expand, widening the exercise of universal benevolence; and if, at length, the idea of a God, a being of every possible moral excellence, the wise and righteous governor of the universe, should be presented; how would his heart be affected? Here his virtuous principles would find occasion for their highest exercise, and would grow into religious devotion. This glorious being would have the highest place in his admiration and love; and the discovery of his universal dominion would produce ineffable joy. Such are the affections of heart which even natural religion teaches, that the knowledge of God's existence and perfections ought to produce.

In God's written Word, we learn our duty in a reverse method. We are not left to trace it out by a slow process, beginning with the first exercise of moral principle in the heart, and rising at length to the infinite God; but the existence and character of God are immediately presented, and the first and chief of all duties is at once announced: "Thou shalt love the Lord thy God with all thy heart." How sublime! how appropriate! The virtuous mind is open to receive such a revelation; and its perfect accordance with the best teachings of natural religion, recommends it to our understandings and our hearts. The second commandment, "Thou shalt love thy neighbor as thyself," is introduced, not as leading to the first, but as subordinate to it. It takes the place which properly belongs to it in a revelation from the supreme authority.

Love has been divided into benevolence, beneficence, and complacence. This division may at first appear inconsistent with the simplicity which has been ascribed to love. Benevolence is the disposition to do good to an object, and beneficence is the conferring of that good. The latter is not properly love, but the effect or manifestation of it. On the other hand, complacence includes the cause of the love together with the affection itself. Love may be exercised toward an unworthy object, as when God loves those who are dead in trespasses and sins. But it may be exercised toward those whose moral character renders them fit objects. In this case, the love being connected with approbation of the character beloved, is called complacence. When love has an inanimate thing for its object, as when Isaac loved savory meat, the term refers to the deriving of enjoyment; but when the object of love is a sentient being, the term always implies the conferring of enjoyment, even when some pleasure has been received, or some enjoyment in return is expected.

Love to God implies cordial approbation of his moral character. His natural attributes, eternity, immensity, omnipotence, &c., may fill us with admiration; but these are not the proper objects of love. If we worship him in the beauty of holiness, the beauty of his holiness must excite the love of our hearts. As our knowledge of these moral perfections increases, our delight in them must increase; and this delight will stimulate to further study of them; and to a more diligent observation of the various methods in which they are manifested. The display of them, even in the most terrible exhibitions of his justice, will be contemplated with reverent, but approving awe; and their united glory, as seen in the great scheme of redemption by Christ, will be viewed with unmixed and never-ceasing delight.

Love to God includes joy in his happiness. He is not only perfectly holy, but perfectly happy; and it is our duty to rejoice in his happiness. In loving our neighbor, we rejoice in his present happiness, and desire to increase it. We cannot increase the already perfect happiness of God, but we can rejoice in that which he possesses. If we delight in the happiness of God, we shall labor to please him in all things, to do whatever he commands, and to advance all the plans, the accomplishment of which he has so much at heart. Love, therefore, includes obedience to his commands, and resignation and submission to his will.

Love to God will render it a pleasing task to examine the proofs of his existence, and to study those glorious attributes which render him the worthy object of supreme affection. Let us enter on this study, prompted by holy love, and a strong desire that our love may be increased.

4

CHAPTER I.

EXISTENCE OF GOD.

THERE IS A GOD.[1] ✓

The doctrine that God exists, is not now to be demonstrated as a new truth. It has been supposed in all the preceding pages; and the proofs of it have been brought to view, in various ways. But, for the sake of systematic arrangement, it will be proper to collect these proofs under one head; and a clearer statement of. them will tend to the confirmation of our faith.

1. Our moral nature demonstrates the existence of God.

Our moral nature is adapted to moral government. We find this government within us administered by conscience, and it meets us from without in the influence which we experience from the moral judgments and feelings of others. It restrains our appetites and passions; and, however unwelcome this restraint may be to our vicious propensities, every one knows that it is conducive to his well-being.

We are social as well as moral beings. The circumstances in which we enter the world, and the propensities which we bring with us, unite to render the establishment of society necessary. The birds congregate in flocks, and the bees in swarms, and their instincts are adapted to the social relations which they form. To man in society, moral principles are indispensable. Banish from every member of human society the restraints which his conscience and the moral sense of the community impose on him, and you will desolate the earth, or convert it into a hell. Brute-force, and diabolical cunning, under the dominion of lawless passions, will take the mastery of the world, and fill it with wretchedness.

From the combined influence of our moral and social principles, civil governments have originated, and their existence has been found by experience indispensable to the well-being of society. These governments have differed very widely in their degrees of excellence; and some of them have been most unrighteously and

---

[1] Gen. i. 1; Ps. xiv. 1; Mark xii. 32; 1 Cor. viii. 6; Heb. iii. 4.

cruelly administered; yet the very worst of them has been considered preferable to wild anarchy.

The notion of moral government, and the feeling of its necessity, spring up naturally in the human mind; but no earthly form of it satisfies our desires, or meets our necessities. Conscience restrains us; and, when we have disregarded its monitions, stings us with remorse; but men are still wicked. Public sentiment stamps vice with infamy; but, in spite of public sentiment, men are vicious. Civil government holds out its penalties, and the ruler brandishes his sword; but men persevere in wickedness, and often with impunity. The voice of nature within us calls for a government free from these imperfections. If, from the idea of a petty ruler over a single tribe or nation, we ascend to that of a moral governor over all intelligent creatures; if, instead of the imperfect moral judgments and feelings which we find in men, we attribute to this universal ruler, all possible moral perfections, if we invest him with knowledge sufficient to detect every crime, and power sufficient to manifest his disapprobation of it in the most suitable and effectual way; and if this exalted sovereign, instead of being far from us, is brought into such a relation to us, that in him we live, move, and have our being; we shall have the most sublime conception of moral government, of which our minds are capable. This conception is presented in the proposition, THERE IS A GOD. The idea of God's existence, as the moral ruler of the universe, accords precisely with the tendencies and demands of our moral nature; and, without admitting it, our moral faculties and the phenomena which they exhibit, are totally inexplicable.

The moral principles of our nature find occasion for development and exercise, in the relations which we sustain to our fellow-creatures. But, for their full development and exercise nothing furnishes opportunity, but the relation which we bear to God, and his universal dominion. This exercise of them constitutes religion. Religion is, therefore, the perfection of morality; and the fundamental doctrine of religion is the existence of God.

2. The existence of the world and the contrivances which it contains, demonstrate the existence of God.

While our moral nature leads us to the conception of God, as the moral governor of the universe, and to the belief of his existence, our intellectual nature approaches him, as the Great First

Cause. Reason traces the chain of cause and effect throughout its links. It finds every link dependent on that which precedes it; and it asks on what does the entire chain depend? It obtains no satisfactory answer to this question, until it has admitted the existence of an eternal, self-existent, and independent being, as the first cause of all things. Here, and here only, the mind finds repose.

The argument which has been most relied on in natural religion, to prove the existence of God, is derived from the indications of contrivance, with which Nature abounds. The adaptation of means to ends, and the accomplishment of purposes by contrivances of consummate skill, are everywhere visible. Contrivance implies a contriver. The intelligence displayed is often found in creatures that have no intelligence; and in other cases, when found in intelligent creatures, it is manifestly not from themselves; because it exists without their knowledge, and operates without their control. The contrivance must be referred to an intelligent First Cause. This argument for the existence of God, is of great practical value, because it is presented to our minds daily, and hourly, in all the works of Nature. We meet it in the sun-beams, which impart to plants and animals, the warmth necessary to life; and, to every eye, the light without which, eyes would be useless. It presents itself in the eyes of every man, beast, bird, fish, insect, and reptile, and is most convincingly exhibited in the arrangements for receiving and refracting the light, and employing it for the purposes of vision; a contrivance as truly mechanical, and conformed to the laws of optics, as that which is seen in the structure of the telescope. We behold it in the descending shower which fertilizes the earth, and causes the grass to grow; and in the bursting germ, the spreading blade, the rising stalk, and the ripening grain, in all which a skilful contrivance is displayed, that infinitely transcends all human art. We discover it in the instincts by which the parent hen hatches her eggs, and takes care of her young; and in the adaptation of every species of animals on land, in air, or in water, to their mode and condition of life. It is seen in the return of day and night, the revolution of the seasons, the wind that sweeps the sky, and the vapor that rises from the ocean, and floats through the atmosphere. We find it in the bones of the body, fitted for their respective motions, and in the muscles which move them; in the throbbing heart, the circulating blood, the digesting stomach, and the heaving lungs. In every thing which the eye beholds, or the mind contemplates, we discover the manifestations of the Creator's wisdom and power. The devotional heart is struck with the evidence of God's existence, so abundantly displayed in all his handiworks, and is incited to admire and adore. The whole universe becomes a grand temple, pervaded with the presence and glory of the deity; and every place becomes an altar, on which may be offered to him the sacrifice of praise and thanksgiving.

3. The doctrine that there is a God, is confirmed by the common consent of mankind.

There have been tribes of men without literature, and, to a great extent, without science and arts; but the notion of an invisible, overruling power, with some form of religious worship, has been nearly, or quite universal. In this particular, man is distinguished from all other animals that inhabit the globe; and if there has been any portion of our race in whom no idea of God and religion has appeared, it may be said of them, that they have so far brutalized themselves, as to hide from view the characteristic distinctions of human nature. Now, however it may be accounted for, that a belief in the existence of God has prevailed so generally among mankind; the fact of its prevalence is an argument for the truth of the opinion. If it is an ancient revelation handed down by tradition, that revelation proceeded from God, and therefore proves his existence; and if it springs up naturally in the human mind, in the circumstances in which we are placed, what Nature universally teaches, may be received as true.

4. Divine revelation dispels all doubt as to the existence of God.

In the Bible, the existence of God is from the very first assumed. "In the beginning, God created the heavens and the earth."[1] The doctrine, though formally declared in scarcely a single passage, is represented as fundamental in religion. "He that cometh to God, must believe that he is;"[2] and the denial of it is attributed to folly; "the fool hath said in his heart, there is no God."[3] The volume of revelation is a light emanating from the Father of lights, and is, of itself, an independent proof of his existence. As we study its pages, in his light we shall see light; and a more realizing

---

[1] Gen. i. 1.   [2] Heb. xi. 6.   [3] Ps. xiv. 1.

and abiding conviction that he, the great Source of light, exists, will occupy our minds.

The perfect harmony between natural and revealed religion, with respect to this doctrine, confirms the teaching of both. "The heavens declare the glory of God, and the firmament showeth his handiwork.   Day unto day uttereth speech, and night unto night showeth knowledge."[1] While heaven and earth, day and night, speak for God, he speaks for himself in his inspired word, confirming the testimony which they give, and completing the instruction which they convey. Revelation never contradicts or sets aside the teachings of natural religion. God affirms, that "the invisible things of him are from the creation of the world clearly seen, being understood by the things that are made; even his eternal power and Godhead."[2] It is no derogation from the authority or perfection of the Scriptures, that we study natural religion. The Scriptures themselves direct us to this study. "Ask the beasts, and they shall teach thee, and the fowls of the air, and they shall tell thee."[3] The same God who speaks to us in his word, speaks to us also in his works; and in whatever manner he speaks, we should hear, and receive instruction.

It is a lamentable proof of human depravity, that men should deny or disregard the existence of God. We read of the fool, who says in his heart, there is no God; of nations that forget God; and of individuals who have not God in all their thoughts. Such persons do not delight in God; and therefore they say, "Depart from us; we desire not the knowledge of thy ways." Of such atheism, the only effectual cure is a new heart. For the occasional suggestion of atheistic doubts, with which a pious man may be harassed, the remedy is, a diligent study of God's word and works, a careful marking of his hand in Providence, and a prayerful and confiding acknowledgment of him in all our ways. If we habitually walk with God, we shall not doubt his existence.

The invisibility of God is one of the obstacles to the exercise of a lively faith in his existence. It may assist in removing this obstacle, to reflect that the human mind is also invisible; and yet we never doubt that it exists. We hear the words, and see the actions of a fellow-man, and these indicate to us the character and state of

---

[1] Ps. xix. 1, 2.   [2] Rom. i. 20.   [3] Job xii. 7.

his mind, so as to excite in us admiration or contempt, love or hatred. If, while we listen to his words, and observe his actions, we clearly perceive the intelligence from which these words and actions proceed, why can we not, with equal clearness, perceive the intelligence from which the movements of nature proceed? If we can know, admire, and love, an unseen human mind, it is equally possible to know, admire, and love an unseen God.

CHAPTER II.

ATTRIBUTES OF GOD.

As we acquire knowledge of other beings, and of the relations which they hold to us, opportunity is given for the development of our moral principles, and the exercise of our moral feelings. It accords with the dictates of individual conscience, with the moral judgments common to mankind, and with the teachings of God's word, that the feelings which we exercise, and the actions which we perform towards others, should have regard to their characters and their relations to us. To understand our duty towards God, we must know his character. It is not enough to believe that he exists, but we should labour to acquire a knowledge of him. Let us, then, reverently inquire, Who is the Lord?

SECTION I.—UNITY.

THERE IS BUT ONE GOD.[1]

The heathen nations have worshipped many gods; but the inspired volume throughout inculcates the doctrine, that there is but one God. Moses said, "Hear, O Israel, the Lord our God is one Lord;"[2] and, in the New Testament, the same truth is taught: "There is one God, and one Mediator;"[3] "To us there is but one God."[4]

---

[1] Deut. vi. 4; Ps. lxxxvi. 10; Mark xii. 29, 32; John xvii. 3; Gal. iii. 20; Eph. iv. 6; 1 Tim. ii. 5; James ii. 19.
[2] Deut. vi. 4.   [3] 1 Tim. ii. 5.   [4] 1 Cor. viii. 6.

It is not clear that the unity of God can be proved by natural religion. In some of the reasonings which have been relied on, the thing to be proved is assumed. The most satisfactory argument is derived from the uniformity of counsel, which appears in the works of creation and providence. The same laws of Nature prevail everywhere; so that, in passing from one region to another, we never feel that we have entered the dominion of another Lord. Light which emanates from the remote fixed stars, possesses the same properties, and obeys the same laws, as that which comes from the sun of our own system.

The proof from revelation is clear and decisive. It is true, that plural names of the deity are frequently used in the Old Testament; but it is manifest that they were not designed to teach the doctrine of polytheism. In Deut. vi. 4, the word "God" is plural, in the original Hebrew; but the whole passage contains the most unequivocal declaration of the unity of God. In Gen. i. 1, the name "God" is plural, but the verb "created" is singular, and therefore bars out all inference in favour of polytheism. In several passages, plural pronouns are used when God speaks of himself. "Let us make man;"[1] "Let us go down;"[2] "The man is become as one of us;"[3] these passages, and especially the last of them, cannot well be reconciled with the doctrine of God's unity, so abundantly taught elsewhere, without supposing a reference to the doctrine of the trinity, which will be considered hereafter.

The unity of God renders his moral government one, uniting the subjects of it into one great empire. It leaves us in no doubt to whom our allegiance is due; and it fixes one centre in the universe to which the affections of all hearts should be directed. It tends to unite the people of God: as we have "one God," so we have "one body, and one spirit."[4]

Section II.—SPIRITUALITY.

GOD IS A SPIRIT.[5]

By our external senses we obtain knowledge of properties which belong to a class of substances called matter; such as extension, solidity or impenetrability, divisibility, figure, color.

---

[1] Gen. i. 26.   [2] Gen. xi. 7.   [3] Gen. iii. 22.
[4] Eph. iv. 4, 6.   [5] John iv. 24; Is. xxxi. 3; Heb. xii. 9.

By consciousness, we have knowledge of our own thoughts and feelings; and these we ascribe to a substance, called mind, which is capable of perceiving, remembering, comparing, judging, reasoning, and willing. The distinction between these two classes of substances is recognised in the judgments of all men. We never attribute thought to fire, air, earth, or water; and we never conceive of mind as round or square, black or white. The properties which we discover in our own minds, we attribute to the minds of others; and we readily conceive the existence of these properties in beings of a different order. The term *spirit* is used to denote an immaterial and intelligent substance, or being; one which is without the peculiar properties of matter, and possesses properties analogous to those of the human mind. In this sense, God is a spirit. He is not extended, solid, and divisible, like a rock, a tree, or a human body; but thinks and wills, in a manner free from all imperfection.

The texts of Scripture which directly teach the spirituality of God, are few. It may be inferred from Isaiah xxxi. 3: "The Egyptians are men, and not God; and their horses flesh, and not spirit." The foundation of the parallelism, in this passage, is that God is a spirit. It may be inferred, also, from the language of Scripture, in which God is called the Father of spirits: " We have had fathers of our flesh, which corrected us, and we gave them reverence; shall we not much rather be in subjection to the Father of spirits, and live?"[1] A father and his children possess a common nature, and, as the fathers of our flesh, are flesh, so, the Father of our spirits, is spirit. There is one passage which teaches the doctrine expressly, " God is a spirit;"[2] and this would be sufficient to prove it, if it were taught nowhere else.

It is no objection to the doctrine of God's spirituality, that bodily parts, as hands, feet, eyes, &c., are ascribed to him. These are manifestly mere accommodations of language, because we have no words more suitable to express the operations of the divine mind. If it were inadmissible to speak of God's eyes, because he has not material organs of vision, as we have, it would also be inadmissible to speak of God's seeing, because he does not see by means of material light, as we do; or to speak of God's thinking, because his thoughts are not as our thoughts.

---

[1] Heb. xii. 9.   [2] John iv. 24.

The practical use of this doctrine is taught by Christ: "God is a spirit, and they that worship him must worship him in spirit and in truth."[1] In offering him homage, it is not sufficient to come before him with a bended knee, or a prostrate body; but our minds, our spiritual nature, must render the homage, or it will be unacceptable to him.

The spirituality of God is the foundation of the second commandment in the decalogue: "Thou shalt not make unto thee any graven image, or the likeness of anything that is in heaven above, or that is in the earth beneath, or that is in the water under the earth; thou shalt not bow down thyself to them, nor serve them."[2] The reason assigned for this commandment is, that the Israelites saw no form when God manifested his presence to them at Mount Sinai.[3] He appeared to them in cloud and fire. A pillar of cloud and fire went before the Israelites in their journey through the wilderness, as a token of the divine presence. This token appeared at the tabernacle; and afterwards in the temple built and dedicated by Solomon. God appeared to Moses in a burning bush. We are not to understand from these things, that God is either cloud or fire. These are material, and not spiritual substances. As what is purely spiritual cannot be perceived by our bodily senses, God was pleased to employ these material symbols to give a sensible demonstration of his presence. For the same reason, he sometimes presented himself in human form. In all these material manifestations of himself, which are recorded in the Old Testament, there is reason to believe that it was the second person in the Godhead, who thus exhibited himself; the same that afterwards appeared in human flesh, in the person of Jesus Christ. He is called the Angel of the Lord, the Angel of the Lord's presence, and yet he is called Jehovah; and the reverence due to Jehovah is claimed for him. A created angel is not entitled to this name, or this honour; but they both belong to the Son of God, the Angel of the Covenant, who, after his incarnation, was God manifest in the flesh. This opinion is confirmed by the teachings of the New Testament: "No man hath seen God at any time; the only begotten Son, which is in the bosom of the Father, he hath declared him."[4] Of the Father, Jesus says, "Ye have neither heard his voice at any time, nor seen

---

[1] John iv. 24.   [2] Ex. xx. 4, 5.   [3] Deut. iv. 12–18.   [4] John i. 18.

his shape;"[1] and he said to his disciples, "He that hath seen me, hath seen the Father."[2] A comparison of these passages may satisfy us, that all the manifestations of the deity to human senses, whether visible or audible, were made in the person of the Son, or Word of God.

The spirituality of God contradicts the pantheistic notion that the universe is God. The universe is not spirit. In its material fabric, intelligence is displayed; but this intelligence does not belong to the material fabric itself, for matter cannot think or know. To present our religious devotions to the universe, is an idolatry not less degrading than that of the most stupid of the heathen nations. They worship stocks and stones; but this philosophy clothes every clod of earth with divinity, and entitles it to our worship. The heathen render divine honors to a few men, whom, for extraordinary merit, they enroll among the gods; but this notion directs our worship to every man, and to every beast of the field. It is a notion perfectly adapted to crush the outflowings of the devotional heart, as they rise to the one, indivisible, spiritual intelligence, to whom alone divine worship is due.

The notion, that God is the Soul of the universe, may not be liable to precisely the same objection. But what does the proposition mean? The only sense in which we can possibly understand that God is the Soul of the universe, is, that he sustains a relation to the universe analogous to that which the human soul sustains to the body with which it is connected. But how extensive is this analogy? The soul did not create the matter of which the body is made; did not form the skilfully wrought parts of the wonderful machinery, or contrive their mysterious movements, which it studies with admiration, and comprehends only in very small part. The soul exercises but a very limited control over the body. The muscles of voluntary motion are under its command, and move at its will; and, in this fact, we may discover a faint analogy to the operation of Him, who worketh *all things* after the counsel of His will, and in whom every creature lives, moves, and has its being. An analogy so meager as this is not sufficient to justify the metaphorical language in which the proposition is stated. Yet, while we reject the proposition, we may derive from it a profitable sug-

---

[1] John v. 37.　　　　　　[2] John xiv. 9.

gestion. In our intercourse with the myriads of mankind, we perceive and acknowledge, in the movements of every human limb, in the changes of every human countenance, and in the words which fall from every human tongue, the power and intelligence of an operating human soul. Equally obvious, and infinitely more extensive, is the control which God exercises, at every moment, over every part of the universe. With a proper view of God's spirituality, and of his operative control over the world and everything in it, our minds would hold intercourse with his mind, as direct and undoubted as that which we hold with the minds of our fellow-men, and one more constant, and more elevating and delightful.

SECTION III.—IMMENSITY, OMNIPRESENCE.

GOD IS EVERYWHERE.[1]

Every material thing in the universe is somewhere. The sun has its place; the earth also, and every grain of sand, and every drop of water. The drops of water may change their place perpetually, but every drop has, for each moment, its own place, to the exclusion of all other matter in the universe.

In our conceptions of the human mind we assign place to it also, though in a different manner. We do not attribute to it length, breadth, and thickness, as to a block of marble, which can be measured by feet and inches; but we conceive of it as present in the human body, with which it is connected, and absent from another, with which it is not connected. Each mind is operated on by impressions made on the organs of sense which belong to its own body; and operates by its volitions on the muscles of motion which belong to that body. In this view, we conceive of each mind as present in its own body, and not elsewhere; and we conceive of changing the place of the mind, while its connection with the body continues, only by a change in the place of the body.

When we conceive of finite spiritual beings as angels, we assign to each some place; because his operation, though not confined like that of the human mind, to a particular material body, is nevertheless limited. Such conception accords with the teaching of Scripture, in which angels are represented as moving from place to place, to execute the will of their Sovereign. So the angel

---

[1] 1 Kings viii. 27 ; Ps. cxxxix. 7; Jer. xxiii. 23.

came to Daniel,[1] and to Peter;[2] and so one is represented as flying through the midst of heaven.[3]

We must not conceive of God's omnipresence as if it were material. We say that the atmosphere is present at every part of the earth's surface; but this is not strictly true. It is not the whole, but merely a small part of the atmosphere, which is present at each place; God is indivisible. We cannot say, that a part of his essence is here, and a part yonder. If this were the mode of God's omnipresence in universal space, he would be infinitely divided, and only an infinitely small part of him would be present at each place. It would not be the whole deity, that takes cognizance of our actions, and listens to our petitions. This notion is unfavorable to piety, and opposed to the true sense of Scripture: "The eyes of the Lord are in every place, beholding the evil and the good."[4] "The eyes of the Lord are over the righteous, and his ears are open unto their prayers."[5]

There are passages of Scripture which speak of God's removing from one place to another; of his approaching and departing; of his dwelling in heaven, and of his coming near to his people, and taking up his abode with them. These are manifestly accommodations of language; just as when eyes or hands are attributed to him. They refer to the manifestations of his presence in his various works, and dispensations, in which such changes take place, as are appropriately and impressively expressed by this language.

When we deny a material omnipresence of God, as if his essence were divided and diffused; and when we maintain that the whole deity is everywhere present by his energy and operation, it is not to be understood that we deny the essential omnipresence of God. In whatever manner his essence is present anywhere, it is present everywhere. What the mode of that presence is, we know not. We know not the essence of the human mind, nor the mode of its presence in the body; much less can we comprehend the essence of the infinite God, or the mode of his omnipresence. To that incomprehensible property of his nature, by which he is capable of being wholly present at the same moment, with every one of his creatures, without division of his essence, and without removal from

---

[1] Dan. ix. 23.   [2] Acts xii. 7.   [3] Rev. xiv. 6.
[4] Prov. xv. 3.   [5] 1 Pet. iii. 12.

place to place, the name immensity has been given. The essence of God is immense or unmeasured, because it is unmeasurable. It is unmeasurable, because it is spiritual, and, therefore, without such dimensions as may be measured by feet and inches; and because, in whatever sense dimensions may be ascribed to it, these dimensions are boundless. Time has a dimension not to be measured by feet and inches: and we may say of time, that it is omnipresent. The same moment exists in Europe and America, at Saturn, and at the centre of the earth. The omnipresence of time does not explain the omnipresence of God, but it may help us to admit the possibility of omnipresence without division of essence, or removal of place. But the omnipresence of time is not immensity; for time has its measure, and a moment is not eternity.

It is not derogatory to the dignity and glory of God, that he is present everywhere. There are foul places where human beings would prefer not to be; but they do not affect the Deity as they affect men. The sun-beams fall on them without being polluted; and the holy God cannot be contaminated by them. There are scenes of wickedness, from which a good man will turn away with abhorrence, and, in the figurative language of Scripture, God is "of purer eyes than to behold evil:"[1] yet, in another place of scripture, language no less figurative teaches us that the eyes of God behold the evil as well as the good.[2] He witnesses, while he abhors.

A man who sincerely believes the omnipresence of God, cannot be indifferent to religion. To realize that the moral Governor of the universe is ever near, in all his holiness and power, and as much present as if he were nowhere else, must awaken solicitude. When a sense of guilt oppresses, the presence of such a companion becomes intolerable. The guilty man strives to flee from the presence of God, as Jonah did; but the doctrine of God's omnipresence teaches him that the attempt is unavailing. The power of conscience tormenting the guilty man, wherever he goes, is terrible; but the presence of the God against whom he has sinned, and whose wrath he dreads, is still more terrible. To the soul, reconciled to God, the doctrine is full of consolation. In every place, in every condition, to have with us an almighty friend, a

---

[1] Hab. i. 13.   [2] Prov. xv. 3.

kind father, is a source of unspeakable comfort and joy. We need not fear, though we pass through fire or flood, if God be with us. Even in the valley of the shadow of death, we may fear no evil. In every circumstance and trial, it conduces to holiness, to know that God is present.

SECTION IV. ETERNITY AND IMMUTABILITY.

GOD IS ETERNAL.[1]

IN our knowledge of the objects which surround us, we include not only their present state, but their continued existence, and the changes which they undergo. Some things pass before our eyes, as visions of the moment; others, as the rocks, the sun, the stars, outlast many generations of men. Few living creatures remain in life as long as man; but the shortness of his life is a subject of daily remark, and of impressive scriptural representation.[2] The duration of the deity is exhibited in contrast thus: " Lord, make me know mine end, and the measure of my days, what it is; that I may know how frail I am. Behold, thou hast made my days as a handbreadth, and mine age is as nothing BEFORE THEE."[3] A thousand years, include many of the ordinary generations of mankind; yet, in comparison with God's duration, they are said to be " as yesterday when it is past, and as a watch in the night."[4] To-morrow, while future, may appear to our view, as a duration of considerable length; but yesterday, when it is past, how short it is! An hour of the day, filled with a great variety of incidents, which it might require many hours to narrate, is lengthened out in our view; but how short, how contracted is a watch of the night, in which we sleep and awake, and know not that time has passed! Such, to the view of God, is the long period of a thousand years. To heighten our conception of God's eternity, it is contrasted with the duration of those natural things which appear to possess the greatest stability: "Thou, Lord, in the beginning, hast laid the foundation of the earth, and the heavens are the work of thy hands; they shall perish, but thou remainest; and they all shall wax old as doth a garment: and as a vesture shalt thou fold them up, and they shall be changed; but thou art the same, and thy

---

[1] Deut. xxxii. 40; xxxiii. 27; Ps. ix. 7; xc. 2; cii. 27; cxlvi. 10; Isaiah lvii. 15; lxiii. 16; Jer. x. 10; Lam. v. 19; 1 Tim. i. 17.
[2] 1 Chron. xxix. 15; Job vii. 6; Job ix. 25, 26. [3] Ps. xxxix. 4, 5. [4] Ps. xc. 4.

years shall not fail."[1] But when we have enlarged our conceptions to the utmost, they still utterly fail to comprehend the vast subject. We stretch our thoughts backward and forward; but no beginning or end of God's existence appears. To relieve our over-stretched imagination, and to stop the unavailing effort to comprehend what is incomprehensible, we bring in the negative idea—no beginning, no end. Duration without beginning and without end, becomes the expression of God's eternity.

That every thing, except God, had a beginning, is a doctrine of revelation: "In the beginning, God created the heavens and the earth.[2] This doctrine, philosophy cannot contradict, and perhaps cannot fully demonstrate. But there are manifestations of design, even in unorganized matter, in the kinds and quantities that exist, and the uses to which they are adapted. If matter is eternal, or a production of chance, why is it not all of one kind; and why are the kinds of it, and the proportionate quantities of each, so apparently the result of design? Revelation answers this by the declaration, "In wisdom thou hast made them all.[3]

In contemplating God as the First Cause, we consider his existence uncaused. As we look back through duration past, till we find one existence that is without beginning, so we look back through the long chain of effect and cause, till we have found one existence that is without cause. Sometimes, however, the conception is clothed in language that has not merely negative import. Not satisfied with the merely negative idea, *without cause*, learned men labor to assign a cause for God's existence, and represent it as the cause of itself, or as including its cause within itself. They express this, by saying, that God is self-existent. This mode of expression accommodates our tendency to philosophize; but it perhaps conveys no other intelligible idea, than that God's existence is without cause.

Another philosophical expression, *God necessarily exists*, seems to possess some deep meaning; but when we labor to explore its depths, we shall, perhaps, find in it no other intelligible idea, than that God exists, and has always existed. His existence has always rendered his non-existence impossible, because it is impossible for anything to be, and not to be, at the same time. If philo-

---

[1] Heb. i. 10, 11, 12.   [2] Gen. i. 1.   [3] Ps. civ. 24.

sophy goes behind the existence of God, in search of a cause necessitating his being, she wanders out of her proper province. We may permit her to trace the relation of cause and effect, as far as that relation is to be found; but when she has arrived at the uncaused existence of the eternal One, we should say to her, thus far shalt thou go, and no further.

The eternity of God has been defined, existence without beginning, without end, and without succession. Time with us, is past, present, and future; but God's existence is believed to be a perpetual now. The subject is beyond our comprehension; but it is most reasonable to conclude, that God's mode of existence differs from ours, as it respects time, as well as space; and that, as he exists equally at every point of space, without division of his immensity, so he equally exists at every moment of time, without division of his eternity. Possibly this may be intimated in the Scripture phrase, "inhabiteth eternity."[1] We dwell in time, a habitation with its various apartments; and we pass from one to another in order; but God's habitation is undivided eternity. Our lifetime has its parts, childhood, boyhood, manhood, and old age; but God's life is as indivisible as his essence.

GOD IS UNCHANGEABLE.[2]

The doctrine of God's eternity, and that of his unchangeableness, are nearly allied to each other; and if his eternity excludes succession, it must also exclude the possibility of change. Unchangeableness applies not only to his essence, but also to his attributes. His spirituality is ever the same, his omnipresence the same, and so of the rest. His purpose, also, is unchangeable; it is called "his eternal purpose."[3] He says: "My counsel shall stand."[4] He is said, in Scripture, to repent; but, in the same chapter[5] in which it is twice said that God repented, it is also stated: "He is not a man, that he should repent." We cannot suppose that the sacred writer intended to contradict himself palpably in the compass of a few verses. In accommodation to our modes of speaking, God is said to repent when he effects such a change in his work as would, in human actions, proceed from repentance. Repentance, in men, implies grief of mind, and change of work. The former is

---

[1] Is. lvii. 15.
[2] Num. xxiii. 19; Ps. cii. 27; Mal. iii. 6; Heb. i. 12; xiii. 8; Jas. i. 17.
[3] Eph. iii. 11.   [4] Is. xlvi. 10.   [5] 1 Sam. xv.

5

inconsistent with the perfection of God, but the latter is not. To destroy the world by the deluge, no more implied a change in God than to create it at first. Each act effected a great change, but in both God remained unchanged. No other language could so impressively represent God's abhorrence of man's wickedness to be the cause of the deluge, as that used by the sacred historian : "It repented the Lord that he had made man on the earth, and it grieved him at his heart."[1]

When we contemplate the shortness of human life, and the incessant change of everything with which we have to do on earth, and of ourselves, as we pass from the cradle to the grave, we may well exclaim, as we look up to the eternal and unchangeable God, "Lord, what is man, that thou art mindful of him." A sense of our comparative nothingness is eminently conducive to humility. A view of God's eternity and unchangeableness is necessary to the due exercise of confidence in him. It is folly to trust in uncertain riches, and in the things which perish in the using of them; but we wisely put our trust in the living God. The men with whom we converse are passing away; the condition of life is perpetually changing; we are, in all our relations to earthly things, as if we were on the surface of a restless ocean; but God is as a rock amidst the fluctuating waters; and, while we repose unshaken confidence in him, our feet stand firmly, and we can look without dismay on the troubled scene around us. Men of age receive our reverence, and the counsels of their long experience are highly prized. Who will not reverence the Ancient of Days, the eternal God; and who will reject the counsel of Him, "whose goings forth have been from of old, from everlasting"?[2]

The immutability of God has been made a pretext for restraining prayer before him; but this is wrong. Even if the giving or withholding of the blessings desired were unaffected by the prayer, there still remains sufficient reason for perseverance in offering the petition. The devotional feeling is acceptable to God, and profitable to the soul. If prayer will not bring God to the soul, it will, at least, bring the soul to God. A man in a boat, on a dangerous water, may be saved by means of a rope thrown to him from the shore. When he pulls, though the rock to which the other end of

---

[1] Gen. vi. 6.   [2] Micah v. 2.

the rope may be fastened does not come to the boat, the boat comes to the rock. So prayer brings the soul to God.

But it is not true, that the giving or withholding of the blessing desired is unaffected by the petition presented. Though God is unchangeable, his operation changes in its effect on his creatures, according to their changing character and circumstances. The same sun hardens clay and softens wax. Adam was in God's favor before he sinned; but afterwards was under his displeasure. When a man becomes converted, he is removed from under the wrath of God into a state of favor with him, and all things now work together for his good. In all this, God changes not. God has, in time past, bestowed blessings in answer to prayer, and his unchangeableness encourages the hope that he will do so in time to come. His whole plan has been so arranged, in his infinite wisdom, that many of his blessings are bestowed only in answer to prayer. The connection between the prayer and the bestowment of the blessing, is as fixed by the divine appointment as that between cause and effect in natural things. The unchangeableness of God, therefore, instead of being a reason for restraining prayer, renders prayer indispensable; for our weak petitions have their effect with God, according to his immutable purpose; and, to deny the possibility of this, would be to deny the efficacy of Christ's intercession.

Section V.—OMNISCIENCE.

GOD KNOWS ALL THINGS.[1]

In their stupidity, men have worshipped gods of wood and stone, which, having eyes, see not, and having ears, hear not; but the deity that the Bible makes known, is a God of knowledge.[2] Even natural religion teaches that the maker and governor of the world must possess intelligence; and the degrading idolatry which worshipped birds, four-footed beasts, and creeping things, was contrary to reason, as well as to revelation.

The MODE of God's knowledge we cannot comprehend. Scripture and reason unite in teaching that his thoughts are not as our thoughts. We derive our best conception of his knowledge from our own mental operations; but we ought to be careful not to think

---

[1] Job xxxvii. 16; Ps. cxlvii. 5; Is. xlii. 9; xlvi. 9, 10; Acts i. 24; Rom. xi. 33; Heb. iv. 13; 1 John iii. 20.   [2] 1 Sam. ii. 3.

of him as altogether such an one as ourselves. As he differs from all creatures, in mode of presence and of duration, so he differs, in mode of knowledge, from all other intelligent beings.

God does not *acquire* knowledge after our mode. We acquire knowledge of external objects by means of our bodily senses; but God has no body, and no organs of sense like ours. We learn the less obvious relations of things by processes of reasoning, which are often tedious and laborious, but God has no labor to acquire knowledge, and suffers no delay in attaining it. All things are naked, and open to his eyes.[1] We learn much by the testimony of others; but God is not dependent for knowledge on information received from any of his creatures. We obtain knowledge of our own mental operations by means of consciousness; and, as this is without any process of reasoning, and not by our bodily senses, or the testimony of others, it may give us the best possible conception of God's mode of knowledge. All things which he knows are before his mind as immediately and completely as the states and operations of our minds are before our consciousness; but our best conceptions fall infinitely short of the incomprehensible subject. As the heavens are higher than the earth, so are his thoughts higher than our thoughts.[2]

God does not *hold* his knowledge *in possession*, after our mode. The great store-house of our knowledge is memory, a wonderful faculty, with which the human mind is endowed. Without it, all knowledge would pass from the mind, as the image passes from a mirror, when the object producing it has gone by. But if God's duration is without succession, there is, with him, no past to remember; and therefore memory, with him, is something wholly different from what it is with us. His whole mode of life differs so widely from ours, that we cannot attribute human faculties to him, without degrading his divinity.

In our study of God's attributes, it is important to remember, at every step of our progress, that they are all incomprehensible to us. We should do this, not only for the sake of humility, but to guard us against erroneous inferences, which we are liable to draw from our imperfect conceptions of the divine nature. It is instructive to notice how far the elements of these conceptions are

---

[1] Heb. iv. 13.   [2] Is. lv. 9.

derived from what we know of our own minds. No combination of such elements can possibly give us adequate conceptions of the eternal and infinite Mind. Even the Holy Scriptures, which reveal God to us, do not supply the elementary conceptions necessary to a perfect knowledge of God. They speak to human beings in human language, and the knowledge which they impart is sufficient for our present necessities, and able to make us wise to salvation; but we should remember, that human language cannot express to us what the human mind cannot conceive, and, therefore, cannot convey a full knowledge of the deity.

Much of human knowledge consists of mere negations. Frequent exemplifications of this occur in our study of the divine attributes. What God's spirituality is, we cannot positively know; but we know that it is *not* matter. What God's eternity is, we cannot comprehend; but, in our labor to comprehend it, we stretch our positive conception of duration to the utmost possible extent, and at length seek relief in the negative ideas — without beginning, without end, without succession. These negations mark the imperfection of our knowledge. God's knowledge is direct and positive, and he seeks no relief in the negations that we find so convenient.

God does not *use* his knowledge after our mode. For the proper directing of actions, knowledge is necessary, both of things actually existing, and of things, the existence of which is merely possible. Our minds possess both these kinds of knowledge to a limited extent, and use them in an imperfect manner. In the study of history and geography we acquire knowledge of things which are, or have been, in actual existence. Arithmetic treats of number, and geometry of magnitude; but these sciences do not teach the actual existence of anything. By reasoning from the abstract relations and properties of things, our minds are capable of determining what would, or might exist, in supposed cases; and, by this process, our knowledge extends into the department of things possible. This knowledge is necessary to choice; and, therefore, to voluntary action. If but one thing were possible, there would be no room for choice; and we must know the things possible, before we can choose. God has perfect knowledge of things possible, and these depend on his power. He has, also, perfect knowledge of things actual, and these depend on his will. He knew how many worlds he could create, and how many kinds of plants and animals; and out of these he chose what worlds, plants, and animals, should exist. According to our mode of conception, the knowledge of things possible precedes the will or purpose of God, and the knowledge of things actual follows it. But we dare not affirm that there is any succession of thought in the divine mind. How God uses his knowledge, in counsel, or in action, we cannot comprehend.

The EXTENT of God's knowledge is unlimited. He knows all things; all things possible, and all things actual. He knows himself perfectly, though unknown by any other being. The attributes which we labor in vain to comprehend, he understands fully. His ways, to us unsearchable, are fully known to him from the beginning of his works. All creatures are known to him, and everything that appertains to them: the angels of heaven, the men who inhabit the earth, and every living thing, even to the sparrow, or young ravens, he knows, and carefully regards. The thoughts of the mind he understands, and the secrets of every heart he fully searches.

All events, past, present, or future, are known to God. Past events are said to be remembered by him; and he claims the foreknowledge of future events, challenging false gods to a comparison with him in this respect.[1] His foreknowledge of future events is proved by the numerous predictions contained in the Bible, that have proceeded from him. It was given to the Israelites,[2] as a rule for distinguishing a true prophet of the Lord, that his predictions should be fulfilled; but a foreknowledge of future events could not be imparted to them from the Lord, if the Lord himself did not possess it.

The *mode* of God's *foreknowledge* we cannot comprehend. He sees present things not as man sees, and remembers the past not in he manner of human memory. It is, therefore, not surprising that we cannot comprehend the mode of his knowledge; and especially of his foreknowledge, in which we, least of all, resemble him. We have some knowledge of the present and the past; but of the future we have no absolute knowledge. We know causes at present existing, from which we infer that future events will take place; but an absolute foreknowledge of these future events we do not

---

[1] Is. xli. 22.   [2] Deut. xviii. 22.

possess. Some cause, of which we are now not aware, may intervene, and disappoint our expectation. The phenomena of nature,
which we expect with the greatest confidence, such as the rising of
the sun, the occurrence of an eclipse, are foreknown only on the
condition that the present laws of nature shall continue to operate,
without change or suspension. But the Author of Nature may
interpose, and change the present order of things. On the supposition that God has a perfect knowledge of all the causes now operating; that there are fixed laws which determine the succession of
events; and that God perfectly understands these laws; we may
comprehend that God can infallibly predict things to come. No
being but himself can interfere with the order of things which he
has established. This mode of foreknowledge we can, in some
measure, conceive; but the supposition which it involves, that all
events take place according to an established order of sequence,
many are unwilling to admit. They maintain that events dependent on the volitions of free agents, do not so occur; and, therefore,
cannot be foreknown after this manner.

Some, who adopt the view last mentioned, deny that God foreknows future events, dependent on human volitions. They nevertheless attribute omniscience to him, and .understand it to be *the
power of knowing all things.* They say that, as omnipotence signifies a power to do all things, without the doing of them, so
omniscience signifies the power to know all things, without the
knowing of them. There is clearly a mistake here in language.
As omnipotence signifies all power, so omniscience signifies all
knowledge; and God does not possess omniscience, if he possesses
merely the power to know, without the knowledge itself. But it
may be questioned, whether, according to the theory, God has even
the power to know. The power of God might have excluded such
contingencies from existence; but, after having opened the door, it
is difficult to understand how any power could foreknow, what things
will enter, if they are in their nature unforeknowable. But the
strongest possible objection lies against the theory, in that it is
opposed to fact. God has predicted very many events dependent
on innumerable volitions of free agents, and, therefore, must have
foreknown them. Those who have advocated this theory, in connection with the opinion, that the duration of God is an eternal
now, and that there is strictly speaking, neither foreknowledge nor

after-knowledge with him; fix narrow limits to the divine omni-science. If God's knowledge is unchangeable, and if he has no foreknowledge of contingencies, he can have no after-knowledge of them. But the whole history of mankind is dependent on contingencies; being filled with them, and events depending on them. All this must be a blank to the view of God. Men may know this history, and it may be written out in ten thousand volumes; but God knows it not, for, though he possesses the power to know, he has determined not to exercise it. How then shall God judge the world?

Human beings have two modes of knowing past events; one, by memory; the other, by inferring their existence from the effects which have followed. One man remembers that a house was burned down, having seen the flames of its combustion; another knows that it was burned down, because he sees its ashes. In one mode, memory runs back along the line of time; in the other, reason runs back along the line of cause and effect. The only mode which we have of knowing future events, is by the reasoning process. Whether God has a method, analogous rather to our memory or perception, than to our reason; it is impossible for us to determine. If he has, we cannot conceive of it, because there is nothing like it in ourselves; but the absence of such a power in us, by no means proves its non-existence in God. Some have imagined that God looks down the vista of time, and sees future events, as we see a traveller approaching when he is yet at a distance from us. But the cases are not analogous. We see the traveller *coming*, not *having come;* what is present, as to time, and not what is future. His arrival, the future event, we know only by a process of reasoning. The supposition is, that God has an immediate perception of the future event, without any intervening process of reasoning. To say that he sees it, expresses this figuratively, but does not explain it.

The doctrine that there is no succession in the eternity of God, neither denies nor explains his foreknowledge. 1. *It does not deny.* Some have maintained that there is, strictly speaking, neither foreknowledge nor after-knowledge with God; and this may be admitted, if foreknowledge necessarily implies succession of thought. But the foreknowledge which we attribute to God, is not knowledge antecedent to something else in the divine mind, but knowledge antecedent to the event foreknown. From God's knowledge predictions of future events have proceeded. Such knowledge, in a human mind, would be foreknowledge; and, in human language, this is its proper name. 2. *It does not explain.* The doctrine teaches that all times and events, past, present, and future, are alike present to God. The overthrow of Babylon by Cyrus, and the prediction thereof by Isaiah, are both historical events; and, as such, are supposed to have been alike present to the mind of God from the beginning of the world. Now, the fact that the overthrow was present to the mind of God, could not be the cause of the revelation made to the prophet, and of the prediction which followed; for, according to the doctrine, the prediction was already as much present to the mind of God as the event predicted; and, therefore, its existence must be as much presupposed in the order of cause and effect. Hence, to account for this, or any other prediction, we are compelled to admit that God has a mode of foreknowledge, into the nature of which the doctrine of the perpetual now gives us no insight.

But why should we indulge ourselves in vain speculations, or exhaust ourselves with needless efforts? We are like children who wade into the ocean, to learn its depth by the measure of their little stature, and who exclaim, almost at their first step, O! how deep! Even Paul, when laboring to fathom this subject, exclaimed, "O the depth of the riches both of the wisdom and knowledge of God! how unsearchable are his judgments, and his ways past finding out!"[1]

In comparison with God's infinite intelligence, how little is all human knowledge! We honor Newton, and other giants of intellect that have appeared in the progress of our race; but their highest glory was, to know a very little of God's ways. Let every power of our minds bend before his infinite understanding, with deep humility and devout adoration. We study our own minds, and find in them much that we cannot explain; and when we use the little knowledge of them to which we can attain, in our labored efforts to understand something of God, an important part of its use consists in convincing us that we cannot find out God, and that his thoughts are not as our thoughts.

As intelligent beings, we may contemplate the omniscience of

---

[1] Rom. xi. 33.

God with devout admiration ; and as guilty beings, we should fear and tremble before it.   He sees the inmost recesses of the heart. The hateful thoughts which we are unwilling a fellow-worm should know, are all known to him, and every thought, word, and deed, he remembers, and will bring into judgment.   How terrible is this attribute of the Great Judge, who will expose the secrets of every heart, and reward every man according to his works, though un-observed or forgotten by men !

But with all the *awe* which invests it, this attribute of the Divine Nature, is delightful to the pious man.   He rejoices to say, Thou, God, seest me.   He prays, Try me, and see if there be any wicked way in me, and lead me into the way everlasting.   Gladly he com-mits himself to the guidance of him who has all knowledge.   Con-scious of his own blindness and darkness, he knows not which way to take, or what is best for him ; but he puts himself, with un-wavering confidence, into the hands of the omniscient God.

Section VI.—OMNIPOTENCE.

GOD IS ABLE TO DO WHATEVER HE PLEASES.[1]

Our first idea of power, is probably derived from the control which we possess over our muscles, and the use which we make of them, to produce effects on things about us.   Our limbs and voice become the instruments of our power; and, in the using of them for effecting our purpose, the notion of power arises.   We transfer this notion, and incorporate it into the conception which we form of other intelligent beings like ourselves; and it thus becomes an element in our conception of the deity.   In the material world, causes are followed by their effects in a manner similar to that in which effects are produced by the motion of our limbs; and the material causes are said to have power.   It is thus we speak of the power of steam, or of an engine.

We know well that our power is limited.   Many things which we attempt we fail to accomplish.   To conceive of omnipotence, we introduce, as in other cases, the negative idea, *without fail*.   This, however, does not exclude the idea of attempt, desire, or will.   It derogates nothing from the omnipotence of God, that he does not accomplish what he has no desire or will to accomplish.   It is im-

---

[1] Gen. xvii. 1; Job. v. 9; Jer. xxxii. 17; Matt. xix. 26; Rev. i. 8; xix. 6.

possible for God to lie, or to deny himself; but these are things which he does not please to do, because they are inconsistent with his moral perfections. Nor would the doing of these things be any indication of supreme power. It is also true, that God cannot do things which imply contradiction in themselves; as, to make a thing to be, and not to be, at the same time; to make a circle to be at the same time a square, &c. If finite power fails to accomplish such things, it fails not because it is finite, but because the things are impossible. No measure of power could come nearer to success. Impotence is as good as omnipotence for accomplishing impossibilities.

We are filled with awe in contemplating the omnipotence of God. When we hear the voice of his thunder in the heavens, or feel the earth quake under the tread of his foot, how do solemn thoughts of things divine fill our minds! From the rending cloud, and the quaking earth, let us look back to the power which brought creation into being, and forward to that display of his power which we are to witness on the last day. Such a being, who will not fear? Our minds exercise their power through our bodies, to which, therefore, the immediate exercise of it is limited; and even over these the power is confined within narrow limits; for we cannot add one cubit to our stature, or make one hair white or black. But God has everything in the universe under his immediate and perfect control. He needs no instruments, no mechanical aid, no series of contrivances; but, at his will the thing is done, whether it be the production of an animalcule, or the creation of a world. At our will, a finger moves; but at the volition of God, a planet is launched in its orbit, with a force of which the cannon-ball gives but a very faint conception. Hurricanes, which sweep the earth, and lift up the dwellings, and the very bodies of men, in the air, have their power. The ocean, which sports with mighty ships, has its power. The volcano, which bursts forth with such awful grandeur, has its power. But when we have combined the force of air, ocean, and subterranean fire, we must multiply it by the number of such agencies which are operating, through all the worlds in the whole of God's vast empire, before we can begin to conceive adequately of his omnipotence. Lo, these are parts of his ways; but the thunder of his power, who can understand?[1]

---

[1] Job xxvi. 14.

Section VII.—GOODNESS.

GOD IS INFINITELY BENEVOLENT.[1]

God's goodness, as exercised towards his creatures, is often expressed in the Scriptures by the term love. Love is distinguished as benevolence, beneficence, or complacence. Benevolence is love in intention or disposition; beneficence is love in action, or conferring its benefits; and complacence is the approbation of good actions or dispositions. Goodness, exercised toward the unworthy, is called grace; toward the suffering, it is called pity, or mercy. The latter term intimates that the suffering, or liability to suffer, arises from the just displeasure of God.

Goodness implies a disposition to produce happiness. We are conscious of pleasure and pain in ourselves, and we know that we can, to some extent, cause pleasure or pain in others. Continued pleasure is happiness; continued pain, misery. God is able to produce happiness or misery, when, and to whatever extent he pleases. Which of these is it the disposition of his infinite nature to produce?

God's goodness may be argued from the manifestations of it in the works of creation. The world is peopled with sentient beings, capable of pleasure; and sources of pleasure are everywhere provided for them. Every sense of every animal is an inlet of pleasure; and for every sense the means of pleasure are provided. What God gives them they gather. His open hand pours enjoyments into their existence at every moment. When we consider the innumerable living creatures that are, at this moment, receiving pleasure from the abundant and varied stores which his creating power has furnished; and when we reflect, that this stream of bounty has flowed incessantly from the creation of the world, we may well consider the fountain from which it has descended as infinite.

It demonstrates the goodness of God, that the pleasures which his creatures enjoy do not come incidentally, but are manifestly the result of contrivance. Food would nourish without the pleasure experienced in eating. We might have been so constituted as to

---

[1] Ex. xxxiv. 6; Ps. ciii. 2–8; Zech. ix. 17; Matt. vii. 11; Luke ii. 14; xii. 32; Rom. v. 8; 1 John iv. 8.

be driven to take it by hunger, and to receive it with pain, but little less than that produced by the want of it. But God has superadded pleasure where it was not absolutely necessary, and has made the very support of animal existence a source of perpetual gratification.

It adds greatly to the force of this argument, that indications of malevolent design are not found in the works of God. Pain is, indeed, often experienced, but it never appears to result from an arrangement specially made for receiving it. There is no organ of our body to which we can point, and say, this was specially designed to give us pain.

Mere animal enjoyment is not the highest that God bestows. To his intelligent creatures he has opened another source in the pursuit and acquisition of knowledge. We need knowledge, as well as food; and we might be driven to seek it by a painful necessity, without deriving any pleasure from it. But here, again, the benevolence of the Creator is manifested. Pleasure is superadded when we acquire necessary knowledge; and, when the progress has reached the limit of our necessities, the pleasure does not cease. The intellectual appetite is never satiated to loathing.

But God has made us susceptible of far higher and nobler pleasure in the exercise of virtue and religion. To this he has adapted our moral nature, rendering us capable both of the exercise and the enjoyment. For the exercise of virtue and religion, the constitution of human society, and the various relations which we sustain in its organization, furnish abundant occasion; and in the moral sense of mankind, and the approbation which virtue extorts, even when the tribute is not spontaneously rendered, a source of enjoyment is opened. In the proper exercise of our moral powers, we are capable of loving and enjoying God; and, therefore, of experiencing a happiness that infinitely transcends all other enjoyment. This ocean of infinite fulness, this source of eternal and exhaustless happiness, gives the full demonstration of God's infinite goodness. And this enjoyment, also, never cloys; but, with the progress, the delight increases.

The doctrine of God's goodness, notwithstanding the abundance of its proofs, is attended with difficulties. Though sentient beings are not furnished with organs purposely prepared for the receiving of pain, they have organs for inflicting it, which are unquestionably the result of contrivance. The fangs of serpents, and the stings of insects, are instances of this kind; and to these may be added the talons and tusks, or beaks, with which carnivorous animals rend their prey. How is the existence of such pain-inflicting contrivances to be reconciled with the infinite goodness of God? How can we explain, in harmony with this doctrine, the suffering which animals endure from the violence of each other, from hunger, cold, and disease? Above all, how can we reconcile the innumerable miseries with which human society is filled, in every rank and condition of life? If God is infinitely good, why is human life begun in pain, and closed in pain, and subject to pain throughout its whole course?

These difficulties are of too much magnitude to be overlooked. They perplex the understanding, and disquiet the heart; and, therefore, demand a careful and candid consideration. The following observations are offered, to guard the heart against their influence.

1. Admit the existence of the difficulties in their full force, and what then? Does it follow that God is a malevolent being? Were he so, the proofs of his malevolence would abound, as those of his goodness now do. We should everywhere find animal senses adapted to be the inlets of misery, and the objects of these senses all adapted to give pain. Does it follow that God is indifferent whether his creatures are happy or miserable? The numerous provisions which are made with a manifest reference to animal enjoyment, forbid this supposition. Does it follow that God is capricious? This conclusion is precluded by the fact, that what suffering there is in the world, runs throughout along with its enjoyments; the happiness and the misery are entwined with each other, and form parts of the same system. By summing up the whole, we discover that animal life has more enjoyment than suffering, and that its pains are, in most cases, incidental. In our daily experience, blessings are poured upon us incessantly; and when suffering comes, we are often conscious that it arises from our abuse of God's goodness, and is, therefore, no argument against it. In many other cases, we find present suffering conducive to future good; and we have reason to believe that it would always be so, if we endured it with a proper spirit, and made a wise improvement of it. It becomes us, therefore, when sufferings occur, the bene-

ficial tendency of which we cannot discover, to remember that we comprehend but a very small part of God's way. We have found every other attribute of his nature incomprehensible to us, and it ought not to surprise us that his goodness is so.

The sufferings which we experience in ourselves, or see in others, become an occasion for the trial of our faith. To the understanding of a child, the discipline of his father may appear neither wise nor kind. Indulgences which are craved may be denied; and toils and privations, exceedingly unwelcome, may be imposed. In these circumstances, it is the child's duty to confide where it cannot comprehend. So we should exercise faith in the wisdom and goodness of our heavenly Father, and believe that his ways are full of goodness, even when they are inscrutable. Enough of his goodness is seen elsewhere to satisfy us of its existence when mystery hides it from view.

2. It cannot be proved that an admixture of pain with the large measure of enjoyment which God bestows on his creatures, is inconsistent with his goodness. The insect of a day, and the immortal near the throne of God, derive their enjoyment from the same infinite goodness. If the short-lived insect should pass its few hours in the sunbeams without pain, and should be annihilated without pain, the difficulty which now embarrasses us would not apply to its case. Its existence, filled with enjoyment, would correspond with our notions of the Creator's goodness; and the finiteness, or very small measure of its enjoyment, would not disprove the source to be infinite from which it proceeds. Now, if a creature of another kind should have enjoyments a hundred fold greater, with an abatement of one measure of pain, its existence, on the whole, is ninety-nine times more desirable than that of the insect. Shall we, then, deny that this existence proceeds from the goodness of the deity? If the pain forms a part of the same system with the pleasure, we must attribute them to the same author; and the animal that has ninety-nine measures of enjoyment remaining, has no more right to complain of the abatement of one by the endurance of pain, than the insect supposed would have to complain of the absence of ninety-nine measures which the more favored creature enjoys. This consideration may satisfy us that the presence of some pain, connected with a far greater amount of enjoyment, is not inconsistent with the doctrine that God is infinitely good.

Furthermore, it is perfectly conceivable that pain itself may, in some cases, enhance our pleasures, as relief from suffering renders subsequent enjoyment more exquisite : and, in other ways, which we are unable to comprehend, pain may produce a beneficial result. In this view, the existence of pain cannot be inconsistent with the goodness of God.

3. Much of the suffering in the world is clearly the effect of sin, and is to be considered an infliction of divine justice. The justice of God claims scope for its exercise, as well as his goodness. The goodness of God is infinite, if it confers happiness as widely as is consistent with the other perfections of his nature. It is a favorite theory with some, that God aims at the greatest possible amount of happiness in the universe ; and that he admits evil, only because the admission of evil produces in the end a greater amount of happiness than its exclusion would have done. According to this theory, justice itself is a modification of benevolence ; and the pain suffered by one being, is inflicted from love to the whole. But whether justice be a modification of benevolence, or a distinct attribute, its claims must be regarded ; and goodness does not cease to be goodness, because it does not overthrow the government of God, or oppose his other perfections.

Some persons attribute all the sufferings of brute animals to the sin of man, but the Scriptures do not clearly teach this doctrine ; and we have shown that the pain which brutes endure, may be otherwise reconciled with the goodness of God. That animals suffer because of man's sin, is clear in the cruelty which they often experience from human hands ; but that all their sufferings proceed from this cause is not so clear. Unless the order of things was greatly changed at the fall of man, hawks had their claws and beaks from the day they were created, and used them before man sinned, in taking and devouring other birds for food ; and, therefore, pain and death, in brute animals, did not enter the world by the sin of man. Brute animals have, on the whole, a happy existence. Free from anxiety, remorse, and the fear of death, they enjoy, with high relish, the pleasures which their Creator has given them ; and it is not the less a gift of his infinite goodness, because it is limited in quantity, or abated by some mixture of pain.

4. It may be, that God's goodness is not mere love of happiness. In his view, happiness may not be the only good, or even the chief

good. He is himself perfectly happy; yet this perfection of his nature is not presented to us, in his word, as the only ground, or even the chief ground, on which his claim to divine honor and worship rests. The hosts of heaven ascribe holiness to him, and worship him because of it; but not because of his happiness. .If we could contemplate him as supremely happy, but deriving his happiness from cruelty, falsehood, and injustice, we should need a different nature from that with which he has endowed us, and a different Bible to direct us from that which he has given, before we could render him sincere and heart-felt adoration. In the regulation of our conduct, when pleasure and duty conflict with each other, we are required to choose the latter; and this is often made the test of our obedience. On the same principle, if a whole life of duty and a whole life of enjoyment were set before us, that we might choose between them, we should be required to prefer holiness to happiness. It therefore accords with the judgment of God not to regard happiness as the chief good; and the production of the greatest possible amount of happiness could not have been his prime object in the creation of the world. We may conclude that his goodness is not a weak fondness which indulges his creatures, and administers to their enjoyment, regardless of their conduct and moral character. It aims at their happiness, but in subordination to a higher and nobler purpose. According to the order of things which he has established, it is rendered impossible for an unholy being to be happy, and this order accords with the goodness of God, which aims, not at the mere happiness of his universe, but at its well-being, in the best possible sense.

If these views are correct, the miseries which sin has introduced into the world, instead of disproving the goodness of God, proceed from it, and demonstrate it. They are means used by the great Father of all, in the discipline of his great family, to deter from the greatest of all evils. Precisely this use the wisdom from above teaches us to make of his judgments and threatenings; and when these awful means have taught us the evil of sin, and have been blessed to us as means of sanctification, we may perceive in them a manifestation of God's goodness.

5. To infer the infinitude of God's goodness from its effects, we must view them in the aggregate. The perfection of his justice appears in its minute and precise adaptation to each particular

6

case. Every part of his administration must, when brought to the line of rectitude for comparison, be found to agree with it precisely. But as in estimating the length of a line, we do not examine its parts, so the infinitude of God's goodness must be judged from the aggregate of its effects, as we learn the power of God, not from a single grain of sand, but from the whole extent of creation.

To comprehend this vast subject, we need the infinite mind of God himself. In events which now appear to us dark and mysterious, the seeds of future benefits to his creatures may be wrapped up, which will bring forth their fruit hereafter, for the use of admiring and adoring intelligences. The parts of the great system are so wonderfully adjusted to each other, that no finite being dare say that this is useless, or that pernicious or hurtful. Why God has made precisely such orders of creatures as inhabit the world with us, and why he has appointed to them their various modes of life, with the advantages and inconveniences peculiar to each, we are wholly unable to say; and, if we undertake to say why he has made any creatures at all, we may assign a reason which we think we understand, but of which, in reality, we know but little. If the united intelligence of the universe could lift up its voice to God, as the voice of one creature, and say, "Why hast thou made me thus?" it would be daring impiety. How unbecoming then for man, who is a worm, to arraign the wisdom and goodness of his Maker!

The goodness of God is the attribute of his nature, which, above all others, draws forth the affection of our hearts. We are filled with awe at his eternity, omnipresence, omniscience, and omnipotence; but we can imagine all these attributes connected with moral qualities which would render them repulsive. But the goodness of God, while it is awful and grand, is at the same time powerfully attractive. It is this, when understood in its proper sense, not as the mere love of happiness, that renders Jehovah the proper centre of the moral universe. It is this that attracts the hearts of all holy intelligences now in heaven, and that is drawing to that high and holy place whatever on earth is most lovely and excellent; and if the hearts of any repel this centre, and recede further from it, they are "wandering stars, to whom is reserved the blackness of darkness forever."

Section VIII.—TRUTH.

GOD IS A BEING OF INVIOLABLE TRUTH.[1]

The truth of God includes veracity and faithfulness:—veracity in his declaration of things as they are, and faithfulness in the exact fulfilment of his promises and threatenings. Men often err in their testimony from mistake of facts, and fail through inability to fulfil promises which they have made with honest intentions. The omniscience of God renders mistake with him impossible; and his omnipotence and unchangeableness render the fulfilment of his intentions certain. Truth, as a moral attribute, is the agreement of what is spoken with the mind of the speaker. We never charge men with want of veracity, when they err in their testimony through mere mistake; or with want of faithfulness, when they fail to fulfil their promises entirely from inability. God's testimony is true, because it agrees perfectly with his view of things, and that this view agrees with the actual state of things, results, not from his truth, but his omniscience. His promises are true because they agree precisely with his intentions; and that these intentions are exactly fulfilled, results from other attributes, as has been explained. Truth is understood for the most part to refer to something spoken or written; but the truth of God may be understood, in a wider sense, to denote the agreement of all the revelations or manifestations which he has made of himself, with his mind and character.

Because God's manifestations of himself are true, it does not follow that they are complete and perfect. He showed his glory to Moses; but it was only a part of his glory that he exhibited, because Moses was unable to bear the full display. All manifestations to his creatures are necessarily limited; and they are made as seems good in his sight. Our knowledge of God, which is necessarily imperfect because of our weakness, is often erroneous, through our misuse of the manifestations which he has made. So the heathen world, when they knew God, glorified him not as God, but changed the truth of God into a lie.

When men abuse the knowledge of God which they possess, and

---

[1] Deut. xxxii. 4; Ps. cxix. 142; John viii. 26; Rom. iii. 4; Tit. i. 2; Heb. vi. 18; Rev. iii. 7.

the means of knowledge which he has afforded them, it is not inconsistent with his character to give them up, in righteous judgment, to their own hearts' lusts. Because they receive not the love of the truth, God shall send them strong delusions,[1] that they should believe a lie. So Ahab desired a false prophecy, and his prophets desired to gratify him, and God gave him up to be deceived.[2] This is expressed, in the prophetic imagery of Scripture, by his sending a lying spirit into the prophets. Ahab was deceived; but it was in spite of the true word of God, by the prophet whom he rejected. Jeremiah complains that God had deceived him; but this, in the most unfavorable construction that can be put on his language, amounts to nothing more than an impatient exclamation of the prophet, under a severe trial.

We can have no knowledge of God, except by the manifestations he has made of himself. When we receive these, however made, as expressing to us the mind and character of God, we exercise faith in God But when we close our understandings and hearts against these manifestations, or, through disrelish of them, misinterpret them in any manner, we are guilty of the great sin of unbelief, which rejects the testimony of God, and makes him a liar.

Section IX. —JUSTICE.

GOD IS PERFECTLY JUST.[3]

Justice consists in giving to every one his due. It has been distinguished into Commutative and Distributive. Commutative Justice is fair dealing in the exchange of commodities, and belongs to commerce. Distributive Justice rewards or punishes men according to their actions, and appertains to government. In either view, justice relates to the distribution of happiness, or the means of procuring it, and presupposes a principle or rule to which this distribution should conform, and, according to which, something is *due* to the parties. Commutative Justice regulates the giving of one means of enjoyment in exchange for another, so as not to disturb the proportion of happiness allotted to each; but Distributive Justice rises higher, and respects the very allotment or distribution of happiness, giving to one, and withholding from another, according

---

[1] 2 Thess. ii. 11.   [2] 1 Kings, xxii.
[3] Job xxxiv. 12; Ps. ix. 4; xcii. 15; Isaiah xxviii. 17; Rom. ii. 6.

to rule. It is in the latter sense only that justice is attributed to God. It implies the existence of moral government; and it is the attribute which secures a faithful and perfect administration of this government.

Some have admitted another distinction, to which the name Public Justice has been given. This determines the character of God's moral government, and the rules according to which it proceeds. It may be regarded as a question of definition, whether the existence and character of God's moral government shall be ascribed to his justice or his goodness. As this government tends to the greatest good of the universe, there appears to be no reason to deny that it originates in the goodness of God; and if it be ascribed to his Public Justice, that justice may be considered a modification of his goodness.

In the moral government of God, men are regarded as moral and as sentient beings, and the amount of their enjoyments is regulated with reference to their moral character. The precise adaptation of this is the province of justice. In the blindness of human depravity, men claim enjoyments as a natural right, irrespective of their moral character and conduct. They reject the moral government of God, and seek happiness in their own way. This is their rebellion, and in this the justice of God opposes them. This is the attribute which fills them with terror, and arrays omnipotence against them. The moral government of God must be overthrown, and the monarch of the universe driven from his high seat of authority, or there is no hope of escape for the sinner. He would gladly rush into the vast storehouse of enjoyments which infinite goodness has provided, and claim them as his own, and riot on them at pleasure; but the sword of justice guards the entrance. In opposition to his desires, the government of God is firmly established, and justice and judgment are the habitation of his throne. Even in the present world, the manifestations of this government are everywhere visible; and it is apparent that there is a God, a God of justice, who judgeth in the earth; but the grand exhibition is reserved for the judgment of the great day. Conscience now, in God's stead, often pronounces sentence, though its voice is unheeded; but the sentence from the lips of the Supreme Judge cannot be disregarded, and will fix the sinner's final doom.

Although there are hearts so hard as to be unaffected by a sense of God's justice, a right view of this awful and glorious attribute inspires that fear of the Lord which is the beginning of wisdom. An abiding assurance that a just God sits on the throne of the universe, is indispensable to the proper exercise of piety.

Section X.—HOLINESS.

GOD IS IMMACULATELY HOLY.[1]

Goodness, truth and justice, are moral attributes of God. Holiness is not an attribute distinct from these; but a name which includes them all, in view of their opposition to contrary qualities. It implies the perfection of the assemblage;—the absence of every thing in it contrary to either of the properties included.

Men are unholy. Even the purest of men have their spots. It is useful to contrast the character of God, in this respect, with that of men. It increases our admiration and love, adds fervor to our devotion, incites to worship him in the beauty of holiness, and to imitate him in our character and lives. "Be ye holy, for I am holy."

Section XI.—WISDOM.

GOD IS INFINITELY WISE.[2]

Knowledge and wisdom, though often confounded by careless thinkers, are different. Wisdom always has respect to action. Our senses are affected by external objects, and perceptions of them arise in the mind, which constitute a large part of our knowledge. We learn their properties and relations, and this knowledge, laid up in the memory, becomes a valuable store, from which we may take what may be necessary for use. But it is in using this store that wisdom is exhibited. When impressions from without have stirred the mental machinery within, that machinery, in turn, operates on things without. It is in the out-goings of the mind that wisdom has place, and is concerned in forming our plans and purposes of action. Our knowledge and moral principles have much influence in directing our conduct, and that man is considered wise, whose knowledge and moral principles direct his conduct well.

---

[1] Ex. xv. 11; Lev. xi. 44; 1 Sam. ii. 2; Job. iv. 18; Ps. v. 4, 5; xxii. 3; Isa. vi. 3; Hab. i. 13; Matt. v. 48; 1 John i. 5; Rev. iv. 8.

[2] Job iv. 18; xxxvi. 5; Ps. civ. 24; Prov. xxi. 30; Rom. xi. 33; 1 Cor. i. 25. 1 Tim. i. 17.

Wisdom is therefore regarded as consisting in the selection of the best end of action, and the adoption of the best means for the accomplishment of this end.

God is infinitely wise, because he selects the best possible end of action. What the end is which Jehovah has in view in all his works, we cannot claim to comprehend. The Scriptures speak of the glory of God as the end of creation and redemption, and we seem authorized to speak of this as the end of all his works; but what is the full import of the phrase, "the glory of God?" We suppose it to signify such a manifestation of his perfections, and especially of his moral perfections, as is supremely pleasing to himself, and therefore to all intelligent beings who are like-minded with him. But we are lost in the contemplation.

God is infinitely wise, because he adopts the best possible means for the accomplishment of the end which he has in view. In creation his wisdom made them all;[1] and in redemption he hath abounded toward us in all wisdom.[2] He worketh all things after the counsel of his will;[3] and he is wise in counsel.

The wisdom of God is an unfathomable deep. His way is in the sea, and his path in the mighty waters. O the depth of the riches both of the wisdom and knowledge of God![4] A child cannot comprehend the plans of a sage statesman; much less can the wisest of men comprehend the plans of the only wise God. We should ever bear this in mind when we undertake to inquire into the reasons of the divine procedure.

The question, why God permitted the entrance of sin into the world, has baffled the wisdom of the wise. As a being of perfect holiness, he hates sin with a perfect hatred. Having infinite power to exclude it from his dominions, why did he permit its entrance? As the benevolent Father of his great family, why did he permit so ruinous an evil to invade it? Was there some oversight in his plan, some failure in the wisdom of his arrangements, that rendered this direful disaster possible? As our faith is often perplexed with these questions, such observations as the following may be of use to assist its weakness.

1. Sin is in the world; and God is infinitely good and wise. The first of these propositions expresses a fact of which we have

---

[1] Ps. civ. 24.   [2] Eph. i. 8.   [3] Eph. i. 11.   [4] Rom. xi. 33.

daily proof, before our eyes and in our hearts; the second is an indubitable truth of natural and revealed religion. Though we may be unable to reconcile these propositions, they are both worthy to be received with unwavering faith. No man, in his right mind, can doubt either of them.

2. The existence of sin is not to be ascribed to weakness in God. He could easily have barred it out of his dominions. He might have declined to make moral agents, and have filled the world with creatures possessing no moral faculties, and therefore incapable of sinning. Or, for aught that appears to the contrary, it was in his power to create moral agents, and so confirm them in holiness from the first, as to render their fall impossible. Or, on the very first appearance of sin in any one of his creatures, he might have at once annihilated the transgressor, and have prevented the evil from spreading, to the ruin of his subjects, or even remaining in his dominions. If we can, for a moment, entertain doubt on this point, his perfect control of the evil, now that it has obtained entrance into his dominion, is sufficient to confirm our faith. It has indeed entered, and the prince of the power of the air is combined with his numerous legions, to give it prevalence and triumph. But, to destroy the works of the devil, the son of God appeared in human nature. He chose the weakness of that nature for the display of his power, in crushing the head of the old serpent. Hence Christ is the power of God. In his deepest humiliation, in the hour while hanging on the cross, he triumphed over his foe, and gave proof of his triumphant power, by plucking the thief, who expired near him, from the very jaws of destruction. The cross exhibits the brightest display of omnipotence.

3. The existence of sin is not inconsistent with the justice of God. It is the province of justice to punish the sinner, but not to annihilate his sin. Justice, in the wide sense in which it is called Public Justice, and coincides with Goodness, will be considered, in its relation to this subject, in the next observation; but, in its ordinary sense, it supposes the existence of moral government, and moral agents, and, therefore, the possibility of transgression. Laws are made with reference to the lawless and disobedient; and the civil ruler would be armed with the sword in vain, if there could be no evil-doers to whom he might be a terror. Justice does not prevent the entrance of sin, but finds in it an occasion for its highest

exercise. This attribute is displayed awfully and gloriously in the punishment of offenders. On seeing the destruction of Antichrist, and the smoke of his torment ascending up for ever and ever, the inhabitants of heaven are represented as saying: "Alleluia; for the Lord God omnipotent reigneth."[1] It is in the exercise of his punitive justice that they understand his government, and wherefore he is seated on the throne. Justice and judgment are the habitation of his throne.

4. The existence of sin is not inconsistent with the goodness of God. Even those who explain goodness to be the love of happiness for its own sake, and understand utility, or the production of happiness, to be the foundation of virtue, do not conclude that God's goodness must necessarily exclude moral evil from the world. On the contrary, they suppose that he will overrule the evil so as ultimately to produce a larger amount of happiness in the universe, than would have existed had moral evil never entered. If this be taken as a mere hypothesis, until it be disproved, it will be sufficient to answer objections; and the hypothesis cannot be disproved by a mind incapable of comprehending the infinite subject. If God's goodness aims at the well-being of the universe, rather than at its happiness, another hypothesis, impossible to be disproved, may be made, that God overrules the existence of sin so as to produce most important moral benefits. What these may be, we cannot be expected to understand; but of one benefit, at least, we can form a conjecture. As God's moral perfections are the glory of his character, so his moral government is the glory of his universal scheme; and it may, therefore, have been pleasing to his infinite mind to permit the entrance of sin, because it gave occasion for the display of his justice and moral government. It may accord best with his infinite wisdom, to confirm his obedient subjects in holiness, not by physical necessity, but by moral influence; and the display of his justice and moral government must be a most important means for the accomplishment of this end. How could the intelligences that are to expand for ever in the presence of his throne, have those moral impressions which are necessary to the perfection of their holiness, if they should for ever remain ignorant of his justice, and hatred of sin?

---

[1] Rev. xix. 6.

In contemplating this subject, it is important to keep in view, that God's goodness is to be estimated by its aggregate effect. As including the love of happiness, it provides enjoyments for his creatures: in this life, innumerable and ever present, though not infinite, or unmixed; and in the life to come, what eye has not seen, or ear heard, or the heart of man conceived. This mass of enjoyment he has not thrown before his creatures, that each may secure to himself what he can; but infinite justice guards the distribution of it. The rule of distribution is that which Public Justice, or God's goodness, considered as the love of well-being, has prescribed in the establishment of his moral government. Infinite goodness secures the greatest possible good from his universal administration, while perfect justice regulates all the details of that administration, in beautiful harmony with the grand design.

5. Although to do evil that good may come is reprobated in God's word, yet to permit evil, which he overrules for good, accords with his method of procedure. It is said: "The wrath of man shall praise thee, and the remainder of wrath thou shalt restrain."[1] In this it is clearly implied that a portion of the wrath is unrestrained, or permitted, and is overruled for good. Paul asks, "What if God, willing to show his wrath, and make his power known, endured with much long-suffering the vessels of wrath fitted to destruction?"[2] Endurance and long-suffering is the permission of the continuance of the evil; and the display of God's justice and power thereby, is manifestly supposed in the Apostle's question. The crucifixion of Christ, a deed perpetrated by wicked hands, was permitted by God. He was even delivered by the determinate counsel and foreknowledge of God. This event has been overruled to good inconceivably great. Why may we not suppose that it accorded with infinite wisdom to permit the entrance of sin, with a view to the glorious scheme of redemption by the blood of Christ? Christ crucified is the wisdom of God. In his cross, the power, goodness, justice, and wisdom of God, are harmoniously and gloriously displayed. While we glory in the cross of Christ, we do not forget that the enemies of the cross are to perish. Mournful as the fact is, our hearts will fully approve the sentence which will be executed upon them, when we shall hear it pronounced by the lips of the righteous judge.

---

[1] Ps. lxxvi. 10.   [2] Rom. ix. 22.

Such was the benevolence of Paul's heart, that he was willing to lay down his life for the salvation of souls; yet so overpowering was his sense of Christ's claim to the love of every human heart, that he did not hesitate to exclaim: "If any man love not the Lord Jesus Christ, let him be anathema maranatha."[1] If it accorded with his love of souls to pronounce this imprecation, it will accord with the benevolence of God to punish the enemies of Christ with everlasting destruction from the presence of the Lord, and from the glory of his power. If our minds now fail fully to approve the awful sentence, it is because we inadequately conceive the glory and loveliness of Christ.

It should fill us with joy, that infinite wisdom guides the affairs of the world. Many of its events are shrouded in darkness and mystery, and inextricable confusion sometimes seems to reign. Often wickedness prevails, and God seems to have forgotten the creatures that he has made. Our own path through life is dark and devious, and beset with difficulties and dangers. How full of consolation is the doctrine, that infinite wisdom directs every event, brings order out of confusion, and light out of darkness, and, to those who love God, causes all things, whatever be their present aspect and apparent tendency, to work together for good.

CONCLUSION.

The doctrine concerning God harmonizes with the affections of the pious heart, and tends to cherish them. The moral nature of those who do not love God, demonstrates his existence and their obligation to love him, and consequently, their nature is at war with itself. There is a conflict within, between conscience and the depraved affections. The moral principle is in the unrenewed heart, overrun with unholy passions; and it cannot be duly developed, until the affections are sanctified. When, by this change, harmony has been produced in the inner man, all that is within will harmonize with the doctrine concerning God. The mind, in its proper and healthy action, joyfully receives the doctrine, and finds in God the object of its highest love. The pious man rejoices that God exists, and that his attributes are what nature and revelation pro-

---

[1] 1 Cor. xvi. 22.

claim them to be. "Whom have I in heaven but thee? and there is none upon earth that I desire beside thee."[1]

The doctrine concerning God not only harmonizes with inward piety, but tends to cherish it. If love to God exists when he is but partially known, it will increase as our knowledge of him increases. As the pious man studies the character of God, the beauty and glory of that character open to his view, and his heart is drawn out towards it with more intense affection. With such soul-ravishing views the Psalmist had been favored, when he exclaimed, "O God, thou art my God; early will I seek thee: my soul thirsteth for thee, my flesh longeth for thee in a dry and thirsty land, where no water is; to see thy power and thy glory, so as I have seen thee in the sanctuary."[2]

The love of God, which is increased by a true knowledge of him, is not a mere feeling of gratitude for blessings received. Many persons talk of God's goodness, and profess to love him, who have no pleasure in contemplating his holiness and justice, and to whom these are unwelcome attributes. When such persons stand before him in the last judgment, there is reason to fear that they will find him to be a different God from that which they loved and praised on earth. Love to the true God is love to the God of holiness and justice, the God in whom every moral perfection is united; and if our love is of this kind, we shall delight to survey the glories of the divine character, and, apart from all views of the benefits received from him, shall be enamored of his essential loveliness.

The love to God which increases by a true knowledge of him, is pervaded with a deep-felt reverence for his character. The familiar levity with which he is sometimes approached and addressed, by no means comports with the awful exhibitions of himself which he has made in his works and in his word. They who, while they profess to love him, have no solemn sense of his infinite grandeur and holiness, have yet to learn the fear of God, which is the beginning of wisdom. The true knowledge of God will rectify this evil in the heart.

The true love of God is accompanied with humility. When we are absorbed in the contemplation of the human mind, we may well be filled with admiration of its powers and capacities. But lately,

---

[1] Ps. lxxiii. 25.   [2] Ps. lxiii. 1, 2

it rose into being, from the darkness of nonentity, a spark so feebly glimmering, that an omniscient eye only could perceive its light. In the short period which has intervened, it has gradually increased in splendor, and has probably astonished the world by its brilliance. What was once the feeblest ray of intellect, has become a Newton, a Locke, a Howard, or a Napoleon. And when we conceive of this immortal mind, as continuing to expand its powers throughout a boundless future, we are ready to form a high estimate of human greatness. But when we remember that man, whatever he is, and whatever he is capable of, is a creature formed by the hand of God, and endowed by him with all these noble faculties; when we consider that, with all his advancement through eternal ages, he will forever be as nothing, compared with the infinitude of God; and when we look back into past eternity, and contemplate God as existing with all this boundlessness of perfection, ages of ages before our feeble existence commenced; we may well turn away from all admiration of human greatness, and exclaim, "Lord, what is man, that thou art mindful of him?"

But the strongest incentive to humility is found in contrasting our depravity with God's holiness. Noble as the human intellect is, it is ruined by its apostasy from God. Every depraved son of Adam, who has studied the attributes of God, and has attained to some knowledge of his immaculate holiness, may well exclaim, in deep humility, "Wo is me! a man of unclean lips; for mine eyes have seen the King, the Lord of hosts."[1]

The true knowledge of God gives confidence in him. In view of his truth, we learn to put unwavering trust in the manifestations of himself which he has made, and the promises which he has given, for the foundation of our hope. There are times when the good man loses his sensible enjoyment of the divine favor, and when the sword of justice appears pointed at his breast; but even then, with the true knowledge and love of God in his heart, he can say, "Though he slay me, yet will I trust in him."

The doctrine concerning God which the Bible teaches, confirms its claim to be regarded as the word of God.

This doctrine, as we have seen, is precisely adapted to man's moral nature, and calls forth the moral and religious principles

---

[1] Isaiah vi. 5.

with which his Creator has endowed him, into their best and noblest exercise. If viewed apart from his relation to God, man, the creature so wonderfully endowed, is an enigma in the universe; but the doctrine concerning God solves the mystery. The tendency of this doctrine to exert a sanctifying influence, at the very origin of all human feeling and action, demonstrates that it comes from God. He who experiences its sanctifying power on his heart, has a proof of its truth that nothing else can give. For this doctrine, we are chiefly indebted to the Bible. Here God, who has dimly exhibited himself in his works, comes forth in a direct communication, and like the sun in the heavens, makes himself visible by his own light. If the religious principle within us acted as it ought, the doctrine of the Bible would be as precisely adapted to us as the light of the sun is to the eye; and we should have as thorough conviction that the God of the Bible exists, as we have that the sun exists, when we see him shining forth with all his splendor in the mid-heavens.

The proof that the Bible is the word of God, will accumulate as we make progress in our investigation of religious truth. We have advanced one step, by our inquiries into the existence and attributes of God; and the glory of the Bible-doctrine concerning God, has shone on our path with dazzling brightness. Let us continue to prosecute our studies, guided by this holy book; and if we open our hearts to the sanctifying power of its truth, we shall have increasing proof, in its influence on our souls, that it comes from the God of holiness.

BOOK THIRD.

DOCTRINE CONCERNING THE WILL AND WORKS OF GOD.

INTRODUCTION.

DUTY OF DELIGHTING IN THE WILL AND WORKS OF GOD.[1]

IF any one supposes that religion consists merely of self-denial and painful austerities, and that it is filled with gloom and melancholy, to the exclusion of all happiness, he greatly mistakes its true character. False religions, and false views of the true religion, may be liable to this charge; but the religion which has God for its author, and which leads the soul to God, is full of peace and joy. It renders us cheerful amidst the trials of life, contented with all the allotments of Divine Providence, happy in the exercises of piety and devotion, and joyful in the hope of an endless felicity. Heaven is near in prospect; and, while on the way to that world of perfect and eternal bliss, we are permitted, in some measure, to anticipate its joys, being, even here, blessed with all spiritual blessings in heavenly places in Christ Jesus.[2] We are enabled, not only to pursue our pilgrimage to the good land with content and cheerfulness, but even to "delight ourselves in the Lord."[3] Our happiness is not merely the absence of grief and pain, but it is positive delight.

---

[1] *Ps.* xxxvi. 4. Delight thyself in the Lord.
Ps. xl. 8. I delight to do thy will, O my God.
Ps. cxix. 47. I will delight myself in thy commandments.
Rom. vii. 22. I delight in the law of God.
Ps.. cvii. 22. Declare his works with rejoicing.
[2] Eph. i. 3.   [3] Ps. xxxvii. 4.

The delight which attends other religious exercises should be felt in the investigation of religious truth, and should stimulate to diligence and perseverance. Divine truth is not only sanctifying, but it is also beatifying. To the ancient saints it was sweeter than honey and the honey-comb;[1] and the early Christians, in "believing" the truth as it is in Jesus, "rejoiced with joy unspeakable and full of glory."[2] If we loved the truth as we ought, we should experience equal delight in receiving it; and the careful investigation of it would be a source of pure and abiding pleasure. It would not suffice to employ our intellectual powers in the discussion of perplexing questions appertaining to religion, but we should find a rich feast in the truth that may be known and read by all. The man who indulges his skeptical doubts, and suffers himself to be detained by questions to no profit, is like one who, when a bountiful feast is spread before him, instead of enjoying the offered food, employs himself in examining a supposed flaw in the dish in which it is served. The glorious truths which are plainly revealed concerning God, and the things of God, are sufficient to enable every one to delight himself in the Lord.

We have before seen that love to God lies at the foundation of true religion. Love, considered as simple benevolence, has for its object the production of happiness, and not the receiving of it. But, by the wise arrangements of infinite goodness, the producing of happiness blesses him that gives as well as him that receives. It is even "more blessed to give than to receive."[3] But when God is the object of our love, as we cannot increase his happiness, we delight in it as already perfect; and all the outflowing of our love to him, finding the measure of his bliss already full, returns back on ourselves, filling us also with the fulness of God. God is love; and to love God with all the heart is to have the heart filled, to the full measure of its capacity, with the blessedness of the divine nature. This is the fulness of delight.

In the existence and attributes of God a sufficient foundation is laid for the claim of supreme love to him; but, for the active exercise of the holy affection, God must be viewed not merely as existing, but as acting. To produce delight in him, his perfections must be manifested. So we enjoy the objects of our earthly love

---

[1] Ps. xix. 10.   [2] 1 Pet. i. 8.   [3] Acts xx. 35.

by their presence with us, and the display of those qualities which attract our hearts. Heaven is full of bliss, because its inhabitants not only love God, but see the full manifestations of his glory. To enjoy God on earth, we must contemplate him in such manifestations of himself as he has been pleased to make to us who dwell on his footstool. These we may discover in the declarations of his will, and in his works, which are the execution of his will. In a contemplation of these, the pious heart finds a source of pure, elevating delight.

When the Son of God consented to appear in human nature for the salvation of man, he said: "I delight to do thy will, O my God." [1] If the same mind were in us that was in Christ Jesus, we, too, would delight in the will of God. We should be able to say with David, "I will delight myself in thy commandments;" and with Paul, "I delight in the law of God." We should yield obedience to every precept, not reluctantly, but cheerfully; not cheerfully only, but with joy and delight. It would be to us meat and drink to do the will of God, as it was to our blessed Lord. Our religious enjoyment would consist not merely in receiving good from God, but in rendering active service to him; like the happy spirits before the throne, who serve God day and night, and delight in his service. Not only should we delight to render personal service to our Sovereign, but we should desire his will to be done by all others, and should rejoice in his universal dominion. "The Lord reigneth, let the earth rejoice."

As the ancient saints delighted in the will and government of God, so they delighted in his works. They saw in them the manifestations of his wisdom, power, and goodness; and they delighted to meditate on them. His glory, displayed in the heavens, and his handy work, visible in earth, they contemplated with holy pleasure. They rejoiced to remember, "It is he that made us;" and, in approaching him with religious worship, they were accustomed to address him as the Creator of all things: "Lord, thou art God, which hast made heaven and earth, and the sea, and all that in them is." [2]

The goodness displayed in God's works awakens gratitude in the pious man. While he enjoys the gift, he recognises the hand which bestows it; and each blessing is rendered more dear, because

---

[1] Ps. xl. 8.   [2] Acts iv. 24.

7

conferred by him whom he supremely loves. He sees in creation a vast store-house of enjoyment, and blesses the author of it. He receives from the providence of God the innumerable benefits which are every day bestowed, and he blesses the kind bestower. God is in every mercy, and his heart, in enjoying it, goes out ever to God, with incessant praise and thanksgiving.

The trial of our delight in God is experienced when affliction comes. The pious man feels that this, too, is from the hand of God. So thought all the saints, of whose religious exercises the Bible gives us an account. They bowed under affliction in the spirit of resignation to God, as the author of the affliction. So Job,[1] "The Lord gave, and the Lord hath taken away; blessed be the name of the Lord." So David,[2] "I was dumb, I opened not my mouth; because thou didst it." So Eli,[3] "It is the Lord; let him do what seemeth him good." So Paul's companions,[4] "We ceased, saying, the will of the Lord be done." The ancient saints believed in an overruling Providence, and they received all afflictions as ordered by him, in every particular; and on this faith the resignation was founded by which their eminent piety was distinguished. To the flesh, the affliction was not joyous, but grievous, and, therefore, they could not delight in it, when considered in itself; but, when enduring it with keenest anguish, they could still say, with Job, "Blessed be the name of the Lord." They firmly believed that the dispensation was wisely and kindly ordered, and that God would bring good out of the evil; and, however oppressed with suffering, and filled with present sorrow, they still trusted in God; and delight in him alleviated their misery, and mingled with their sorrows.

Let love to God burn in our hearts while we contemplate his existence and attributes. Let delight in him rise to the highest rapture of which earthly minds are susceptible, while we study his will and works. The grand work of redemption, into which the angels especially desire to look, and which is the chief theme of the song of the glorified, is fitted to produce higher ecstasy; but even the themes of creation and providence may fill us with delight, if we approach them as we ought. When the foundations of the earth were laid, the morning stars sang together, and all the sons of God

---

[1] Job i. 21.   [2] Ps. xxxix. 9.   [3] 1 Sam. iii. 18.   [4] Acts xxi. 14.

shouted for joy; and angels now delight to be the ministers of God's providence. Let us, with like devotion to Almighty God, delight in his will and works.

CHAPTER I.

WILL OF GOD.

THE term *will*, which always imports desire, is variously applied, according to the object of that desire.

1. It denotes intention or purpose to act. It is said of Apollos "His will was not at all to come at this time,"[1] *i. e.*, he had not formed the intention or purpose to come. In this sense, the will of God is spoken of: "According to the purpose of him who worketh all things after the counsel of his own will."[2] Purpose or intention may exist before the time of action arrives. When it has arrived, the mind puts forth an act termed volition, to produce the desired effect. In human beings, purposes may be fickle, and may undergo change before the time for action comes; but God's purpose or intention is never changed; and when the time for producing the purposed effect arrives, we are not to conceive that a new volition arises in the mind of God; but the effect follows, according to the will of God, without any new effort on his part.

2. It denotes a desire to act, restrained by stronger opposing desires, or other counteracting influences. Pilate was "willing" to release Jesus;[3] but other considerations, present to his mind, overruled this desire, and determined his action. We are compelled to conceive of the divine mind, from the knowledge which we possess of our own; and the Scriptures adapt their language to our conceptions. In this way, a desire to act is sometimes attributed to God, when opposing considerations prevent his action. "I would scatter them, were it not that I feared the wrath of the enemy."[4] "How often would I have gathered, &c., and ye would not."[5]

---

[1] 1 Cor. xvi. 12.   [2] Eph. i. 11.   [3] Luke xxiii. 20.   [4] Deut. xxxii. 27.
[5] Matt. xxiii. 37.

3. It is used with reference to an external object that is desired, or an action which it is desired that another should perform. "Sacrifice and offering thou wouldst not."[1] "Be it unto thee as thou wilt."[2] "Ask what ye will."[3] "What will ye, that I should do."[4] In this sense, as expressing simply what is in itself desirable to God, will is attributed to him. "Not willing that any should perish, but that all should come to repentance."[5] "I have no pleasure in the death of the wicked, &c."[6] "This is the will of God, even your sanctification."[7]

4. Closely allied to the last signification, and perhaps included in it, is that use of the term *will*, in which it denotes *command*, *requirement*. When the person, whose desire or pleasure it is that an action should be performed by another, has authority over that other, the desire expressed assumes the character of precept. The expressed will of a suppliant, is petition; the expressed will of a ruler, is command. What we know that it is the pleasure of God we should do, it is our duty to do, and his pleasure made known to us becomes a law.

Will of Command.

It is specially important to distinguish between the first and last of the significations which have been enumerated. In the first, the will of God refers exclusively to his own action, and imports his fixed determination as to what he will do. It is called his will of purpose, and always takes effect. In the last sense, it refers to the actions of his creatures, and expresses what it would be pleasing to him that they should do. This is called his will of precept, and it always fails to take effect when the actions of his creatures do not please him, i. e., when they are in violation of his commands. The will of purpose is intended, when it is said, "According to the purpose of him who worketh all things after the counsel of his own will,"[8] and, "He doeth according to his will in the army of heaven, and among the inhabitants of the earth."[9] The will of precept is intended, when it is said, "Thy will be done in earth, as it is in heaven.[10] Let it be noted that, in the former case, God only is the agent, and the effect is certain; in the latter, his

---

[1] Heb. x. 5.   [2] Matt. xv. 28.   [3] John xv. 7.   [4] Mark xv. 12.
[5] 2 Peter iii. 9. [6] Ezek. xxxiii. 11. [7] 1 Thess. iv. 3.   [8] Eph. i. 11.
[9] Dan. iv. 35.   [10] Matt. vi. 10.

creatures are the agents, and the effect is not an object of certain expectation, but of petition.

GOD'S WILL OF COMMAND, HOWEVER MADE KNOWN TO US, IS OUR RULE OF DUTY.[1]

The Scriptures make the will of God the rule of duty, both to those who have the means of clear knowledge, and those who have not. The disobedience of the former will be punished with many stripes, that of the latter with few. No man will be held accountable, except for the means of knowledge that are within his reach; but these, even in the case of the benighted heathen, are sufficient to render them inexcusable. We have no right to dictate to God in what manner he shall make his will known to us; but we are bound to avail ourselves of all possible means for obtaining the knowledge of it; and, when known, we are bound to obey it perfectly, and from the heart.

Various terms are used to denote the will of God, as made known in the Holy Scriptures, statutes, judgments, laws, precepts, ordinances, &c. The two great precepts, which lie at the foundation of all the laws, are, thou shalt love the Lord thy God with all thy heart, and thou shalt love thy neighbor as thyself. The first of these is expanded into the four commandments, which constitute the first table of the decalogue; the second into the six commandments, which constitute the second table. The decalogue was given for a law to the children of Israel, as is apparent from its introduction. "I am the Lord thy God, which have brought thee out of the land of Egypt, out of the house of bondage."[2] It was, however, distinguished from the other laws given to that nation, by being pronounced audibly from Sinai with the voice of God, and by being engraved with the finger of God on the tables of stone. When we examine its precepts, we discover that they respect the relations of men, as men, to God and to one another; and we find, in the New Testament, that their obligation is regarded as extending to Gentiles under the gospel dispensation.[3] We infer, therefore, that the decalogue, though given to the Israelites, respected them as men, and not as a peculiar people, and is equally obligatory on all men.

The ceremonial law respected the children of Israel as a wor-

---

[1] Ps. xl. 8; cxliii. 10; Matt. vi. 10; Rom. ii. 18; Ex. xx; Rom. ii. 12–15; Eccl. xii. 13.   [2] Ex. xx. 2.   [3] Rom. xiii. 8, 9; Eph. vi. 2.

shipping congregation, called "the Congregation of the Lord." It commenced with the institution of the passover, and ended when Christ our passover was sacrificed for us, and when the hand-writing of ordinances was nailed to the cross. Then its obligation ceased. Baptism and the Lord's Supper are ceremonies of the Christian dispensation, obligatory on the disciples of Christ, to the end of the world.

The judicial law was given to the Israelites as a nation, and is not obligatory on any other people. The principles of justice on which it was based, are universal, and should be incorporated into every civil code.

Will of Purpose.

GOD WILLS WHATEVER HE DOES.[1]

God is a voluntary agent. There are many powers in nature which operate without volition. Fire consumes the fuel, steam moves the engine, and poison takes away life; but these have no will. Even beings that possess will, sometimes act involuntarily, and sometimes against their will, or by compulsion from a superior power. God acts voluntarily in every thing that he does; — not by physical necessity; not by compulsion from any superior power; not by mistake, or oversight, or power unintentionally exerted. Men may plead in apology for their acts, that they were done in thoughtlessness, or through inadvertence; but God has never any such apology to make. Known unto him are all his works from the beginning of the world,[2] and therefore they have been duly considered.

GOD DOES WHATEVER HE WILLS TO DO.[3]

God is not omnipotent, if he absolutely wills or desires to do anything, and fails to accomplish it.

WHATEVER GOD DOES IS ACCORDING TO A PURPOSE THAT IS ETERNAL, UNCHANGEABLE, PERFECTLY FREE, AND INFINITELY WISE.[4]

That God has a purpose, none can deny, who attribute wisdom to him. To act without purpose is the part of a child, or an idiot. A wise man does not act without purpose, much less can the only wise God. Besides, the Scriptures speak so expressly of his pur-

---

[1] Job xxiii. 13; Dan. iv. 35; Eph. i. 11.   [2] Acts xv. 14.
[3] Job xxiii. 13; Dan. iv. 35; Eph. i. 11; Isa. xlvi. 10; Dan. xi. 36.
[4] Job xxiii. 13; Isa. xl. 14; xlvi. 10; Jer. li. 29; Rom. viii. 28; Eph i. 11; iii. 11; 2 Tim. i. 9.

pose, that no one, who admits the authority of revelation, can reject the doctrine, however much he may misinterpret or abuse it. The term implies that God has an end in view in whatever he does, and that he has a plan according to which he acts.

The purpose of God is eternal and unchangeable. A wise man, in executing a purpose, may have many separate volitions, which are momentary actings of his mind; but his purpose is more durable, continuing from its first formation in the mind to its complete execution. The term will, as applied to the act of the divine mind, does not, in itself, imply duration; but the purpose of God, from the very import of the phrase, must have duration. God must have had a purpose when he created the world; and the Scriptures speak of his purpose before the world began. But the duration of it is still more explicitly declared in the phrase, "the eternal purpose."[1] The term is never used in the plural number by the inspired writers; as if God had many plans, or a succession of plans. It is one entire, glorious scheme; and the date of it is from everlasting. Its eternity implies its unchangeableness; and its unchangeableness implies its eternity; and its oneness accords with both these properties.

The purpose of God is perfectly free. It is not forced upon him from without; for nothing existed to restrict the infinite mind of him who was before all. It is the purpose which he hath "purposed in himself."[2] It is his will; and must, therefore, be voluntary. The term purpose and will apply to the same thing in different aspects of it, or according to different modes of conceiving it. If *purpose* more naturally suggests the idea of duration, *will* suggests its freeness. It is not the fate believed in by the ancient heathens, by which they considered the gods to be bound, as truly as men.

The purpose of God is infinitely wise. We have argued, that God must have a purpose because he is wise; and, therefore, his wisdom must be concerned in his purpose. It is not an arbitrary or capricious scheme; but one devised by infinite wisdom, having the best possible end to accomplish, and adopting the best possible means for its accomplishment.

Writers on theology have employed the term Decrees, to denote

---

[1] Eph. iii. 11.   [2] Eph. i. 9.

the purpose of God. It is an objection to this term, that there is no inspired authority for its use in this sense. When the Scriptures use the term decree, they signify by it a command promulged, to be observed by those under authority. It is the will of precept, rather than the will of purpose. And further, its use in the plural number does not accord so well with the oneness of the divine plan.

Scarcely any doctrine of religion has given so much occasion for cavil and stumbling as that of God's decrees. As if men would be wiser than God, they refuse to let him form a plan, or they find fault with it when formed; and very few have so much humility and simplicity of faith, as to escape wholly from the embarrassment which the objections to this doctrine have produced. They, therefore, need a careful examination.

Objection 1. — The purpose of God is inconsistent with the free-agency of man.

It is a full answer to this objection, that a mere purpose cannot interfere with the freedom of any one. When a tyrant designs to imprison one of his subjects, until the design is carried into execution, the liberty of the subject is not invaded. He roams as free as ever, untouched by the premeditated evil. The infringement of his liberty commences when the purpose begins to be executed, and not before. So, in the divine government, the purpose of the Supreme Ruler interferes not at all with the liberty of his subjects, so long as it remains a mere purpose. The objection which we are considering, is wholly inapplicable to the doctrine of God's purpose. Its proper place, if it has any, is against the doctrine of God's providence; and, under that head, it will be proper to meet it. It was God's purpose to create man a free-agent; and he did so create him. Thus far, neither the purpose, nor the execution of it, can be charged with infringing man's moral freedom; but they unite to establish it. It was God's purpose to govern man as a free-agent; and has he not done so? If every man feels that the providence of God, while it presides in the affairs of men, leaves him perfectly free to act from choice in every thing that he does, what ground is there for the complaint, that the purpose of God interferes with man's free-agency? If the evil complained of is not in the execution of the purpose, it is certainly not in the purpose itself.

This objection often comes before us practically. When we are called upon for action to which we are averse, the argument presents itself; if God has fore-ordained whatever comes to pass, the event is certain; and what is to be, will be, without our effort. It is worthy of remark, that this argument never induces us to deviate from a course to which we are inclined. If some pleasure invites, we never excuse ourselves from the indulgence, on the plea, that, if we are to enjoy it, we shall enjoy it. The fact is sufficient to teach us the insincerity of the plea, when admitted in other cases It prevails with us only through the deceitfulness of sin; and, however specious the argument may appear, when it coincides with our inclinations, we never trust it in any other case. No man in his senses remains at ease in a burning dwelling, on the plea, that, if he is to escape from the flames, he will escape. The providence of God establishes the relation between cause and effect, and gives full scope for the influence of the human will. To argue that effects will be produced without their appropriate causes, is to deny the known arrangement of Providence. He who expects from the purpose of God, that which the providence of God denies him, expects the purpose to be inconsistent with its own development. He charges the plan of the Most Wise, with inconsistency and folly, that he may find a subterfuge for criminal indulgence.

Objection 2. — If God purposed the fall of angels or men, he is the author of their sin.

Before we proceed to answer this objection, it is necessary to examine the terms in which it is expressed. In what sense did God purpose the fall of angels or men, or any sinful action? There is a sense, familiar to the pious, in which any event that takes place, under the overruling providence of God, is attributed to him, whatever subordinate agents may have been concerned in effecting it. The wind, the lightning, the Chaldeans, the Sabeans, were all concerned in the afflictions that fell on the patriarch Job; but he recognised the overruling hand of God in every event, and piously exclaimed: "The Lord gave, and the Lord hath taken away; blessed be the name of the Lord."[1] So Joseph, when sold by his brethren in Egypt, saw the hand of God in the event, and explained the design of his providence: "For God did send me before you to preserve life."[2] In precisely the same sense in which God's

---

[1] Job. i. 21.   [2] Gen. xlv. 5.

providence is concerned with such events, his purpose is concerned with them; and in no other.

With this explanation, let us proceed to consider the objection. Did Joseph design to charge on God the authorship of his brethrens' sin? Nothing was further from his mind. They had been truly guilty of their brother's blood; and their own consciences charged them with it. They felt that they were responsible for the sin, and Joseph knew the same; and nothing that he said was designed to transfer the responsibility from them to God. Yet he saw and delighted to contemplate the purpose of God in the event. That purpose was, "to save much people alive." This purpose was executed; and God was the author, both of the purpose and the beneficial result. So, in every case, the good which he educes out of moral evil, and not the moral evil itself, is the proper object of his purpose. It should ever be remembered, that his purpose is his intention to act; and that, strictly speaking, it relates to his own action exclusively. It does, indeed, extend to everything that is done under the sun, just as the omnipresence of God extends to everything; but it extends to everything, no otherwise than as he is concerned with everything; and what God does, and nothing else, is the proper object of his purpose. "HE WORKETH all things after the counsel of his own will."[1] "I WILL DO all my pleasure."[2] "HE DOETH according to his will in the army of heaven, and among the inhabitants of the earth."[3] It cannot be too carefully noticed, that the purpose of God relates strictly and properly to his own actions. Now, God is not the actor of sin, and therefore his purpose can never make him the author of it.

The objection, though it may appear to have greater force when applied to the first sin of man, is not, in reality, more applicable to this, than to every sin which has been since committed. God made Adam, and all his descendants, moral and accountable agents, preserved them in being, and sustained their moral powers; he permitted their sin; and he overrules the evil, from the beginning throughout, to effect a most glorious result. In all this, what God has done, and is doing, he purposed to do. In all, his action is most righteous, wise, and holy; and, therefore, his purpose is so.

---

[1] Eph. i. 11.   [2] Isaiah xlvi. 10.   [3] Dan. iv. 35.

He is the author, not of the moral evil which he permits, but of the good of which he makes it the occasion.

The distinction between the permission and the authorship of sin some have denied; but, in so doing, they have not the countenance of God's word. The whole tenor of the inspired volume leads us to regard God as the author of holiness, but not of sin. We are taught that in him is no sin;[1] that "he is light, and in him is no darkness;"[2] that "every good and perfect gift," not sin, "cometh down from the Father of lights;"[3] that God is not tempted of evil, neither tempteth he any man.[4] In such language we are taught to consider God as the author and source of holiness; and it is as contrary to the doctrine of the holy word to attribute sin to him, as darkness to the sun. Yet this same word teaches his permission of evil. "He *suffered* all nations to walk in their own way."[5] His long-suffering, of which the Scriptures speak so much, implies the permission of sin. But of that which is highly displeasing to him, even when he bears with it, he cannot be the author.

Objection 3. — If God purposed the final condemnation of the wicked, he made them on purpose to damn them.

This objection, which impiety loves to present in the most repulsive form, it becomes us to approach with profound reverence for him whose character and motives it impugns. Let us imagine ourselves present at the proceedings of the last day. The righteous Judge sits on his great white throne, and all nations are gathered before him. The books are opened, and every man is impartially judged, according to the deeds done in the body. The award is made up, and the sentence pronounced. The wicked are commanded to "depart into the fire prepared for the devil and his angels;" and the righteous are welcomed into "the kingdom prepared for them from the foundation of the world." The scene is past, and the mysterious economy of God's forbearance and grace is now finally closed. Is there anything in the transactions of that day which is unworthy of God? Is there anything which the holy inhabitants of heaven, throughout their immortal existence, can ever remember with disapprobation? Not so. The Judge, while

---

[1] 1 John i. 5.   [2] Ibid.   [3] James i. 17.
[4] James i. 13.   [5] Acts xiv. 16.

he punishes the wicked with everlasting destruction, from the presence of the Lord and the glory of his power, is glorified in his saints, and admired in all them that believe;[1] and he will ever appear glorious in the decisions of that day. If God's action on that day will be so glorious to him, will it be any dishonor to him that he has purposed so to act?

The idea, were any one disposed seriously to entertain it, that God will be taken by surprise at the last judgment, and compelled to pass an unpremeditated sentence, is for ever set aside by the fact that, as early as the days of Enoch, the seventh from Adam, the great day, and especially the fearful doom of the ungodly, were foretold. "Behold the Lord cometh, with ten thousand of his saints, to execute judgment upon all; and to convince all that are ungodly among them, of all their ungodly deeds."[2] This fact also demonstrates that the Lord will not punish for the mere pleasure of punishing. Why does he give warning of that day? Why are his messengers sent to warn men to flee from the wrath to come? Why are these messages delivered with so earnest entreaty and expostulation, so that his servants say, "As though God did beseech you by us, we pray you, in Christ's stead, be ye reconciled to God."[3] As creatures, formed by his hand, he has not, and cannot have, any pleasure in rendering them unhappy; but, as rebels against his authority, enemies to his character and government, and the good order of his universal empire, and obstinate rejecters of his scheme of mercy and reconciliation, he will take pleasure in inflicting on them the punishment which his justice requires. The reward of the righteous is a kingdom prepared for them from before the foundation of the world; but the fire into which the wicked will be driven, is said to be prepared, not for them, but for the devil and his angels.[4] In this significant manner, God has been pleased to teach us, that his punishments are prepared, not for his creatures, as such, but only for sinners, and in view of *sins* already committed. Must he, to secure himself from disgrace and reproach, be able to plead that he has been taken by surprise, and that, from the beginning of the world, he had never expected the fearful result? If the proceedings of this great day will be so glorious to God that he will regard them with pleasure through all

---

[1] 2 Thes. i. 9, 10.   [2] Jude 14, 15.   [3] 2 Cor. v. 20.   [4] Matt. xxv. 34, 41.

future eternity, why may he not have regarded them with pleasure through all eternity past ?

The objection, originating in dislike of God's justice, wholly misrepresents the character of his righteous judgment. It leaps from the creation of man to the final doom of the wicked, and wholly overlooks the intermediate cause of that doom. It proceeds as if sin were a very inconsiderable matter, and as if it must have been so regarded by God; and, therefore, it represents the punishment inflicted for it as if inflicted for its own sake. The sentence pronounced will be, in the judgment of God, for just and sufficient cause; and, in all the purpose of God respecting that sentence, the cause has been contemplated. What God does, and why he does it, are equally included in the divine purpose; and this connection the objection wholly overlooks. God did not regard sin as a trifling thing, when, on account of it, he destroyed the old world with the flood; and, as if to answer the very objection now before us, and convince men that he did not make them for the pleasure of destroying them, it is recorded: " God saw that the wickedness of man was great in the earth, and that every imagination of the thoughts of his heart was only evil continually. And it repented the Lord that he had made man on the earth; and it grieved him at his heart." [1]

Our best judgment decides that the world ought not to have been made without a purpose, and that, for its mighty movements now to proceed without any purpose, is infinitely undesirable. The best work of human hands that we contemplate with any pleasure, has been formed with some purpose; and no intelligent being can view the works of God with satisfaction, if he can imagine them to have been undertaken and executed without design. Who would not grieve to think that this vast machinery is moving to accomplish no end; that the planets are hurled through space wildly, guided in their course, and controlled in their velocity, by no wise counsel; that the sun shines, that animals exist, that immortal man lives, moves, and has his being, without purpose ? In this view, what an enigma is our life ? Our understandings may consent not to comprehend the purpose for which the world was made, but to consent that it was made for no purpose, they cannot. Our intelligent natures wholly reject the thought.

---

[1] Gen. vi. 6, 7.

The doctrine of God's purpose, while it recommends itself to our understandings, applies a test to the moral principles of our hearts. If God has a purpose, we should delight to study it, and rejoice in the accomplishment of it; and our hearts and lives should be regulated in harmony with it. When we prefer that God should have no purpose, or that it should be different from what it is, our hearts cannot be right in his sight. If we loved him as we ought, we should rejoice in the accomplishment of his will, and view with pleasure the unfolding of his grand designs. Holy angels study the mystery of redeeming love, and learn, from the dispensations toward the Church, the manifold wisdom of God.[1] If right principles prevailed in our hearts, we would not presume to dictate to the Infinitely Wise, nor find fault with his plans, but wait with pleasure on the development of his will: and when we cannot see the wisdom and goodness of his works, we should, in the simplicity of faith, rest assured that his plan, when fully unfolded, will be found most righteous and most wise.

CHAPTER II.

WORKS OF GOD—CREATION.

GOD CREATED ALL THINGS OUT OF NOTHING.[2]

Originally, nothing existed but God; no matter, out of which visible things were formed, and no spiritual substance, out of which angels and human souls were made; but God gave to all things that exist their entire being.

It has been argued that matter cannot be eternal, because self-existence is too noble a property to be attributed to an inferior nature; but this argument is not satisfactory. Why may not a small thing exist without a cause, as well as a greater? The producing of some particular effect we may conceive to be easier for a

---

[1] Eph. iii. 10.

[2] Gen. i.; Neh. ix. 6; Job ix. 9; Ps. lxxxix. 11; xcv. 5; ciii. 19; civ. 4, 19; Col. i. 16; Rev. iv. 11; Heb. iii. 4; xi. 3; Acts xvii. 24.

higher nature than a lower; but, in self-production, the effect is equal to the cause, and the difficulty of producing it must be as great for the one nature as for the other. In all such *à priori* reasoning, we are liable to deceive ourselves; and perhaps the danger is greatest where the reasoning appears most profound. For aught that philosophy can teach us, an atom of matter is absolutely indestructible; and, on philosophical principles, if it must exist through future eternity, it may have existed through past eternity. The miracle of creation is as far beyond the demonstrations of philosophy as the miracle of annihilation. When we have proved the existence of a God, able to work miracles, a probability arises that matter may be a production of his power, and we may see creative intelligence displayed in the properties and quantities of the various kinds of matter, and their adaptedness to beneficial purposes. But, for decisive proof that all things were made out of nothing, we turn to the word of God, and receive it as a truth of faith, rather than of reason. "Through faith we understand that the worlds were framed by the word of God, so that things which are seen were not made of things which do appear."[1]

In the text just quoted, the doctrine of creation is not expressed in the language in which it is most commonly stated. It is not said the world was made out of nothing; but the same idea is expressed in a different manner. When we see a statue, we see the marble of which it consists; and when we see a house, we see the materials of which it is constructed. Paul teaches that the world which we see was not made of the visible substances that we behold, *i. e.*, it was not formed of pre-existent matter, but the materials of which it now appears to be formed, were brought into existence at the time when the things themselves were created.

The work of creation was performed without effort. God spake, and it was done. He said, let there be light, and there was light. After working six days, he rested on the seventh; not because he was weary, but that the seventh day might be sanctified, and made a day of rest for man. Wherefore it is said, the sabbath was made for man.[2]

---

[1] Heb. xi. 3. [2] Mark ii. 27.

From an examination of the earth's crust, geologists have discovered, as they think, that animals and plants existed long before the Mosaic date of creation. Methods have been proposed to reconcile the account, as contained in the first chapter of Genesis, with these professed discoveries. Some have supposed each of the days of creation to have been a long period of years. The seventh day of rest, or cessation from the work of creating, they understand to have continued to the present time, though nearly six thousand years have passed; and they suppose that each of the preceding days may have included an equally long period. Others understand "the beginning" mentioned in the first verse of the history, to refer to a time long anterior to that referred to in the second verse, "the earth was without form, &c." A similar transition, though not so sudden, is made in the first chapter of John: "In the beginning was the word;—and the word was made flesh."[1] Many divines have been disposed to regard the science of geology with suspicion, and to consider its deductions as inimical to the faith. But there can be no just ground to fear science, in any of its departments, so long as it pursues its investigations legitimately, and makes its deductions with becoming modesty. The Author of the Bible is the maker of the world, and the author of all truth; and his works and his word must harmonize, for truth is always consistent. Passages in his word have been thought to be inconsistent with each other; but a more careful examination has shown their harmony, and we need not fear but that due investigation will show the word to be consistent with all the legitimate deductions of science.

The undesigned coincidences which have been discovered in the Scripture narratives, constitute a highly satisfactory part of the internal evidence which the bible contains, that its records are true. The proof which these furnish is always the more satisfactory, the more manifest it is that the coincidence was undesigned. When two portions of Scripture, which appeared to disagree with each other, have been found, on careful investigation, to be perfectly harmonious, a coincidence has been discovered, that has the best possible evidence that it was undesigned. In this way the supposed discrepancies, which at first embarrassed us, turn out to

---

[1] John i. 1–14.

the establishment of our faith; and when some still remain which we have not yet learned to harmonize, we are taught to wait patiently, with the confident expectation that these dark places also will at some time be illuminated. The same faith and patience should be exercised when science and Scripture are supposed to disagree. The infidel delights to point out apparent discrepancies in Scripture, and he exults when he can announce some supposed discovery of science inconsistent with the word of revelation. While the infidel triumphs, men of weak faith stagger; but it is truly a weak faith that cannot withstand such a shock. We might as well doubt whether the sun shines, when his brilliance is eclipsed by a passing cloud. The mass of evidence that the Bible is the true word of God, is so great that we can well afford to wait till the temporary cloud passes, with the confident expectation that the light will again shine, perhaps with increased splendor. Geology is yet a recent science. What it will do ultimately for the cause of truth, future years must decide, and it is unwise to fear the result. We may trust that the ark of God will be carried through safely. Already, to some extent, the discoveries of the new science have turned out to the establishment of the faith. It has penetrated a very small distance below the earth's surface, and, in the successive deposits of animal remains, it has found a record from which it professes to read the order in which the various species of animals came into being. Between this record and that of Moses, there is an undesigned coincidence. It is especially remarkable that, by the general consent of geologists, human remains are found only in the last of the animal deposits. This fact points to a time agreeing well with the Mosaic date of creation, when men began to exist, and when, of course, a creating power was exerted. If geology can establish that, previous to this, a convulsion of nature desolated the earth, and buried a whole generation of inferior animals in its caverns, be it so. We will listen to her arguments, and weigh them well; but we cannot omit to notice the agreement of her facts with the faithful record of inspiration. If geology were to carry back the origin of the human race to a date long anterior to that of Moses, she would contradict, not only the Bible, but all history, written and traditionary. It cannot be accounted for, that our knowledge of ancient history should be limited to so recent a period, if the race had previously existed

8

through thousands of generations. The progress in the settlement of the world, the establishment of ancient kingdoms, and the building of cities, are spread out before us on the pages of history, and geology does not contradict the record.

Although science will never contradict Scripture, it may correct erroneous inferences from it, and, in doing this, may incidentally demonstrate the wisdom from which the Bible emanated. When we have arrived at mature years, we call to mind instructions that we received in our childhood from a wise father, and that were adapted to the purpose for which they were designed. They did not teach the sciences which we have since learned, but they taught us nothing contrary; and we are now able to see, in what was said and what was omitted to be said, that the father fully understood the sciences, which it was then no part of his design to teach us. Had he not understood them, he would have employed other forms of speech, and we should be able to recollect some word or words that would betray his ignorance. So the false revelations of the heathen world contradict science. Some of them contradict the very first lessons in geography, and a child in a christian school can prove them to be false. But science, in all its advancement, though it has made its greatest attainments in the lands where the Bible is most known, has found nothing in the Bible to contradict. The only rational way to account for this, is to suppose that the Author of the Bible understood the sciences. We nowhere read in this work that the earth is supported by an elephant, and that the elephant stands on a tortoise; but we read, " He hangeth the earth upon nothing,"[1] a statement which, made in the very infancy of revelation, may satisfy us that the author of the Bible understood the mechanism of the universe. In a past age of ignorance, men supposed that Joshua's command to the sun to stand still, disproved the Copernican system of astronomy; but this childish inference from the language of Scripture, is now well understood to be unwarranted. Men of science, who firmly believe the Copernican system, speak as freely of the sun rising and the sun setting, as those who never have heard that these appearances are owing to the earth's rotation. Future science may teach us to correct other erroneous inferences which many have drawn from

---

[1] Job xxvi. 7.

the Scripture; and we should be content to learn. The result will give further proof that the Author of Nature is the author of the Bible.

Our hearts receive a strong impression of the power, wisdom and goodness of the Lord, when we dwell on the thought that he made the heavens and the earth, with all that they contain. Above all, when we reflect that he made us, and not we ourselves, we are constrained to acknowledge his right to require what service, praise and glory we are capable of rendering. He is the former of our bodies, and the father of our spirits; and shall we not render to him that which is his own? Shall we not serve and glorify him with our bodies and our spirits, which are his? His right, by virtue of redemption, may present stronger claims, but his right by virtue of creation, is sufficient to establish our obligation, and we ought to recognise its force.

CHAPTER III.

WORKS OF GOD. — PROVIDENCE.

LET us approach nearer to the object of our supreme love. Such a being as God would be worthy of our hearts' best affection, if we were wholly under the dominion of another Lord, and owed our existence to another creative power. Like the Queen of Sheba, when she heard of the wisdom and glory of Solomon, we might, with great propriety, desire to visit the remote palace of Jehovah, that we might learn his character, and the arrangements of his empire. If God, after creating the world, had left the management of it in other hands, and had withdrawn to employ himself in other works, our inquiries might well follow him, and we might laudably seek to know our Creator. But God is not far from us. He did not, on making the world, leave it to itself, or commit it into other hands; but it is an object of his constant care, and his hand is concerned in all its movements. Whether we look on the right hand, or on the left, we can see where he doth work; and, in the display of his wisdom, power, and goodness, which at every moment meets our eyes, we find continued incitements to adore and love.

God's care of his creation, is termed Providence; and includes Preservation and Government.

SECTION I.—PRESERVATION.

ALL CREATED THINGS ARE KEPT IN BEING BY THE WILL AND POWER OF GOD.[1]

We can as little understand the act of Providence, as that of creation; but we know that both are acts of God, implying both his will and power. That a continued preserving act is necessary to keep his creatures in being, ought not to be doubted. . The expression, "upholding all things,"[2] clearly denotes such an act. An architect may build a house, which, when once completed, may stand, independent of his labor and skill, a monument of both, when he has fallen by the hand of death; and we are prone to conceive that the work of God might equally stand, if left to itself, without his constant care and support. But the cases are widely different. The human architect finds the materials which he uses already in existence; and his whole work consists in changing their form, and combining them in a new order. The substances used did not receive their existence from him; and the independent being which they possessed before the architect touched them, they retain after his hand has been withdrawn. But the very substance, as well as the form, of all created things, came from the hand of God; and the withdrawal of that hand would leave their being unsupported, or the expression, "upholding all things," has no appropriate meaning.

Many have maintained that the preserving act not only has the same author as the creating act, but is identical with it. They consider it philosophically true that preservation is a perpetual creation. All created existence is conceived to terminate at every moment by its natural tendency to annihilation, and to be reproduced by a new creative act. But, notwithstanding the ingenious arguments which have been advanced in support of this opinion, philosophy perseveres in distinguishing between the two acts, regarding creation as miraculous, and preservation, as conformed to

---

[1] Job i. 21; v. 18; Ps. xxxiii. 10–15; ciii. 3–5, 10; civ. 27–30; cxxvii. 1, 2; Prov. xvi. 9; Matt. v. 45; x. 29; Luke xii. 6; Acts xvii. 28.
[2] Heb. i. 3.

the laws of nature. We are prone to conceive, that, to bring from non-existence into existence, differs from the preservation of existence already bestowed. It is enough, for every practical purpose, to attribute the preservation of all things to the power and will of the same being that originally created them. At his will, the world came into existence; and, at his will, it continues to exist.

SECTION II.—GOVERNMENT IN GENERAL.

ALL CREATED THINGS ARE SO UNDER GOD'S CONTROL, THAT THEIR CHANGES TAKE PLACE ACCORDING TO HIS PURPOSE.[1]

Created things are perpetually operating on each other in the relation of cause and effect. The properties and powers by which they so operate, were given to each of them in their creation, and are continued in the act of preservation. It follows, therefore, that all created things operate on each other, and produce changes in each other, by the will and power of God. If they are dependent for their existence, they must be, for their properties and powers, and, of consequence, for their operations.

God's control over all events that happen, is abundantly taught in the Scriptures; which represent the wind,[2] the rain,[3] pestilence,[4] plenty,[5] grass,[6] the fowls of the air,[7] the hairs of the head,[8] &c., as objects of his providence.

The Scriptures not only attribute events to the overruling hand of God, but they represent him as ordering them for the accomplishment of some purpose. The grass grows, that it may give food.[9] Pestilence is sent, that men may be punished for their sins.[10] Joseph was sent into Egypt, to preserve much people alive.[11] Nor are there a few events only which are so ordered; but it is said, He worketh all things after the counsel of his own will. The declaration, "All things work together for good,"[12] &c., could not be true, if God's control were not alike extended to all events, causing them all to co-operate in the fulfilment of his purpose.

Some persons are unwilling to attribute to God the care and

---

[1] 2 Chron. xx. 6; Ps. civ. 4, 7, 10, 13, 14, 19, 32; Prov. xvi. 9; Ps. lxxvi. 10; Dan. iv. 35; Rom. viii. 28; Eph. i. 11.

[2] Jonah iv. 8.   [3] Matt. v. 45.   [4] Lev. xxvi. 25.   [5] Gen. xxvii. 28.
[6] Matt. vi. 30.   [7] Matt. vi. 26.   [8] Matt. x. 30.   [9] Ps. civ. 14.
[10] 2 Sam. xxiv. 15.   [11] Gen. xlv. 7.   [12] Rom. viii. 28.

management of minute and unimportant events. They consider it
beneath his dignity to be concerned about such trivial matters.
They believe in a General Providence over the affairs of the world,
exercised by general laws; but a Particular Providence, exercised
over every particular incident of every man's life, enters not into
their creed. But the Scriptures are plain on this subject. The
fall of a sparrow is a very trivial event, yet it is affirmed by the
teacher from heaven, to be not without our heavenly Father.[1] If
great events happen according to general laws, it is equally true
of small ones; and the operation of these laws, in the latter case,
must be as well understood, and as perfectly controlled, as in the
former. Moreover, it often happens, that very important events
depend on others that are in themselves trivial and unimportant.
The King of Israel was slain,[2] and God's prophecy concerning him
was fulfilled, by an arrow shot at a venture. How many very
minute circumstances must have concurred in this act! That the
arrow was shot at all—that it was then shot—that it was precisely
so directed, and with precisely the necessary force—and that it
met no obstacle on its way: all these concurred, and all these
must have been under the control of Him, in whose hand was the
life of the king. As God's greatness permitted him to create the
minutest of his works, so it permits him to take care of them; and
this care is as easy and undistracting to him, as if his whole energy
were directed to the care and benefit of a single man or angel.

The objects of God's Providence are all created things, animate
and inanimate, rational and irrational. Some of these, as angels
and men, are moral agents. All others, viewed as causing change
of any kind, may be classed together as natural agents. With
reference to this division of the agencies under his control, the
government of God may be divided into natural and moral.

Section III.—NATURAL GOVERNMENT.

Among our earliest lessons, we learn that the relation of cause
and effect exists, and that events occur because of this relation in
an established order of sequence. Were the order of succession
not established, or were we ignorant of it, we should be unable to

---

[1] Matt. x. 29.   [2] 1 Kings xxii. 34.

manage the most common concerns of life. If food sometimes nourished, and sometimes poisoned, or if we were incapable of learning whether the nutritive quality belonged to bread, or to arsenic, we should be unable to regulate the process of eating, so necessary to the preservation of life. But our Creator has made us capable of observing the sequences of nature, and of learning the order in which they occur, and the relation of cause and effect, which the parts of the succession sustain to each other. The study of these sequences is the business of philosophy; but philosophy is not confined to the university, or the lecture-room. It is found in every man's walk, and in the every-day experience of life. The child begins to learn it in the cradle; and without some knowledge of it, men would not know how to shun the flood, the flames, or the precipice.

In all departments of knowledge we classify the things known; and the sequences of nature, classified, become what we call laws of nature. These are only the regular modes in which the sequences of nature occur. In the phrase, law of nature, the term law is used in a transferred sense. When employed in morals, it implies an authority commanding, and a subject bound to obey. But nature is not a being possessing authority; and natural things are not capable of obedience in the proper sense. In morals, laws given may be disobeyed; but the processes of nature always conform to what are called the laws of nature. The laws of nature may be regarded as the modes in which the providence of God operates. His will has determined the relation of cause and effect; and, therefore, the laws of nature are the orders of sequence, in which it is his will, that the changes of natural things should occur.

When we contemplate the order which prevails in the natural world, we behold the exhibition of the wisdom which God's providence displays. His natural government, as well as his moral, abounds with wisdom. All his reasons for planning the system of things precisely as it is we cannot presume to understand; but the advantage resulting from its order meets us in every experience of life. It would be to no purpose that we have been so made as to be capable of observing the sequences of nature, if these sequences took place without order. If chaos reigned in the succession of events, philosophy would be impossible, and equally impossible the most common arts of life. Reason would be an unavailing gift;

and, if human life were not filled with perpetual terror, the exemption would arise rather from inability to comprehend its danger, than from the circumstances of its situation.

Section IV.—MORAL GOVERNMENT.

A voluntary agent, with a sense of right and wrong, we call a moral agent. Such an agent is a proper subject of moral law. He may be commanded, and he can obey or disobey. He can feel the force of moral obligation, and be affected by self-approbation or remorse.

Moral law is not an established order of sequence, as the laws of nature are. Some have sought to find an agreement between them in this particular, by referring to the fact, that a moral action has consequences inseparably connected with it, which result from its moral quality. But the connection of these consequences with the moral action belongs rather to the class of natural sequences. Like other natural sequences, the order is inviolable. But moral law may be violated. The order of sequence which moral law aims to regulate, is that which subsists between the command and the action, not between the action and its consequences. In the first of these sequences, not in the last, the obedience or disobedience of moral law appears. If moral law were an established order of sequence, as natural law is, none but God could violate it, as none but he can work miracles. But, while God cannot commit sin, which is a transgression of moral law, it may be committed by angels and men, as sad experience has proved.

The distinction which has been drawn between natural and moral law must be kept in view, to understand the difference between natural and moral government. Moral government is a department of God's universal administration, specially adapted to moral agents, furnishing scope for the exercise of their moral agency, as, also, on God's part, for the exercise of his justice. It is not inconsistent with the rest of his administration, but is distinct from the rest, and is the holy of·holies, in which the great Supreme manifests his highest glory. It is true, that in this the will of God is not invariably done; whereas, in his natural government, he worketh all things after the counsel of his will; but it must be remembered that the term will is used in different senses. The will which is violated in moral government is the will of precept; that which is invariably executed in natural government is the will of purpose. The whole of God's moral government perfectly accords with his purpose. It was his purpose to institute it; to create moral agents, to give them a moral law, a will of precept, which they, as free agents, might violate or not; to permit the violation, and to hold them responsible for it. All this God purposed, and all this he has accomplished. Because the term will is used in two senses, manifestly distinct from each other, it becomes necessary, in our use of it, to keep the distinction in view, lest our reasonings be confused.

The general proposition, under the head of Government, page 117, was stated thus: "All God's creatures are so under his control, that their changes take place according to his purpose." The truth of this, with respect to his natural government, will be readily admitted. An important part of the changes which take place in the world, consists of the actions performed by moral agents. In applying the proposition to these, it becomes necessary to distinguish between the efficient and permissive purpose of God. Even the most sinful action cannot take place without his permission; and, in this view, the proposition extends to the moral, as well as to the natural government of God.

Section V.—FREE AGENCY.

What is free agency? If it signifies freedom from accountability to a higher power, there is no free agent but God. This, however, is not the sense in which the term is technically employed, and in which it denotes voluntary agency — agency without compulsion.

A creature who acts voluntarily, and knows the difference between right and wrong, is a proper subject of moral government. The common sense of mankind holds such an one accountable for his actions. We do not enter into a metaphysical inquiry to ascertain by what mental process the volition was formed; but it is enough for us to know that it was formed. If a man does what he did not intend to do, we admit the plea of involuntariness; but, when the intention to perpetrate the deed is proved, together with the knowledge of its criminality, no metaphysical subtleties exempt him, in the uniform judgment of mankind, from being held accountable.

Some have maintained that, in order to responsible agency, it is necessary that the will should have a self-determining power. It is, they maintain, not only necessary that the agent should have acted voluntarily, but he should have the power to will otherwise than he did. That he should have had the power to *act* otherwise than he did, is implied in his acting voluntarily, *i. e.* without compulsion, and is, therefore, necessary to his accountability; but the power to *will* otherwise than he did, is a superaddition to voluntariness, which the common sense of mankind does not inquire into; yet, as a metaphysical perplexity, it claims our attention.

Self-determining power of the will.—It is inconsistent with philosophical accuracy to speak of the will as determining or deciding. The faculties of the mind are not distinct agents, possessing a separate existence from the mind itself. We may say that a man understands or wills, or that his mind understands or wills; but to say that his understanding understands, or his will wills, is bad philosophy. If it be conceived that the will determines itself, as the magnetic needle determines its position, without reasoning, and without choice, a supposition is admitted which will not at all accord with the views of those who advocate the self-determining power of the will. But, if it be conceived that the will determines by choice, or any other mental process, then the will is represented as a distinct agent, having a mind of its own.

Power of the will.—Here is another incongruity. In the external acts of men, power and will are concomitants necessary to the act. Without either, the act cannot be. But to an act of willing, what is necessary besides the will itself? What power must be conjoined with it? What a supposition it would be, that the will has a will to put forth a volition, but has not the power! Yet something like this must be conceived, to give a distinct and intelligible meaning to the phrase, "self-determining *power* of the will."

Section VI.—MORAL NECESSITY.

If a number of dice be put into a box and thrown out on a table, it is certain that every one will take some position, and will lie on some one of its six sides; but no one can foretell what the several positions will be, or on which of the six sides each one will lie. These positions are attributed to chance; and, in a calculation of chances, this case may be adduced as an appropriate example. But

[handwritten marginalia: see Hodge vol. 2. p. 295. *]*

[handwritten: Certainty (see Hodge vol. 2 p. 65 *]*

[handwritten at foot: * moral or philosophical necessity or Certainty versus Necessity. Fatalism & mechanical necessity *]*

though no one will undertake to foretell what position each die will assume, yet every one believes that all its motion, till its final position is assumed, is in accordance with the laws of nature, and that the fall from the box is not more determined by these laws than the final position. A mind which could go through the calculation, and estimate the precise effect of the forces applied, from the beginning to the end, on each die, from the position in which it started, might determine the result with as much certainty as the astronomer feels in computing an eclipse. The position of the die is not more the effect of chance than the occurrence of the eclipse. Chance is, in this case at least, a relative term — having reference to our ignorance.

That a large part of the events which we esteem contingent are so merely with reference to our ignorance, everybody will admit; but it is still a question, whether there is any absolute contingency in the world. Are there any events which occur that do not conform to an established order of sequence?

The doctrine of necessity denies the existence of absolute contingency, and maintains that the relation of cause and effect, with its established order of sequence, is not only general, but universal. In opposition to this doctrine, many maintain that human actions do not conform to an established order of sequence; and it is argued that such conformity would render man a mere machine, moving as he is moved, and, therefore, not accountable for his actions. To this argument it is replied, that the doctrine fully admits the distinction between man as a living, thinking, willing, and moral being, and a mere machine, which neither lives nor thinks; and that this difference is the foundation of his accountability. It is argued, that if his actions did not follow from his volitions, by an established order of sequence, they would not be voluntary, and he would not be accountable for them. The validity of this argument, so far as it goes, probably no one will deny; and the question becomes narrowed down to this: Do human volitions occur as effects of antecedent causes, in an established order of sequence? The question is one of great difficulty; and, though the minds of the ablest reasoners have been employed on it, no solution has been reached that gives general satisfaction. The very difficulty of it may satisfy us that our benevolent Creator has not made the solution of it necessary, either to our faith or our duty; and we might leave the puzzling investigation to those powerful minds that are best fitted to grapple with such abstrusities, were it not that the subject is intruding itself into the minds of all inquirers, and, to some extent, affecting their theological opinions. It is, therefore, desirable to ascertain, if possible, wherein the difficulty of the subject consists, and how far it is connected with our faith or practice.

Analogy favors the doctrine of necessity. A regular order of sequence is admitted to exist throughout the material world. It is admitted to exist also, to some extent, in the operations of the human mind. Impressions on the organs of sense produce their appropriate sensations in the mind, according to fixed laws. Perceptions follow, and judgments, and trains of reasoning, all of which so far conform to fixed laws, that the order of their succession is studied with a view to find out these laws; and the science of mental philosophy proceeds on the supposition that such laws exist, and employs itself in finding them out. The train of mental operations, beginning with the sensation which immediately follows the impression on the organs of sense, terminates with the volition which immediately precedes muscular action. A regular order of sequence may be traced from the first, through much of the mental process that is moving on toward the ultimate volition. Thence onward we again espy the line of succession in the action which follows, and in all its effects. At most, but a few links only in the chain can be wanting; and analogy favours the conclusion that these are not absent, but that they exist even if we cannot trace them.

An argument for the doctrine of necessity may be drawn from the fact that human volitions are every day made a subject of calculation. A man who would not attempt to calculate the position which a thrown die will assume, will judge what a known individual will determine to do in given circumstances; and so much does he rely on the correctness of his calculation, that he will be governed by it in some of his most important concerns. It is thus that a sagacious general often anticipates the movements of his enemy. All this would be impossible if the sequences of human volitions were wild and lawless.

The doctrine of necessity has been argued from God's foreknowledge. The more sagacious any one is, the more successfully he can judge beforehand what a known individual will do in given circumstances. As a wise man may foreknow, much more can the all-wise God. If all events are contained in their causes, and are to be developed in due time, in conformity to an established order of sequence, we can conceive that the Omniscient One sees these events in their causes, and foreknows their future development with infallible certainty. On the other hand, if there is absolute contingency in the world, it is out of our power to conceive how even God himself can foreknow it, and it is alleged that he may be disappointed, and perhaps defeated in some of his plans by its occurrence.

The leading arguments against the doctrine are, that it is inconsistent with the free agency of man, and that it makes God the author of sin.

It is argued that the doctrine is inconsistent with the free agency of man. While we see the material world moving around us in obedience to the laws of nature, we are conscious that our acts are not directed by such a necessity. We choose every day which of two courses we will take, and the very choice, of which we are conscious, implies the power to take either. The faculty of choosing would be possessed in vain, if we were restricted to one of the courses by invincible necessity. There is no free agency where an individual is bound to one way, and can take no other.

To this the advocates of necessity reply, the freedom of our actions, of which consciousness testifies, is fully admitted in their doctrine. Freedom of action consists in doing what we please. Compulsion to act against our will is physical necessity. The moral necessity which is contended for, respects, not the relation of the volition to the subsequent action, but its relation to antecedent causes. When a man's volitions are known to be determined by strong ruling principles of action, it is maintained that his free agency is as perfect as if they were the result of long continued deliberation, or proceeded from no known cause. While we are conscious that we act from choice, and are therefore free agents, we are equally conscious that our choice itself is, in many cases, determined instantly and firmly by strong ruling principles; and that this fact, instead of detracting from the free agency and virtue of our deeds, is our highest praise.

It is further argued, that the doctrine makes God the author of sin. The laws of nature, in the material world, are viewed as God's mode of operation. If the sun shines, and the rain descends, it is God who gives light to his creatures, and fertilizes the ground for their benefit; and when storms rage, and hurricanes sweep over the land, these, arising according to the laws of nature which he has established, are still regarded as God's operation. In every case the cause of the cause is the cause of the effect. If fixed laws govern with like necessity in the department of morals, it is argued that God must be viewed as the author of all that happens in obedience to these laws. Having himself established them, and created the causes which contain all the effects to be developed in the established order of sequence, he is as truly the author of these effects as if they proceeded immediately from his hand. It can no longer be said that sin has place by his permission, any more than it can be said that a storm arises by his permission. Even sin must, like the storm, be viewed as God operating. This is the argument which the advocates of necessity find it most difficult to answer.

The philosophical arguments on this question appear to me to preponderate on the side of necessity. Indeed, how philosophy could decide against it, cannot well be conceived. She begins her investigations with the assumption that laws of nature do exist, and she makes it her business to find out what these laws are. If she observes any events that do not conform to known laws, she still assumes that there is a law which governs them, and she renews her effort to find it out. Hence, for philosophy to decide that there are events which conform to no law, would be to abandon the foundation on which she has ever stood. If such events ever occur, they belong to a department of nature which is beyond the walks of philosophy.

As a theological question, the doctrine of necessity is seriously embarrassed by the difficulty respecting the authorship of sin. The whole subject of God's providence over sin, is exceedingly difficult. A future section will be devoted to the consideration of it.

Truth, whether ascertained by philosophy or theology, must be consistent with itself. But it ought to be remembered, that the tests by which philosophy ascertains truth, are unequal to those which theology applies. Philosophy allows conclusions to be drawn from an induction of particulars, which is unavoidably incomplete. As far as our individual observation has extended, gravitation is found at every part of the earth's surface. From the testimony of others, we know that it exists wherever human foot has trodden. This induction is sufficient for philosophy, and she draws her conclusion that gravitation exists at every part of the earth's surface, even in the regions denied to the habitation or approach of men. If some voyagers should testify that, on a certain island in the Pacific, gravitation ceases to operate at the distance of ten feet above the earth's surface, the announcement, if deemed worthy of credence, would startle the whole race of philosophers, who would hasten to institute the experiments necessary to determine the truth or false-hood of the strange report. Should it be found, on trial, that all bodies thrown ten feet into the air, on that island, go off into un-known space, philosophers would inquire into the cause of this phenomenon, that is, would endeavor to find a law to which it con-forms. Thus philosophy often finds it necessary to rectify her previous conclusions, because these were formed from an incom-plete induction of particulars. To Siamese philosophy, it was impossible for water to become solid, so as to bear up carriages of burden. So, much of our wisest philosophy may be the erroneous conclusions of our ignorance. God's knowledge is perfect, and with him mistake is impossible. If human testimony can suffice to rectify a conclusion of philosophy, much more ought the testimony of God to be sufficient. A "thus saith the Lord," is a better foundation for faith than all the deductions of human philosophy, and then only is faith divine, when it stands on this foundation.

Let us imagine all created things to have been brought into being, and left, for a time, in a wild state, before the laws of nature were enacted. In this chaos, the atoms would not regard the very first law of philosophy, which enjoins that matter at rest shall continue at rest; and, when put in motion, shall move forward in a right line with uniform velocity. All the affinities and elective attrac-tions, now so familiar to the chemist, would be unknown to the various species of matter, and unobserved by them. Particles would dance and rest alternately in the most capricious manner. They would attract each other for a time, and then repel with un-accountable inconstancy. They would remain for a period in close embrace, and then divorce each other with the changeableness of fickle lovers. If, when the fiat of Jehovah reduced this confusion to order by subjecting all the movements to regular laws, it was his pleasure to except some little region of his vast empire from the operation of these laws, what can philosophy say against it? If such exception was made, it was doubtless made for wise reasons; perhaps to show to his celestial school of intelligences the benefit of order by retaining a memorial of the ancient chaos; as the manna was laid up in the ark for the benefit of the Israelites. If such a region was permitted to remain, it was doubtless so bounded and shut in, that its lawless confusion cannot disturb the order of the universal empire. Now, if it should be discovered that the link of connection between volition and the cause or causes antecedent, is the place, and the only place that God has left without law, philosophy must be dumb. If God says that it is so, we are bound to believe it; and we may infer that he so keeps this lawless connection under control, that it shall not subvert his government.

If the views which have been presented are correct, the following conclusions may be considered established :— 1. The doctrine of moral necessity is not inconsistent with the free-agency and accountability of man. 2. The doctrine cannot be disproved by human philosophy. 3. We ought not to admit any inference from it as an article of faith, unless it be supported by the authority of the Holy Scriptures.

Section VII.—DESIGNS OF PROVIDENCE.

In the view which we have taken of God's providential government, we have included the fact, that he so orders the events which occur, as to accomplish his purpose. This is called predestination. The purpose of God respects the end which he has in view; and also the means which he uses for the accomplishment of this end.

The doctrine of predestination teaches that no event comes to pass, which is not under the control of God; and that it is so ordered by him as to fulfil his purpose. If it would thwart his purpose, the event is prevented; or if, in part only it would conduce to his purpose, only so far is it permitted to happen. This divine control extends over all agents, animate and inanimate, rational and irrational; and is exercised over each in perfect accordance with its nature, and with all the laws of nature as originally established. Physical agents are controlled as physical agents; and moral, as moral agents. The latter act as freely as if no providence over them existed. Their ends are chosen, their means adopted, and their accountability exists, just as if there were no predestination of God in the matter. Yet God is not unconcerned in any of these acts, but overrules each and all of them according to his pleasure.

The holy men of ancient times were accustomed to view the hand of God in everything with which they had to do; and the passages of Scripture are numerous, in which God's direction of man's affairs and actions is taught. " A man's heart deviseth his way; but the Lord directeth his steps." [1] " The king's heart is in the hands of the Lord, as the rivers of water; he turneth it whithersoever he will." [2] The gardener has his rivulet, with which he waters his beds; and, by cutting a channel here, and damming up there, he directs the fertilizing stream to whatever part of his garden he pleases; while the water, however directed, moves according to its own natural tendency. So the king's heart moves according to its own inclination; but the directing hand of God guides his movements, though freely made, to the accomplishment of such ends as infinite wisdom has designed. The passages are also numerous, which show that this direction of events is for the accomplishment of some purpose. God meant it unto good. [3] All things work together for good. [4] Each particular event accomplishes some purpose; and the whole combined accomplishes the grand purpose, to which the particular purposes are subordinate. So he who builds a house, has, in adjusting each timber, a purpose subordinate to the general or final purpose for which the whole work was undertaken; and, to the accomplishment of which, the whole is directed.

The possibility that God should possess this complete control of all things, cannot be doubted by any who admit the doctrine of necessity. Even if human volitions are absolutely contingent, his control of overt acts must be conceived to be as perfect, as on the other hypothesis. As length and breadth are necessary to constitute area, as weight and velocity are necessary to constitute force; so volition and power are necessary to constitute action. He does not act, who has the will without the power, or the power without the will. Now, the power is in the hand of God, and under his

---

[1] Prov. xvi. 9.   [2] Prov. xxi. 1.   [3] Gen. l. 20.   [4] Rom. viii. 28.

9

perfect control; and, therefore, whatever the will may be, no overt act can be performed but by his permission; and consequently, no influence can be brought to bear on any part of God's dominions, so as to disturb his administration. This hook God has in the nose of every rebellious subject; so that, however filled with rage, he cannot move but by God's permission.[1]

Again, even if human volition is absolutely contingent, it is still true, that men often fortell it with sufficient certainty or probability, to know how to direct their actions with respect to it. A sagacious sovereign knows the character of his subjects, and the parties which exist in his government; and he adapts the measures of his administration to meet the exigencies as they arise. Why cannot God, on the throne of the universe, manage the affairs of his government with equal skill? A human sovereign sometimes fails for want of time to deliberate. His enemies form their schemes, and their plots proceed to their accomplishment before he is aware of their designs; and, when they are discovered, he cannot command his resources, or digest his plan, in time to meet the emergency. But God sees every budding volition; and, as all his power may be exerted at any point of space, so all the resources of his infinite wisdom can arrange his plan, while the volition is taking its form as wisely and completely as if it were the result of an eternity of deliberation. God is verily able to govern the world; and who doubts that he is willing? And our belief that God governs the world, and predestinates its various events to accomplish the counsel of his will, is not dependent on a metaphysical speculation.

SECTION VIII.—PROVIDENCE OVER SIN.

Providence has been explained to be the care which God exercises over the world. Though this care is watchful and kind, sin has entered, bringing innumerable evils in its train, and is now mingling in the whole current of human enjoyment, and spreading havoc and death, where peace, order, life, and happiness, would have reigned undisturbed. How all this comes to pass, under the government of a God, infinitely wise, powerful, and good, is a question of great difficulty. The observations which follow, will not clear away the darkness in which the subject is involved; but

---

[1] 2 Kings xix. 28.

they may suffice to assist our faith, and guard our hearts from unworthy thoughts of the deity.

1. The fact of God's providence over sin, is incontrovertible, whatever difficulties attend its explanation. If there were anything from which he would stand aloof, it would be sin, the abominable thing which he hates; but nothing so clearly shows his providence to be universal as the abundant proof which is furnished, that it extends over sin. Indeed, if it kept at a distance from everything sinful, it would abandon all human affairs, which are thoroughly mixed with sin. The Scriptures speak, in very clear and strong terms, of God's control over sinful agents. He brought the Chaldeans against Jerusalem,[1] and stirred up the Medes against Babylon.[2] These were nations composed of wicked men, and could not have been moved by the providence of God, if wicked agents were not under his control. Wicked men are called the rod, the staff, the ax, the saw, in his hand;[3] and are therefore moved by him as these instruments are, by the hand of him who uses them. The Scriptures descend with still greater particularity to the very acts of wicked agents, in which their wickedness is exhibited, and attributes these to God. So Shimei's cursing of David[4] and Absalom's lying with his father's wives;[5] wicked as these acts were, are, in the words of inspiration, ascribed to the God of holiness. Why is this, if it be not designed to teach us that the providence of God extends over sinful actions. So strong are some of the representations contained in the holy word, that, like the ascribing of repentance to God, they need to be explained by the general tenor of the sacred teachings. He blinds the eyes,[6] and hardens the hearts[7] of sinful men; and sends them strong delusions,[8] that they should believe a lie, and be damned; and he raised up[9] Pharoah, and hardened his heart,[10] that he might show his power in him. Such language was certainly designed to make a strong impression on our minds, that God exercises a perfect control over every sinful agent in all his acts; and it is not more clearly revealed, that God hates the wicked acts of wicked men, than that he controls and directs them to the accomplishment of his purpose. All this we are

---

[1] Hab. i. 6. [2] Isaiah xiii. 17; Jer. li. 11. [3] Isaiah x. 5–15.
[4] 2 Sam. xvi. 11. [5] 2 Sam. xii. 12. [6] John xii. 40. [7] Rom. ix. 18.
[8] 2 Thess. ii. 11. [9] Ex. ix. 16. [10] Ex. vii. 13.

bound to believe, whatever mystery may attend it; and what we know concerning any subject, is not the less true, or the less firmly to be believed, because there are other things involved in it which we know not.

2. What we know not concerning God's providence over sin, respects him rather than ourselves; and we may, therefore, safely leave it for him to interpret. How to govern a world of sinful agents, is a problem which it is not necessary for us to solve, as the task has not been assigned us. Had God imposed the duty on us, he would doubtless have taught us how to perform it. But he has reserved it to himself; and he giveth no account of his matters. Instead, therefore, of being surprised that there are things in God's government which are inscrutable to us, we should have reason for surprise if it were otherwise. Earthly governments have their secrets, and these may especially relate to the management of the hostile. We must, without taking offence, permit the Sovereign Ruler of all to have his secrets, and to make known his ways only so far as he pleases. We are often, in appearance at least, exceedingly anxious to relieve the character of God from foul aspersions; but we may safely leave him to vindicate himself. We shall do well to look to it, that our very officiousness does not betray an unwillingness to repose entire confidence in the wisdom and goodness of his ways, when they are past our comprehension. Let the very darkness in which he leaves them be improved by us to the trial and strengthening of our faith.

3. The distinction between God's permission of sin, and his being the efficient cause of it, is one which we appear authorized to use to free our thoughts from embarrassment when we contemplate this subject. More than mere permission is implied in many of the expressions found in Scripture, that refer to the influence by which the current of sinful propensity is directed into this channel, rather than that. But the notion that God is the efficient agent in producing the sinful propensity, we are unable to reconcile with our ideas of his character; and it does not appear to be taught in the sacred volume. God is a sun, and moral darkness arises from the absence, rather than from the presence of his beams. We dare not doubt that, had it been his pleasure, he might have poured forth such a flood of holy influence from himself as would have effectually preserved the human race from all possibility of defilement;

and, that he did not do so, is his permission of sin. But every one readily conceives of this as very different from a positive efficiency in the production of moral evil. It is a good maxim, to consider all our good as coming from God, and give him the praise of it; and all our evil as our own, and give ourselves the blame of it. In like manner, when we see sin in others, and know that God is over-ruling it for good, we can blame them for the evil, and praise God for the good which he educes from it.

4. We should restrain our philosophy within due bounds, and not give ourselves up to its deductions when they would disturb our faith. We have already shown that philosophy is compelled to rely on inductions which are incomplete, and that her inferences have not equal authority with the declarations of God. We are so constituted that we rely on the uniformity of nature's laws, and therefore believe that they will operate in the future as they have operated in the past. This constitutional propensity is wisely given, fitting us to shape our course in the world; and, for all the purposes for which it was given, it does not deceive us; but there are limits within which the propensity must be restrained. A child asks the cause of something which he notices, and when we have answered, he asks, What is the cause of that? and when, in answering his successive inquiries, we have led his mind up to God as the First Cause, he asks, Who made God? We may very wisely tell him that God is self-existent; but this means nothing more than that his inquisitive philosophy must stop here, having reached its utmost bounds. Now, whether we can metaphysically account for it or not, there is a propensity in the human mind to regard each moral agent as a sort of original source of action, somewhat as we conceive of God. This propensity, perhaps as universal as the propensity to rely on the uniformity of nature's laws, may have been given us for the very purpose of checking our philosophy when it would presume to explain the origin of evil in the heart of a moral agent. Accustomed, as it is, to contemplate the relation of cause and effect, operating in an established order of sequence, it does not submit to consider man an original source of action, but labors to account for the moral evil in him by causes operating from without, and ultimately traces it to God. It may be well to inquire whether philosophy, when it pushes the doctrine of necessity into the inmost arcana of this subject, does not assume in the

premises from which it reasons, that there is a natural inertia in mind, as in matter; or, rather, a sort of natural immutability. Among the arguments in favor of moral necessity, it was stated that the volitions of a known individual under given influences, are often the subject of calculation; but, for successful calculation, the individual must be *known;* and in this, it is implied that he must possess some-fixed character. A change in him, all the circumstances being the same, makes a change in the result. A chemical experiment now operates precisely as it would have done before the flood, because every atom of matter has precisely the same properties now that it had then. Matter has a natural immutability; but can this be predicated of mind? And does not philosophy assume it when it applies the doctrine of necessity to mental phenomena without any limitation, and boldly carries back the authorship of sin to God, as the First Cause. There is a tendency in the human mind to a fixed state of virtue or vice, by the power of habit; but a natural immutability of the mind, anterior to the formation of habits, philosophy ought not to assume. Matter, in each atom, is immutable; and it is mutable only in its combinations. The mind of man, though an uncompounded essence, is not immutable. God has made matter immutable; or operates immutably in matter. But if he has not chosen to operate in the same manner in mind, but has made each mind, in some sort, an original source of action, philosophy must submit to push her orders of sequence with confidence only where she has firm ground to stand on.

To illustrate the distinction attempted in the last paragraph, let us suppose a metallic globe placed on the sharp point of a pyramid. No human art could so adjust it that it would not fall to one side. Mathematically we may demonstrate the possibility of such an adjustment that the power of gravity, operating equally on every side, would retain it for ever in the same position. But, in spite of mathematics, the globe would fall to one side; and philosophy will seek to account for its fall as arising from some failure in the adjustment, or some external cause, as a breath of air, operating from without, and not from any changeableness in the globe itself. When once started in the descent, the globe has a tendency to motion in the direction taken, but it does not pass from rest to motion except from external influence. Now, if philosophy equally denies that motion can originate in the mind, and maintains that its doctrine of necessity is applicable to the mind, not only when acting under the influence of habit, but as existing before habits were formed, does not philosophy assume a natural immutability of mind. in attributing the first start in the wrong way to a failure in God's adjustment, or to the operation of external causes, which have been brought into being and action by him? If philosophy assumes this in the premises from which it reasons, its conclusions are not to be trusted.

CONCLUSION.

Genuine piety in the heart prompts the inquiry which burst forth from the lips of the converted Saul of Tarsus, "Lord, what wilt thou have me to do?" It asks to know the will of God, for the purpose of doing it, as naturally as the infant's appetite craves the appropriate food. The men of the world walk in their own ways, and fulfil the desires of their own minds; but the man of piety desires to walk in the way of the Lord, and to do that which is pleasing to him. Hence he delights to meditate on his law. The Bible would not be a book adapted to the state of his mind, if it did not contain precepts for the regulation of his conduct.

The infant's appetite not only craves food, but appropriate food; and this fact is alluded to in the words of Peter, "As new-born babes, desire the sincere milk of the word, that ye may grow thereby.[1] The Bible, the word of God, supplies the sincere milk which the child of grace needs and craves. It not only gives precepts, but precisely such precepts as are adapted to the holy affections of the new-born soul, and tend to increase and strengthen them. Paul delighted in the law of God, not simply because it was his law, but because it was holy, just and good.[2] The pure morality of Christ and his doctrine, even infidels acknowledge; and precisely the same morality appears in the decalogue, and in the two great precepts on which hang all the law and the prophets. The decalogue, written on the tables of stone by the finger of God, has been thought by some to be the first specimen of alphabetical writing known in the world. Whether this be true or not, it is certainly among the earliest specimens of which we have any know-

---

[1] 1 Peter ii. 2.   [2] Rom. vii. 12.

ledge. The fact, that at so early a period a law so pure and perfect was given to mankind, is very remarkable, and can be satisfactorily accounted for only on the supposition that it emanated from God. The intrinsic excellence of this law corresponds well with the solemnity and grandeur of its promulgation from Sinai. The pious man admires its perfection and delights in its holiness, and sees in it a proof that the Bible which contains it is indeed the word of God.

When the desires are properly regulated within, all the out-goings of the soul will be in accordance with the will of God; and they will be so adapted to the circumstances of our being, as to show that the power which made the things that are without, is the same that works within us to will and to do. All the works of God, in heaven above, where the sun, moon and stars declare his glory, and in the earth beneath, which is full of his goodness, are fitted to excite our admiration and gratitude. We admire the habitation which our Creator has provided for us, so splendid and so richly furnished, and we sit, with overflowing gratitude, at the table which his Providence has spread before us with such profusion and variety.

The doctrine of General Providence suffices for the exercise of gratitude in the pious heart. The general arrangements of the world in which we are placed, show the benevolence of him who planned them; and we should have just cause of gratitude to him for the wise and beneficial arrangements, even if we conceived of him as leaving the world to the operation of the general laws which he has instituted, and giving no direction to them in the minute details of our daily experience. But genuine piety is no less dis-played by resignation in the hour of suffering, than by gratitude in the general experience of enjoyment. Yet resignation to God under afflictions would be impossible, if they were not viewed as coming from the hand of God. Job was resigned under his afflic-tion, because he considered it sent by God. "Shall we receive good at the hand of God, and shall we not also receive evil?" To the exercise of resignation, a belief in particular Providence is necessary. The general arrangements of Providence, which, be-cause of their benevolence, have called forth our gratitude, may fail, in the particular exigency of our present condition, to meet our necessities. We suffer in consequence of this failure, and piety prompts us to bear the suffering with resignation to the will of God; but this would be impossible if we did not believe that the particular event happens according to the will of God. We must view Providence, not merely as instituting general laws, but as directing the times and circumstances in which the operation of these laws shall cross our path.

In order to the further exercise of piety, the providence in which we believe must not only be particular, but it must be exercised with design. Resignation to blind fate is not piety. We must not only feel the hand of God in our affliction, but we must realise that it has been laid on us with design. We have to do, not so much with our Father's hand as with our Father's heart. It is not necessary to the exercise of piety, that we should be able to penetrate his design; but we must believe its existence. We are not required to understand or explain all the mystery attendant on the doctrine of predestination; but a belief of the doctrine is necessary to an intelligent exercise of pious resignation. A wise Providence, and to such only is intelligent piety resigned, operates with design.

Human depravity is prone to make an improper use of divine truth. The doctrine concerning God's will of purpose is made a pretext for neglecting his will of command, and an apology for past disobedience. The transgressor pleads, "who hath resisted his will?" But sincere piety leaves God to execute his will of purpose in his own way, and makes the will of precept its rule of duty. It leaves God to his work, and delights in it as the work of God. Where it cannot comprehend his design, it still trusts in him, and rejoices in the assurance that he does all things well. It recognises him as operating in all things without; and, in viewing all these operations, finds occasion for admiration, gratitude and resignation. But whenever a question of duty arises, it is decided, not by the inquiry, What has God done? or, What has he purposed to do? but, What has he commanded? The union of resignation and obedience in the same heart, is a test of true piety. Happy is he in whom their influence is combined. He can delight to do the will of God, and find a heaven in his obedience; and he can rejoice even in tribulation, and feel a bed of thorns, if God has laid him on it, to be a bed of down.

BOOK FOURTH.

DOCTRINE CONCERNING THE FALL AND PRESENT STATE OF MAN.

INTRODUCTION.

DUTY OF REPENTANCE.[1]

WE have seen that religion is not confined to the intellect, but brings into exercise the strongest feelings of the heart. Love to God, and delight in his will and works, have been shown to be essential elements; and these are affections which do not play on the surface, but move the soul from its lowest depths. If, in our study of religious truth, we have proceeded thus far without feeling, without strong feeling, our labor has been unprofitable, and we would do well to begin anew. No time should be lost in securing the main end for which God's truth should be studied; and if heretofore we have treated it as we do the truths of other science, we should persevere in this course no longer, lest the profane use of sacred things become habitual, and provoke God to deny us his illuminating grace.

Love to God, and delight in his will and works, are holy and pleasurable exercises of the mind; but religion in a sinful being is necessarily attended with pain. To be at ease in sin, is a proof that the heart is dead, "dead in trespasses and sins." Every one whom the spirit of God quickens, becomes sensible of sin, and feels the pang of a broken heart on account of it. The anguish of

---

[1] *Matt.* iii. 2. Repent, for the kingdom of heaven is at hand.

Acts xvii. 30. The times of this ignorance God winked at, but now commandeth all men everywhere to repent.

remorse may be alleviated by a sense of pardoning mercy; but the joy of pardon cannot stop the flow of penitence. Like the woman to whom much had been forgiven, the believer, while receiving his pardon with overflowing joy, does not lose his sense of sin, but is ready to wash the feet of his Lord with tears. These tears have their sweetness.

The necessity of repentance is abundantly taught in the sacred volume. The language of Christ is explicit, "Except ye repent, ye shall all likewise perish."[1] We have no right to consider ourselves in the way to eternal life, if we are strangers to repentance. Nor will it suffice to have been at some time alarmed about our sin. A false repentance, which needs to be repented of, satisfies many a deluded soul. Genuine repentance is a deep-felt and abiding sense of sin, a condemnation of ourselves before God on account of it, a turning away from it with abhorrence and loathing, and a fixed purpose of soul never again to commit it, or be at peace with it. This sense of sin drives the soul to Christ, and unites with the exercise of faith in Christ, to distinguish genuine religion from the counterfeits with which the world abounds.

Reason teaches that it is the duty of men, as sinners, to repent of their sins. When one man has given just occasion of offence to another, by the common consent of mankind it is his duty to be sorry for his offence. If we have no sorrow for having offended God, we treat him with less respect than is due to a fellow-worm. Not to be sorry is to justify the offence, and virtually to repeat it. God searches our hearts, and knows our inmost thoughts; and, if we remain impenitent after having sinned against him, it is as if we told him to his face that we did right to treat his authority with contempt. Our impenitence insults the majesty of heaven, and defies his wrath.

But the duty of repentance is not left to be inferred from the common sense of mankind. It is true, that no command to repent is found in the decalogue. That summary of duty was given to men as men, and not as sinners. It was not designed to restore men to the favor of God, and, therefore, did not treat with them as sinners. But when the gospel began to be preached, its first proclamation was, "Repent ye, for the kingdom of heaven is at hand."[2] In all the ministry of the gospel, this is the first duty

---

[1] Luke xiii. 3.   [2] Matt. iii. 2.

required of men. Without it, not a step can be taken in the way
of return to God; and, without it, there is no possibility of obtaining the divine favor. "Except ye repent, ye shall all likewise
perish." It is, therefore, of the very highest importance to understand what repentance is, and to have such views of truth as will
tend to produce it in our hearts.

When we approach a fellow-man whom we have offended, to offer
to him our confessions, and seek his pardon, it is expected that we
shall be sensible of having done wrong, shall regret the deed, blame
ourselves for it, acknowledge his right to be displeased, and resolve,
perhaps promise, to do so no more. All this must exist in repentance toward God, if we do not mean to repeat our insults to the
Searcher of hearts. We may deceive a man like ourselves with
professions of penitence that are insincere, and designed merely
to propitiate him, but God cannot be deceived, and to attempt it is
to mock him.

In order to sincere repentance toward God, it is indispensable
that we should understand that we have sinned against him. Men
do not usually compare their actions with his righteous law, but
with the actions of other men. We walk according to the course
of this world, and are satisfied if we conform to such rules of conduct as are esteemed reputable among men. Multitudes pass
through life without any proper conviction of sin, and die impenitent, who have never examined and tried their conduct by a higher
rule. To undeceive such persons, and to strip them of such false
and delusive pleas, it is necessary to convince them that the course
of this world is downward and wicked, and that their conformity to
it should alarm rather than satisfy them. The doctrine of universal total depravity, is therefore conducive to true repentance.

We do not truly repent of an offence to a fellow-man, and sincerely ask pardon, unless we believe that he has just cause to be
offended. If his displeasure has arisen from mere mistake, we expect to appease him by giving such information as will correct his
mistake. If he has become displeased through mere captiousness,
we may justify ourselves before him, and convict him of the wrong.
In order to the exercise of genuine repentance towards God, we
must know that he has a right to be displeased with us, that he
has made no mistake in the matter, and that every attempt of ours
to convict him of wrong in the case, will be abortive. To impress

all this deeply on our minds, it is only necessary we should be fully convinced that we are under just condemnation from God, and that all our pleas in self-justification are without foundation.

Good men have been accustomed to draw motives to penitence from the doctrines that have been mentioned. David humbled himself before God, with a confession of his natural depravity. "Behold, I was shapen in iniquity; and in sin did my mother conceive me."[1] He viewed his sin with the greater abhorrence, as he saw and confessed the justice of the condemnation which it received from his Judge. "That thou mightest be justified when thou speakest, and be clear when thou judgest."[2]

True penitence is rendered more deep and pungent by a view of the wretchedness and helplessness which sin has brought upon us. So Paul exclaimed, "O wretched man that I am; who shall deliver me from the body of this death?"[3]

CHAPTER I.

ORIGINAL STATE OF MAN.

THE FIRST MAN AND WOMAN WERE CREATED HOLY, AND, FOR A TIME, SERVED THEIR CREATOR ACCEPTABLY.[4]

How long the first pair continued in their original state of innocence and happiness we have no means of knowing; but that they did so continue for a time, is apparent on the face of the sacred record. A free intercourse with their Maker existed, and the token of the divine favor, the fruit of the tree of life, was not denied until a period arrived, distinctly marked in their history, when they first violated the covenant of their God.

The fact that the first pair continued, for a time, to serve God acceptably, proves that their Creator had endowed them with the powers necessary for this service. The possession of these endowments is implied in the phrase, "God created man in his own

---

[1] Ps. li. 5.   [2] Ps. li. 4.
[3] Rom. vii. 24.   [4] Gen. i. 27, 31; Ecc. vii. 29.

image."[1] To interpret this as referring to the form of the human body, is wholly inconsistent with the spirituality of God. It is true, that God was afterwards manifested in human form; but the Scriptures represent the Son of God, in his assumption of our nature, as "made like his brethren," and, therefore, to suppose his human body to have been the pattern after which the body of Adam was formed, would change the order presented in the divine word. The phrase, "image of God," as explained by Paul,[2] includes "knowledge, righteousness and true holiness." It, therefore, refers to their mental endowments, by which they were fitted for the service of God.

Intelligence was necessary to render the service to God for which man was designed. A vast world had been created, abounding with creatures which exhibited, in their wonderful structure, the wisdom and power of their Creator, and, in the bountiful provision made for the supply of their wants, his goodness was richly displayed; but not one of all these creatures was capable of appreciating this wisdom, power, and goodness. They had eyes to see the light of the material sun; but, though the heavens declared the glory of God, and the earth was full of his goodness, to that glory and goodness all were totally blind. A creature was wanted capable of knowing God, and this knowledge our first parents possessed.

Something more than mere intellectual endowments was necessary to fit our first parents for acceptable service to God. These were possessed by the angels that had not kept their first estate, and yet they were enemies of God, and cast out from his presence. Purity of heart was needed; and, accordingly, Adam and Eve were endowed with righteousness and true holiness. They not only knew God, but they loved him supremely. Every natural desire which they possessed was duly subordinated to this reigning affection. Even their love to each other, pure and unalloyed, was far inferior to that which they both felt to him, who daily favored them with his visits, and taught them to see his glory in all his works by which they were surrounded.

We may interpret the phrase, "image of God," as including, also, the dominion with which man was invested over all inferior creatures. When representing man as the head of the woman,

---

[1] Gen. i. 27.   [2] Col. iii. 10; Eph. iv. 24.

Paul speaks of him, in this relation, as "the image and glory of God."[1] This investiture of authority gives him a likeness to God, the Supreme Ruler. In the state of innocence, man possessed this authority without fear from any of the creatures. Until he had rebelled against his God, they were not permitted to rebel against him. As the appointed lord of the lower world, all creatures rendered him homage; and, as it were in their name, he stood, the priest in the grand temple, to offer up spiritual worship and service to the God of the whole creation. From every creature which Adam named he could learn something of God; and, with every new lesson, a new tribute of adoring praise was rendered to the Maker of all.

In the particulars which have been mentioned, the image of God is "renewed" in those who experience the regenerating influences of the Holy Spirit, and are created in Christ Jesus unto good works. The word "renewed" carries back our thoughts to man's original state. A new creation is effected by the Spirit, restoring the regenerate to the knowledge, righteousness, and holiness from which man has fallen. In their renewed state, the effects of the fall still appear, and will remain until the last enemy, death, shall be destroyed; but their connection with the second Adam secures the completion of the good work begun, and assures them that they shall ultimately bear the likeness of the heavenly, who is the image of God.

The human soul bears likeness to God, "the Father of spirits," in its spirituality and immortality. Also, the happiness which Adam and Eve enjoyed, while their innocence remained, was a rill from the fountain of blessedness, which is in the eternal God. In this happiness the image of God appeared, until it became sadly effaced by transgression. The spirituality and immortality of the soul remain, but the happiness of Eden has never revisited the earth; and it is again to be enjoyed only in the celestial paradise. Spirituality and immortality, without knowledge, righteousness, holiness, and communion with the blessed God, would constitute us immortal spirits in eternal woe.

We may profitably look back to the holy and happy state in which our first parents stood when they came from the hand of their

---

[1] 1 Cor. xi. 7.

Creator; and we may, with good effect, remember from whence we have fallen. A due contemplation of this subject will recommend to our acceptance the gracious plan of restoration which the gospel unfolds, in the person and work of the second Adam. What a Sabbath was that, when God, resting from the six days' work of creation, held communion with man, the last work of his hands; and when man, unstained by sin, poured forth the first offering of praise from the newly-created earth, free and acceptable to the Creator! Such a Sabbath the earth does not now know; but such a Sabbath remains to the people of God, and blessed are they who shall enter into this rest.

CHAPTER II.

THE FALL.

THE FIRST MAN, HAVING BEEN PLACED UNDER A COVENANT OF WORKS, VIOLATED IT, AND BROUGHT ITS PENALTY ON HIMSELF AND HIS DESCENDANTS.[1]

The narrative of the Fall, as given in the book of Genesis, is to be considered, not as a mythical representation, but as proper his_tory. It is always so referred to in subsequent parts of the sacred volume; and its connection with other historical events is such as excludes the supposition, that it was anything else than simple fact.

The revelation of God's will to Adam, as recorded in the book of Genesis, is not there called a covenant; and some have doubted the propriety of using this term to denote it. If the word, in the Scripture use of it, signified, as it does in human transactions, a bargain made between equals, who are independent of each other, we might well reject the application of it to this subject. But in the sacred Scripture, it is used in a more extended signification. It denotes, 1. *An immutable ordinance.*[2] Under this sense may be included *an irrevocable will or testament.*[3] 2. *A sure and sta-*

---

[1] Gen. ii. 17; iii. 6, 16, 17, 18, 19; Rom. v. 12, 15, 16, 17, 18, 19.
[2] Jer. xxxiii. 20.   [3] Heb. ix. 15–17.

ble promise.[1] 3. *A precept.*[2] 4. *A mutual agreement.*[3] With this latitude of meaning, the word must be considered applicable in the present case; yet there would be no necessity to insist on its use, were it not that the Scriptures have used it in this application. See Hosea vi. 7, which may be more properly rendered than in the common version, "They, like Adam, have transgressed the covenant." So the same Hebrew phrase may be understood in Job xxxi. 33; Ps. lxxxii. 6, 7.

As the term covenant is sometimes applied to a free promise, in which no condition is stipulated; it is proper to characterize that which was made with Adam as a covenant *of works.* It was a law, with a penalty affixed. "Of every tree of the garden, thou mayest freely eat; but of the tree of knowledge of good and evil, thou shalt not eat of it; for in the day that thou eatest thereof, thou shalt surely die."[4] No promise was given, that Adam would continue to enjoy the divine favor if he continued obedient; but this may be understood to be clearly implied. Whether higher favor than he then enjoyed, would have been granted on condition of his persevering in obedience through a prescribed term of probation, we are not informed. We have reason to conclude, that a continuance in well-doing, would have received stronger marks of divine approbation according to its progress; and, from what we know of the power of habit, as tending to establish man in virtue or vice, (a tendency which it has, because God has so willed it) the conjecture is not improbable, that, had Adam persevered in his obedience, he would, after a time, have been confirmed in holiness. But, where the Scriptures are silent, we should not frame conjectures and make them articles of faith.

It is vain and sinful, to arraign God at the tribunal of our reason, for having prescribed such a test of obedience, as the eating of an apple. We may so far forget the reverence due to God, as to call in question the wisdom and goodness, of making so much ado about so little a matter; but in this we betray great impiety. Shall not the Judge of all the earth do right? It is enough that God has done it. God's acts are not little, when he creates the

---

[1] Acts iii, 25; xxxiv. 10; Isaiah lix. 21.   [2] Ex. xxxiv. 28.
[3] Gen. xxxi. 44; xxvi. 28, 29; 1 Sam. xviii. 3.   [4] Gen. ii. 16, 17.

10

minutest atom; and God's requirements are not to be contemned, when he gives one of the least of his commandments. The very simplicity of the thing, though human folly may scoff at it, may best agree with the wisdom of God. Had Adam made an attempt to dethrone his Maker, human reason would admit the magnitude of the crime; but no greater evil would have been inflicted on omnipotence by his puny effort, than when he ate the forbidden fruit. What difference, then, is there, in the magnitude of the crimes? None, in their effect; and none in their principle. To disobey, is, as far as the creature can go, to dethrone. Shall men mock God by permitting him to occupy the seat of universal authority, while they refuse obedience to that authority? Be not deceived; God is not mocked. He that disobeys God, rejects his reign; and so God views it. The test of obedience prescribed to Adam was easy; and this very fact makes the transgression the more inexcusable. It showed the greatness of Abraham's faith, that it stood so severe a test when he was required to offer up his son Isaac; and it proves the greatness of Adam's sin, that it was committed, when he might so easily have avoided it.

What kinds of fruit the tree of life, and the tree of the knowledge of good and evil, bore, we have no means of knowing; and the knowledge, if we could attain to it, would do us no good. Some have asked, whether one fruit had a natural efficacy to produce immortality, and the other to produce death; but this also is an unprofitable question. Nature has no other efficacy than the will of God, and his appointment of these trees, for the use which it was his pleasure they should serve, was as efficacious as any law of nature.

The sacred narrative informs us that the garden of Eden, in which the innocent and happy pair were placed, abounded with trees, yielding all sorts of pleasant fruits. In the midst of the garden, were two trees distinguished from all the rest, and designed for special use. What that use was, may be inferred from their names. The tree of life, of which they were permitted to eat, secured to them immortality, or exemption from the penalty of the covenant. The tree of knowledge of good and evil, was designed for a different purpose; and its fruit was prohibited. Not to know good and evil, is a distinction ascribed to children.[1] Good and

---

[1] Deut. i. 39; Heb. v. 14.

evil, when spoken of in contrast, may refer to the moral quality of actions; but they are not restricted to this signification. When Job said, "Shall we receive good at the hand of God, and shall we not receive evil?" he did not refer to the moral distinction between actions, but to enjoyment and suffering. When Barzillai declined to accompany David to Jerusalem, and live with him there, and assigned as a reason his inability to distinguish between good and evil; his reference was to enjoyment, not to moral quality.[1] Eve decided to eat of the forbidden fruit, because "she saw that it was *good*," not in a moral sense, but "for food." Children, who have not the knowledge of good and evil, are instructed by their parents, both what to do, and what to enjoy; and it is their duty and interest to follow the instructions received. The first human pair stood in the relation of children to their Creator; and, while they abstained from the forbidden fruit, they acknowledged their inability to know good and evil, and their dependence on the guidance of infinite wisdom. In abstaining, they acknowledged the prerogative of God, to decide for them what was good, and what was evil. The two trees were very significantly placed near to each other, and in the midst of the garden. The tree of life was the symbol of the divine favor; and the other tree, the symbol of the divine prerogative. The trees of the garden, generally, yielded fruit that was pleasant and life-sustaining; but the fruit of the tree of life was distinguished from the rest, as a special pledge of the divine favor. Yet the proximity of this tree to that which bore forbidden fruit, perpetually reminded the subjects of this probation, that the favor of God could be enjoyed only by respecting his prerogative. This token of the divine authority was in the midst of the garden; to remind them, that they held the privilege of eating all the pleasant fruits, by the grant of the Supreme Lord; and that their desire and enjoyment of natural good, was to be regulated by the decision of him, whose prerogative it was to know good and evil.

The departure of Eve from the straight line of duty is distinctly marked in the sacred narrative. "When the woman saw that the tree was good for food,"[2] &c. When *she saw*. She judged for herself what was good. God's account of the transgression is:

---

[1] 2 Sam. xix. 35.   [2] Gen. iii. 6.

"Behold, the man has become as one of us, to know good and evil;"[1] he has usurped our prerogative. This was the first transgression. The desire of natural good was made the rule of action. "When she saw," &c. The desire of natural good prevailed over reverence for the authority of God; and, in the transgression may be seen not only a desire of the pleasant fruit, but also a desire to be exempt from the necessity of referring to God's decision as the rule of conduct — "a tree to be desired to make one wise;"[2] to make one independent of God's wisdom. Such was the first transgression. It cast off the authority of God, usurped his prerogative, and gave the mind up to the dominion of natural desire.

Because of his violation of the covenant, man was excluded from the symbol of the divine favor. A cherub, with a flaming sword, was placed to guard the approach to the tree of life, lest he should eat thereof and live for ever. He had incurred the threatened penalty, and it began at once to be inflicted on him.

What was the precise import of *death*, as the penalty threatened to Adam, is a question of some difficulty. If it imported the death of the body, the threat was not executed at the time designated: "In the day that thou eatest thereof thou shalt surely die." He did not literally die on the day of his transgression. Some have accounted for this by supposing that the mediation of Christ interposed, and prevented the execution of the threat. That God's purpose of mercy, through Christ, was kept in view in his dealings with Adam, we have no reason to doubt; but the Scriptures nowhere explain that it rescued man from the threatened penalty. If immediate literal death was the proper import of the threatened penalty, and if Adam was rescued from it by the mediation of Christ, he was delivered from a less evil to endure far greater. He was spared to live a life of depravity, and to die, if he died impenitent, under the wrath of God, and be doomed to eternal misery. If it be said that eternal misery would have followed his death had it taken place immediately, how can it be accounted for that this dreadful consequence of transgression was not intimated in the threatening? If it be said that the term death included this also, then the literal interpretation of it is abandoned, and its chief import is made to relate to another matter, of far greater magnitude

---

[1] Gen. iii. 22.   [2] Gen. iii. 6.

than the dissolution of the body. The Holy Spirit is the best expositor on this subject; and, after stating that death was introduced into the world by the sin of Adam,[1] sets this death in contrast with the eternal life procured by Christ: "The wages of sin is death; but the gift of God is eternal life, through Jesus Christ our Lord."[2] As eternal life does not consist in exemption from literal death, so its opposite does not consist in the mere loss of life to the body.

We may understand that the threatened penalty was executed on Adam, in its proper import, when he was denied approach to the tree of life. This had been to him the symbol of the divine favor. What notion he had of death, as pertaining to the body, we know not; and he may never have been taught anything on this subject until he heard the sentence, "Dust thou art, and unto dust shalt thou return."[3] But Adam, besides having a body made of dust, had received from God "a living soul," which could not suffer dissolution. Some idea of this living principle, which distinguished him from the brutes around him, must have formed a part of that "knowledge" with which he was endowed, and in which the image of God in part consisted. What was death to his living soul? He knew, by happy experience, what it was to have the communion and favor of the living God; and to be cut off from these was the most dreadful death, and the only death of which the immortal spirit was capable. This penalty was inflicted in its awful import. The separation of the body from the soul, to which the name death is given, bears some likeness to the separation of the soul from God; and the dissolution of the body, whether by worms, or the funeral fire, leads the mind to the worm that dieth not, and the fire that is not quenched, which are consequences of the second death. Of this full and most momentous import was the death of the soul. If Adam became a believer in Christ,.he was delivered from under the penalty, and not merely prevented from falling under it. The dissolution of the body, which is the extension of the penalty to the material part of his constitution, he was not prevented from enduring; but from this, too, he will be redeemed at the resurrection.

The fallen pair were not only excluded from the tokens of God's

---

[1] Rom. v. 12.   [2] Rom. vi. 23.   [3] Gen. iii. 19.

favor, but they began to suffer positive inflictions of his displeasure. They were banished from Eden, the home of their innocence and joy. Its pleasant shades, its beautiful flowers, its fragrant odors, its delicious fruits, they are compelled to leave for ever. The delightful employment of dressing and keeping the garden, which yielded sustenance without painful toil, was to be exchanged for hard labor in cultivating a cursed soil, yielding briers and thorns; and bread, hardly earned by the sweat of the face, was to be their food. On the woman, first in the transgression, a woe was denounced: "In sorrow shalt thou bring forth children."[1] The first pain, thus intimated, became the model pain of exquisite suffering. These denunciations foretold a sad future. Stung with remorse, harassed with fears, God offended, and their souls undone, they bade farewell to their late blissful abode, and became wanderers on the earth, until their bodies, sinking under the weight of the ills inflicted, should crumble into dust. What other evils were included in that dreadful penalty, death; what the full import of the word, they and their posterity were to learn by woeful experience.

CHAPTER III.

MAN'S PRESENT STATE.

THE evils consequent on the disobedience of our first parents were not confined to them personally, but have fallen on their descendants also. Adam had been created in the image of God; but when that image had been lost by transgression, he begat a son in his own likeness.[2] So all his descendants since have borne the image of the earthly, fallen progenitor, and have been like him, not only in character, but in condition. The subject will be examined further in the following sections.

SECTION I.—ACTUAL SIN.

MEN OF ALL AGES AND NATIONS HAVE, IN THEIR ACTIONS, VIOLATED THE LAW OF GOD.[3]

The sacred volume, in describing the state of the world before

---

[1] Gen. iii. 16.   [2] Gen. v. 3.   [3] Rom. iii. 9–19; 1 John v. 19; Eph. ii. 2, 3.

the flood, says that "the earth was filled with violence."· The history of the period before the flood is very brief; yet we find, in the beginning of it, the murder of Abel by his brother;[2] in the progress of it, the bigamy of Lamech,[3] and the murder which he confessed to his wives; and, in the close of it, this account of the complete corruption of the earth, and the general prevalence of violence. The flood was sent in wrath for the transgressions of men; but its waters did not cleanse the earth from sin. Iniquities prevailed after the flood, as they had done before; and the condition of mankind, in all nations, was such as Paul has described in the first chapter of his Epistle to the Romans. The children of Abraham were separated from the rest of mankind, and made a peculiar people to God; but, notwithstanding the religious advantages which they enjoyed, their history is little else than a record of rebellions against God, and judgments inflicted on them for their provocations. So common is wickedness in the earth, that it is called "the course of this world,"[4] and it is said, "the whole world lieth in wickedness."[5]

From this universal corruption no man is exempt. "There is no man which sinneth not."[6] All whom the Spirit of God brings to a knowledge of themselves confess, "In many things we offend all;"[7] and they pray, "Forgive us our sins."[8] If others make no confessions of sin, and no petitions for pardon, it is because of the blindness and hardness of their hearts.

He who looks into the state of society around him, finds proof of man's wickedness. Crimes abound everywhere; and the earth is filled with violence, as it was of old. Laws restrain the crimes and violence of men; but the very·necessity of laws demonstrates the wickedness of mankind. War and oppression make up, in great measure, the history of our race; and innumerable deeds of wickedness, which never find a place in the historic record, are written in God's book of remembrance, and will be brought to light in that day, when men shall be judged according to the deeds done in the body.

The actual transgressions of men consist in doing what God has forbidden, and in leaving undone what he has commanded. The

---

[1] Gen. vi. 11.   [2] Gen. iv. 8.   [3] Gen. iv. 19–23.
[4] Eph. ii. 2.   [5] 1 John v. 19.   [6] 2 Ch. vi. 36.
[7] James iii. 2   [8] Luke xi. 4.

latter are called sins of omission; the former, sins of commission. With both these kinds of transgression all men are more or less chargeable. They who abstain from grosser crimes have, nevertheless, committed many sins, and omitted many duties. But sin, in the overt act, constitutes only a very small part of man's sinfulness, as will appear in the next section.

SECTION II.—DEPRAVITY.

ALL MEN ARE BY NATURE TOTALLY DEPRAVED.[1]

The depravity which we have to lament in mankind, respects their principles of action as moral beings. As merely sentient beings, external objects produce on them the proper effects; and, as rational beings, they draw conclusions in science with correctness. The disease and debility which are the consequence of moral evil, may impair both sense and reason; but we cannot affirm of these powers that they are totally depraved. Moral depravity shows itself in outward acts of transgression; but, atrocious as these often are, it is chiefly in the heart that God beholds and hates it. " God saw that the wickedness of man was great in the earth, and that every imagination of the thoughts of his heart was only evil continually."[2] In the heart it was that God saw the great wickedness of the earth. The heart is a metaphorical term, denoting those mental affections which are the principles or beginnings of action. Here depravity exists at the very fountain from which all human action flows.

The depravity of man is total. We do not mean by this that his conduct is as bad as it could be, or that no amiable affections have a place in his heart. The young man who addressed our Redeemer with most respectful inquiry how to attain eternal life, appears to have been unconverted, yet he possessed so amiable qualities that it is recorded, " Jesus, beholding him, loved him."[3] The goodness of God is great, even to the unthankful and evil; and he has been pleased to implant natural affections in hearts which desire not to retain him in their knowledge, and so to balance the propensities, even where there is no holiness, that life and human society have

---

[1] Gen. vi. 5; viii. 21; Ps. xiv. 2, 3; li. 5; Rom. i. 21–25; iii. 9–23; vi. 17, viii. 5, 6, 7, 8; Eph. ii. 1; 1 John v. 19.

[2] Gen. vi. 5.   [3] Mark x. 21.

many enjoyments. When our first parents permitted natural desire to prevail over the authority of God, human depravity began to flow, and what it was at the fountain-head, it has been in all the streams that have spread through the earth. Men seek good at their own choice, and walk in their own ways, regardless of the authority of God. The love of God is dethroned from the heart, and therefore the grand principle of morality is wanting, and no true morality exists. A total absence of that by which the actions should be controlled and directed, is total depravity. Hence the strong language of Scripture, already quoted, is properly descriptive of human nature in its fallen state: "Every imagination of the thoughts of his heart was only evil continually."

Human depravity is universal. In heathen nations, men did not delight to retain God in their knowledge, and their very religion became filled with abominable rites. In lands blessed with the light of revelation, men love darkness rather than light, and give melancholy proof that they have not the love of God in them. The rich and the poor, the learned and the unlearned, the young and the old, all give evidence that, to serve and please God, is not their chief delight, their meat and their drink. A few, converted by divine grace, differ from the rest of mankind, and esteem it their pleasure and honor to obey God; but these very men testify that it is God who has made them to differ, and that, in themselves, they are like other men. "Such were some of you; but ye are washed, but ye are sanctified, but ye are justified, in the name of the Lord Jesus, and by the Spirit of our God."[1] "I know that in me, that is, in my flesh, dwelleth no good thing."[2]

Depravity is natural to man; it is born with him, and not acquired in the progress of life. It is not to be ascribed to evil habit, or evil example. Evil habits are formed by evil doing; and evil doing would not be, if there were no evil propensity. Evil example would not everywhere exist, if human nature were not everywhere corrupt; and the tendency to follow evil example would not be so common, and so much to be guarded against, if it were not natural to man. The Scriptures clearly teach this doctrine. "Behold, I was shapen in iniquity, and in sin did my mother conceive me."[3] The psalmist did not mean to charge his

---

1 Cor. vi. 11.　　　　[2] Rom. vii. 18.　　　　[3] Ps. li. 5

mother with crime in these his humble confessions, but manifestly designs them to be an acknowledgment that his depravity was inwoven in his nature, and bore date from the very origin of his being. The Saviour taught, that which is born of the flesh, is flesh.[1] The term flesh, which is here opposed to spirit, signifies, as it does in other places, our depraved nature. It traces human depravity up to our very birth.

As every individual of our race is born of depraved parents, and brings depravity with him into the world, we are led to conceive of it as propagated from parent to child. This accords with the representations of Scripture: "Adam begat a son in his own likeness."[2] It accords also with analogies to which we are familiar.

Plants and animals propagate their like; diseases are often hereditary, and the peculiarities of temper and mind by which parents were distinguished, often appear in their children. In our proneness to find fault with God's arrangements, we ask, why was the fallen nature of Adam propagated, rather than the original nature which he received from the hand of God. But we might as well complain that the ascent from the state of sin to that of innocence, is not as easy as the descent was found to be. Virtue fits the creatures of God for society, and for its most beautiful exhibitions opportunity is presented in the social relations. All these give one creature an influence over another, according to the character of the relation between them. Even angels, who were created independent of each other, had an influence on each other, so that the chief apostate in the great rebellion led followers after him. When man was created, it appeared good, in the view of Infinite Wisdom, to institute closer social relations than subsisted among angels. From these resulted a more extended influence than was known in the angelic ranks. Now, if Adam had transmitted his original nature, as created by God, the effect would have been the same as if the son had been immediately created by the divine hand, and the peculiarity designed to distinguish the human race would have been virtually abolished.

Another complaint which sometimes rises in our murmuring minds is, that pious men do not propagate their piety, but their natural depravity. We might as well complain that men of great

---

[1] John iii. 6.   [2] Gen. v. 3.

scientific attainments do not transmit their knowledge to their children as a natural inheritance. This complaint would have even greater appearance of propriety, for their attainments are, in a sense, their own; but whatever of holiness is found in man, is not a natural endowment or attainment, but a special gift of divine grace.

When we have discovered that the propagation of depravity in the human race accords with analogies found in nature, our minds seem to obtain relief; but, in reality, the matter has not been explained. Nature is not some superior rule to which God was compelled to conform, but it is an institution of his own, and cannot be right in the whole, if its parts are not right. If the propagation of human depravity is not in itself right, all the analogies of nature could not make it so. The true benefit of tracing these analogies is, that we may perceive all the arrangements to be from the same divine mind, and may the more reverently bow our judgment to the decision of Infinite Wisdom, and hush our murmurs into the more profound silence.

Our natural inquisitiveness takes occasion from this subject to indulge in unprofitable speculations. As the depravity which is propagated belongs more properly to the soul than to the material frame, we ask whether the soul is propagated. Some have preferred to consider the soul as a production immediately proceeding from the creating power of God. They suppose this to be intended when the Scriptures say, that he formeth the spirit of man within him.[1] They regard the body as all that is propagated, and suppose the Creator to form a spirit within it, as he breathed the spirit of life into the inanimate body of Adam, when he became a living soul. They view propagation as belonging to the material part of our nature, and consider it impossible, in the nature of things, that this should generate an immaterial spirit. The latter argument, which is merely philosophical, has to struggle with the fact that all animals generate something more than mere matter, in the powers with which they are endowed, and which bear a strong resemblance, in many respects, to the mental endowments of man. The preceding argument, from Scripture, fails in this, that God is equally said to form the body of the child in the womb of the

---

[1] Zech. xii. 1.

mother,[1] and yet we never regard that body as a production of
immediate creation. It is true that the body of Adam was lifeless
for a time; but it was not, as lifeless, that he begat a son in his
likeness. We would not argue, from this case, that all life, whether
in plants or animals, is a production of immediate creation, and
not of propagation; and it does not appear that a more valid
argument can be deduced from it, to prove the immediate creation
of every human soul. After all, what does the question amount
to? If the preservation of all things is strictly a perpetual creation, the distinction is wholly annihilated; for the soul is, at the
first moment of its being, and at every subsequent moment throughout its whole existence, an immediate creation. But if this view
be not admitted, it is still true that preservation is as dependent
on the efficacious will of God, as creation. God willed that the
soul of Adam should exist, and it came into being; this we call
creation. God willed that Adam should propagate a son, and that
this son should, like the father, have both a soul and a body. The
progeny came into being according to the will of God. This work
differs from the former, in that it is not singular, but conforms to
what we call a law of nature; but nature's laws have no efficacy
in themselves; and when we attribute the work to the efficacious
will of God, it is a mere question of classification, whether we refer
it to creation or Providence.

An objection to the doctrine of natural depravity is founded on
the fact, that Jesus referred to little children, as examples for his
disciples. This fact, however, will not authorize the inference,
that little children are not depraved. The same teacher said to
his disciples, "Be ye wise as serpents, and harmless as doves."[2]
As something may exist, proper to be imitated in animals which
have no moral character, and even in serpents, notwithstanding
their venom, so, something for imitation could be pointed out in
children, notwithstanding their depravity. Another objection is
drawn from the statement of Scripture, concerning children that
had not done either good or evil.[3] But the doctrine does not
affirm that all have committed overt acts of transgression. It
refers to the first spring of action in the heart; and a fountain
may be corrupt, before it has sent forth streams, as truly as after-

---

[1] Job xxxi. 15; Is. xliv. 2.   [2] Matt. x. 16.   [3] Rom. ix. 11.

wards. No objection, worthy of consideration, can be drawn from Paul's statement, that the children of the Corinthian Christians were holy;[1] for this manifestly relates to their fitness for familiar intercourse.

Vain it will be, to receive the doctrine of human-depravity into our creed, if it is not received into our hearts. A thorough conviction of our total depravity is necessary to humble us before God, and drive us to the fountain opened for sin and uncleanness. No genuine Christian experience can exist, where this is not felt and operative.

Section III.—CONDEMNATION.

ALL MEN ARE BORN UNDER THE JUST CONDEMNATION OF GOD.[2]

The depravity of mankind unfits them for the favor and enjoyment of God; and that separation from him, in which the death of the soul consists, would be the necessary result, even if no declaration to that effect were made by the Supreme Judge. But this sentence has been declared. The voice of *Providence* loudly leclares it. The pain with which our first breath is drawn; the sickness and suffering which attend on the cradle; the sorrows and toils of our best years; the infirmities of age; and lastly death, which, if it does not terminate our course earlier, after threatening us at every step, and keeping us all our life-time in bondage, finally triumphs over us; all these proclaim, in language not to be misunderstood, that we are under the displeasure of God. The curse of God rests on the very ground that we tread; and his wrath is poured out on our race in the wars, famines, and pestilence, with which the nations are often visited. The sentence is pronounced by the voice of *conscience* within us, which is to us as the voice of God; "For if our heart condemn us, God is greater than our heart, and knoweth all things."[3] God speaks in *his holy word*, proclaiming the sentence; "Cursed is every one that continueth not in all things which are written in the book of the law to do them."[4] "What things the law saith, it saith to them who are under the law, that every mouth may be stopped, and all the world become

---

[1] 1 Cor. vii. 14.
[2] Ps. vii. 11; Mark xvi. 16; John iii. 36; Rom. i. 18; ii. 5, 6; iii. 19; v. 12–21.   [3] 1 John iii. 20.   [4] Gal. iii. 10.

guilty before God." [1]   The view which is here presented of man's
condition, relates not merely to his transgressions, but to his natural state.   Hence it is said, "And were by nature, the children
of wrath." [2]

These manifestations of God's displeasure are of early date,
commencing with the first woes of mankind.   They may be traced
to the first sentence pronounced on our guilty parents, when they
were expelled from Eden.   Paul has explained, that we were all
included in this sentence, and this is the proper date of our condemnation.   "By the offence of one, judgment came upon all men
to condemnation." [3]   *From* that hour, the descendants of Adam,
their habitation, their employments, and their enjoyments, have all
been under the curse.   Blessings have, indeed, been poured out in
rich profusion on our guilty race; but our very basket and store
have been cursed, and the cup of mercies has been mingled with
bitterness.   The forbearance and long-suffering of God are manifested; but the hand of his wrath is uplifted.

The condemnation under which we are born is just.   It is God's
sentence; and all his judgments are righteous.   It is not unusual
for those who are condemned by human laws, to complain of their
sentence; and we show our want of reconciliation to the justice of
God, by our hard thoughts of God, when we either suffer or fear
his displeasure against us.

Our rebellious hearts deny the justice of our condemnation, on
the ground that God made us, and not we ourselves.   If he did
not create our souls directly with depraved propensities, he brought
them into being, in circumstances which made their depravity certain.   He gave us existence at his own pleasure; and over the
circumstances of our origin we had no manner of control.   It is
therefore unjust, says the carnal heart, to condemn and punish us,
for the sinful propensities which we bring with us into the world,
or for the sinful deeds which naturally and necessarily proceed
from them.   In this manner, we are prone to transfer the blame
of our iniquities from ourselves to our Maker.   So did Adam;
"The woman whom *thou* gavest to be with me, she gave me of the
tree, and I did eat," [4] and so do all his descendants.   Every one is
probably conscious that such reasonings have at some time had a

---

[1] Rom. iii. 19.   [2] Eph. ii. 3.   [3] Rom. v. 18.   [4] Gen. iii 12.

place in his mind; and that it is difficult to exclude them wholly. On this account, they need a full and sober examination.

A consideration which ought to silence our accusing thoughts of God, is, that however much we may condemn him, we do not thereby acquit ourselves. If we admit that Adam would not have eaten the forbidden fruit had not God given him a wife; and if we even admit that God was to blame for giving him a wife who might become his tempter: still this does not exculpate Adam. His wife was certainly to blame for tempting him; and yet the guilt of his transgression is not the less on that account. Every agent is responsible for himself. Distributive justice, which gives to every man his due, has no other rule, and can have no other. Human courts do not excuse culprits, because of the corrupting influences which have led them to violate the law. The law takes direct cognizance of the agent and his deed. This accords with the common sense of mankind. So divine justice condemns the wicked man, and cannot do otherwise than condemn him, however he may have become wicked, and whoever else may be to blame for his being so. This principle we should hold fast in all our reasonings on that subject.

A difficulty in holding fast the principle just laid down, and applying it steadily to the case, arises from the circumstance that the Judge by whom we are condemned is also our Creator. To free our thoughts from embarrassment on this account, let us suppose the case were otherwise. Let us imagine that, after "the Sons of God had shouted for joy," at seeing the foundations of the earth laid, and its finished surface covered with verdure and beauty, the Most High was pleased to appoint one of this joyful choir to the honorable service of populating this new world, and to confer on him creative power for this purpose. Let us imagine that, just as this chosen agent was proceeding to execute his commission, he conceived the thought of making himself the god of the world he was about to people; and, for this purpose, filled it with unholy inhabitants, willing to join him in rebellion against the Supreme Ruler. This case, though merely imaginary, will serve to test the principle under consideration; and the question which it presents for adjudication, is, how, according to the rule of eternal and immutable justice, ought this world of rebels to be treated.

Perhaps it will be said, that the agent who abused the creative

power conferred on him ought to be punished, and that the creatures that he had brought into being ought to be annihilated.
But this is not the plea which is set up for the human race.   The
plea which the sons of Adam present before the Judge of the earth,
is, not that we ought to be annihilated, but that we ought not to
be condemned and punished; this new order of creatures might
object to annihilation, and think themselves as much entitled to
life and impunity as we do.   They might say, that annihilation is
only a scheme to get the question out of court, and to free the
Judge from difficulty; but they might insist on right, and claim, as
they were created immortal· by the commission granted to him by
whom they were made, they have a right to immortality; and that
this immortality, since their depravity is natural to them, ought to
be free from all punishment.   Now, the Judge might, for wise reasons, not chose to evade the responsibility of adjudicating the case;
What, then, would the righteous sentence be?   Even to annihilate
them against their will, would be a punishment; that ought not to
be inflicted, if the plea not guilty, because depravity is natural, can
be sustained.   The plea before an earthly judge would not stand
a moment.   Who could bear that a criminal should be acquitted
and turned loose on the community, because he was born wicked,
had grown up wicked, and it was as natural for him to commit
theft, murder, and all manner of crimes, as it was to breathe?
Such a plea, which the justice of men will not admit, the justice
of God will not admit.   The new order of creatures must be treated
as they deserve; and Infinite Wisdom, instead of annihilating them,
must adopt some other expedient, to counteract the diabolical intentions of the agent that created them.

The case which has been supposed is not so wholly imaginary as
at first view it may have appeared.   Though it is not true that an
angel of light was commissioned to create a population for the
earth, something else was done which, for all the purposes of the
present discussion, amounts to the same.   Adam and Eve, while
yet in innocence, were commissioned to procreate a race of immortals, that should people the new world.   This power, Satan, ambitious of divine honor, availed himself of to make himself the god
of the world.   By temptation he gained over the first pair to his
design; and so completely is the procreating power with which they
were invested, turned to his account, that the offspring of it are

called the "children of the devil."[1] So complete is his control of them, that he is called "the spirit that worketh in the children of disobedience,"[2] and they "are taken captive by him at his will;"[3] and the death which comes on them for disobedience is attributed to his power: "That through death he might destroy him that had the power of death, that is the devil."[4] The imaginary case, therefore, is substantially our own; and, if rebellion against God, subserviency to Satan, and confederacy with him to overthrow the government of the King Eternal, cannot be justified at the tribunal of divine justice, we are verily guilty, and justly condemned.

But our accusing thoughts of God are suppressed with difficulty. We have seen that the whole world is guilty before him; and yet every mouth is not stopped. We still entertain hard thoughts, and vent hard words against him; and the thing formed says to him that formed it, Why hast thou made me thus?[5] Of such impiety it becomes us to beware. We should feel that our depravity is our own, however we came by it; that it renders us wholly unfit for the society and enjoyments of the holy place where God dwells, and for his favor, service, and communion; and that it ought to be loathsome in our own view, and must be so in the view of the holy God. If our own hearts condemn it, we shall be ready to admit, without complaint, that God also condemns it. And what can we say against God in the matter? What wrong has he done? His distributive justice does no wrong in treating the unholy according to their character. If he has done any wrong, it must relate to the department of public justice, which, as formerly explained, seeks the greatest good, and is the same as universal benevolence. Now, who will say that God's plan will not produce the greatest good? Who is wiser and better than God, to teach him a preferable way? When Satan gained his conquest over our first parents, God could have confined him at once in the pit, and inflicted on him the full torment yet in store for him; and he might have annihilated the whole race of man in the original pair. This would have terminated the difficulty by an act of power; but who will affirm that it would have been wisest or best? God would have appeared disappointed and defeated. Distributive justice would have ap-

---

[1] 1 John iii. 10; John viii. 44.   [2] Eph. ii. 2.   [3] 2 Tim. ii. 26.
[4] Heb. ii. 14.   [5] Rom. ix. 20.

11

peared relieved rather than developed. Satan triumphed by arti-
fice, and God has chosen to defeat him by the counsel of his wisdom. Satan exalted himself to dominion over the world; God
chose to overcome him, not by power, but by humiliation. Satan
gained his success by means of the first Adam; God, in the second
Adam, bruised the serpent's head. Satan, by his success, gained
the power of death; God, by death, the death of Jesus Christ, has
destroyed him and his power.[1] Who will dare affirm that God's
way is not best? It becomes us to feel assured, whatever darkness
may yet remain on this subject, that God would not have given up
his Son to free us from condemnation, if that condemnation had
not been just; and that he would not have made so great a gift, so
costly a sacrifice, if the scheme had not been worthy of his infinite
wisdom; or if some other, by which the sacrifice might have been
spared, would have been preferable.

When the question has been settled, and the principle established,
that men may be held responsible for their own sins, without inquiring how they became sinners, a difficulty still remains as to the
date of the condemnation under which we all lie, and the ground
of the original sentence. When the mind becomes perplexed with
subtle reasonings, it is well to keep facts steadily in view, and to
hold fast the plain testimony of inspired truth. It is expressly
said, in the unerring word, "By the offence of one judgment came
upon all men to condemnation;" and again, "The judgment was
by one [offence] to condemnation."[2] It is here clearly taught that
one judgment, one sentence, included all men, and that this judgment was made up and the sentence pronounced on one offence of
one man. With this express teaching of Scripture facts agree.
The indications of God's displeasure against the race are not post-
poned until each individual has been born into the world. Every
mother is not carried back to Eden before she brings forth a son,
that he may, in his own person, receive the sentence of condemnation, be denied access to the tree of life, driven from the garden of
delights, and doomed to sorrow, toil, and death. Whatever our
reasonings may say on the subject, it is fully ascertained to be the
will of God, before an individual is born into the world, that, when
born, he shall be in the condition in which the curse left the father

---

[1] Heb. ii. 14.   [2] Rom. v. 16, 18.

of the race. The Bible, and the voice of Nature, speak alike on this point; and if our reasonings say that the Author of Nature and the Bible has done wrong, we should suspect that we have erred in our inferences, or in the premises from which they are drawn. And if it could be shown that a separate sentence is pronounced on each individual as he comes into the world, his condition would be no better. Being depraved by nature, we are "by nature children of wrath."[1] Wrath is still our inheritance; and if the antiquity of the sentence which appointed it be admitted, the measure of that wrath is not thereby increased, nor the endurance of it made earlier. As to these results, the question is one of no importance whatever. Its relation, as exhibited in Scripture, to the doctrine of justification by the obedience of Christ, constitutes its chief claim to our careful consideration.

The sentence, "Dust thou art, and unto dust shalt thou return," was pronounced on Adam in the singular number; yet he appears to stand under this sentence as the representative of his descendants, on all of whom the sentence takes effect. So Eve was addressed in the singular number, "In sorrow shalt thou bring forth children;" but she stood, in this sentence, as the representative of all her daughters, on whom this penalty falls. As the natural parents, Adam and Eve stood together as the head of the race; but there was a peculiar sense in which that headship pertained to Adam. Though Eve was first in the transgression, it is not said by one woman, but "by one man sin entered into the world." The judgment was not by the two offences of the two natural parents of the race, but by the one offence of the one man; the previous offence of the woman being left out of the account. In this headship Adam is contrasted with Christ, being called "the figure of him that was to come."[2] This comparison is further brought to view in 1 Cor. xv. 45, 47, where Christ is called the second Adam; and in verse 22, where it is said, "As in Adam all die, even so in Christ shall all be made alive." On Adam, who was first formed, the responsibility of peopling the new world with a race of holy immortals specially rested; and, though Satan artfully directed his first assault against the woman, his scheme would have failed had not Adam been gained over to his interest. This divinely ap-

---

[1] Eph. ii. 3. [2] Rom. v. 14.

pointed headship of Adam made his disobedience the turning point
on which the future condition of his posterity depended; and Paul
takes occasion from this to illustrate the dependence of believers
on the obedience of the second Adam, for justification and life.

To this view it is objected, that, according to the principles of
justice, the guilt of one man cannot be transferred to another, and
no man can be justly condemned for that of which it is impossible
for him to repent. No man living can repent of Adam's sin, and
the guilt of Adam's sin cannot justly be imputed to any other
person.

What are here so confidently assumed as axioms, may well be
called in question. We must believe the Scriptures, when they
say, "The Lord hath laid on him the iniquity of us all."[1] "He
bore our sin in his own body on the tree."[2] And we know that men
cannot repent of deeds which they have wholly forgotten, and yet
they are responsible for them. But there is a much shorter way
of getting at this question, than by a tedious examination of these
assumed axioms. No man understands that the guilt of Adam was
transferred. It still remained his, and was closely and inseparably
bound about him. But every one knows that there may be union
and confederacy in crime. In commercial affairs, if twenty men
owe one hundred dollars, each may pay five dollars, and the obligation of the whole will be cancelled. But in morals, if twenty
subjects confederate to assassinate their king, each one is guilty of
the whole crime, because each one has the full intention of it.
Only one of the band may plunge the dagger to the monarch's
heart; but his crime may be justly imputed to them all, though his
guilt may not be transferred to another. Now, we may inquire,
whether such union does not exist between Adam and his descendants, as justifies the imputation of his sin to them; or, in
other words, shows it to be in accordance with justice. Paul, in
comparing Adam and Christ as public heads, has, in the fifth chapter of Romans, pointed out disagreements as well as agreements.
Death comes from the disobedience of the one; and life from the
obedience of the other; and in Rom. vi. 23, he teaches that there
is an important difference as to the mode in which these results
follow. Death is wages, a thing deserved; life is a gift. The

---

[1] Is. liii. 6.   [2] 1 Pet. ii. 24.

benefits of righteousness and life, received from Christ, are by faith; and " It is of faith, that it might be by grace." [1] The condemnation and death which are from Adam, are not gratuitous and arbitrary, but come on us justly. We inquire, then, whether there is such a connection between Adam and his descendants, as renders the imputation of his sin to them, an act of justice.

1. There is a moral union between Adam and his descendants. His disobedience unfurled the banner of rebellion, and we all rally around it. We approve the deed of our father, and take arms in maintaining the war against heaven, which his disobedience proclaimed. He is the chief in this conspiracy of treason, but we are all accessories. As to the outward act, the eating of the forbidden fruit, we did not commit it; but, regarding it as a declaration of independence and revolt, we have made it our own, and it may be as justly set to our account, as if we had personally committed the deed. In this view, if we cannot, strictly speaking, repent of Adam's sin, we may most cordially disapprove the whole revolt from God, in which our race is engaged; may most bitterly regret that it was ever commenced; and may take guilt and shame to ourselves in deep humiliation before God, that we have been engaged in it. With such feelings pervading our hearts, the doctrine that Adam's sin is imputed to us, will not be rejected as inconsistent with justice. If we cannot, strictly speaking, repent of it, we may at least take the guilt of it to ourselves, in a sense which perfectly accords with the feelings of true penitence; and when the Holy Spirit has taught us to impute it to ourselves, we shall not complain that God imputes it.

2. There is a natural union between Adam and his descendants. He is their natural parent; and, because of this relation, they inherit a depraved nature. Our moral union with him renders our condemnation just, from the moment we possess separate existence, because of our personal depravity; and our natural union with him rendered it proper, that our condemnation should be included in the general sentence.

3. There is a federal union between Adam and his descendants. We have before seen that a covenant, not in the common, but the Scripture sense of the term, was made with Adam. This covenant,

---

[1] Rom. iv. 16.

this arrangement or constitution of things, made the future character and condition of his descendants dependent on his obedience.
He was, in this respect, their federal head. Some maintain that
the covenant with Adam was the covenant of nature, and that
there was no federal headship, different from the natural headship
which belonged to him as the first parent. Happily for us, a decision of this question is not indispensable to our present discussion.
The natural and moral union which we have already considered, is
a just ground for the divine sentence against the whole race, in the
person of their first parent; but a further examination of this
question may be conducive to a better understanding of the subject.

Since nature is not something different from God operating, it
cannot be of much importance to determine how much of the transaction with Adam was natural, and how much beyond the proper
province of nature. The revelation of God's will in the garden
was as much above nature, as the subsequent revelation from Sinai;
and so also was the judgment pronounced after the transgression.
But the including of children with their parents, in the penalty inflicted for the sins of their parents, is seen in the providence of God,
both in ordinary and extraordinary dispensations. Every one
knows that poverty and suffering are brought on children by the
intemperance and other crimes of their parents. The evils of war,
famine, and pestilence, judgments inflicted for the sins of men, fall
on children as well as their parents. In the deluge, and the burning of Sodom, children were destroyed with their parents. On
this point, the word of God agrees with his providence. We are
sometimes jealous for the Lord's reputation, and are afraid to
speak of his visiting the sins of parents on their children, but we
are more cautious than the Lord himself. He proclaimed from
Sinai, with his own voice, and recorded in stone with his own finger,
" I, the Lord thy God, am a jealous God, visiting the iniquity of
the fathers upon the children, unto the third and fourth generation
of them that hate me." [1] And when he showed his glory to Moses,
and proclaimed his name, instead of being jealous to conceal this
fact, he was jealous rather to make it known: " Visiting the iniquity of the fathers upon the children. [2]

God's solemn declarations on this point not only explain his

---

[1] Ex. xx. 5.   [2] Ex. xxxiv. 7.

providence, but, in the most impressive manner, exhibit the great responsibility of parents. To bring an immortal into being, and to form his character for time and eternity, is a responsibility most momentous. This responsibility devolves on men, and it is proper they should feel it. To awaken them to a sense of it, God addresses them in the solemn language which has been quoted.

While the Scriptures stir up parents to a sense of their responsibility, they leave to children no pretext with which to cover their iniquities. Some have said, " The Lord's ways are not equal. Our fathers have eaten sour grapes, and the children's teeth are set on edge." [1] To these complainers God said, " Behold all souls are mine; as the soul of the father, so also the soul of the son is mine; the soul that sinneth, it shall die." [2] This is not a law repealing the decalogue, but is to be explained in harmony with it. The sins of parents affect both the character and the condition of their children, and for all this they are responsible; but the condition of the children is not worse than their character, and therefore the Lord's ways are equal, and their complaints against him groundless.

The case of Adam differed from that of all fathers since. These may transmit peculiar tempers and propensities, and may influence their children by instruction and example, but they cannot bring them into the world free from the depravity and condemnation which the transgression of Adam brings upon them. But, though the responsibility on Adam was greater, it is still true, as in the other cases, that his descendants are responsible for themselves, and not one of them will suffer beyond the demerit of his personal character. Such is the union between Adam and his descendants, that depravity and condemnation pass from him to them, not separately, but as one inheritance. His sin, for which they suffer, is their own as well as his, and it is imputed to them because it belongs to them — is justly theirs.

After all the explanations that have been made, it may be that our hearts still accuse God, and secretly say that, had we been in his stead, we would have dealt more kindly with the human race than he has done. These accusations of God, he hears; these

---

[1] Ez. xviii. 2.   [2] Ezek. xviii. 4.

most secret whispers of the heart, he fully understands. What impiety does he see therein ! That we, who know so little of his ways, should presume to be wiser or better than he, is daring impiety ; and if nothing else will convince us that we deserve the wrath of God, let this impiety suffice. Let us accuse no more, but lay our hands on our mouths, and in deep silence before him, confess our guilt.

Section IV.—HELPLESSNESS.

MEN ARE UNABLE TO SAVE THEMSELVES.[1]

The inability of men to save themselves, respects both their condemnation and their depravity.

1. Men are unable to free themselves from condemnation.

The justice by which we are all condemned is immutable. It is an attribute in the nature of God, who is not only the first cause of all things, but the very standard of all perfection. When we inquire whether God's ways are right, we have only to ask whether they correspond with his own perfections, for there is no higher standard by which they may be tried. As the perfections of God are immutable, the standard of right is immutable. A change in the law by which we are condemned is therefore impossible. God has sometimes, from regard to the peculiar circumstances of some men, given special commands to them, which have not been obligatory on all ; but the obligation to obey him, whatever his commands may be, is universal and perpetual, and no act of disobedience can ever be justified under his righteous government.

The sentence of condemnation has been duly pronounced. It was not a rash decision, needing to be revised. The Omniscient Judge knew well all the facts in the case, all the circumstances which may be pleaded in extenuation, all the effects of his decision on us, and all the bearings of it on his own character and government. His determination to create the world was not made with greater deliberation, or on surer ground ; and we may as soon expect him to annihilate all the creatures that he has made, as to reverse the sentence by which we are condemned.

---

[1] Jer. xiii. 23 ; John iii. 3 ; vi. 44 ; Rom. iii. 19, 20 ; viii. 7, 8 ; Gal. iii. 10 ; Heb. x. 4 ; xii. 14.

The Scriptures affirm, that by the deeds of the law there shall no flesh be justified.[1] The law requires perfect and perpetual obedience, and can be satisfied with nothing less. Law is converted into mere advice, when its requirements are not obligatory. To claim the privilege of violating the law, or coming short of its requirements, is to claim, so far, exemption from its authority, and therefore from the moral government of God. Such exemption divine justice will not allow. Its language is, " Cursed is every one that continueth not in all things which are written in the book of the law to do them."[2] "What things the law saith, it saith to them who are under the law, that every mouth may be stopped, and all the world become guilty before God."[3] The view which is here presented of man's condition, relates not merely to his transgressions, but to his natural state. Hence it is said, "And were by nature the children of wrath."[4] So much has God the maintenance of his law at heart, that he who was in the bosom of the Father, and well understood all his counsels, has with solemnity assured us : " Verily I say unto you, till heaven and earth pass, one jot or one tittle shall in no wise pass from the law till all be fulfilled."[5]

There is a method of rescue from condemnation ; but it is not one of man's devising or executing. To effect it required a display of wisdom, power and love, infinitely beyond the highest efforts of man. It is God's work, challenging the admiration of angels, and demanding gratitude, praise, and joyful acceptance from every human being.

2. Men are unable to free themselves from depravity.

The first element of this inability is seen in the fact that men lack the necessary disposition. By nature we love darkness rather than light, sin rather than holiness. To be free from depravity is to be holy, and no man can desire holiness or perfect conformity to the law of God, who does not delight in that law. But experience and Scripture unite in teaching us that the carnal mind is not subject to the law of God, neither indeed can be.[6] The cause of this exists in the fact, that the carnal mind is enmity

---

[1] Rom. iii. 20   [2] Gal. iii. 10.   [3] Rom. iii. 19.   [4] Eph. ii. 3.
[5] Matt. v. 18.   [6] Rom. viii. 7.

against God. Men love the ways of transgression, and desire not the knowledge of God's ways; and, therefore, they lack the disposition necessary to free themselves from depravity, and render themselves strictly conformed to the law of God.

Another element which renders the inability complete, is, that if men had the disposition, they have not the power. Men have the power to perform such external acts as the law of God requires of them. If they were wholly disposed to perform such acts, and failed through mere physical inability, that inability would be a valid excuse. God accepteth according to what a man hath.[1] We are commanded not to forsake the assembling of ourselves together; but the man who is fastened to his bed by palsy is not required to meet in the house of God. Depravity does not consist in external acts, but belongs to the heart; and the affections of the heart are not subject to volition, as the motions of the limbs are. Hence the Apostle says, "Ye cannot do the things that ye would."[2] Every converted man knows the meaning of this language. The current of depraved affections in our hearts, which has been flowing in the wrong direction from the beginning of our being, and gathering strength by the power of habit, does not stop at our bidding. A volition cannot stop it with as much ease as when it moves a finger. If any man thinks he has the power to be holy at will, let him try it, and he will find his mistake.

The inability last described, which is usually called moral, must be distinguished carefully from that physical inability which excuses outward acts. Physical inability would prevent the action, even if the whole heart were bent on performing it. It excuses the failure to act; but it will not excuse a corrupt or a divided heart. The paralytic may be excused for not attending at the house of God; but he is not excused for preferring to be absent, or for possessing no longing for the courts of the Lord. The moral inability of men consists in having either a divided heart, or a heart fully set in them to do evil. The former every converted man laments, and blames himself for; and the latter is descriptive of unconverted or natural men. This includes the lack, both of disposition and power, and renders the inability complete. This inability is

---

[1] 2 Cor. viii. 12.   [2] Gal. v. 17

not an excuse for the depravity, but is the depravity itself, in its
full influence over all the powers of the soul.

The Scripture representations of men's inability are exceedingly
strong. They are said to be without strength,[1] captives,[2] in bond
age,[3] asleep,[4] dead,[5] &c. The act by which they are delivered from
their natural state, is called regeneration, quickening or giving life,
renewing, resurrection, translation, creation; and it is directly ascribed to the power of God, the power that called light out of darkness, and raised up Christ from the dead.

Our views concerning our character and condition by nature are
wholly incorrect, if we imagine that a little work, which we can
effect at pleasure, will set all right. Thousands postpone the concerns of the soul from this vain imagination. A true sense of our
inability would drive us to him who is able to save.

CONCLUSION.

A careless admission that men are sinners is often made by persons who give themselves little concern about religion; and even
acrimonious complaints may be freely vented by them against the
iniquities of others. But such is the stupefying effect of human
depravity, that men have very little complaint to make against
themselves; and their condition, as sinners against God, awakens
very little uneasiness. Occasionally conscience may be aroused,
and produce alarm; but, through the deceitfulness of sin, its re-
bukes and warnings become unheeded, and men are again lulled to
sleep in carnal security. Until this fatal slumber is broken, and a
thorough, deep-rooted conviction of sin seizes the mind, and allows
the man no quiet, his spiritual state exhibits no favorable indications.

Conviction of sin has sometimes produced very disquieting effects
in the minds of heathen men, destitute of the true knowledge of
God. Costly sacrifices and painful austerities have been resorted
to for the purpose of appeasing their offended deities. Nature
teaches men their danger, but cannot show them the way of escape.
In these circumstances, how welcome is the light which the Bible

---

[1] Rom. v. 6.   [2] 2 Tim. ii. 26.   [3] 2 Pet. ii. 19; Rom vi. 16, 17.
[4] 1 Thes. v. 6.   [5] Eph. v. 14; Col. ii. 13.

throws on our path! It gives a far clearer discovery of our danger, and, at the same time, opens before us the door of hope.

Conviction of sin may at first respect merely our overt acts of wickedness; but, if thorough and effectual, it will extend to the depraved heart, from which evil actions proceed. It will open to our view this fountain of corruption, this deep sea casting up mire and dirt. To explore the deep windings of depravity, dark and filthy, we need the torch of revelation. Its use in making us acquainted with ourselves, demonstrates the divinity of its origin. The woman of Samaria said of Jesus, "Come see a man which told me all things that ever I did; is not this the Christ?"[1] And the Bible, which tells us so exactly all that is in our hearts, must be from God, the Searcher of hearts. The world of iniquity within us was formerly to us a land unknown; but we have now explored it in part, and we can testify that the only correct map of it is in the Holy Scriptures. As we make progress in the knowledge of ourselves, throughout our course of religious experience, what we read in our own hearts and what we read in the Bible agree perfectly, and we ever carry with us a proof that the doctrine of the Bible is the truth of God.

Many who profess to regard the Bible as a revelation from heaven, do not receive its doctrine concerning the present state of man. They cannot conceive the human heart to be so deceitful and desperately wicked as the Bible declares it to be; and especially they do not so conceive of their own hearts. We hence know that such men could not have written the Bible. When the light of truth has produced in us a thorough conviction of sin, we read the Bible with new eyes, and we discover in it the handwriting of him who said, "I the Lord search the heart."[2]

The exceeding sinfulness of sin appears when it is viewed as committed against God. David said, "Against thee, thee only, have I sinned."[3] While under genuine conviction of sin, a view of God's perfections renders the conviction overwhelming. To have sinned against so glorious and excellent a being; to have rebelled against the rightful Sovereign of the universe, and aimed at dethroning him; to have violated his law, holy, just, and good; to

---

[1] John iv. 29.　　　　[2] Jer. xvii. 10.　　　　[3] Ps. li. 4.

have trampled his authority under our feet, insulted his majesty, despised the riches of his forbearance and goodness; to have persevered in our course, notwithstanding the calls of his mercy; and, in spite of all his warnings and threatenings, to have, feeble worms as we are, defied his omnipotent vengeance: when such views of sin are presented, in the light of God's word, our souls are filled with anguish, and in the depth of sorrow and self-condemnation we adopt the publican's prayer, "God be merciful to me a sinner."[1]

The word of God, which pierces to the dividing asunder of soul and spirit, and of the joints and marrow, and is a discerner of the thoughts and intents of the heart,[2] often gives pain by its probings, but their tendency is salutary. They are unwelcome to hypocrites and false professors; but the man of sincere piety prays, "Search me, O God, and know my heart; try me, and know my thoughts; and see if there be any wicked way in me, and lead me into the way everlasting."[3]. The Bible tears the mask from the hypocrite, and shows to the Pharisee that all his righteousnesses are but filthy rags;[4] but, humiliating as these wholesome instructions are, the true penitent rejoices to receive them. He fears to be deceived; and he blesses God for the light of truth, by which his true character is revealed.

When men's eyes are opened to see their spiritual danger, they generally attempt, in their own strength, to work out their salvation. These efforts prove unavailing; and they learn, by experience, that they have no help in themselves. This truth, though clearly taught in the Bible, they never really believed until it was thus learned. Here arises, in the heart of Christian experience, another confirmation of Bible doctrine. A truth which no man sincerely believes until the Spirit of God has taught him, by inward experience, must have proceeded from God. In the whole progress of our spiritual life we become increasingly convinced of our utter helplessness and entire dependence on strength divine; and the Bible doctrine on this subject acquires perpetually increasing confirmation.

Genuine Christian experience commences with conviction of sin; but, blessed be God, it does not end here. The knowledge of our

---

[1] Luke xviii. 13.   [2] Heb. iv. 12.   [3] Ps. cxxxix. 23, 24.   [4] Is. lxiv. 6.

depravity, condemnation, and helplessness, would fill us with despair, were it not that salvation, precisely adapted to our necessities, has been provided by the mercy of God, and revealed in the gospel of his Son. The very truth, which would otherwise fill us with anguish and despair, prepares for the joyful acceptance of salvation by Christ. He who rejects this truth does not feel the need of Christ; and, therefore, does not come to him for life. They that be whole need not a physician.[1] Let the truth of this chapter be received deep in the heart, and we shall be prepared for the profitable study of the next subject.

---

[1] Matt. ix. 12.

BOOK FIFTH.

DOCTRINE CONCERNING JESUS CHRIST.

INTRODUCTION.

DUTY OF BELIEVING IN JESUS CHRIST.[1]

In close connection with repentance for sin, the Word of God enjoins the duty of believing in Christ: "Repent ye, and believe the Gospel:[2] "Testifying repentance toward God, and faith in our Lord Jesus Christ."[3] Both the duties relate to men as sinners, and without the performance of them, escape from the penalty of sin is impossible. The requirement of faith, in addition to repentance, proves that mere sorrow for sin will not suffice; and the passages of Scripture are numerous in which faith is expressly declared to be necessary to salvation: "Preach the Gospel to every creature. He that believeth and is baptised shall be saved: but he that believeth not, shall be damned."[4] "Without faith it is impossible to please him."[5] "He that believeth on the Son hath everlasting life; and he that believeth not, shall not see life; but the wrath of God abideth on him."[6] "He that believeth not, is condemned already, because he hath not believed in the name of the only begotton Son of God."[7]

---

[1] Acts xvi. 31. Believe on the Lord Jesus Christ, and thou shalt be saved. John ix. 35. Dost thou believe on the Son of God? Who is he, that I might believe on him?

[2] Mark i. 15.   [3] Acts xx. 21.   [4] Mark xvi. 15, 16.
[5] Heb. xi. 6.   [6] John iii. 36.   [7] John iii. 18.

(175)

These clear proofs that faith is necessary to salvation, render it important to understand the nature of faith. And since the saving benefit does not result from every kind or exercise of faith, but only from faith in Christ, what it is to believe in Jesus Christ, is an inquiry of highest interest.

Every one who reflects on the operations of his own mind, will perceive that faith lies at the foundation of every mental affection, and of every purpose to act. The testimony of our senses must be believed, before external objects can awaken any emotion in the mind; and the uniformity of nature's laws, and the deductions of our reason, must be believed before we can resolve to shun a precipice, or to labor for a future crop. In the ordinary affairs of life, faith is the basis of action. The man who believes that his house is on fire, or that a rich treasure is buried under it, acts accordingly. It is equally true that faith lies at the foundation of every religious affection and of every religious duty. He who loves God, and delights in his will and works, must believe that he is, and that the will and works in which he delights are realities, and possess the qualities which his mind attributes to them. He who repents of sin, must believe that the sin of which he repents has been committed, and that it possesses the evil nature which he condemns and loathes. So, in everything else, faith is the foundation of all religion.

In the view which has been taken, faith is merely intellectual, and does not imply any emotion, either pleasurable or painful. It may immediately excite emotions, pleasurable or painful, according to the character of the truth believed, and the state of mind in which it is received. The belief of one truth gives pleasure; and another, pain; and the belief of the same truth may give pleasure to one mind and pain to another. So, the truth of God, which a man dislikes while he is unconverted, is delighted in after his heart has been changed.

Faith, in this general sense, is necessary to the obedience of holy creatures, and mingles with all the holy exercises of their minds. But holy beings are incapable of repentance, because they have no sin to repent of: and they are unable to approach to God through Christ as guilty beings, seeking pardon. The Gospel addresses men as sinners, and presents Christ to them as the

Saviour of sinners; and the faith in Christ which it requires, is the receiving of the truth which it declares concerning Christ.

Although faith may be contemplated as merely intellectual, and as antecedent to all emotion; it is not, in this abstract view of it, that faith in Christ is enjoined in the Gospel, and has the promise of salvation. Men must receive "the love of the truth, that they may be saved,"[1] as well as the truth itself. A merely intellectual faith, without the love of the truth believed, cannot produce the proper fruits of faith; for "faith worketh by love;"[2] and it cannot secure the blessings promised to faith; for "with the *heart* man believeth unto righteousness."[3] A faith which dwells exclusively in the intellect, and leaves the heart untouched and cold, is the dead faith which the apostle James describes.[4]

Faith in Christ, is faith in the declarations of the Gospel concerning Christ; and it is faith in these as coming from God. It is the receiving of God's testimony concerning his Son; and, in this view of it, we see the great sinfulness of unbelief; for he who believeth not, hath made God a liar.[5] We see, also, how firm a foundation is laid for strong faith. The Gospel is the Word of God that cannot lie. Our senses may deceive us; and the deductions of our reason may be false. Relying on these, we may err, in things pertaining to the present life; but, in laying hold on life eternal, we may believe the truth of God with unwavering confidence. His word cannot fail.

Faith *in Christ* is necessary to salvation. We may believe many things that God has said in his Holy Word, without believing in Christ; and we may believe many truths concerning Christ, without possessing that faith in him which has the promise of eternal life. True faith receives Christ entire, as he is presented in the Gospel. If any part of his character, of his offices, or of his doctrine, is unwelcome to the heart, true faith does not dwell there. A perfect knowledge of Christ is not necessary to true faith: otherwise true faith would be impossible: for the riches of Christ are unsearchable,[6] and his love passeth knowledge.[7] But the true believer delights in Christ, just so far as he has knowledge

---

[1] 2 Thess. ii. 10.   [2] Gal. v. 6.   [3] Rom. x. 10.
[4] James ii. 26.   [5] 1 John v. 10.   [6] Eph. iii. 8.
[7] Eph. iii. 19.

12

of him; and desires to know more of him, that he may be more
filled with his love. The revelation made to the Old Testament
saints was obscure; but, so far as they could see Christ, in the
light which was afforded them, they rejoiced to see his day and
were glad.[1]

From the necessity of faith in Christ may be inferred the
greatness of Christ's character. When Jesus said, "If ye believe
not that I am he, ye shall die in your sins,"[2] he claimed an
importance to which Isaiah or Paul could never have aspired.
When the ministers of his religion taught, "There is none other
name under heaven given among men, whereby we must be saved,"[3]
they ascribed to him an office of exceeding greatness. If we
believe in Christ, according to the Scriptures, we fully justify all
that he claimed for himself, and all that his apostles claimed for
him; and we rejoice to render to him all honor and praise.

We may consider the question proposed to us: "Dost thou
believe on the Son of God?" On the decision of this question
our eternal all depends. As guilty sinners we are under condemnation, and the wrath of God abides on us. Among all the beings
in the universe, no deliverer can be found, except Jesus Christ,
and there is no salvation possible, except by faith in him. It is,
therefore, an inquiry of infinite importance whether we believe in
him. The man, to whom the question was proposed by the Saviour,
very pertinently asked in turn, "Who is he, that I might believe
on him?" We are about to institute the inquiry, Who is he?
While we search the Holy Scriptures, to find the answer, let us
take heed to it that we believe in him with all our hearts. Let us
rejoice to discover that he is mighty to save; and that he is, in
every particular, just such a Saviour as we need. While we study
his character and works, let us receive him into our hearts, and
yield ourselves up to him, as bought with his blood, and seek to
glorify him with our bodies and spirits, which are his.

---

[1] John viii. 56.   [2] John viii. 24.   [3] Acts iv. 12.

CHAPTER I.

THE PERSON OF CHRIST.

Section I.—HUMANITY.

JESUS CHRIST WAS A MAN.[1]

The manner of Christ's conception was peculiar. Without a human father, he was conceived in the womb of his virgin mother, by the power of the Holy Ghost. How far the son of Mary, conceived in this peculiar manner, resembled the sons born of other mothers, in the ordinary mode of generation, and how far he differed from them, we cannot certainly know from the circumstances of his conception. The divine power, which formed a man out of the dust of the ground, could also form a man in the womb of the virgin: but whether this extraordinary production should be a man, or a being of some other order, depended entirely on the will of God. For the knowledge of what Jesus Christ was, we are wholly indebted to the testimony concerning him given in the sacred Scriptures.

The testimony of the inspired Word on this point is very explicit. Whatever else Jesus Christ may have been, he was certainly a man; for so innumerable passages of Scripture declare. "Jesus of Nazareth, a man approved;"[2] "One mediator, the man Christ Jesus."[3]

Jesus Christ had a human body. His was not a mere shadowy form of humanity; for, even after his resurrection, he said to his disciples, "Handle me and see me, for a spirit hath not flesh and bones, as ye see me have."[4] It was a real body that bore the weight of the cross, and was afterwards nailed to it. It was a real body that was pierced by the spear; and real blood and water

---

[1] John i. 14; Phil. ii. 7, 8; Heb. ii. 14–17; Mark ix. 12; 1 Tim. ii. 5; Matt. i. 18–25; Luke i. 28–35; Gal. iv. 4; Matt. iv. 2; xxi. 18; John iv. 6, 10; Matt. viii. 24; xxi. 18; Mark ix. 12; Isaiah liii. 3; John xi. 35; Luke xix. 41; Matt. xxvi. 37, 38; Luke xxii. 44; Matt. iv. 1; Mark i. 13; Luke iv. 2; Heb. ii. 18; iv. 15; Luke ii. 10, 52; Matt. iv. 11; Luke xxii. 43; Mark xv. 34.
[2] Acts ii. 22.   [3] 1 Tim. ii. 5.   [4] Luke xxiv. 39.

issued from the wound. It was a real body that was embalmed with spices and laid in the tomb; and that afterwards rose from the dead. This body was human. It had the appearance and organs common to human bodies; was sustained by food, was subject to hunger and weariness, and needed the rest of sleep, like the bodies of other men.

Jesus Christ had a human soul. If the divine nature had dwelt in his body as a mere tabernacle of flesh, and supplied to it the place of a human soul, it could not have been said that "Jesus increased in wisdom."[1] The mere material fabric could have no wisdom, and the wisdom of the divine nature was not susceptible of increase. Nor was it some created spirit of angelic or super-angelic nature that animated his body. He was made in all things like his brethren;[2] and he would not have been a brother, one of the family, made like the rest, if the spirit that dwelt in his human flesh had not also been human. Without this he would not have been a man. If he had not possessed a soul, he could not have said, "My soul is exceeding sorrowful;"[3] nor could it have been said, "When thou shalt make his soul an offering for sin."[4] And if his soul had not been human, it would not have been a suitable offering for the sin of human beings. He took not on him the nature of angels, but the seed of Abraham.[5] He must be made like those whose law-place he assumed, and for whom he made himself a sacrifice.

The soul of Christ was unlike the souls of ordinary men, in being without the taint of sin. The mention of this exception proves more strongly the likeness in other respects. "He was in all points tempted like as we are, yet without sin."[6] Had the divine nature served as the soul of Christ, a statement of this exception would have been needless and inappropriate. Christ could be a man without being depraved; for Adam was a man before he fell. In the comparison between Christ and Adam as public heads, Adam is called the first man, and Christ the second man.[7] The humanity of the latter is as real as that of the former.

In the working of miracles God has shown that he is able to

---

[1] Luke ii. 52.   [2] Heb. ii. 17.   [3] Mark xiv. 34.
[4] Isaiah liii. 10.   [5] Heb. ii. 16.   [6] Heb. iv. 15.
[7] 1 Cor. xv. 47.

suspend the laws of nature; and he could have suspended that law of nature by which depraved parents generate depraved children. Had it been his pleasure, Jesus Christ might have had a human father as well as a human mother; and have been, nevertheless, without sin; for with God all things are possible. But it was not the pleasure of God that he should be so born; and the reason for his conception by the power of the Holy Ghost, is given in the words of the angel to his virgin mother: " *Therefore*, that holy thing which shall be born of thee shall be called the Son of God."[1] Ordinary generation would have made him the son of man: but his generation was extraordinary, because he was also the son of God. The conception by the Holy Ghost did not give the offspring an intermediate nature between the divine and the human, such as the demigods of the heathen were supposed to possess. In that case, Christ, as the son of God, would have been the son of the Holy Ghost, and not of the Father. But the Holy Spirit was the agent in preparing the body in which the sacrifice was to be made; and such was the union between it and the divinity, that the name, Son of God, belonged to the entire person so constituted.

Section II.—DIVINITY.

JESUS CHRIST WAS GOD.[2]

As the humanity of Christ, conceived by the power of the Holy Ghost, could not be known but from the testimony of the Scriptures; so his divinity, considering that he was born of a human mother, could not be known but from the testimony of the same unerring word. The conception by the Holy Ghost is sufficient to intimate that he was not to be an ordinary man; and the declaration that, in consequence of it, he was to be called the Son of God, leads the mind to conceive that, in some sense, he was to partake of the

---

[1] Luke i. 35.

[2] Mic. v. 2; Heb. i. 8; xiii. 8; Rev. i. 8, 18; John ii. 24; x. 15; xxi. 17; Acts i. 24; Rev. ii. 23; Matt. xviii. 20; xxviii. 20; John i. 48; Col. ii. 3; Jude 25; Matt. iii. 17; Luke i. 35; x. 22; John v. 23; 1 John v. 20; Matt. xxviii. 19; Isaiah xl. 3; Zech. ii. 8, 10; iv. 8; Mal. iii. 1; Matt. iii. 3; 1 Cor. xv. 47; Rev. xix. 16; Isaiah ix. 6; John i. 1; Rom. ix. 5; 1 Tim. iii. 16; Heb. i. 8; 1 John v. 20; Phil. ii. 6; Matt. xxviii. 9; Luke xxiii. 42; Acts vii. 59; Rev. v. 12; John i. 3, 10; Col. i. 16; Heb. i. 10; Neh. ix.

divine nature. Demigods, according to the heathen, had an intermediate nature between that of gods and men. But we have seen that Jésus Christ was properly a man, according to the testimony of the Scriptures; and we have now to appeal to the same testimony to learn whether he was also properly God.

The proofs on this point are abundant, and will be produced under several distinct heads.

I. The names of God are ascribed to Jesus Christ.

"The Word was God."[1] This testimony of the beloved disciple is the more important, because it was his design to inform us who his divine Master was. As he opens his First Epistle with an account of Jesus Christ, as the "eternal life which was with the Father,"[2] so he opens his Gospel with an account of him as the Word which was with God, and which was God. The subsequent part of the chapter clearly shows that this Word became flesh,[3] in the person of Jesus Christ, and the name Word is given elsewhere, by the same writer, to Jesus Christ.[4] Now it is incredible that the Gospel should open with a declaration which has misled its readers, in all ages, into a belief that Jesus Christ is God, if he were nothing more than a mere man. To no purpose has this apostle said most earnestly, "Little children, keep yourselves from idols,"[5] if his own teachings are such as must inevitably lead to idolatry. His language is usually very plain and simple: but in this case it needs the torture of most ingenious criticism, if it does not teach the deity of Christ. He has written that we might believe in Christ, and, believing, might have life through his name;[6] but if he has so written as to lead our souls into the sin of idolatry, our faith must be to death rather than life.

"Who is over all, God blessed for ever."[7] Christ is here called God; not in some subordinate sense, but over all, and blessed for ever. His possession of human nature is signified in the phrase, "Of whom, as concerning the flesh, Christ came." In contrast with this, his divinity is distinctly brought to view. What he was, *according to the flesh*, is not all that he was; but above that, he

---

[1] John i. 1. [2] 1 John i. 1. 2. [3] John i. 14.
[4] Rev. xix. 13. [5] 1 John v. 21. [6] John xx. 31.
[7] Rom. ix. 5.

was over all, God, blessed for ever. All the criticisms which have been tried on this text leave its testimony plain and decisive.

"My Lord and my God."[1] These words of Thomas are a brief, but very expressive declaration of his faith; and were so received by his Master: "Thomas, because thou hast seen me, thou hast believed."[2] So, the unfolding of Christ's true character to the mind of Nathaniel, drew forth his declaration of faith, "Thou art the Son of God.[3] So this confession of Thomas was elicited by the opening of the Saviour's character to his mind. Both of them were doubtless taught by the same Spirit which revealed Christ's character to Peter;[4] and the faith of both was accepted, and publicly approved. If Christ had not been God, it behoved him to correct his disciple, and save him from idolatry.

"Thy throne, O God, is for ever."[5] In this place, as in the first chapter of John, the inspired writer is designedly stating who Jesus Christ was. He has represented him as superior to the prophets, by whom God spake in times past to the fathers;—as superior to the angels;—as the proper object of angelic worship;—and finally closes the account with quotations from the Old Testament, applied to him, in which he is called God, and Lord, and said to have made the heavens and earth, and to endure for ever. If he was not God, Paul was mistaken.

To these texts in which the name God is applied to Jesus Christ, we may add the following: "The Church of God, which he hath purchased with his own blood."[6] "God was manifest in the flesh."[7] "We are in him that is true, even in his Son Jesus Christ; this is the true God, and eternal life."[8] "So then every one of us must give account of himself to God;"[9] compared with the preceding verse. "He that built all things, is God,"[10] considered in connection with the context, which shows that the Son is the builder here intended.

Several other passages may be cited as pertinent examples, if the translation of them, given in our common English version, be amended. "The appearing of our great God and Saviour, Jesus

---

[1] John xx. 28. [2] John xx. 29. [3] John i. 49.
[4] Matt. xvi. 17. [5] Heb. i. 8. [6] Acts xx. 28.
[7] 1 Tim. iii. 16. [8] 1 John v. 20. [9] Rom. xiv. 12.
[10] Heb. iii. 4.

Christ."[1] "The grace of our God and Lord, Jesus Christ."[2] "In the kingdom of the Christ and God," *i. e.* of him who is both Christ and God.[3] "Before the God and Lord, Jesus Christ."[4] "The righteousness of our God and Saviour, Jesus Christ."[5] These emendations of the translation are not made arbitrarily, but are required by a rule of criticism, founded on the usage of Greek writers, as to the repetition of the article, when prefixed to two nouns connected by a conjunction.

II. The attributes of God are ascribed to Jesus Christ.

Eternity.—In a prediction concerning him by Isaiah, it is said : "His name shall be called Wonderful, Counsellor, the Mighty God, the Everlasting Father, the Prince of Peace."[6] The phrase "Everlasting Father" may be rendered the *Father of Eternity*. Were this name given to him by erring men, we might suppose it inappropriate : but it is given to him by the infallible Spirit that spoke in the ancient prophets. In another prophecy concerning him, it is said : "Whose goings forth have been from of old, from everlasting."[7] We know that this prophecy referred to Christ ; for it is expressly applied to him in Matt. ii. 6. In the book of Proverbs, ch. viii., Wisdom is introduced, saying : "I was set up from everlasting, from the beginning, or ever the earth was. * * Then I was with him, as one brought up with him ; and I was daily his delight, rejoicing always before him ; rejoicing in the habitable part of the earth ; and my delights were with the sons of men."[8] The most consistent interpretation of this passage, applies it to Christ, the Eternal Word, who is called "the Power of God, and the Wisdom of God."[9] To these passages, we may add the words of Christ : "Before Abraham was, I am."[10] As his human nature was not fifty years old, these words could not refer to it. They attribute existence to him of more ancient date than the time of Abraham ; and, in affirming that pre-existence, the present tense, I am, is employed. This very extraordinary mode of speaking, agrees precisely with Old Testament language, describing the self-existent Jehovah : "I am that I am." "I am hath sent me."[11]

---

[1] Titus ii. 13. [2] 2 Thess. i. 12. [3] Eph. v. 5.
[4] 1 Tim. v. 21. [5] 2 Peter i. 1. [6] Isaiah ix. 6.
[7] Micah v. 2. [8] Prov. viii. 23–31. [9] 1 Cor. i. 24.
[10] John viii. 58. [11] Ex. iii. 14.

The Jews who heard Jesus speak thus concerning himself, understood him to claim divinity; and if he did not design to do so, it is undeniable that he employed language well calculated to mislead them.

Immutability.—"Jesus Christ, the same yesterday, to-day, and for ever."[1] "They shall wax old as doth a garment, and as a vesture shalt thou fold them up, and they shall be changed, but thou art the same."[2]

Omnipresence.—Christ promised to be with his disciples always, even to the end of the world,[3] and, not only at all times, but at all places: "Where two or three are met together in my name, there am I in the midst of them."[4] To fulfill this promise, he must be omnipresent. The same is implied in the words, "No man hath ascended up to Heaven, but he that came down from Heaven, even the Son of man which is in Heaven."[5] His body was on earth, when he spoke these words; and yet he declares himself to be in Heaven. This could not be true, if he were not omnipresent.

Omniscience.—Jesus knew the thoughts of men, even while shut up in their own breasts. Other prophets had this knowledge communicated to them, by special revelation, on particular occasions; but Jesus had his knowledge at all times. "He knew all men, and needed not that any one should testify of man; for he knew what was in man."[6] To know the secrets of the heart, belongs peculiarly to Jehovah. "Who can know it? I, the Lord, search the heart."[7] Yet the power of searching the heart, is expressly ascribed to Jesus. "I am he which searcheth the reins and hearts."[8] Peter appealed to Christ, as knowing the secrets of his heart, and expressly ascribes omniscience to him. "Lord, thou knowest all things; thou knowest that I love thee."[9] Christ claimed omniscience in the words, "No man knoweth the Son, but the Father, neither knoweth any man the Father, save the Son, and he to whomsoever the Son will reveal him."[10] Without omniscience, Christ would not be qualified to judge the world.

Omnipotence.—Paul, feeling his own weakness, desired the power of Christ to rest upon him;[11] and he conceived of that power

---

[1] Heb. xiii. 8.
[2] Heb. i. 11, 12.
[3] Matt. xxviii. 20.
[4] Matt. xviii. 20.
[5] John iii. 13.
[6] John ii. 25.
[7] Jer. xvii. 10.
[8] Rev. ii. 23.
[9] John xxi. 17.
[10] Matt. xi. 29.
[11] 2 Cor. xii. 9.

as infinite, when he said: "I can do all things, through Christ which strengtheneth me."[1] The omnipotence of Christ is manifested in the works which he performs, of which we shall presently speak more particularly. He claimed like omnipotence with the Father: "My Father worketh hitherto, and I work."[2] "What things soever the Father doeth, these also the Son doeth likewise."[3] "Neither shall any man pluck them out of my hand. No man is able to pluck them out of my Father's hand."[4] In the prophecy already quoted from Isaiah, he is called "the Mighty God;" and in Rev. i. 8–11, he is called "the Almighty."

III. Divine works are ascribed to Christ.

Creation.—"All things were made by him, and without him was not anything made that was made."[5] "By him all things were created that are in heaven and that are in earth, visible and invisible."[6] We may admit, that the word "by" frequently denotes an instrument used in a work; but this is not its invariable meaning. It is applied to God the Father. "It became him, of whom are all things, and by whom are all things, in bringing many sons to glory to make the captain of their salvation perfect through suffering."[7] If Christ was a created instrument, used in the creation of everything else, he was himself created without such instrumentality, and the words of John were not true, "Without him was not anything made that was made." God created all things by Jesus Christ,[8] not as a mere instrument, or as an inferior agent; otherwise it could not be said, "All things were created by him and for him."[9] An inferior agent, employed to do a work, performs it not for himself, but for the superior who employs him. The Son co-operated with the Father in the work of creation, as supreme God. The word "by" implies no inferiority. When it is said of Christ, he by himself purged our sins,[10] himself does not denote an agent inferior to Christ.

Providence.—All things are kept in being by the power of Christ, and he must, therefore, be God. "Upholding all things by the word of his power."[11] All the powers of the universe are

---

[1] Phil. iv. 13.   [2] John v. 17.   [3] John v. 19.
[4] John x. 27, 28.   [5] John i. 3.   [6] Col. i. 16.
[7] Heb. ii. 10.   [8] Eph. iii. 9.   [9] Col. i. 16.
[10] Heb. i. 3   [11] Heb. i. 3.

under his management, and therefore all the workings of providence are directed by him.

Giving of life.—Christ raised the dead to life during his personal ministry, not as prophets and apostles did, in the name and by the power of another. The apostles wrought miracles, not by their own power, but in the name of Jesus Christ.[1] Jesus, on the contrary, claimed the power which he exercised in the working of miracles. "The Son quickeneth whom he will."[2] He claimed to exercise his power, both in the quickening of souls dead in sin, and in the resurrection of the body. "The hour is come, and now is, when the dead shall hear the voice of the Son of God, and they that hear shall live."[3] "The hour is coming in the which all that are in their graves shall hear his voice, and shall come forth."[4] The power of raising the dead, is attributed by Paul to Christ, and is called the working whereby he is able to subdue all things to himself.[5]

IV. Numerous passages of the Old Testament, which unquestionably speak of Jehovah, the Supreme God, are, in the New Testament, applied to Jesus Christ. Isaiah vi. 3, compared with John xii. 41; Isaiah xl. 3, compared with Matt. iii. 1, 3; Isaiah xlv. 21–23, compared with Phil. ii. 9–11; Zach. xii. 10, compared with John xix. 37.

V. Divine worship was commanded to be rendered, and was rendered, to Jesus Christ. The angels were commanded to worship him. "When he bringeth in the first begotten into the world, he saith: 'Let all the angels of God worship him.'"[6] Men are commanded to believe in him, trust in him, which are acts of divine worship. This has more force when compared with the declaration: "Cursed is the man that trusteth in man, and maketh flesh his arm."[7] Christ permitted himself to be worshipped as the Son of God.[8] He was worshipped by his disciples, after his ascension to Heaven.[9] They were accustomed to call on his name,[10] that is, to address prayer to him. So the dying Stephen prayed: "Lord Jesus, receive my spirit."[11] The administering or receiving of

---

[1] Acts iii. 12; iv. 10. [2] John v. 21. [3] John v. 25.
[4] John v. 28, 29. [5] Phil. iii. 21. [6] Heb. i. 6.
[7] Jer. xvii. 5. [8] John ix. 38. [9] Luke xxiv. 52.
[10] Acts ix. 14. [11] Acts vii. 59.

baptism in his name, is an act of religious worship, in which he is honored equally with the Father, and the Holy Spirit.[1]

VI. The equality of the Son with the Father, is taught by Paul, in Phil. ii. 9. His example, in humbling himself, and taking on himself the form of a servant, is proposed for our imitation; but there was no humiliation in his taking on himself the form of a servant, if that had been the only character that he could rightfully assume. But he had a right to claim equality with God, and this fact showed the greatness of his humiliation. A parallel passage is found in 2 Cor. viii. 9: "Though he was rich, for our sakes he became poor."

VII. If Jesus Christ was not God, he was justly condemned to death.

It is difficult to state and unfold this argument, without an appearance of irreverence. To charge the divine Jesus with crime, even hypothetically, is grating to the feelings of those who love and adore him. But it must be remembered that he who is, by this argument, proved to be chargeable with crime, is the Jesus of another gospel, a mere man, whose character and conduct are to be judged like those of other men.

Jesus was condemned to death by the Jewish Sanhedrim. That council reported to Pilate, "We have a law, and by our law he ought to die, because he made himself the Son of God."[2] On a former occasion, Jesus said unto them: "My Father worketh hitherto, and I work."[3] And they charged him with blasphemy, because he made God his [own] Father, thereby making himself equal with God. It was in this peculiar sense that the charge of making himself the Son of God was construed, or it would not have amounted to blasphemy. The high priest who was the president of the council, put Christ on his oath, "I adjure thee by the living God;"[4] and propounded to him two questions which, though mentioned together by Matthew and Mark, are by Luke stated as proposed separately. "Art thou the Christ?" and "Art thou the Son of God?" It was the affirmative reply of Jesus to the last of these questions, which was the ground of his condemnation. Jesus knew the sense in which the question was propounded; and

---

[1] Matt. xxviii. 19.   [2] John xix. 7.
[3] John v. 17.   [4] Matt. xxvi. 62.

he was bound, on correct principles of morals, in answering the question, to answer it honestly and truly in the sense in which he knew that the high priest meant it. He therefore affirmed on oath, at that tribunal, that he was the Son of God, in this high sense. For this he was condemned to death; and if he was not what he claimed to be, he was guilty of perjury and of his own death. On this charge he was condemned to death, by the Council, but God justified him by raising him from the dead. "Declared to be the Son of God, with power, according to the spirit of holiness, by the resurrection from the dead."[1] This proved that his condemnation was unjust; and that he was truly what he had claimed to be, the Son of God, in the sense which the Jews accounted blasphemy.

The last argument exhibits the importance of this doctrine in a strong light. According to the law of Moses, any one who enticed to idolatry was to be punished with death.[2] The council before which Jesus was tried, was the court which had cognisance of this offence. A mere man, who should claim divine honor to himself, was guilty of this capital crime; and although the Romans had taken away from the Jews the power of inflicting capital punishment, the council might, with perfect propriety, report to the governor concerning such a man, "By our law he ought to die." This was their decision, as reported to Pilate, concerning Jesus; and, if he was not entitled to the divine honor which he claimed, the decision was just.

Two accusations were brought against Jesus. Before the Roman governor he was charged with treason against Cæsar, by making himself king. Into this accusation the governor inquired, asking Jesus, "Art thou a king?" Jesus answered in the affirmative, as in the other case: but, that he might not convict himself of a crime of which he was not guilty, he explained, "My kingdom is not of this world."[3] His reply was satisfactory to the governor, who acquitted him on this charge. In the other case he not only claimed to be the Son of God, but accompanied the claim with no explanation, to prevent the passing of the sentence. He might have said, I am the Son of God, but not in such a sense as to claim divine honor. He made no such explanation. If Jesus was not entitled to divine honor, he knew it; and he knew also that

---

[1] Rom. i. 4.   [2] Deut. xiii. 6, 8.   [3] John xviii. 36.

he deserved death, under the decision of this court, for claiming it. To make the claim before the court, was to be guilty of the crime. To answer as he did, on oath, if he did not mean to make the claim, was perjury. And to permit the sentence against him to pass, without any effort to explain, was to be guilty of his own death. It follows, therefore, that Jesus Christ, if not entitled to divine honor, was a wicked man and a deceiver.

We might suppose the possibility of mistake, concerning Christ's claim of divine honor before the court that condemned him, if he had habitually disclaimed such honor in his previous ministry. But, instead of this, he had taught, "It is the will of God, that all men should honor the Son, even as they honor the Father."[1] He claimed superiority to the law of the Sabbath, and the right of working every day, as his Father did: "My Father worketh hitherto, and I work."[2] He claimed to have been before Abraham, in language which appropriately intimates self-existence: "Before Abraham was, I am."[3] He claimed to be one with the Father: "I and my Father are one."[4] Moreover, he never rejected divine honor, when offered him. Paul and Barnabas, at Lystra, indignantly repelled those who approached to do them honor as gods;[5] and the angel hastily prevented John from worshipping him: "See thou do it not. Worship God."[6] When the people were minded to take him by force, and make him king, he escaped from them. He refused to be "a judge or divider,"[7] and declined all civil honor, in perfect consistence with his disclaimer of it before Pilate. But in equal consistence with his claim of divine honor before the Sanhedrim, he never rejected it when offered by any one. The man to whom he had given sight worshipped him as the Son of God,[8] without rebuke; and Thomas addressed him, "My Lord and my God;" not only without rebuke, but with approbation.[9] To all this we may add, that the disciples to whom he taught the principles of his religion, and who believed that they had the mind of Christ, were accustomed to render him divine honor. Many proofs of his deity have been cited above, from their writings. That Paul did not consider him a mere man, is most clear from

---

[1] John v. 23. [2] John v. 17. [3] John viii. 58.
[4] John x. 30. [5] Acts xiv. 15. [6] Rev. xxii. 9.
[7] Luke xii. 14. [8] John ix. 38. [9] John xx. 28, 29.

Gal. i. 1 : Paul an apostle, not of men, neither by man, but by Jesus Christ;" and the whole tenor of his writings shows, that he felt such obligations to Christ, and reposed such trust in him, as are utterly inconsistent with the belief that he was a mere creature.

From these facts, we must believe that the deity of Christ is an essential doctrine of Christianity. As there can be no religion without the existence of God; so there can be no Christian creed in which the doctrine of Christ's deity is not a fundamental article.

But, clear and abundant as the proofs on this subject are, the humble inquirer into the truth as it is in Jesus, is sometimes perplexed with difficulties respecting it. The more common of these it will be proper briefly to consider.

Obj. 1. This doctrine is inconsistent with the Unity of God. This objection will be considered hereafter, under the head of " The Trinity."

Obj. 2. In various passages Jesus Christ is spoken of as distinct from God, and sometimes in such a manner as seems to deny his proper deity.

Before we proceed, under this head, to examine particular passages, we may premise that the Scriptures speak of a two-fold connection between the Godhead and the man Jesus Christ—a personal union and an indwelling. The personal union is not with the whole Godhead, but with one person or subsistence therein. It was not the whole Godhead that was made flesh; but the Word that was with God, and was God. God sent forth, not the whole Godhead, but his Son, made of a woman.[1] On the other hand, the indwelling is of the whole Godhead. In him dwelleth all the fullness of the Godhead bodily.[2] The Father dwelt in him,[3] and the Spirit was given to him without measure.[4] This indwelling did not make him one person with the Father and the Holy Spirit. His body was a temple for the whole Godhead. As the Holy Ghost, in the prophets, was distinct from the prophets; so the Godhead, dwelling in Jesus Christ, was distinct from the person of Jesus Christ.

John xvii. 3. "This is life eternal, that they might know thee

---

[1] Gal. iv. 4.   [2] Col. ii. 9.
[3] John xiv. 10.   [4] John iii. 34.

the only true God; and Jesus Christ whom thou hast sent." The Father is here addressed, as the representative of the Godhead. The Godhead that sent Christ is distinct from the person of Jesus Christ; but the person sent was nevertheless divine. His divinity, though not affirmed in the passage, may be inferred from the fact that the knowledge of him was necessary to eternal life.

1 Cor. viii. 6. "To us there is but one God, the Father, of whom are all things, and we in him; and one Lord Jesus Christ, by whom are all things, and we by him." Here, again, the Father is the representative of the entire Godhead, which is in him, as the object of ultimate worship, and is one. "Of whom are all things." The same Godhead is in Jesus Christ as the medium of manifestation. "By whom are all things." This text does not affirm that Jesus Christ is a divine person; but his qualification to be universal Lord implies it. This text no more denies Jesus Christ to be God, than it denies the Father to be Lord.

In the same manner other similar passages may be explained.

Obj. 3. The various passages which speak of Jesus Christ as inferior to the Father, as sent by the Father, and as working by the power of the Father, appear to deny his proper deity.

The explanation of all these passages is given by Paul in Phil. ii. 5–8. "Let this mind be in you, which was also in Christ Jesus; who, being in the form of God, thought it not robbery to be equal with God; but made himself of no reputation, and took upon him the form of a servant, and was made in the likeness of men; and being found in fashion as a man, he humbled himself, and became obedient unto death, even the death of the cross."

The Son of God, though truly divine, and entitled to divine honor, humbled himself; and, by his union with human nature, was made under the law. He was not originally under the law, but was made under it. Hence we read of his inferiority to the Father, his subjection to the Father's authority, &c. Inferiority of office does not require inferiority of nature. A subject is inferior in authority to his king; though he is equal to him in nature, and may surpass him in intellectual and moral worth. Jesus Christ is inferior to the Father in his human nature, and his mediatorial office; but in his divine nature he is God over all.

Obj. 4. Jesus Christ appears, in Luke xviii. 19, to admit that he had not the goodness peculiar to God; and, in Mark xiii. 32 to deny that he had omniscience.

"Why callest thou me good? none is good save one, that is God." These words are a question. Questions sometimes imply strong affirmation; but, in such cases, the reason of asking them must be apparent. In the present case there is nothing in the whole context indicating that it was Christ's design to explain his own character; and we may therefore conclude that the question was asked for another purpose. The young ruler thought himself to be a good man, and addressing Christ as another good man, from whom he was willing to receive instruction, asked, in the spirit of self-righteousness, "What *good* thing shall I do?"[1] The whole of Christ's discourse with this young man was designed to convince him of his self-righteousness, and the question with which it commenced was precisely adapted to this purpose. It was calculated to lead his mind to the humbling reflection that all human goodness, such as he trusted in, and such as he had attributed to Christ, was insignificant and worthless when brought into comparison with God. Whether divine goodness belonged to Jesus Christ is here neither affirmed nor denied. This question the ruler never thought of, and Christ made no reference to it, and said nothing about it.

Mark xiii. 32. "Of that day and that hour knoweth no man; no, not the angels of heaven; neither the Son, but my Father only." This passage must be explained in harmony with other Scriptures. Were Gen. xviii. 21 the only passage of Scripture from which we could learn anything respecting the extent of God's knowledge, we should conclude that it is not unlimited; and, in like manner, if Mark xiii. 32 were the only text from which we could learn the extent of Christ's knowledge, we should infer that he is not omniscient. But the proofs of his omniscience, as before adduced, are so abundant, that we are obliged to seek an explanation of this passage which shall be consistent with them. When we consider that it was the spirit of Christ in the ancient prophets, that enabled them to make their numerous predictions—that he personally predicted so many things, and so much in particular concerning this very day,[2] and that this day is emphatically called

---

[1] Matt. xix. 16.   [2] Phil. i. 6.

13

the day of Christ, the day of the Lord,[1] it seems improbable that he should be wholly ignorant of the time of its coming. He describes himself as a lord, coming unexpectedly on his servants after a season of absence. Now, although we can see a propriety that the servants should not know when their lord would come, no reason appears why the lord himself should not know it. These facts, therefore, favor an interpretation of the passage which will be consistent with the doctrine of Christ's omniscience.

The most obvious method of interpreting the passage in harmony with other Scriptures, is to suppose that it refers to the knowledge which Christ's humanity possessed. In this nature he was not omniscient; for it is said[2] that Jesus increased in wisdom. The Holy Spirit communicated to his human soul, from time to time, such knowledge as was necessary; but not *all* knowledge, for human nature could not be made omniscient. There is, however, an objection to this interpretation, on the ground that Christ could not, with truth, deny of himself any knowledge which either nature possessed. This objection would be embarrassing, if it were not true that Christ, in the passage, has placed his knowledge and that of his Father in contrast. In the same manner he has denied omnipotence of himself, in John v. 30; not absolutely, but as distinct from his Father. "I can, of mine own self, do nothing." In the same verse, he, in the same sense, speaks of himself as without omniscience also: "As I hear, I judge." The question, "When shall these things be?" was proposed by the disciples[3] to Christ as visible before them in his human nature. It was not proper that they should receive an answer; for it was intended that they should watch: "Watch ye therefore; for ye know not when the master of the house cometh."[4] As the human nature of Christ was the medium through which the disciples received their instruction, and as this was one of the times and seasons which the Father had reserved in his own power,[5] we may suppose that the Holy Spirit had not communicated, and the holy humanity of Jesus had not sought this knowledge, which was unnecessary to any of the purposes of his present ministry. In this view it was well calculated to check the inquisitiveness of his

---

[1] Cor. v. 5.   [2] Luke ii. 52.   [3] Mark xiii. 4.

[4] Mark xiii. 35.   [5] Acts i. 7.

disciples into this matter which it was not the will of God that they should know, for him to inform them, that though the infinite stores of his Father's knowledge were ever accessible to him, he had not chosen, in his distinct character, in which he revealed the counsels of God to them, to inquire into the matter, and could not, therefore, communicate to them the knowledge which their unprofitable curiosity led them to desire.

Some have thought it a more satisfactory solution of the difficulty to take the word know in the sense *to make known*. This sense it is alleged to have in 1 Cor. ii. 2; but this may be doubted. It seems more proper to regard the language as a common rhetorical figure, according to which the cause is put for the effect. So David said, "I was dumb;"[1] meaning, "I was as silent as if I had been dumb." So Paul determined, in his ministry among the Corinthians, to be as though he knew nothing but Christ crucified. In the same manner, the words of Christ may be interpreted as if he had said, "Your inquiries into the precise time of my coming will all be in vain. No source of information will be available, to give you this knowledge. As to the effect, it will be to you as if the knowledge were possessed by none but the Father; who will make it known, not by the ministry of men, angels, or his Son; but by his own hand, in the execution of his purpose."

The two views of this passage which have been presented, differ somewhat from each other; but the inquirer is not bound to decide on their comparative merit, or to accept either as unquestionably correct. A perfect understanding of every difficult text, though desirable, is not indispensable to the exercise of piety.

Obj. 5. Jesus Christ is called "the beginning of the creation of God;" and "the firstborn of every creature." These passages, while they attribute a high character to him, nevertheless speak of him as a creature.

Rev. iii. 14. "The beginning of the creation of God." This text may be explained by others in the same book: Rev. i. 8; xxi. 6; xxii. 13. When Jesus Christ is called "the beginning and the end, the first and the last," we are not to understand that he was created before other creatures, and that other creatures will be annihilated, leaving him to survive them. The sense is, that

---

[1] Ps. xxxix. 9.

all things are from him and to him; or, as Paul says, "All things were created by him and for him."[1]   He is the original and the first cause of all things.   His being the beginning, is explained " He is before all things."   In this sense he is the beginning of the creation of God, *i. e.* its original cause.

Col i. 15.   " The first born of every creature."   The clause " first born of every creature," may be grammatically construed in two different ways.   The genitive "of every creature" may be governed by the word " first born," as a noun ; or by the word " first," as an adjective of the superlative degree in composition.   The objection assumes that the last of these is the true construction. Having decided on this, it then infers that Christ is one of the creatures, because the superlative degree usually compares one thing of a group with the rest of that group.   But this usage of the superlative, though general, is not invariable : for this same word " first" is twice used in the first chapter of John,[2] where the comparison is of a different kind, and our translators have, on this account, rendered the word as if it had been in the comparative, instead of the superlative degree : " He was *before* me."   In proof that Paul did not design to group Christ with the creatures, as one of them, the following arguments may be adduced.   The descriptive terms employed do not accord with this supposition. To make him one of the group, Christ should have been called the first *created* of all creatures, or the first born of all born : but the distinction between being born and being created, excludes him from the group of creatures.

2. There is a further incongruity in the use of the word " every."   We could not say, Solomon was the wisest of every man.   Yet the objection makes Paul use this mode of speech.   It is true that this incongruity may be in part removed by translating the clause thus : " the first born of all creation."   But even this would not naturally express the idea supposed to be intended.   A plural noun is needed, to denote the group of which Christ is supposed to be one of the constituent parts.

3. The context proves that Paul did not design to compare Christ with created things, as one of the number.   He says, " All things were created by him and for him; and he is before all

---

[1] Col. i. 16.   [2] John i. 15, 30.

things, and by him all things consist."[1] This language clearly excludes him from the number of created things.

If we admit that the genitive is governed by the adjective, the arguments adduced should satisfy us that the adjective must be understood, as in the places referred to in the first chapter of John. But the construction, which takes the genitive to be governed by the noun, is preferable. According to this, we may translate the clause, "the whole creation's first born." God said, "I will make him my first born, higher than the kings of the earth."[2] The term "first born" here denotes superiority of dignity, in comparison with the kings of the earth. To the first born belonged, not only superior dignity, but superior right of inheritance. Christ, as the Son, was appointed "heir of all things."[3] In respect both of dignity and inheritance, he is "the creation's first born," the king and heir of the whole creation.

From the fact that the same Greek word is used in v. 18, some have supposed that this verse is explanatory of the former, and that Christ is the first born of every creature, because he is the first born from the dead. Others, by accenting the Greek word in v. 15 on a different syllable, make it to signify "first begetter," or "first producer."

Some, who admit the proper deity of Christ, suppose that his human soul was created before all other creatures, and continued without a human body until the incarnation in the womb of the virgin. But, according to this opinion, Christ was not "made like his brethren." Moreover, as that human soul, being a creature, must have been under law to God from the beginning of its existence, it was not true that he was made under the law, when he was made of a woman, as is taught in Gal. iv. 4. We have seen that the texts do not require such a hypothesis to explain them.

Obj. 6. Jesus, in John x. 35, 36, explained his use of the phrase, "Son of God," as not implying proper deity. "If he called them gods unto whom the word of God came, and the Scripture cannot be broken; say ye of him whom the Father hath sanctified and sent into the world, Thou blasphemest; because I said, I am the Son of God?"

---

[1] Col i. 16, 17.   [2] Ps. lxxxix. 27.   [3] Heb. i. 2.

As this objection opposes a very strong argument for the divinity of Christ, it will be proper to give it a careful examination.

In examining the tenth chapter of John, in which these words are found, we may observe the following facts:

1. The claim to be the Christ was not that on which the charge of blasphemy was founded.

While Jesus was walking in Solomon's porch, the Jews gathered round him, and asked, "How long makest thou us to doubt? If thou be the Christ, tell us plainly." They had asked John the Baptist, "Art thou the Christ?" The Jews were in expectation that their Messiah would make his appearance about this time; and, from the manner in which these questions were proposed, it is plain that the claim to be the Christ could not necessarily be blasphemous. It only needed to be sustained by proper proof, and the proposing of the question intimated a readiness to admit the claim. Jesus did not directly answer their question, but charged them with rejecting the testimony which he had previously given concerning himself, and the proofs which he had adduced. All this they bore, without charging him with blasphemy.

2. The charge of blasphemy was founded on the claim to be the Son of God.

This point is clear from the words of Christ, "Say ye, Thou blasphemest, because I said, I am the Son of God?" He had spoken of God as his Father in a peculiar relation, according to which he could say, "I and my Father are one." This was said after such declarations concerning the power by which his sheep were kept, as represented himself omnipotent as well as his Father. His oneness with the Father was, therefore, such a unity as implied his possession of divine attributes. So the Jews understood him; and this they distinctly declared to be the ground of their charge: "For a good work we stone thee not, but for blasphemy; because thou being a man, makest thyself God." On a former occasion they had made out the same charge against him on the same ground. He had spoken of God as his father in a peculiar sense, which implied co-operation with the Father, beyond what a mere creature could claim; and they who heard him, understanding the high claim which he set up, charged him with blasphemy, because "he called God his Father, making himself equal

with God."[1] It was precisely on this ground that he was reported
to Pilate, by the Jewish Sanhedrim, as worthy of death : "By our
law, he ought to die, because he made himself the Son of God."[2]
They also reported to Pilate that "he made himself Christ a
king;" but they do not say that for so doing he deserved to die
by their law. They said, "Whosoever maketh himself a king
speaketh against Cæsar."[3] This was an offence of which the
Roman law might take cognisance, and which Pilate might judge;
but the other offence was a sin of which the Roman law would
take no cognisance. The charge of blasphemy was investigated
by the Jewish court, and was not made out on the claim to be
"Christ a king."

3. Jesus knew that the charge of blasphemy would be left without foundation, if he should explain that, in claiming divine Sonship, he did not mean to claim divine attributes or honors.

The charge of blasphemy was, for making himself God, and
equal with God. Now, the Jews called God their Father; and
believers and angels are called sons of God. To claim sonship in
this sense could not be blasphemy. Jesus knew all this, and
showed himself able to avail himself of the plea which might be
based on this distinction. He referred to the Scripture use of the
term "gods," in its application to Hebrew magistrates; and showed
clearly, that, if the words which he had used were to be justified
by availing himself of this distinction, he understood well how to
do it.

4. Jesus did not plead, that in making himself the Son of God,
he did not intend to claim divine attributes or honors.

What has been supposed to imply this, is merely a question,
which affirms nothing: "Say ye?" In this aspect, it is like the
question proposed to the young ruler: "Why callest thou me
good?" Jesus was not now on trial before a regular court, but
was addressed by a company of malignant and captious men, to
whom he did not feel bound to give answers and explanations at
their demand. When they asked to know plainly, whether he was
the Christ, instead of answering them, he charged them with
rejecting the testimony and proofs which he had already given, and
with murderous intentions towards him. So, when they state their

---

[1] John v. 17, 18.   [2] John xix. 7.   [3] John xix. 12.

charge of blasphemy, he charged them with inconsistency in making it out. They were desirous to condemn him. When he was finally delivered to the Roman governor, "Pilate knew that the chief priests had for envy delivered him to them."[1] Jesus, who knew what was in man, fully understood that their pretended jealousy for the divine honor, was hypocritical. Some of them, as members of the great council, could readily have found Scripture for being themselves styled "Gods," yet they would give no patient attention to the proofs which Jesus offered, to sustain his claim to the dignity he assumed.

5. Instead of leaving the matter to rest on the plea which these words have been supposed to imply, Jesus reasserted his intimate union with the Father: "That ye may know and believe that the Father is in me, and I in him."[2] After this, it is added, "therefore they sought again to take him." It is manifest that the Jews did not understand him to retract the claim which had given them offence.

The Jewish magistrates, though called gods, in a subordinate sense of the term, had nothing of that intimate union with the Father which Jesus claimed. They were, after all, mortal men. "I have said ye are gods, and all of you are children of the Most High; but ye shall die like men."[3] But concerning himself, Jesus had said: "As the Father hath life in himself, so hath he given to the Son to have life in himself."[4] "The Son quickeneth whom he will."[5] "The dead shall hear the voice of the Son of God."[6] The Father hath committed all judgment to the Son."[7] "I and my Father are one."[8] If, after making these high claims, Jesus had quailed before his enemies, and sought shelter in likening himself to mortal judges, called gods, he would not have closed his address by re-asserting that which had given them offence. "Believe me, that I am in the Father, and the Father in me."

We should remember that Jesus was not now on trial. These words were not spoken before the Sanhedrim, where the plea which they are supposed to contain, was needed, if needed at all. When formally arraigned before that tribunal, Jesus did not object to

---

[1] Matt. xxvii. 18.   [2] John x. 38.   [3] Ps. lxxxii. 6 7.
[4] John v. 26.   [5] John v. 21.   [6] John v. 25.
[7] John v. 22.   [8] John x. 30.

their jurisdiction, nor to the oath administered by the high priest. He answered directly and plainly the question which the high priest propounded, though he knew well that the answer which he gave would, in the judgment of the court, convict him of blasphemy. Where now is the plea which he is supposed to have made on the former occasion? He then understood its bearing on the point. Has he forgotten it now? The plea urged on a former occasion, at a different place, to a different company, when not on trial, and not on oath, cannot avail now, unless repeated in due form. Besides, when before made, if made at all, it was obscure, and hidden under the form of a question. It is now needed in plainness and by direct affirmation. But Jesus does not produce the plea. Let those who urge the objection we are considering, account for his silence.

Section III.—UNION OF NATURES.

The two natures of Jesus Christ, the divine and the human, are united in one person.[1]

The name Son of God, properly denotes his divine nature; and the name Son of Man, his human nature. He frequently called himself the Son of God; more frequently, the Son of Man. Both these names were used as denoting one and the same person. The whole use of them indicates this; but there are some passages which show it more clearly than others. After speaking of himself as the Son of God, he says the Father hath given him authority to execute judgment, because he is the son of man.[2] Here the same person is manifestly called the Son of God, and the Son of Man. In other cases, attributes or works which belong to one nature, are ascribed to his person, denoted by the name which is derived from the other nature. "No man hath ascended up to Heaven, but he that came down from Heaven, even the Son of Man, which is in Heaven."[3] Here he is named from his human nature, the Son of Man; while omnipresence is ascribed to him, which belongs to his divine nature. Another example of like kind is, "The Son of Man is Lord also of the Sabbath."[4] The superiority to the Sab-

---

[1] John iii. 13; Rom. i. 4; ix. 5; 1 Cor. ii. 8; Matt. i. 23.
[2] John v. 27.   [3] John iii. 13.   [4] Mark ii. 28.

bath belongs to his divine nature, but the name by which he is designated belongs to the human. On the other hand, he is called God, and the Lord of Glory, when his blood and his crucifixion, things pertaining to his human flesh, are the subjects of discourse. "They would not have crucified the Lord of Glory."[1] "The Church of God, which he hath purchased with his own blood."[2]

How two natures so widely different, should be so united, we cannot understand. In the union of the body and soul of man in one person, there is a similar fact which we are unable to comprehend; but if we should disbelieve it, we should reject the testimony of our own consciousness. We have, therefore, no plea for rejecting the doctrine now before us, on the ground of its mysteriousness.

The union of the two natures does not confound the properties peculiar to each. The humanity is not deified, nor the divinity humanized. So, the body of man does not become spirit, by its union with the soul; nor does the soul become matter, by its union with the body.

The union of Christ's divinity with his humanity, is a different thing from the indwelling of the Godhead in him. The Holy Ghost dwells in believers, so that their bodies are called his temple, but this union does not constitute them one person. So, though Jesus said, "The Father is in me, and I in him," he addressed his Father, and spoke of him, as a distinct person. The same is true of the Holy Spirit which dwelt in him, being given to him without measure.

The personal union is more than a mere manifestation of the divine nature through the human. God manifests himself in the works of creation. But this manifestation is not a personal union; otherwise, the universe must be God.

This union is indissoluble. Jesus will ever be the Lamb in the midst of the throne,[3] and will for ever appear, in his glorified humanity, to the worshipping saints, who, with adoring praise, will for ever sing, "Worthy is the Lamb that was slain, to receive power and riches, and wisdom and strength, and honor and glory and blessing."[4]

---

[1] 1 Cor. ii. 8.
[3] Rev. vii. 17.
[2] Acts xx. 28.
[4] Rev. v. 12.

CHAPTER II.

STATES OF CHRIST.

Section I.—ORIGINAL GLORY.

BEFORE HIS INCARNATION, THE SON OF GOD WAS IN INTIMATE COMMUNION OF GLORY AND BLESSEDNESS WITH THE FATHER.[1]

The existence of Christ, previous to his appearing in the world, is proved by passages of Scripture, that do not expressly declare his divinity.

If we had no further teaching on the subject, we might suppose that he was a created spirit, had enjoyed honor and happiness in the presence of God, and had consented to appear, in obedience to the will of God, in the person of Jesus Christ. But the proofs which have been adduced from other parts of Scripture, clearly show that this pre-existent spirit was God, and not a creature.

Several names are ascribed to the pre-existent divinity of Jesus Christ. John calls him the Word of God.[2] He is more frequently called the Son of God. Various passages speak of him as the Son of God, antecedent to his coming into the world. He is called the Angel of the Lord, the Angel of the Lord's presence, the Angel of the Covenant, the Captain of the Lord's hosts. It is also supposed that he is intended to be designated, in the 8th chapter of Proverbs, by the name Wisdom.

To ascertain the precise import of these several names, is attended with difficulty. He appears to be called the Angel or Messenger, because he is sent to make known, or to execute, the will of God. He is probably called the Word of God, because he is the medium through which the mind of God is made known. Why he is called the Son of God, is a question on which divines

---

[1] John i. 15, 30; iii. 13, 17, 31; vi. 38; viii. 58; xvii. 5; 1 Cor. xv. 47; Gen. xviii.; xxii. 15; xxxii. 30; Ex. iii.; xx.; Acts vii. 30, 35, 38; John i. 3; Col. i. 16; Heb. i. 2, 10; Mic. v. 2; John viii. 58; Heb. i. 8; xiii. 8; Rev. i. 8, 18.

[2] John i. 1.

have differed. His miraculous conception, his mediatorial office, his resurrection from the dead, and his investiture with supreme dominion, have been severally assigned, as the reason of the title; but these appear rather to declare him to be the Son of God, or to belong to him because of that relation, than to constitute it. The phrases first-born, first-begotten, only-begotten, seem to refer to the true ground of the name, Son of God: but what these signify, it is probably impossible for us to understand. The ideas of peculiar endearment, dignity, and heirship, which are attached to these terms, as used among men, may be supposed to belong to them, as applied to the Son of God; but all gross conceptions of their import, as if they were designed to convey to our minds the idea of derived existence, and the mode of that derivation, ought to be discarded as inconsistent with the perfection of Godhead. Some have considered the titles Christ, and Son of God, as equal and convertible; but the distinction in the use of them, as pointed out in our examination of the charges brought against the Redeemer, shows the error of this opinion. When Saul at Damascus,[1] and Apollos in Achaia,[2] preached to the Jews that Jesus was the Christ, the aim was to convince them that Jesus was the Messiah, long expected by their nation. But when Saul preached " Christ, that he is the Son of God,"[3] and when the eunuch professed his faith, " I believe that Jesus Christ is the Son of God,"[4] more than the mere messiahship of Jesus is manifestly intended. Christ or Messiah is a title of office: but the phrase " Son of God," denotes, not the mere office, but the exalted nature which qualified for it.

The possession of proper deity is alone sufficient to show that the Son of God was glorious and happy eternally; but we may learn the same truth from the language of Scripture directly referring to this subject. "And now, O Father, glorify thou me with thine own self, with the glory which I had with thee, before the world was."[5] "For ye know the grace of the Lord Jesus Christ, that though he was rich, yet for your sakes he became poor, that ye through his poverty might be rich."[6] "Then I was by him, as one brought up with him; and I was daily his delight, rejoicing always

---

[1] Acts ix. 22. 	[3] Acts xviii. 28. 	[3] Acts ix. 20.
[4] Acts viii. 37. 	[5] John xvii. 5. 	[6] 2 Cor. viii. 9.

before him."[1] "Who, being in the form of God, thought it not robbery to be equal with God."[2] "The only begotten Son, which is in the bosom of the Father."[3] The full communion of the Son with the Father, in all the glory and blessedness of the Godhead, is to be inferred from these passages.

Section II.—HUMILIATION.

THE SON OF GOD ASSUMED HUMAN NATURE, AND IN THAT NATURE LIVED A LIFE OF TOIL AND SORROW, AND DIED AN IGNOMINIOUS AND PAINFUL DEATH.[4]

The full history of this wonderful humiliation, is given by the four Evangelists; and is often referred to in the New Testament, and sometimes in the prophetic declarations of the Old.

In contemplating this mystery of "God manifest in the flesh," we are not to suppose that the divine nature underwent any real change. God cannot cease to be God. The change was in the manifestation, and not in the nature. In this manifestation, even the angels were concerned, for it is a part of the mystery that "God manifest in the flesh" was "seen of angels;"[5] but so wonderful was this new mode of manifestation, that the angels could not readily know their God, in this humble form, as the babe of Bethlehem, and the man of sorrows. Hence, they needed a special command from the eternal throne, before they could render him divine worship: "When he bringeth the first-begotten into the world, he saith, 'Let all the angels of God worship him.' "[6] But this fact, it may be objected, shows it to have been a concealment, rather than a manifestation. This, to some extent, is true; but it is a concealment resembling that by which God showed himself to Moses in the cleft of the rock, concealing the beams of insufferable brightness, that the favored servant might see the back parts of his glory. So the angels, while they behold the Godhead veiled in human nature, obtain views of the divine glory, which would otherwise have been impossible. These are the things "into which the angels desire to look."[7] "Unto the principalities and powers

---

[1] Prov. viii. 30. [2] Phil. ii. 6. [3] John i. 18.
[4] 2 Cor. viii. 9. [5] 1 Tim. iii. 16. [6] Heb. i. 6.
[7] 1 Pet. i. 12.

in heavenly places, might be known by the Church."—by the redemption and salvation of the Church, through the humiliation and death of Christ,—"the manifold wisdom of God."[1]

The lowest point of Christ's humiliation, was his death by crucifixion, and his being held for a time under the power of death, as a prisoner in the grave. Some have thought that he descended into hell; but this opinion has arisen from misinterpretation of the Scripture, "It was said, Thou wilt not leave my soul in hell:"[2] but the word "hell" signifies in this place, as it does in many others, the unseen world, or the state of departed spirits. When it is said, "He went and preached unto the spirits in prison,"[3] the meaning is, that he, by his spirit, in the ministry of Noah, who was a preacher of righteousness, preached to the antediluvians, who, being disobedient, and rejecting the ministry, were swept away by the flood, and were, when these words were penned, spirits in prison.

The glorious benefits resulting to us from the deep humiliation of Christ, are intimated in the words of Paul: "that ye through his poverty might be rich."[4] The extent of the riches which we shall acquire by his poverty, eternity must disclose.

Section III.—EXALTATION.

The Son of God, in human nature, was raised from the dead, ascended to heaven, and was invested with supreme dominion over all creatures.[5]

The facts of Christ's exaltation, like those of his humiliation, are related in the Scripture narrative, and referred to in various parts of the sacred volume.

The exaltation, like the humiliation, produced no real change in his divine nature. It affected the manifestation of it, and also wrought a real change in the condition of the human nature. This nature is now perfectly happy. Jesus has received the joy that was set before him;[6] and saints, who are to be happy with

---

[1] Eph. iii. 10. [2] Ps. xvi. 10. [3] 1 Pet. iii. 19.
[4] 2 Cor. viii. 9.
[5] Matt. xxviii.; Mark xvi.; Luke xxiv.; John xx.; Acts i. 11; vii. 56; ix. 4; 1 Cor. xv. 4–8; Phil. ii. 9, 10, 11.
[6] Heb. xii. 2.

him for ever, are said to "enter into the joy of their Lord."[1] On this nature rests, also, the full glory of the Godhead, "the glory of God in the face of Jesus Christ."[2] As through him the brightest manifestations of the divine glory are made to intelligent creatures, so through him they receive the commands of supreme authority. "He is head of principalities and powers." "He raised him from the dead, and set him at his own right hand in the heavenly places, far above all principalities and powers, and might and dominion, and every name that is named, not only in this world, but also in that which is to come."[3]

The glory to which Christ has been exalted, is not a subject of idle speculation, in which we have no interest. In his address to his Father, he said, in allusion to his disciples, "The glory which thou hast given me, I have given them."[4] Hence, while we suffer with Christ,[5] and for Christ, in this world, we may rejoice in the hope of being glorified with him.

CHAPTER III.

OFFICES OF CHRIST.

JESUS CHRIST IS THE MEDIATOR BETWEEN GOD AND MEN.[6]

A mediator is a middle person between two parties. The term is especially applied to one who interposes between parties at variance, with a view to effect a reconciliation. Men are under the displeasure of God, on account of their sins, and are in rebellion against him, and enemies in mind by wicked works. Christ appears as mediator, to effect a reconciliation.

The duty of a mediator differs, according to the relation of the parties. When the variance between them arises wholly from misunderstanding, an explanation is all that is necessary to effect a reconciliation. In this case a mediator is simply an interpreter.

------

[1] Matt. xxv. 21.　　[2] 2 Cor. iv. 6.　　[3] Eph. i. 20, 21.
[4] John xvii. 22.　　[5] Rom. viii. 17.
[6] 1 Tim. ii. 5; 2 Cor. v. 18; Col. i. 20; 1 John ii. 1; Gal. i. 4; iii. 13; Tit. ii. 14.

When an offence has been given, but such a one as may be pardoned on mere entreaty, the mediator becomes an intercessor. But when the circumstances are such as to require satisfaction for the offence, the mediator must render that satisfaction or become surety for the offender. On God's part, as he has committed no wrong, nothing more is required than an Interpreter,[1] to show to man his uprightness. But, on the part of guilty man, it is necessary that the Mediator should be both Intercessor and Surety.

The union of two natures in Christ qualifies him for the work of mediation. As man, he sympathizes with us, is accessible, both when we desire to present petitions and to receive instruction; and he is capable of standing as our substitute or surety, and of making the requisite satisfaction to divine justice. As God, he understands fully the claims against us, has ready access to the offended Sovereign, has all the knowledge which it can be necessary to communicate to us, and can give dignity and value to the satisfaction offered in our behalf. These qualifications are found in no other person, and accordingly "There is none other name under heaven, given among men, whereby we must be saved."[2]

In the one office of Mediator three offices are included, which need separate consideration: those of Prophet, Priest, and King.

Section I.—PROPHET.

JESUS CHRIST, AS PROPHET, MAKES REVELATION FROM GOD TO MEN.[3]

Among the revelations made by prophets, the foretelling of future events has held a conspicuous place: but this does not constitute the whole of the office. The word prophesy does not always refer to future events, as is apparent from an incident in the injurious treatment which our Redeemer received at his trial. When blindfolded he was struck by one of the attendants, who contemptuously demanded, "Prophesy who is he that smote thee."[4] From this example we learn that the term was not exclusively used

---

[1] Job xxxiii. 23.   [2] Acts iv. 12.
[3] Isaiah lxi. 1; Luke iv. 18, 23; Heb. ii. 3; 1 Pet. i. 11; Deut. xviii. 18; John iii. 34; xvi. 1; Rev. i. 1.
[4] Matt. xxvi. 68.

for the foretelling of future events, but was applied to the making of any declaration which required superhuman knowledge.

Jesus Christ, as a Prophet, was superior to all other prophets. Moses was so far distinguished above the rest, that it was said no prophet had arisen like him;[1] but Moses foretold the coming of Jesus Christ, in these words: "The Lord, thy God, will raise up unto thee, a prophet from the midst of thee, of thy brethren, like unto me; unto him ye shall hearken."[2] Elijah was a prophet, highly distinguished in his day, and was translated to heaven, without tasting death: but Moses and Elijah appeared on the mount of transfiguration, to lay down their prophetical office and honors at the feet of Jesus, when the voice from heaven said, "This is my beloved Son, hear ye him."[3] Moses and Elijah were to be heard in their day; but the voice from the excellent glory singled out Jesus as the superior prophet, whose instructions we are commanded to receive.

Not only was Christ superior to the prophets of the former dispensation, but it was he who qualified them for their office, and spoke through them."[4] This fact accords with his statement, "No man hath seen God at any time: the only begotten Son which is in the bosom of the Father, he hath declared him."[5] He is, in this view, the only Prophet, the only Revealer of the mind of God. Before his personal ministry commenced, he made revelation by prophets whom he inspired; during his ministry, he spoke as one from the bosom of the Father; and after he left the world, he continued to make revelation, through his apostles and others, to whom he gave his Spirit. The last book of the Bible is a revelation which he gave to his servant John;[6] and the whole Bible is now to us as the word of Christ. His truth he still uses, as the Prophet of the Church, instructing his people into the knowledge of God.

God has sometimes been pleased to make known his will by the ministry of angels; but the prophets, whom he ordinarily employed, were men of like passions with ourselves. There was peculiar fitness, as well as condescending kindness, that the great Prophet of the Church should be one in our own nature. Though

---

[1] Deut. xxxiv. 10.   [2] Deut. xviii. 15.   [3] Matt. xvii. 5.
[4] 1 Pet. i. 11.   [5] John i. 18.   [6] Rev. i. 1.

14

it was true, "Never man spake like this man,"[1] it was still true, that he spoke with the voice of a man; and, instead of the terrific thunders heard from Sinai, addressed those who were willing to receive his instructions, in the accents of tenderness, as an affectionate friend. But such affection might have existed, without the knowledge necessary to make known the whole mind of God. This qualification his divine nature supplied. Paul asks, on one occasion, "Who hath known the mind of the Lord? and who hath been his counsellor?[2] But, it had been predicted of Jesus, that he should be called Wonderful, Counsellor.[3] He was the wisdom of God, from the bosom of the Father, and was therefore fully qualified to reveal the mind and counsel of God to men.

At the feet of this Prophet let us sit, that we may learn the knowledge of God. With Mary, let us take our place there, leaving the cumbering cares of the world, and opening our ears and our hearts to receive his heavenly instructions. Peter, James, and John, who saw his glorious form in the holy mount, when the bright vision had passed away, were left in possession of the divine command: "Hear ye him." Let us take this direction as the guide of our way, until we shall be admitted to the brighter vision of his glory, of which the former was but a shadow.

Section II.—PRIEST.

JESUS CHRIST, AS PRIEST, MADE AN EFFICACIOUS SACRIFICE FOR THE SINS OF HIS PEOPLE, INTERCEDES FOR THEM AT THE RIGHT HAND OF GOD, AND BLESSES THEM WITH ALL SPIRITUAL BLESSINGS.[4]

A prophet approaches men with revelations from God; but a priest approaches God in behalf of men. His chief business is to offer sacrifice, and make intercession. Priests have existed in the various religions of the heathen world; but in the forms of worship instituted by divine authority for the observance of the Hebrew nation, we find the most instructive exposition of the priestly

---

[1] John vii. 46.   [2] Romans xi. 34.   [3] Isaiah ix. 6.
[4] Ps. cx. 4; Zech. vi. 13; Heb. iv. 14, 15; v. 6; vi. 20; vii. 24, 26; viii. 1; ix. 11, 12, 14, 26; x. 12, 14; Isaiah liii. 5, 7, 12; John i. 29; x. 15; 1 Cor. v. 7; Eph. v. 2; 1 Tim. ii. 6; Heb. ix. 26; x. 5; xiii. 12; 1 Pet. ii. 24; iii. 18; 1 John i. 7; Rev. v. 9; vii. 14; Rom. viii. 34; Heb. vii. 25; ix. 24.

office. The Epistle to the Hebrews explains the design of this institution, and sets forth the Levitical priests as types of Christ in his priesthood. It is there stated to be the duty of the priest to offer gifts and sacrifices for sins.[1]

The text last quoted refers to two kinds of offerings which the priest presented: one for thanksgiving, the other for propitiation. Various offerings were prescribed as expressions of gratitude for mercies received, and others to make atonement for sins. Christians make their offerings of praise and thanksgiving through Christ, as their high priest; but the only atoning sacrifice is the offering which he made of himself, when he gave his life a ransom for us.[2]

All propitiatory sacrifices involve the idea of substitution. The animal offered represented the offerer, and bore his sins, which were confessed, over its head.[3] So Christ bore our sins,[4] our iniquities being laid on him. With reference to the use of lambs in sacrifice, he is called "the Lamb of God, that taketh away the sin of the world."[5] The idea of substitution is clearly conveyed in such passages as these: "For a good man some would dare to die; but God commendeth his love toward us, in that, while we were yet sinners, Christ died for us."[6] "He who knew no sin was made sin for us."[7]

Those who deny the divinity of Christ, deny also the doctrine of his vicarious sacrifice. When he is said in Scripture to die for us, they understand the import of the language to be, that he died for our benefit; but they exclude the idea of his suffering in our stead, bearing the penalty due to our sins, that we might be released from it. He is supposed to have died for our benefit, in that he gave us an example of patience and resignation in suffering, confirmed the doctrine that he taught, and, by rising from the dead, established the truth of the soul's immortality, and the resurrection of the body. These several benefits, all will admit, are derived from the death and resurrection of Christ: but they do not fully come up to the import of the strong language which the Scriptures employ in relation to this subject. The ancient mar-

[1] Heb. v. 1.
[4] 1 Pet. ii. 24.
[7] 2 Cor. v. 21.
[2] Matt. xx. 28.
[5] John i. 29.
[3] Lev. xvi. 21.
[6] Romans v. 8.

tyrs generally set us a noble example of patience and resignation
in suffering and death.   Many of them exhibited a fortitude and
triumph in the prospect of their dying agonies, not seen in the
example of our Redeemer.   In the garden, his soul was exceedingly sorrowful in the prospect of his sufferings, and he thrice
prayed that the cup might pass from him; and, on the cross,
though he was all submissive to his Father, and yielded his spirit
at last into his Father's hands, yet he exhibited none of that joyful exultation which has often shone forth in the martyr's last
moments, but he seemed oppressed, shrouded in gloom, and
mourning the withdrawal of his Father's presence.   All this may
be accounted for, if we consider that his death was unlike that of
the martyrs, because he endured in it the wrath of the Father,
due to our transgressions.   If his death had been merely to set
us an example, it might be said, with greater propriety, that
Peter, Paul, and other Christian martyrs, died for us: but Paul
will not admit this; for he says, in a manner which implies a
strong denial, "Was Paul crucified for you?"[1]

The sincerity of the ancient Christians was demonstrated by
their readiness to suffer and die, rather than renounce the faith
which they professed.   Christ's death may be said to confirm his
sincerity in the same way; but if this is what is meant by his
dying for us, Stephen, James, Peter, and Paul died for us in this
sense.   But though the death of Jesus may be understood to
establish his sincerity for the confirmation of his doctrine, he was
accustomed to refer, for this purpose, not to his death, but to his
miraculous works and his resurrection.   It was his resurrection
also, rather than his death, which established the truth of the
soul's immortality and of the resurrection of the body.   If, therefore, these confirmations of truth for our benefit are what is intended
by Christ's dying for us, it would be more correct to say, that he
wrought miracles and rose from the dead for us.   But his death
has so prominent a place in the Scriptures, as that to which we
are indebted for eternal life, that we are compelled to seek for a
higher sense of the phrase, "Christ died for us."

The humble disciple of Jesus, who is willing to learn, as a little
child, in what sense his Lord and Master died for him, needs only

---

[1] 1 Cor. i. 13.

to read with attention the passages of Scripture which have been quoted, and which fully establish the doctrine, that Christ's death was an atoning sacrifice for our sins. This doctrine is essential to Christianity. It is the grand peculiarity of the Christian scheme. Hence Paul determined to know nothing but "Christ crucified,"[1] to glory in nothing but "the cross of Christ."[2] The gospel was the preaching of Christ crucified.[3] It was a stumbling block to the self-righteous Jews, and foolishness to the philosophical Greeks; but to those who received it to the salvation of their souls, it was Christ, the power of God, and the wisdom of God.[4] It was not Christ transfigured on Mount Tabor; not Christ stilling the tempest, and raising the dead; not Christ rising triumphantly from the grave, and ascending gloriously, amidst shouts of attendant angels, to his throne in the highest heavens: but Christ on the cross, expiring in darkness and woe, that the first preachers of the Gospel delighted to exhibit to the faith of their hearers. This was their Gospel; its centre, and its glory. It was faith in this Gospel that controlled the hearts of their converts, and made them ready to die for him who had, by his death, procured for them eternal life. In this faith they exclaimed, "God forbid that I should glory save in the cross of our Lord Jesus Christ."[5] To this they referred when they said, "I am crucified with Christ; nevertheless I live; yet not I, but Christ liveth in me; and the life which I now live in the flesh, I live by the faith of the Son of God, who loved me, and gave himself for me."[6]

The doctrine of Christ's atoning sacrifice explains the Old Testament dispensation. To what purpose were its victims brought to the altar, and the rites of its worship all stained with blood? Was God really pleased with the slaughter of animals, and the smell of their sacrifice? Paul has explained, that these were a shadow of good things to come;[7] but the body is of Christ. As mere types of Christ's atoning sacrifice, they are intelligible. This they prefigured. "Christ also hath loved us, and given himself for us; an offering and a sacrifice to God of sweet smelling savor;"[8] and it was only because of their reference to this sacrifice,

[1] 1 Cor. ii. 2.　　[2] Gal. vi. 14.　　[3] 1 Cor. i. 23.
[4] Rom. i. 16.　　[5] Gal. vi. 14.　　[6] Gal. ii. 20.
[7] Heb. x. 1.　　[8] Eph. v. 2.

that the sacrifices of the preceding times were acceptable to the Lord.

The general prevalence of sacrifices, in the religions of the world, is a fact which it is difficult to account for. If it be supposed to arise from principles implanted in human nature, it will furnish a strong argument to prove that human nature has ever felt, and must feel, the necessity for such a sacrifice as is made by the death of Christ. If the prevalence of sacrifices be accounted for by tracing them to an ancient institution, given to our race by revelation from God, an argument, still stronger in favor of our doctrine, is furnished by the fact. It appears, from this view of the subject, that the institution is not only more ancient than the laws of Moses, but has come down from the time when Abel offered to God a more acceptable sacrifice than Cain.[1] As this sacrifice, like all subsequent ones which were offered by faith, had reference to the sacrifice of Christ, the whole institution of sacrifice bears testimony to it.

The sacrifice of Christ, which is the object of Christian faith on earth, will be the song of glorified saints in heaven. The Lamb, in the midst of the throne, will appear in their view, not as once honored and powerful, but as having been made a sacrifice, "a lamb that had been slain."[2] He was once the victim on the sacrificial altar, but he will be the object of adoration in the everlasting song, "Unto him that loved us,"[3] &c.

When the birth of Jesus was announced by the angel, it was said, "His name shall be called Jesus, for he shall save his people from their sins."[4] This was the grand design of his coming into the world: "The Son of man is come to seek and to save that which was lost."[5] To effect this salvation, a sacrifice was demanded; and, that he might make the required sacrifice, it was necessary that he should assume human nature: "When he cometh into the world, he saith: Sacrifice and offering thou wouldest not, but a body hast thou prepared me."[6] "It was necessary that this man have somewhat to offer."[7] His humanity was the victim laid on the altar, for which reason it is said, "He bore our sins in his own body, on the tree."[8] "The Captain of our salvation must be made

---

[1] Heb. xi. 4.   [2] Rev. v. 6.   [3] Rev. i. 5.
[4] Matt. i. 21.   [5] Luke xix. 10.   [6] Heb. x. 5.
[7] Heb. viii. 3.   [8] 1 Pet. ii. 24.

perfect through suffering;"[1] and he must, therefore, have a nature capable of suffering: "For this cause, he was made lower than the angels, that, for the suffering of death, he might be crowned with glory and honor."[2]   There is, doubtless, also a peculiar fitness in the arrangement, by which the Redeemer is the near-kinsman of the redeemed; and the sacrifice made in the nature that had sinned.   Had the Son of God undertaken the salvation of angels, there would have been a fitness in his taking on him the nature of angels: but as he came to save men, he took on him human nature, and was made in all points like his brethren.[3]

While the fact of the sacrifice depended on the assumption of a nature capable of suffering, the undertaking of the work, the efficacy of the sacrifice, the power to lay down his life, and the power to take it again, depended on the divine nature of Christ. The divine nature, alone, could not be made under the law: and the human nature, alone, could not have originally consented to be made under the law; and would not thereby, had it been possible, have exhibited any humiliation, any voluntary impoverishing of himself, that we might be made rich.   The question has sometimes been proposed, how much obedience did the human nature of Jesus Christ owe for itself, and how much did it render for the benefit of others? but this is a useless question, and is asked on a mistaken apprehension of the facts concerning Christ's assumption of our nature.   The man Christ Jesus never had an existence separate from the divine nature.   The Word did not enter into flesh previously existing; but "the Word was made flesh."[4] Had the Word entered into a previously existing man, we might conceive of the obligations which that man had previously owed to the law, and the continuance of those obligations.   But the Son of God was made of a woman, made under the law, to redeem them that were under the law.[5] As the obligations were assumed for their benefit, the whole fulfilment of them must have been for their benefit.   As the assumption of human nature was designed for the salvation of his people, all that he did and suffered in that nature, is to be viewed as a part of the great design, and constituting a part of the work.

---

[1] Heb. ii. 10.   [2] Heb. ii. 9.   [3] Heb. ii. 16, 17.
[4] John i. 14.   [5] Gal. iv. 5.

We are not permitted to suppose that the divine nature of Jesus Christ could, in itself, endure the sufferings necessary to make atonement, or that it did, in the proper sense, suffer with the human nature. We cannot conceive that the perfect blessedness of God can consist with the endurance of suffering, any more than we can conceive the divine immensity shut up within the limits of a human body. Yet we are authorized to conclude, that whatever Jesus did or suffered, does, in some manner, represent to us the mind of God. To think God to be altogether such an one as ourselves,[1] is a gross and sinful view of him, which he resents: but we are, nevertheless, compelled to form our conceptions of his mind from the knowledge which we have of our own. This mode of conception his word authorizes. The pity of a father for his children, is made by God himself the image in which we are to see his pity for those who fear him.[2] Pity, as exercised by human beings, may be a very painful emotion; but, when we attribute it to God, we must conceive of it as posesssing all that is excellent in human pity, but without the imperfection of pain. So, the mind of the holy Jesus exhibits to us the mind of God. The pity which he felt, however painful it may have been to his human soul, is an image in which we are permitted to see the compassion of God. Could we have before our contemplation all the affections and emotions that the holy soul of Jesus ever experienced, we might learn therein more of the mind of God than is otherwise discoverable: and if we understood the affections and emotions of which he was the subject in his last hours, we should probably understand, better than in any other way, how the divine perfections were concerned in his atoning sufferings. It is our duty to look to Jesus, who endured the cross,[3] and to study his character, that the same mind may be in us, and we feel the stronger obligation to study with what mind he suffered death; because Paul prayed to have fellowship with his sufferings, and to be conformed to his death.[4]

What, then, were the emotions of Jesus in his last sufferings? When he consented to make the sacrifice in the body prepared for him, he said, "Thy law is within my heart."[5] He doubtless

---

[1] Ps. l. 21.   [2] Ps. ciii. 13.   [3] Heb. xii. 2.
[4] Phil. iii. 10.   [5] Ps. xl. 8.

retained this law in his heart, through his intensest agony, and approved it, even while he was undergoing its dire penalty. In this particular Paul had fellowship with him, for he could say, "I delight in the law of God after the inward man."[1] When Jesus bore our sins in his body on the tree, it is reasonable to suppose that his human soul had a sense of the great evil of sin; otherwise we cannot understand how it should approve the law under which he was suffering the penalty for sin. Whatever other emotions had a place in his mind, we are authorized to conclude that he had a deep sense of the evil of the sins which he bore, and of the excellence of the law which those sins opposed. While love, stronger than death, identified him with his people, who were under the sentence of the violated law, he loved also that law with all his heart. These contending affections painfully struggled together in his breast. The sins of his people were not offences which he had personally committed; and therefore remorse, in the proper sense, was not an ingredient in his suffering. But an affectionate husband, who loves his wife as his own flesh, would, when grieving for a crime which she has committed, feel nearly the same agony as if he had personally committed it; so, when Christ loved the Church, and gave himself for it, he felt the sins of the Church as if they had been his own. In this sense of the evil of sin, which was an element in the sufferings of Jesus, it was lawful for Paul to desire fellowship with him. The Scripture teaches that Jesus offered himself to God, through the eternal Spirit.[2] This Spirit produces love to God and his law in the hearts of believers, and gives them a sense of the evil of sin; in both which particulars they have fellowship with Christ in his sufferings. Now, if we suppose that the Spirit, which was given to Christ without measure, opened to his view, when hanging on the cross, the full glory of the divine law which the Church, his bride, had violated; and the full enormity of the sins which his people had committed; what intense agony would these discoveries produce! No agony of the deepest penitence could surpass it. Yet all this Jesus probably felt; and in all this we may well pray to have fellowship with him.

If the view which we have taken, gives us any just insight into the emotions which rent the holy soul of Jesus, when he hung on

---

[1] Rom. vii. 22.   [2] Heb. ix. 14.

the cross for us, it should make us feel, deeply feel, the moral power of that cross. To think as he thought, and feel as he felt, is enough to constrain us to live to him who died for us. No higher motive to holiness can be needed, than that which proceeds from the cross.

The denial of Christ's divinity, and that of his atonement, consistently accompany each other. We should have little need of a divine person, to fulfil the offices ascribed to Christ, if that of making an efficacious sacrifice for sin be not included. The system in which these two cardinal doctrines are omitted, is another gospel, which Paul, and the first ministers of the Christian religion, knew not; and which cannot meet the necessities of lost men. It is worthy of special remark, that the two positive institutions of Christianity—baptism and the Lord's supper, refer to these two doctrines, and silently and significantly preach them. In baptism, we devote ourselves to the Father, the Son, and the Holy Spirit; acknowledging the divinity and authority of each person in the Godhead: and the divinity of the second person is more especially acknowledged in those brief accounts of baptism, in which persons are said to have been baptised in the name of Christ. In the Lord's supper, the doctrine of atonement is clearly set forth. "This is my blood of the New Testament, which is shed for many for the remission of sins."[1] The two ordinances have, from the days of the apostles, been observed by the great body of professing Christians; though their form and use have not been kept pure, as they were originally delivered, and the two doctrines which they set forth, have been maintained in the great body of Christian professors, in all ages; though accompanied with much corruption.

The Scriptures plainly teach that the propitiatory sacrifice of Christ was necessary to render the justification of a sinner consistent with the justice of God. "Whom God hath set forth to be a propitiation through faith in his blood, to declare his righteousness for the remission of sins that are past, through the forbearance of God; to declare, I say, at this time, his righteousness, that he might be just, and the justifier of him which believeth in Jesus."[2]

Had it not been absolutely necessary, we cannot account for it, that God should have inflicted such suffering, or even permitted it

---

[1] Matt. xxvi. 28.   [2] Rom. iii. 25, 26.

to fall, on his beloved Son, who was "holy, harmless, undefiled, and separate from sinners." The death of Christ, if he was not a divine person, was, as we have before shown, the effect of perjury and suicidal prevarication on his part; and if it was not an atoning sacrifice indispensably necessary to satisfy divine justice, it is difficult to show that it was not, on the part of the Father, a display of injustice and cruelty towards the Son of his love. Why was his ear deaf to the thrice-repeated petition, "Let this cup pass from me"? Why had the sorrows of Gethsemane, and the bloody sweat of the agonized, but innocent, sufferer, no effect to move the pity of the Father, to whom Christ had said: "I know that thou hearest me always."[1] The resigned language of the suffering Jesus, and the condition on which he bases the petition, furnish the answer: "O my Father, if it be possible, let this cup pass from me; nevertheless, not as I will, but as thou wilt."[2]

Whatever views of propriety may be entertained by short-sighted mortals, it is manifestly the teaching of sacred Scripture, that God could not, consistently with his justice, forgive our sins on our mere asking, or even on our penitential acknowledgments. We are required to forgive offences till seventy times seven, when a brother acknowledges his trespass; but sins against God are not private offences, to be remitted in the same manner. A judge who should pardon a criminal, that, according to law, ought to be condemned, and turn him loose on the community, would be false to his sacred office. So God sustains the character of a righteous Judge; and, sooner than disregard the claims of law, and overthrow his moral government, he is willing to plunge the sword of justice into the heart of his beloved Son. And such is the reverence of the Son, for the law of his Father and the claims of justice, that he patiently consents to be led as a lamb to the slaughter, that his death may justify God in forgiving and saving the guilty.

How the death of Christ rendered full satisfaction to divine justice, is a question which we shall have occasion to consider, under the head of Justification.

Those who oppose the doctrine of atonement, have viewed it as inconsistent with justice, that the innocent should suffer for the guilty. Their views, however, are plainly at variance with those

---

[1] John xi. 42.   [2] Matt. xxvi. 39.

which are presented in the Book of God. "He suffered, the just for the unjust."[1] "He hath made him to be sin for us, who knew no sin; that we might be made the righteousness of God in him."[2] Even in human affairs, sureties are allowed to pay the debts of others; and, with reference to this well-known arrangement among men, Christ is called the surety of the better covenant.[3] To render such suretyship consistent with justice, his voluntary consent must be given, and he must have had a perfect right to dispose of himself. The right he possessed, because of his divinity; and the consent was given in the covenant of grace which he made with the Father.

A part of the priest's office consisted in making intercession for the people. The high priest did this in a special manner, when he went into the holy of holies. Jesus interceded, when he prayed for Peter that his faith might not fail; and when he poured forth to his Father the beautiful prayer recorded in John xvii. But now, in the holy of holies, the immediate presence of God, he ever liveth to make intercession for us.[4] How that intercession is carried on, we cannot undertake to explain. What his mode of asking is, we know not; but in some mode, he asks, and the heathen are given to him for an inheritance, and the uttermost parts of the earth for a possession.[5] In some mode, while he sympathises with his suffering followers on earth, he asks grace for them, to help them in their trials and sorrows, and his intercession prevails.

The remaining part of the priest's office consisted in blessing the people.[6] The high priest did this, on his return from the holy of holies. This, also, our great High Priest will do, in the most public manner, when he shall return from the heavens which he has entered, and meet his people in the great congregation at the last judgment. It is of little importance, whether we refer this act of blessing to the priestly or the kingly office of Christ. It was anciently said, that the priest's lips should keep knowledge, and they should seek the law at his mouth.[7] Yet we refer Christ's teaching to his prophetical, rather than to his priestly office. So, though the ancient priests blessed the people, yet, as the priest's

---

[1] 1 Pet. iii. 18.   [2] 2 Cor. v. 21.   [3] Heb. vii. 22.
[4] Heb. vii. 25.   [5] Ps. ii. 8.   [6] Num. vi. 22–27.
[7] Mal. ii. 7.

office was to approach God, in behalf of men; rather than to approach men with either revelations or blessings from God; we may consider the blessings conferred on the obedient subjects of Christ's reign, as the bestowments of his royal munificence; and, therefore, as appertaining to his kingly office. This accords with the language of Scripture: "Then shall the King say: 'Come, ye blessed of my Father.' "[1] But all Christ's offices yield blessings to his people; and were undertaken by him for their sake.

Section III.—KING.

JESUS CHRIST, AS THE MEDIATOR BETWEEN GOD AND MEN, EXERCISES KINGLY AUTHORITY OVER ALL CREATURES, TO THE GLORY OF GOD, AND THE GOOD OF HIS PEOPLE.[2]

The superscription which Pilate placed on the cross, was, "Jesus of Nazareth, the King of the Jews." This writing expressed a truth of which its author was not aware. Jesus of Nazareth was the Messiah, foretold by the Hebrew prophets, and expected by the nation as the king who would rule over them, and raise them to great prosperity.

The Hebrew word Messiah, to which the Greek word Christ corresponds, signifies the Anointed. When kings and priests were introduced into office among the Israelites, it was usual to anoint them with oil. We have one example, in which a prophet was set apart to his work, by the same ceremony.[3] Jesus was the Anointed, because he sustained all these offices; and, although he was not introduced into either of them, by a literal anointing with oil, he had the unction of the Holy Spirit, of which the literal unction with oil was a type. The words of Isaiah, read by him in the synagogue of Nazareth, were applied to himself: "The Spirit of the Lord God is upon me, because he hath anointed me to preach,"[4] &c. Here the anointing must be understood as referring to his prophetical office. The same reference seems to have been made with taunt and derision by the individual who smote Jesus, and said:

---

[1] Matt. xxv. 34.

[2] Num. xxiv. 17; Ps. ii. 6; Isaiah xxxii. 1; Zech. ix. 9; Matt. xxi. 5; John xviii. 36; Matt. xxv. 34; Heb. ii. 9; Rev. v. 13; 1 Tim. vi. 15; Rev. xvii. 14; xix. 16; Eph. i. 20–23; v. 23; Phil. ii. 9, 10.

[3] 1 Kings xix. 16.   [4] Isaiah lxi. 1.

"Prophesy, thou Christ, who is he that smote thee?"[1]   In this taunt, it was implied, that the Christ was expected to be a prophet. But from the common use of anointing, we are led to refer the term Christ rather to the priestly and kingly offices, with which Jesus was invested.   The most common reference, is to his kingly office. He was reported to Pilate, as making himself "Christ, a king."[2] In expecting their Messiah, the Jews looked for a king, who was to rule over them and deliver them from their enemies.   Many of the prophecies concerning the Christ, relate to his reign as king over Israel: and when he, before the Jewish council, claimed to be the Christ, he referred to the future manifestation of his kingly power and glory, "Hereafter shall the Son of man sit on the right hand of the power of God."[3]

A proof that Jesus was the promised Messiah, is found in the fact, that the prophecies were fulfilled in him.   The time and place of his birth, and the tribe and family from which he was to spring, were particularly foretold; and the events corresponded to the predictions.   Many prophecies of events in his life, sufferings, death, burial, and resurrection, were exactly fulfilled.   Jesus appealed with confidence to the Scriptures, for proof of his claims: "Search the Scriptures; for they are they that testify of me."[4]   And the apostles said: "To him give all the prophets witness."[5]

Further proof that Jesus was the Christ, is furnished by the testimony of John the Baptist,[6] by the voice of the Father at his baptism,[7] and at his transfiguration in the mount;[8] by his works, to which he often appealed in proof of his claim; and by his claim itself, which was made repeatedly during his ministry; and finally before the Jewish council, and before Pilate, and which was sustained by his miracles, and ultimately by his resurrection from the dead.

To all these proofs it may be added, that the Jews have found no other Messiah.   They have confidently expected one, and the time for his coming has long passed.   Either Jesus of Nazareth is the Messiah foretold, or the prophecies were false, and the religion of which they were a part was not from God.

---

[1] Matt. xxvi. 68.   [2] Luke xxiii. 2.   [3] Luke xxii. 69.
[4] John v. 39.   [5] Acts x. 43.   [6] John iii. 28.
[7] Matt. iii. 17   [8] Matt. xvii. 5.

Jesus Christ, as the Supreme God, had, of original right, sovereign authority over all creatures. But when the Word was made flesh, he took on him the form of a servant; and, for a time, appeared divested of divine power and glory. But, after having humbled himself, and completed the service for which his humiliation was necessary, it pleased God to reward that service by exalting him to supreme authority over all creatures. "All power is given unto me in heaven and in earth."[1]

A peculiarity of Christ's dominion as Mediator, is, that it is exercised by him in human nature. Why it was the pleasure of God to exalt human nature to a dignity so high, it is impossible for us fully to comprehend. We see in it the complete defeat of Satan, the apostate angel, who aimed to bring our inferior nature entirely under his power. He triumphed over the first Adam: but the second Adam has triumphed over him, and will bring him into complete subjection, with all the hostile powers that he has set in array; and will, in the very nature over which Satan triumphed, bring them into subjection under his feet. This dominion over principalities and powers Jesus Christ exercises, with a reference to the good of his people, redeemed from among men. To secure this benefit, the exercise of his dominion in human nature doubtless contributes. The redeemed are one with him, as he is one with the Father. That wonderful prayer is fulfilled, "that they all may be one; as thou, Father, art in me, and I in thee, that they also may be one in us."[2] They are admitted to a communion with God, far more intimate and glorious than could otherwise be enjoyed; and are exalted to such honor, that they are said to reign with Christ. This dignity is nowhere ascribed to angels. Jesus Christ is Lord, to the glory of God the Father. This exercise of divine authority, through the human nature of Jesus Christ, will manifest the glory of God in its richest displays; and angels and men will here learn, through eternal ages, the perfections of the divine nature, and will for ever admire and adore, with ineffable joy.

Another peculiarity of this dominion, is, that it opens a new dispensation to rebellious men. When the angels, that kept not their

---

[1] Matt. xxviii. 18.   [2] John xvii. 21.

first estate, sinned against God, they were driven from his presence, and condemned to hopeless woe. No mediator was provided for them; and no gospel of salvation was ever proclaimed in their ears. Such an administration of divine authority, as gives hope of pardon to offenders, was unknown in the government of the world until man sinned; and this administration constitutes a distinguishing feature of Christ's mediatorial reign. Hence, he is the Mediator between God and men, and not between God and angels; and hence the Mediator is emphatically called "the man Christ Jesus."[1] On earth, the Son of man had power to forgive sins;[2] and in heaven he sits on a throne of grace, to which we are permitted and invited to come, that we may obtain mercy, and find grace to help in every time of need. When God displayed his glory to Moses, and proclaimed his name in the hearing of that favored servant, his forgiving mercy had a conspicuous place in the revelation: "The Lord God, merciful and gracious, long suffering,"[3] &c. So, in heaven, where his full glory is seen, the dispensation of his mercy from the throne of grace on which the exalted Mediator sits, constitutes the most lovely and attractive exhibition of the divine glory that the happy worshippers are permitted to behold.

Of the two peculiarities which have been mentioned as distinguishing the mediatorial dominion of Christ, the first could not exist until the humanity of Christ was exalted to the throne. Then the mediatorial reign, in its full development, commenced, when the Father said, "Sit thou at my right hand, until I make thine enemies thy footstool."[4] But the second peculiarity existed in an incomplete administration of this mediatorial reign, which was exercised from the time of man's fall. Before the efficacious sacrifice for sin was made, in which the humanity of Christ became the victim, the merits of that sacrifice were anticipated; and, through its virtue, pardons were bestowed on believers, from the days of Abel. It is now made known to us, that these pardons were bestowed through the second person in the Godhead, who had engaged, as the surety for sinners, to do the work which he has since performed: and the inquiries of angels, and the faith of Old Testament saints, were all directed forward to the coming of Christ,

---

[1] 1 Tim. ii. 5.   [2] Matt. ix. 6.
[3] Ex. xxxiv. 6.   [4] Ps. cx. 1.

for explanation of that mysterious dispensation by which rebels obtained mercy.

Jesus Christ is head over all things to the Church. He exercises his supreme authority for the benefit of his people, for whose sake he sanctified himself to undertake the work of mediation. He is head over principalities and powers; and angels honor and obey him, and are sent forth as ministering spirits, to minister to the heirs of salvation. He is Lord over all the earth; and regulates every agent and every event in the world, so that "all things work together for good to them that love God." If Christ is ours, all things are ours; for all things are in his hands, and he holds them for the benefit of his people.

In the few words which Jesus spoke respecting his kingdom, when he stood before Pilate, the most important instruction is conveyed. We cannot too much admire the wisdom with which he accurately described, in so few words, the kingdom that he came to establish: "My kingdom is not of this world. If my kingdom were of this world, then would my servants fight."[1] The kings of the earth maintain their authority by force. The coerced obedience which they procure, is often reluctantly rendered. The proper subjects of Christ's kingdom are a willing people,[2] who voluntarily give themselves up to his authority, and serve him with delight. In extending his kingdom he has not allowed carnal weapons to be used; but such only as are powerful, through God, to bring the heart into subjection: "Every one that is of the truth, heareth my voice."[3] He who receives the truth, hears the voice of the king, and acknowledges his authority. To believe the truth, is to obey the Gospel; and this is to be subject to Christ as king. The Jews had expected the Messiah to set up a kingdom, which would be like the kingdoms of the earth, and surpass them in glory. The disciples of Jesus entertained similar views; and hence arose the request to sit on his right hand, and on his left, in his kingdom. Hence, too, arose their despondency when they saw him crucified. They had thought that it was he who was to restore the kingdom to Israel;[4] and his death darkened their prospects, and cut off their hopes. The faith of the expiring thief recognised

---

[1] John xviii. 36.
[2] Ps. cx. 3.
[3] John xviii. 37.
[4] Luke xxiv. 21; Acts i. 6.

15

the expiring Jesus as king; and prayed, "Lord, remember me, when thou comest into thy kingdom:"[1] but the mourning disciples of Jesus could not see the bright prospect of his kingdom, through the darkness of the grave. Yet, the death of Jesus was necessary to the establishment of his kingdom: "For obedience unto death, he was crowned with glory and honor."[2] And the dying love of Christ is the constraining power which brings the heart into subjection to his authority.

Wrong views respecting the nature of the Messiah's kingdom, have been productive of much evil. The princes of this world crucified the Lord of glory, because they could not recognize him in the person of Jesus of Nazareth, who came into the world to bear witness to the truth, and not to introduce his kingdom with the pomp which the carnal mind is pleased with. And Christ has been crucified afresh, and put to open shame, by his professed followers, because of their wrong notions respecting his kingdom. A visible ecclesiastical organization, distinguished by the observance of external forms, has claimed to be the kingdom of Christ; and its power has been extended and wielded by means far different from those which Jesus authorized. To banish this corrupt Christianity from the earth, correct views respecting the kingdom of Christ must prevail.

The Messiah was to rule in the midst of his enemies; and his iron sceptre was to break in pieces, as a potter's vessel,[3] all who are disobedient, and do not obey the truth: but those who obey the truth are "the children of the kingdom;" and to them the benefits and blessings of his reign belong. In this restricted sense, none but regenerate persons enter into his kingdom.[4] We are translated into the kingdom of God's dear Son,[5] when we receive his truth into our hearts. In this sense, no profession of religion, and no observance of external forms, can bring any one into the kingdom of Christ. The tares may resemble the wheat: but the tares are the children of the wicked one; and the good seed only are the children of the kingdom;[6] and when the Son of man shall gather out of his kingdom whatever is offensive to him, the tares will, equally with the briars and thorns, be rejected, as not belong-

---

[1] Luke xxiii. 42.   [2] Phil. ii. 8, 9; Heb. ii. 9.   [3] Ps. ii 9.
[4] John iii. 5.   [5] Col. 1. 13.   [6] Matt. xiii. 38.

ιng properly to his kingdom, and doomed to be burned. Let it then be distinctly understood, that the kingdom of Christ is not a great visible organization, consisting of good men and bad, who are bound together by some ecclesiastical tie. He rules over all; but he accounts all as the enemies of his reign who do not obey the truth: and the hypocrite and formalist have no more part in his kingdom than Herod and Pontius Pilate.

Some obscurity has arisen in the interpretation of Scriptures in which the word kingdom occurs, from supposing that it always refers to the territory or subjects that are under the government of a king. *King-dom* is king dominion, king jurisdiction. The primary idea is kingly authority. In this primary sense it is used in Luke xix. 12: "A certain nobleman went into a far country to receive for himself a kingdom." See also Rev. xvii. 12. This radical idea the word retains everywhere; but it becomes so modified by the connection in which it is used, as to refer to the time, place, or circumstances in which kingly authority is exercised; to the persons over whom it is exercised; and, sometimes, to the benefits resulting from its exercise. An example of this last use is found in Rom. xiv. 17: "The kingdom of God is righteousness, peace, and joy in the Holy Ghost." The phrases, "kingdom of heaven," "kingdom of God," "kingdom of Christ," "kingdom of God's dear Son," are used with reference to the reign of the Messiah. They denote *God's exercise of kingly authority in the person of the Messiah;* and this radical idea, as before stated, becomes modified by the connection in which the phrases are used. When parables are introduced with the words "The kingdom of God is like," we are to understand that some fact or truth connected with the reign of the Messiah is illustrated by the parable. It will be impossible to make sense of many passages, if the term be understood always to signify the *subjects* over whom Christ reigns. How, in this signification of the term, can the kingdom be like a merchantman,[1] a net,[2] a treasure?[3] "The kingdom of heaven is like to a man which sowed good seed in his field."[4] Here, no comparison can be intended between the *subjects* of Christ's reign and the man that sowed the seed. But the parable illustrates important

---

[1] Matt. xiii. 45.
[2] Matt. xiii. 47.
[3] Matt. xiii. 44.
[4] Matt. xiii. 45

truth connected with the reign of the Messiah. It teaches that the world, represented by the field, is under his dominion; that, for a time, the good and bad are permitted to remain together; but that a separation will finally be made, and the blessings of his reign will be enjoyed by those only who are "the good seed," sown by himself, and who only are "the children of the kingdom."

The mediatorial reign of Christ will include the judgment of the great day. It is said, "We must all stand at the judgment seat of Christ;" and also, in describing the sentences pronounced, "Then shall the king say," &c. Then they who condemned and crucified Christ the king, and all who would not have him to reign over them, shall stand at his tribunal. The decisions of that day will be made according to the relation which each individual has borne to Christ. What men have done to the least of his disciples, he will regard as done to him; and, according to the dispositions so evinced, will be every man's final doom.

Will the mediatorial reign of Christ continue after the transactions of the great day? An important change will doubtless then take place in the manner of his reign. All his enemies will have been subdued, all his ransomed people brought home, and his last act of pardoning mercy performed. Yet, we are informed that the glory of God and the Lamb will be the light of the New Jerusalem;[1] that the Lamb will be in the midst of the throne; and that he will feed the redeemed, and lead them to the fountains of living water.[2] From these representations, we appear authorized to conclude that Christ will remain the medium of communication through which the saints will for ever approach God, and receive glory and bliss from him. The language of Paul in 1 Cor. xv. 25, is not inconsistent with this opinion: "He must reign, until he hath put all enemies under his feet." When it is said, "Until the law, sin was in the world,[3] we are not to conclude that sin was not in the world afterwards: so, when it is said, "He must reign until," &c., we must not infer that he will not reign after this time. It will not accord with his own representation of the subject, if, when those who would not have him to reign over them, shall have been slain before his face,[4] he himself shall cease to reign. When it is

---

[1] Rev. xxi. 23
[2] Rev. vii. 17.
[3] Rom. v. 13.
[4] Luke xix. 27.

said, "then shall the Son be subject to the Father,[1] we are not to understand that this subjection excludes the idea of reigning; otherwise it would be implied that his previous reign had not been in subjection to the Father. Christ now reigns in subjection to the Father; but the harmony of his administration with the will and perfections of God, cannot fully appear while rebels go at large under his government; but when all enemies have been subdued, the harmony of his administration with the government of God, absolutely considered, will be made apparent. The coincidence of the two modes of government will be fully manifested. This will be the time of the restitution of all things.[2] He must reign until his enemies are subdued; and the heavens must receive him until the time of the restitution of all things; but he will not, then, either forsake heaven or cease to reign.

CONCLUSION.

"WHAT think ye of Christ?" We may now, with great propriety, consider this question solemnly addressed to us. We have contemplated the person, states, and offices of Christ. What impression does the contemplation leave in our minds? What emotions has it produced? Have the words of the prophet been fulfilled in our case: "He hath no form nor comeliness; and when we shall see him, there is no beauty that we should desire him"? Or, can we say, "He is the chief among ten thousands, and altogether lovely"? According as Christ appears in our view, the evidence of our spiritual state is favorable or unfavorable; and by this test, we may try our hope of acceptance through him, and of reigning with him for ever.

In the ordinary experience of mankind, the affections are attracted most strongly by objects near at hand. To the imagination, distance may lend enchantment; but the affections of the heart play around the fireside, and fix their firmest hold on those with whom we converse most familiarly. In accordance with this

---

[1] 1 Cor. xv. 28. [2] Acts iii. 21.

tendency of our nature, the Son of God attracted the hearts of men, by dwelling among them, and exhibiting himself in familiar intercourse with them, and in the endearing relations well known in human society. We see him, as the affectionate brother and friend, weeping in the sorrows of others, and alleviating their sufferings by words and acts of kindness. The tenderness with which, when hanging on the cross, he committed his mother to the care of his beloved disciple, is an example of filial love, which cannot be contemplated with an unmoved heart. In the simple narratives of his life, which have been given for our instruction, we trace his course in his daily walk as a man among men, going about doing good, and the traits of character exhibited in this familiar intercourse, call forth our love. The heavens have now received him out of our sight, but we know that, in fulfilment of his promise, he is always with us; and we are taught to regard him, not only as near at hand, but also as sympathizing with our infirmities, having been tempted in all points as we are. In the humanity of Jesus, we see the loveliness of the divine perfections familiarly and intelligibly exhibited.

It sometimes happens, in the experience of mankind, that persons of extraordinary merit remain for a time in obscurity, and that those who have been most intimate with them have been taken by surprise, when the unsuspected greatness of their character has been disclosed. Writers of fiction know how to interest the feelings, by presenting great personages under disguise, and unveiling them at a fit moment, to produce impression. But incidents, infinitely transcending all fiction, are found in the true history of Jesus Christ, in which the concealed majesty of his divinity broke forth, and caused surpassing astonishment. The humble sleeper in the boat on the Lake of Tiberias, comes forth from his slumbers, and stills the raging water; and the beholders of the miracle exclaim: "What manner of man is this?" The weary traveller arrives at Bethany, and claims to be the resurrection and the life, and demonstrates the truth of his claim, by calling the dead Lazarus from the tomb. As a condemned malefactor, he hangs on the cross, and expires with such exhibitions of divinity, that the astonished Roman centurion cried: "Truly this man was the Son of God." We have contemplated the divinity of Jesus Christ, not merely in these transient outbursts which occurred while he was on earth, but in the full demonstration which has been given since he ascended to heaven, and the impression on our hearts ought to be strong and abiding. The disciples who attended on his personal ministry loved and honored him; but when they saw him ascend to heaven, being more deeply impressed with his divinity, they worshipped him. Let us devoutly join in rendering him divine honor.

We read with interest the history of men who have passed through great changes in their condition, and who, in every condition, have displayed great and noble qualities. But no changes of condition possible to men, can equal those which the Son of God has undergone. Once rich in his original glory, he became so poor that he had not where to lay his head: and from this depth of poverty, he has been exalted to supreme dominion, and made proprietor and ruler of all worlds. Through these changes he has ever exhibited such moral perfections as have been most pleasing to God. In whatever condition we view him, let us delight in him, as did his Father.

The offices which Christ sustains toward us, are such as have been in highest repute among men. Prophets, priests, and kings have always been accounted worthy of honor. We should give the highest honor to Christ, who, as a prophet, is superior to Moses; as a priest, superior to Aaron; and as a king, the Lord of David. These offices, as exercised by Christ, deserve our honor, not only because of their excellence, but also because of their adaptedness to us. We are, by nature, ignorant, guilty, and depraved. As ignorant, we need Christ, the prophet, to teach us; as guilty, we need Christ, the priest, to make atonement for us; and as depraved, we need Christ, the king, to rule over us, and bring all our rebellious passions into subjection. These offices of Christ are also adapted to the graces which distinguish and adorn the Christian character. The chief of these, as enumerated by Paul, are faith, hope, and love; in the exercise of *faith*, we receive the truth, revealed by Christ, the prophet; in the exercise of *hope*, we follow Christ, the priest, who has entered into the holiest of all, to appear before God for us; and we submit to Christ, the king, in the exercise of *love*, which is the fulfilling of the law, the principle and sum of all holy obedience.

In the theology of the ancient Christians, Christ held a central and vital place. If we take away from the epistles of Paul all that is said about Christ, what mutilation shall we make? If, when we have opened anywhere to read, as at 1 Cor. ch. i., we expunge Christ, what have we left? Paul, while in ignorance and unbelief, thought that he did God service, by persecuting Jesus of Nazareth. But when his eyes were opened, to see that the despised Nazarene, whom his nation had crucified, was the Lord of Glory, when he learned that in him are the treasures of wisdom and knowledge, unsearchable riches, and the fulness of grace, the heart of the persecutor was changed, and he became devoted to the service of him whom he had sought to destroy. Henceforth, he counted all things but loss, for the excellency of the knowledge of Christ Jesus. Has our knowledge of Christ produced a like effect on us? If our hearts are in unison with that of the great Apostle, we are prepared to say, from the inmost soul, "Though we, or an angel from heaven, preach any other gospel," a gospel of which Christ is not the centre and the sum, "let him be accursed."[1]   "If any man love not our Lord Jesus Christ, let him be be anathema maranatha."[2]

In our investigation of religious truth, we have found four sources of knowledge: our own moral feelings, the moral feelings and judgments of others, the course of nature, and the book of divine revelation. The first three of these can give us no knowledge of Jesus Christ and his great salvation. For this knowledge we are wholly indebted to the Bible. Yet, when we have learned our lost and helpless state by nature, the scheme of salvation which the Bible reveals is so perfectly adapted to our condition, that it brings with it its own evidence of having originated in the wisdom of God.

When Paul preached the gospel of salvation, he knew nothing but Jesus Christ, and him crucified. He gloried in nothing, save the cross of our Lord Jesus Christ. We have tarried long in our meditations on the doctrine concerning Jesus Christ; and, before we dismiss the subject, it may be profitable to linger yet a little time at the cross, that we may again survey its glory, and feel its soul-subduing power.

In the cross of Christ, all the divine perfections are gloriously and harmoniously displayed. Infinite love, inviolable truth, and inflexible justice are all seen, in their brightest and most beautifully

---

[1] Gal. i. 8.   [2] 1 Cor. xvi. 22.

mingled colors. The heavens declare the glory of God; but the glory of the cross outshines the wonders of the skies. God's moral perfections are here displayed, which are the highest glory of his character.

The cross of Christ is our only hope of life everlasting. On him who hangs there, our iniquities were laid, and from his wounds flows the blood that cleanses from all sin. Our faith views the bleeding victim, and peacefully relies on the great atoning sacrifice. It views mercy streaming from the cross; and to the cross it comes to obtain every needed blessing.

In the cross, the believer finds the strongest motive to holiness. As we stand before it, and view the exhibition of the Saviour's love, we resolve to live to him who died for us. The world ceases to charm. We become crucified to the world, and the world crucified to us. Sin appears infinitely hateful. We regard it as the accursed thing which caused the death of our beloved Lord; and we grow strong in the purpose to wage against it an exterminating war. By all the Saviour's agonies, we vow to have no peace with it for ever. The cross is the place for penitential tears. We look on him whom we have pierced, and mourn. Our hearts bleed at the sight of the bleeding sufferer, murdered by our sins; and we resolve that the murderers shall die. The cross is a holy place, where we learn to be like Christ, to hate sin as he hated it, and to delight in the law of God which was in his heart. In the presence of the cross, we feel that omnipotent grace has hold of our heart; and we surrender to dying love.

The wisdom of man did not devise the wonderful plan of salvation. As well might we suppose that it directed the great Creator, when he spread abroad the heavens, and laid the foundations of the earth. But as in the heavens and earth, human reason may see the power and wisdom of God, so, to the Christian heart, Christ crucified is the power of God, and the wisdom of God. The doctrine of the cross needs no other demonstration of its divine origin, than its power to sanctify the heart, and bring it into willing and joyful subjection to Christ.

BOOK SIXTH.

DOCTRINE CONCERNING THE HOLY SPIRIT.

INTRODUCTION.

DUTY OF LIVING AND WALKING IN THE HOLY SPIRIT.[1]

WE live, move, and have our being in God. His presence is ever with us; and by his power, we are, at every moment, upheld in being, and the faculties and powers, from which all movements, corporeal or mental, proceed, are preserved in existence and action. Such is our constant and immediate dependence on God. We are, in like manner and degree, dependent on the Holy Spirit, for the existence of spiritual life, and for the faculties and powers necessary to all spiritual action. Our dependence on the Holy Spirit extends still further. The very disposition to holy action, proceeds from the Spirit; and the production of this disposition, is his peculiar work in sanctification. In our natural actions, we live and move in God; in our spiritual actions, we live and walk in the Holy Spirit.

The Scripture representations of our dependence on the Holy Spirit, are full and strong. Our spiritual life comes from him, for it is the Spirit that quickeneth;[2] and he is called the Spirit of Life.[3] When the prophet saw the dead bones in the valley, he prayed: "Come from the four winds, O breath, and breathe upon these slain, that they may live;"[4] and the spirit of life entered into them.

---

[1] Gal. v. 25. If we live in the Spirit, let us also walk in the Spirit.
[2] John vi. 63.   [3] Rom. viii. 2.   [4] Ez. xxxvii. 9.

So souls, dead in trespasses and sins, are quickened by the Holy Spirit.   And we live in the Holy Spirit as dependent on him for spiritual life, as the body is dependent for animal life on the atmosphere which we breathe.   Hence proceed the earnest prayers, that the Holy Spirit may be granted, and may not be taken away.[1] And hence the bestowment of the Holy Spirit is regarded as the giving of all good.[2]   The importance of the Holy Spirit's influence in the exercises of the spiritual life, may be inferred from such passages as the following: "Led by the Spirit;"[3] "Mind the things of the Spirit;"[4] "Filled with the Spirit;"[5] "The Spirit lusteth against the flesh;"[6] "If ye through the Spirit do mortify the deeds of the body, ye shall live;"[7] "The Spirit helpeth our infirmity;"[8] "Changed into the same image by the Spirit;"[9] "The Spirit beareth witness with our spirits."[10]

No believer, who has any just sense of his dependence on the Holy Spirit, for the divine life which he enjoys, and all its included blessings, can be indifferent towards the Agent by whom all this good is bestowed.   He cannot willingly "grieve the Holy Spirit, by whom he is sealed to the day of redemption."   He will seek to know, in all things, what is the mind of the Spirit; and, to him, the communion of the Holy Spirit will be the sweetest foretaste of heaven, that can be enjoyed on earth.   And to him, therefore, the study of the Holy Spirit's character and office, will be a source of delight.

---

[1] Ps. li. 11, 12.
[2] Compare Matt. vii. 11 with Luke xi. 13
[3] Gal. v. 18.
[4] Rom. viii. 5.
[5] Eph. v. 18.
[6] Gal. v. 17.
[7] Rom. viii. 13.
[8] Rom. viii. 26.
[9] 2 Cor. iii. 18.
[10] Rom. viii. 16.

CHAPTER I.

PERSONALITY OF THE HOLY SPIRIT.

THE HOLY SPIRIT IS A PERSON, DISTINCT FROM THE FATHER AND THE SON.[1]

The Holy Spirit is a person, and not a mere influence or operation. This may be proved by the following arguments:

1. When Christ promised his coming as another Comforter, the language clearly refers to him as a person: "I will pray the Father, and he shall give you another Comforter that he may abide with you."[2] "The Comforter whom the Father will send in my name, he shall teach you."[3]

2. Things are, in the Holy Scriptures, attributed to the Holy Spirit, which can be true only of a person: "He divideth to every man severally as he will;"[4] "Separate me Barnabas and Saul for the work whereunto I have called them;"[5] "Why hath Satan filled thine heart to lie to the Holy Ghost;"[6] "Grieve not the Holy Spirit."[7]

3. The commission given to the apostles required them to baptize in the name of the Father, and of the Son, and of the Holy Ghost.[8] A mere influence or virtue, could not thus be associated with the Father and the Son; nor would it accord with the language of Scripture, to speak of the *name* of an influence; or with the analogy of faith, to administer baptism in the name of an influence. In the apostolical benediction, the Holy Spirit is connected, in a similar manner, with the Father and the Son: "The grace of our Lord Jesus Christ, the love of God, and the communion of the Holy Ghost, be with you all."[9] In 1 Cor. xii. 4–6, the Holy Spirit is introduced, together with God the Father, and the Lord Jesus Christ, as *a personal* agent equally with them.

---

[1] Isaiah xlviii. 16; Matt. iii. 16; John xiv. 16, 26; xvi. 7; Acts x. 19, 20; xiii. 2; xv. 28; xx. 28; Eph. iv. 30; Matt. xxviii. 19.

[2] John xiv. 16. [3] John xiv. 26. [4] 1 Cor. xii. 11.

[5] Acts xiii. 2. [6] Acts v. 3. [7] Eph. iv. 30.

[8] Matt. xxviii. 19. [9] 2 Cor. xiii. 14.

To these arguments, it may be opposed, that the Scriptures frequently use the words Spirit, Holy Spirit, to denote divine influence. But it is very common, in language, for an influence to be designated by the name of the source from which it emanates. We say: "This plant thrives in the shade; that, in the sun;" but by the word sun, we mean, not the body of the luminary, but the light and heat emanating from it. So, when it is said: "He will report that God is in you of a truth,"[1] the general omnipresence of God is not meant; for this is equally true of all persons and places. A peculiar presence, implying special divine influence, is intended. It would be improper to argue from this passage, that God is nothing but *an influence;* and it is, in the same manner, improper to argue that the Holy Spirit is not a person, because the name is used in the Scriptures for the influence which he, as a personal agent, exerts.

The frequency with which the name is used to denote the influence exerted, may perhaps be accounted for, from the fact, that the name is given to the agent, because of his influence. It cannot denote anything peculiar in the nature of the agent; for the first and second persons in the Godhead, are, in their nature, spirit, and holy, as truly as the third. The name must, therefore, be regarded as distinguishing him with reference to his operation. He is called holy, because he is the immediate agent in the production of holiness; and he is called the Spirit, the Spirit of God, because he is the immediate agent in exerting the invisible, life-giving, divine influence which proceeds from God.

The Holy Spirit is distinct from the Father and the Son. The same passages which prove his personality prove this also. He could not be another Comforter, if he were not distinct from the Son; nor sent by the Father, if he were not distinct from the Father. In the commission to baptise, and in the benediction, his personality is not more manifest than the distinction from the Father and the Son, with whom he is named.

---

[1] 1 Cor. xiv. 25.

CHAPTER II.

THE DIVINITY OF THE HOLY SPIRIT.

THE HOLY SPIRIT IS GOD.[1]

When we have ascertained that there is a person to whom the name Holy Spirit is applied, we can have little difficulty in arriving at the conclusion that he is a divine person. The following arguments establish this truth.

1. In the commission he is equally included with the Father and the Son, in the name into which we are baptised. If he is not God, when we devote ourselves to him in our baptism, we are guilty of idolatry. It is no objection to this argument, that Paul says the Israelites were baptised unto Moses.[2] A formal baptism in the name of Moses is neither affirmed nor intended. An analogy is exhibited between the course of a believer who dedicates himself to Christ in baptism, and the course of the Israelites, who gave themselves up to the guidance of Moses, from the Red Sea to the promised land: but an analogy only is all that is intended. The Corinthians were not baptised in the name of Paul;[3] though it was their duty to follow him as he followed Christ: and the Israelites were not baptised in the name of Moses; though they followed him as their leader. The Angel, in whom the name of God was, went before them, in the pillar of cloud and fire; and Moses, equally with all the rest, followed his guidance, and acknowledged his authority.

2. In the benediction, the Spirit is named, equally with the Father and the Son, and regarded as the source of spiritual blessings. The words may be considered a prayer to the Holy Spirit, for the bestowment of these blessings.

3. When the bodies of believers are called the-temple of the

---

[1] Matt. xxviii. 19; Heb. ix. 14; Ps. cxxxix. 7; 1 Cor. vi. 19; 2 Cor. vi. 16; Acts v. 3, 4.

[2] 1 Cor. x. 2.   [3] 1 Cor. i. 13.

Holy Ghost,[1] the deity of the Holy Ghost is recognised. They to whom temples of wood or stone were erected, were regarded as deities: and he to whom the bodies of the saints are temples, must be God. But we are not left to our own inference on this subject. Paul has drawn the conclusion for us: for after having stated that the bodies of the saints are the temples of the Holy Ghost, he speaks of them as belonging to God;[2] and in another place, when speaking of the saints as a temple, he calls the building a "habitation of God through the Spirit."[3] The same view is presented in 1 Cor. iii. 16: "Know ye not, that ye are the temple of God, and that the spirit of God dwelleth in you? If any man defile the temple of God, him shall God destroy: for the temple of God is holy, which temple ye are." So the heathen deities were imagined to dwell in the temples dedicated to them; and so God was in his holy temple at Jerusalem.

4. The heinousness of the sin against the Holy Ghost, is proof of his divinity. When Ananias and Sapphira lied to the Holy Ghost, Peter explained the enormity of their sin in these words: "Thou hast not lied to men, but to God.[4] To sin against the Holy Ghost, is to sin, not against a creature, but against God. This argument acquires greatly increased force, when we consider the words of Christ: "All manner of sin and blasphemy shall be forgiven unto men; but the blasphemy against the Holy Ghost shall not be forgiven unto men.[5] Whatever be the reason that renders blasphemy against the Holy Ghost unpardonable, it must include in it that he is God. If he is not God, sin committed against him would be less heinous than that committed against the Father and the Son.

5. Passages of the Old Testament which speak of Jehovah, the Supreme God, are, in the New Testament, applied to the Holy Ghost.[6]

6. The attributes of God are applied, in Scripture, to the Holy Spirit.

---

[1] 1 Cor. vi. 19.   [2] 1 Cor. vi. 20.   [3] Eph. ii. 22.
[4] Acts v. 3, 4.   [5] Matt. xii. 31.
[6] Ex. xvii. 7 compared with Heb. iii. 9; Isaiah vi. 8, with Acts xxviii. 25; Jer. xxxi. 31–34, with Heb. x. 15–17.

Eternity. "Who through the eternal Spirit offered himself without spot to God."[1]

Omnipresence. "Whither shall I go from thy Spirit? and whither shall I flee from thy presence?"[2]

Omniscience. "The Spirit searcheth all things; yea, the deep things of God."[3]

7. Divine works are ascribed to the Holy Spirit.

Creation. The Spirit of God moved on the face of the waters."[4] "By his Spirit he garnished the heavens.[5]

Providence. "Thou sendest forth thy Spirit, they are created; and thou renewest the face of the earth."[6]

Miracles. "If I cast out devils by the Spirit of God, then the kingdom of God is come unto you."[7] "To another is given the working of miracles by the same Spirit."[8]

Resurrection of Christ. "Declared to be the Son of God with power, according to the spirit of holiness, by the resurrection from the dead."[9] Being put to death in the flesh, but quickened by the Spirit."[10]

Resurrection of believers. "If the Spirit of him that raised up Jesus from the dead dwell in you, he that raised up Christ from the dead shall also quicken your mortal bodies by his Spirit that dwelleth in you."[11]

---

[1] Heb. ix. 14.   [2] Ps. cxxxix. 7.   [3] 1 Cor. ii. 10.
[4] Gen. i. 2.   [5] Job xxvi. 13.   [6] Ps. civ. 30.
[7] Matt. xii. 28.   [8] 1 Cor. xii. 10.   [9] Rom. i. 4.
[10] 1 Pet. iii. 18.   [11] Rom. viii. 11.

CHAPTER III.

OFFICE OF THE HOLY SPIRIT.

The Holy Spirit is the Sanctifier and Comforter of God's people.[1]

The Holy Spirit is the author of holiness in all those who are saved: "Through sanctification of the Spirit."[2] "Ye are washed, ye are sanctified by the Spirit of our God."[3] He is the author of the new or spiritual life which is produced in regeneration.[4] Not only the beginning of the new life, but its whole progress, is dependent on the Spirit: wherefore, believers are said to live in the Spirit,[5] to walk in the Spirit, to be led by the Spirit,[6] and to be filled with the Spirit;[7] and, for this reason David prayed, "Take not thy Holy Spirit from me."[8] As it is his office to change the soul, and from a state of death in trespasses and sins, bring it into a new life, so it is his office to change our vile body, and fashion it like the glorious body of Christ: "He that raised up Jesus from the dead, shall also quicken your mortal bodies by his Spirit that dwelleth in you.[9] As both body and spirit are redeemed by Christ, so both body and spirit are changed by the Holy Spirit, and fitted for the presence and enjoyment of God.

The Holy Spirit is the Comforter of God's people. By his teaching, the knowledge of salvation by the remission of sins is obtained. The Saviour promised: "He shall take of mine, and shall show it unto you."[10] In fulfilment of this promise, the Spirit makes known the sufficiency and suitableness of Christ as a Saviour, and the efficacy of his blood to cleanse from sin. By the Holy Spirit the promises of the divine word are applied to the heart. Hence, peace and joy are called the fruit of the Spirit.[11] These spiritual enjoyments, which are a foretaste of heaven, are called

---

[1] Ps. li. 10–12; Ezek. xxxvi. 27; John xiv. 26; Acts ix. 31; Rom. v. 5; viii. 13, 16, 26; 1 Cor. vi. 11; 2 Cor. i. 22; iii. 18; Gal. v. 22; 2 Thes. ii. 13.

[2] 1 Pet. i. 2.   [3] 1 Cor. vi. 11.   [4] John iii. 6.
[5] Gal. v. 25.   [6] Gal. v. 18.   [7] Eph. v. 18.
[8] Ps. li. 11.   [9] Rom. viii. 11.   [10] John xvi. 15.
[11] Gal. v. 22.

16

"the earnest of the Spirit."[1]   And, as the earnest is given by him, we have reason to conclude that the full possession will be given by him.   As Christ will be the medium through which the felicity of the future world will be bestowed; so, the Holy Spirit will be the immediate agent in bestowing it.   The first comfort here below, and the full bliss and glory of heaven, are alike his work.

CONCLUSION.

ADAM became a living soul when God breathed into him the breath of life :[2] and from that time, the process of breathing is evidence that life exists.   Prayer may be regarded as the breathing of the spiritual man.   Sufficient proof was given that Saul of Tarsus had been converted, when the Lord said, "Behold, he prayeth."[3]   True prayer proceeds from the Holy Spirit, imparting spiritual life, and enkindling those spiritual desires which find their vent in prayer.   These desires are breathed into the bosom of God, in the exercise of filial confidence in him; and, being in accordance with the will of God,[4] they are regarded by him with favor, and obtain answers of grace and peace.

From this view of prayer, we may see the propriety of the Apostle's injunction : "Pray without ceasing."[5]   The cessation of prayer would be the cessation of spiritual life.   A form of words may not be incessantly used; but spiritual desires must ever have place in the heart; and the habit must ever exist, of looking to God for the fulfilment of these desires.   This constant intercourse with God is the life of faith.   We live with him, converse with him, and enjoy communion with him, through the Holy Spirit which dwelleth in us.

We often complain that our prayers are not answered; but it would be profitable to inquire, what those unanswered petitions were.   Did we ask for wealth, power, and long life?   If so, our desires were carnal, and did not proceed from the Spirit of God.

---

[1] Eph. i. 13, 14; 2 Cor. i. 22.   [2] Gen. ii. 7.   [3] Acts ix. 11.
[4] Rom. viii. 27.   [5] 1 Thess. v. 17.

We must learn to regulate our desires by the will of God, and our prayers will be sure to obtain a gracious hearing.

Sincere prayer begins with the very commencement of spiritual life. An infant's cries express its wants, before it knows how to express them in words; and the tender mother will understand this inarticulate language. So the desires of the spiritual infant may be signified by groanings which cannot be uttered:[1] but the Lord understands these groans, and knoweth what is the mind of the Spirit, who maketh intercession for them. As the lamb in the bosom of the kind shepherd; as the babe on the breast of its tender mother; so the spiritual babe reposes on the bosom of eternal love; and in that bosom breathes all its desires.

Spiritual life, evidenced at first by the breathing of prayer, is afterwards indicated by spiritual growth. To be spiritual, we must not ever remain babes in religion. Paul said to the Corinthians, "I could not speak unto you, as unto spiritual, but as unto carnal, even as unto babes in Christ."[2] Spiritual life is progressive, and tends to make us men, strong men in Christ Jesus. The truth of God supplies the milk for babes, and the strong meat for those who have attained to greater age.[3] We have been engaged in the study of this truth; and it will be well for us to inquire whether our spiritual life has been nourished by it, and whether we are growing in faith, and love, and every grace. Unless the truth strengthens the inner man, and gives increased vigor in the Christian life, our study of it has been in vain.

---

[1] Rom. viii. 26.   [2] 1 Cor. iii. 1.   [3] 1 Pet. ii. 2; Heb. v. 12.

BOOK SEVENTH.

DOCTRINE CONCERNING DIVINE GRACE.

INTRODUCTION.

DUTY OF GRATITUDE FOR DIVINE GRACE.[1]

As love is the affection which should arise in our hearts, from a view of God's character, so gratitude is the affection which should be produced, by a view of the benefits that he confers. The stream of his benefits flows incessantly so that our cup is ever full. To receive the benefits thoughtlessly, like the brutes that perish, and to enjoy them without thanksgiving to him from whom they come, is demonstration complete of human depravity. Such demonstration is given daily and hourly in the conduct of mankind, and by it God is offended and his wrath provoked. The unthankful man is the evil man,[2] and the enemy of God. Hence, when we are called on to love our enemies, the example proposed for our imitation is the bestowment of God's providential blessing on the unthankful.

Love your enemies, and do good, and lend, hoping for nothing again, and your reward shall be great, and ye shall be the children of the Highest; for He is kind unto the unthankful and to the evil.

---

[1] 2 Thess. ii. 13. We are bound to thank God alway for you, brethren, beloved of the Lord, because God hath from the beginning chosen you to salvation, through sanctification of the Spirit and belief of the truth.

1 Cor. xv. 10. By the grace of God, I am what I am.

2 Cor. ix. 15. Thanks be to God for his unspeakable gift.

[2] Luke vi. 35.

We are bound to thank God for the blessings of providence so incessantly and so richly bestowed; but far higher obligations to gratitude, arise from the grace that bringeth salvation.[1] This grace includes God's gift of his Son, a gift so great that no name for it can be found. " God *so* loved the world, that he gave his only begotten Son, that whosoever believeth in him should not perish, but have everlasting life."[2]. The love of the Son, which demands our gratitude, is not less unmeasured, than the love of the Father: whence Paul labored to explore " the height, the length, the breadth and the depth of the love of Christ, which passeth knowledge."[3] And our gratitude is not complete till we acknowledge and celebrate also, the love of the Spirit,[4] by whom believers are fitted for the enjoyment of God, and brought into fellowship with him.

In exercising and cultivating our gratitude for the blessings of salvation, we must distinctly recognise that they come from God, and that they are intentionally bestowed. When we trace them to their source, the infinite love of the triune God; and when we receive them, as conferred according to his eternal counsel, we are prepared while we enjoy the benefit, to return thanks to its Author, and to exclaim with liveliest emotion, " Bless the Lord, O my soul, and forget not all his benefits."[5]

That our gratitude to God may be proportional to the blessing received, we should count his mercies over, and survey their magnitude. Unmeasurable! unspeakable! passing knowledge !—yet we should labor to know them ; and as we make progress in this spiritual knowledge, our gratitude should swell and fill the enlarged capacity of the mind.

In order to the full exercise of gratitude to God it is necessary to be thoroughly impressed with the conviction that the blessings received are wholly undeserved, and proceed entirely from the mere mercy and grace of God. When we feel that we are less than the least of all God's mercies, that our only desert is hell, and that if salvation is bestowed on us, it will be of his own good pleasure ; we are prepared to give thanks for the unspeakable gift, and to say, " Not unto us, O Lord, not unto us, but unto thy name give glory."[6]

---

[1] Tit. ii. 11.   [2] John iii. 16.   [3] Eph. iii. 18, 19.
[4] Rom. xv. 30.   [5] Ps. ciii. 2.   [6] Ps. cxv.

CHAPTER I.

THE TRINITY.

THE FATHER, SON, AND HOLY SPIRIT, ARE THREE PERSONS IN ONE DIVINE ESSENCE.[1]

The unity of God is a fundamental doctrine of religion; and no doctrine can be true which is inconsistent with it. All admit that the Father is God; and we have seen that the Son is God, and the Holy Spirit is God, according to the teachings of the sacred Scriptures. To reconcile the proper deity of these three, with the strict unity of God, is a matter of great difficulty. All admit that they cannot be three and one in the same respect; and divines have usually held that they are three in person, and one in essence.

The doctrine of a three-fold distinction in the Godhead, belongs especially to the economy of grace, and is therefore more clearly revealed in the New Testament than in the Old. Some intimations of it, however, may be found in the Hebrew Scriptures. In the very first verse of the Bible, the name of God is plural, and the verb "created," with which it is construed, is singular. This countenances the opinion, that there is plurality as well as unity in the Godhead. But since words which are plural in form, are sometimes used to denote objects which are singular, this argument for a plurality in the Godhead cannot be regarded as in itself conclusive. It derives strength, however, from two considerations: 1. The Hebrew scriptures guard the doctrine of God's unity with great care; and if all plurality were inconsistent with it, this important purpose of the revelation made to the Hebrews, would have been better subserved if none but singular names for the deity had been admitted, yet plural names are very commonly employed. And in one remarkable case, the Hebrew name *Elohim*, is used in an express declaration of the divine unity. "Hear, O Israel, Jehovah, our Elohim, is one Jehovah."[2] Why was the

---

[1] Matt. xxviii. 19; 2 Cor. xiii. 14; Rev. i. 4; Gen. i. 26; iii. 22; xi. 7; Isaiah xlviii. 16; John xiv. 16; Matt. iii. 16, 17.

[2] Deut. vi. 4.

plural name here introduced? The declaration of the divine unity would have been complete without it. If it was introduced to guard against an improper inference from the use of plural names, it shows the use of such names to have been dangerous, and therefore difficult to reconcile with the wisdom of revelation. If the name Jehovah be understood to refer to the divine essence; and the name Elohim, to the three divine persons; the passage may be interpreted consistently and beautifully, and it becomes an explicit declaration of the New Testament doctrine. 2. The Hebrew scriptures contain other intimations of a plurality in the Godhead. Plural pronouns are applied to God, and consultation is attributed to him. "Let us make man."[1] "Let us go down and confound their language."[2] A consultation with created beings cannot here be supposed. The opinion that God spoke in these cases, after the pompous manner of eastern monarchs, besides being, on other accounts, wholly improbable, is completely set aside, by the passage, "Behold, the man is become as one of us."[3] No eastern monarch ever spoke of his individual unity, in this style. No consistent interpretation of this language can be given, without admitting a plurality in the Godhead; and this admission explains the use of plural names for God.

That the plurality in the Godhead is three-fold, has been inferred from the three-fold ascription of holiness[4] to God, and the three-fold benediction of the High Priest.[5] A more satisfactory argument is derived from passages in which the three divine persons are distinctly brought to view.[6]

This doctrine is more clearly revealed in the New Testament. In the formula of Christian baptism it is clearly exhibited.[7] We are baptised into one name, because God is one; but that is the name of the Father, and of the Son, and of the Holy Ghost, because it belongs alike to each of these divine persons. Here, this doctrine meets us, at our very entrance on the profession of the Christian religion. If Christ was not God, he was justly condemned to death, and his religion is false; and the Holy Spirit, the Comforter whom he promised, is as little entitled to regard as

---

[1] Gen. i. 26.   [2] Gen. xi. 7.   [3] Gen. iii. 22.
[4] Isaiah vi. 3.   [5] Num. vi. 24–26.
[6] Isaiah xlviii. 16; lxi. 1; lxiii. 7–10.   [7] Matt. xxviii. 19.

he was. If Christ and the Holy Spirit are not God, the form of baptism should be rejected, as of a piece with the false religion into which it introduces us. No man can consistently receive Christian baptism, without believing the doctrine of the Trinity.

We have spoken of this doctrine as belonging especially to the economy of grace. It is here that it is most clearly unfolded to our view, and without this doctrine, the covenant of grace, and its developments in the great work of salvation, cannot be understood. Yet there are fainter exhibitions of the doctrine in other works of God. This is true of creation. The consultation at the creation of man has already been noticed, as a proof of plurality in the Godhead. Moses says, "The Spirit of God moved on the face of the waters." Job says, "By his Spirit he garnished the heavens. John says, "By him (the Word) all things were made."[1] All the divine persons, therefore, were concerned in creation: and other passages teach that they are also concerned in providence.[2]

The most sober-minded divines admit that there is incomprehensible mystery in the doctrine of the Trinity. All attempts to explain it have failed. Two methods which have been proposed to bring it within our comprehension, deserve special notice.

Some who are called Sabellians, maintain, that the distinction between the Father, the Son, and the Holy Ghost, is official and not personal. They hold that God is one in person, as well as in essence; but that he manifests himself in three different ways, and that the three different names denote these three modes of manifestation. This simplifies the doctrine; but it does not accord with the Scriptures. According to this view of the doctrine, we might paraphrase the words of Christ, in John, xiv. 16, thus: "I, who am the same person with the Father, will pray the Father, who is no other than myself, in a different office, or mode of manifestation, and he shall give you another comforter, who is not another, but the same person as my Father and myself." We see, from this specimen, that this explanation of the doctrine is at variance with the word of God.

Others admit the distinction of persons in the Godhead, and

---

[1] Gen. i. 2; Job xxvi. 13; John i. 3.   [2] Heb. i. 3; Isaiah xxxiv. 15, 16.

explain that the three possess one essence, just as three men, Peter, James, and John, possess one nature. This is Tritheism. It makes the Father, Son, and Holy Ghost, three Gods, just as Peter, James, and John, are three men. If we may call the three persons one God, merely because they are alike in their nature; we may, with equal reason, call all mankind one man; and we may maintain that Jupiter, Neptune, Pluto, and all the heathen deities were one God. Paul's distinction, "There are gods many; but to us there is but one God,"[1] is a distinction without a difference; for the many gods are one, in the same sense in which the three divine persons are supposed to be one. This explanation must, therefore, be rejected, as inconsistent with the proper unity of God.

Attempts have frequently been made, to illustrate the mystery of the Trinity, by means of material objects. One of these may be cited as a specimen of the rest. Water, ice, and snow, it is said, are different things, and yet they are but one. For aught that appears, it would have served quite as well, to illustrate the mystery, by three separate glasses of water, all in the liquid form. The distinction between them would have been as perfect; and the identity of nature would have been as real, and more apparent. All such illustrations darken counsel with words without knowledge. What shall we liken unto the Lord?

These efforts to explain the doctrine, are not simply fruitless, but they lead to error. If the mind receives satisfaction from them, it is by a false view of God's mode of existence, and thinking him such an one as ourselves. It is far wiser to admit, that none by searching can find out God; and to abstain from unavailing efforts to comprehend what is incomprehensible to our finite minds. What God tells us on the subject, we ought to believe; and with this measure of knowledge, we ought to be satisfied; and all beyond this is human speculation, of which it is our duty and interest to beware. Nor are we justly liable to the reproach of believing what we do not understand. The teaching of divine revelation, we may understand, and we should labor to understand; and the mystery which remains unrevealed to our understanding, is not an object of our faith. The proposition, *God is incomprehensible*, is

---

[1] 1 Cor. viii. 5, 6.

simple and intelligible, and our faith embraces it. God is the subject of this proposition; and, if a full understanding of the subject were necessary to faith, a belief of this proposition would be impossible. Though we do not comprehend God, we comprehend the meaning of the proposition; and this is what we believe. So the doctrine of the Trinity, as an object of our faith, may be expressed in propositions, each one of which is intelligible, notwithstanding the incomprehensibility of the subject.

The view which has been presented, is important, to strengthen our faith in the doctrine of the Trinity. So long as we imagine that a full comprehension of the subject is necessary to the exercise of faith, we must embrace the truth feebly. But let us examine the propositions, in which the doctrine may be expressed, and we shall find each one of them perfectly intelligible. The Father is God;—the Son is God;—the Holy Ghost is God;—there is but one God. All these propositions, we may understand, and receive with unwavering faith; while we are well assured that our understandings fall infinitely short of comprehending the great subject, and that, in harmonizing the last proposition with the preceding three, there is a difficulty which finite intelligence cannot explain.

In receiving a truth which is attended with difficulty, our faith may be assisted, by noticing that other truths, which we are compelled to admit, are attended with equal difficulty. The Omnipresence of God, may be shown to be as incomprehensible as the Trinity. If, at the same moment, a ball of matter is here, a ball there, and a ball yonder, we know that there are three balls. If, in the illustration, we substitute an angel for the ball, we know that there are three angels in the three places, and not one and the same angel. Yet the doctrine of God's omnipresence teaches, that a whole deity is here, a whole deity there, and a whole deity yonder; and yet it is one and the same deity which is present at each place. If an entire deity may dwell, at the same time, in three separate places, and yet be but one, why may not an entire deity dwell in the three separate persons, the Father, the Son, and the Holy Ghost, and yet be but one God? There is, perhaps, no analogy between the two cases, except in this, that they alike confound our arithmetic; but this analogy is sufficient for our present purpose. Were God's mode of existence like that of created things, either material or spiritual, he could not be in several places at the same time, or in three distinct persons; and yet be an undivided unit. We are compelled to admit the omnipresence of God, and we should admit, with equal faith, on the authority of God's word, the doctrine of the Trinity, ascribing the difficulty of the subject to the incomprehensibility of the divine nature.

The doctrine of God's omnipresence has, in one particular, greater difficulty, than that of the Trinity. The latter has a relief not discoverable in the other, arising from the consideration, that God is not three and one in the same respect. God is three in person, one in essence; and, although we may be unable to explain the precise difference between person and essence, the fact that there is a difference, relieves the doctrine from the charge of inconsistency.

We study the human mind in the phenomena which it exhibits. The operations of memory, imagination, reasoning, &c., differ widely from each other; but we refer them all to the one indivisible substance, called mind, of which we have no knowledge, except what we acquire from the phenomena. What we know of God, we learn from the manifestations which he has made of himself, in his works and word. In these manifestations, we discover the personal distinction of Father, Son, and Holy Ghost; yet, as taught by the divine word, we refer all the manifestations to the one indivisible essence, in which the unity of God consists. It is not a threefold manifestation of the same person, as the Sabellians hold; but a manifestation of three distinct persons, counselling and covenanting with each other, one sending another, one speaking to another, and of the third, &c. Nothing like this appears in the phenomena of one human mind: but we cannot thence infer, that it cannot be in the manifestations of one divine mind.

The word Trinity is not in the Bible, and objection has therefore been made to its use. As signifying tri-unity, three in one, it is an expressive name for the doctrine. As a convenient word, we are at liberty to use it, as we do many other words not found in the Bible; and the propriety of using it is the greater, because there is no single word in the Bible, which can be substituted for it. But we are under no obligation to contend for the name, which is human, provided we firmly maintain the doctrine, which is divine.

The word *person*, also, which is used in stating this doctrine, is without Scripture precedent. Some have cited, as authority for its use, the passage in Heb. i. 3: "Who being the brightness of his glory, and the express image of his person." Here, it is alleged, the person of the Father is mentioned; and, as the Son is his express image, we must conclude that he, also, is a person; and, having established the personal distinction between the Father and the Son, no doubt can remain, that the Holy Spirit is a third person. To all this, it may be answered, that the word *person* is not a good rendering of the Greek word here used, the sense of which would be better expressed by the word *substance*. The passage properly interpreted, refers to the full display of the Godhead, made through Jesus Christ as mediator, and not to the relation subsisting among the divine persons. But though there is no Scripture precedent for the use of the word, must it therefore be abandoned? A scrupulosity, which should refuse to use any word not found in the Bible, would be unwise, and lead to no good result. No one would refuse to apply the word *person* to Jesus Christ, and speak of him as a holy and just person, an extraordinary or wonderful person; or to say that his divine and human natures are united in one person: yet it would be difficult to produce Scripture precedent for this application of the term. Paul does speak, in 2 Cor. ii. 10, of "the person of Christ;" but a better rendering of this passage would be, "in the presence of Christ;" and Pilate's wife said, Mat. xxvii.: "Have thou nothing to do with this just person;" but the word *person* is here supplied by our translators, and has no word corresponding to it in the original text. Yet our translators, in applying this word to Christ, have conformed to the common usage of the word, adopted and sustained by the common sense of mankind. Now, if Jesus Christ was a person, in the common acceptation of the term; and if he addressed his Father, and spoke of the Holy Spirit, as one human person would address another, and speak of a third, it must be an excessive scrupulosity, which refuses to apply the term to the Father, and the Holy Spirit, as well as to the Son. Some have preferred to substitute the word *manifestation;* but this is equally without Scripture precedent; and to say, that one manifestation speaks to another, and of a third: would be unintelligible. We may, therefore, defend the use of the term person, provided we remember that it is a human expedient to avoid circumlocution. But if any one proceed to draw from the term, an inference which will affect the doctrine, he must be reminded that the word is human. If any one should infer, when we speak of the three divine persons, that they are as distinct from each other, in every respect, as the three human persons, Peter, James, and John, he is building an inference on a foundation not authorized by the word of God.

CHAPTER II.

COVENANT OF GRACE.

THE THREE DIVINE PERSONS CO-OPERATE IN MAN'S SALVATION ACCORDING TO AN ETERNAL COVENANT.[1]

On a former occasion, it was shown that the Scriptures use the term covenant with great latitude of meaning. The propriety of its use in the present case, cannot well be questioned. We have three divine persons, who are parties in this covenant; and the doctrine of God's unity cannot exclude the notion of a covenant, without, at the same time, excluding the distinction of persons in the Godhead. We are not to imagine, as included in this covenant transaction, a proposal of terms by one party, and a deliberation, followed with an acceptance or rejection of them, by the other parties. These things occur, in the making of human covenants, because of the imperfection of the parties. In condescension to our weakness, the Scriptures use language taken from the affairs of men. They speak as if a formal proposal had been made, at the creation of man, addressed by one of the parties to the others: "Let us make man;" but this is in accommodation to our modes of conception. An agreement and co-operation of the divine persons, in the creation of man, is what is taught in this passage. This agreement and co-operation extend to all the works of God: "Who worketh all things after the counsel of his will."[2] The idea

---

[1] Ps. ii. 8; xl. 6–8; lxxxix. 3; Isaiah xlix. 3–12; John xvii. 6; Heb. xiii. 20; Titus i. 2.

[2] Eph. i. 11.

of *counsel* in all these works, accords with that of consultation which is presented in the account of man's creation. In every work of God, the divine persons must either agree or disagree. As they alike possess infinite wisdom, disagreement among them is impossible. The salvation of men is a work of God, in which the divine persons concur. It is performed according to an eternal purpose; and in this purpose, as well as in the work, the divine persons concur; and this concurrence is their eternal covenant. The purpose of the one God, is the covenant of the Trinity.

In the work of salvation, the divine persons co-operate in different offices; and these are so clearly revealed, as to render the personal distinction in the Godhead more manifest, than it is in any other of God's works. Beyond doubt, these official relations are severally held, by the perfect agreement of all; and, speaking after the manner of men, the adjustment of these relations, and the assignment of the several parts in the work, are the grand stipulations of the eternal covenant.

That the covenant is eternal, may be argued from the eternity, unchangeableness, and omniscience of the parties, and from the declarations of Scripture which directly or indirectly relate to it: "Through the blood of the everlasting covenant."[1] "His eternal purpose in Christ Jesus."[2] "In hope of eternal life promised before the world began."[3] "Grace given in Christ Jesus before the world began."[4]

Although God's purpose is *one*, we are obliged, according to our modes of conception, to view it, and speak of it, as consisting of various parts. So, the eternal covenant is one; but it is revealed to us in a manner adapted to our conceptions and to our spiritual benefit. The work of redemption by Christ is presented in the Gospel as the great object of our faith; and the stipulation for the accomplishment of this work, is the prominent point exhibited in the revelation which is made to us respecting the covenant of grace. The agreement between the Father and the Son is conspicuously brought to view, in various parts of the sacred volume: "Thine they were, and thou gavest them me."[5] "Ask of me, and I will give thee the heathen for thine inheritance, and the uttermost

---

[1] Heb. xiii. 20. [2] Eph. iii. 11. [3] Tit. i. 2
[4] 2 Tim. i. 9. [5] John xvii. 6.

parts of the earth for thy possession."[1] "Sacrifice and offering thou didst not desire. Then said I, Lo, I come, in the volume of the book it is written of me, I delight to do thy will, O God;"[2] and in Isaiah, chapter xlix., the stipulations between the Father and the Son are presented, almost as if they had been copied from an original record of the transaction.

According to the covenant arrangement, the Son appeared in human nature, in the form of a servant; and, after obeying unto death, was exalted by the Father to supreme dominion. The Holy Spirit also is revealed as acting in a subordinate office, being sent by the Father and by the Son. The Father alone is not presented as acting in a subordinate office; but appears as sustaining the full authority of the Godhead, sending the Son, giving him a people to be redeemed, prescribing the terms, accepting the service, rewarding and glorifying the Son, and sending the Holy Spirit. In all this the Father appears as the representative of the Godhead, in its authority and majesty. The Son also sustains a representative character. The promise of eternal life was made, before the world began, to the people of God, in him as their representative. The reconciliation between God and men is provided for by the covenant engagement between the Father and the Son; the Father acting as the representative of the Godhead, and the Son as the representative and surety of his people. The Holy Spirit concurs in this arrangement, and takes his part in the work, in harmony with the other persons of the Godhead. His peculiar office is necessary to complete the plan, and to reward the obedience of the Son by the salvation of his redeemed people. The promises of the Father to the Son include the gift of the Holy Spirit; and, therefore, the sending of the Spirit is attributed to the Son;[3] and sometimes to the Father at the petition of the Son.[4]

In this order of operation, inferiority of nature is not implied, in the subordination of office to which the Son and the Spirit voluntarily consent. The fulness of the Godhead dwells in each of the divine persons, and renders the fulfilment of the covenant infallibly sure, in all its stipulations. The Holy Spirit, in the execution of his office, dwells in believers; but he brings with him

---

[1] Ps. ii. 8. [2] Ps. xl. 6–18.

[3] John xvi. 7. [4] John xiv. 16.

the fulness of the Godhead, so that God is in them, and they are the temple of God, and filled with the fulness of God. The Son or Word, in the execution of his office, becomes the man Jesus Christ; but the fulness of the Godhead dwells in him; so that, in his deepest humiliation he is God manifest in the flesh, God over all, blessed for ever.

The order of operation in this mysterious and wonderful economy, can be learned from divine revelation only. Here we should study it with simple faith, relying on the testimony of God. In the representation of it here exhibited, we may discover that the blessings of grace, proceeding from God, appear to originate in the Father, "of whom are all things," to be conferred through the Son, "by whom are all things," and by the Spirit, who is the immediate agent in bestowing them, the last in the order of operation. The approach to God, in acts of devotion, is in the reverse order. The Spirit makes intercession *in* the saints, moving them, as a spirit of supplication, and assisting their infirmities, when they know not what to pray for. Their prayers are offered through Christ, as the medium of approach; and the Father, as the highest representative of the Godhead, is the ultimate object of the worship. Through him [Christ] we have access by one Spirit to the Father.[1] The Spirit moves us to honor the Son and the Father: and for this purpose takes of the things of Christ and shows them to us, that we may believe in him, and through him approach the Father. In this work he acts for the whole Godhead, and therefore his drawing is ascribed to the Father: "No man can come to me, except the Father, which hath sent me, draw him."[2] When we come to Jesus Christ, the whole Godhead meets us again in the person of the Mediator: for "God is in Christ reconciling the world unto himself."[3] And when we address the Father, as the ultimate object of our worship, the whole Godhead is there, and receives our adorations. In the covenant of grace, the triune God is so presented to the view of the believer, that he may worship without distraction of thought, with full confidence of acceptance, and with a clear perception that God is to him all and in all. In the retirement of the closet, the devotional man addresses God as present in the secret place, and holds communion with him, as a

---

[1] Eph. ii. 18.   [2] John vi. 44.   [3] 2 Cor. v. 19.

friend near at hand. When he comes forth into the busy world, he sees God all around him, in the heavens, and in the earth; and holds converse with him in this different manifestation of himself. When he lifts his thoughts to the high and holy place where God's throne is, and prays, "Our Father which art in heaven," his mind is directed to the highest and most glorious manifestation of the Deity. In all this he suffers no distraction of thought. The same omnipresent, One is addressed, whether conceived to be in the closet, or in the world, or in the highest heavens. With equal freedom from distraction we may worship the Infinite One, whether we approach him as the Holy Spirit, operating on the heart; or as the Son, the Mediator between God and men; or as the Father, representing the full authority and majesty of the Godhead. We worship God, and God alone, whether our devotions are directed to the Father, the Son, or the Holy Spirit; for the divine essence, undivided and indivisible, belongs to each of the three persons.

To guard against mistake, it should be observed, that the covenant which we have been considering is not identical with the new covenant of which Paul speaks in the epistle to the Hebrews. The latter is made, according to the prophecy which he quotes, "with the house of Israel and the house of Judah;"[1] whereas the covenant of which we have treated, is not made with man. There is, however, a close connection between them. In the eternal covenant, promises are made to the Son, as the representative of his people: in the new covenant, these promises are made to them personally, and, in part, fulfilled to them. The promises are made to them: "I will be to them a God, and they shall be to me a people:"[2] and they are, in part, fulfilled. "I will put my law in their minds, and write it in their hearts."

---

[1] Heb. viii. 8.   [2] Heb. viii. 10.

17

CHAPTER III.

BLESSINGS OF GRACE.

THE SALVATION OF MEN IS ENTIRELY OF DIVINE GRACE.[1]

Grace is unmerited favor. Paul distinguishes, in Rom. iv. 4, between the reward of grace and the reward of debt. When good is conferred because it is due, it is not of grace. Whatever may be claimed on the score of justice, cannot be regarded as unmerited favor. Justice gives to every man according to his works; and if salvation were of works, it could not be of grace. Paul has made this matter very plain: "To him that worketh, is the reward not reckoned of grace, but of debt. If by grace, then it is no more of works; otherwise grace is no more grace. But if it be of works, then it is no more grace; otherwise work is no more work."[2]

For the same reason that salvation is not of works, it is not of the law. The law is the rule of justice, and takes cognisance of men's works. If it gave life to men, it could be only on the ground of their obedience to its requirements; for its language is, "The man that doeth these things shall live by them."[3] Salvation by the law is declared to be impossible: for if there had been a law given which could have given life, verily righteousness should have been by the law.[4] The Scriptures represent grace and law as opposed to each other: "The law was given by Moses; but grace and truth came by Jesus Christ."[5] "Received ye the Spirit by the works of the law, or by the hearing of faith?"[6] "It is of faith, that it might be by grace."[7] Sometimes the term *law* is used in an extended sense; as when the law of faith is opposed to the law of works;[8] and the law of the spirit of life, to the law of sin and death.[9] Hence we read of "the perfect law of liberty,"[10] which cannot be the rule of justice: that says, "Cursed is every one

---

[1] Eph. ii. 5, 7, 8; 2 Tim. i. 9; Rom. iii. 24; viii. 23; xi. 5, 6; ix. 15, 16.
[2] Rom. xi. 6. [3] Rom. x. 5. [4] Gal. iii. 21.
[5] John i. 17. [6] Gal. iii. 2. [7] Rom. iv. 16.
[8] Rom. iii. 27. [9] Rom. viii. 2. [10] James i. 25.

that continueth not in all things which are written in the book of the law to do them."[1] When the term *law* is used in this extended sense, it denotes the method of salvation by grace through faith, and is carefully distinguished from "the law of works."

The doctrine that salvation is of grace, is taught in the sacred Scriptures with great clearness. In the second chapter of the epistle to the Ephesians, the declaration is twice made, " By grace ye are saved." Paul ascribed his own salvation to grace: " By the grace of God, I am what I am."[2] He traces the blessing of salvation to "the grace given in Christ Jesus, before the world began:"[3]—to "the riches of his grace:"[4]—to " the exceeding riches of his grace."[5]

Salvation is entirely of grace. The passages already quoted show that salvation is not partly of grace and partly of works. Grace and works are so opposed to each other, that, when it is affirmed to be of grace, it is denied to be of works: " Not of works; otherwise grace is no more grace." " Not according to our works; but according to his own purpose and grace."[6] The exclusion of all boasting,[7] was, that the blessing bestowed is entirely of grace: "Not of works, lest any man should boast."[8] Our works are wholly excluded; because they are all sinful, and can deserve nothing but the wrath of God. Faith renounces all reliance on our own works, all expectation of favor on their account; and asks and receives every blessing as the gift of divine grace through Jesus Christ. When salvation is so received, all boasting is effectually excluded.

That salvation is entirely of divine grace, may be argued from the condition in which the Gospel finds mankind. We are justly condemned, totally depraved, and, in ourselves, perfectly helpless. All this has been fully proved in a former chapter; is verified in the experience of every one who is awakened to a just view of his lost state; and precisely accords with the language of God to his ancient people: " O Israel, thou hast destroyed thyself, but in me is thy help."[9] The second chapter of the epistle to the Ephesians describes the condition of men by nature: " Children of wrath,"

---

[1] Gal. iii. 10. [2] 1 Cor. xv. 10. [3] 2 Tim. i. 9.
[4] Eph. i. 7. [5] Eph. ii. 7. [6] 2 Tim. i. 9.
[7] Rom. iii. 27. [8] Eph. ii. 9. [9] Hosea xiii. 9.

"dead in trespasses and sins," "without hope and without God;" and it attributes their deliverance from this wretched and hopeless condition, to the grace of God, who is rich in mercy: "But God, in his great love, wherewith he loved us even when we were dead in sins, hath quickened us together with Christ (by grace ye are saved), and hath raised us up together; and hath made us sit together in heavenly places in Christ Jesus. For by grace ye are saved through faith, and that not of yourselves, it is the gift of God." In the eagerness of his desire to impress the minds of the Ephesian Christians with a sense of their obligation to divine grace, before he reaches the conclusion of his argument, as if impatient to express the thought with which his own mind was so deeply impressed, he introduced it parenthetically, by anticipation, "By grace ye are saved." Afterwards, when his argument is completed, he repeats the declaration, and expands it to the utmost fulness of meaning, when he adds that faith itself is the gift of God. If the blessing bestowed is of faith, that it might be by grace, and if faith itself is the gift of God, it must be emphatically true that salvation is of grace.

The blessings which are bestowed in salvation, demonstrate that it is entirely of grace. We shall proceed to a particular consideration of these, in the sections which follow: but we may here, in a general view, comprehend them under two gifts, namely, of Christ, and of the Holy Spirit.

The gift of Christ, to die for us, and to become to us the author of eternal salvation, is entirely of grace: "God so loved the world that he gave his only begotten Son."[1] "God commendeth his love toward us, in that, while we were yet sinners, Christ died for us."[2] "He that spared not his own Son, but delivered him up for us all; how shall he not with him also freely give us all things?"[3] Without the death of Christ, our salvation was impossible: and we had no claim on God to draw forth from him the gift of his well-beloved. He was freely given, of God's great love, wherewith he loved us: and as he was freely given, so all the blessings which flow through him are freely given also. If any man feels that Christ was under obligation to die for him, or that God was bound to give his Son to make the needed sacrifice for

---

[1] John iii. 16.   [2] Rom. v. 8.   [3] Rom. viii. 32.

sin, he totally mistakes, on a point of vital importance to the salvation of his soul. The doctrine that salvation is of grace, is not
a useless speculation; but it enters into the very heart of Christian
experience; and the faith which does not recognise it, does not
receive Christ as he is presented in the Gospel. It is, therefore,
a matter of unspeakable importance, that our view of this truth
should be clear, and that it should be cordially embraced by every
power of our minds.

As the Son of God was freely given to effect our salvation by
his death; so the Holy Spirit is freely given, to apply the salvation which the Son has wrought out: "The love of God is shed
abroad in our hearts by the Holy Ghost which is given unto us."[1]
We receive the Holy Spirit as a gift of the Father's love, who
bestows it, as earthly parents give good things to their children.[2]
And this gift is not bestowed because of merit in the recipient.
Paul asks, "Received ye the Spirit, by the works of the law, or
by the hearing of faith?"[3] From this inquiry we learn that this
gift also is of faith, that it might be by grace.[4] The Spirit is
given in answer to the prayer of Christ: and being thus bestowed
through Christ, it is one of the good things freely given together
with Christ. We are encouraged to pray that God would give us
his Holy Spirit: but our prayer cannot be acceptable, and will not
be heard, if we ask the blessing as one which is justly due, and
which we may demand as a right. When our humbled hearts plead
that God would, in the exceeding riches of his grace, grant us his
Holy Spirit, to renew and sanctify us, and fit us for his service,
our petitions rise with acceptance to the ear of the Lord of hosts.

An objection to the views which have been presented, may arise
from the fact, that, in the last day, men will be judged according
to their works.[5] But the good works of the saints are the fruit
of grace bestowed; and, although the sentence in the great day
will be according to their works, the reward will nevertheless be
of grace, and not of debt. Their works will be an evidence of
their faith; and Christ, the Judge, will refer to them, as proof of
love to him. The kingdom which he will bestow, will be, not a
reward for the merit of their works, but an inheritance prepared

---

[1] Rom. v. 5.   [2] Luke xi. 13.   [3] Gal. iii. 2.
[4] Rom. iv. 16.   [5] Rev. xx. 12.

for them before the foundation of the world.[1] It will be as true
on that day, as it is now, and it will be felt to be true by all the
saints, that eternal life is the gift of God through Jesus Christ.[2]

Section I.—PARDON.

ALL WHO REPENT OF SIN OBTAIN FORGIVENESS THROUGH JESUS
CHRIST.[3]

Forgiveness implies deliverance from the penalty due to sin.
The wrath of God is revealed from heaven against all ungodliness:
and when men become sensible of the danger to which they are
exposed, deliverance from the impending wrath becomes an object
of intense solicitude. Hence arises an anxious desire to obtain
forgiveness. To persons in this state of mind, the doctrine that
there is forgiveness with God, is most welcome.

All forgiveness is bestowed through Jesus Christ. It is he who
delivers from the wrath to come.[4] In him " we have redemption
through his blood, the forgiveness of sins, according to the riches
of his grace."[5] He had power on earth to forgive sins ;[6] and he is
now exalted a Prince and a Saviour, to give repentance to Israel, and
remission of sins.[7] That we might be delivered from the penalty
due to our sins, it was necessary that Christ should bear it for us.
Hence it is true, that without the shedding of blood, there is no
remission ;[8] and hence, in the teachings of Scripture, the forgiveness of sins stands connected with redemption by the blood of
Christ. With this agrees the language of the redeemed : "Unto
him that loved us, and washed us from our sins, in his own blood."[9]

The blessing of forgiveness is bestowed on all who truly repent
of their sins. This is taught in various passages of Scripture.
" Repent ye, and be converted, that your sins may be blotted out.[10]
" If we confess our sins, God is faithful and just to forgive us our
sins."[11] Repentance and remission of sins[12] were preached in the
name of Christ, and are associated blessings, bestowed by " the
exalted Prince and Saviour."[13] When Jesus said, " Except ye

---

[1] Matt. xxv. 34.   [2] Rom. vi. 23.
[3] Isaiah lv. 7 ; Jer. iii. 12, 22 ; Luke xxiv. 46, 47 ; Acts ii. 38 ; iii. 19 ; v. 31.
[4] 1 Thess. i. 10.   [5] Eph. i. 7.   [6] Matt. ix. 6.
[7] Acts v. 31.   [8] Heb. ix. 22.   [9] Rev. i. 5.
[10] Acts iii. 19.   [11] 1 John i. 9.   [12] Luke xxiv. 47.
[13] Acts v. 31.

repent, ye shall all likewise perish,"[1] it was implied that, if they repented, they would escape. God, in the gospel, commands all men everywhere to repent, in view of the approaching judgment.[2] The hope of escape in that great day, is clearly held out to those who obey the command, and sincerely repent of their sins.

Forgiveness is sometimes represented in the Scriptures, as received by faith in Christ: "To him give all the prophets witness, that through his name whosoever believeth in him shall receive remission of sin."[3] Repentance and faith are twin graces, proceeding from the same Holy Spirit, and wrought in the same heart; and, although they may be contemplated separately, they exist together, and the promise of forgiveness belongs to either of them.

In the New Testament, a connection appears, between the remission of sins and the ordinance of baptism. John preached the baptism of repentance for the remission of sins;[4] and Ananias commanded Saul, "Arise, and be baptised, and wash away thy sins, calling on the name of the Lord."[5] In the Old Testament, a similar connection appears, between remission and the sacrifices of that dispensation. "Almost all things were by the law purged with blood, and without the shedding of blood is no remission."[6] Yet Paul has taught us that the blood of bulls and goats cannot take away sin;[7] that these offerings were only figures of things to come; and that the only effectual removal of sin is by the blood of Christ. Baptism under the gospel, is as truly a figure, as the sacrifices were under the law. In the ceremonies instituted by Moses, the death of Christ was prefigured by the death of the slaughtered victims; and in the gospel ceremony, the burial and resurrection of Christ are figured forth in the ordinance of baptism: and in both cases, the remission connected with the ceremony is merely figurative. Our sins are washed away in baptism, in the same sense in which we eat the body and drink the blood of Christ, in the ordinance of the Lord's supper.[8] Baptism and the Lord's supper are duties to be performed under the gospel

---

[1] Luke xiii. 3.   [2] Acts xvii. 30.   [3] Acts x. 43.
[4] Mark i. 4.   [5] Acts xxii. 16.   [6] Heb. ix. 22.
[7] Heb. ix. 13.   [8] 1 Cor. x. 16.

dispensation; as the various ceremonies instituted by Moses, were duties under the former dispensation; but the figures ought not, in either case, to be confounded with the things which they represent. In a figure, baptism washes away sin: in reality, "The blood of Jesus Christ cleanses from all sin." We must be careful not to rely on the figure, instead of the reality which it represents.

To escape the wrath to come, is the first desire of the awakened sinner; and mercy, mercy, forgive, forgive, are the first words uttered in his earnest prayers. Forgiveness is bestowed on repentance, and repentance is the first duty enjoined in the gospel. It is fit that the first blessing of grace which the sinner anxiously seeks, should be connected with the first duty required of him. It shows, on the one hand, the holiness of God, who will not pardon sin, except on the condition of the sinner's return to obedience; and, on the other, God's readiness to forgive, inasmuch as his wrath is averted at the first step of the sinner's return. He might have required that the sinner should undergo a long discipline of painful penance, and a long course of laborious service, as a condition of release from the indignation and wrath so long provoked. But God's readiness to forgive, is beautifully illustrated in the parable of the prodigal son, by the conduct of the father, who, while his son was yet a great way off, ran, and fell on his neck, and kissed him,[1] with free and full assurance of pardon and acceptance. Such is the love which God manifests to the returning sinner. It hastens to receive him on the first indication of true penitence. Nor is it a partial forgiveness which is then bestowed. The storm of divine wrath, which had been gathering over the sinner's head, during all his life of impenitence, is at once dispelled, and his sins, as a thick cloud, are at once blotted out.[2] To show the completeness of his pardon, his iniquities are represented as buried in the depths of the sea;[3] not in some shallow place, where an ebbing tide might leave them uncovered; but in the depths of the ocean, where, if they should be sought for, they could never be found. Such is God's forgiveness. Why are sinners so averse to seek it?

Although, on the first movement of a sinner in his return to God, the first blessing of divine grace is bestowed on him, so full,

---

[1] Luke xv. 20.   [2] Isaiah xliv. 22.   [3] Mic. vii. 19.

so freely, so gloriously; it does not follow, that he may safely stop short in his progress. The doctrine of the saints' final perseverance, which we shall hereafter consider, is misunderstood and misapplied; if men take encouragement from it, to relax in their efforts to advance in the way of holiness. The blessing of forgiveness, and the exercise of repentance, are connected with each other, at the beginning of the divine life; and their connection remains throughout its progress. We have occasion to pray for forgiveness, as often as we pray for our daily bread,[1] and the prayer cannot be presented with a well grounded hope that it will be heard and answered, unless it proceed from a penitent heart. Penitence is as necessary to pardon, in the saint who is just finishing his warfare, and taking his departure for the other world, as it was in the first moment of his drawing near to God. Christ was exalted "to give repentance and remission of sins;" and if these do not accompany each other, they do not come from Christ. He who believes that all his sins, past and future, were forgiven at his first conversion, in such a sense that he may dispense with all subsequent penitence, and rest satisfied with his first forgiveness, has need to learn again the first principles of the doctrine of Christ.

Section II.—JUSTIFICATION.

ALL WHO BELIEVE IN CHRIST, ARE JUSTIFIED BY HIS RIGHTEOUSNESS IMPUTED TO THEM.[2]

Justification is the act of a judge acquitting one who is charged with crime. It is the opposite of condemnation. In Deut. xxv. 1, the judges of Israel were commanded, in the discharge of their official duty, to justify the righteous, and condemn the wicked.

Justification is a higher blessing of grace, than pardon. The latter frees from the penalty due to sin, but it does not fully restore the lost favor of God. A pardoned criminal, and a just man who has committed no crime, stand on different ground. The distinction between pardon and justification may be illustrated by these words

---

[1] Matt. vi. 11, 12.

[2] Acts xiii. 39; Rom. iii. 21, 22, 25, 26; x. 4; Gal. ii. 16; iii. 22, 24; Phil. iii. 8–10.

of Job, "God forbid that I should justify you."[1] If, in this passage, we should substitute the word pardon for justify, every one would perceive an important change in the meaning. This change shows the difference between pardon and justification. Such is the greatness of divine grace to the sinner who returns to God through Jesus Christ, that he is treated as if he had never sinned; and this is imported in the declaration that he is justified. We are, however, not to conceive of these as separate blessings. It is not true that one sinner is justified, and another merely pardoned: but every penitent believer is both pardoned and justified. As repentance and faith are duties mutually implying each other, so pardon and justification are twin blessings of grace, bestowed together through Jesus Christ. All whom Jesus delivers from the wrath to come are freely justified from all things, and presented faultless before the presence of his glory.

Justification is attributed, in the Scriptures, to the blood and the obedience of Christ: "Being justified by his blood, we shall be saved from wrath through him."[2] "By the obedience of one, shall many be made righteous."[3] Both his blood and his obedience were necessary to magnify the law, and make it honorable. His blood signifies the endurance of its penalty; and his obedience, the fulfilment of its precepts. On his endurance of the penalty, our deliverance from wrath is based; and on his fulfilment of the precepts, our complete justification before God. Justification, however, could not be complete, without deliverance from the penalty; and it therefore required both the blood and the obedience of Christ; or, in the language of Scripture, "his obedience unto death."

Justification is by faith. On this point, the Scriptures are explicit. "Being justified by faith, we have peace with God."[4] By him all that believe are justified from all things.[5] Faith does not justify, because of its own merit. Other graces co-exist with it in the heart of the believer; as repentance, love, &c. And these have equal claim to merit; and especially love, which is the fulfilling of the law,[6] but faith is selected as the justifying grace; and Paul assigns the reason, "It is of faith, that it might be by

---

[1] Job xxvii. 5.
[2] Rom. v. 9.
[3] Rom. v. 19.
[4] Rom. v. 1.
[5] Acts xiii. 39.
[6] Rom. xiii. 10.

grace."[1] In the very exercise of faith, merit is renounced, and the sole reliance is placed on the merit of Christ. Hence faith is opposed to works: "To him that worketh not, but believeth on him that justifieth the ungodly, his faith is counted for righteousness."[2] In faith, the sinner as ungodly comes to God, who justifies the ungodly,[3] through Christ, who died for the ungodly.[4] He presents no plea, and entertains no hope, founded on personal merit, but relies wholly on the blood and obedience of Christ. Faith is an exercise of the believer's mind; and, as such, it is as much a work as repentance or love, and it produces other works: for, "Faith worketh by love."[5] But it is not as a work, or as producing other works, that faith justifies; but as renouncing all personal merit and self-reliance, and receiving salvation as a gift of free grace through Jesus Christ.

In justification, righteousness is imputed, accounted, or reckoned. "David describeth the blessedness of the man unto whom God imputeth righteousness.[6] Abraham believed God, and it was counted unto him for righteousness:[7] "For us, also, to whom it shall be imputed, if we believe."[8]

How God can justly account an ungodly man righteous, is a problem which it required infinite wisdom to solve. How it was solved Paul has informed us. Him hath "God set forth to be a propitiation through faith in his blood, to declare his righteousness for the remission of sins that are past through the forbearance of God; to declare I say at this time his righteousness, that he might be just, and the justifier of him that believeth in Jesus."[9] The propitiatory sacrifice of Christ, and faith in that sacrifice, are the means which God employs for the solution of the difficult problem: and these solve it completely; God himself, the perfectly just one, being judge. We may not be able fully to understand the solution, and perceive all its fitness and beauty; but we may learn much respecting it, from the light which the Scriptures throw on it; and, where we fail to comprehend, we ought patiently to wait for the further light which eternity will disclose.

When the Scriptures speak of justification by the obedience or

---

[1] Rom. iv. 16.   [2] Rom. iv. 5.   [3] Rom. iv. 5.
[4] Rom. v. 6.   [5] Gal. v. 6.   [6] Rom. iv. 6.
[7] Rom. iv. 3.   [8] Rom. iv. 24.   [9] Rom. iii. 25, 26

blood of Christ, faith is supposed; otherwise, those passages which
speak of justification by faith, would be without meaning. And
in like manner, when they speak of justification by faith, the
obedience and blood of Christ are supposed; otherwise, it would
be unmeaning to say, "Justified by his blood:" "By his obedience many are made righteous." What Christ did and suffered,
and also our faith in Christ, are necessary to effect our justification; and the part which each of these has in the process, is an
interesting subject of inquiry.

We have already seen that faith does not justify as a meritorious
work. If it justified on the ground of merit, it would need to
possess sufficient merit to satisfy all the demands of the law, both
preceptive and penal; and in that case the obedience and sufferings
of Christ would be unnecessary. It is not jointly meritorious with
the obedience and sufferings of Christ; for they are in themselves
perfect: and, without addition from the works of the sinner, magnify the law and make it honorable. Christ, and Christ alone, is
the end of the law for righteousness, to every one that believeth.[1]
Faith disclaims all merit of its own, but receives Christ as the propitiation that God has set forth, and, as the end of the law, fully
satisfying all its claims. Faith distinguishes those to whom righteousness is imputed: "it is unto all, and upon all them that believe;"[2] but it is not, in itself, either in whole or in part, the meritorious cause of justification.

But merit is ascribed, in the word of God, to the obedience and
sufferings of Christ. His blood is represented as a price paid, and
a price of such value, that our deliverence from under the law may,
on the ground of it, be justly claimed: "Ye were not redeemed
with corruptible things, as silver and gold; but with the precious
blood of Christ."[3] "He was made under the law, to redeem them
that were under the law."[4]

"Ye are not your own: ye are bought with a price."[5] As a com-
modity may be claimed, when its full value has been paid, and the
purchase completed; so our deliverance from the condemnation of
the law, and our justification before God, may be claimed on the
merits of Christ's obedience and sufferings. Avenging justice is

---

[1] Rom. x. 4.   [2] Rom. iii. 22.   [3] 1 Pet. i. 18, 19.
[4] Gal. iv. 5.   [5] 1 Cor. vi. 19, 29.

satisfied: "He is the propitiation for our sins."[1] "The Lord is well pleased for his righteousness' sake."[2] He gave himself an offering and a sacrifice to God of sweet smelling savor."[3]

When the Scriptures speak of Christ's blood as the ground of our justification, his obedience is supposed: and, on the other hand, when his obedience is mentioned, his sufferings are supposed. His obedience to the precepts of the law would not have sufficed, if he had not also endured its penalty: and if, while enduring his sufferings, he had not loved God with all his heart, his sacrifice would have been polluted. A lamb without spot was needed; and perfect obedience was therefore necessary to render his offering acceptable. His active and passive obedience are both necessary to make a complete salvation; and when only one is mentioned in the Scriptures, the other is supposed.

In being made under the law, Christ became our substitute; and his obedience and sufferings are placed to our account, as if we had personally obeyed and suffered, to the full satisfaction of the law. We are thus justified by the righteousness of Christ imputed to us: "He who knew no sin, was made sin for us, that we might be made the righteousness of God in him."[4] Our sins were imputed to Christ when he died for them; and his righteousness is imputed to us when we receive eternal life through him. He was treated as if he had personally committed the sins which were laid on him: and all who believe in him are treated as if they had personally rendered that satisfaction to the law which was rendered by his obedience and sufferings.

Nothing can be accounted the meritorious cause of justification, but the obedience and sufferings of Christ: yet faith is indispensable: "He that believeth not the Son shall not see life; and the wrath of God abideth on him."[5] By him all that believe are justified.[6] Faith, then, is the turning point, by which a sinner's condition is determined. In God's method of grace, all the benefits of Christ's satisfaction to the law are made over to the sinner, as soon as he believes: and faith, therefore, serves to him instead of a perfect personal obedience to the law. On his believing in Christ, he is treated as if he had personally rendered a perfect

---

[1] 1 John ii. 2. [2] Isaiah xlii. 21. [3] Eph. v. 2.
[4] 2 Cor. v. 21. [5] John iii. 36. [6] Acts xiii. 39.

obedience to the law: and this is the import of those Scriptures which say that faith is imputed to him for righteousness. It is not so imputed, because of any merit which it possesses; but because it is that which the Gospel recognises in the sinner as entitling him to the full satisfaction that Christ has rendered. When faith is said to be imputed for righteousness, the obedience and sufferings of Christ, on which faith lays hold, are viewed as connected with it, and constituting the meritorious ground of its acceptance.

That the sin or righteousness of one should be imputed to another, has been thought by some to be inconsistent with the principles of justice, the province of which is, to give to every man his due. From some cause, the notion of imputation has prevailed in all ages, in the sacrifices which have been offered, both by divine authority and by heathen worshippers. This notion has the full authority of God's word, and evidently lies at the foundation of the salvation which infinite wisdom and goodness have provided for guilty men. It would, therefore, be extreme folly in us to reject this salvation because of an objection which may arise to our erring reason, in determining the abstract principles of justice. There is no higher rule of justice than God himself; and what the Judge of all does, must be right.

In explaining the imputation of Adam's sin, we showed that there is a threefold union between Adam and his posterity, rendering the imputation of his sin to them an act of justice. There is, in like manner, a threefold union between Christ and his people, rendering the imputation of their sin to him, and of his righteousness to them, consistent with justice.

1. There is a union *of consent.* Christ consented to the righteousness of the law, in its condemnation of his people, and to the necessity of satisfaction: and they do the same. He consented to become a substitute for them, and render the required satisfaction in their behalf: and they joyfully accept the favor. While in impenitence and unbelief, they do not approve the law, or its sentence, and do not acknowledge the obligation to make satisfaction. When they become sensible of this obligation, the first effort is to make satisfaction in their own persons. In this state of mind their consent with Christ is only partial; and the Gospel does not pronounce them justified. But when they become con-

vinced of their utter inability to render satisfaction in their own persons, they give themselves up to Christ, and not only consent, but pray to be found in him, not having their own righteousness, but the righteousness which is of God by faith.

How the union of Christ and his people rendered it just in God to inflict the penalty of their sins on him, and to justify them, we cannot claim fully to understand. God knows well what his moral government requires; and as he has approved the arrangement, we may be sure it must be right. We may hope to obtain further knowledge of this glorious mystery when the counsels of infinite wisdom are unfolded to our view in the future world.

But even here we may see, in part, a fitness in the procedure. Without the consent of Christ, we cannot suppose that justice would have laid our iniquities on him: and, without the consent to be saved by him, which faith yields, we cannot understand how justice would have been honored in our being justified. As the consent of Adam's descendants to the deed of their father, in rebelling against the law of his Sovereign, justifies the imputation of his sin to them; so the consent of Christ and his people to the divine scheme of grace, justifies what is done to them both in the execution of the scheme.

2. There is a *spiritual* union. As Adam was the natural head of his posterity, so Christ is the spiritual head of his people. Adam's descendants are born from him according to the flesh, and possess the nature which existed in him as its beginning or fountain. Christ's people are born of the Spirit, and possess the spirit which was in Christ without measure; so that, "If any man have not the spirit of Christ, he is none of his."[1] This union is like that of the head and members of the human body: and by one spirit believers are all baptised into this one body."[2] It is like the union of the vine and its branches; through all which the same vitalizing and fructifying sap circulates. This union secures the perfect consent, which has already been noticed, between Christ and his people; and further illustrates the fitness of that arrangement by which they are regarded as one in the administration of God's moral government.

3. There is a *federal* union. As Adam was the federal head

---

[1] Rom. viii. 9.   [2] 1 Cor. xii. 13.

and representative of his descendants; so Christ stood, in the covenant of grace, as the federal head and representative of all whom the Father gave to him. For their sakes he undertook the work of mediation; and for their sakes he did and suffered all that was necessary to the full execution of the work. Justice, and every other attribute of the divine nature, concurred in the arrangement, by which he was to see of the travail of his soul and be satisfied; and by the knowledge of him to justify many.[1] And now, justice, and every other attribute of the divine nature, fully sanction the arrangement, by which his righteousness is imputed to all his elect people, on their believing in him. "Who shall lay anything to the charge of God's elect? It is God that justifieth. Who is he that condemneth? It is Christ that died."[2]

The imputation of Adam's sin to his posterity, is an act of justice; the imputation of Christ's righteousness to believers, is an act of grace. The former is on the proper level of justice; but the latter rises above it. Justice has nothing to say against it, but, on the contrary, is fully satisfied and abundantly honored by it; yet the plan did not originate in the justice, but in the love, of God, which provided the needed sacrifice. This distinction ought never to be forgotten. If our condemnation, in our natural state, is not just, our deliverance from it is of debt, and not of grace. When we feel, in every power of our minds, that we are justly condemned before God, and that his wrath is our righteous due; we can then receive Christ and salvation by him, as the gift of God, the free gift, the unspeakable gift, of his grace.

The Apostle James says: "A man is justified by works, and not by faith only."[3] In this he appears, at first view, to contradict the words of Paul: "A man is justified by faith, without deeds of the law."[4] James has assigned a reason, which furnishes a clue that leads to a perfect reconciliation of this apparent contradiction: "For," says he, "faith without works is dead."[5] Faith alone, is dead faith; and dead faith, according to his teaching, does not justify; and this doctrine, Paul does not contradict. The justifying faith of Paul, is living, working faith. He says expressly: "Faith works by love."[6] James does not exclude faith from justification;

---

[1] Isaiah liii. 11.   [2] Rom. viii. 33, 34.   [3] James ii. 24.
[4] Rom. iii. 28.   [5] James ii. 17.   [6] Gal. v. 6.

but, on the contrary, introduces works, not as excluding faith, but as making it perfect: "By works was faith made perfect."[1] As thus perfected, faith justifies, according to his teaching: and this is precisely what Paul teaches. The works which Paul excludes, are not works of faith, but works of law—not works, evidencing the genuineness and vitality of faith; but works, claiming to be, in whole, or in part, the meritorious cause of justification. Such works are excluded, because they would imply an imperfection in Christ's work, and give the sinner a ground of glorying. It is manifest that James insists on works, merely as evidences of faith: "Show me thy faith without thy works, and I will show thee my faith by my works."[2] Even words, as well as works, are necessary, to give evidence of faith: "With the heart, man believeth unto righteousness; and with the mouth, confession is made unto salvation."[3] So far as words prove the presence or absence of faith, it is true, that, "By thy words thou shalt be justified; and by thy words thou shalt be condemned."[4] But words without works, avail nothing; for Christ teaches that, "Not every one that saith Lord, Lord, shall enter into the kingdom of heaven: but he that doeth the will of my Father who is in heaven."[5] And words and works together, avail nothing, without faith; for, whatever a man may say or do, if he believe not, he "shall be damned."

A difference of opinion has existed as to the proper date of justification. Some have regarded the day of judgment as its proper date. It is an act of God, as Judge; and, in the judgment of the great day, the Judge will publicly pronounce, on every individual, the sentence which will determine his condition through eternity. Then God's judgments will be fully revealed; but a partial revelation of them is made in the present life: "Even now, the wrath of God is revealed from heaven against all ungodliness, and unrighteousness of men, who hold the truth in unrighteousness."[6] It is true, "He that believeth not, *shall be* damned;"[7] but it is also true, "He that believeth not, *is condemned already*."[8] In like manner, it is true that Christ will publicly own his people in the great day, and pronounce the final sentence in their favor;

---

[1] James ii. 22.   [2] James ii. 18.   [3] Rom. x. 10.
[4] Matt. xii. 37.   [5] Matt. vii. 21.   [6] Rom. i. 18.
[7] Mark xvi. 16.   [8] John iii. 18.

18

but it is also true, that they are justified in the present life. Hence Paul says: "Ye *are justified* in the name of our Lord Jesus Christ."[1] "All that believe *are justified* from all things."[2] The same rule by which the eternal state of men will be determined in the great day, is now made known on the authority of him who will sit on the throne of judgment then, and who is now the Judge of all the earth. By this revelation, men are already condemned or justified, according to their character. That character is often secret here. In the great day, God will judge the secrets of all hearts; but he will not establish a new rule of judgment: so far as that rule has been correctly applied here, its decision will be confirmed in the last day by the final sentence.

Some have dated justification in eternity past, regarding it as grace given in Christ Jesus before the world began. Justification is not a secret purpose in the bosom of God, but a revelation from him, and therefore it cannot be eternal. It implies, not only the accounting of the sinner righteous, but the declaring of him righteous; otherwise, it would not be the opposite of condemnation; and neither justification nor condemnation can be from eternity. God's purpose to justify is eternal, and so is his purpose to glorify; but it is as improper to say that believers are justified from eternity, as to say that they are glorified from eternity. It is clearly the doctrine of Scripture, that, on believing in Christ, men pass from a state of condemnation into a state of justification.

Section III.—ADOPTION.

GOD ADOPTS, AS SONS, ALL WHO BELIEVE IN JESUS CHRIST.[3]

In adoption, as practised among men, an individual receives the son of another into his family, and confers on him the same privileges and advantages, as if he were his own son. In this sense, God adopts all who believe in Jesus Christ: "We are all the children of God by faith in Jesus Christ."[4] "Behold what manner of love the Father hath bestowed on us, that we should be called the sons of God."[5] This blessing of grace rises higher than justifi-

---

[1] 1 Cor. vi. 11.   [2] Acts xiii. 39.
[3] John i. 12; Rom. viii. 17; Gal. iii.26; 1John iii. 1, 2.
[4] Gal. iii. 26.   [5] 1 John iii. 1.

cation. Though a judge may fully acquit one who is arraigned before him on a charge of crime, he does not confer, on the man so acquitted, any of the privileges or advantages which belong to a son. But the believer in Jesus is permitted to regard God, not only as a justifying Judge, but as a reconciled and affectionate Father. The problem, how he can be put among the children,[1] has been solved. Though once afar off, he has been brought nigh by the blood of Christ, and made of the household of God.[2]

Among the privileges and advantages which adoption secures, we may enumerate the following:

1. The love of God, as a kind Father, is secured to believers. The Scriptures frequently exhibit the love of God to his people, under the figure of a Father's love to his children: "As a Father pitieth his children, so the Lord pitieth them that fear him."[3] "If ye, being evil, know how to give good gifts to your children, how much more shall your heavenly Father give good things to them that ask him."[4] "Your Father knoweth that ye have need of these things."[5] Corresponding with this encouraging and delightful exhibition of God's love, is the confidence with which the believer in Christ is inspired to approach his heavenly Father: "Because ye are sons, God has sent forth the Spirit of his Son into your hearts, crying Abba, Father."[6] Hence Christ habitually spoke to his disciples of God as their Father, and, before he left them, said, in language full of endearment and encouragement: "I ascend to my Father and your Father;"[7] and hence he taught them to say, in their daily prayers: "Our Father, who art in heaven."[8]

2. The discipline of God, as a kind and wise Father, is secured to all who believe in Jesus: "Whom the Lord loveth, he chasteneth and scourgeth every son whom he receiveth."[9] "We have had fathers of our flesh which corrected us, and we gave them reverence. Shall we not much rather be in subjection to the Father of Spirits and live?"[10] "For they verily for a few days chastened us after their own pleasure; but he for our profit, that we might be

---

[1] Jer. iii. 19.　　[2] Eph. ii. 13, 19.　　[3] Ps. ciii. 13.
[4] Matt. vii. 11.　　[5] Matt. vi. 32.　　[6] Rom. viii. 15.
[7] John xx. 17.　　[8] Matt. vi. 9.　　[9] Heb. xii. 6.
[10] Heb. xii. 9.

partakers of his holiness."[1] Inestimably rich is this blessing of divine discipline. Let the wealthy and noble of the earth rejoice in the advantages which give them distinction among men, and supply them with the means of carnal enjoyment; but let the afflicted believer in Jesus, rejoice in the lot which God has assigned him, because it has been chosen for him by a Father who knows what is best for him, and who loves him so tenderly as to withhold from him no good thing. Having all good in heaven and earth at his disposal, he has selected that portion for each of his children on earth, which will best promote their highest interest.

3. Believers in Christ are made heirs of God: "If children, then heirs of God, and joint heirs with Jesus Christ."[2] God, the creator of all things, is the proprietor of all things, and his adopted children are made heirs of this vast estate. "He that overcometh, shall inherit all things."[3] "All things are yours, and Christ is appointed heir of all things; and believers are co-heirs with him."[4]

The inheritance of God's children, is frequently represented as a kingdom: "Fear not, little flock, it is your Father's good pleasure to give you the kingdom."[5] "Come, ye blessed of my Father, inherit the kingdom."[6]

The adoption of believers does not take full effect in the present life: "We are waiting for the adoption, the redemption of the body;" "waiting for the manifestation of the sons of God."[7] Flesh and blood cannot inherit the kingdom; and, therefore, this vile body must be changed, and fashioned like the glorious body of Christ, before we can receive the glory and joy which God has prepared for us. Yet the title to the inheritance is made sure, since we are co-heirs with Christ; and the promise and oath of God, two immutable things in which it is impossible for God to lie,[8] give to the heirs of promise, the strongest possible assurance, that they shall receive the inheritance: "Beloved, now are we the sons of God; and it doth not yet appear what we shall be; but we know, that when he shall appear, we shall be like him, for we shall see him as he is."[9] Though now in exile, and pilgrims and strangers in the earth, perhaps despised and forsaken, we are the children

---

[1] Heb. xii. 10.
[2] Rom. viii. 17.
[3] Rev. xxi .7.
[4] 1 Cor. iii. 22.
[5] Luke xii. 32.
[6] Matt. xxv. 34.
[7] Rom. viii. 19.
[8] Heb. vi. 18.
[9] 1 John iii. 2.

of God, and heirs of an inheritance which is incorruptible, undefiled, and fadeth not away. Even now, whatever may be our
poverty, affliction, or reproach, we are the objects of our Father's
care, and he gives us, as an earnest of the future inheritance, so
much of it in present enjoyment, as he sees to be best for us. All
things within the boundless dominion of Jehovah, work together
for good, to them that love God.[1]

Section IV.—REGENERATION.

In all who are finally saved, the Holy Spirit produces
a great moral change, by which they become inclined to
holiness.[2]

In our natural state we are totally depraved. No inclination to
holiness exists in the carnal heart; and no holy act can be performed,
or service to God rendered, until the heart is changed. This change,
it is the office of the Holy Spirit to effect. Pardon, justification,
and adoption, are changes in a man's condition; but if no other
change were wrought, the man would remain a slave to sin, and
unfit for the service and enjoyment of God. Grace, therefore,
does not stop with a mere change of condition, but it effects also
that change in the character, without which the individual could
not participate in the holy enjoyments of heaven, or be fitted for
the society of the blessed.

Various forms of expression are employed in the Scriptures, to
denote the change of heart; and they signify it with various
shades of meaning. It is taking away the heart of stone, and
giving a heart of flesh;[3] giving a new heart;[4] putting the law in
the heart;[5] quickening or making alive;[6] a resurrection from the
dead; an illumination;[7] a conversion, or turning back to God.[8]
So great is the change produced, that the subject of it is called a
new creature,[9] as if proceeding, like Adam, directly from the

---

[1] Rom. viii. 28.

[2] John iii. 5, 6; Ezek. xi. 19; xxxvi. 26, 27; xxxvii. 14; Tit. iii. 5; James
i. 18; 2 Cor. v. 17; 1 John iv. 8.

[3] Ezek. xxxvi. 26.   [4] Ezek. xviii. 31.   [5] Heb. viii. 10.

[6] John vi. 63; Eph. ii. 1; Rom. vi. 11, 13.   [7] Heb. x. 32.

[8] Ps. li. 13; Matt. xviii. 3; Ps. xxv. 16; Isaiah lix. 20.

[9] 2 Cor. v. 17; Gal. vi. 15.

creating hand of God; and he is said to be renewed,[1] as being restored to the image of God, in which man was originally formed. With reference to the mode in which the descendants of Adam come into the world, the change is denominated regeneration;[2] and the subjects of it are said to be born again.[3]

The change is moral. The body is unchanged; and the identity of the mind is not destroyed. The individual is conscious of being the same person that he was before; but a new direction is given to the active powers of the mind, and new affections are brought into exercise. The love of God is shed abroad in the heart by the Holy Ghost.[4] No love to God had previously existed there; for the carnal heart is enmity against God. Love is the fulfilling of the law, the principle of all holy obedience; and when love is produced in the heart, the law of God is written there. As a new principle of action, inciting to a new mode of life, it renders the man a new creature. The production of love in the heart by the Holy Spirit, is the regeneration, or the new birth; for " he that loveth, is born of God.[5]

The mode in which the Holy Spirit effects this change, is beyond our investigation. All God's ways are unsearchable; and we might as well attempt to explain how he created the world, as how he new-creates the soul. With reference to this subject, the Saviour said, " The wind bloweth where it listeth, and thou hearest the sound thereof, but canst not tell whence it cometh, or whither it goeth; so is every one that is born of the Spirit."[6]

We know, from the Holy Scriptures, that God employs his truth in the regeneration of the soul. " Of his own will begat he us with the word of truth."[7] Love to God necessarily implies knowledge of God, and this knowledge it is the province of truth to impart. But knowledge is not always connected with love. The devils know, but do not love; and wicked men delight not to retain the knowledge of God,[8] because their knowledge of him is not connected with love. The mere presentation of the truth to the mind, is not all that is needed, in producing love to God in the

---

[1] Col. iii. 10; Rom. xii. 2; Tit. iii. 5.   [2] Tit. iii. 5.
[3] John iii. 3, 7; 1 Pet. i. 23.   [4] Rom. v. 5.
[5] 1 John iv. 7.   [6] John iii. 8.   [7] James i. 18.
[8] Rom. i. 28.

heart. What accompanying influence the Holy Spirit uses, to render the word effectual, we cannot explain: but Paul refers to it, when he says, "Our gospel came not unto you in word only, but also in power, and in the Holy Ghost."[1]—"but in the demonstration of the Spirit, and with power."[2]

The term regeneration is sometimes used in a comprehensive sense, as including the whole formation of the Christian character. At other times it is used for the first production of divine love in the heart. In the latter sense, the work is instantaneous. There is a moment known only to God, when the first holy affection exists in the soul. Truth may enter gradually, and may excite strong affections in the mind, and may for a time increase the hatred of God which naturally reigns in the heart. So Paul says, "Sin, taking occasion by the commandment, wrought in me all manner of concupiscence."[3] But, in his own time and manner, God, the Holy Spirit, makes the word effectual in producing a new affection in the soul: and, when the first movement of love to God exists, the first throb of spiritual life commences.

Faith is necessary to the Christian character; and must therefore precede regeneration, when this is understood in its widest sense. Even in the restricted sense, in which it denotes the beginning of the spiritual life, faith, in the sense in which James[4] uses the term, may precede. But a faith which exists before the beginning of spiritual life, cannot be a living faith. Yet some have maintained that faith produces love. This opinion is of sufficient importance to demand a careful consideration.

The power of faith over the actions, the conscience, and the affections of the heart, every one must admit. Confidence placed in a treacherous man, has often led to a course of action ruinous in its effects on the condition and character. A belief in false principles of morality blinds the conscience, and causes it to approve the wrong, and condemn the right. We may love or hate an individual, under a mistaken view of his character; and our affection towards him may be completely changed, by a better acquaintance with him. Now, it may be asked, does not dislike

[1] 1 Thess. i. 5. [2] 1 Cor. ii. 4.
[3] Rom. vii. 8. [4] James ii. 17.

of God proceed from a wrong view of his character, and will not a true knowledge of him infallibly produce love?

That hatred of God, and a wrong view of his character, accompany each other, no one can deny; but which of these produces the other, ought not to be assumed without investigation. We readily judge well concerning those whom we love, and ill concerning those whom we dislike. Men's interests pervert their judgments. In a deliberative assembly, parties are formed, according to the interests of individuals; and men take sides according to the circumstances which influence the heart. In these cases, the affections control the faith. The affections and the faith mutually influence each other, and if either be wrong, the other cannot be perfectly right. The enmity to God which rules in the hearts of unregenerate men, renders their view of his character incorrect. A perfectly correct view cannot co-exist with enmity to him: and yet it does not follow that love to him may be produced, by giving right views of his character.

Some have maintained the opinion that a revelation of God's love to us is sufficient to produce love to him. That it ought to do so, cannot be denied; and in a heart under no evil bias, it would produce this effect. We may rather say, that a heart in which no evil bias exists, will love God, on receiving a revelation of his general character, without waiting for evidence of special favor. If our love to God proceeds from a belief that he loves us in particular, it is merely a modification of self-love. Such love has no moral excellence in it; for "sinners love those that love them."[1] Some have supposed, that the faith of devils differs from the faith of Christians in the circumstance, that it sees in God no manifestation of love towards them; and therefore can produce no love in their hearts towards God. But this opinion regards the faith which distinguishes the people of God, and purifies their hearts, as possessing no moral excellence in its nature. The circumstances in which it is exercised, do not make its nature better. If it may consist with perfect hatred to God, it cannot have moral excellence in itself, or tend to produce moral purity.

An inspired writer has said, "We love him, because he first loved us:"[2] but these words do not teach, that our love to God

_____

[1] Luke vi. 32.   [2] 1 John iv. 19.

originates in the conviction that we are the favorites of his love. The love of God towards us, operates both as an efficient, and as a motive. 1. As an efficient cause. "For his great love wherewith he loved us,[1] when we were dead in sin, hath quickened us together with Christ." Here is an operation entirely distinct from that of mere motive. The dead body of Christ in the grave, was quickened by the Spirit; and a like power quickens the dead soul. "We believe according to the working of his mighty power, which he wrought in Christ, when he raised him from the dead."[2] Here faith itself is ascribed to this divine operation. All this operation proceeds from God's great love wherewith he hath loved us. It is plain, therefore, that this love operates as an efficient cause, before it operates as a motive to holiness. It cannot operate as a motive without faith; and faith is produced by its efficient power. After this efficiency has quickened the dead soul, the love of God towards us then operates. 2. As a motive. The goodness of God leads to repentance, and every attribute and act of God has a tendency to call forth the love of the heart, when in the right state. Nothing so effectually melts the heart, as a view of God's great love towards us, while we were yet sinners: and of Christ's love in giving himself for us: but many a heart has felt this melting influence, without having in view the personal benefit to be received from this love. Our love to God does not produce a disregard to our own happiness, but it rises above the consideration of it. It is, therefore, not a modification of self-love.

This divine operation, which is additional to the motive power of truth, proceeds from what has been called the direct influence of the Spirit. Truth, as contained in the Holy Scriptures, is a revelation from the Holy Spirit; and as men's words, whether spoken or written, have an influence on the minds of other men, so the words of the Holy Spirit have an influence on the minds of all who read the Bible, or hear the gospel preached. In this indirect way, the Holy Spirit operates on men's minds, as the author of a book operates on all who read his work. But this indirect influence is by means of truth as a motive power; and no mere motive, operating on the sinner's heart, can induce him to love God for his own sake. While self-love rules in the mind, all

---

[1] Eph. ii. 4, 5.   [2] Eph. i. 19. 20.

motives derive their power from their relation to the ruling principle; and cannot, therefore, establish a higher principle of action. This change, by which true love to God is produced, results from the direct influence of the Holy Spirit, accompanying his word, and making it effectual. It was this direct influence which rendered the word so effectual on the day of Pentecost,[1] which opened Lydia's heart,[2] so that she attended to the things that were spoken by Paul ;—which gave the increase when Paul planted, and Apollos watered,[3]—and which has ever brought the word to the heart, in demonstration of the Spirit, and with power.[4]

The doctrine of the Holy Spirit's direct influence, is a fundamental truth of the gospel dispensation. That Jesus Christ has come in the flesh, and completed the great work for which he assumed our nature, is a truth that lies at the foundation of Christianity. The gospel reveals to us the Spirit as well as the Son. When about to leave the world, Jesus promised another Comforter, who should dwell with his disciples for ever. The Holy Spirit, as God, had always been in the world: but he was now to be present by a peculiar manifestation and operation. This manifestation and operation attended the ministry of the Word on the day of Pentecost, and the gospel has always been the sword of the Spirit,[5] the instrument with which he operates in the fulfilment of his office for which he has come into the world, in answer to the prayer of Christ.

The experience of mankind, before the coming of Christ, prepared the way for the introduction of his religion. The wise men of the world had sought to know God, but their laborious research had been ineffectual. Some other means of knowledge was, by their failure, proved to be necessary: "After that in the wisdom of God, the world by wisdom knew not God, it pleased God by the foolishness of preaching to save them that believe."[6] While an experiment was made in the heathen world, demonstrating the necessity of revelation, another was in progress among the people of Israel, under the Mosaic dispensation, demonstrating the inefficiency of revelation, unless accompanied by direct influence of the Holy Spirit. The Israelites had this great advantage over the

---

[1] Acts ii.   [2] Acts xvi.   [3] 1 Cor. iii.
[4] 1 Cor. ii. 4.   [5] Eph. vi. 17.   [6] 1 Cor. i. 21.

heathen world, that to them were committed the oracles of God.[1] The Scriptures, given by inspiration from God, were in their possession: and God spoke to them at sundry times and in divers manners, by prophets whom he raised up among them, and inspired to declare his will. That these prophets, with their burdens of divine messages, might arrive in due time, God represents himself as rising up early and sending them.[2] So abundant were the means of religious knowledge granted them, that God said, "What could have been done more to my vineyard, that I have not done in it?"[3] Yet, with all this advantage, they turned away from the God of Israel, and provoked him to anger. Another influence was needed, to produce love and obedience to God. Hence it was said, by the prophet Jeremiah, "Behold, the days come, saith the Lord, that I will perform that good thing which I have promised unto the house of Israel, and to the house of Judah."[4] This new covenant is explained in the Epistle to the Hebrews,[5] to be the spiritual dispensation of the gospel. Its grand peculiarity is, that the law of God is written in the heart. The Israelites had the revelation from God written on stone and parchment, but it was not in their hearts; and a new divine influence was needed to put it there. This new divine influence was promised by the prophet, and the promise has been fulfilled in the direct influence of the Holy Spirit, the gift of which characterizes the gospel dispensation as the ministration of the Spirit.[6] The saints of God, under the former dispensation, received this influence of the Holy Spirit, and to them also was the gospel preached.[7] The privileges and blessings of the future dispensation, were, by anticipation, bestowed on them; and the Christ to come was made their Saviour, as if he had already appeared and fulfilled his work. But the abundant influence of the Holy Spirit was reserved for the times following the ascension of Christ, and from that day he dwells in the Church, and makes the bodies of believers his temple. This peculiar presence implies the peculiar influence by which the truth is put into the heart; that is, by which men are made to love the truth. The whole Mosaic dispensation was an experiment, demonstrating the

---

[1] Rom. iii. 2.　　　[2] Jer. xxxii. 33.　　　[3] Isaiah v. 4.
[4] Jer. xxxiii. 14.　　[5] Heb. viii.　　　[6] 2 Cor. iii. 8.
[7] Heb. iv. 2; Gal. iii. 8.

necessity of this peculiar influence. That covenant did not promise this blessing, and God found fault with it, because it did not secure the obedience of his people. The experiment was made, in his wisdom, not for his information, but for our benefit; and, by the failure of that covenant, we are enabled better to estimate the value of the blessing that distinguishes the covenant founded on better promises.

That philosophy which shuts God out of his creation, and substitutes laws of nature for his ever-present influence and operation, stands ready to deny the doctrine of the Holy Spirit's direct influence. It admits not the possibility of any influence, but that which the means employed naturally tend to produce. But means have no natural efficiency apart from the will of God. By the will of God, the truth has its regenerating and sanctifying power; for he works in us to will and to do, according to his pleasure.[1] It belongs to the Holy Spirit, in the economy of grace, to produce divine life in the soul, as he brooded over the face of the waters, at creation, reducing the chaotic mass to order, and filling it with life. He is pleased to work with means; and he employs the truth as his instrument of operation. This instrument he wields at his pleasure, and he renders it effectual by his divine power: "My word shall not return unto me void, but it shall accomplish that which I please, and it shall prosper in the thing whereto I sent it."[2] By the ordinary providence of God, the Bible operates in the world, and influences the minds of men: but this providence equally existed in the former dispensation, in which the oracles of God were possessed by the Israelites, but held by them in unrighteousness. An influence above the ordinary providence of God is needed, to the regeneration of the soul. The coming of Christ into the world, and the coming and abiding of the Holy Spirit, belong to a dispensation which is above the ordinary providence of God. Into this new economy we are ushered, when we are translated into the kingdom of God's dear Son. Here we recognise both the Son and the Spirit, as specially given of God. It is contrary to the faith of the gospel to regard Christ and his redeeming work, as things of God's ordinary providence; and it is equally

---

[1] Phil. ii. 13.   [2] Isaiah lv. 11.

contrary to faith to consider the Spirit and his work in the heart as merely natural influence of the truth on the heart.

Section V.—SANCTIFICATION.

THE HOLY SPIRIT CONTINUES TO SANCTIFY THOSE WHOM HE HAS REGENERATED, AND FINALLY PREPARES THEM FULLY FOR THE HOLY SERVICE AND ENJOYMENT OF HEAVEN.[1]

Regeneration is the beginning of sanctification, but the work is not completed at the outset. A new affection is produced in the heart, but it does not govern without opposition. The love of the world, the love of self, and all the carnal appetites and passions, have reigned in the heart; and the power of habit gives them a controlling influence, which is not readily yielded. Hence arises the warfare of which every regenerate man is conscious: the flesh lusting against the Spirit, and the Spirit against the flesh.[2] In this struggle, the carnal propensities often threaten to prevail, and they would prevail, if God did not give a supply of the Spirit of Jesus Christ. "Without me," said Jesus, "ye can do nothing."[3] If severed from the living vine, the branches are sapless, fruitless, dead. But "he that is joined to the Lord is one Spirit;"[4] and the Spirit of life from Christ, the head, flows through all the members of his body, and gives and preserves their vitality. This Spirit in them lusteth against the flesh, and enables them to carry on their warfare, and gives them final victory: "He that hath begun a good work in you, will perform it until the day of Jesus Christ."[5]

As in the beginning, so in the progress of the work, the Holy Spirit operates by direct and by indirect influence. The indirect influence is by means of the truth. With reference to this, the Saviour prayed: "Sanctify them through thy truth;"[6] and, with reference to it, the Scriptures connect "belief of the truth," with "sanctification of the Spirit;"[7] and speak of the heart being purified by faith.[8] The direct influence fixes the affections on the truth; or, in the language of Scripture, "writes the law in the heart."[9]

---

[1] 2 Thess. ii. 13; 1 Pet. i. 2; 1 Cor. vi. 11; 2 Cor. iii. 18; Mal. iii. 3; Eph. v. 26; Tit. ii. 14; Prov. iv. 18; Phil. i. 6; 1 John iii. 2.
[2] Gal. v. 17.　　　　[3] John xv. 5.　　　　[4] 1 Cor. vi. 17.
[5] Phil. i. 6.　　　　[6] John xvii. 17.　　　　[7] 2 Thess. ii. 13.
[8] Acts xv. 9.　　　　[9] Heb. x. 16.

The mode in which this direct influence is exerted, we cannot explain; but the result is, that the truth produces its proper effect, which otherwise it would fail to accomplish, through the depravity of the heart. Our carnal affections tend to shut out the truth from the heart; hence Christ said: "How can ye believe, which receive honor one of another, and seek not the honor that cometh from God only ?"[1]   While carnal affections tend to prevent the proper influence of the truth, the Spirit exercises an opposite influence, and "lusts against the flesh." As this influence gives the word an efficacy which it would not otherwise possess, it is something superadded to the intrinsic power of the word. For this direct influence, the Psalmist prays: "Open thou mine eyes, that I may behold wondrous things out of thy law;"[2] and for this, the prayers recorded in the New Testament were offered: "Lord, increase our faith."[3]   "Lord, I believe; help thou mine unbelief."[4] This influence operated on the two disciples, when their understandings were opened, that they understood the Scriptures.[5] This influence is prayed for by every child of God, when, as he opens the Bible, he prays that what he is about to read, may be blessed to the good of his soul. And it is prayed for by the faithful minister of the gospel, and by every devout hearer, when at the beginning of a sermon, they ask God to make his truth effectual.

Besides the word of truth, the dispensations of Providence are used by the Holy Spirit, as means of sanctification. Afflictions are often blessed to the spiritual good of God's people. David says: "Before I was afflicted, I went astray; but now have I kept thy word."[6] These afflictions are chastisements which our heavenly Father employs, to make us partakers of his holiness."[7]   In themselves, afflictions have no sanctifying efficacy, and many who are tried by them, are incited to greater hatred of God; but the Holy Spirit accompanies them to the believer with a sanctifying power, and uses them to wean his affections from the world, and fix them on God. When outward things either cease to give him enjoyment, or produce positive grief and pain, he finds within him a source of happiness, in the exercise of faith and hope in God. Hence, in his darkest hours, as to worldly prosperity, the believer

---

[1] John. v. 44.   [2] Ps. cxix. 18.   [3] Luke xvii. 5.
[4] Mark ix. 24.   [5] Luke xxiv. 45.   [6] Ps. cxix. 67.
[7] Heb. xii. 10.

sometimes finds his prospects of heaven most clear, and his foretaste of future blessedness most delightful.

SECTION VI.—FINAL PERSEVERANCE.

We have said, that the Holy Spirit continues to sanctify those whom he has regenerated. In consequence of this, they persevere in a course of holy obedience to the end of life. Whatever struggles it may cost, and whatever temporary departures from the straight line of duty may mark their course, they are graciously preserved from total and final apostacy. This truth may be proved by the following arguments:

1. By the will of God, as revealed in the Holy Scriptures, that which is produced in regeneration, is immortal. This is signified by the language of the Scriptures: "The hidden man of the heart, in that which is not corruptible."[1] "Being born of the incorruptible."[2] "Whosoever is born of God, doth not commit sin, for his seed remaineth in him."[3] Grace in the heart is here represented as incorruptible and abiding, and as securing its possessor from sin, that is, from a life of sin, such as unregenerate men pursue. The same truth is taught in these words of Christ: "He that believeth, hath everlasting life, and shall not come into condemnation, but is passed from death unto life."[4] The new life which grace produces, is in the present possession of the believer, and is here called everlasting. Its perpetuity is asserted in another form, in the words "Neither shall he come into condemnation." If one who has been made a new creature, and justified by faith, can return to the state from which divine grace has rescued him, he will come again into condemnation; but this is declared in these words of the infallible teacher, to be impossible: "If they who have passed from death to life, may return again to death, their present life is not everlasting;" and the assurance, neither shall come into condemnation, is groundless. The same truth is exhibited in another light, in these words of Paul: "Knowing that Christ, being raised from the dead, dieth no more, death hath no dominion over him; likewise reckon ye yourselves to be dead indeed unto

---

[1] 1 Pet. iii. 4.
[2] 1 Pet. i. 23.
[3] 1 John iii. 9.
[4] John v. 24.

sin, but alive unto God, through Jesus Christ, our Lord."[1] Here
believers are taught to account the new life which they have
received, to be like the life of Christ, raised from the dead. As
death hath no more dominion over him, the resemblance would fail
in a most important particular, if their spiritual life were not
immortal. As death can have no more dominion over the risen
Saviour, so, death can have no more dominion over those who, in
regeneration, have passed from death to life, and have been raised
up together with Christ.

2. The union of believers with Christ is indissoluble. His love
holds them fast. "Who shall separate us from the love of Christ,"
&c.[2] "Having loved his own, he loved them to the end."[3] "His
power holds them fast; neither shall any pluck them out of my
hand."[4] Such is their union to him, that their life is said to be in
him, and he is called their life.[5] The life of the risen Jesus, is the
life of his people, and such is their union with him, as to render
this life operative in them: "If when we were enemies, we were
reconciled to God by the death of his Son, much more, being
reconciled, we shall be saved by his life."[6] As his death was
efficacious to bring us into a state of reconciliation with God, his
life, now that he has been raised from the dead, and is ever living
to make intercession for us, and is the source of our life, hid in the
Godhead, will much more preserve us in this state of reconciliation,
and secure our final and complete salvation.

3. The promises of God secure our preservation in Christ.
When the new covenant is made with believers, by writing the law
in their hearts, the accompanying promise is: "I will be to them
a God, and they shall be to me a people."[7] It is true that the
Israelites were once accounted the people of God; and that they
departed from God, and were rejected by him; and the same
departure and rejection might happen to believers in Christ, if they
were under the same covenant. But God found fault with the old
covenant precisely on this ground, that it did not secure his people
from disobedience and rejection: "Because they continued not in
my covenant, and I regarded them not."[8] Having found fault
with this covenant, which did not put the law in their hearts, and

---

[1] Rom. vi. 9, 11.   [2] Rom. viii. 35–39.   [3] John xiii. 1.
[4] John x. 28.   [5] Col. iii. 3, 4.   [6] Rom. v. 10.
[7] Heb. viii. 10.   [8] Heb. viii. 9.

secure them from rejection, he abolishes that covenant, and makes
a new one, founded on better promises: "I will put my fear in
their hearts, that they shall not depart from me."[1] "Believers
are kept by the power of God through faith unto salvation;"[2] and
the power which keeps them through faith, keeps that faith in
existence and exercise, or it would fail to preserve them. This
preservation of their faith, follows from the intercession of Christ,[3]
who prayed for Peter, that his faith should not fail; and as he ever
liveth to make intercession,[4] the preservation of faith is secured by
the continued supplies of his grace, which otherwise would not be
sufficient for his people. It is manifest that Paul entertained these
views, when he wrote to the Philippians: "Being confident of this
very thing, that he which hath begun a good work in you, will
perform it until the day of Jesus Christ."[5]

4. Final apostasy, when it does occur, is accounted for, in the
Scriptures, on the ground that there was an absence of true
religion. This is clearly expressed by John: "They went out
from us, but they were not of us; for if they had been of us, they
would no doubt have continued with us; but they went out, that
they might be made manifest that they were not all of us."[6] With
this agrees the teaching of Christ, in the parable of the seed sown
in different kinds of ground, and explained by him of the word in
its effect on different classes of hearers. The stony ground hearers
"in time of temptation fell away,"[7] because the seed had not much
depth of earth. There may be much appearance of religion where
it does not really exist. Some, the Saviour has informed us, will
seek to enter in, saying: "Lord, Lord, have we not prophesied in
thy name, and in thy name have cast out devils? and in thy name
have done many wonderful works?" These applicants are rejected,
not on the ground that their plea was false. Their profession of
Christ, and their prophesying, and working of miracles, in his
name, are not denied: but the ground of this rejection is stated in
these words: "Depart from me, ye that work iniquity. I never
knew you."[8] Now, if any of them had ever been true followers

---

[1] Jer. xxxii. 40.   [2] 1 Pet. i. 5.   [3] Luke xxii. 32.
[4] Heb. vii. 25.   [5] Phil. i. 6.   [6] 1 John ii. 19.
[7] Luke viii. 13.   [8] Matt. vii. 23.

19

of Christ, he must have known them as such, and therefore he could not say: "I *never* knew you."

The text last considered, may assist us in explaining a passage in which many have found difficulty: "It is impossible for those who were once enlightened, and have tasted of the heavenly gift, and were made partakers of the Holy Ghost, and have tasted the good word of God, and the power of the world to come, if they shall fall away, to renew them again unto repentance."[1] Apostasy, after great attainments in religion, is here supposed; but these apostates had never been true disciples of Christ, distinguished by love to him, and works of holy obedience. In immediate connection with his account of them, Paul addresses true Christians thus: "Beloved, we are persuaded better things of you, and things which accompany salvation, though we thus speak, for God is not unrighteous to forget your work and labor of love."[2] The work and labor of love will be acknowledged by him in the great day, when the workers of iniquity will be rejected, whatever knowledge of divine things they may have possessed, and whatever miraculous gifts they may have been endowed with. The superiority of love to all knowledge, miraculous gifts, and all outward works, however costly and self-denying, is clearly taught in 1 Cor. xiii., and we are assured that all these, where love is wanting, will avail nothing. Hence all these, if without love, will not preserve from apostasy in this life, nor from rejection in the last day.

In a practical use of this and some other passages, the minds of many have been distressed with the apprehension that they had committed the unpardonable sin. For their relief, it is important to observe, that the difficulty in the way of the salvation of the apostates here described, consists in the impossibility of renewing them again to repentance. No humble penitent, therefore, has any ground to fear. Whatever his backslidings may have been, if he now truly repents of his sin, and implores pardon through the blood of the cross, he may feel assured that the way of salvation is open to him. The renewal to repentance has, in his case, been accomplished; and he may therefore know that he is not in the number of those, to whom this renewal is impossible.

The confessions of men eminent for piety, prove that they are

---

[1] Heb. vi.   [2] Heb. vi. 9.

not free from sin; and the cases of David, who committed adultery, and Peter, who denied his master, prove that true saints have sometimes fallen into gross sins. But David was renewed to repentance, and the record of his penitential acknowledgments has been transmitted to us in the 51st Psalm. A look of Jesus melted Peter's heart, and he went out, and wept bitterly. But the apostates, who are described in the passage which we have been considering, are given over to hardness of heart: "It is impossible to renew them again to repentance." The difficulty is, not that the blood of Christ is insufficient to atone for sins so atrocious, but that it is impossible to renew them again to repentance. God never bestows the grace of repentance on such characters. But when one who has been born of God, falls into sin, this impossibility of renewing to repentance does not exist; but his seed remaineth in him; and divine grace brings him back from his wanderings, and restores him to the paths of righteousness. The fire of divine love in the heart, though its flame may be smothered for a time, is more easily rekindled than when first produced; and it is never true of him, as it is of an unregenerate man who falls away, that the last state is worse than the first.

Several other passages of Scripture, which have been understood to imply the apostasy of true believers, require consideration.

"Every branch in me that beareth not fruit, he taketh away."[1] This figurative representation, which the Saviour has employed, teaches that there is a sense, in which persons are "in" him, who do not bring forth the fruits of holiness. Such persons do not abide in him.[2] Their connection is not vital, but professional. They are among his disciples, but not of them; for if they had been of them, they would no doubt have continued with them. The process of separating them, described by the words, "he taketh away," corresponds well with the removing of a branch which has been grafted into a stalk, but has failed to become vitally connected with it. The perseverance of true saints is taught in the remaining part of the verse: "Every branch that beareth fruit, he purgeth it, that it may bring forth more fruit."

"If we sin wilfully after that we have received the knowledge of the truth, there remaineth no more sacrifice for sins; but a

---

[1] John xv. 2.   [2] John xv. 6.

certain fearful looking for of judgment and fiery indignation which shall devour the adversaries."[1]   This passage has sometimes severely tried the faith of weak believers.   When conscious of having committed sins to which their will has consented, these words present themselves in dreadful array, and seem to deter them from all further approach to the atoning sacrifice of Jesus, from which they once obtained peace.   In such times of trial, the language of faith is, "Though he slay me, yet will I trust in him."[2] While this awful text fills with terror, the existence of an humble abiding trust in God is thus demonstrated, and, in view of it, other texts authorize encouragement and hope.   With these encouraging and consolatory texts, the passage now under consideration, if properly understood, cannot be inconsistent.   It describes the sin of those Hebrews who, after embracing the gospel of Christ, forsook the assembly of Christians,[3] and turned back to Judaism. To them no efficacious sacrifice for sin remained, in the abolished ceremonies of the Mosaic dispensation; and if that of Christ were renounced, no other could be found.   But these words were never designed to deter any humble penitent from free approach to the atoning sacrifice of Christ, whatever sins he may have committed.   The assurance that Jesus has given, "Him that cometh to me, I will in no wise cast out,"[4] is sufficient to banish all fear from those who put their trust in him.   The same invitation which first made them welcome, and the same assurance which first gave them peace, remain to encourage their continued confidence in his power and grace.

"Of how much sorer punishment suppose ye shall he be thought worthy, who hath trodden under foot the Son of God, and hath counted the blood of the covenant wherewith he was sanctified, an unholy thing; and hath done despite to the spirit of grace?"[5]   The difficulty in this passage is found in the phrase "wherewith he was sanctified."   Do these words teach that persons who have been sanctified may apostatise?   Let it be observed that the word sanctify, among the Hebrews, was used to denote external consecration to God.[6]   This consecration, under the former dispensation, to which the Hebrews had been accustomed, was by the blood

---

[1] Heb. x. 26, 27.   [2] Job xiii. 15.   [3] Heb. x. 25.
[4] John. vi. 37.   [5] Heb. x. 29.   [6] Ex. xiii. 2; xix. 10, 22, 23, &c

of animals. In professing Christianity, they had turned from the blood of animals to the blood of Christ; and their consecration to the service of Christ was by professed faith in his blood. In returning to Judaism, they rejected this precious blood, and accounted it an unholy thing, as if it had been the blood of a vile impostor. But it is better to interpret the phrase by referring the pronoun "he" to the last antecedent, "the Son of God." The Son of God was sanctified and sent into the world;[1] and as the priests of the law were consecrated with blood, Jesus, as our great High Priest, may be said to have been consecrated with the blood of the new covenant.

"The just shall live by faith; but if any man draw back, my soul shall have no pleasure in him."[2] In this verse our translators have supplied the words, "any man," which have no corresponding word in the Greek. The regular translation would be, "If he draw back," &c. Thus rendered, the pronoun "he" naturally refers to the just man, mentioned in the preceding clause; and the words seem to imply that a just man may draw back, so that God will have no pleasure in him. An argument for supplying the words "any man," may be drawn from the fact that these words are quoted from the Septuagint version of Habakkuk ii. 6, in which the last clause occurs first; and the man who draws back is manifestly distinguished from the just man. The same distinction is made by Paul in the words which immediately follow: "We are not of them who draw back to perdition, but of them who believe to the saving of the soul." The introduction of the words "any man," may therefore give a correct exposition of Paul's words: still, they are an exposition, and not a translation. Paul has inverted the order of the two clauses written by the prophet: and, in so doing, he was doubtless guided by the Holy Spirit, for some wise purpose; and it becomes us to learn from his words, as they have been given by the Spirit for our instruction and admonition. The prophet's warning was, "If any man draw back, my soul shall have no pleasure in him." This warning Paul places in such order, as to make it apply to the just man. What is true of any man, must be true of the just man; and Paul will not deny to the just man the benefit of this admonition. Such admonition,

---

[1] John x. 36.   [2] Heb. x. 38.

in the apostle's view, was not inconsistent with the doctrine of the saints' final perseverance.

"When a righteous man turneth away from his righteousness, and committeth iniquity, and dieth in them; for his iniquity that he hath done, shall he die."[1] These words are to be understood in the same manner as the words of Paul which have just been considered. The terms "just" and "righteous" are of like import, and are descriptive of those who obey God's commands, and enjoy his favor. Such persons need the admonitions contained in these passages; and they are given in language precisely adapted to the case. To all, except the Searcher of hearts, there is an uncertainty respecting men's character in his sight; and, on the ground of this uncertainty, opportunity is given for the needed admonition. Paul spoke with confidence, that the Hebrews whom he addressed were "of those who believe to the saving of the soul:" yet, without relying on his own estimate of their character, or deriving from it an assurance of their perseverance, he warned them earnestly against apostasy.

"If, after they have escaped the pollutions of the world, through the knowledge of the Lord and Saviour Jesus Christ, they are again entangled therein, and overcome, the latter end is worse with them than the beginning."[2] These words describe men who have been reformed in their conduct by the influence of the gospel, but without a thorough change of heart. This appears from the proverb applied to them: "The dog has returned to his vomit, and the sow that was washed, to her wallowing in the mire."[3] As the temporary change of the dog and the sow had not altered their natural propensities, so it was with these men. Their change, though a reform, had not made them new creatures.

"Whosoever of you are justified by the law, ye are fallen from grace."[4] These words describe a change in their doctrinal views as to the method of salvation. They had turned from salvation by grace to salvation by the law. But how far the state of their hearts was influenced by their doctrinal creed, either before or after the change here described, the passage does not inform us.

"Concerning faith having made shipwreck."[5] "Overthrow the

---

[1] Ezek. xviii. 26. [2] 2 Pet. ii. 20. [3] 2 Pet. ii. 22.
[4] Gal. v. 4. [5] 1 Tim. i. 19.

faith of some.""[1] Wrong views had been inculcated by these men respecting the resurrection of the dead. It may be that neither they, nor those who were misled by them, had ever received the love of the truth. On this point the passage says nothing.

" Through thy knowledge shall the weak brother perish for whom Christ died?"[2] When the stronger Christian will not, for the sake of a weak brother, deny himself a carnal indulgence, he exhibits a criminal disregard of his weak brother's spiritual interest. The tendency of his conduct is the ruin of his weak brother; and the criminality is to be judged by its tendency; and is the same, whether the tendency goes into effect, or is prevented by the interposition of divine grace. The question propounded does not affirm what the result will be; but impressively exhibits the guilt of the offender by contrasting his conduct with that of Christ. Christ died for the weak brother; and would you cause him to perish, rather than deny yourself a trifling gratification?

" I keep under my body and bring it into subjection, lest that by any means when I have preached to others, I myself should be a castaway."[3] These words contain a manifest reference to the Grecian games, in which the herald, who announced them, took no part in the contest, or the previous preparation for it; and therefore did not receive the crown. Paul was not only a herald, making the gospel proclamation, but he entered the lists as a combatant, and made diligent preparation for the conflict, by keeping under his body. He did this, knowing that his preaching, or acting the herald, to others, would not secure a crown to himself. He prepared diligently for the combat, that he might receive the crown, and not be a castaway, or one rejected by the Judge.

The explanation which has been given of this passage, removes all appearance of inconsistency between it and the doctrine of the saints' final perseverance; yet it admits that Paul was stimulated to activity and perseverance in the Christian conflict, by the belief that his obtaining of the crown depended on his perseverance and success in the struggle. They who understand the doctrine of perseverance to imply that God's people will obtain the crown without the struggle, totally mistake the matter. The doctrine is, that God's people will persevere in the struggle; and to suppose

---

[1] 2 Tim. ii. 18.   [2] 1 Cor. viii. 11.   [3] 1 Cor. ix. 27.

that they will obtain the crown without doing so, is to contradict the doctrine. It is a wretched and fatal perversion of the doctrine, if men conclude that, having been once converted, they will be saved, whatever may be their course of life. God's word plainly declares, that " he who soweth to the flesh shall of the flesh reap corruption :" and every man who does not keep under his body, and bring it into subjection, and who does not endure to the end, in this spiritual conflict, will assuredly fail to receive the crown. Without this, no conversion which he may have undergone, and not even a call to apostleship, will secure the approbation of the final Judge.

We have said that the new creature produced in regeneration, is immortal; but this immortality is dependent on the will of God, and is secured by means which God has provided. Adam, in his primeval innocence, was immortal; but his life was sustained, under God, by the fruits of the garden which had been assigned to his use. So God has appointed necessary means for preserving the divine life in the soul, and the use of these means is as indispensable to the accomplishment of the purpose, in this, as in all other cases in which he has chosen to work by means. The doctrine of final perseverance, when properly understood, does not teach that God's people are in no sense in danger of final apostasy. Paul tells us that he had often been in perils of waters.[1] One of these times of danger was the shipwreck which he experienced in his voyage to Rome. He, and all his companions in the vessel, were in great danger; and they could not have been saved, if the necessary means for their preservation had not been used. Yet God had both purposed and promised their deliverance. The righteous, notwithstanding the purpose and promise of God, are scarcely saved.[2] They succeed at last, as by a narrow escape. Through danger, imminent danger, they are at last delivered: and, in order to that deliverance, the use of the appointed means is as necessary as the appointment itself;—as necessary as the purpose of God.

The warnings which the Scriptures give to the people of God, constitute an important part of the means which God has appointed for their perseverance in holiness to eternal life. As the rock in

---

[1] 2 Cor. xi. 26.   [2] 1 Pet. iv. 18.

the mariner's chart guards him from being dashed to pieces, so these warnings preserve the spiritual mariner from destruction. The awful warnings given by Paul to the Hebrews, were designed to guard them against final apostasy. They therefore imply that there was danger of such apostasy. The heirs of promise might have strong consolation, in the hope founded on the oath and promise of God, that they would be brought safely through the danger. In the wisdom of God, the warnings are so given, as to secure their proper effect, without destroying that confidence in God, which is the Christian's hope and joy. To make this clear, and to derive the proper benefit from these warnings, let us briefly review them.

The warning given in Heb. vi. 4–7, was designed for real Christians. Every clause in the description of the persons, whose apostasy is declared to be fatal, would in other connections be understood to denote true Christians. The Hebrew Christians are elsewhere described as persons "illuminated."[1] The first particular in the description here, is, "who were once enlightened." Other particulars are added, agreeing with well known peculiarities, which distinguished the followers of Christ. These words, therefore, contain a general description of Christians; and the warning which they contain was applicable to Christians, and designed for their benefit. With these features of the Christian character, which are so vividly portrayed, and which were so well known in the days of primitive Christianity, there was generally connected a love to the truth, which was necessary to the full and proper effect of divine instruction. When this operated, the warning here proposed had its proper effect. These persons were like the fruitful ground, which received blessing from God;[2] and this love the apostle believed to exist in those to whom his epistle was directed.[3] They who possessed this love were moved by his warning, to make advance in spiritual attainments, according to his exhortation in the beginning of the chapter. But this result did not invariably follow the instructions and warning, which were given to those who possessed the general features of the Christian character. Apostasy sometimes occurred; and apostasy which was final and hopeless. This fact gave just occasion for the warning.

Heb. x. 32.   [2] Heb. vi. 7.   [3] Heb. vi. 9, 10.

Similar remarks may be made on the passages in the 10th chapter of Hebrews. That they were designed as warnings to true Christians, may be seen in the fact that Paul includes himself in the number. "If *we* sin wilfully,"[1] &c., and in the further fact that the just "are warned against drawing back."[2] The alarming consequences of apostasy are exhibited in the absence of all further sacrifice for sin; in the sore punishment which is deserved;—and in the perdition to which the apostate draws back. All these consequences were set before the Christians, who are addressed, and the apostle again expresses his confidence, that they, with himself, will, in the belief and love of the truth, receive the warning and be saved.

The warnings against apostasy, and the exhortations to perseverance, were not addressed to false professors, as such. The apostle was not solicitous that these should persevere in their false profession. They to whom his epistle was directed, were all exhorted to hold fast their profession, on the supposition that it had been honestly made. All had exhibited the appearances of true religion, and were treated accordingly. The plant which springs from seed sown in stony places, does not differ from that which is sown in good ground, except in not having much depth of earth; and this defect becomes manifest, when it withers under the beams of the sun. So those who afterwards apostatise, agree in the profession which they make, and all the appearances of religion which they exhibit, with those who endure to the end. The difference is, that the word has not a deep place in their hearts; and this is discovered only by their apostasy. "They went out from us, that they might be made manifest, that they are not all of us."[3] Hence, until their apostasy occurs, the same means of spiritual cultivation are employed for their benefit, as for others; the same hopes are entertained for them; and the same language is used in describing them. The tendency of this spiritual cultivation is to render them fruitful, like the rest; but it fails to produce this effect, because they have no sincere and abiding love of the truth.

The doctrine of final perseverance, properly understood, gives no encouragement to sluggishness or negligence in duty; much less does it lead to licentiousness. He who takes occasion from it to

---

[1] Heb. x. 26.   [2] Heb. x. 38.   [3] 1 John ii. 19.

sin against God, or to be indolent in his service, not only misunderstands, and misapplies the doctrine, but has reason to fear that his heart is not right before God. Perseverance in holiness is the only infallible proof that the heart is right; and he who ceases to persevere, on the presumption that his heart is right, believes without the proper evidence, and is wofully hazarding his eternal interests on his presumption. The doctrine is, that grace in the heart will produce perseverance to the end; and where the effect is not produced, the cause does not exist. Every man, therefore, whatever his past professions and attainments may have been, has reason to take alarm, if he finds his heart inclined to depart from Christ: and the greater his past attainments may have been, the greater is the occasion for alarm; because his case, if he falls away, will so much the more resemble that in which renewal to repentance is impossible.

To reject the doctrine of final perseverance, tends to fix the hope of salvation on human effort, and not on the purpose and grace of God. If, in God's method of salvation, no provision has been made, which secures the safe keeping of the regenerate, and their perseverance in holiness, their salvation is left dependent on their own efforts, and their trust must be in that on which success depends. All that God has done for them, will fail to bring them through, if this effort, originating in themselves, be not superadded; and the eye of hope is necessarily directed to this human effort, as that on which the momentous issue depends. Thus the denial of the doctrine draws off the heart from simple trust in God, and therefore tends to produce apostasy. The just shall live by faith.[1] Simple trust in God, is necessary to preserve the spiritual life; and to trust in man, and make flesh our arm,[2] is to fall under the curse, and draw back to perdition. In our first coming to Christ, we renounce all confidence in self, and put our entire trust in the mercy and power of God: and in the same faith with which we began, we must persevere to the end of our course. Worldly wisdom may encourage self-reliance, and regard it as necessary to success: but the wisdom that is from above teaches us to renounce and avoid it as ruinous to the soul.

Convinced of his weakness and helplessness, the believer learns more and more in this life of faith to trust God, and to have no

---

[1] Heb. x. 38.   [2] Jer. xvii. 5.

confidence in himself. He learns, by daily experience, the treachery of his own heart, and is increasingly weaned from the folly of trusting in it. It becomes his more earnest prayer, as he makes greater progress in the knowledge of himself and the way of salvation. " Hold thou me up."[1] He looks forward to the temptations and trials through which he has to pass; and, unwilling to trust himself in the least degree, asks God, earnestly and importunately to keep him to the end. This prayer he may hope that God will answer, if the doctrine of final perseverance be true. If the grace to persevere is a gift of God, it is a proper subject of prayer; and that doctrine best accords with God's method of salvation, which teaches us to come boldly to the throne of grace, for the mercy and grace to help in every time of need. We cannot now ask with confidence, for grace to help us through all future times of need, and to incline and strengthen us to persevere to the end, if the bestowment of such persevering grace is not within God's plan of salvation.

The doctrine of final perseverance is full of consolation to the believer, when ready to faint in his spiritual warfare. So far as he finds, in a careful examination of his heart, evidence that the love of God has been shed abroad there by the Holy Spirit, he is enabled to regard this grace as an earnest of the future inheritance, and to rejoice in hope of obtaining that inheritance in full possession, at the time appointed of his heavenly Father. If doubts arise, they spring not from a view of incompleteness in God's method of salvation, but they refer exclusively to the question whether his heart has been brought to put simple and exclusive trust in that divine method, and the provision of mercy which it includes. As the best termination of these doubts, he views the way open for him to come now, if never before, and cast himself on this mercy, so richly provided, and so gloriously adapted to his necessities.

Section VII.—PERFECTION.

The process of sanctification, which is continued during the present life, is completed when the subjects of it are perfectly fitted for the service and enjoyments of heaven. In this work of

---

[1] Ps. cxix. 117.

the Spirit, the resurrection of the body is included, and the fashioning of it like the glorious body of Christ. Having been predestinated to be conformed to the image of God's dear son,[1] the purposed work of grace is not completed until we appear in glory, with our bodies like the glorious body of the Redeemer. For this perfect conformity, the saints on earth long, and to it they look as the consummation of their wishes and hopes: "Then shall I be satisfied, when I awake with thy likeness."[2] This was the object of Paul's earnest desire, the prize for which he put forth every effort. He refers to it in these words: "If by any means I might attain unto the resurrection of the dead: not as though I had already attained, either were already perfect; but I follow after, if that I may apprehend that for which also I am apprehended of Christ Jesus. I press toward the mark, for the prize of the high calling of God in Christ Jesus."[3]

The work of grace will not be completed until the second coming of Christ: "He which hath begun a good work in you, will perform it until the day of Jesus Christ."[4] Then the last change will be made, which will fit us for the eternal service and enjoyment of God, in his high and holy place. Then we shall be like him; for we shall see him as he is." "Now we know in part; but then we shall know even as also we are known." "Then that which is perfect will have come;" and until then every saint must say with Paul: "Not as though I had already attained, or were already perfect."

Besides this final perfection, to which the saints are taught to aspire, there are stages in their progress to which the name perfection is, in a subordinate sense, applied in the Holy Scriptures. The disembodied saints, now in the presence of God, though they have not attained to the resurrection of the body, are nevertheless called "just men made perfect."[5] They are free from the body of death, free from sin, free from all the tribulations and sorrows of this world, and are present with the Lord, and in the enjoyment of his love.

Even in the present life there are stages in the Christian's progress to which the term perfection is applied. When they have

---

[1] Rom. viii. 29.   [2] Ps. xvii. 15.   [3] Phil. iii. 11, 12, 13.
[4] Phil. i. 6.   [5] Heb. xii. 23.

attained to an enlarged knowledge of divine truth, they are said to be perfect, or of full age, to distinguish them from those who have learned only the first principles of the doctrine of Christ.[1] Men who make a full and consistent exhibition of the religious character, by a godly life, are called perfect. So Job was " perfect and upright, fearing God and eschewing evil."[2] To Christians generally the term " perfect" appears to be applied, in the exhortation of Paul: " Let us, as many as be perfect, be thus minded."[3] He here includes himself among the perfect; and yet, in the same chapter,[4] he affirms that he was not already perfect. It is clear, therefore, that the words are used in different senses in the two places.

No perfection to which the people of God attain in the present life, includes perfect freedom from sin. Job, though a perfect man, said, " If I justify myself, mine own mouth shall condemn me. If I say, I am perfect, it also shall prove me perverse."[5] Paul, though numbering himself among the perfect, said, " When I would do good, evil is present with me."[6] " I am carnal, sold under sin."[7] John says, " If we say that we have no sin, we deceive ourselves;"[8] and Solomon, " There is not a just man upon earth that doeth good and sinneth not."[9] With these declarations of God's word, the experience of Christians in all ages has agreed; and they have found need for the daily prayer, " Forgive us our trespasses."

In the precept, " Be ye perfect, even as your Father in heaven is perfect,"[10] we may take the term in its highest sense. As we are commanded to love God with all the heart—to be holy because he is holy; it is our duty to be perfectly free from sin; and to come up to this standard, should be our constant aim and effort. We cannot attain to a perfect knowledge of God in the present life; but we may follow on to know him.[11] So we cannot attain to a perfect likeness in holiness, yet we may be " changed into the same image from glory to glory."[12] Progress in the divine life is full of reward, and full of encouragement, even while we are fighting the good fight of faith, and before we obtain the victor's crown. The

---

[1] Heb. vi. 1; v. 14.   [2] Job i. 1.   [3] Phil. iii. 15.
[4] Phil. iii. 12.   [5] Job ix. 20.   [6] Rom. vii. 21.
[7] Rom. vii. 14.   [8] 1 John i. 8.   [9] Eccl. vii. 20.
[10] Matt. v. 48.   [11] Hosea vi. 3.   [12] 2 Cor. iii. 19.

promise of grace to help in every struggle, of continued success in every conflict, and of final victory, is sufficient encouragement to put forth every effort. We should ever press toward the mark, ever keep the high standard of perfection in view, and aim to reach it. " Having these promises, dearly beloved, let us cleanse ourselves from all filthiness of flesh and spirit, perfecting holiness in the fear of God."[1]

The indication is fearful when a man excuses sin in himself, on the ground that perfection is not attainable in the present life. A true Christian may have a besetting sin; but any one who has an indulged, allowed, or excused sin, has reason to fear that the love of sin has never been crucified in his heart. And he who satisfies himself with any standard below absolute perfection in holiness, is so far allowing sin in himself, and giving the indication which ought to alarm him.

In the spiritual warfare, of which every believer is conscious, the love of God in the heart is in conflict with other affections which are not duly subordinated to it. Growth in grace implies an ascendancy of the holy affection over those with which it contends. That gains strength, and those grow weaker, as the house of David waxed stronger, and the house of Saul weaker,[2] in their struggle for the dominion over Israel. It is therefore our duty, that we may grow in grace, to cherish the holy affections, which rise heavenward, and to mortify the carnal affections, which are earthward in their tendency. No man on earth can justly claim that the affections of his heart are perfectly regulated according to the high standard of God's law. The internal conflict between the law in the members and the law in the mind, does not cease till God calls away the spirit from its union with the mortal body. The phrase "law in our members,"[3] does not imply that our sin belongs properly to our material bodies; but it nevertheless apparently suggests that the conflict between the law in the members and the law in the mind, may be expected to continue as long as the members and the mind have their present relation to each other. Just men are made perfect[4] when they become disembodied spirits. When absent from the body, they are present with the Lord;[5] and

---

[1] 2 Cor. vii. 1. [2] 2 Sam. iii. 1. [3] Rom. vii. 23.
[4] Heb. xii. 23. [5] 2 Cor. v. 8.

they are then holy; for without holiness no man shall see the Lord.[1]

We should not attribute to death the efficiency of our final deliverance from sin. It is only an instrument which the Holy Spirit uses in his work, just as he has used the many afflictions which have preceded death, and of which death is the termination. As this is the last suffering which the righteous will endure, the last enemy which remains to be destroyed, it is appropriately used as the last instrumentality which the Holy Spirit will employ in his work. And it is a most suitable instrumentality. Death introduces us into the full knowledge of God, which is necessary to the perfect love of him. It opens to our view the unseen things of the eternal world, that they may have their full and proper influence on our minds. It separates us for ever from the things of earth, to which our affections have been so strongly inclined to cleave. The death of a beloved friend has often been blessed as a means of our sanctification: but when we die, all our surviving friends die to us at once. The loss of property has weaned us from the world: but at death we lose all our earthly possessions at a single stroke. God may have burned down our dwellings and consumed in the flames the coffers which contained our gold, when he graciously designed to direct our thoughts to the house not made with hands, and to the treasure which cannot be consumed. What, then, when the earth itself, which he has given for the habitation of men, and all therein which he has given them to enjoy, shall be burned up in the last conflagration; or shall be shown to us as prepared to be cast into that funeral fire? This is well adapted to eradicate from the heart the love of the things that perish. This fit instrumentality the Spirit employs in completing his work of sanctification. Yet, as in all our afflictions, the efficiency is not in the means employed, but in the divine power which employs them to fulfil his gracious purpose.

---

[1] Heb. xii. 14.

CHAPTER IV.

SOVEREIGNTY OF GRACE.

GOD BESTOWS THE BLESSINGS OF HIS GRACE, NOT ACCORDING TO THE WORKS OF THE RECIPIENT, BUT ACCORDING TO HIS OWN SOVE-REIGN PLEASURE.[1]

God is sovereign in doing what he pleases, uncontrolled by any other being. "He doth according to his will, in the armies of heaven, and among the inhabitants of the earth, and none can stay his hand, or say unto him: 'What doest thou?'"[2] No superior being exists, who can dictate to Jehovah what he should do, or hinder him from the execution of his pleasure, or call him to account for anything that he has done.

Sovereignty is to be distinguished from arbitrariness. In the latter, the will of the agent directs the action, without reference to a wise or good purpose to be accomplished. When God acts, it is according to his good pleasure. His pleasure is good, because it is always directed to a good end. He is sovereign in his acts, because his acts are determined by his own perfections. He has a rule for what he does; but this rule is not prescribed to him by any other being, nor does it exist independently of himself. It is found in his own nature. In his acts, his nature is unfolded and displayed.

In some respects the divine nature is so far made known to us, that we are able to understand the rule to which his acts conform. We so far understand his justice, that the distribution of rewards and punishments according to the works of men, is a process for which we can account, and the result of which we can in part foretell. But there are mysteries in the divine nature which are too deep for us to fathom: and hence we are unable to assign a rule for the divine proceedings. These are the cases which we specially refer to the sovereignty of God. He is not less sovereign in his justice, than in the dispensations for which he has given us

---

[1] 2 Tim. i. 9; Rom. ix. 16; Phil. ii. 13, Matt. xi. 25; Luke x. 21; Eph. ii. 4–9.

[2] Dan. iv. 35.

20

no reason. But we bow before his sovereignty, in the best exercise of simple confidence in him, when we are least able to account for his doings; and it has been his pleasure, to leave much of his proceedings involved in mystery, that we may have occasion for the exercise of this confidence, which is pleasing to him, and profitable to ourselves.

We are prone to demand the reason or rule of God's acts, and to prescribe rules according to which God should act; but the Scriptures teach us to restrain this propensity. "Shall the thing formed, say to him that formed it: 'Why hast thou made me thus?'"[1] "He giveth not account of any of his matters."[2] But though the Scriptures do not explain those dispensations of God which we are compelled to refer to his inscrutable sovereignty, they teach us that God is not governed by such rules as human wisdom would prescribe. His ways are above our ways, and his thoughts above our thoughts, as high as the heavens are above the earth.[3]

Men often complain that God's ways are not equal, and charge him with partiality in his dealings with his creatures. When this charge is brought against him, in such a manner as to imply injustice in anything which he does, he repels the charge: "Are not my ways equal? Are not your ways unequal?"[4] But in bestowing the blessings of his grace, God claims the right to do what he will with his own.[5] He is not bound to give to every one an equal measure of undeserved favor; or to measure his freely bestowed blessings, according to the works of those on whom they are bestowed. This is clearly taught in the inspired word: "He hath saved us and called us with a holy calling, not according to our works, but according to his own purpose and grace which was given us in Christ Jesus before the world began."[6] "Not of works, but of him that calleth."[7] "Not of him that willeth, nor of him that runneth, but of God that showeth mercy."[8]

In the condition of the creatures that God has made, we observe a diversity to which we can assign no limits. In the vegetable kingdom, we find productions varying from the cedar of Lebanon to the minute blade of grass, some beautiful and fragrant, or adapted

---

[1] Rom. ix. 20.
[2] Job xxxiii. 13.
[3] Isaiah lv. 9.
[4] Ez. xviii. 29.
[5] Matt. xx. 15.
[6] 2 Tim. i. 9.
[7] Rom. ix. 11.
[8] Rom. ix. 16.

to great utility, and others without any quality in which we can perceive a reason for their having been made. Among animals, a boundless variety appears, in their size, modes of life, and capacity for enjoyment. In the condition of human beings, the system of diversity continues. As the human species differs from every other species, so the condition of each individual man differs from that of every other individual belonging to the species. One man passes his days in affluence and ease, and another drags out his miserable existence in poverty and toil. One enjoys almost uninterrupted health, while another, from the beginning to the end of his life, is oppressed with disease and pain. One possesses intellect susceptible of the highest cultivation, and is favored with all the necessary means of cultivation; while another gropes his way in mental darkness, either from the natural imbecility of his mind, or from the disadvantageous circumstances in which his lot of life is cast. Why is all this diversity? We must answer in the words of Christ: "Even so, Father, for so it seemed good in thy sight."[1] To some extent the sufferings and enjoyments of men in the present life are attributable to their personal conduct; and so far the reason for the divine dispensation towards them is apparent; but, to a far greater extent, no cause can be assigned by human reason; and we are compelled to ascribe the mysterious arrangement to the sovereignty of God. As he is sovereign in creation and providence, so he is sovereign in the dispensations of his grace. "He divides to every man severally as he will."[2] He withholds from the wise and prudent, and reveals unto babes, as it seems good in his sight.[3] When the question arises: "Who made thee to differ from another?" the proper answer is: "It is not of him that willeth, nor of him that runneth, but of God that showeth mercy;"[4] and "By the grace of God, I am what I am."[5] In the dispensations of grace, full regard is had to justice, and nothing unjust is done to any one; but grace rises high above justice, and gives ample room for the display of the divine sovereignty, in the distribution of blessings to which no individual has the slightest claim.

Among the rules which human officiousness prescribes to God

---

[1] Matt. xi. 26. [2] 1 Cor. xii. 11. [3] Matt. xi. 25.
[4] Rom. ix. 16. [5] 1 Cor. xv. 10.

for the regulation of his conduct, we are prone to insist that the blessings of his grace should be distributed according to men's works. We do not presume to say, that they should be given *for* men's works, for this would render them rewards of debt, and not of grace. Scripture and reason unite in checking the presumption which would claim all that God bestows, as due on the ground of merit: but, while we relinquish the claim on the ground of positive merit, we are yet prone to conceive that there is a fitness in conferring the blessings of grace on those who have the negative merit of being less wicked than others. In this method of dispensation, which human wisdom would recommend, the blessings are conferred, not *for* men's works, but *according to* their works: but the wisdom of God rejects the counsel of human wisdom in this particular. A Saul of Tarsus, though chief of sinners, is made a happy recipient of divine grace, while an amiable young ruler, who had kept the law from his youth up, is left to perish in his self-righteousness. Publicans and harlots enter the kingdom of heaven; while multitudes, less wicked than they, are left to the course to which natural depravity inclines them. These cases exemplify the explicit declarations of Scripture, which teach, that "we are saved and called, not according to our works."

It is true, that in the last day, men will be judged according to the deeds done in the body. But it must be remembered that salvation begins in the present life. To the present life the calling of men from darkness to light is limited; and the salvation and calling of the present life, are not according to men's works. As men are called "to be holy," the holiness which they exhibit as a consequence of the salvation and calling which they receive from the grace of God, distinguishes them from other men, and becomes a proper rule for the decisions of the last day. We see, therefore, that the last judgment will be according to the deeds done in the body; while it nevertheless remains, that we are saved and called, not according to our works, but according to the purpose and grace of God.

Section 1.—ELECTION.

ALL WHO WILL FINALLY BE SAVED, WERE CHOSEN TO SALVATION BY GOD THE FATHER, BEFORE THE FOUNDATION OF THE WORLD, AND GIVEN TO JESUS CHRIST IN THE COVENANT OF GRACE.[1]

The doctrine of election encounters strong opposition in the hearts of men, and it is therefore necessary to examine thoroughly its claim to our belief. As it relates to an act of the divine mind, no proof of its truth can be equal to the testimony of the Scriptures. Let us receive their teachings on the subject without hesitation or distrust; and let us require every preconceived opinion of ours, and all our carnal reasonings, to bow before the authority of God's holy word.

The Scriptures clearly teach, that God has an elect or chosen people. "Who shall lay any thing to the charge of God's elect."[2] Elect according to the foreknowledge of God.[3] "Shall not God avenge his own elect."[4] "Ye are a chosen generation."[5] "God hath chosen you to salvation."[6] "According as he hath chosen us in Christ."[7] Whatever may have been our prejudices against the doctrine of election as held and taught by some ministers of religion, it is undeniable, that, in some sense, the doctrine is found in the Bible; and we cannot reject it, without rejecting that inspired book. We are bound by the authority of God, to receive the doctrine; and nothing remains, but that we should make an honest effort to understand it, just as it is taught in the sacred volume.

The Scriptures teach expressly, that God's people are chosen to salvation. "Beloved, we are bound to give thanks always to God for you, because he hath from the beginning chosen you to salvation."[8] Some have been chosen by God[9] to peculiar offices; as Paul was a chosen vessel, to bear the name of Christ to the Gentiles, and David was chosen to be the King of Israel. The whole nation of Israel was chosen out of all nations to be a peculiar people to the Lord: but it is very clear that the eternal

---

[1] Eph. i. 4, 5; 2 Thess. ii. 13; 1 Pet. i. 2; ii. 9; John vi. 37; Rom. viii. 33; John x. 27–29.

[2] Rom. viii. 33. [3] 1 Pet. i. 2. [4] Luke xviii. 7.
[5] 1 Pet. ii. 9. [6] 2 Thess. ii. 13. [7] Eph. i. 4.
[8] 2 Thess. ii. 13. [9] Acts ix. 15.

salvation of every Israelite was not secured by this national election; for to some of them Christ said, " Ye shall die in your sins; and whither I go ye cannot come."[1] The election to salvation is shown by the words of Paul in Rom. ix. 6, to be different from this national election : " They are not all Israel that are of Israel." " There is a remnant according to the election of grace."[2] The national election comprehended all Israel, according to the flesh : but the election of grace included those only who will finally be saved. It is not a choice merely to the means of salvation, for these were granted to all the nation of Israel : but it was a choice to salvation itself, and therefore respected the " remnant," and not the whole nation.

The Scriptures plainly teach that the election of grace is from eternity. " God hath, from the beginning, chosen you to salvation."[3] " According as he hath chosen us in him from the foundation of the world."[4] " According to his own purpose and grace, which was given us in Christ Jesus before the world began."[5] Election is a part of God's eternal purpose. Had it been his purpose to save all the human race, there would have been no elect from among men ; no peculiar people, no redeemed out of every nation. But his purpose to save did not include all the race ; and therefore, on some principle yet to be inquired into, some of the race have been selected, who will receive the kingdom prepared for them from the foundation of the world. The eternity of God's election ought not to excite in our hearts any objection against it. If, in the final judgment, God will distinguish between the righteous and the wicked, whatever he will then do in righteousness, it was right for him to purpose to do from all eternity. In his final sentence, all his preceding dispensations toward the children of men, and all their actions under these dispensations, will be carefully reviewed, and the final doom of every one will be pronounced in righteousness. All that will then be present to the divine mind, was before it from all eternity ; and what God will then do, he purposed to do from the beginning ; and the reasons for which he will do it, are the reasons for which he purposed to do it. There can be no wrong in the purpose, if it does not exist in the execution. If

---

[1] John viii. 22, 24.   [2] Rom. xi. 5.   [3] 2 Thess. ii. 13.
[4] Eph. i. 4.   [5] 2 Tim. i. 9.

God can fully justify at the last day, before the assembled universe, all his dispensations toward the children of men; all these dispen sations must be right, and the purpose of them from eternity must have been right: and if a division of the human race can then be righteously made, that division was righteously made in the purpose of God; and consequently God's election was made in righteousness.

The Scriptures teach that election is of grace, and not of works. "Not of works, lest any man should boast;"[1] and if it be of works, then grace is no more grace.[2] The subject is illustrated by the case of Jacob and Esau, of whom Jacob was chosen, before the children had done either good or evil; and in applying this illustration, Paul says: "That the purpose of God according to election might stand; not of works, but of him that calleth."[3] In the last day, God will discriminate between the righteous and the wicked, according to their works: and it was the eternal purpose of God, that this discrimination should then be made on that ground; but the purpose of God includes an earlier discrimination made in effectual calling; whence we read of those who are "the called according to his purpose."[4] This discrimination, made at the time of calling, is not according to men's works, for it is expressly said, "who hath saved us and called us with a holy calling, not according to our works, but according to his own purpose and grace, which was given us in Christ Jesus, before the world began;"[5] calling is a blessing of grace, not conferred for previous works, nor according to previous works. Why is this benefit bestowed? The answer is, "not of works, but of him that calleth."[6] "Not of him that willeth, or of him that runneth, but of God that showeth mercy."[7] It is God that worketh in us to will and to do, of his good pleasure."[8] The first actual separation of God's people from the rest of mankind, is made when they are called out of darkness into his marvellous light; and this calling is not according to men's works, but according to the good pleasure of God. A discrimination is then made, for reasons wholly unknown to mortals; not according to the works of men, but on a ground which infinite wisdom approves. The reason of the procedure is laid deep in the counsels of the divine

---

[1] Eph. ii. 9.
[2] Rom. xi. 6.
[3] Rom. ix. 11.
[4] Rom. viii. 28.
[5] 2 Tim. i. 9.
[6] Rom. ix. 11.
[7] Rom. ix. 16.
[8] Phil. ii. 13.

mind; and we are compelled to say respecting it, "How unsearchable are his judgments, and his ways past finding out!"[1] This actual separation of God's people from the rest of mankind, made in their effectual calling, is like everything which he does, the fulfilment of his eternal purpose. "He worketh all things after the counsel of his will;"[2] and "known unto him are all his works from the beginning."[3] The purpose to effect this first actual discrimination, is God's election; and the ground of the discrimination when it actually takes place, is nothing different from that of the purpose to discriminate; that is, it is the ground of election. The discrimination, when actually made, is approved by the wisdom of God; and all the consequences of it will be approved in the last day, and throughout all coming eternity; and therefore the election, or purpose to discriminate, was approved by infinite wisdom, in the counsels of eternity past. When we object to the act, or the purpose, we presume to be wiser than God.

From the views which have been presented, it necessarily follows, that election is not on the ground of foreseen faith or obedience. On this point, the teachings of Scripture are clear. They are chosen not because of their holiness, but that they may be holy;[4] not because of their obedience, but unto obedience.[5] As the discrimination made in effectual calling is God's work, and antecedent to all holiness, faith, or acceptable obedience; the purpose to discriminate could not be on the ground of acts foreseen, which do not exist as a consideration for the execution of the purpose. The discriminating grace which God bestows, is not on the ground of faith and obedience previously existing, but for a reason known only to God himself. This unrevealed reason, and not foreseen faith and obedience, is the ground of election.

The Scriptures teach that election is according to the foreknowledge of God.[6] We are, however, not to understand the foreknowledge here mentioned, to be foreknowledge of faith or good works. Faith and good works do not exist, before the grace consequent on election begins to be bestowed; and therefore a foresight of them is impossible. Moreover, the objects of this divine foreknowledge are the persons of the elect, and not their

---

[1] Rom. xi. 33.   [2] Eph. i. 11.   [3] Acts xv. 18.
[4] Eph. i. 4.   [5] 1 Pet. i. 2.   [6] 1 Pet. i. 2.

faith or good works. "Whom he foreknew, them he also did predestinate."[1] In this foreknowledge of persons, according to the Scripture use of terms, a peculiar regard to them is implied. It is said, "Hath God cast away his people, whom he foreknew."[2] If simple knowledge, without any peculiar regard, were all that is here implied, it would be equally true that God foreknew the heathen nations, as well as the nation of Israel.

This case of national election may serve also to illustrate the ground of election to salvation. God's choice of the Hebrew nation arose from a peculiar regard to them, not founded on their superiority to other nations,[3] but on his own sovereign pleasure. He loved them, because he would love them. So the election of grace is according to God's foreknowledge of his people; a foreknowledge implying a peculiar regard not founded on any superiority in the objects of it, but arising from the sovereign pleasure of God.

Election is ascribed to God the Father, redemption to God the Son, and sanctification to God the Holy Spirit: "Elect according to the foreknowledge of God the Father, through sanctification of the Spirit, unto obedience, and sprinkling of the blood of Jesus Christ."[4] The Father, as sustaining the authority of the Godhead, is represented as giving the elect to Christ in the covenant of grace: "Thine they were, and thou gavest them me."[5]

The choice of them was with reference to Christ, and that they might be given to him, and rendered accepted in him. Hence they are said to be "chosen in Christ."[6] The election, or setting of them apart to salvation, is, in Jude, attributed to God the Father, by the use of the word sanctify, which signifies to set apart: "Sanctified by God the Father." The next clause of this verse, "preserved in Christ Jesus," may denote that a special divine care is exercised over the elect, because of their covenant relation to Christ, even before their being called by the Holy Spirit. "Preserved in Christ Jesus, and called."

Those who are not included in the election of grace, are called, in Scripture, "the rest,"[7] and "vessels of wrath."[8] Why they are not included, we are as unable to explain as why the others are

---

[1] Rom. viii. 29.   [2] Rom. xi. 1, 2.   [3] Deut. vii. 7
[4] 1 Pet. i. 2.   [5] John xvii. 6.   [6] Eph. i. 4.
[7] Rom. xi. 7.   [8] Rom. ix. 22.

included; and we are therefore compelled to refer the matter to the sovereignty of God, who, beyond all doubt, acts herein most wisely and righteously, though he has not explained to us the reasons of his procedure. His absolute sovereignty, in the discrimination which he makes, is expressed by Paul in these words: "He hath mercy on whom he will have mercy; and whom he will he hardeneth."[1] The natural tendency of human depravity is such, that the heart grows harder under the general mercies which God bestows, unless he superadds to all the other benefits which he confers, the renewing grace of the Holy Spirit, by which the heart is changed. This renewing grace he gives or withholds at his sovereign pleasure. This sovereignty, in so bestowing mercy as to soften the hard heart, is unquestionably taught by the words just quoted, however we may interpret the phrase "he hardeneth." It is not necessary to understand these words as implying a positive act of God, exerted for the purpose of producing hardness of heart, and directed to this end. When Paul speaks of the vessels of mercy, he says that God hath "afore prepared" them for glory; but when he speaks of the vessels of wrath, as fitted for destruction, he does not say that God has fitted them for this end.[2] As the potter, out of the same mass, makes one vessel to honor and another to dishonor;[3] so God, out of the same mass of mankind, prepares some for glory, as vessels of mercy; while others, whatever benefits they may receive from him, being left without renewing grace, abuse the mercies which he bestows, and, growing harder by the influence of their natural depravity, are vessels of wrath fitted for destruction.

Divines have used the term "reprobate" as equivalent to "non-elect;" but this is not the Scripture use of the term. Paul says, "Examine yourselves whether ye be in the faith, prove your own selves. Know ye not your own selves, how that Jesus Christ is in you, except ye be reprobates?[4] Here all are regarded as reprobates in whom Christ does not dwell by faith; and, of consequence, the elect themselves are reprobates so long as they remain in unbelief. Reprobation, as a positive act of God, is no other than the condemnation under which all unbelievers lie.

---

[1] Rom. ix. 18.   [3] Rom. ix. 22, 23.
[2] Rom. ix. 21.   [4] 2 Cor. xiii. 5.

From a state of condemnation, God, according to his purpose in election, delivers some by his renewing grace, and this is no injury or disadvantage done to the rest.

The doctrine of election is generally opposed by unrenewed men: and even in the minds of those whose hearts have been renewed by grace, such objections to it often arise as to prevent the cordial reception of it. The most common of these objections it will be proper here to consider.

Obj. 1. The doctrine of election offers no inducement to human effort. Under the belief of it men conclude that, if elected, they will be saved, do what they will; and if not elected, they will be damned, do what they can. Hence they decide that all effort on their part is useless, and that it will be as well to live as they please, and dismiss all concern about their destiny, over which they can have no control.

That some men, who profess to believe the doctrine of election, make a bad use of it, cannot be denied; but it cannot be affirmed that all who receive the doctrine reason or act in the manner stated in the objection. On the contrary, multitudes, eminent for holiness of life and self-denying labors in the cause of Christ, not only cordially receive the doctrine, but ascribe all their holiness and self-denying labors to that grace which they have received from God's electing love. Many who reject and hate the doctrine, determine to live as they please, and to give themselves no concern for the things of God and religion: and the same cause will produce the same effect, in unregenerate men who admit the doctrine, and pervert it by their carnal reasonings to a use to which it has no legitimate tendency.

This objection to election applies equally to every part of the divine purpose, and proceeds on the supposition that God has predetermined the end without reference to the means by which it is to be accomplished. God has his purpose in providence, as well as in grace; and works all things in each department of his operations, after the counsel of his own will: but no wise man will say, "If I am to have a crop, I shall have it, whether I plough and sow, or not; and therefore I need not labor, or give myself concern to obtain bread to eat." The purpose of God leaves men at equal liberty, and gives them equal encouragement to labor for the meat that perisheth not, as for that which perisheth. · God's purpose does not sever the connection between the means and the end, but establishes it; and there is nothing, in a proper view of God's sovereignty, whether in providence or in grace, to induce the belief that the end may be obtained without the use of the appropriate means; or that the end need be despaired of if the appropriate means be used. The word of God assures us, that " he who believes in Christ shall be saved, and he who believes not shall be damned;" and there is nothing in God's purpose, or in a proper view of his purpose, to annul these declarations of his word. The purpose of God determines his own action; but his revealed word is the rule of ours; and if we so act as to have his promise on our side, we may be sure that his purpose also will be on our side: but his purpose cannot secure the salvation of any who remain in impenitence and unbelief, and under the condemnation of his revealed word.

It is true, however, that election discourages such human effort as is made in a wrong direction. It prostrates all human hope at the feet of a Sovereign God, and teaches the prayer, "Lord, if thou wilt, thou canst make me clean." It discountenances all effort to save ourselves by our own works of righteousness; but brings the sinner to commit himself at once to the sovereign mercy of God. He who, knowing himself to be condemned and helpless, gives himself, from the heart, into the hands of God as a sovereign, and trusts entirely to his grace for salvation, will find no reason to prefer that this grace should be conferred according to some present determination of the divine mind, rather than according to the counsel of eternal wisdom. The objection to the latter, if thoroughly analyzed, will be found to contain in it some lurking idea that it is safer to trust in something else than in God's absolute mercy. As such lurking trust is dangerous to the soul, the doctrine of election has a salutary tendency to deliver us from it. It tends to produce precisely that trust in God, that complete surrender of ourselves to him, to which alone the promise of eternal life is made; and if we reject the doctrine, we ought to consider whether we do not, at the same time, reject our only hope of life everlasting.

Obj. 2. The doctrine of election is unfavorable to the interests of morality. If men believe that God has appointed them to salvation or damnation, at his own pleasure, without regard to their works, the motive to good works which is drawn from the expectation of future reward or punishment, will cease to influence them.

At the last day men will be judged according to their works. God's choice of men to holiness and obedience, and the grace bestowed on them to render them holy and obedient, do not change the rule by which the final judgment will be pronounced: they, therefore, leave the expectation of future retribution to have its full effect on the minds of men. No one will be condemned at the mere pleasure of God; but every sentence of condemnation will be for sins committed. Hence the fear of future punishment ought to deter men from the commission of sin. None have a right to expect acceptance in the great day who do not, in the present life, serve God in sincerity and with persevering constancy. A belief that God, by his grace, inclines some men to serve him, and that he determined, from eternity, to bestow this grace upon them, cannot diminish, in any well-disposed mind, the proper influence arising from the expectation of future retribution, or produce indifference to the claims of morality. In electing men to salvation, God has devised no method of accomplishing his gracious purpose respecting them, but by rendering them holy and obedient; and therefore the doctrine of election teaches the indispensable necessity of holiness and obedience, in order to salvation. The doctrine is perverted and abused when men take occasion from it to indulge in sin.

Obj. 3. The doctrine of election represents God as partial, and is, therefore, inconsistent with the Scripture, which teaches that "The wisdom which is from above, is without partiality."[1]

The wisdom from above, which James declares to be without partiality, dwells in the minds of Christian men, and is exercised in their intercourse with mankind. It does not incline or require them to feel equal affection toward all, or to do good equally to all. Within the limits of justice, it requires that every man shall have his due; and here, all partiality is injustice. In the department of benevolence, the Christian man is not bound to bestow his favors with equality, on all his fellow creatures. The wisdom from above guides him, in the distribution of his favors, by other rules. So

---

[1] James iii. 17.

God, the source of this wisdom, is without partiality in the dispensation of his justice; but, in bestowing his grace, he acts as a sovereign, and claims and exercises the right to do what he will with his own. Partiality in a judge, when professing to administer justice, is a great wrong; but the same judge may bestow special favor on his children, or near friends, or on chosen objects of charity, without any just imputation of wrong; and to charge God with partiality, because he bestows his favors as he pleases, is to pour contempt on his sovereignty, and covertly to deny his right to do what he will with his own. He may well say to man who makes this charge: "Is thine eye evil, because I am good?"

Obj. 4. The doctrine of election represents God as a respecter of persons; but Peter affirmed that "God is not a respecter of persons."[1]

The same phrase has different significations, according to the connection in which it is used. We may affirm that God is, in one sense of the phrase, a respecter of persons, for his word states, that "he had respect unto Abel and his offering."[2] The first Christians were taught, not to have respect of persons, by giving superior places, in their religious assemblies, to those who were rich, and wore gay clothing.[3] The Hebrew judges were required not to have respect of persons, by favoring any one in his cause.[4] In this objectionable sense, God is not a respecter of persons. Before him, the rich and great of the earth are as nothing: yet he has respect to his saints, however humble and despised among men. When Peter affirmed that God is not a respecter of persons, he was addressing the first company of uncircumcised persons to whom the Gospel was preached; and his words manifestly imported the equal admission of Gentiles with Jews, to the privileges and blessings of the Gospel. "God is not a respecter of persons; but in every nation, he that feareth God, and worketh righteousness, is accepted with him."[5] The words express nothing contrary to what Peter elsewhere says: "Ye are a chosen generation, a royal priesthood, a holy nation, a peculiar people, that ye should show forth the praises of him who hath called you out of darkness into his marvellous light."[6]

---

[1] Acts x. 34.   [2] Gen. iv. 4.   [3] James ii. 3.
[4] Lev. xix. 15.   [5] Acts x. 34, 35.   [6] 1 Pet. ii. 9.

Obj. 5. The doctrine of election represents God as insincere. He invites all men to participate in the blessings of the gospel; and yet, if this doctrine is true, the blessings of the gospel are not designed for all.

If God's word teaches the doctrine of election, and if it contains commands or invitations to all men to seek salvation through Christ, it is highly presumptuous in us to charge God with insincerity, because we cannot reconcile the two things with each other. We ought to remember that we are worms of the dust, and that it is criminal arrogance in us to judge and condemn the infinite God. But, in truth, there is no ground whatever for this charge of insincerity. God requires all men to believe in Christ; and this is their duty, however unwilling they may be to perform it. The fact that they are unwilling, and that God knows they will remain unwilling, unless he change their hearts, abates nothing from the sincerity of the requirement. God proves his sincerity, by holding them to the obligation, and condemning their unbelief. He promises salvation to all who believe in Christ; and he proves his sincerity, by fulfilling his promise in every instance. The *bestowment* of special grace, changing the hearts of men, and bringing them to believe in Christ, is, in no respect, inconsistent with any requirement or promise that God has made. While men regard the call of the gospel as an invitation which they may receive or reject at pleasure, it accords with their state of mind to institute the inquiry, whether God is sincere in offering this invitation: but when they regard it as a solemn requirement of duty, for which God will certainly hold them accountable, they will find no occasion for calling his sincerity in question.

Obj. 6. The doctrine of election confines the benevolence of God to a part of the human race; but the Scriptures teach, that "the Lord is good to all, and his tender mercies are over all his works."[1]

God is kind to the unthankful and evil, and bestows blessings on the just and the unjust; but his benevolence, though infinite, does not produce in every one of his creatures the highest degree of happiness. The world which we inhabit abounds with misery, and the Scriptures have warned us, that there is a world of

---

[1] Ps. cxlv. 9.

unmitigated torment, into which wicked men will be driven, to be punished for their sins, with the devil and his angels. The justice of God limits the exercise of his benevolence; and, if we deny the doctrine of election, it still remains true, that the benevolence of God will effect the salvation of a part only of the human race. Now, unless it can be shown that the election of grace lessens the number of the saved, no objection can lie against it, on the ground of its relation to God's benevolence. Paul did not regard it as lessening the divine benevolence. According to his view of the subject, all Israel would have been cast away, had not God reserved a remnant according to the election of grace.[1] What was true of this nation, is true of all other nations. There are causes, apart from election, which intercept the flow of God's benevolence to sinful men : and election, instead of increasing the obstacles, opens the channel in which the mercy of God can flow, to bless and save the lost.

Obj. 7. The doctrine of election, by teaching that God has reprobated a part of the human race to hopeless misery, represents him as an unamiable being.

Sinful men are indeed reprobated, not by the election of grace, but by the justice of God; but their reprobation is not hopeless, so long as the gospel of salvation sounds in their ears. But the only hope on which they are authorized to lay hold, springs from the electing love of God. Instead of covering men's prospects with the blackness of darkness, the doctrine of election sends a ray of hope, the only possible ray, to enlighten the gloom.

The justice of God will hereafter doom the finally impenitent, as it has already doomed the fallen angels, to hopeless misery. The unamiable feature, which the objection we are considering finds in the divine character, is the justice so horrible to the workers of iniquity. The election of grace, if it wholly annihilated the justice of God, would receive the praises of unconverted men; but it cannot do this. The infinite benevolence of God cannot do this. If men will pronounce the character of God unamiable, because he is just, and dooms sinful beings to hopeless misery, they prove thereby that they do not love the God whom the Scriptures reveal, and by whom they are to be judged. Their quarrel with the

---

[1] Rom. xi. 2–5.

doctrine of election is, in truth, a quarrel with the justice of God, from which that election has not delivered them.

Of the laborers in the vineyard, who received every man his penny, they who had borne the heat and burden of the day, complained that those who had labored but one hour, received equal wages with them. The occasion for this complaint would not have existed, if no one had received more than was due to him, in strict justice, according to the amount of service rendered. So, if all grace were withheld from the human race, and every one received from God what his deeds in strict justice deserve, no occasion would exist for the objection which is urged against God's election. But, would men be better off? or would God be more amiable? The lord in the parable met the objection thus: " Friend, I do thee no wrong. Is it not lawful for me to do what I will with mine own? Is thine eye evil, because I am good?"[1] We are taught hereby how to silence objections to the sovereignty of divine grace. While God does wrong to no man, though he does as he will with his own, it becomes us to bow to his sovereignty, and acknowledge him infinitely amiable in all his perfections.

Not content with the God whom the Bible reveals, and who does according to his pleasure in the army of heaven, and among the inhabitants of the earth, we carve out to ourselves a deity more amiable, in our view, than he. If we dare not strip him of his justice, and secure thereby the salvation of all men, we endeavor to devise for him a method of salvation less exposed to human cavil. We aim to free him from the responsibility of determining who shall be saved; and we form the plan, and fix the terms of salvation, with the design of rendering the result contingent on the actions of men. Our method of grace, we admit, will not secure the salvation of all men. If the infinitely wise God should adopt it, he would foreknow all its results, and precisely how many persons, and what persons, would finally be saved by it. Now, if he should make our plan his own, with this foreknowledge of its results, it would then be his plan, fixing as definitely the salvation of those who will be saved, as the plan on which he at present proceeds, and equally leaving the residue of mankind to the awful doom to which his justice will consign them. Our preferred plan

---

[1] Matt. xx. 13, 15.

may accord better with the views of finite worms, like ourselves, who know not the end from the beginning; but if God should adopt it, he would be responsible for it, in all its workings, to the final issue: responsible, though not to any other being, yet to himself; for his acts must accord with his perfections, and must receive his own approbation. In selecting his present plan, he has chosen it with a full knowledge of all its results. As the plan is his chosen plan, so the people whom it will save are his chosen people. We must prove that our plan would be better, before we can maintain that the deity of our imagination would be more amiable than the God of the Bible.

Every proposed method of salvation that leaves the issue dependent on human volition, is defective. It has been always found, that men *will* not come to Christ for life. The gospel is preached to every creature; but all, with one consent, ask to be excused. The will of men must be changed; and this change the will itself cannot effect. Divine grace must here interpose. Unless God work in the sinner to will and to do, salvation is impossible. God knows the force of opposition which his grace will encounter in each heart, and the amount of spiritual influence necessary to overcome it. He gives or withholds that influence at his pleasure. He has his own rule of acting in this matter—a rule infinitely wise and good. With full knowledge how his rule will affect every particular case, he perseveres in acting according to it, however men may cavil: and the rule which infinite wisdom adopts must be the best; nor can it be any objection to it, that infinite wisdom knows perfectly its final result.

Obj. 8. The doctrine of election does not recommend itself to the general acceptance of mankind; but is received only by those who believe themselves to be in the number of the elect; and who are therefore interested judges.

The truth or falsehood of a religious doctrine cannot be determined by the acceptance which it obtains among men. What God says, is true, whether men receive or reject it. The gospel, which is preached on the authority of God's truth, is rejected by a large part of mankind; and those who do receive it are exposed to the charge of being interested judges, because they expect God's blessing through their belief of it. All that the objection says of election is true of the gospel. It does not prove the gospel untrue;

and it ought not, in the least degree, to impair and weaken our faith in the doctrine of election.

According to God's method of grace, as revealed in his holy word, the salvation of men is made dependent on their belief of the gospel. It is a test of genuine faith, that it cordially receives those parts of divine truth which are least acceptable to the carnal heart. Hence it arises, that the doctrine of election, or, which is the same thing, of God's sovereignty in the bestowment of his grace, often becomes the point at which a sinner's submission to God is tested. When this doctrine is cordially received, the sinner's rebellion against God ceases. When he yields to the sovereignty of God in bestowing eternal life at his pleasure, he admits that sovereignty in everything else. How much soever he may permit the monarch of the universe to do what he pleases in smaller matters, if he refuses to yield to his sovereignty in the matter of highest importance, his submission to God is partial, and the spirit of rebellion has not departed.

. Many examples of Christian experience might be adduced, in which a submission to God's sovereignty in bestowing the blessings of grace, became the deciding point of a sinner's acceptance of Christ.

Though the objection which we have considered contains no valid argument against the doctrine of election, it may suggest an important lesson to those who admit this doctrine into their creed. If men, as interested judges, decide in favor of the doctrine, and regard it with pleasure merely because they suppose themselves to be among the favorites of heaven, their faith will be unavailing. No submission to God is implied in our approving of his supposed favoritism toward us. The gospel calls on every sinner to give himself up, through Christ, into the hands of his offended sovereign; and to do this as a guilty creature, and not as a supposed favorite of Heaven. In this complete surrender, the heart becomes fully reconciled to the doctrine of election.

Section II.—PARTICULAR REDEMPTION.

THE SON OF GOD GAVE HIS LIFE TO REDEEM THOSE WHO WERE GIVEN TO HIM BY THE FATHER IN THE COVENANT OF GRACE.[1]

The Scriptures teach that the Son of God, in coming into the world and laying down his life, had the salvation of a peculiar people in view : " Thou shalt call his name Jesus, for he shall save his people from their sins."[2]   " The good Shepherd giveth his life for the sheep."[3]   " Husbands, love your wives, even as Christ also loved the Church, and gave himself for it, that he might sanctify and cleanse it with the washing of water by the word, that he might present it to himself a glorious church."[4]   The Scriptures also teach that the expectation of the Redeemer will be fully realized, and that not one of all whom the Father gave him will fail to be saved : " He shall see his seed.   He shall see of the travail of his soul and be satisfied."[5]   " All that the Father giveth me, shall come to me ; and him that cometh to me I will in no wise cast out."   " And this is the Father's will which hath sent me, that of all which he hath given me I should lose nothing, but should raise it up again at the last day."[6]   " Father, I will that they also, whom thou hast given me, be with me where I am."[7]

And finally, when all shall be congregated, he will say, " Behold, I, and the children which God has given me."[8]   In presenting to the Father all who had been given to him, in the covenant of grace, to be redeemed out of every kindred, tongue, nation, and people, the Saviour will have the full reward of his obedience unto death.

Redemption will not be universal in its consummation ; for the redeemed will be *out of* every kindred, tongue, nation, and people ;[9] and therefore cannot include all in any of these divisions of mankind.   And redemption cannot have been universal in its purpose ; otherwise the purpose will fail to be accomplished, and all, for which the work of redemption was undertaken, will not be effected.

---

[1] Eph. v. 25–27 ; Tit. ii. 14 ; John x. 11 ; Rev. i. 5, 6 ; Acts xx. 28 ; Heb. x. 14 ; Isaiah liii. 5, 11.

[2] Matt. i. 21.	[3] John x. 11.	[4] Eph. v. 25–27.
[5] Isaiah liii. 10, 11.	[6] John vi. 37, 39.	[7] John xvii. 24.
[8] Heb. ii. 13.	[9] Rev. v. 9.	

Besides God's will of purpose, we have seen that he has a will of precept. According to the latter, he commands all men everywhere to repent; he requires all to believe in Jesus Christ; and it is his will that all men should honor the Son. To all who obey his will in these particulars, he gives the promise of eternal life. The precept and the promise are both included in the revealed will of God. It is the revealed will of God that the gospel should be preached to every creature, and that every creature who hears should believe, and that all who believe shall receive life everlasting. The revealed will is the rule of our faith, duty, and hope; and by it those who preach the gospel, and those who hear it, are authorised and bound to regulate every thought and action. In it, Christ is exhibited as the Saviour of the world;[1] the only name under heaven given among men whereby we must be saved;[2] and sinners, without exception, are invited and commanded to believe in Christ. As the gospel is preached to all men without distinction, and all are called upon to come to Christ for life; and nothing but man's rejection of the gospel prevents the extension of its blessing to all who hear it; it accords with the design of God's revealed word, to speak of the offices and work of Christ, according to men's obligations respecting them. It must be remembered, however, that the gospel promises its blessings to those only who obey it; and, as the promise, not the precept, is the proper measure of the benefits which it secures, its benefits are limited to particular persons, even when the limitation in its extent does not appear in the language employed. Christ is called the Saviour of the world,[3] the propitiation[4] for the sins of the whole world; and the free gift through him is said to come on all men unto justification of life.[5] These, and other like expressions of Scripture, represent the facts as they would be, on the supposition that all men did their duty. But notwithstanding these general expressions, the revealed will of God secures blessings only to the obedient, and is therefore narrower in its limit than the purpose or secret will of God, which not only provides all needed grace for the obedient, but also, for all the elect, the grace necessary to render them obedient.

The remarks which have been made may suffice to show that

---

[1] John iv. 42. [2] Acts iv. 12. [3] John iv. 42.
[4] 1 John ii. 2. [5] Rom. v. 18.

redemption is not universal, in any view which can properly be taken of it. It is particular in its consummation, and in its purpose; and it is equally so in the revelation of it, which is made in the gospel. The general terms "all men," "the whole world," &c., which the Scriptures employ in speaking of its extent, cannot be understood to secure its benefits to the impenitent and unbelieving. According to God's secret will, or will of purpose, redemption is secured by the death of Christ to all the elect; according to his revealed will, it is secured to those only who believe.

The adaptedness of Christ's death to serve as a ground for universal gospel invitations, constitutes it in the view of some persons a universal redemption. But no one can with propriety be said to be redeemed, who does not obtain deliverance, and who never will obtain it. Other persons who maintain the doctrine of particular redemption, distinguish between redemption and atonement, and because of the adaptedness referred to, consider the death of Christ an atonement for the sins of all men; or as an atonement for sin in the abstract. In Rom. v. 11, the only place in the New Testament where the word atonement occurs, the Greek word for which it stands, is the same that is rendered *reconciling—reconciliation*, in other places.[1] The reconciliation is not between God and sin in the abstract, for such a reconciliation is impossible. It is a reconciliation of persons; and such a reconciliation as secures eternal salvation. "If, when we were enemies, we were reconciled to God, by the death of his Son, much more, being reconciled, we shall be saved by his life."[2] In Paul's view, all those for whom Christ's death made reconciliation or atonement, will certainly be saved; and therefore atonement cannot be universal, unless salvation be universal. It is possible to use the word atonement in such a sense, as to render the question respecting the extent of the atonement one of mere definition: but it is best to use the words of Scripture in the Scripture sense.

In reconciling the vicariousness of Christ's death with the universal call of the gospel, a difficulty arises, which may be stated thus:—

An unrestricted invitation to all who hear the gospel, to come to Christ for life, seems to imply that universal provision has been

---

[1] Rom. xi. 15; 2 Cor. v. 18, 19.   [2] Rom. v. 10.

made in him; and in order to the making of universal provision, it appears necessary that he should have borne the sins of all men.

But the supposition that he bore the sins of the whole human race, is attended with much difficulty. Multitudes died in impenitence before he came into the world, and were suffering for their sins in the other world, while he was hanging on the cross. How could he be a substitute for these, and suffer the penalty for their sins, when they were suffering it in their own persons? And if he endured the penalty for the sins of all who have since died, or shall hereafter die in impenitence, how shall they be required to satisfy justice a second time by personal suffering?

For a solution of this difficulty, with which the minds of many have been much perplexed, it has been supposed that the amount of suffering necessary to make an atoning sacrifice, is not increased or lessened by the amount of sin to be atoned for. This hypothesis is entitled to respect, not only because of the relief which it affords the mind, but also because it has recommended itself to the general acceptance of learned and pious men. Nevertheless, like every other hypothesis invented for the removal of difficulty, it should not be made an article of faith, until it has been proved.

In support of the hypothesis, it has been argued that since the wages of sin is death, Christ must have died for a single sin, and he needed only to die, in making atonement for the sins of the whole world.

This argument does not sustain the hypothesis, unless it be assumed that death is the same in every supposable case. But death may be an easy and joyful transition from this world to the world of bliss. Such was not the death of Christ. Death, as the wages of sin, includes more than the mere dissolution of the body: and Christ, in dying for sin, endured an amount of sorrow which was not necessary to mere natural death. In this suffering, the expiatory efficacy of his death chiefly consisted; and we dare not assume that the amount of it must be the same in every supposable case. The sufferings of Christ derive infinite value from his divine nature; but, being endured by his human nature, their amount could not be infinite; hence it is supposable that the amount might have been different in different circumstances. The inhabitants of Sodom and Gomorrah will, in the last day, be doomed to the second death, equally with the more guilty inhabitants of Chorazin and Bethsaida: but the anguish attendant will be more intolerable in one case than in the other. Analogy would seem to require, that Christ, suffering for the sins of the whole world, must endure more than if suffering for only one sin.

The advocates of the hypothesis urge, that the atonement is moral, and not commercial; and they object, that the notion of so much suffering for so much sin, degrades it into a mere commercial transaction. According to an illustration before given, if twenty men owe one hundred dollars, commercial justice is satisfied when each man has paid five dollars; but when twenty men have conspired to commit murder, moral justice, or rather distributive justice (for commercial justice is also moral), holds every man guilty of the deed, and as deserving of capital punishment as if he alone had committed the crime. On the same principle, it is maintained, moral justice does not divide the death of Christ into parts, accounting so much for each offence; but regards it as equally sufficient for many offences, as for one; and equally sufficient for the sins of the whole world, as for the sins of the elect.

The argument is not conclusive. It is not true, that the principle of distributive justice repels the notion of so much suffering for so much sin. Justice has its scales in government, as well as in commerce; and an essential part of its administration consists in the apportionment of penalties to crimes. It does not account the stealing of herbs from a neighbor's garden, and the murder of a father, crimes of equal magnitude; and it does not weigh out to them equal penalties. The justice of God has a heavier penalty for Chorazin and Bethsaida, than for Sodom and Gomorrah. Everything of which we have knowledge in the divine administration, instead of exploding the notion of so much suffering for so much sin, tends rather to establish it. The objection that it is commercial, is not well founded. Though justice in government, and justice in commerce, may be distinguished from each other, it does not follow, that whatever may be affirmed of the one, must necessarily be denied of the other. Distributive justice is not that which determines the equality of value, in commodities which are exchanged for each other: but it does not therefore exclude all regard to magnitudes and proportions. In the language of Scripture, sins are *debts*,[1] the blood of Christ is a *price*,[2] and his people are *bought*.[3] This language is doubtless figurative: but the figures would not be appropriate, if commercial justice, to which the terms *debt*, *price*, *bought*, appertain, did not bear an analogy to the distributive justice which required the sacrifice of Christ.

In the case adduced for illustration, every accomplice in the murder is held guilty of the crime, because every one has the full intention of it. Justice, viewing the crime in the intention, accounts each one guilty, and requires the penalty to be inflicted on him. It does not admit that the punishment of one will be equivalent to the punishment of all: but, in this very case, employs its scales to give to every one his due, and apportions the amount of penalty inflicted, to the amount of crime.

This examination of the argument discovers, that it is not conclusive. If the atonement of Christ excludes all regard to the amount of sin to be expiated, the exclusion does not arise from the abstract principles of distributive justice, as distinguished from commercial, but from something peculiar in the great transaction. No transaction like it with which it may be compared, has ever occurred. The wisdom and justice of God have decided this single case, and have decided it right. Christ did endure just *so much* suffering, as would expiate the sins that were laid on him. What amount of suffering would have been necessary, if he had expiated but one sin, is a question which, so far as we know, has never been decided in the court of heaven. When we confidently decide it, we are in danger of intruding into those things which do not belong to us. If the Holy Scriptures teach us nothing on the subject, we should not seek to be wise above what is written.

The Scriptures, so far as I know, contain no proof of the hypothesis. The best argument in its favor is drawn from Hebrews ix., in which it is taught that, if the sacrifices of the old dispensation had been efficacious, they would not have needed to be repeated. This seems to involve the principle, that an efficacious sacrifice for sin, when once made, will suffice for all sin, however it may be multiplied in all future time; and this principle, if established, establishes the hypothesis before us. But the clause "then would they not have ceased to be offered," may be taken without

---

[1] Matt. vi. 12.   [2] 1 Cor. vi. 20; 1 Pet. i. 18.   [3] 1 Cor. vi. 20.

an interrogative point following, and the argument of Paul will be, that the sacrifices of the Old Testament dispensation, if efficacious, would have continued to be offered from year to year, making atonement for the sins of each year as it passed, and would not have been superseded by another covenant, as the Lord had foretold by his prophet. So interpreted, the argument of Paul, instead of establishing the hypothesis, subverts it. But if the clause be read with the interrogative point, it may still be understood to refer to the remembrance from year to year continually of the *same sins*, that had once been atoned for. When the sins of one year had been atoned for, why should the very same sins be brought into remembrance the second, third, and fourth years, and the offering for them repeated, if the first offering had been efficacious? So understood, the apostle's argument does not establish the principle involved in the hypothesis.

If, after a thorough examination of the hypothesis, we should, instead of making it an article of faith, be inclined to abandon it; and if the difficulty which it was invented to remove should perplex us; we may obtain relief, as we are compelled to do in other cases, by receiving the whole of God's truth on his authority, even though the harmony of its parts is not apparent to our weak understandings. In this way, theological difficulties furnish an opportunity for the exercise of confidence in the divine veracity: and our state of mind is never better or safer than when, in simple faith, we take God at his word.

So far as we have the means of judging, the sufferings of Christ, when viewed apart from the purpose of God respecting them, were in themselves as well adapted to satisfy for the sins of Judas as of Peter. But we cannot affirm this of every act which Christ performed in his priestly office. His intercessions for Peter were particular and efficacious; and these, as a part of his priestly work, may be included with his sufferings, as constituting with them the perfect and acceptable offering which he, as the great High Priest, makes for his people. The atonement or reconciliation which results, must be as particular as the intercessions by which it is procured.

Some have maintained that, if the atonement of Christ is not general, no sinner can be under obligation to believe in Christ, until he is assured that he is one of the elect. This implies that no sinner is bound to believe what God says, unless he knows that God designs to save him. God declares that there is no salvation, except through Christ; and every sinner is bound to believe this truth. If it were revealed from heaven, that but one sinner, of all our fallen race, shall be saved by Christ, the obligation to believe that there is no salvation out of Christ, would remain the same. Every sinner, to whom the revelation would be made, would be bound to look to Christ as his only possible hope, and commit himself to that sovereign mercy by which some one of the justly condemned race would be saved. The abundant mercy of our God will not be confined to the salvation of a single sinner; but it will bring many sons to glory through the sufferings of Jesus, the Captain of our salvation. Yet every sinner, who trusts in Christ for salvation, is bound to commit himself, unreservedly, to the sovereign mercy of God. If he requires some previous assurance that he is in the number of the elect, he does not surrender himself to God, as a guilty sinner ought. The gospel brings every sinner prostrate at the feet of the Great Sovereign, hoping for mercy at his will, and in his way: and the gospel is perverted when any terms short of this are offered to the offender. With this universal call to absolute and unconditional surrender to God's sovereignty, the doctrine of particular redemption exactly harmonizes.

Section III.—EFFECTUAL CALLING.

THE HOLY SPIRIT EFFECTUALLY CALLS ALL THE ELECT TO REPENT AND BELIEVE.[1]

The gospel calls all who hear it to repent and believe. This call proceeds from the Holy Spirit, who qualifies the ministers of the gospel for their work, and gives them the written word. But men resist and disobey this call of the Spirit, and remain under condemnation. "Ye do always resist the Holy Ghost; as your fathers did, so do ye." "Which of the prophets have not your

---

[1] John vi. 37; Rom. viii. 26, 30; 1 Cor. i. 24; 2 Tim. i. 9; 1 Pet. ii. 9; Jude 1, 2; 1 Cor. ii. 4; 1 Thess. i. 4–6.

fathers persecuted?"[1] "He shall be revealed, taking vengeance on all them that obey not the gospel."[2]

· Besides the call which is external, and often ineffectual, there is another, which is internal and effectual. This always produces repentance and faith, and therefore secures salvation. The former external call is intended in such passages of Scripture as the following: "Because I have called, and ye refused."[3] "Many be called, but few chosen."[4] The internal and effectual call is designed in the following passages: "Who hath saved us, and called us with a holy calling."[5] "Whom he predestinated, them he also called; whom he called, them he also justified."[6] "Called to be saints."[7] "Among whom are ye also the called of Jesus Christ."[8] "To them who love God, who are the called according to his purpose."[9] It is not true of all who receive the external call, that they are predestinated to life, justified and saved. Whenever these blessings are represented as belonging to the called, the internal and effectual call must be meant.

We have before distinguished between the direct and the indirect influence of the Holy Spirit. The external call being by means of the written or preached word, belongs to the indirect influence of the Spirit. To render this call effectual, the direct influence is superadded; and the gospel is then said to come, not in word only,[10] but in demonstration of the Spirit and with power.[11] The external call is disobeyed, because men will not come to Christ that they may have life: the internal call operates on the will itself, working in men to *will* and to do, and rendering God's people *willing* in the day of his power. As distinguished from the external call, the internal is always unresisted. In the process of conversion, the Holy Spirit is violently resisted; but this resistance is directed against the outward means. The internal grace softens and subdues the heart, and brings it into peaceful subjection to the gospel of Christ.

The internal grace, which renders the outward call effectual, is the grace of regeneration. Hence regeneration, considered as the

---

[1] Acts vii. 51, 52.   [2] 2 Thess. i. 7, 8.   [3] Prov. i. 24.
[4] Matt. xx. 16.   [5] 2 Tim. i. 9.   [6] Rom. viii. 30.
[7] Rom. i. 7.   [8] Rom. i. 6.   [9] Rom. viii. 28.
[10] 1 Thess. i. 5.   [11] 1 Cor. ii. 4.

work of the Holy Spirit, is the same as effectual calling; considered as the change of the sinner's heart, it is the effect of this calling. The calling is effectual, because it produces regeneration in the subject on whom it operates.

In effectual calling, the Holy Spirit displays his omnipotence. " We believe according to the working of his mighty power, which he wrought in Christ, when he raised him from the dead."[1]   The same power which created the world, and said, " Let there be light, and there was light," is needed in the new creation of the sinner. " God, who commanded the light to shine out of darkness, hath shined in our hearts."[2] " We are his workmanship, *created* in Christ Jesus unto good works."[3] " According as his divine power hath given unto us all things that pertain unto life and godliness, through the knowledge of him that hath called us to glory and virtue."[4] His power in creating the world was unresisted; and equally unresisted is the power by which he new-creates the heart.   The outward means which the Spirit sends may be resisted; but when the Spirit himself comes in the omnipotence of his grace, resistance vanishes.

In effectual calling, the Holy Spirit acts as a sovereign.   In bestowing the various gifts which he conferred on the ancient Christians, he acted as a sovereign: " All these worketh that one and the self-same Spirit, dividing to every man severally as he will."[5] He is equally sovereign in giving regenerating grace. " Of his own will begat he us with the word of truth."[6] Grace is sovereign in election by the Father, redemption by the Son, and effectual calling by the Holy Spirit.   The discrimination which grace makes among the children of men, first appears in effectual calling.   This work of the Holy Spirit leads up, through the redemption of Jesus Christ, to God the Father, to whose electing love we are taught to ascribe all the blessings of eternal salvation.   In this reverse order we look back, along the stream of mercy, to the fountain from which it flows.   This reverse order is observed in the precept, "Make your calling and election sure."[7]   Our calling proceeds

---

[1] Eph. i. 19, 20.   [2] 2 Cor. iv. 6.   [3] Eph. ii. 10.
[4] 2 Pet. i. 3.   [5] 1 Cor. xii. 11.   [6] James i. 18.
[7] 2 Pet. i. 10.

from our election; but we ascertain our election by first ascertaining our calling.

In effectual calling, the Holy Spirit operates on the elect. These are "sanctified by God the Father, preserved in Christ Jesus, and called."[1] They whom the Spirit calls are "chosen in Christ from the foundation of the world."[2] "As many as were ordained to eternal life believed."[3] The Spirit's effectual calling fulfils the word of Christ, "All that the Father giveth me, shall come to me."[4] "Other sheep have I, which are not of this fold; them also I must bring."[5]

It has been asked, for what purpose does God send his outward call to the non-elect, since it will be ineffectual, unless accompanied with his omnipotent grace. We might as well ask for what purpose does God give men his law, when they will not obey it; or why does he institute a moral government over them, when they will not submit to it. Instead of demanding God's reasons for what he does, it becomes every man rather to inquire, what reason he can render to God, for violating his holy law, and rejecting the call of his gospel. We may be sure that God will do right, and will be able to vindicate his ways before the intelligent universe; and we should regard our propensity to call in question the wisdom and righteousness of his procedure, as an alarming evidence of our want of submission to his will.

Objection. If repentance and faith are gifts of grace bestowed by the Holy Spirit in effectual calling, men on whom this grace is not conferred, are not blameworthy for being impenitent and unbelieving.

The objection virtually assumes, that men are under no obligation to serve God further than they please; or that if their unwillingness to serve him can be overcome by nothing less than omnipotent grace, it excuses their disobedience. Let the man who makes to himself this apology for his impenitence and unbelief, consider well, with what face he can present his plea before the great Judge. "I did not serve God, because I was wholly unwilling to serve him; and so exceedingly unwilling that nothing less

---

[1] Jude 1.　　[2] Eph. i. 4–13　　[3] Acts xiii. 48.
[4] John vi. 37.　　[5] John x. 16.

than omnipotent grace could reconcile me to the hated service." Who will dare offer this plea on the great day?

The efficacious grace which renders the gospel successful, is the grand peculiarity of the gospel dispensation.

This grace was bestowed in a smaller measure, before the coming of Christ, and during his personal ministry; but the abundant outpouring of it was reserved for the Pentecost that followed the Saviour's ascension, and the times succeeding. The apostles were commanded to remain in Jerusalem, until they were endued with power from on high, and the power of the Holy Spirit which fell on them rendered their preaching far more successful than the ministry of Christ himself had been. Had God bound himself, by rule, to give an equal measure of grace to every human being, and to leave the result to the unaided volitions of men, the extraordinary success which marked the first period of Christianity would not have existed. It must be ascribed to the efficacious grace of the Holy Spirit, whom the Saviour promised to send after he should go to the Father.. To the power of the Spirit, the success of the word, in all ages, must be attributed: and the glorious millennial day so long expected by the church will not come, until the Spirit be poured out from on high.[1] Hence, all good men looking forward to this glorious day, have not relied for its coming on the superior morality and religious tendency of future generations, but have prayed for it and have hoped for success, only through the abundant influence of the Holy Spirit.

CONCLUSION.

OUR Saviour frequently rebuked those who trusted in themselves that they were righteous, and despised others. This self-righteous temper prevailed in the sect of the Pharisees; and Paul, who was a Pharisee, was obliged to renounce it, when he became a follower of Christ. He then prayed to be found, not having his own righteousness, but the righteousness which is of God by faith. In

---

[1] Isaiah xxxii. 15.

his strong desire and earnest prayer for the salvation of his countrymen, the Jews, he regarded it as their great and fatal error, that, "being ignorant of God's righteousness, they went about to establish their own righteousness."

Self-righteousness is offensive to God. The king, in the parable, was displeased, because one of the guests appeared at the marriage, not having on a wedding garment. But when we array ourselves in our own righteousness of filthy rags, and present ourselves in the assembly of the saints, before the God of holiness, and claim his approbation and smile, because we are thus arrayed, we offer insult to the King Supreme. We evince that we have no right appreciation of his holiness and justice : and while we profess to honor him as God, we so degrade his moral perfections as to make him altogether such an one as ourselves. This temper of mind rejects the mediation and righteousness of Christ, and thereby sets at nought the counsel of God, in the great scheme of salvation. The Father is well pleased with the Son, for his righteousness' sake ; and he cannot be well pleased with those who despise that righteousness, and choose to appear in their own.

Self-righteousness is ruinous to the soul. It may be highly esteemed among men ; for the Pharisees, who loved the praise of men more than the praise of God, obtained their reward, in being honored for their great sanctity. But God searches the heart, and in his view the outward sanctity avails nothing, while all within is rottenness. Yet the disguise cheats mankind, and cheats him who wears it. Blindly and stupidly trusting to his own righteousness, he is at ease, and cries Peace, Peace, until sudden destruction comes upon him. It is one of Satan's most successful artifices, to lull men to sleep in their own righteousness. Many who have been alarmed by a view of their outward sins, have reformed their lives ; and, relying on their morality, have, without any heart-religion, without any true faith in Christ, fatally dreamed their life away in the vain hope that all will be well at last. So difficult is it to rouse men from this delusion, that publicans and harlots entered into the kingdom of heaven before the self-righteous Pharisees.[1]

The doctrine of grace is the remedy for self-righteousness. It

---

[1] Matt. xxi. 31.

is a remedy which the unholy heart greatly dislikes, but if once received, it proves an effectual antidote to the evil. It slays all self-dependence, and lays the guilty sinner prostrate at the feet of mercy. He turns from his own righteousness, as from his sins, with loathing and abhorrence, and pleads, and trusts, and hopes for mercy only for the sake of Christ. In this method of salvation there is no compromise with the self-righteous spirit; no reliance is admitted either on absolute merit, or on comparative merit. Every one is required to come to Christ, as most guilty and vile, and to seek mercy as the chief of sinners. He must bring no plea that he is more worthy, or less unworthy than his neighbor. So long as he relies on such a plea, the door of mercy is shut against him. He is taught to receive salvation as a free gift, absolutely free, without money and without price.

The doctrine of grace completely excludes all human boasting. This was Paul's view of it. "Where is boasting then? It is excluded. By what law? Works? Nay, but by the law of faith."[1] Its tendency to humble men before God, and teach them to glory in the Lord alone, is an excellence which the inspired apostle highly prized. This endeared the doctrine to him, and should endear it to us. We are prone to think of ourselves above what we ought to think: but we have the means at hand for humbling our pride, in the interrogatory, "Who made thee to differ from another? and what hast thou, that thou didst not receive?"[2]

This doctrine presents the strongest motive to holiness. It has been charged against it, that it leads to licentiousness; and this charge is as old as the days of the apostles. It was then asked, "Shall we continue in sin, that grace may abound?"[3] and it was falsely asserted that they taught, "Let us do evil, that good may come."[4] If, in advocating this doctrine, we meet with similar charges, we may rejoice in the proof thus furnished, that we stand on apostolic ground. But the whole charge is without foundation. Men may be self-righteous Pharisees, and, at the same time, live in sin; but when self-righteousness is destroyed by the Spirit of grace, the man becomes dead, not only to the law, but also to sin, and, being dead to sin, he can live no longer therein. Men may, in a

---

[1] Rom. iii. 27.   [2] 1 Cor. iv. 7.
[3] Rom. vi. 1.   [4] Rom. iii. 8.

self-righteous spirit, abstain from sin, while they love it. But the doctrine of grace, when received into the heart, destroys the very love of sin. A sense of obligation for free and unmerited mercy, occupies the heart, and constrains to holy obedience.

This doctrine is honorable to God. All flesh is humbled before him, and he alone is exalted. The cross of Christ is elevated; and men are attracted to it, and taught to glory in it alone. The full salvation, as it comes forth from the triune God, in its completeness, and perfect adaptedness to our wretched and lost condition, becomes the object of our admiring delight, and calls forth our joyful ascriptions of praise.

This doctrine unites the people of God. All come to Christ on the same level. The rich, the poor, the learned, the unlearned the bond, the free; all come to him, without distinction of rank, or of merit. All melt before him into penitence and love, and their hearts become one. Under the full influence of this doctrine, no man can glory in men, or treat with contempt a fellow member of Christ, a weak brother whom Christ has received.

This doctrine prepares us to join the song of the redeemed in heaven. Even here we learn to sing, "Not unto us, not unto us, but unto thy name give the glory,"[1] and the same shall be our song, when we stand before the throne. "Salvation, and glory, and honor, and power, unto the Lord our God."[2] The celestial harps cannot sound a self-righteous note. It would disturb the heavenly harmony. Every heart feels, and every song declares, that "Salvation is of the Lord."[3]

---

[1] Ps. cxv. 1.　　　　　[2] Rev. xix. 1.　　　　　Jonah ii. 9.

BOOK EIGHTH.

DOCTRINE CONCERNING THE FUTURE WORLD.

INTRODUCTION.

DUTY OF PREPARING FOR THE FUTURE WORLD.[1]

THE people of God have ever been strangers and pilgrims in the earth. Though in the world, they are not of the world; and, both by their professions and their deportment, they declare plainly, that they seek another country, as their final home. Hence, they walk not according to the course of this world, and are deaf to its enticements, and appear to have their eyes fixed on objects that the world sees not. So Moses endured, as seeing him who is invisible.[2] So he turned his back on the pleasures of sin, and the treasures of Egypt, and had respect unto the recompense of the reward, to be obtained in the future world. So patriarchs, prophets, apostles, and martyrs, have lived for eternity, and have left their testimony to mankind, that they were not of this world, and that their treasure, their hearts, and their final home to which they journeyed, were in heaven. These examples call on us for imitation, and, if we possess the wisdom and spirit by which they were actuated, we too shall make it the business of our lives, to prepare for the future world.

The precepts of revelation call on us to prepare for eternity.

---

[1] Amos iv. 12. Prepare to meet thy God.

2 Cor. iv. 18. We look not at the things which are seen and temporal, but at the things which are unseen and eternal.

[2] Heb. xi. 27.

(339)

"Prepare to meet thy God." "Set your affections on things above."[1] "Lay not up for yourselves treasures on earth, but lay up for yourselves treasures in heaven; for where your treasure is, there will your heart be also."[2] "O that they were wise, that they would consider their latter end."[3] All revelation calls as with one voice, as with a voice from heaven, a voice of warning, expostulation, and earnest entreaty, to quit this perishing world, to flee from the wrath to come, to lay hold on eternal life, and to seek a continuing city, an enduring portion, in the world to come. With reference to this future world, every duty is enjoined, every promise made, every motive presented, and he whose eye is not steadfastly fixed on that world, has no reason to hope that he will secure the inheritance of the saints.

Since the motives to holiness, and to diligence in the pursuit of it, are drawn so abundantly from the future world, a knowledge of that world is of great importance to all men. Every man knows that the time of his continuance on earth is short and uncertain; and while fully assured that he must leave this world, and that the time of his departure is just at hand, to make no inquiry concerning the world to which he is going, or to disregard authentic information concerning it, and the means of obtaining happiness there, is folly in the extreme. It is therefore wise to study the doctrine concerning the future world, and to study it as a subject of momentous personal interest. At every step in our progress, we should ask, how does this truth affect my heart? Am I so running as to obtain? Are my prospects clear? Ought I not to renew my diligence, and to seek more earnestly the guidance and help needed, that I may finish my course with joy?

---

[1] Col. iii. 2.   [2] Matt. vi. 19, 20, 21.   [3] Deut. xxxii. 29.

CHAPTER I.

IMMORTALITY AND SEPARATE STATE OF THE SOUL.

WHEN THE HUMAN BODY DIES, THE SOUL, WHICH IS IMMORTAL, CONTINUES TO EXIST IN A SEPARATE STATE.[1]

When the body dies, the atoms of which it consisted are not annihilated; but they separate from each other, and continue to exist in a different state, or in new combinations. The mind, which had previously existed in connection with the body, and had, in that connection, exhibited phenomena, superior to matter, and peculiar to mind, now disappears, and no longer manifests itself as formerly. Though it has disappeared, analogy suggests, that it has not been annihilated. The same philosophy that teaches the indestructibility of the atoms which compose the body, gives its sanction to the doctrine, that the soul is immortal. As the soul is not a compound substance, like the body, it is not susceptible of decomposition, and, therefore, if it continues to exist, it must exist entire, with the properties peculiar to it.

Though philosophy gives its sanction to the doctrine of the soul's immortality, it arrives at the truth through so many perplexing difficulties, that it grasps it finally with but a feeble faith. Plants are bodies of peculiar organization; and are endowed with vitality, either arising from, or connected with, their organization. Brute animals possess organized bodies, endowed with vitality, and, in connection with this vitality, properties are exhibited, which resemble those of the human mind. In surveying the order of beings, from the most imperfect plant, through the rising scale, up to man, the most exalted of animals, philosophy asks, whether man alone is immortal. This question, with which philosophy is embarrassed, natural religion comes in to answer. The moral faculty of

---

[1] Luke xvi. 22, 23; xxiii. 43; Matt. xxii. 31, 32; Luke xx. 37, 38; Rev. xiv. 13; Heb. xii. 23; 2 Cor. v. 6, 8; Phil. i. 23; 1 Thess. v. 10; Eccl. xii. 7.

man, and its adaptedness to religion, separate him widely from all other animals, and justify the conclusion that he alone, of all the creatures that inhabit the earth, is destined to immortality.

Philosophy and natural religion have, after all, only an obscure view of this important truth. Life and immortality are brought to light by the gospel.[1] Divine revelation was needed, to make the truth clear; and that revelation, in the light of the gospel, has so exhibited the truth, that he who does not see it, is wilfully blind. In the dawn of revelation under the former dispensation, so much light was thrown on this truth, that believers of that age regarded themselves as pilgrims and strangers in the earth, and declared plainly that they sought a continuing city, a place of everlasting abode, in another world. But the gospel of Jesus Christ has poured the light of noonday on this momentous truth. The doctrine of Jesus, and the resurrection of Jesus, have lifted the veil that hid the invisible world from our view, and we are now permitted to look into it, with the full assurance of hope.

When the soul leaves its mortal tenement, we are taught by the Scriptures that it is not companionless. The departing spirit of Lazarus was borne by angels to Abraham's bosom.[2] This discourse of our Saviour concerning the rich man and Lazarus, was designed to give us knowledge of the future world. It is not called a parable, but if we regard it as such, it should be remembered, that the parables of Jesus were not like the fables of Æsop, in which beasts and birds spoke and reasoned, but were representations drawn from nature, and conformed to the existing properties of things. In this view, though we are not obliged to regard the account of the rich man and Lazarus, as the actual history of two individuals, it is such a representation as our divine teacher was pleased to employ, to give us some knowledge of the unseen world. In this representation, the angels, who, according to sacred teaching in which is no parable, are ministering spirits,[3] sent forth to minister to them who are heirs of salvation, are hovering around the despised beggar, in his last suffering, and receiving his released spirit, to bear it to its final happy abode. Death, to the departing saint, is not a journey through a solitary way. He is no sooner separated from earthly friends, than he finds himself in a company

---

[1] 2 Tim. i. 10.   [2] Luke xvi. 22.   [3] Heb. i. 14.

of celestial spirits, who offer themselves as his attendants and guides, to his eternal and blissful home.

Paul has taught us, that believers, who depart from the dissolving tabernacle, when absent from the body, are present with the Lord.[1] The promise made to the dying thief, is fulfilled to every expiring saint: "To-day, thou shall be with me in paradise."[2] More than this, he has promised: "I will come again, and receive you unto myself, that where I am, there ye may be also."[3] ·As the Lord descended on Mount Sinai, with ten thousands of his angels, so he comes with these attendant spirits, to the chamber in which the Christian dies. As he enters the unseen world, he can joyfully exclaim: "I will fear no evil, for thou art with me." In company with his blessed Lord, and borne by ministering spirits, the departing saint is conveyed to the mansion which Jesus has prepared for him in the Father's house. Here, he is brought into Abraham's bosom, into intimate communion with the Father of the faithful, and all the holy patriarchs, prophets, and apostles, and with all the spirits of just men made perfect.

The paradise to which the departing spirit goes, is not a place distinct from the heaven in which God makes the most glorious manifestation of himself, and in which the glorified body of Christ has been received until the restitution of all things. The idea, that the disembodied spirit has a separate existence in sheol or hades, shut out from the glorious assembly near the throne, has originated from a misinterpretation of Scripture. Sheol or hades means the unseen world into which the spirit enters, when it leaves the body; but nothing is determined, by the use of the term, respecting the place or condition of the departed. The rich man and Lazarus alike went to the unseen world; but the rich man was "in torment," and Lazarus "in Abraham's bosom."

When separated from the body, the soul does not lose the mental powers which belong to it. The power of perception remains: for the rich man, though the eyes of the body were closed and in the grave, lifted up other "eyes" in hell, and saw Abraham afar off. The power of memory remains: for Abraham said: "Son, remember that thou," &c. The capacity of enjoying and suffering remains: for Lazarus was comforted, and the rich man tormented. It

---

[1] 2 Cor. v. 8.   [2] Luke xxiii. 43.   [3] John xiv. 3.

appears, also, from the discourse between Abraham and the rich man, that disembodied spirits not only know each other, but are allowed to hold converse with each other. Doubtless their modes of perceiving, and of communicating with each other, differ widely from ours; and all attempts to understand what is entirely beyond our experience and conception, must necessarily fail. What the Scriptures teach on the subject, is all that we can possibly know; and they explicitly declare that the instruction which they give on the subject, leaves our knowledge imperfect: "We know in part."[1] "We see through a glass darkly."[2]

The Scriptures teach us that the departed spirit of the saint is free from suffering. It no longer groans, being burdened.[3] Lazarus is comforted.[4] Together with freedom from suffering, it enjoys freedom from sin. The spirits of just men, when separated from the bodies in which they groaned, are "made perfect."[5] They are admitted into the high and holy place, where nothing impure can enter.

The souls of the wicked, as well as of the righteous, are immortal, and survive the body. They, too, have their companions; for the devil, by whom they have been led captive, and his angels, with whom they are to suffer everlasting punishment, receive them into their society. Their mental powers and capacities remain, to see heaven and glory at a distance, to remember and bitterly regret their sin against God, and the opportunity of mercy despised, and to endure torments without mitigation, or hope of relief.

Some persons have supposed that departed spirits become angels, and have cited, in proof of this opinion, the words of the angel to John: "I am thy fellow-servant, and of thy brethren, the prophets."[6] They understand that the angel declares himself to be the spirit of one of the ancient prophets. But this is an erroneous interpretation of the passage, which may be correctly interpreted thus: "I am the fellow-servant of thee, and the fellow-servant of thy brethren, the prophets." The angels are spirits, but not human spirits. They were never redeemed by the blood of Christ; and therefore, in their joyful announcement to the shepherds of Bethlehem, they said: "Unto you," not unto us, "is born this day in

---

[1] 1 Cor. xiii. 9. [2] 1 Cor. xiii. 12. [3] 2 Cor. v. 4.

[4] Luke xvi. 25. [5] Heb. xii. 23. [6] Rev. xix. 10.

the city of David, a Saviour."[1] Hence the song of redemption, when heard in heaven, is described as a *new* song,[2] having never been sung by the angelic choirs. Paul has clearly distinguished between the innumerable company of angels,[3] and "the spirits of just men made perfect," though they are named together, as component parts of the great society into which men are introduced, when they become believers in Christ.

CHAPTER II.

RESURRECTION.

THE BODIES OF ALL WHO DIE, WILL BE RAISED FROM THE DEAD, AND RE-UNITED TO THEIR SPIRITS, FOR THE JUDGMENT OF THE GREAT DAY.[4]

Philosophy and natural religion may attain to an obscure discovery of the soul's immortality; but we should have remained ignorant concerning the resurrection of the body, if we had not been instructed by divine revelation. From God's book we learn that the body is redeemed,[5] as well as the soul; and that the body shall be delivered from the bondage of corruption. That no doubt may remain on the subject, the body which is to be raised again, is described as the corruptible, the vile body, the body deposited in the grave:[6] "This corruptible shall put on incorruption."[7] "Who shall change this vile body."[8] "All that are in their graves shall hear his voice, and shall come forth."[9] Paul urges not to use the members of the body for sinful purposes, because the body is the temple of the Holy Ghost;[10] and, with reference to the same body he says, "If the Spirit of him that raised up Jesus from the dead dwell in you, he that raised up Christ from the dead, shall also quicken your mortal bodies, by his Spirit that

---

[1] Luke ii. 11.   [2] Rev. v. 9.   [3] Heb. xii. 22, 23.

[4] John v. 28, 29; Dan. xii. 2; Job xix. 25-27; Ps. xvii. 15; Acts iv. 2; xxiv. 15; xxvi. 8; Rom. viii. 11; 1 Cor. xv. 12-54; 1 Thess. iv. 14-17; Rev. xx. 6, 12, 13.

[5] 1 Cor. vi. 20.   [6] John v. 28.   [7] 1 Cor. xv. 53.

[8] Phil. iii. 21.   [9] John v. 28.   [10] 1 Cor. vi. 19.

dwelleth in you.''[1] No doubt can remain that the Scriptures teach the resurrection of the mortal body, the body that dies, and enters the grave.

The resurrection of the body is not only taught in the Scriptures, but it is exemplified in the resurrection of Jesus Christ. The fact that he was raised from the dead, is testified by many witnesses, who saw him, and conversed, and ate and drank with him, after his resurrection; and who confirmed the truth of their testimony by astonishing miracles and sufferings. On this grand fact the truth of Christianity depends; and therefore the doctrine of the resurrection is fundamental and vital to the Christian system. If it is not true, Christ is not risen; and, if Christ is not risen, Paul admits "our preaching is vain, and your faith is vain, and we are found false witnesses of God.''[2]

As the resurrection is a desirable privilege to the just, only, it is treated of, in some passages of Scripture, as if it appertained to them exclusively: but other passages teach that it will be universal: "There shall be a resurrection of the just and of the unjust.''[3] "All that are in their graves shall hear his voice, and come forth, they that have done good to the resurrection of life, and they that have done evil to the resurrection of damnation.''[4] The only exception to its universality will be in the case of those who shall be found alive at Christ's second coming. Concerning these, Paul has taught us that they will undergo a change[5] equivalent to that which they pass through who shall have died and risen again. Their case, therefore, is virtually no exception to the general rule: "It is appointed unto all men once to die.''[6] "As in Adam all die, even so in Christ shall all be made alive.''[7]

The power by which the dead are raised, is God's. To the Sadducees, who erred respecting the resurrection, the Saviour said, "Ye do err, not knowing the Scriptures, nor the power of God.''[8] It is a work which nothing short of omnipotence could accomplish. The Son of God is represented as the immediate agent, "Who shall change our vile body, that it may be fashioned like unto his own glorious body, according to the working whereby he is able

---

[1] Rom. viii. 11.   [2] 1 Cor. xv. 14, 15.   [3] Acts xxiv. 15.

[4] John v. 28, 29.   [5] 1 Cor. xv. 52.   [6] Heb. ix. 27.

[7] 1 Cor. xv. 22.   [8] Matt. xxii. 29.

even to subdue all things unto himself."[1] Even when he was on earth, weak and despised, he claimed this power: "The hour is coming, when all that are in their graves shall hear his voice [the voice of the Son of God], and shall come forth."[2] At his com-mand, who said, "Lazarus, come forth," the dead shall quit their graves, and assemble at his tribunal: and the power which he will manifest, in bringing them before him, will demonstrate his right to judge them.

The resurrection, though it will require the same power that created the world out of nothing, will not be another creation. The glorified body will not be created out of nothing, but will be formed out of the vile and mortal body which the spirit once in-habited: "Who shall *change* our vile body, that it may be fash-ioned," &c.[3] The same body of Jesus which was nailed to the cross and laid in the tomb, was raised from the dead, and was seen by the disciples ascending from Mount Olivet. It had been trans-figured on Mount Tabor, and rendered glorious in the view of the dis-ciples who were present; and now it is crowned with glory and honor, in the presence of all the celestial hosts. It is now the "glorious body," into the likeness of which he will fashion our vile bodies, when he fits them to inhabit the mansions that he has prepared.

How the "vile body" will be changed, we know not. We are under no obligation to suppose that all the gross matter of which it consists, will be included in the glorious body into which it will be fashioned. The corruptible body is perpetually losing, in the daily waste which it undergoes, the atoms of matter which compose it, and having their place supplied by other atoms, received from the nourishment taken in to supply the waste. The nails are pared away, and the hair shorn off; and other growth succeeds, to take the place of that which is lost. The bones, muscles, and all other parts of the body, undergo a change as real, though not so appar-ent, and as unceasing. The fluid parts of the body change more rapidly; and the solid parts are absorbed and renewed by the de-posit of other matter, in the processes of nutrition and assimila-tion. It is not necessary to suppose that all the matter thus lost, during a life of fourscore years, will be gathered again. The

---

[1] Phil. iii. 21.　　　[2] John v. 28.　　　[3] Phil. iii. 21.

identity of the body during life did not imply an identity of the atoms composing it: and much less is an identity of atoms necessary to be preserved, when it is changed into the glorious. Paul's teaching on this point is explicit: "Thou sowest *not that* body that shall be, but bare grain; but God giveth it a body as it hath pleased him." What is deposited in the ground, is bare grain; but the body which God giveth consists of the blade, the ear, and the full corn in the ear. The body deposited, dies; that is, it is decomposed, and ceases to be the bare grain deposited. Part of its matter is lost, and part enters into the composition of the new plant, and God adds other matter, constructing such a body as pleases him. Such is the illustration which this inspired writer gives of the process by which the dead will be raised; and we are certainly freed by it from the obligation of regarding a philosophical identity of atoms, as necessary to be preserved in the resurrection of the dead.

Yet, let us observe the relation which the glorious body has to the vile body. It is not another body, but the vile body changed. In Paul's illustration, he says: "God giveth it a body as it hath pleased him, and to every seed his own body."[1] So, every man who rises from the grave, will come forth with his own body. However changed, he will recognise himself, and will be recognised by others, as the same. When wheat, rye, barley, and other grains, are sown in the ground, a grain of each may be deposited in the same bed; and when they spring up together, though all have bodies differing from the bare grain that was sown, they differ also from each other. Every seed has "his own body;" and it may be determined with certainty which is the wheat, which the rye, which the barley, &c. The illustration is doubtless incomplete: but the wisdom of inspiration has given it, to assist our conceptions of this mysterious subject; and our faith, without presuming to be wise above that which is written, should thankfully receive the instruction graciously imparted.

What will be the form and the properties of the glorified body, it is impossible for us to know. Even the beloved disciple who lay on the bosom of Jesus did not claim to know this:—"Beloved, it doth not yet appear what we shall be: but we know that when he

---

[1] 1 Cor. xv. 37, 38.   [2] 1 Cor. xv. 38.

shall appear, we shall be like him, for we shall see him as he is."[1] It ought to satisfy us that we shall be fashioned like the glorious body of Christ. But though this general information ought to be sufficient, the Scriptures, while they do not attempt to describe a glorified body, have given us some information respecting it.

It is incorruptible. Our bodies here undergo perpetual decay and perpetual renewal; and they finally suffer decomposition, and return to dust. The glorified body will suffer no decomposition, no waste, and, therefore, will not need renewal. The process of nutrition by food, and the organs of digestion, will not be needed. "Meats are for the belly, and the belly for meats; but God shall destroy both it and them."[2] The glorified body will be adapted to all the purposes for which it will be used; but, as our mode of life will be entirely different, corresponding changes will be made in the members and organs, to adapt the body to the mode of life into which it enters.

It will be spiritual. Paul affirms this. He says, "It is sown a natural body, it is raised a spiritual body. There is a natural body, and there is a spiritual body."[3] What a spiritual body is, we are unable to say. We shall not be pure or uncompounded spirit, as God is; for we shall have a "body," which God cannot be said to have. But that body will be "spiritual," as distinguished from the natural or grossly material bodies that we now possess. It will be freed from the inactivity, the ponderableness that now binds us to the earth; and will be fitted for swift motion, similar to that of which angelic spirits are capable.

It is immortal. "Now this mortal must put on immortality."[4] As there will be no need to supply a daily waste in each individual body, or to preserve it from corruption, so there will be no need to supply a waste of the race by death. "They neither marry, nor are given in marriage; neither can they die any more; for they are equal unto the angels."[5] In a state of being so different from the present, we shall need bodies of far different construction and properties; and, from the likeness which we are to bear to the angels, we may infer that our spiritual bodies will resemble, to some extent, the spirituality of these holy and immortal beings.

---

[1] 1 John iii. 2.   1 Cor. vi. 13.   [3] 1 Cor. xv. 44.
[4] 1 Cor. xv. 53.   [5] Luke xx. 35, 36.

The true and perfect pattern to which we shall be conformed, is the glorious body of the Redeemer, who, though once dead, now liveth for ever, and who will give us to share his own immortality. "Because I live, ye shall live also."[1]

With what body the wicked will come, and to what likeness they will be conformed, the Scriptures do not tell us. As they will be raised, to stand in the judgment, and receive the sentence under which they will suffer everlasting punishment, in the fire prepared for the devil and his angels; we may conclude that, both in body and spirit, they will be fitted and capacitated for the everlasting endurance of the torments inflicted. We know that their bodies will not be "glorious," for their resurrection will be "unto shame and everlasting contempt."[2] Conjecture, on points which revelation has not enlightened, must be unprofitable.

CHAPTER III.

THE LAST JUDGMENT.

IN THE LAST DAY JESUS CHRIST WILL COME TO JUDGE THE WORLD; AND, HAVING ASSEMBLED ALL MEN BEFORE HIM, WILL PASS SENTENCE ON THEM ACCORDING TO THEIR WORKS.[3]

Natural religion leads us to expect future retribution; and of course some sort of judgment, by which that retribution will be awarded. Even the heathen mythology had its judges, Æacus, Minos, and Rhadamanthus, by whom the dead had their place and condition assigned to them in the other world. But the doctrine of a public, general judgment, is peculiar to revelation. This teaches, that, besides the judgment passed on each individual when he leaves this world, there will be a final judgment, in which all men will stand at the judgment seat of Christ, and receive their final sentence from his lips. "God hath appointed a day, in which he will judge the world in righteousness, by that man whom he hath

---

[1] John xiv. 19.   [2] Dan. xii. 2.
[3] Rev. xx. 11, 12; Acts xvii. 30, 31; Eccl. xi. 9; xii. 14; Matt. xii. 36;
1 Pet. iv. 4, 5; 2 Cor. v. 10.

ordained."[1] "It is appointed unto all men once to die, and after this the judgment."[2]

As the condition of each soul will be determined, when it leaves the body, another judgment may, to our finite minds, appear to be unnecessary; but the wisdom of God has determined otherwise. All the reasons for this divine appointment, we cannot presume to understand; but we are able to conceive of some important advantages which may arise from a general judgment.

The general judgment will publicly and impressively vindicate the ways of God, in the view of all intelligent beings. The mystery of the divine administration will then be fully unfolded; the wisdom and righteousness of all God's dispensations will then be made apparent; the justice of the sentences then pronounced will be rendered perfectly clear; and, on every creature, as he leaves the tribunal, to go to the place assigned him, an impression will have been made, which will last throughout eternity. It is for the glory of God, that his perfections should thus be displayed, in the view of his intelligent creatures; and the remembrance of this great day will constitute an important element in the happiness or misery to which each individual will be adjudged.

The general judgment will be honorable to Jesus Christ. It is called "the day of Christ."[3] When Jesus stood, as an arraigned malefactor, before the Jewish council, he claimed, in their presence, to be the Christ, and he referred to this day as the time when his claim would be acknowledged. This will be the day of Christ, the day when every knee shall bow to him,[4] and every tongue confess that Jesus Christ is Lord, to the glory of God the Father.[5]

The general judgment will extend to the bodies of men. The previous judgment, at the death of each individual, affects the spirit only. But men are to be judged according to the deeds done in the body, and it is fit that they should be judged in the body, and especially inasmuch as the body is to participate in the final retribution.

The general judgment will suitably mark the final victory over all God's enemies. Among men, days of triumph have been observed, when wars have terminated, and victory has been attained.

---

[1] Acts xvii. 31. [2] Heb. ix. 27. [3] Phil. i. 6; 2 Thess. ii. 2.
[4] Rom. xiv. 11. [5] Phil. ii. 11.

In the great day of the Lord, all the enemies of God will have been subdued; the kingdom, which, as rebels against him, they have seized and claimed, will have been fully restored; and universal peace and order will have been established in Jehovah's empire.   At this day of triumph, it is suitable that all creatures should be present, to do honor to the victory, and to him by whom it has been achieved.

The judge on the last day will be Jesus Christ, the same who was condemned at the bar of Caiaphas and of Pilate.   How changed the scene!   They who then condemned him to death, will now tremble before him, and be condemned by him to death eternal. "The Father has committed all judgment to the Son."[1]   The transactions of the great day will form a part of his mediatorial administration.   Having undertaken to restore order to God's empire, in which the rebellion of the human race had broken out, and having assumed the office of Mediator for this purpose, it will be proper, in this office, to complete the work; and therefore Christ the Mediator will be the Judge in the last great day: "We must all stand before the judgment seat of Christ."[2]

At the day of judgment Christ will make his second coming. This coming is frequently spoken of in the Holy Scriptures.   He instituted the Lord's supper, to be observed until he come.[3]   Believers are described as looking for his appearing.[4]   As men look for a beloved friend who has gone away, leaving a promise of return; so believers in Christ look for the return of their Lord, who has promised, "I come quickly;"[5] and they pray, "Even so, come, Lord Jesus."[6]   He came, formerly, *with* sin; not sin of his own, but the sin of his people, which the Lord laid on him.   Having fully expiated this by his death, he will come, the second time, without sin unto salvation."[7]   On this great and terrible day, Christ will come to the salvation of his people, and will, at the same time, take vengeance on them that know not God, and obey not the gospel.   In a subordinate sense, he is said to come, when he displays his power, either in the deliverance of his people, or in the destruction of his enemies.   But all these times are over-

---

[1] John v. 22.   [2] Rom. xiv. 10.   [3] 1 Cor. xi. 26.
[4] Heb. ix. 28.   [5] Rev. xxii. 12.   [6] Rev. xxii. 20.
[7] Heb. ix. 28.

looked in the computation, when, with reference to his appearing for judgment, it is said, "he will come the *second* time." This will be the great day of deliverance and of wrath. There are other comings mentioned in Scripture, not included in this computation, which are only preparatory and subordinate.

An impression has often prevailed among the followers of Christ, that his second coming was near at hand. This impression, when soberly entertained, has a salutary influence. Compared with the eternity which is to follow, the interval until the day of judgment is exceedingly short; and but a very little part of this short interval is included in the life of any one individual; whose preparation for judgment must be completed before he is called away by death. It is therefore true concerning every one, that the time is short,[1] and that the Judge standeth before the door.[2] But the expectation that Christ's coming will be so hastened as not to leave time for the fulfilment of prophecy, or for the measure of duty and suffering to which he has appointed us, is of injurious tendency. An erroneous impression on this subject had so disquieted the minds of the Thessalonian Christians, that Paul thought it necessary, in his second epistle to them, to free them from its influence: "Be not shaken in mind, or troubled, as that the day of Christ is at hand."[3] It may be that they had mistaken his design, when, in his first epistle to them, he said, "We which are alive and remain unto the coming of the Lord, shall not prevent them which are asleep."[4] They may have understood him to intimate, by his use of the word "we," that he expected to be alive and remain when Christ should appear. He may have used this word as including himself, in interest, in the number of those who will be alive at the second coming; or he may intimate that believers of each successive generation should regard themselves as placed, for the time, on the watch-tower, to look for the coming of Christ, and that, compared with those who had fallen asleep, all who at any time are alive and remain, should regard themselves, though looking for his coming, as having no advantage to prevent [go before, or get the start of] those that are asleep. Whatever may have been Paul's design in using this mode of speech, it is clear, from

---

[1] 1 Cor. vii. 29.   [2] James v. 9.
[3] 2 Thess. ii. 2.   [4] 1 Thess. iv. 15.

23

his second epistle, that he did not mean to make the impression that the coming of Christ was so near at hand. He stated explicitly, that the day will not come, "unless there be a falling away first, and the man of sin be revealed."[1] It was necessary that time should be allowed for the Romish apostasy. So now, there are various prophecies remaining to be fulfilled; as, the calling of the Gentiles, the conversion of the Jews, and the millennial state of the Church. All these must be accomplished before the coming of Christ; and, while these prophecies remain unfulfilled, believers should not permit themselves to be troubled in mind by those who would persuade them that the end of the world is just at hand.

Some suppose that the coming of Christ, and the resurrection of the righteous dead, will precede the millennium, and that the resurrection of the wicked will be at the end of the thousand years. This opinion, according to which the reign of Christ will be personal, is founded chiefly on Rev. xx. 4, 5: "And I saw the souls of them that were beheaded for the witness of Jesus, and for the word of God, and which had not worshipped the beast, neither his image, neither had received his mark upon their foreheads, or in their hands; and they lived and reigned with Christ a thousand years. But the rest of the dead lived not again until the thousand years were finished. This is the first resurrection." In carefully examining this passage, we may observe that the first resurrection here mentioned does not include all the righteous dead, but only the martyrs; and that it is not a resurrection of their bodies, but of their souls: "I saw the souls of them, and they lived," &c. Making due allowance for the boldly figurative language employed in this prophetical book, we may understand this passage to mean, that generations of holy men will arise, at the time here referred to, who will so much resemble the ancient martyrs in zeal and devotion to the service of God, that it will be as if the souls of these martyrs had returned in new bodies. So Elijah reappeared, in the person of John the Baptist; not literally, but in the figurative sense in which we may interpret the passage before us; which, so understood, teaches a spiritual, and not a personal reign of Christ. It is true that Paul says, "the dead in Christ shall rise first:"[2] but the meaning of this is, that the dead in Christ shall rise before

---

[1] 2 Thess. ii. 3.   [2] 1 Thess. iv. 16.

the living saints shall be changed. The interval, however, he represents to be exceedingly short: "In a moment, in the twinkling of an eye, the trumpet shall sound, and the dead shall be raised incorruptible, and we shall be changed."[1] Whether the wicked dead will be raised at the precise moment at which the righteous dead will be raised, we are not expressly informed; but, from the representations of the scene which are given in the Scriptures, we may infer that one voice, one trumpet will call forth all the dead, and that one hour[2] will suffice for the resurrection of all. In one and the same day,[3] the great day of the Lord, he will be revealed in flaming fire, taking vengeance on them that know not God; and will come, to be glorified in his saints, and admired of all them that believe.[4]

The place of the final judgment will be on earth. Here Jesus was humbled, condemned, and crucified; and here he will be glorified, and sit in judgment over all the world. When he ascended from the earth, it was foretold that he would return as he had ascended.[5] A cloud received him out of the sight of his disciples,[6] who were gazing after him as he went up; and, on his return, he will be seen coming in the clouds of heaven, with power and great glory.[7] A multitude of angels and the spirits of the just will attend him. The bodies of his saints, called forth from their graves, will rise to meet him in the air, and reunited with their spirits, will appear before him. The living saints will be changed and form a part of the company at his right hand. The wicked dead will be raised, and will stand on the left hand of the Judge. On what part of the earth the Saviour may choose to fix the throne of judgment, we are not informed, nor is it a matter of any moment. Why Sinai was selected for the giving of the law, Calvary for the crucifixion, and Olivet for the ascension, we know not. It is enough for us to know, that he will come, and that we must appear before him.

In the description of the great day, contained in the book of Revelation, it is said, that the Judge will be seated on a great white throne, and that the books will be opened; and that another book will be opened, which is the book of life: and the dead will be

---

[1] 1 Cor. xv. 52. [2] John v. 25. [3] Acts xvii. 31.
[4] 2 Thess. i. 8–10. [5] Acts i. 11. [6] Acts i. 9.
[7] Matt. xxiv. 30; Rev. i. 7.

judged out of the things which are written according to their works.[1] The representation is doubtless figurative, but we may learn from it that the decisions will be made in perfect justice; and that the acquittal of the righteous will be an act of grace. Their names will be found in the Lamb's book of life. They will be accepted in that day, because they belong to Christ, and in proof of their attachment to him, their work and labor of love in his cause, and towards his people, will be brought into remembrance.[2]

In the transactions of this great day, notwithstanding the greatness of the multitude that will be assembled, no individual will feel himself lost in the immense throng, or concealed from the view of the omniscient Judge. Every one will be brought to judgment, as if he were the only creature present, and every one will give account of himself, and receive sentence for himself with as much discrimination and perfection of justice, as if the judge were wholly absorbed in the consideration of his single case. So rapidly do our minds move, even now while bound to our sluggish bodies, that we can review our past history in a few moments, and judge and condemn ourselves before God. With a rapidity beyond our present conception, the deeds, words, and thoughts of our whole lives will pass in review before us on that day, and we shall realize that the eye of God is fixed on each particular with as thorough knowledge of it, as if that deed, word, or thought, were the only one on which he sat in judgment. How can we bear a scrutiny so severe, a knowledge so perfect? How shall we abide a judgment so strict? Who shall be able to stand?

---

[1] Rev. xx. 11, 12. [2] Matt. xxv. 34–40.

CHAPTER IV.

HEAVEN.

THE RIGHTEOUS WILL BE TAKEN TO HEAVEN, AND MADE PER-
FECTLY HAPPY FOR EVER IN THE PRESENCE AND ENJOYMENT OF
GOD.[1]

Godliness has the promise of the life that now is, and of that
which is to come. It often happens that the believer in Christ has
an afflicted lot in the present world; but, in the midst of tribulations, he is enabled, through grace, to rejoice in hope of the glory of
God. So much does the happiness of his present life depend on
the hope of a better portion hereafter, that he is said to be " saved
by hope."[2] This hope has for its object an inheritance that is
incorruptible, undefiled, and that fadeth not away.[3] He is taught
by the doctrine of Christ, to look for this portion, not in this world
of sin, not in the pursuits and enjoyments of carnal men, but in
another and better world, to which his faith and hope are ever
directed.

The believer's portion is laid up in heaven.[4] That heaven is a
place, and not a mere state of being, we are taught by the words
of Christ, who said, " I go to prepare a place for you;"[5] but in
what part of universal space this happy place is situated, the Bible
does not inform us. It is sometimes called the third heavens,[6] to
distinguish it from the atmospheric heaven, in which the fowls of
heaven have their habitation, and from the starry heavens, which
visibly declare the glory of God. The glory of the third heavens
is invisible to mortal eyes; and the place may be far beyond the
bounds within which suns and stars shine, and planets revolve.
Some have imagined that it is a vast central globe, around which

---

[1] Matt. xxv. 34; Luke xii. 32; John xiv. 2; Col. iii. 4; 1 Thess. iv. 17;
Luke xxii. 29, 30; Acts xiv. 22; Rev. iii. 21; vii. 15–17; xiv. 4; 1 Pet. i. 3, 4;
Matt. xxv. 21; John xvii. 24; Rev. xxi. 4; xxii. 3.

[2] Rom. viii. 24.   [3] 1 Pet. i. 3, 4.   [4] Col. i. 5.

[5] John xiv. 2.   [6] 2 Cor. xii. 2.

the stars of heaven are making their slow revolutions, carrying with them their systems of attendant planets. There is something pleasing in this conjecture, which connects astronomical science with the hopes of the Christian : but it must be remembered that it is mere conjecture. No telescope can bring this glorious place within the reach of human view. "Eye hath not seen, nor ear heard, neither have entered into the heart of man, the things which God hath prepared for them that love him."[1] Yet, though science cannot give us a knowledge of this happy world, divine revelation has made us to some extent acquainted with it. Paul adds to the words just cited, " but God hath revealed them to us by his Spirit." By faith, which is the evidence of things not seen, we look at things unseen and eternal. The light of revelation brings the glories of the distant land before the eyes of our faith ; and in the spiritual enjoyment which we are made to experience, even in this land of exile, we have an earnest[2] and foretaste of heavenly joy. These drops of heaven sent down to worms below, unite with the descriptions found in God's holy word, to give such ideas of heaven as it is possible for us to form; but at best, we know only in part. " It doth not yet appear, what we shall be," or where we shall be, or in what our bliss will consist. But though in looking forward to the inheritance in prospect, we are compelled to see through a glass darkly, we may yet discover that the future happiness of the saints will include the following elements :

1. *An intimate knowledge of God.* Now we know in part, but then we shall know even as we are known.[3] Heaven is " the high and holy place, where God resides, the court of the great King." He says, " heaven is my throne."[4] Though present everywhere throughout his dominions, he manifests himself in a peculiar manner in this bright abode, of which the glory of God and the Lamb are the light. Here the blessed are permitted to *see* God. To see God, as human eyes now see material objects, by means of reflected light, will be as impossible then as it is now, for God is a spirit : but we shall have such a discovery of God, as is most appropriately expressed by the word see; otherwise, the promise

---

[1] 1 Cor. ii. 9.   [2] Eph. i. 14.
[3] 1 Cor. xiii. 12.   [4] Isaiah lxvi. 1.

of Christ would not be fulfilled. "Blessed are the pure in heart · for they shall see God."[1] The knowledge of God will be communicated through the Mediator. "No man hath seen God at any time; the only begotten Son, who is in the bosom of the Father, he hath declared him."[2] Though God dwells in light which no man can approach unto, and is a Being whom no man hath seen, or can see;[3] yet the light of the knowledge of the glory of God, in the face of Jesus Christ, the same that shines into the hearts of God's people on earth, fills the world of bliss. There no sun or moon shines; but "the glory of God did lighten it, and the Lamb is the light thereof." The glory of God is the illumination, and the Lamb is the luminary from which it emanates. Jesus will still be our teacher there, and through him we shall acquire our knowledge of the perfections and counsels of God.

Our knowledge of God will be for ever increasing. On earth, believers "grow in the knowledge of God and our Saviour Jesus Christ," and the advantages for attaining to higher knowledge, instead of ceasing at death, will be far greater in heaven. The perfections and counsels of the infinite God, will be an exhaustless source of knowledge, a boundless subject of investigation; and the Mediator, the equal of the Father, and his bosom-counsellor, will be our all-sufficient instructor; and our glorified spirits will be fitted to prosecute the study through eternal ages. It follows, that we shall continue to grow in the knowledge of God, while immortality endures.

The angels diligently study the dealings of God with his people on earth, and, by this means, acquire knowledge of God's manifold wisdom. They saw his creative skill and power displayed, when the creation sprang forth from his hand in its unmarred beauty; and they rejoiced in songs and shoutings. They learned the justice of God, when some of their number were driven from heaven for their transgression, and doomed to interminable woe. While the angels have been making the dispensations of God's providence and grace their delightful study, we cannot suppose that the spirits of the just, who are their companions in glory, have been indifferent to these subjects; which interested them so deeply while on earth. It must be, that they continue to make

---

[1] Matt. v. 8. [2] John i. 18. [3] 1 Tim. vi. 16.

progress in the knowledge which, while here below, they so earnestly desired to acquire, and in which they made a small beginning. Here, the ways of God appear dark and mysterious, and the doctrine taught us in his word, is attended with difficulties, which our finite minds labor in vain to remove. We desire instruction on these points; and Jesus has said, "What I do, thou knowest not now, but thou shalt know hereafter."[1] We wait now for the fulfilment of this promise; and we hope hereafter, with the spirits that are before the throne, to drink in the knowledge which we are here so desirous to obtain, which we so greatly long to acquire.

How far the learning of the future world will include the sciences which are taught in the schools on earth, it is of little use to inquire. It will certainly include whatever is necessary to the knowledge of God. We shall study his works, his moral government, and the mysterious scheme of redemption. New truths, of which we have now no conception, will be unfolded to our view; and the truths of which we have now some knowledge, will be exhibited in new relations, and with new attractions. The truths which now appear discordant with each other, will have light thrown on their connecting links; and the whole will be seen, in one grand system of beautiful proportion and perfect harmony, and in everything God will be displayed. All our knowledge will be the knowledge of him.

2. *Perfect conformity to God.* The first man was made in the image of God; and the subjects of regeneration are renewed, after the image of God. But the likeness given in creation has been lost; and that which is reproduced in regeneration is incomplete. God's people are striving and praying for a higher degree of conformity; and they are looking to the future world for the consummation of their wishes: "Then shall I be satisfied, when I awake in thy likeness."[2] They are predestinated to be conformed to the image of God's Son,[3] who is the image of the invisible God.[4] As they study the divine character here, they grow in conformity to it: "We, beholding as in a glass, the glory of the Lord, are changed into the same image, from glory to glory, even as by the

---

[1] John xiii. 7.   [2] Ps. xvii. 15.
[3] Rom. viii. 29.   [4] Col. i. 15.

Spirit of the Lord.''[1] The same transforming influence which the knowledge of God exerts in this life, will continue in the future world. As we make progress in the knowledge of God, we advance from glory to glory, in the likeness of God; and this progress will be interminable, through all our immortal existence. We shall be like him; for we shall see him as he is.''[2]

In being conformed to God, who is love, we shall love the display of divine perfection, of which we shall obtain increasing discoveries, in our study of the character, works, and government of God. As our knowledge enlarges, our love to the things learned will become more intense, and the new developments which will be made at every stage of our endless advancement will be increasingly ravishing. What would be subjects of barren speculation to merely intellectual beings, will be to us as moral beings, having a moral likeness to God, sources of ineffable bliss, ever rising higher and higher in its approach towards the perfect and infinite blessedness of God.

3. *A full assurance of divine approbation.* In this world we groan, being burdened. A sense of sin, and God's displeasure on account of it, often fills the mind with gloom. We see, in the gospel of Christ, how God can be just, and the justifier of the believer in Jesus: but our faith is often weak. We are conscious of daily offences against infinite love; and the bitterness of grief possesses the soul. Oh! to see our Father's face, without a cloud between, and to feel that perfect love occupies the full capacity of our hearts, and governs every emotion! We pant after God, the living God. We long for heaven; because there we shall dwell for ever in the light of his countenance. The sentence of the last judgment, "Come, ye blessed of my Father," will give an eternal assurance of divine acceptance, and perfect love in the heart will for ever exclude all fear.

4. *The best possible society.* Paul thus describes this society: "Ye are come unto Mount Zion, and unto the city of the living God, the heavenly Jerusalem, and to an innumerable company of angels, to the general assembly and church of the first born, which are written in heaven, and to God, the Judge of all, and to the spirits of just men made perfect, and to Jesus the Mediator of the new covenant."[3] Our brethren who have gone before us, with some of whom we

---

[1] 2 Cor. iii. 18. [2] 1 John iii. 2. [3] Heb. xii. 22-24.

took sweet counsel here, and went to the house of God in company, are there waiting to welcome our arrival. The angels that attend on us as ministering spirits, during our pilgrimage here, will convey us, when we leave the world, to the glorious abode, in which they ever behold the face of our Father in heaven, and will form part of the happy society into which we shall be introduced. There we shall be with Jesus, the Mediator, who loved us, and gave himself for us, in whose blood we shall have washed our robes, and made them white; there we shall approach to God, the Judge of all, who is our Father, the object of our love, and the source of our joy. In such society we shall spend eternity. We are travelling to our final home, through a desert land, a waste howling wilderness, but we seek a city; and God is not ashamed to be called our God, for he hath prepared for us a city.[1] A city is a place where society abounds. The rich and noble resort to cities, that they may enjoy life. Here they display their wealth, erect magnificent palaces for their residence, and multiply the means of enjoyment to the utmost possible extent. In our eternal home, we shall not be lonely pilgrims; but we shall dwell in the city of our God; where the noblest society will be enjoyed, where the inhabitants will be all rich, made rich through the poverty of Jesus, and all kings and priests to God; and where the King of kings holds his court, and admits all into his glorious presence.

5. *The most delightful employment.* The future happiness of the saints is called a rest: but it is not a rest of inactivity; which, however desired it may sometimes be, by those who inhabit sluggish bodies, is not suited to spiritual beings. The rest resembles the Sabbath, the holy day, in which the people of God now lay aside their worldly cares and toils, and devote the sacred hours to the worship of God. Such a sabbatism remains for the people of God, when the cares and toils of this life shall have ceased for ever. To the glorified saints, inaction would be torture, rather than bliss. Their happiness will not consist of mere passive enjoyment. They will *serve* God day and night; and, in this service, will find their highest enjoyment. They pray now, that his will may be done on earth, as it is done in heaven; and when they are themselves taken to heaven, they will delight to do his will, as it is

---

[1] Heb. xi. 16.

done by all the heavenly host. The worship of God, and the study of his holy word, form a part of the delightful employment of the saints on the earthly Sabbath. So, to worship God with joyful songs of praise and suitable ascriptions of glory, constitutes, according to the Scripture representation, a part of the saints' employment in glory. The subjects of their transporting songs, and rapturous ascriptions of praise and glory, will be supplied by their continually fresh discoveries of the divine perfections, the study of which will also form an important part of their blissful employment.

6. *The absence of everything which could mar their happiness.* Sin, which here pollutes all our joys, will never enter there; for nothing entereth that defileth.[1] Devils and wicked men will be confined in their eternal prison, and will be able to molest no more. The sorrows and afflictions of this world will have passed away. There will be no more sickness, no more curse; and death, the last enemy, will have been destroyed.

7. *A free use of all the means of enjoyment.* Future happiness is promised as a kingdom: "Fear not, little flock, it is your Father's good pleasure to give you the kingdom."[2] " Come, ye blessed of my Father, inherit the kingdom."[3] A king is superior to all the nobles of his realm, and holds the highest place of dignity in his dominions. Christ, as king, is crowned with glory and honor; and believers also will be exalted to glory, honor, and immortality. The subjects of earthly despots are often deprived of their possessions by the injustice of those who have power over them; but the king is above the reach of such injustice. He commands the resources of his dominions, and makes them contribute to his pleasure. Hence, to minds accustomed to regal government, royalty conveys the idea of the most abundant resources, and the highest measure of undisturbed enjoyment; hence the language of Paul: "Now ye are full; now ye are rich; ye have reigned as kings."[4] In this view, the children of God will be made kings. Besides the honor to which they will be exalted, their enjoyments will be boundless. All the resources of creation will be made tributary to them, and no one will dispute their claim, or hinder

---

[1] Rev. xxi. 27.
[3] Matt xxv. 34.
[2] Luke xii. 32.
[4] 1 Cor. iv. 8.

their enjoyment. Earthly crowns are often tarnished by the iniquity of those who wear them, but the crown bestowed on the children of God is a crown of righteousness, not only because it is righteously conferred, but because, without any unrighteous violence, the wearers will have all the honors and enjoyments of royalty secured to them for ever.

CHAPTER V.

HELL.

THE WICKED WILL BE CAST INTO HELL, WHERE THEY WILL SUFFER EVERLASTING PUNISHMENT FOR THEIR SINS.[1]

Natural religion teaches the doctrine of future retribution; and even the heathen had their notions of punishment to be endured in another world, for crimes committed in this. Conscience in every man's breast, as the agent of him who placed it there, inflicts torture, often intolerably severe, for iniquities perpetrated, and it teaches the transgressor, when he hears God's voice in the thunder, or beholds any remarkable display of the divine power, to tremble in the apprehension of suffering the wrath of heaven. Though conscience often sleeps, for a long period, over the sinner's guilty deeds, yet some special dispensation of Providence sometimes awakens it, and calls upon it to inflict its tortures. So Joseph's brethren, when brought into difficulties in Egypt, were reminded of their cruelty to their brother, and filled with anguish by the remembrance.[2] But conscience, in some hardened transgressors, sleeps undisturbed, while life lasts; and natural religion, in view of the proofs that a great God reigns, infers that it will be awakened in another life which is to follow. Moreover, in the allotments of the present life, a partial disclosure of God's moral government is made, in the rewarding of virtue, and the punishing of vice; but it

---

[1] Ps. ix. 17; Matt. x. 28; xiii. 40–42; xxiii. 29, 33; xxv. 41–43; Mark ix. 43; 2 Thess. i. 7–9; 2 Pet. ii. 4, 9, 10; Jude 7; Rev. xiv. 11; xx. 10, 14, 15; xxi. 8.

[2] Gen. xlii. 21.

is so incomplete, as here seen, that we are compelled to conclude, that, either the Governor of the Universe is not perfectly righteous, or his distribution of rewards and punishments reaches into a future state. Hence, the expectation of future punishment for crimes committed in this life, accords with the dictates of conscience and reason.

But the strongest and most impressive proof of this momentous truth, is furnished by divine revelation. In God's book, the lessons of natural religion are taught with clearness and force; and the wrath of God is revealed from heaven against all ungodliness and unrighteousness of men. From this infallible word, we learn that wicked men treasure up wrath against the day of wrath, and the revelation of the righteous judgments of God.[1] We know that this day of God's wrath will be, when he shall be revealed in flaming fire, taking vengeance on all them that know not God, and obey not the gospel of our Lord Jesus Christ, who shall be punished with everlasting destruction from the presence of the Lord and from the glory of his power.[2] This day of judgment and wrath will not be in the present life: for " it is appointed to all men once to die, and after this the judgment."[3] " The rich man died, and in hell lifted up his eyes, being in torments."[4] Men will be called from their graves to the judgment; and from the judgment, the wicked will be sentenced to everlasting punishment. God is to be feared, because, beyond the destroying of the body, he can destroy both soul and body in hell.[5] Vain are the dreams of infatuated mortals, who suppose that the only punishment to be endured for sin is in the present life. Conscience and reason unite their voice, to awaken them from their delusion; and revelation depicts the future retribution before their eyes so clearly, that they must see it, unless wilfully and obstinately blind.

The magnitude of the evil included in damnation may be inferred from the importance which the Scriptures attach to salvation. It was a great work which Christ undertook, when he came to seek and to save them that were lost;[6] to save his people from their sins;[7] not to condemn the world, but to save the world;[8] to deliver from the wrath to come.[9] If wrath and damnation had been trivial

---

[1] Rom. ii. 5. [2] 2 Thess. i. 8. [3] Heb. ix. 27.
[4] Luke xvi. 23. [5] Matt. x. 28. [6] Luke xix. 10.
[7] Matt. i. 21. [8] John iii. 17. [9] 1 Thess. i. 10.

matterś, the sending of God's only son into the world, the laying of our sins upon him, and the whole expedient adopted to deliver us from these inconsiderable evils, would have been unworthy of infinite wisdom. It would not deserve to be called "a great salvation;"[1] and the intelligence of the Saviour's birth, brought by the angels, would not deserve to be called "good tidings of great joy."[2] Paul declared, "It is a faithful saying, and worthy of all acceptation, that Christ Jesus came into the world to save sinners;"[3] and Paul was of this mind, because he believed the salvation of a sinner to be a work of vast magnitude. In this view of it, he said: "My heart's desire and prayer to God for Israel is, that they might be saved."[4] In this view, he relinquished every earthly hope, and gave himself to the ministry of the gospel, enduring all hardships and sufferings, if by all means he might save some.[5] Why did he labor thus, why suffer thus, if wrath and damnation are evils of little magnitude? Paul understood the matter otherwise, when he, said, "Knowing the terror of the Lord, we persuade men."[6] It is said in the Scripture, "Who knoweth the power of thine anger? Even according to thy fear, so is thy wrath."[7] The utmost dread with which any finite mind can regard the wrath of God, will be realized, and more than realized, when that wrath is poured out on him. The power of God's anger, finite intelligence cannot conceive; but God understands it well, and the full estimate of it was regarded, in the deep counsels which devised the scheme of salvation. An almighty Saviour, able to save to the uttermost, was chosen, because salvation was a work requiring such an agent for its accomplishment. The gospel is sent forth into the world, with the declaration of its great Author, "He that believeth and is baptised shall be saved, and he that believeth not shall be damned."[8] Every sound of the glorious gospel speaks of salvation and damnation. Every accent of mercy, inviting the sinner to come to Christ for life, is a warning to flee from the wrath to come. Diminutive views of sin, and of the wrath of God due to sin, permit the sinner to sleep in neglect of the great salvation that God has provided.

The human heart is prone to doubt the doctrine of eternal dam-

---

[1] Heb. ii. 3.   [2] Luke ii. 10.   [3] 1 Tim. i. 15.
[4] Rom. x. 1.   [5] 1 Cor. ix. 22.   [6] 2 Cor. v. 11
[7] Ps. xc. 11.   [8] Mark xvi. 16.

nation. The facts reported in the gospel, that Christ came into the world, died, and rose again, are so abundantly attested, that few have the hardihood openly to deny them. These are past facts, which rational men cannot well permit themselves to doubt; but eternal woe is something future, unseen, and unfelt. The apprehension of it disquiets men, and disturbs their enjoyments; and hence they are prone to drive it from them. The threat of indignation and wrath, tribulation and anguish, is fearful; but if they listen to it, and interpret it in its full import, they cannot remain at ease. Hence arises a criminal and fatal tendency not to take God at his word, in these fearful warnings and denunciations; but to persuade ourselves that they will never be executed. Some relieving method of interpretation is adopted, or some view taken of God's benevolence and mercy, by which the sinner may be permitted to remain at ease, and hope that all will be well. Hence we see the astonishing fact, that multitudes practically neglect the gospel, who dare not openly deny it. If they verily believed that the wrath of God abides on them; that the treasures of wrath are daily increasing, and that the accumulated vengeance is just ready to burst on their heads in a fearful tempest; they would not, they could not remain at ease. To appreciate justly and fully the gospel of eternal salvation, we must believe, thoroughly believe, the doctrine of eternal damnation. All our misgivings, as to the truth of this doctrine, proceed from an evil heart of unbelief; and lead to a neglect of the great salvation.

Some have sought relief, in the apprehension of future misery, from the idea that the language of Scripture, which describes it, is figurative. The descriptions of future happiness in heaven, are figurative; but the figures convey very imperfect ideas of the reality. So it is with the figures which describe future misery. The fire prepared for the devil and his angels;[1] the lake of fire;[2] unquenchable fire;[3] the worm that dieth not, and the fire that is not quenched;[4] are terrific descriptions; but they are not exaggerations. They are figures; but they come short of the reality. When God punishes, he punishes as a God. Who knoweth the power of thine anger? What omnipotent wrath can accomplish,

---

[1] Matt. xxv. 41.
[2] Rev. xx. 10.
[3] Matt. iii. 12.
[4] Mark ix. 44.

all language fails to describe, and all finite minds are unable to conceive.

Of what elements future misery will consist, we cannot tell; but it will include poignant remorse, and a sense of divine wrath, with the absence of all enjoyment, and of all hope. It will produce, in the subjects of it, weeping, wailing, and gnashing of teeth. They will realize that they are shut out for ever from the kingdom of heaven, into outer darkness; and they will remember the good things which they once enjoyed, never more to be enjoyed again; and the opportunities of mercy, once neglected, never more to return. They will be tormented in the flame, without a drop of water to cool their tongues. Their hatred of God will be complete; and they will blaspheme his name, while they feel themselves grasped in the hand of his almighty wrath, without power to extricate themselves. Devils, and wicked men, all under the same condemnation, will be their eternal companions: and the companionship, instead of affording relief, will be an aggravation of their woe. The whole throng, hateful, and hating one another, will be tormentors of one another. The malignant passions, which, on earth, caused wars, assassinations, cruelty, oppression, and every species of injury, will be let loose without restraint to banish peace and brotherhood for ever from the infernal society; and the passions which burn in the hearts of wicked men on earth, and destroy all internal peace, and sometimes drive to suicide, will then be unrestrained, and do their full work of torture; and relief by suicide, or self-annihilation, will be for ever impossible. O, who can endure such torments? Who will not, with every energy, and at every sacrifice, seek to escape from devouring fire and everlasting burnings?

As heaven is a place, so is hell. Judas went to his own place;[1] and the rich man desired that his brethren might not come to this place of torment.[2] In what part of universal space this place is situated, we know not. Heaven is above, and hell beneath; but astronomy has taught us, that, in consequence of the earth's diurnal rotation, the up and down of absolute space is not to be determined by the position of the little ball which we inhabit. If the third heaven, where God resides, be a region of perfect light and

---

[1] Acts i. 25.   [2] Luke xvi. 28.

glory, beyond the limits within which stars and planets revolve; and if its inhabitants see the sun and stars, as beneath their feet: the region of outer darkness may be in the opposite extreme of space, where sun and stars shine not, and where the glory of God is for ever unseen. But, wherever it is, the broad way that sinners go, leads to it; and they will at length certainly find it.

The duration of future misery will be eternal. This is expressly declared in Scripture. "These shall go away into everlasting punishment; but the righteous into life eternal."[1] The words everlasting and eternal are renderings of the same Greek word, which is applied alike to the future state of the righteous and the wicked. The punishment of these, and the happiness of those, will be of equal duration. Both will be eternal or everlasting. The criticism which would take the word in a different sense, in one case, from that which it is admitted to have in the other, is rash and dangerous. The same truth is taught in other passages of Scripture:—"Where their worm dieth not, and their fire is not quenched."[2] "The smoke of their torment ascendeth up for ever and ever."[3] "Suffering the vengeance of eternal fire."[4] The last passage, inasmuch as it refers to the cities of Sodom and Gomorrah, which were destroyed by fire from heaven, may contain an allusion to that fire; but this, viewed in itself, was not eternal fire. It was a type of future wrath, and may be regarded as its beginning, and first outbursting. The fire which consumed the cities of the plain, has long since ceased to burn; but the wrath due to their guilty inhabitants did not then cease to burn: for the day of judgment will find Sodom and Gomorrah,[5] with guilty Chorazin, Bethsaida, and Capernaum, all doomed to suffer, according to their several measures of guilt, the vengeance of eternal fire. These cities, in their fearful overthrow, are set forth as an example; and from the visible beginning of their awful doom, we may faintly conceive what will be the end. But it will be more tolerable for Sodom and Gomorrah in the day of judgment, than for those who hear and reject the gospel of Christ; who must, therefore, suffer the vengeance of eternal fire, in its fiercest burnings, and in its everlasting duration.

---

[1] Matt. xxv. 46. [2] Mark ix. 44. [3] Rev. xiv. 11.
[4] Jude i. 7. [5] Matt. xi. 21.

24

Future misery will not be purifying in its effect. The afflictions which the righteous endure in this world are fatherly chastisements, inflicted in love, and God designs them for the profit of his children, that they may be partakers of his holiness.[1] Future misery will be inflicted not on the children of God, but on the enemies of God; not in love, but in wrath. And it will not be designed for the profit of its subjects, but for the vindication of the law and justice of God, " to show his wrath and make his power known."[2] Affliction purifies the righteous, not by any inherent tendency which it possesses, but by the accompanying influence of the Holy Spirit. The wicked, even in the present life, grow hardened under affliction, and sometimes blaspheme God, while they gnaw their tongues with pain.[3] In the world to come, the Holy Spirit will send forth no sanctifying influence to render future torments purifying. Many of the wicked he gives up to hardness of heart, even in the present life; and to all of them the day of grace will be past for ever.

The opinion that they will be ultimately restored to the favor of God, and taken to heaven, is not authorized by the Scriptures.[4] On the contrary, it teaches that the Master of the house will " shut the door;" that there is a great gulf[5] between the two worlds, rendering passage from one to the other impossible; that the unjust and filthy will remain unjust and filthy still.[6] Jesus said to some, " Ye shall die in your sins; and whither I go ye cannot come:"[7] and he said concerning Judas Iscariot, " It had been good for that man if he had not been born."[8] The last words cannot be true, if Judas at any future time, however remote, shall be taken to heaven, to enjoy for ever the perfect happiness of that world: for the eternal weight of glory which will then be awarded to him, will far more than outweigh all his previous sufferings. The Scriptures teach that the heavens have received Jesus Christ, " until the restitution of all things:"[9] but if his restitution implied a restoration of all to the favor of God, Christ's second coming would be deferred until its accomplishment. But as Christ will come from heaven to judge the world, and will in

---

[1] Heb. xii. 10.   [2] Rom. ix. 22.   [3] Rev. xvi. 10, 11.
[4] Luke xiii. 25.   [5] Luke xvi. 26.   [6] Rev. xxii. 11.
[7] John viii. 21.   [8] Matt. xxvi. 24.   [9] Acts iii. 21.

the judgment, condemn the wicked to everlasting punishment, we must conclude that the restitution of all things will be regarded as complete and for ever fixed; when the final judgment shall have decided the eternal state of all, and the order which had been disturbed by the enemies of God, shall have been fully restored in his kingdom.

Future misery will not be *annihilating* in its effect. It is called death, the second death: but the first death does not imply annihilation of either soul or body; and neither does the second. It is called destruction: but as the men of Sodom and Gomorrah were destroyed[1] in the overthrow of those cities, but are nevertheless to appear in the day of judgment,[2] destruction does not imply annihilation. An immortal spirit suffers destruction when it is separated from God and happiness, and doomed to eternal misery. So the wicked shall be punished with everlasting destruction, from the presence of the Lord, and from the glory of his power.[3] Besides death and destruction, the word corruption is used as the opposite of life. "They that sow to the flesh, shall of the flesh reap corruption, and they that sow to the Spirit, shall of the Spirit reap life everlasting."[4] Corruption is not annihilation. The death of the body is followed by corruption and the worm; so that we may say to corruption, Thou art my father; and to the worm, Thou art my mother and sister.[5] Hence, corruption, and the worm that dieth not, are figures employed to denote the consequences of the second death. By the flesh, to which men sow, and of which they reap corruption, we do not understand the material body, but the depraved mind. The corruption of this is its moral disorganization, or utter loss of holiness. Were annihilation intended, the worm that dieth not, would cease to have anything on which to feed; and the fire that cannot be quenched, would cease to burn for want of fuel. If the wicked are to be destroyed by instantaneous annihilation, that destruction, instead of being an infliction of torment, will be a termination of all suffering. This does not accord with the Scripture representations of the future portion of the wicked: and no good reason can be assigned for raising the bodies of the wicked, if they are to be immediately annihilated.

---

[1] Luke xvii. 29. [2] Matt. x. 15. [3] 2 Thess. i. 9.
[4] Gal. vi 8. [5] Job. xvii. 14.

If destruction is to be a process, whether rapid or lingering, by which annihilation is to be produced, it will not be everlasting destruction, or everlasting punishment; for the process and the punishment will sooner or later cease. To no purpose can it be called eternal punishment, when the subjects of it shall have eternally ceased to exist. To no purpose can any be said to suffer the vengeance of eternal fire, when the fire itself shall have eternally terminated their suffering. And to no purpose will the smoke of their torment ascend for ever and ever, when the torments themselves shall have eternally ceased.

Some understand the words, " Every one shall be salted with fire,"[1] to import, that the fire of hell, instead of consuming its victims, will, like salt, preserve them. Whether this be its meaning or not, there is no reason to doubt that the vessels of wrath fitted for destruction, will be adapted to the suffering which they will undergo. Instead of wasting away under its influence, or having their powers of endurance benumbed, we may rather conclude, that, as the righteous will perpetually ascend in bliss, the wicked will perpetually sink in woe. Their deep is bottomless,[2] and being banished from the presence of God, they may continue to recede from him for ever. Their capacity for suffering, their tormenting passions, their hatred of God, and of one another, may all increase indefinitely, through eternal ages. As wandering stars, to whom is reserved the blackness of darkness for ever, they will continue to fly further and further from God, the eternal source of light and happiness, into deeper, and still deeper darkness and woe. O, that men would seek the Lord, while he may be found.

Obj. 1. The justice of God does not require, and will not permit, the infliction of eternal torments for the sins committed in the short period of human life. If eternity be divided by the number of sins which any man commits, during the whole course of his probation on earth, the quotient will be eternity: and it follows, that future misery cannot be eternal, unless an eternity of torment be inflicted for every sin. An eternity of woe for one transgression, shocks all the sense of justice which God has implanted in the human breast.

---

[1] Mark ix. 49.   [2] Rev. xx. 3.

This objection proceeds on the radical mistake, that men cease to be moral agents, bound by the law of God, when they have passed into the world of woe. God's dominion is universal; and the inhabitants of hell are as much bound to love and obey him, as those of heaven or earth. Men who die in their sins, will carry with them not only the guilt accumulated during the present life, but the inclination, confirmed by habit, to continue in sin. They will hate God and blaspheme his name, and their sins cannot cease to be offensive to God, because their moral character has become fixed and unalterable. A sinner cannot become innocent by being confirmed in sin. Were it so, the inhabitants of hell would be innocent beings; their habitation would be as pure as the high and holy place where God dwells; and their blasphemies would be as little offensive to God and all holy beings, as the songs of angels. All this is manifestly absurd. Sin continued, will deserve and provoke continued wrath; and the future condition of the wicked is chiefly terrible, because they are abandoned by God to the full exercise and influence of their unholy passions, and the consequent accumulation of guilt for ever and ever.

If God's justice will not permit him to punish sinners with banishment from his presence, and confinement in the regions of woe, beyond a limited period of time; then it will follow, that when this limited period of suffering shall have passed, justice will not only permit, but will absolutely require, that they should be released. Who can believe that, after a thousand years spent in blaspheming God, and strengthening their enmity to his character and government, they shall be turned loose, to roam at large in God's dominions, and to visit at pleasure the holy and happy place where nothing entereth that defileth ?"[1] Who can believe that God's justice will demand this, and will authorize them to demand it ? Yet all this will follow, if the ground assumed in the objection be not false.

Obj. 2. God's benevolence will not permit him to inflict such misery on his creatures. He claims them as his offspring, and represents himself as their Father: and, as no human parent would so treat his children, it is not to be supposed that the benevolent Father of all will be so unfeeling and unmerciful.

---

[1] Rev. xxi. 27.

This objection, while it claims to honor God's benevolence, dishonors his veracity. Our inferences from God's benevolence may all be mistake; but God's word must be true: and he who, relying on the deductions of his own reason, rejects the warnings that God has graciously given him, will find, in the end, that he has acted most foolishly and wickedly.

The objection assumes what is inconsistent, not only with the truth of God's declarations as to the future, but also with known and undeniable facts of the past and present. Had the objector been present when man came forth in his original purity from the hand of his Maker, he would, on the principle assumed in his objection, have predicted, with confidence, that God would never permit this fair production of his creative power and skill to become involved in the fall and its consequent evils. Had he been present in the garden of Eden, when the serpent said, " Ye shall not surely die," he would, in his professed honor of God's benevolence, have confirmed the declaration made by the father of lies. The misery endured by the human race in every age, from the fall to the present moment, in every region of the globe, in every tribe, in every family, in the daily and hourly experience of every individual, is all inconsistent with the principle assumed in the objection. If, at the creation, it would have denied the possibility of what we know has occurred, how can we trust it when it now denies the possibility of what God says shall be? When our inferences oppose fact, and the truth of God, we may be assured that they are wrong.

When pestilence is desolating a land, God sees the wretchedness that is produced, and hears the cries of the suffering, and could, with one breath, drive far away the cause of the fatal malady. When a ship is wrecked in the raging ocean, God hears the cries of the sinking mariners, and understands well their terror and anguish, and could, without effort, bear the shattered vessel at once to its destined port in safety. Were the objector in God's stead, would he be deaf to the cries of his children? Would he not promptly afford the needed relief? He would. What then? Is he benevolent, and is God unfeeling and unmerciful? So the objection would decide; and we know, therefore, that it is not according to truth.

God is of right the Father of his creatures: but he says, " If I be a father, where is my honor?"[1] and he complains, "I have nourished and brought up children, and they have rebelled against me."[2] By their rebellion, men have become the children of the wicked one. Christ said, "If God were your Father, ye would love me;"[3] implying that those whom he addressed were not the children of God. To such men God is not a Father, but an offended and insulted moral Governor. He is benevolent; but his benevolence does not overthrow his moral government. On the contrary, it enforces the claims of justice. To turn loose the guilty, and to permit the lawless to roam at large through his dominions, to disturb the peace and order of his government, and render the obedient unhappy, would not be benevolence. God's benevolence is against the sinner; and when the walls of the infernal prison are broken down, and its guilty inmates are permitted to fill the universe with crime and wretchedness, it will no longer be true that God is love.

In contemplating the awful subject of future misery, and its relation to God's benevolence, our minds may find some relief in regarding the misery as the natural and proper effect of sin. God has so constituted the nature of man, that he feels remorse for crime; and he has so constituted the nature of external things, that drunkenness, and many other sins, produce poverty and suffering. We have not the hardihood to complain that this constitution of things is not benevolent. He who, knowing that fire will burn, voluntarily puts his hand into the flame, has no right to charge God with want of benevolence, because he has made it the nature of fire to burn. Much of future misery may be regarded as the natural effect of sinful passions, tearing the soul by their violence, or of an upbraiding conscience, gnawing within, as the worm that dieth not. "God is a consuming fire," ever present to the workers of iniquity; and his nature must change if his wrath cease to burn against sin. The nature of things, as constituted by God, and as including the nature of God himself, must render the sinner miserable. If he would cease to be miserable, he must escape from himself, and must find another God, and another universe.

---

[1] Mal. i. 6.　　　　[2] Isaiah i. 2.　　　　[3] John viii. 42.

CONCLUSION.

THIS world is not such a habitation as a wise man would desire to live in for ever. The young and thoughtless expect to find happiness in it; but experience teaches that the expectation is vain and delusive. Disappointment, care, and sorrow form a large part of human life; and as men approach the end of their course, they can adopt the language of the patriarch Jacob: "Few and evil have been the days of my pilgrimage."[1] This sad experience results from the fact, that God's curse rests on the world, because it is full of sin: and what wise man would wish to live for ever in a habitation that God has cursed?

If this were the only world, it would be well for us to make the best of it: but we have abundant proof that another world exists; and a revelation from it has been made, by which we may learn how to obtain a portion there, that will be full of unmixed happiness, and will endure for ever. We are called on to relinquish our delusive hope of earthly good, and lay hold on the hope set before us, that is sure and certain: to give up our pursuit of the unsatisfying and short-lived pleasures of the present life, and to seek the substantial and eternal joys of the life to come. It is certainly the part of wisdom to obey this call.

Another fact needs to be considered. Whether we will or not, we are compelled to leave this world, and take up our eternal abode in another habitation, either of joy or woe. If we had all possible enjoyment here, it would be but momentary, and would not deserve a thought in comparison with eternal happiness and misery. We are rapidly passing through this world, to our eternal home. Whether, in this lodging place of wayfaring men, our comforts shall be few or many, is a matter of very little moment, and unworthy of anxious care: but it is extreme folly to be unconcerned about the world to which we are hastening, and where our condition will be fixed for ever.

---

[1] Gen. xlvii. 9.

There are some things in religion which are hard to be understood, and about which some persons are inclined to be skeptical: but is there any other thing so incredible, as that intelligent and immortal beings should make the things of this fleeting world their chief care, and give themselves no concern about eternity? If the fact were not daily before our eyes, who could believe it? Were the Bible to inform us that there are intelligent immortals in a remote planet who thus act, the skeptic would appear almost excusable who should doubt the truth of the statement; but that book tells us of men, intelligent and immortal men, who are blinded by the god of this world, and led captive by him at his will, and who do not consider their latter end, but rush on to destruction, as the ox goeth to the slaughter. This testimony, than which the Bible contains nothing more incredible, is verified by the whole history of mankind. From this reigning folly even Christian men are but partly delivered. Even they perpetually need the exhortation, "Be not conformed to this world;"[1] and, to preserve them from the fascinating power of "the things seen, which are temporal," they should look habitually at "the things which are unseen and eternal." For this purpose, the doctrine concerning the future world is to them very important. "This is the victory that overcometh the world, even our faith:"[2] and faith, being "the substance of things hoped for, and the evidence of things not seen,"[3] must lay hold on the realities of the invisible and future world.

The doctrine concerning the future world teaches us to set a proper value on earthly good. If the honors of the world tempt us, let us remember that, in the grave, the king and the meanest of his subjects will lie on the same level, and mingle with the same dust; and that, in the resurrection, the noble of the earth, who have not sought the honor that cometh from God, will rise to shame and everlasting contempt. If the pleasures of the world invite, let us conceive of them as the bait with which Satan would ensnare our souls, and lead them into everlasting torments. If our hearts incline, at any time, to covetousness, let us contemplate the rich man in hell, stripped of all his possessions, and unable to procure a drop of water to cool his parched tongue. So let us keep eter-

---

[1] Rom. xii. 2.   [2] 1 John v. 4.   [3] Heb. xi. 1.

nity directly in view; and, in its light, the honors, pleasures, and wealth of this world will lose their lustre, and cease to charm.

This doctrine teaches us how to bear the afflictions of life. The heaviest affliction that can crush the spirit here, is far lighter than the weight of wrath which falls on the wicked in the world to come. Why, then, should a living man complain, a man for the punishment of his sins?[1] So long as he still lives, out of torment, out of hell, his suffering, however severe, is inconceivably less than his sins deserve. Moreover, his afflictions, if endured with humble resignation to God, are conducing to his holiness. Though light and momentary, they work out for him a far more exceeding and eternal weight of glory.[2] With eternity in view, the heaviest and most enduring anguish of this life appears light and momentary; and we can rejoice to endure it, because of the glorious effects which it will produce in the eternal world.

This doctrine teaches the value of religion. Learning and talent, agreeable manners and amiable disposition, are all worthy to be prized; but they do not secure eternal blessedness. Religion is the one thing needful, the good part that will never be taken from us.[3] Let sinners despise religion and curl the lip with scorn, when you speak of its claim on their regard: but even they, when eternity is near in prospect, learn the value of what once they despised. With eternity in view, how precious is religion! how precious the Bible which teaches it!

This doctrine endears Christ to believers. He is precious, for what he is in himself; but this preciousness is enhanced by the consideration, that it is he who delivers us from the wrath to come, who is preparing a place for us in the world of bliss, who will come and take us to himself, an.[3] for ever lead us to the fountains of living waters, in that lan.. of everflowing delight.

This doctrine consoles us, under the loss of Christian friends. We follow them to the tomb, and our tears flow freely: but we sorrow not as those who have no hope. They are not lost to us, but have only gone home before us; and we are waiting to be sent for, when it shall be the pleasure of our heavenly Father. Our separation from them is short, for we are fast approaching our

---

[1] Lam. iii. 39.   [2] 2 Cor. iv. 17.   [3] Luke x. 42.

journey's end, and then we shall join them again, never more to part.

This doctrine, if received in lively faith, enables the Christian to meet death with joy. When a man repents of sin, and believes in Christ, he is prepared to die safely; but he may nevertheless, through the weakness of his faith, be afraid to die. To meet death without fear, requires strong faith in Christ, as the Saviour of sinners. To meet death with joy, requires strong faith in the doctrine concerning the future world. When we can stand, like Moses on Pisgah's top, and view the good land in all its beauty, our hearts leap forward, with strong desire, to go over Jordan, and possess it. We long to join the happy company, who dwell for ever in the presence of our God. O to be free from sin, as they are;—to behold the face of Jesus, as they do;—to partake of their bliss, and unite in their everlasting hallelujahs!

Reader, what are your prospects in the future world? Have you received the love of the truth, that you may be saved? Does the truth as it is in Jesus enter your heart, with sanctifying power? Are you daily striving, by a holy life, to adorn the doctrine of God our Saviour in all things?

THE END.

MANUAL OF THEOLOGY.

SECOND PART.

A TREATISE ON

CHURCH ORDER.

BY

J. L. DAGG.

That thou shouldst set in order the things that are wanting, and ordain elders in every city.—Titus i. 5.

The rest will I set in order when I come.—1 Cor. xi. 34.

CHARLESTON, S. C.:
SOUTHERN BAPTIST PUBLICATION SOCIETY.
RICHMOND, VA.: S. S. & PUBLICATION BOARD.
MACON, GA.: B. B. & COLPORTEUR SOCIETY·
SELMA, ALA.: B. B. & BOOK DEPOSITORY.
NEW ORLEANS: B. B. DEPOSITORY.
1859.

PREFACE.

In the Preface to the " Manual of Theology," published last year, it was said :—" This volume contains nothing respecting the externals of religion. The form of godliness is important, as well as its power, and the doctrine respecting it is a component part of the Christian system; but I have been unable to include it in the present work." The defect here acknowledged, the following treatise on Church Order, including the ceremonies of Christianity, is intended in part to supply.

In all religious investigations, the Holy Scriptures are our chief source of knowledge. This is especially true in regard to positive institutes, which derive all their obligation from the revealed will of the lawgiver. The present work, therefore, relies wholly on the Bible for proof of its positions, so far as they relate to subjects on which the Bible professes to give instruction. But the volume of inspiration was not given to teach us the meaning of words, or the facts of ecclesiastical history after the times of the apostles. When these subjects come under investigation, I have made such reference to human authority as the case seemed to require. It has been my aim, however, so to lay the facts before the mind of the reader, as to give full scope for the exercise of private judgment, and a consciousness that he is not bowing to the decisions of any fallible master.

In most of the investigations attempted in these pages, the sacred volume sheds its light on our path, and enables us to tread the way with confidence; but, at a few points, the light seems to shine with less clearness. Here, the inquiry becomes appropriate, whether the very silence of Scripture is not instructive? We may infer that whatever is not clearly revealed, must be of less importance; and that difference of judgment respecting it ought not to divide the people of God.

The objections and opposing arguments which this work encounters, are such as appear to me most likely to embarrass an inquirer. They are generally expressed in my own language; but, in the discussions on baptism, I am in a few instances indebted for the language, as well as the thoughts, to the Lectures of Dr. Woods. In controverting the opinions of Baptist authors, I have, in some instances, thought it best to present these opinions in the form of direct quotation.

The preparation of this treatise has yielded less religious enjoyment to the Author, than was experienced in writing the "Manual." The subject has less to do with the heart, and furnished fewer occasions for those emotions in which religious enjoyment consists. But the work has been prosecuted under a calm conviction of duty; and if it shall tend to produce, in those who read it, a scrupulous adherence to the precepts of Christ, with expansive love to all who bear his image, the Author's labor will not be in vain. With a hope that it may contribute somewhat to this result, it is commended to the blessing of him whose will it attempts to unfold.

Gratitude requires that I should acknowledge my obligations to the Rev. G. W. Samson, of Washington City, and the Rev. A. M. Poindexter, of Richmond, Va. These brethren have kindly made suggestions, from which the work has received valuable improvements; and Mr. Samson has directly contributed the chief article in the Appendix.

July 31, 1858.

CONTENTS.

(v)

CHURCH ORDER.

INTRODUCTION.

OBEDIENCE TO CHRIST.

To love God with all the heart is the sum of all duty. Love must be exercised according to the relations which we bear. When a parent loves his child, he feels bound to exercise parental authority over it for its benefit; but the love of a child towards a parent requires obedience. So love to God produces obedience; for it is impossible to love God supremely without a supreme desire to please him in all things. Hence this one principle contains, involved in it, perfect obedience to every divine requirement.

The loveliness of the divine character is not abated, by being exhibited in the humble nature of man, in the person of Jesus Christ. In him the glory of the Father appears, claiming our supreme affections; and he is invested with the Father's authority, to which perfect obedience is due. The divine perfections are rendered more intelligible to us by his mediation; and, in proportion to the clearness of the discovery, the obligation to love and obey becomes increased.

A powerful motive, to love and obey Christ, is drawn from the love which he has manifested in dying for us. Paul felt this in an overpowering degree, when he said, "I am crucified with Christ, nevertheless I live; yet not I, but Christ liveth in me; and the life which I now live in the flesh, I live by the faith of the Son

(9)

of God, who loved me, and gave himself for me."[1] The same overpowering impulse to love and obedience, is brought to view in another declaration of this apostle: "The love of Christ constraineth us; because we thus judge, that if one died for all, then were all dead; and that he died for all, that they which live should not henceforth live unto themselves, but unto him which died for them, and rose again."[2] When our love to the Saviour grows cold, we should repair to his cross, and fix our thoughts on the exhibition of love there presented. And when we feel our hearts melt, the recollection that the suffering Saviour is God over all, must produce a full purpose to yield to him the obedience of all our powers during our whole existence. From the cross we come forth to be Christ's, resolved to glorify him with our bodies and our spirits, which are his.

Jesus said to his disciples, "If ye love me, keep my commandments." This claim of obedience is cordially admitted by every true disciple. When the first emotion of love to Christ throbbed in the heart of the persecuting Saul, he inquired, "Lord, what wilt thou have me to do?"

The first disciples were required to serve their Lord and Master by strenuous efforts to spread his religion through the world; and the same obligation devolves on us. He came to be the Saviour of the world; and, notwithstanding the humility of his appearance, and the feebleness of the instrumentality which he chose, the religion of the despised Nazarene must prevail over the earth, and bless every nation of mankind. The conquest of the world has not yet been achieved, but the work is before us; and, if we are loyal subjects of Zion's King, we must give ourselves to its accomplishment.

The means which our King employs, for diffusing the blessings of his reign, are not such as human wisdom would have adopted. It has pleased the Lord, "by the foolishness of preaching, to save them that believe." It has seemed good to infinite wisdom, that the religion which is to bless mankind, should be propagated by the simple instrumentality of the Christian ministry and the Christian churches. If we seek military force, or legislative enactments, to accomplish the work, we turn away from the simplicity of Christ,

---

[1] Gal. ii. 20.   [2] 2 Cor. v. 14, 15.

and convert his kingdom into one of this world; and, whenever human wisdom has attempted, in any particular, to improve the simple means that Christ ordained, the progress of truth and righteousness has been impeded.

Much that has existed, and that now exists, among the professed followers of Christ, cannot be contemplated by one who sincerely loves him, without deep distress. Different creeds, and different ecclesiastical organizations, have divided those who bear his name into hostile parties, and Christianity has been disgraced, and its progress retarded. The world has seen hatred and persecution where brotherly love ought to have been exhibited; and Christ has been crucified afresh, and put to open shame, by those who claim to be his disciples.

For these evils, what shall be the remedy? Shall we look to the wisdom of this world, to devise the cure? Human wisdom did not originate the institutions of Christianity; and it is now unable to give them efficiency. We must return to the feet of our divine Master, and again receive his instructions. Let us, in the spirit of obedient disciples, inquire for the good old paths, that we may walk therein. No individual can accomplish everything; but it is his duty to do what he can. Let each one show that he possesses the spirit of Christ, and carefully obey all the commands of Christ. If he cannot cure the existing evils, he will, at least, not increase them; and the influence of his example may produce salutary effects beyond his most sanguine hopes.

The true spirit of obedience is willing to receive the slightest intimations of the divine will. All the truths of Revelation are not equally clear; yet none of them may be disregarded because of difficulty in their investigation. If some most needful to be known, are presented prominently on the inspired pages, and written in characters so large that he who runs may read; there are others which are discoverable only by diligent search. Yet the truths, thus discovered, are precious gems dug from an exhaustless mine; and even the very labor of discovery brings its own reward in the mental and spiritual discipline which it furnishes. The diligent student of the Scriptures derives an abundant recompense for his toil, not only from the enlarged and clearer views of divine truth to which he attains, but also from that constant exercise of humility and faith, for which he finds occasion at every step of his progress.

As the truths of revelation differ in the clearness with which they are exhibited, so our faith embraces them with different degrees of strength. A man who does not investigate for himself, may receive, with unwavering confidence, and maintain, with obstinate pertinacity, every dogma of his party: but he who uses his own powers in the search after truth, will find some things to be received as undoubted articles of faith, others as opinions to be held with various degrees of confidence, according to the strength of evidence with which they have been severally presented to the mind. By not furnishing overpowering evidence on every question of faith and practice, the divine wisdom has given scope for the moral dispositions of men to exert their influence. A careful inquiry respecting the minutest portions of duty, and a fixed determination to observe the will of God in every particular, may exhibit proofs of obedience more strong and decisive, than would be possible, if all truth and duty were discovered by intuition.

Our obedience to Christ should be universal. The tithing of mint, anise, and cummin, is of less moment than the weightier matters of law, judgment, mercy, and faith; but it is not therefore to be disregarded. Christ taught that both were to be observed. "These ought ye to have done, and not to leave the other undone."[1] Church order and the ceremonials of religion, are less important than a new heart; and in the view of some, any laborious investigation of questions respecting them may appear to be needless and unprofitable. But we know, from the Holy Scriptures, that Christ gave commands on these subjects, and we cannot refuse to obey. Love prompts our obedience; and love prompts also the search which may be necessary to ascertain his will. Let us, therefore, prosecute the investigations which are before us, with a fervent prayer, that the Holy Spirit, who guides into all truth, may assist us to learn the will of him whom we supremely love and adore.

---

[1] Matt. xxiii. 23.

CHAPTER I.

BAPTISM.

Section I.—PERPETUITY OF BAPTISM.

WATER BAPTISM IS A CHRISTIAN ORDINANCE OF PERPETUAL OBLIGATION.

The commission of Christ to his apostles reads thus: "Go, teach all nations, baptizing them in the name of the Father, and of the Son, and of the Holy Ghost; teaching them to observe all things whatsoever I have commanded you; and lo, I am with you alway, even unto the end of the world."[1] It is not expressly stated in these words that water must be used in the baptizing which is enjoined; but so common is the use of water, that a command to immerse, wash, or sprinkle, naturally implies the use of it, unless something in the circumstances of the case, or connection of the word, suggests the use of some other liquid. The word baptize is often used in Scripture where water is implied without being expressly mentioned. The apostles had been accustomed to the administration of water baptism. They had been chosen to be Christ's attendants and witnesses, from the baptism of John;[2] and, in all probability, many of them saw their Master baptized in the Jordan. They had witnessed John's baptism in other cases; and some, if not all of them, had been baptized by him. After Jesus entered on his ministry, it was said that he "made and baptized more disciples than John."[3] Water baptism must be intended here; and we are expressly informed that the disciples, and not Jesus himself, administered it. This they did while they were under the imme-

---

[1] Matt. xxviii. 19, 20.   [2] Acts i. 22.   [3] John iv. 1.

diate direction of their Master, and were his personal attendants. His ministry, and their baptisms, were confined to the nation of Israel. The commission quoted above enlarged the field of their operation. The presence of their Master was promised, though his body was about to be removed from them; and the command to teach or make disciples, and to baptize, would naturally be interpreted by them according to the use of terms to which they had been accustomed. In their subsequent ministry, they preached and baptized; and the record, called the Acts of the Apostles, contains frequent mention of baptisms. In these, no reasonable doubt can exist that water was used: and sometimes it is expressly mentioned.

The commission was given, just before Christ ascended to heaven, and was designed for the dispensation which was to follow. The apostles, before proceeding to execute it, were commanded to tarry in Jerusalem until they should be endued with power from on high. This promised power was given when the Holy Spirit was poured out upon them on the day of Pentecost. It is clear, therefore, that, in the view of the Lord Jesus, water baptism was not inconsistent with the spiritual dispensation which the day of Pentecost introduced.

Besides its literal use, the word baptize is sometimes employed figuratively, when spiritual influence, or overwhelming sufferings, are intended. In such instances there is always something in the context, or circumstances of the case, directing to the proper interpretation. When there is nothing that directs to a figurative interpretation, we are required, by a well known law of criticism, to take the word in its literal sense. According to this law, we are bound to interpret literally the language of plain command used in the commission; and, if "baptizing" must be taken literally, no doubt can exist that the use of water was intended in the command.

Since the ascension of Christ, no change of dispensation has occurred by which the commission could be revoked. The promise which it contains, of Christ's presence until the end of the world, implies its perpetuity. Under this commission the ministers of Christ now act, and by it they are bound, according to the manifest intention of his words, to administer water baptism.

In different ages of Christianity some persons have denied the obligation of water baptism. The modern sect, called Quakers, are of this number. The objections which they urge deserve our attention.

Objection 1.—The proper rendering of the commission, is, "baptizing into the name of," &c. The name of God signifies his power, or some influence proceeding from him. The baptism *into* spiritual influence cannot be water baptism.

We admit the correction of the translation, but not the inference drawn from it. The same Greek preposition is used in other passages which forbid the inference now drawn. John said, "I baptize you unto [into] repentance." Repentance is a spiritual duty: but baptism into repentance is not, therefore, a spiritual baptism; for the words of John fully quoted, are: "I baptize you *with water into* repentance." In another passage it is said, "John preached the baptism of repentance for [into] the remission of sins:" and Peter, on the day of Pentecost, commanded, "Repent and be baptized for [into] the remission of sins." The remission of sins is a spiritual blessing, but it does not follow that baptism into the remission of sins must be a spiritual baptism. John's we know was water baptism; and when those who received Peter's command are said to have been baptized, the sacred historian employs the simple language of plain history: "Then they that gladly received his word were baptized."[1] These examples prove that the use of the preposition *into*, is not inconsistent with the literal interpretation of the commission.

Objection 2.—The baptism of John is, in the Scriptures, carefully distinguished from the baptism of Christ; the former being with water, the latter with the Spirit. The apostles were to act for Christ, and the commission authorized them to administer *his* baptism. Parallel texts may be found, in which the apostles are said to impart spiritual gifts.

Although John had predicted, that Christ would baptize with the Holy Spirit; yet the disciples made by Christ during his personal ministry, were baptized with water. This was administered by his disciples, and doubtless with his sanction. The careful mention by the evangelist that Jesus did not himself baptize, shows that baptism with the Holy Spirit is not in this case intended. John's words, "He shall baptize you with the Holy Ghost," describe spiritual baptism as Christ's peculiar personal work, and we do not

---

[1] Acts ii. 41.

find any passage of Scripture which speaks of the apostles, or any other ministers of Christ, *baptizing* with the Holy Spirit. Such baptism as they had been accustomed to administer, in the presence, and by the authority of Christ, the commission required them to administer.

It is true that Paul was sent to the Gentiles, to open their eyes, and to turn them from darkness to light, and from the power of Satan unto God; but these things are mentioned as the effects of his mission, and not as things directly commanded. The duty commanded, was to preach the gospel. The blessing of God on his ministry rendered his mission effectual to open the eyes of the Gentiles, and to confer the spiritual benefits mentioned in the special commission which he received. But the baptizing mentioned in the commission given to the other apostles, is a commanded duty, and the command must be understood according to the literal import of the words.

Objection 3.—Paul teaches that there is one baptism. Now, there is a baptism of the Spirit; and if water baptism is a perpetual ordinance of Christianity, there are two baptisms, instead of one.

Paul says, "One Lord, one faith, and one baptism." As he uses the words Lord and faith in their literal senses, so he uses the word baptism in its literal sense. In this sense there is but one baptism. John the Baptist foretold that Christ would baptize with the Holy Spirit: and Jesus said to his disciples, "Ye shall be baptized with the baptism that I am baptized with." Both these baptisms were known to Paul. These figurative baptisms were two in number; while the literal baptism was but one. He must, therefore, have intended the latter.

Objection 4.—Peter has defined the true Christian baptism, both negatively and positively. It is ("not the putting away of the filth of the flesh, but the answer of a good conscience toward God), by the resurrection of Jesus Christ."[1] The first clause denies that it is water baptism; and the second affirms that it is spiritual baptism. This is confirmed by the fact that it is said to *save*, which water baptism cannot do. Moreover, the words "the like figure," should be rendered *the antitype*. When spiritual things are compared to literal, the literal are the type, and the spiritual the antitype. Hence, as baptism is called the antitype, spiritual baptism must be intended.

---

[1] 1 Peter iii. 21.

Water baptism, as a Christian rite, is not administered to cleanse the flesh, either literally or ceremonially. It figuratively represents the burial and resurrection of Christ, on which the believer relies for salvation. The answer of a good conscience is obtained by faith in the finished work of Christ, represented in the rite. In the language of Scripture, a thing is said *to be* that which it represents: thus, "The field *is* the world." "This *is* my body." "This cup *is* the new testament." So Paul was said to wash away his sins in baptism, because it represented their being washed away: and so in this passage, baptism is said to save, because it represents our salvation, which is effected by the burial and resurrection of Christ; not by the removing of any corporeal defilement.

The criticism on the word antitype is inaccurate. The antitype is that which corresponds to the type; but it is not necessarily spiritual. The earthly sanctuary is, in one place, called the antitype of the heavenly, "which are the figures [antitypes] of the true."[1] In this passage "the holy places made with hands" are the antitype; and heaven is the type to which the antitype corresponds. This relation between the type and antitype, reverses the order which the objection assumes to be universal.

Objection 5.--The Jews had divers baptisms, which Paul calls "carnal ordinances imposed on them till the time of reformation."[2] An ordinance is not rendered carnal by the time when it is observed; but by its own nature. The Jewish baptisms were commanded by God, and were significant of spiritual things. Water baptism cannot have higher authority, or be more significant; and is, therefore, a carnal ordinance in its own nature, and not suited to Christ's spiritual dispensation. It belonged properly to John's dispensation, and was designed to be superseded by Christ's spiritual baptism, according to the words of John, "He must increase, but I must decrease."[3]

In speaking of the Jewish ceremonies, Paul says, " Which stood in meats and drinks, and divers baptisms, and carnal ordinances." This passage does not confound baptisms, with carnal ordinances, but seems rather to distinguish between them. Nevertheless, as the Jewish baptisms sanctified to the purifying of the flesh, there may be a propriety in denominating them carnal. Christian baptism is not administered for this purpose; and, therefore, is not

---

[1] Heb. ix. 24.   [2] Heb. ix. 10.   [3] John iii. 30.

carnal in the same sense. But, whatever it may be called, if
Christ instituted it for the observance of his followers, we dare not
account it unsuitable to his dispensation. The Jewish dispensation abounded with ceremonies; but amidst them all, a spiritual
service was required; for even then the sacrifices of God were
a broken spirit.[1] The ceremonies were wisely adapted to promote spirituality, rather than to hinder it. Our more spiritual dispensation needs fewer helps of this kind: but we are yet in the
body, and God has judged it fit to assist our faith by visible representations. To reject their use, is to be wiser than God.

Water baptism was not superseded by the baptism of the Spirit.
While Peter was preaching to Cornelius, and those who were in
his house, the Holy Ghost fell on them. The apostle did not consider this a reason for. omitting water baptism; but, on the contrary, argued the propriety of administering it, from this very
fact: "Can any man forbid water, that these should not be baptized which have received the Holy Ghost, as well as we?"[2] Contrary to all his previous views, the Holy Spirit had guided the
apostle to preach the gospel to these uncircumcised gentiles, and
to admit them to Christian baptism. If this rite had been designed
for Jews only, or to be superseded by the baptism of the Spirit,
Peter committed a mistake in commanding these first Gentile converts to be baptized with water. It is true that he had been mistaken before, in confining his ministry to the circumcised; and it
may be argued, that he may have been again mistaken in commanding water baptism to the uncircumcised. But the Holy
Ghost was now correcting the first error, and it is wholly improbable that in doing this, he should have led him into a second. The
propriety of admitting gentile converts had not been determined,
as it afterwards was, by a council of the apostles; but Peter followed the teaching of the Holy Spirit, and the subsequent council
justified his act. Now, if he had again mistaken the mind of the
Spirit in commanding the use of water baptism, it is unaccountable, and inconsistent with the perfection of the Scriptures, that
neither he nor the council, in reviewing the transaction under the
influence of the Holy Spirit, discovered the mistake; and that no

---

[1] Ps. li. 17.   [2] Acts x. 47.

correction, such as was made of the former error, is anywhere to be found in the inspired writings.

When John spoke the words, "He must increase, but I must decrease," the Jews had said to him, "Rabbi, he that was with thee beyond Jordan, behold the same baptizeth, and all men come to him."[1] The baptism which they reported must have been water baptism, and so far as John's words applied to it, they must denote that water baptism, instead of ceasing under Christ's dispensation, would be greatly extended.

Objection 6.—Paul states in 1st. epistle to the Corinthians, "Christ sent me not to baptize, but to preach the gospel;" and he thanked God that he had baptized so few of them. Now, as he was not a whit behind the chief of the apostles, water baptism would not have been omitted in his commission, if it had been designed to be a perpetual ordinance; and if it was as much his duty to baptize as to preach, he would not have thanked God that he had baptized so few. He would as soon have thanked God that he had preached so little. He baptized some, as he circumcised Timothy, accommodating himself to the weakness of men; but he was thankful that such acts of accommodation had been seldom needed. As he was the chief opponent of the prevailing judaizing tendency, he was thankful that, in the matter of baptizing, he had yielded to it in so few instances.

In this quotation from Paul, the word baptize stands alone, without the mention of water. The objection very properly assumes that water baptism is meant; but, in so doing, it confirms our rule, that the word baptize, when alone, implies the use of water. If the word, when standing alone in such a sentence, could mean the baptism of the Spirit, and if Paul and the other apostles had been commissioned to administer this baptism, he could not have declared with truth, "Christ sent me not to baptize."

Paul claimed to be an apostle, not of men, neither by man, but by Jesus Christ. An apostle is one sent, and Paul was sent by Jesus, who said "to whom I now send thee." He claimed to be an apostle in the highest sense, because he had received his commission directly from Christ: "Am I not an apostle? have I not seen Jesus Christ?"[2] Now, in the commission which he received directly from Christ, he was not commanded, either to be baptized himself or to baptize others. He received the gospel which he

---

[1] John iii. 26.   [2] 1 Cor. ix. 1

preached without human instrumentality; but he did not so receive baptism. He submitted to it, at the command of Ananias, who was not himself one of those originally commissioned to administer it. In this act, Paul acknowledged the obligation to perpetuate the ordinance, and the right of Ananias to administer it by authority derived from the other apostles. At Antioch he was set apart with fasting, prayer, and imposition of hands, for ministerial labor; and, whether this was done with reference to the missionary service on which he immediately entered, or whether it was his first ceremonial investiture with the ministerial office, we learn, from what was done, that his direct commission from Christ, was not designed to set aside the Church order which had been previously established by the other apostles. Both in receiving his own baptism, and in being set apart to the work to which the Holy Ghost had called him, Paul acted as an ordinary Christian. His apostleship for preaching the gospel was directly from Christ, and not by man; but his baptism, and his authority to baptize, were received by man, and in a way which respected and honored the established order of things among the disciples of Christ. While he said with truth, "Christ sent me not to baptize," it was nevertheless true, that the baptisms which he did administer were not unauthorized. He considered the administration of the ordinance not his proper apostolic work; and since the Corinthians had divided themselves into parties, claiming Paul, Apollos, and Cephas, for their leaders, he was thankful that so few of them could claim him as their leader on the ground of having received baptism from him.

Paul did not baptize out of mere accommodation to the weakness of others. Because of the Jews who were in that quarter, he circumcised Timothy, whose mother was a Jewess; but when the judaizers desired to have Titus also circumcised, who was a Greek, he steadfastly and successfully opposed them. As a minister of the uncircumcision, he watchfully and zealously defended the gentile converts in the enjoyment of liberty from the Jewish yoke of bondage. But not a word can be found in all that he said or wrote, claiming for them freedom from the obligation of Christian baptism. On the contrary, he uses considerations derived from their baptism, to urge them to walk in newness of life. The rule of interpretation, confirmed by the very objection which we are considering, requires us to understand literal baptism to be meant, when it is said, "So many of us as were baptized into Jesus Christ, were baptized into his death;"[1] and again, when it is said, "As many of you as have been baptized into Christ, have put on Christ."[2] A public profession of Christ was, in the view of Paul, the design of this ceremony, involving an acknowledged obligation to be his, and to walk in newness of life. All that Paul taught, like his own example, tends to establish the perpetuity of Christian baptism.

Section II.—MEANING OF BAPTIZE.

To BAPTIZE IS TO IMMERSE.

We have seen that the commission which Christ gave to his apostles, instituted baptism as an ordinance to be observed by his disciples to the end of the world. It becomes important, therefore, to ascertain the meaning of the word "baptizing," by which this duty is enjoined.

The commission has come down to us in the Greek language; and the word translated "baptizing," is a participle of the Greek verb βαπτιζω. Our present inquiry is, what does this Greek verb mean?

In the ordinary process of translating the writings of a Greek author, when we wish to ascertain the meaning of some word that he uses, we satisfy ourselves, for the most part, by consulting a Greek lexicon.[3]

The laws of interpretation require us to take the primary signification of words, unless there be something in the context, or nature of the subject, inconsistent with this signification. As there

---

[1] Rom. vi. 3.   [2] Gal. iii. 27.

[3] The Lexicons of Donnegan, and of Liddell and Scott, are in common use and high repute. They give the meaning of the word as follows:—

Donnegan.—"To immerse repeatedly into a liquid; to submerge, to soak thoroughly, to saturate; *hence* to drench with wine *Met.*, to confound totally; to dip in a vessel and draw.—Pass. Perf. βεβαπτισμαι, to be immersed, &c."

Liddell and Scott.—"To dip repeatedly, to dip under. *Mid.* to bathe; *hence* to steep, wet; *metaph.* οἱ βεβαπτισμενοι, soaked in wine; to pour upon, drench, εισφοραις οφλημασι βεβ. over head and ears in debt. Plut. μειρακιον Βαπτιζομενον, a boy overwhelmed with questions. Heind. Plat. Euthyd.—to dip a vessel, draw water—to baptize. N. T."

is no such difficulty in the present instance, our first decision, if we follow the lexicons, must be in favor of the sense *to immerse.*

When, from any cause, the decision of lexicons is unsatisfactory, the ultimate recourse is to Greek authors who have used the word in question. We search out the various examples of its use; and, by an examination of these, we learn in what sense the authors used the word. Since use is the law of language, the sense in which Greek authors used a word is its true meaning. The lexicons themselves yield deference to this law, and cite examples from authors in proof of the significations which they assign to words.

Our search of Greek authors, for the use of βαπτίζω, is greatly facilitated by the labors of learned men who have preceded us in the investigation.

Professor Stuart[1] has collected, from different Greek writers, a number of examples in which βαπτίζω, and its primitive, βάπτω, occur, with a view to determine the meaning of the words. To his collection, which he considered sufficiently copious for the purpose, I have added many other examples, from a similar collection by Dr. Carson, and a few others, from a smaller collection by Dr. Ryland. All these are included in the following tables, which may, therefore, be regarded as a fair exhibition of the use made of these words in Greek literature. The examples are so classified as to render the examination of them easy. In rendering the words in question, I have not closely followed the learned men of whose labors I have availed myself, but have aimed at a more literal and uniform translation. This is always put in italics; and the reader may consider the spaces, occupied by the italicized words, as so many blanks which he may fill with any other rendering that he may think better fitted to express the author's meaning. Let it be regarded as a problem to be solved, how these several blanks shall be filled, so that the supply may fit every example, and, at the same time, be consistent, throughout the table, as the meaning of the same word.

In a few of the examples the italicized words are marked with an asterisk. In these cases they are renderings, not of the verbs

---

[1] Dissertation on the question, "Is the mode of Christian Baptism prescribed in the New Testament?"

themselves, which are placed at the head of the tables, but of substantives or adjectives derived from them, and involving the same signification. In the English prepositions which are construed with the verbs, I have sometimes followed Professor Stuart, when, without his authority, I should have been inclined to adopt other renderings. This remark applies especially to the use of "with," in Class III. of Table II. A different rendering would correspond more exactly with the idea of immersion; but it has been my wish to give immersion no advantage to which it is not clearly entitled.

TABLES OF EXAMPLES.

TABLE I.

EXAMPLES OF ΒΑΠΤΩ.

CLASS I.

TO DIP LITERALLY AND STRICTLY.

§ 1. *For the purpose of imbuing or covering.*—1. He took a thick cloth and *dipped* it in water.[1] 2. *Dipping* sponges in warm water.[2] 3. And a clean person shall take hyssop, and *dip* it in the water, and sprinkle it upon the house.[3] 4. Send Lazarus, that he may *dip* the tip of his finger in water.[4] 5. Cakes *dipped* in sour wine.[5] 6. *Dip* thy morsel in the vinegar.[6] 7. One of the twelve that *dippeth* with me in the dish.[7] 8. Who *dippeth* his hand in the dish.[8] 9. And when he had *dipped* the sop.[9] 10. *Dipping* hay

---

[1] 2 Kings viii. 15. [2] Hippocrates. [3] Num. xix. 18.
[4] Luke xvi. 24. [5] Hippocrates. [6] Ruth ii. 14.
[7] Mark xiv. 20. [8] Matt. xxvi. 23. [9] John xiii. 26.

into honey, they give it them to eat.[1] 11. Venus *dipped* the arrows in sweet honey.[2] 12. He put forth the end of the rod that was in his hand, and *dipped* it in a honeycomb.[3] 13. Ye shall take a bunch of hyssop, and *dip* it in the blood which is in the basin.[4] 14. The priest shall *dip* his finger in the blood, and sprinkle of the blood.[5] 15. The priest shall *dip* his finger in the blood of the bullock, and sprinkle it.[6] 16. He *dipped* his finger into the blood.[7] 17. And shall *dip* them and the living bird in the blood.[8] 18. And he shall *dip* it into the blood.[9] 19. The Greeks *dipping* the sword and the Barbarians the spear-head [in blood.[10]] 20. Having *dipped* a crown into ointment.[11] 21. The priest shall *dip* his right finger in the oil that is in his left hand.[12] 22. *Dip* the probes in some emollient.[13] 23. *Dipping* the rag in white sweet-smelling Egyptian ointment.[14] 24. *Dipping* the rags in ointment.[14] 25. By reason of heat and moisture, the colors enter into the pores of things *dipped* into them.[15] 26. They *dip* it [into the dye-stuff.[16]]

§ 2d. *For the purpose of filling, or of drawing out, the verb sometimes taking the sense to dip out.*—27. The youth held the capacious urn over the water, hasting to *dip* it.[17] 28. Take a vessel, ancient servant, and having *dipped* it into the sea, bring it hither.[18] 29. The bucket must be first *dipped* and then be drawn up again.[19] 30. The lad directed his large pitcher towards the water, hastening to *dip* it.[20] 31. He *dipped* his pitcher in the water.[21] 32. Instead of water, let my maid *dip* her pitcher into honeycombs.[22] 33. Bubbling water *dipped* up with pitchers.[23] 34. To-day, ye bearers of water, *dip* not [from the river Inachus].[24] 85. *Dip up* the sea-water itself.[25]

§ 3. *For the purpose of cleansing.*—36. The Egyptians consider the swine so polluted a beast, that if any one in passing touch a swine, he will go away and *dip* himself with his very garments,

---

[1] Aristotle. [2] Anacreon. [3] 1 Sam. xiv. 27.

[4] Ex. xii. 22. [5] Lev. iv. 6. [6] Lev. iv. 17.

[7] Lev. ix. 9. [8] Lev. xiv. 6. [9] Lev. xiv. 51.

[10] Xenophon. [11] Ælian. [12] Lev. xiv. 16.

[13] Hippocrates. [14] Hippocrates. [15] Aristotle.

[16] Plato. [17] Theocritus. [18] Euripides.

[19] Aristotle. [20] Theocritus. [21] Hermolaus.

[22] Theocritus. [23] Euripides. [24] Callimachus.

[25] Nicander.

going into the river.[1] 37. It shall be *dipped* into water: so shall it be cleansed.[2] 38. First they *dip* the wool in warm water, according to ancient custom.[3]

§ 4. *For the purpose of hardening.*—39. The smith *dips* a hatchet into cold water.[4] 40. Iron *dipped.*[5]

§ 5. *For other purposes.*—41. Bring the torch, that I may take and *dip* it.[6] 42. They cannot endure great changes, such as that, in the summer time; they should *dip* into cold water.[7] 43. If the crow has *dipped* his head into the river.[8] 44. The feet of the priests that bare the ark were *dipped* in the brim of the water.[9] 45. Of which the remedy is said to be a certain stone which they take from the sepulchre of a king of ancient times, and having *dipped* it in wine, drink.[10] 46. If any one *dips* anything into wax, it is moved as far as he *dips.*[11] 47. Having melted the wax, he took the flea, and *dipped* its feet into the wax.[12] 48. With his own hand, he shall *dip* his sword into the viper's bowels.[13] 49. He *dipped* his whole chin into the belly of the ram.[14] 50. The one *dipped* his spear between the other's ribs, who at the same moment [dipped his] into his belly.[15] 51. Taking his sounding scimitar from the dead, he *dipped* it into the flesh.[16]

CLASS II.

TO DIP IN A LESS STRICT SENSE.

§ 1. *In appearance.*—52. If the sun *dip* himself cloudless into the western flood.[17] 53. Cepheus *dipping* his head or upper part into the sea.[18]

§ 2. *In effect.*—54. From the dew of heaven, his body was *dipped* [as wet as if it had been dipped.][19] 55. Having *dipped* [wetted or filled as if he had dipped] the hollow of his hand, he sprinkles the tribunal.[20] 56. He was clothed with a vesture *dipped* [colored as if it had been dipped] in blood.[21]

---

[1] Herodotus.	[2] Lev. xi. 32.	[3] Aristophanes.
[4] Homer.	[5] Plutarch.	[6] Aristophanes.
[7] Aristotle.	[8] Aratus.	[9] Josh. iii. 15.
[10] Aristotle.	[11] Aristotle.	[12] Aristophanes.
[13] Lycophron.	[14] Philippus.	[15] Dionysius of Halicarnassus.
[16] Euripides.	[17] Aratus.	[18] Aratus.
[19] Dan. iv. 33, v. 21.	[20] Suidas.	[21] Rev. xix. 13.

CLASS III.

TO COLOR.

§ 1. *By dipping.*—57. The color of things *dyed* is changed by the aforesaid causes.[1] 58. The *dyers,** when they are desirous to *dye* wool so as to make it purple; . . . and whatever may be *dyed* in this manner, the thing *dyed* becomes strongly tinctured. If any one *dye* other colors. That they may receive the laws in the best manner, as a *dye,** that their opinion may be durable. And those streams cannot wash out the *dye,** although they are very efficient to wash out.[2] 59. Some *dyed* with hyacinth, and some with purple.[3] 60. Thou hast well *dyed* thy sword against [in close conflict with] the Grecian army.[4] 61. For the wife has deprived each husband of life, *dyeing* the sword by slaughter.[5]

§ 2. *Without regard to mode.*—62. When it drops upon the garments, they are *colored.*[6] 63. Nearchus relates that the Indians *color* their beards.[7] 64. He endeavored to conceal the hoariness of his hair by *coloring** it. 65. The old man with the *colored* hair.[8] 66. Does a patron affect to be younger than he is? Or does he even *color* his hair?[9] 67. This garment, *colored* by the sword of Ægisthus, is a witness to me.[10] 68. He fell, without even looking upward, and the lake was *colored* with blood.[11] 69. Garments of variegated appearance, *colored** at great expense. 70. A *colored** bird.[12] 71. Lest I *color* you with a Sardinian hue.[12] 72. Then perceiving that his beard was *colored*, and his head.[13] 73. The physiologists, reasoning from these things, show that native warmth has *colored* the above variety of the growth of the things before mentioned.[14] 74. Using the Lydian music or measure, and making plays, and *coloring* himself with frog-colored [paints.][15]

---

[1] Aristotle.   [2] Plato.   [3] Josephus.
[4] Sophocles.   [5] Æschylus.   [6] Hippocrates.
[7] Arrian.   [8] Ælian.   [9] Nicolas of Damascus.
[10] Æschylus.   [11] Homer.   [12] Aristophanes.
[13] Plutarch.   [14] Diodorus Siculus.   [15] Aristophanes.

CLASS IV.

METAPHORICAL USE.

§ 1. *Allusion to dipping.*—75. Let him *dip* his foot in oil.[1] 76. Thy foot may be *dipped* in the blood of thine enemies.[2] 77. Thou hast *dipped* me deeply in filth.[3] 78. They are all *dipped* in fire.[4] 79. *Dipping up* pleasure with foreign buckets.[5]

§ 2. *Allusion to coloring.*—80. *Dyer*, who *dyest* all things, and dost change them by thy colors; thou hast *dyed* poverty also, and now appearest to be rich.[6] 81. For the soul is *colored* by the thought : *color* it then by accustoming yourself to such thoughts.[7]

TABLE II.

EXAMPLES OF BAΠTIZΩ.

CLASS I.

TO IMMERSE LITERALLY AND STRICTLY.

§ 1. *Sinking ships.*—1. Shall I not laugh at the man who *immerses* his ship by overlading it ?[8] 2. Such a storm suddenly pervaded all the country, that the ships that were in the Tiber were *immersed.*[9] 3. When the ship was about to be *immersed.*[10] 4. For our ship having been *immersed* in the midst of the Adriatic Sea.[11] 5. The wave high-raised *immersed* them.[12] 6. They were *immersed* with the ships themselves. 7. How would not his ship be *immersed* by the multitude of our rowers.[13] 8. They were either *immersed*, their ships being bored through.[14] 9. Those from above *immersing* them [ships] with stones and engines.[15] 10. They *im-*

---

[1] Deut. xxxiii. 24. [2] Psalms lxviii. 23. [3] Job ix. 31.
[4] Moschus. [5] Lycophron. [6] Helladius.
[7] Marcus Antoninus. [8] Hippocrates. [9] Dion Cassius.
[10] Josephus. [11] Josephus. [12] Josephus.
[13] Dion Cassius. [14] Dion Cassius. [15] Dion Cassius.

mersed many of the vessels of the Romans.[1]   11. The ships being in danger of being *immersed*.[2]   12. Many of the Jews of distinction left the city, as people swim away from an *immersing* [sinking] ship.[3]   13. Whose ship being *immersed*.[4]   14. As you would not wish, sailing in a large ship adorned and abounding with gold, to be *immersed*.[5]

§ 2. *Drowning.*—15. He would drive him from the bank, and *immerse* him headlong, so that he would not be able again to lift up his head above water.[6]   16. He may save one in the voyage that had better be *immersed* in the sea.[7]   17. The boy was sent to Jericho by night, and there by command, having been *immersed* in a pond by the Galatians, he perished.[8]   18. Pressing him down always as he was swimming, and *immersing* him as in sport, they did not give over till they entirely drowned him.[9]   19. The river being borne on with a more violent stream, *immersed* many.[10]   20. Killing some on the land, and *immersing* others into the lake with their boats and their little huts.[11]   21. The dolphin, vexed at such a falsehood, *immersing* him killed him.[12]   22. Many of the land animals *immersed* in the river perished.[13]

§ 3. *For purification.*—23. Naaman *immersed* himself seven times in Jordan.[14]   24. He that *immerseth* himself because of a dead body.[15]   25. He marveled that he had not first *immersed* before dinner.[16]   26. Except they *immerse*, they eat not.[17]   27. Divers *immersions*.[18]*   28. She went out by night into the valley of Bethulia, and *immersed* herself in the camp at the fountain of water.[19]   29. He who is *immersed* from a dead [carcass] and toucheth it again, what does he profit by his washing?[20]   30. The *immersion** of cups and pots, &c.[21]

§ 4. *Other cases.*—31. The person that has been a sinner, having gone a little way in it [the river Styx], is *immersed* up to the head.[22]   32. He breathed as persons breathe after being

---

[1] Polybius.	[2] Æsop.	[3] Josephus.
[4] Diod. Siculus.	[5] Epictetus.	[6] Lucian.
[7] Themistius.	[8] Josephus.	[9] Josephus.
[10] Diodorus Siculus.	[11] Heliodorus.	[12] Æsop.
[13] Diodorus Siculus.	[14] 2 Kings v. 14.	[15] Ecclus. xxxiv. 30
[16] Luke xi. 38.	[17] Mark vii. 4.	[18] Heb. ix. 10.
[19] Judith xii. 7.	[20] Ecclus. xxxiv. 25.	[21] Mark vii. 8.
[22] Porphyry.		

immersed.[1]   33. Then *immersing* himself into the Lake Copais.[2]
34. *Immerse* yourself into the sea.[3]   35. They marched a whole
day through the water, *immersed* up to the waist.[4]   36. The bitu
men floats on the top, because of the nature of the water, which
admits of no diving; nor can any one who enters it *immerse* himself, but is borne up.[5]   37. But the lakes near Agrigentum have
indeed the taste of sea water, but a very different nature, for it
does not befall the things which cannot swim to be *immersed*, but
they swim on the surface like wood.[6]   38. If an arrow be thrown
in, it would scarcely be *immersed.*[7]   39. As when a net is cast
into the sea, the cork swims above, so am I *unimmersed.*[8]*   40.
When a piece of iron is taken red hot out of the fire and *immersed*
in water, the heat is repelled.[9]   41. Thou mayest be *immersed*, O
bladder! but thou art not fated to sink.[10]   42. Having *immersed*
some of the ashes into spring water, they sprinkled.[11]   43. I found
Cupid among the roses; taking hold of him by the wings I *immersed* him into wine.[12]   44. The sword was so *immersed* in blood
that it was even heated by it.[13]   45. He set up a trophy, on which,
immersing his hand into blood, he wrote this inscription.[14]   46.
They are of themselves *immersed* and sunk in the marshes.[15]   47.
He *immersed* his sword up to the hilt into his own bowels.[16]

CLASS II.

TO IMMERSE IN A LESS STRICT SENSE.

§ 1. *In appearance.*—48. But when the sun *immerses* himself
in the water of the ocean.[17]

§ 2. *In effect.*—49. Certain uninhabited lands which at the ebb
are used not to be *immersed* [covered over as if they had been
immersed], but when the tide is at the full, the coast is quite inun-
dated.[18]   50. And were all *immersed* [surrounded on all sides as if
they had been immersed] unto Moses in the cloud and in the sea.[19]

---

[1] Hippocrates.
[2] Plutarch.
[3] Plutarch.
[4] Strabo.
[5] Strabo.
[6] Strabo.
[7] Strabo.
[8] Pindar.
[9] Heraclides Ponticus.
[10] Plutarch.
[11] Josephus.
[12] Anacreon.
[13] Dionysius.
[14] Plutarch.
[15] Polybius.
[16] Josephus.
[17] Orpheus.
[18] Aristotle.
[19] 1 Cor. x. 2.

CLASS III.

METAPHORICAL USE.

§ 1. *For drunkenness.*—51. I am one of those who *immersed* yesterday [who drank wine freely].[1] 52. Having *immersed* Alexander with much wine.[2] 53. Seeing him in this condition, and *immersed* by excessive drinking into shamelessness and sleep.[3] 54. They easily become intoxicated before they are entirely *immersed.*[4] 55. *Immersed* with wine.[5] 56. *Immersed* by drunkenness.[6] 57. He is like one dizzy and *immersed.*[7]

§ 2. *For afflictions.*—58. Perceiving that he was altogether abandoned to grief and *immersed* in calamity.[8] 59. Since the things you have met with have *immersed* you.[9] 60. Iniquity *immerses* me.[10] 61. I have an *immersion** to be *immersed* with.[11] 62. *Immersed* by misfortune.[12] 63. Else what shall they do who are *immersed* for the dead?[13] 64. Are you able to be *immersed* with the *immersion** that I am *immersed* with?[14]

§ 3. *Other uses.*—65. The mind is *immersed* [drowned like plants by excessive watering] by excessive labor.[15] 66. *Immersed* with business.[16] 67. *Immersed* with innumerable cares—having the mind *immersed* on all sides by the many waves of business, *immersed* in malignity.[17] 68. *Immersed* into sleep.[18] 69. He [Bacchus] *immerses* with a sleep near to death.[19] 70. When midnight has *immersed* the city with sleep.[20] 71. *Immersed* with sins.[21] 72. But the common people they do not *immerse* with taxes.[22] 73. They *immersed* [sunk as a ship] the city.[23] 74. This as the last storm *immersed* [sunk as a ship] the tempest-tossed young men.[24] 75. Being *immersed* in debts of fifty millions

---

[1] Aristophanes.	[2] Plato.	[3] Josephus.
[4] Philo Judæus.	[5] Chrysostom.	[6] Justin Martyr.
[7] Lucian.	[8] Heliodorus.	[9] Heliodorus.
[10] Isa. xxi. 4.	[11] Luke xii. 50.	[12] Heliodorus.
[13] 1 Cor. xv. 29.	[14] Mark x. 38.	[15] Plutarch.
[16] Plutarch.	[17] Chrysostom.	[18] Clemens Alexandrinus.
[19] Evenus.	[20] Heliodorus.	[21] Justin Martyr.
[22] Diod. Siculus.	[23] Josephus.	[24] Josephus.

of drachmæ.[1] 76. He shall *immerse* you in the Holy Spirit.[2] 77. In one spirit have we been *immersed* into one body.[3]

The chief difficulty in classifying Table I., respects Class III. Under it I have placed all the examples in which the sense *to color* is given to the word, either by Professor Stuart, or Dr. Carson. Many of these examples might have been placed in Class I., § 1; and others in Class II., § 2.

To color.—Some learned men have maintained that the verb never signifies *to color*, *without regard to mode*. It is possible to explain the examples in which it appears to have this signification, like Ex. 56. Here the translators of the English Bible supposed the word, though denoting color, to be used with a reference to its primary meaning. But when we consider how many words from the root BAP were used for things pertaining to the dyer's art; and how frequently the verb βαπτω was used to denote *to color;* it seems most probable, that when employed for this purpose, it suggested to the minds of the Greeks in their familiar use of it, the idea of color directly, without that process of thought which was necessary to deduce this meaning from its primary sense *to dip*.

To smear.—Professor Stuart has assigned *smear*, as a secondary sense of the verb, and cites in proof from the Greek classic writers, Ex. 60, 61, 74. To the first two of these the rendering to *smear* is quite inappropriate. The warrior in battle does not redden his sword by *smearing* over it the blood of his enemies, but by *plunging* it into their bodies. In the other example, the rendering is less objectionable; but even here caution is necessary lest it mislead us. The verbs dip, plunge, immerse, wash, wet, pour, sprinkle, and smear, are construed with reference to two substances: one a solid, and the other a liquid. The first five have the solid for their direct object: *to pour* has the liquid for its direct object. We say to dip the hand in water, and to pour water on the hand; but not to dip water on the hand, or to pour the hand with water. The last two verbs, to sprinkle and to smear, admit both constructions. We say, to sprinkle the floor with

---

[1] Plutarch.   [2] Matt. iii. 11; Acts i. 5.   [3] 1 Cor. xii. 13.

water, and to sprinkle water on the floor; to smear the body with paint, and to smear paint over the body. In both these constructions, they always denote an application of the liquid to the solid, agreeing in this particular with the verb *to pour*. The verb βαπτω is always construed with the solid as its direct object. Throughout the table of examples, there can be found but one exception, which will be noticed hereafter. Even when it signifies *to color*, the verb takes for its object the solid, and does not signify that the color is produced by applying the coloring matter, as is done in the process of smearing. Hence, the rendering *to smear* is liable to mislead us into the belief that βαπτω, like *to smear*, may signify an application of the liquid to the solid. The verb never signifies this process. It may signify the effect of it, but never the process itself.

To dip out.—The exception above referred to, is Ex 85. In this, which is Nicander's comment on the preceding example, the verb takes the liquid for its direct object, and assumes the sense *to dip out*. In the metaphoric use of the word, Ex. 79 conforms to this construction. It is worthy of remark that the English verb *to dip* is used in the same way, taking the liquid for its direct object, contrary to its usual construction; thus: He dips water from the pool. We never say, He plunges, or immerses water from the pool. In this sense of abstracting a part of the liquid from the rest, the verb βαπτω, when it takes the solid for its direct object, may be construed with the genitive of the liquid, either with, or without the preposition απω. This remark will explain Ex. 13, 15, 21; to which Professor Stuart has given the sense *to smear*, because the verb is construed with απω. They do not signify *to smear* with *blood* or oil by applying it; but to dip into it so as to bring away a part of it from the rest.

RELATION BETWEEN βαπτω AND βαπτιζω.

Our search is for the meaning of βαπτιζω. This is a derivative from βαπτω; and because some aid in ascertaining its meaning, has been expected from the primitive word, examples in which this occurs, have been introduced in the preceding collection. Some lexicographers have regarded βαπτιζω as a frequentative, and have rendered it *to immerse repeatedly*. Robinson says it "is frequentative in form, but not in fact." Professor Stuart has examined this question at length, and decides "that the opposite opinion, which makes βαπτίζω a *frequentative* (if by this it is designed to imply that it is necessarily so by the laws of formation, or even by actual usage), is destitute of a solid foundation, I feel constrained, on the whole, to believe. The lexicographers who have assigned this meaning to it, appear to have done it on the ground of theoretical principles as to the mode of formation. They have produced no examples in point. And until these are produced, I must abide by the position that a *frequentative* sense is not necessarily attached to βαπτίζω; and that, if it ever have this sense, it is by a specialty of usage of which I have been able to find no example." The termination ίζω, is, with greater probability, supposed by others to add to the primitive word the signification of *to cause*, or *to make*, like the termination *ize* in *legalize*, to make legal; *fertilize*, to make fertile. According to this hypothesis, if βαπτω signifies *to immerse*, βαπτίζω signifies *to cause to be immersed*. This makes the two words nearly or quite synonymous. But, however nearly two words may agree with each other in their original import, it seldom happens that they continue to be used in practice as equally fitted for every place which either of them may occupy. We must, therefore, examine the usus loquendi, to ascertain the peculiar shades of meaning which they acquire. In studying the preceding table of examples, the following things may be observed:—

1. βαπτω more frequently denotes slight or temporary immersion, than βαπτίζω. Hence, the English word *dip*, which properly denotes slight or temporary immersion, is more frequently its appropriate rendering. In nearly one-half of the examples in which βαπτίζω occurs in the literal sense, it signifies the immersion which attends drowning, or the sinking of ships.

2. Βαπτω appears, in some cases, to be used in the secondary sense *to color*, without including its primary signification *to immerse*. No example occurs in which βαπτίζω has lost the primary meaning. A similar fact may be observed in the use of the English words *older* and *elder*. The words have the same primary meaning; or, rather, they are different forms of the same word: yet, while *older* has inflexibly retained its primary meaning, *elder* has

3

adopted a secondary signification, in which it denotes an officer without regard to age.

8. Βαπτω sometimes signifies *to dip up:* βαπτιζω never takes this sense.

DEDUCTION FROM TABLE II.

Though lexicographers frequently assign numerous significations to a word, they regard one as the primary or radical meaning from which all the rest are derived. If meanings have no relation to each other, they do not belong to the same word: hence *to lie,* signifying to be recumbent; and *to lie,* signifying to speak falsehood, though agreeing in orthography and pronunciation, are accounted different words, because their significations are independent of each other. No one imagines that there are two Greek verbs, βαπτιζω. We must, therefore, seek for one primary or radical meaning, and endeavor to account by it for all the uses to which the word is applied.

An important distinction needs to be made between the proper meaning of a word, and the accidental signification which it may obtain from the connection in which it is used. This distinction may be illustrated by the following passage:—"If I wash myself with snow water, and make my hands never so clean; yet thou shalt plunge me in the ditch, and mine own clothes shall abhor me."[1] In this sentence the word *plunge,* besides its proper meaning, obtains the signification *to defile,* from the connection in which it is used. This accidental signification is the most prominent and important idea conveyed by the word; yet it is not, strictly speaking, any part of its meaning. We may substitute *defile* for it, and the general sense of the passage will be conveyed; yet *to plunge* and *to defile* are different things. We must not conclude that we have ascertained the meaning of a word, when we have found another word which may be substituted for it in a particular sentence.

Since the lexicons give *immerse* for the primary meaning of βαπτιζω, let us try the meaning in the examples in which the word occurs, that we may ascertain whether this signification will suffice to account for all the uses to which the word is applied.

In the several examples, in which the word is applied to sinking ships, it obtains the accidental signification to *cause to sink to the*

---

[1] Job ix. 30, 31.

bottom. On this account it has been explained, in such connections, by the word βυθίζω, *to throw into the deep.* But the fact that immersed ships sink to the bottom is not affirmed by the word βαπτίζω. It is a natural consequence of their immersion. There is no necessity for supposing it to be included in the meaning of the word. The same distinction must be made in the examples which relate to drowning. The drowning is a consequence of the immersion, and is not included in the meaning of the word βαπτίζω. In several of the examples the immersion denoted by the word is clearly distinguished from the effect produced by it. So in § 3, we must distinguish between the immersion and the purification resulting from it. The immersion only is properly denoted by the word. All the other examples in Class I. perfectly agree with the sense *to immerse;* and some of them clearly require it. From Ex. 36, 37, 38, 39, it appears that substances which float on water are not baptized. This proves conclusively that *the mere application of water to a part of the surface does not satisfy the meaning of the word.* Ex. 41 proves that sinking to the bottom is not necessary to its meaning; but the other examples just referred to, prove that descent below the surface is indispensable.

The examples in Class II. require the meaning *to immerse.* The same is true of the examples in Class III. The propriety and force of the metaphorical allusions cannot be understood, if the word does not signify *to immerse.*

After thoroughly examining the collection of examples, we find that they fully establish the meaning *to immerse.* Christ, in giving the commission, must have employed the word in its usual sense. The commission is given in the language of plain command, and every other word in it is used in its ordinary signification. We are not at liberty to seek for extraordinary meanings, but are bound to take the words according to their ordinary import, where no reason to the contrary exists. What they mean, according to the ordinary rules of interpretation, is the meaning of Christ's command; and, if we do not receive and observe it in this sense, we are disobedient to his authority.

Let us now re-examine the collection of examples, trying any of the other significations which have been proposed, as, to wash, to purify, to wet, to sprinkle, to pour. The experiment will soon convince us that none of these is the proper meaning of the word.

Immersion, and nothing but immersion, will always satisfy its demands.

The correctness of our deduction is confirmed by the circumstances which attended some of the baptisms recorded in the Bible. The forerunner of Christ is called "the Baptist," because he administered this rite. He was sent to baptize, and it must be supposed that he understood the meaning of the word. Now, if a small quantity of water will suffice, why did John resort to the Jordan for the administration? The reason must have been that which the inspired historian has expressly assigned for his baptizing in Enon, near to Salim; namely, "because there was much water there." The people were baptized by John in the Jordan. In this river our Lord was baptized, and his own example explains the meaning of his command.

The baptism of the Ethiopian eunuch is very circumstantially described. The style in which he travelled forbids the supposition that he had no drinking vessel, in which a sufficient quantity of water might have been brought into the chariot to wet the hand of the administrator. But, if they chose not to perform the rite in the chariot, there was certainly no need for both of them to go into the water, if the mere wetting of Philip's hand was sufficient. Why did they both go into the water? and why did the sacred historian so particularly state this fact? "They both went down into the water, both Philip and the eunuch, and they both came up out of the water." These circumstantial facts are described in language which no one ought to misunderstand, and which no one ought to overlook, who desires to know his duty.

The Greek language continued to be spoken for many years after the times of the apostles. During all this period they, to whom the word βαπτιζω was vernacular, understood it to signify *immerse;* and immersion has always been the practice of the Greek church to the present day. The Greeks must have understood the meaning of their own word. The Latin fathers also understood the word in the same way; and immersion prevailed in the western as well as in the eastern churches, until near the time of the reformation. Affusion was allowed instead of immersion, in case of sickness; but it was accounted an imperfect baptism. The testimony to these several facts I prefer to give in the words of Professor Stuart :—

"In the writings of the apostolic fathers, so called, *i. e.*, the writers of the first century, or, at least, those who lived in part during this century, scarcely anything of a *definite* nature occurs respecting baptism, either in a doctrinal or ritual respect. It is, indeed, frequently alluded to; but this is usually in a general way only. We can easily gather from these allusions that the rite was practised in the church; but we are not able to determine, with precision, either the manner of the rite or the stress that was laid upon it.

"In the Pastor of Hermas, however, occurs one passage (Coteler. Patr. Apostol. I., p. 119, sq.), which runs as follows: 'But this seal [of the sons of God] is water, *in quam descendunt homines* morti obligati, *into which men descend* who are bound to death, but those ascend who are destined to life. To them that seal is disclosed, and they make use of it that they may enter the kingdom of God.'

"I do not see how any doubt can well remain, that in Tertullian's time the practice of the African church, to say the least, as to the mode of baptism, must have been that of *trine immersion*.

"Subsequent ages make the general practice of the church still plainer, if, indeed, this can be done. The Greek words καταδυω and καταδυσις were employed as expressive of *baptizing* and *baptism*, and these words mean *going down into the water*, or *immerging*.

"The passages which refer to immersion are so numerous in the fathers, that it would take a little volume merely to recite them.

"But enough. 'It is,' says Augusti (Denkw. VII., p. 216), 'a thing made out,' viz., the ancient practice of immersion. So, indeed, all the writers who have thoroughly investigated this subject conclude. I know of no one usage of ancient times which seems to be more clearly made out. I cannot see how it is possible for any candid man who examines the subject to deny this.

"That there were cases of exception allowed, now and then, is, no doubt, true. Persons in extreme sickness or danger were allowed baptism by affusion, &c. But all such cases were manifestly regarded as exceptions to the common usage of the church."

BURIAL IN BAPTISM.

The significancy of baptism requires immersion. Paul explains it: "Know ye not that so many of us as were baptized into Jesus Christ, were baptized into his death? Therefore we are buried with him by baptism into death; that, like as Christ was raised up from the dead by the glory of the Father, even so we also should walk in newness of life."[1] And again: "Buried with him in baptism, wherein also ye are risen with him through the faith of the operation of God, who hath raised him from the dead."[2] Peter alludes to the same import of the rite, when he says: "The like figure whereunto even baptism doth also now save us (not the putting away of the filth of the flesh, but the answer of a good conscience toward God) by the resurrection of Jesus Christ."[3]

The faith which we profess in baptism is faith in Christ; and the ceremony significantly represents the great work of Christ, on which our faith relies for salvation. We confess with the mouth the Lord Jesus, and believe in the heart that God has raised him from the dead.[4] His burial and resurrection are exhibited in baptism, as his broken body and shed blood are exhibited in the supper. In both ordinances our faith is directed to the sacrifice of Christ. Under the name of sacraments they have been considered outward signs of inward grace; and, in this view of them, they signify the work of the Holy Spirit within us. But faith relies, for acceptance with God, on the work of Christ. It is a perverted gospel which substitutes the work of the Spirit for the work of Christ as the object of our faith; and it is a perverted baptism which represents the faith that we profess, as directed, not to the work of Christ, the proper object of faith, but to the work of the Holy Spirit in our hearts.

Objection 1.—There is an antithesis between the burial and resurrection which are here mentioned. The resurrection is moral, being to newness of life; and the same appears in the parallel passage in Colossians, where it is said to be "by the faith of the operation of God." If the resurrection is moral, the antithetic burial cannot be physical.

---

[1] Rom. vi. 3, 4.　　　[2] Col. ii. 12.　　　[3] 1 Peter iii. 21.
[4] Rom. x. 9.

If consistency of interpretation requires the burial to be moral the baptism must also be moral. The Quakers suppose that the baptism first mentioned in the passage is moral: " So many of us as were baptized into Christ." But Pedobaptists admit that physical baptism is intended in this clause. Now, in passing from physical baptism at the beginning of the passage, to moral resurrection at its close, there must be a point in the progress where we pass from what is physical to what is moral. Where is that point? some have imagined that it stands between the clause last quoted, and that which immediately follows, "were baptized into his death;" they suppose that "to be baptized into Christ," is physical; but that to be baptized into his death is moral. The passage in Galatians has been quoted as parallel: "For as many of you as have been baptized into Christ, have put on Christ." The first clause in this verse, they say refers to physical baptism; and the last to moral. But this is an erroneous interpretation. To put on Christ, is to put on his religion by outward profession, the profession which is made in baptism. The baptism and the profession are alike, in implying a moral change in the subject, only so far as he is sincere. Some are physically baptized, who do not morally put on Christ; but this, though unquestionably true, is directly contradicted by the passage, if the proposed interpretation of it is correct. So in the passage under consideration, it is affirmed that the same persons, and the same number of persons that are baptized into Christ, are baptized into his death. This could not be true, if the first baptism is physical, and the second moral. Between these two clauses, therefore, there is no place for a division between what is physical and what is moral.

We extend our examination further to find a place for the division, and we find it plainly marked by the word "should;" even so we also should walk in newness of life. Here the obligation to suitable morals is deduced from what goes before. This obligation is deduced from the physical baptism with which the passage begins, and everything in the passage, until we arrive at the word "should," is closely connected with this physical baptism, and explanatory of it. These intermediate links of explanation are necessary to connect the moral obligation at the close, with the physical baptism at the outset of the passage. If these intermediate links were moral, the proper position for the word "should," would be in the first sentence—thus, so many of us as are baptized into Christ, *should* be baptized into his death.

In the parallel passage referred to in Colossians, the expression is "Buried with him in baptism." The word baptism stands without adjuncts. It is not *baptism into death; but simply baptism.* If the word baptism, thus standing alone, can signify something wholly moral, it will be difficult to reject the Quaker interpretation of these passages, and of "baptizing" in the commission. In the preceding verse, circumcision is mentioned; but that we may know physical circumcision not to be intended, it is expressly called "the circumcision made without hands;" and "the circumcision of Christ." No such guard against misinterpretation attends the mention of baptism; and when it is recollected that Christians are not bound to receive physical circumcision, but are bound to receive physical baptism, we must conclude that physical baptism is here intended. The completeness of Christians requires the moral change denoted by circumcision, and also the obedience rendered in physical baptism. In all who are thus complete, this physical act is performed "in faith of the operation of God." This passage does not, like that in Romans, deduce moral obligation from baptism; and, therefore, the word *should* is not introduced: but it affirms the completeness of true believers in their internal moral change, and in their very significant outward profession of it.

Objection 2.—Everywhere else in Scripture, water is an emblem of purification; and it violates all analogy to suppose that in baptism it is an emblem of the grave, which is the place of putridity and loathsomeness.

That water in baptism is an emblem of purification, is clear from the words "Arise, and be baptized, and wash away thy sins." But that water is an emblem of nothing but purification, cannot be affirmed. In numerous passages it is an emblem of afflictions, of deep afflictions, without any reference to purification. When the Saviour said, "I have a baptism to be baptized with;" an immersion is intended, not into a means of purification, but into sufferings and death.

The grave is a place of putridity and loathsomeness, but not until the corruptible body is deposited in it; and when it leaves the grave, the corruptible will put on incorruption. Even the grave, therefore, is a place of regeneration and purification; and, instead of bearing no analogy to the purifying water of baptism, the analogy is striking.

Some of the Scripture allusions to baptism, are made to it as a purifying rite, but this is not true of all. An exception is found in 1 Cor. x. 2. On this Professor Stuart remarks: "Here, then, was the cloud which first stood before them, and then behind them; and here were the waters of the Red Sea, like a wall on their right hand and on their left. Yet neither the cloud nor the waters touched them. 'They went through the midst of the sea upon *dry* ground.' Yet they were *baptized in the cloud and in the sea*. The reason and ground of such an expression must be, so far as I can discern, a surrounding of the Israelites on different sides by the cloud and by the sea, although neither the cloud nor the sea touched them. It is, therefore, a kind of figurative mode of expression, derived from the idea that baptizing is surrounding with a fluid. But whether this be by immersion, affusion, suffusion, or washing, would not seem to be decided. The suggestion has sometimes been made, that the Israelites were *sprinkled* by the cloud and by the sea, and this was the baptism which Paul meant to designate. But the cloud on this occasion was not a cloud of rain; nor do we find any intimation that the waters of the Red Sea sprinkled the children of Israel at this time. So much is true, viz., that they were not *immersed*. Yet, as the language must evidently be figurative in some good degree, and not literal, I do not see how, on the whole, we can make less of it, than to suppose that it has a tacit reference to the idea of *surrounding* in some way or other." This author urges the objection which we are considering, as his "principal difficulty in respect to the usual exegesis;" yet we have here, according to his own exposition, an allusion to baptism, without any reference to purification. Another such reference is found in 1 Peter iii. 21, and again in the words of Christ before quoted, "I have a baptism to be baptized with."

Objection 3.—Very little resemblance can be found, between a man's being dipped in water, and Christ's being laid in a sepulchre hewn out of a rock. The supposed allusion requires resemblance.

Positive proof of allusion must be attended with difficulty; because, if it be mere allusion, it is always made without express affirmation. The proof of allusion must therefore be circumstantial; yet there may be circumstances which exclude all rational doubt of its existence.

If there is no resemblance between immersion and Christ's burial, the passage before us contains no allusion. If the resemblance is so slight, that but few persons are able to perceive it, the probability is, that the supposed allusion exists only in the fancy of those who imagine they see it. But if men have generally believed that allusion exists in the passage, the fact goes far to prove, that there is resemblance.

Have men generally believed in the existence of the supposed allusion? It is not necessary to examine the writings of authors attached to every different creed, and differing from each other in their views of baptism. Professor Stuart tells us their opinion in few words: "Most commentators have maintained, that συνεταφημεν has here a necessary reference to the mode of literal baptism, which they say, was by immersion; and this, they think, affords ground for the employment of the image used by the apostle, because immersion (under water) may be compared to burial (under the earth). It is difficult, perhaps, to procure a patient rehearing for this subject, so long regarded by some as being out of fair dispute." Now this general agreement of commentators, answers the objection which we are considering, far more successfully than any efforts of ours to point out the resemblance, which these commentators have perceived. The fact that it is seen is the best proof that it exists. The Scripture nowhere affirms that Paul, in this passage, alluded to a resemblance between immersion and Christ's burial; and, therefore, "the common exegesis" cannot be sustained by positive proof from Scripture; but it finds proof, the best proof that the nature of the case admits, in the fact that men generally have seen and felt the allusion.

Although positive proof of the common exegesis cannot be found in Scripture, a circumstantial proof may be drawn from the passage itself, amounting to little less than full demonstration. After making mention of baptism into Christ's death, Paul, before he refers to Christ's resurrection, goes out of the usual course to speak of Christ's burial. This was not necessary for the moral instruction which he designed to convey, if nothing but moral conformity to Christ's death was intended. It was not necessary for the purpose of finding an antithesis to the resurrection of Christ. The Scriptures usually speak of Christ's rising *from the dead, not from the grave:* and his death is the common antithesis to his resurrection. An example occurs in the present chapter, "If we have been planted together in the likeness of his death, we shall be also in the likeness of his resurrection." In Colossians, after the passage "Buried with him in baptism," the antithesis is again made, between the death (not the burial) of Christ, and his resurrection: "Wherefore if ye be dead with Christ, from the rudiments of the world, why, as though living in the world, &c."[1] "If ye then be risen with Christ, seek those things which are above," &c. "For ye are dead, and your life is hid with Christ in God."[2] Why did the apostle step out of the usual course, in two different passages to mention the burial of Christ? and to mention it in connection with baptism? It cannot be accounted for if the common exegesis be rejected.

The objection states that little resemblance can be found between immersion and Christ's burial: and the same might be said with respect to the resemblance between a loaf of bread, and the body of Christ. A well executed picture of the crucifixion, such as may be seen in Catholic chapels, has much more resemblance to the body of Christ, than is furnished by a piece of bread; yet, considering all the ends to be answered by the Eucharist, the divine wisdom has determined that we should keep Christ's death in memory, not by looking at a crucifix, but by the eating of bread. In like manner, some means might have been devised for representing the burial and resurrection of Christ, supplying a nearer resemblance than is furnished by immersion in water. But when we consider that baptism not only represents the burial and resurrection of Christ, but also our fellowship with him in both, and the consequent removal or washing away of our guilt, nothing could more conveniently, aptly, and instructively accomplish all these ends at once.

---

[1] Col. ii. 20.   [2] Col. iii. 1,—3.

ARGUMENTS FOR ANOTHER MEANING.

Argument 1.—There are many reasons for supposing that βαπτιζω, being a derivative from βαπτω, has a less definite and less forcible sense than the original. And yet even βαπτω does not always signify a total immersion. This is perfectly evident from Mat. xxvi. 23 : " He that dippeth his hand with me in the dish." Mark has it 'ο εμβαπτομενος, he that dippeth himself. Now, whatever liquid the dish contained, it cannot be supposed, that Judas plunged his hand all over in that liquid ; much less that he dipped his entire person.

What the " many reasons" are, for supposing that βαπτιζω has a less definite and less forcible signification than βαπτω, the argument does not inform us. The mere fact that it is a derivative, furnishes not the slightest proof ; for derivatives may be amplificative or intensive. To assume that they must be diminutive, would be utterly fallacious. The termination ιζω, whether it be frequentative, or causative, is not diminutive. Our examination of the preceding tables has shown, that the primitive generally denotes a slight and temporary immersion ; but that the derivative, in nearly one-half of the examples in which it is used, literally signifies total and permanent immersion. This fact is decisive against the supposition, that βαπτιζω is less definite and forcible.

But if the less forcible primitive βαπτω had been used in the commission, no sufficient reason would exist, for supposing anything less than dipping to be intended. The meaning even of this word, is clearly to dip. The numerous examples of its use which have been adduced, establish this point ; and even the very example brought forward in the argument, proves it. Judas dipped his hand in the dish. He did not wash, purify, wet, sprinkle, or pour his hand ; but he dipped it. To dip, therefore, according to this very example, is the meaning of βαπτω ; and if this word had been employed in the commission, the command would have been, " Go teach all nations, dipping them." Dipping was commanded in many of the ceremonies prescribed in the Old Testament, and the word βαπτω expresses the duty enjoined. No one imagines that it signifies, in these cases, to sprinkle or pour. Had this word been used in the commission, Christian worshippers would be less obedient than the Israelites, if they satisfied themselves with any thing less than dipping.

But it is alleged, that the word does not always denote total immersion. On re-examining the Table of Examples, we find that frequently, in the use of βαπτω, less frequently in the use of βαπτιζω, the immersion is not total; but, in no case, does this arise from any defect in the meaning of either verb. When a teacher directs his pupil to dip his pen in the ink for the purpose of writing, no one understands that an immersion of the whole pen is intended. When we read, "Send Lazarus, that he may dip the tip of his finger in water, and cool my tongue;"[1] every one understands that the whole of the part designated, *the tip of the finger*, is to be immersed. The difference in the two cases does not arise from any difference in the meaning of the verb dip. It is the same word in both cases, and has the same meaning; but the purpose for which the act is to be performed determines the extent to which the immersion is to proceed. If the pupil should stupidly mistake the teacher's design, the command would be explained, "Dip the nib of the pen in the ink;" and this is all that the first command meant. The greater definiteness of the last command, does not arise from any greater definiteness given to the verb *dip*. It is definite in the last case, and was equally definite in the first; but in the first, by a very common figure of speech, the whole pen was put for a part. The teacher relied on the nature of the case to limit the meaning of his command, and language is always sufficiently definite, so long as there is no danger of being misunderstood. We say that a pen is dipped, when in strict language the nib only is dipped; but the nib is totally immersed, and hence, in its proper meaning, to dip signifies total immersion. In all cases where the command is to dip, so far as depends on the meaning of the word, total immersion must be understood; and if we had received the commission in English, Go teach all nations, dipping them, it might safely be left to the common sense of mankind to determine whether partial or total immersion was intended.

The middle voice of Greek verbs is used, when an agent acts for his own benefit. This sufficiently explains Mark's use of εμβαπτομενος in the example cited in the argument. What Judas

---

[1] Luke xvi. 24.

dipped in the dish, is said by Matthew to have been his hand. A hand may be totally immersed in the cavity of an empty dish, or of a dish containing solids; but the probable meaning in the present case is, that something which the hand held, was dipped in a liquid which the dish contained. The hand, by a figure of speech, is put for what it held; and the dish, by a like figure, is put for what it contained: but amidst these figures, the word dip retains its literal and proper meaning; and nothing was literally and properly dipped, except what was totally immersed.

If the reader will again look through the examples in which βαπτίζω occurs, he may observe that, with very few exceptions, they are all cases of total immersion. Among the few exceptions, there are three (Ex.'s 31, 35, 49) in which the immersion is partial by expressed limitations: "up to the head;" "up to the waist;" "up to the hilt." The fact that these limitations are expressed, demonstrates that without them, the word would signify total immersion. This is the word which is used in the commission, without any limiting clause, and without anything either in the context, or the nature of the subject, to suggest that partial immersion was intended. Because an example may be found, in which, from the nature of the case, the immersion denoted is partial, we are not justified in inferring that partial immersion is here intended. The humble and teachable disciple desires to know and do what his divine Master meant that he should do; and the language of the command is as definite, as if it had been expressed in English, "Go, teach all nations, immersing them." It does not read *totally* immersing; but if any one will refuse total immersion until he finds this expressly written, we must leave him to his own conscience, and to the judgment of Him who gave the command.

Argument 2.—Βαπτίζω does indeed signify *to immerse* but it also signifies *to wash*, and under this last meaning, ceremonial purification is included. The Syrian leper was commanded to wash in Jordan; and the act of obedience to this command, is expressed by βαπτίζω. A dispute between the Jews and John's disciples about his baptism, is called "a question about purifying."[1] The Hebrew purifications were performed in various ways; chiefly by sprinkling consecrated water. Among their rites,

---

[1] John iii. 25.

"divers baptisms" are mentioned.[1] The word *divers* is the same that is applied to spiritual gifts in Rom. xii. 6, and signifies, *of different kinds.* Now, the baptisms could not be of different kinds, if they were all performed by immersion. Moreover, one of these kinds is expressly stated in the context to be "sprinkling."[2] Further, the Pharisees are said to have baptized themselves, after returning from market, when nothing more than the washing of hands is intended. They are also said to have held the baptism of pots, cups, brazen vessels, and tables; or, as the last word should have been translated, of beds, or the couches on which they reclined at meals. That all these purifications, and especially of the beds, were performed by immersion, is wholly incredible.

If *to immerse,* and *to wash* or *purify,* are two different senses of βαπτιζω, the question arises, in which of these senses did Christ use the term in the commission? We are not at liberty to take either of them at our pleasure. When a teacher commands his pupil to "dip the pen in the ink," the pupil may, by turning to Johnson's Dictionary, find that the word dip has four senses; and that one of these is *to wet, to moisten.* This sense is exemplified by a quotation from Milton:

"A cold shuddering dew dips me all o'er."

With so high authority for this interpretation of *dip,* the pupil may conclude to wet or moisten the pen, by putting the ink into it in some other way: and he may adopt this conclusion with the less hesitation, because all the purpose for which he understands the command to have been given, will be as well accomplished. But when he has filled his pen in some other mode, has he obeyed his teacher's command? Every one knows that he has not. But why? Does not the word dip signify to wet or moisten? We answer, it does not usually signify this; and the usual sense, is that in which the teacher employed the term. So Christ used the word βαπτιζω in its usual sense; and we as truly disobey his command, if we do not obey it in the sense which he intended, as if we substituted some other command in its place. What the usual sense of the word was, the examples which have been adduced fully establish.

But does βαπτιζω signify *to wash?* Lexicographers say that it

---

[1] Heb. ix. 10.   [2] Ver. 13.

does, just as Johnson says that *to dip* signifies *to wet* or *moisten.*
Words acquire secondary or accidental significations, from peculiar
connections, or tropical usage; and these are enumerated by lexicographers as distinct meanings. Nor are they to be censured for
this. Their design is, to give a view of the language, and not a
mere collection of primary meanings. Our care, however, should
be, when strict accuracy is required, to distinguish what is merely
accidental in the signification of a word, from what is its true and
proper meaning. • *To immerse* and *to wash*, cannot both be the
primary meaning of βαπτίζω. The last meaning cannot account
for the use of the word, in the various examples in which it occurs;
and the other meaning, *to immerse* could not well be derived from
it. On the other hand, to immerse, accounts fully and satisfactorily for every use of the word. It must therefore be the
primary sense; and so lexicographers have decided. The secondary sense, which is unknown to a large part of the examples, is,
in strict criticism, merely the purpose for which the immersion
happens to be performed. When the immersion is designed for
the purpose of washing, or of ceremonial purification, the accidental
signification to wash or purify is ascribed to the word : but its
proper meaning remains unchanged, just as the proper meaning
of βαπτω, in Job ix. 30, remains unchanged, by the accidental
signification, *to defile*, which it acquires. In sound criticism, such
accidental significations of words are not, strictly speaking, any
part of their meaning, as was stated on p. 34. They are ideas,
not expressed by the words, but suggested by the connection in
which they are used.

A further proof that βαπτίζω does not signify to wash, to purify,
to wet, to sprinkle, or to pour, may be drawn from the fact, that
the copiousness of the Greek language supplies distinct words to
express all these several ideas. If Jesus designed to command
any one of these acts, why did he not use the proper word for
denoting it ? Why did he employ a word which properly denotes
a different act, and which, therefore, could not convey his meaning,
or must convey it very doubtfully ?

The Syrian leper was commanded to wash in Jordan, and, for
this purpose, he immersed himself in the river. The word βαπτίζω,
denotes the immersion; and informs us, not only that he obeyed

the command, but also how he obeyed it. He did not wash, by sprinkling a few drops on his face.

We are informed that "there arose a question between some of John's disciples and the Jews about purifying."[1] What the precise question was, we are not told; and it is impossible to determine, what its relation was to John's baptism. But the passage contains no proof, that to *baptize* and to *purify* are identical.

Paul says of the Hebrew worship: "Which stood in meats, and drinks, and divers baptisms, and carnal ordinances." It is true, as stated in the argument, that the same word "divers" is applied to the gifts mentioned in Rom. xii. 6; but these "gifts" were all *gifts*. They were gifts of various kinds; but the variety did not cause any of them to cease to be gifts. In like manner, the divers baptisms, or immersions, mentioned in this passage, are all *immersions*. Their variety does not change them into something different from *immersions*. The immersion of divers persons and things, at divers times, under divers circumstances, and for divers kinds of uncleanness, constitutes divers immersions, without the supposition that some of them were performed by sprinkling. Had the phrase been, divers sprinklings, instead of divers immersions, no one would have inferred that some of these sprinklings were performed by immersion.

But it is alleged, that Paul has informed us in the context, that some of these divers baptisms were performed by sprinkling. This is a mistake. Paul mentions in the context, "the sprinkling of the ashes of an heifer, sanctifying to the purifying of the flesh." He classifies the various rites under four heads: 1. Meats. 2. Drinks. 3. Divers immersions. 4. Carnal ordinances, or ordinances concerning the flesh. Under the last of these heads, the sprinkling which sanctified to the purifying of the flesh, was manifestly included. The assumption that it was one of the divers baptisms, is unauthorized and erroneous.

In maintaining that sprinkling and immersion are divers baptisms, the argument opposes the position usually taken by the advocates of sprinkling. Jewish baptisms were divers; but Christian baptism Paul declares to be one: "One Lord, one faith, one baptism." In explaining this passage, the advocates of sprinkling

---

[1] John iii. 25.

4

allege that sprinkling and immersion are merely different *modes* of the same rite; but different modes of one baptism do not constitute divers baptisms. If sprinkling is really a different baptism, how can the use of it be reconciled with the unity of the Christian rite?

The word βαπτιζω, in Mark vii. 4, does not signify the mere washing of the hands. This act is expressed in the preceding verse, by νιπτω, the proper word for denoting it. Instead of confounding the meaning of the two words, the sense of the passage requires that they should be carefully distinguished. The act which one of them denotes, was performed on ordinary occasions; but the act denoted by the other, was performed on extraordinary occasions: "when they came from the market." Some understand an immersion of the things brought from the market; some, an immersion of the arm up to the elbow; and some, an immersion of the whole body. I suppose the last to be the true meaning; but, for our present purpose, there is no necessity of deciding between these interpretations. According to either of them, the word retains its usual signification to immerse.

What has been said on this passage, will assist in explaining a similar one in Luke: "When the Pharisee saw it, he marvelled that he had not first washed [baptized] before dinner."[1] Jesus had been mingling with a crowd of people, who had "gathered thick"[2] around him; and the danger of ceremonial defilement was as if he had come from the market. Hence, the Pharisee expected him to use immersion before dinner, as necessary to the proper sanctity of a religious teacher.

The immersion of beds, the argument rashly pronounces incredible. Dr. Gill, in his comments on the passage, has proved that such immersions were practised, by quoting at length the regulations of the Rabbins respecting them. To pronounce the statements of the Bible incredible, unless the words be taken in an unusual sense, is not honorable to divine inspiration.

Argument 3.—The Jewish rites were of two kinds; some, atoning; others, purifying. The Christian sacraments are a summary of the Jewish rites: the eucharist corresponding to those which were atoning, and baptism to those which were purifying. If both of them took the place of the atoning rites, by referring to the

---

[1] Luke xi. 38.   [2] Ver. 29.

work of Christ, the Christian system would be defective, in having
no ceremony to represent the purifying work of the Holy Spirit.
But if baptism represents this, it is sufficient to perform it in any
mode that will represent purifying; and especially by sprinkling,
which is the mode that was commonly employed for this purpose.

It is better to learn the design of the Christian rites, from the
Holy Scriptures, than from our own reasonings, as to what is
necessary to render the Christian system complete. The supper
represents the atoning work of Christ, and it, at the same time, represents our feeding on Christ by faith, which is produced by the
influence of the Holy Spirit. Because the supper represents the
atoning work of Christ, we have no right to confine it to this single
purpose, and refuse to eat and to drink, because these acts do not
represent a part of Christ's work. Baptism represents our purification from sin; but it, at the same time, represents our fellowship
with Christ in his burial and resurrection; and if we so perform it
as to make it serve one of these purposes only, we do what no one
claims the right to do with respect to the other Christian ceremony.
We mutilate an ordinance of Christ, and render it unfit to fulfil all
the purposes which his wisdom had in view.

Argument 4.—The language of the New Testament, although
written in Greek letters, is not the Greek of classic authors; but
modified by peculiarities of Hebrew origin. On this account, it
avails but little, in ascertaining the sense of βαπτίζω in the New
Testament, to collect examples of its use by profane authors.
The examples in which the word has reference to purification, Cl.
I. § 3, are numerous in the Greek Scriptures. As the primitive
βαπτω loses the original sense *to dip,* when it takes the secondary
sense *to color;* so βαπτίζω was used by the Hebrews in the sense
to purify, without regard to the primary sense *to immerse.* By
profane writers, the word was usually construed with the preposition εἰς; but, in the Scriptures, it is usually construed with the preposition ἐν, and sometimes with the dative without a preposition.
This peculiarity of construction may be regarded as proof, that the
sense of the word is not identical with that in which it is employed
by Greek classic authors.

We cheerfully admit that the Greek of the New Testament contains many Hebrew idioms. It is also true, that some of the
words are used to denote things which were unknown to writers
unacquainted with the religion of the Hebrews; and these words
must therefore be used in a peculiar sense. But notwithstanding

all this, the language of the New Testament is Greek. This language, because of its general prevalence, was wisely selected to be the vehicle of the New Testament revelation. The Holy Spirit made the revelation for the benefit of mankind, and not for the Jews exclusively. The selection of a language which was generally understood among the nations, was in accordance with this design; provided the words were generally employed in their known signification. But if the words were used in senses to which men were unaccustomed, the prevalence of the language was a strong objection to its use. Men would unavoidably be misled, by taking words which were familiar in the customary sense.

Βαπτίζω did not denote something peculiar to the Hebrew religion or customs, but an act which had no necessary connection with religion, and which was as well known in every heathen land as it was in the land of Judea. If a peculiar use of it could be proved to have prevailed in Judea, it might still be questioned, whether, in a revelation designed for all nations, the Holy Spirit would have conformed to this peculiar usage. But no such proof exists. Not a single passage can be found, either in the Septuagint, or the New Testament, in which the word departs from its ordinary signification. When it denoted immersion, performed for the purpose of ceremonial purification, the meaning of the word was precisely the same, as if the immersion had been performed for any other purpose. Βαπτω frequently occurs in the Old Testament in commands which enjoin religious observances. Yet no one concludes that this word had a Hebrew sense different from that which it obtained among the Gentiles; and the supposition that βαπτίζω had a peculiar Hebrew sense, is destitute of foundation.

The language of Christ, "I have a baptism to be baptized with," cannot be explained, on the supposition that the Hebrew mind attached the sense *purify* to the word *baptize*. To render the phrase intelligible and expressive, we must admit the classical sense *immerse*.

Josephus was a Jew, and wrote soon after the time of Christ. From his use of the word, we may learn what it signified to the mind of a Jew. Table II. contains several examples from this author, in not one of which does the supposed Hebrew meaning *to purify* appear; but the meaning in all is precisely the same as in the Greek of gentile authors.

That the Hebrews attached the ordinary meaning to the word, may be learned from Jewish proselyte baptism. All admit that this was immersion. Many have maintained that this baptism was practised as early as the time of Christ. If it was, the fact decides what the word meant in that age and country. But if, as is more probable, the practice did not originate till the second century, the proof is still decisive, that the Jews had not been accustomed to a different sense of the word.

The use of immersion for the purpose of purifying, was not confined to the Hebrew nation. One design of bathing, a process which classic Greek sometimes expresses by βαπτίζω, is the cleansing of the body. The dipping denoted by βαπτω, in Ex. 36 and 38, is clearly for the purpose of cleansing. The peculiarity in the Hebrew use of these words is, that the immersion which they signify, was performed for the purpose of *religious* purification. This resulted from the religious character of the nation, and not from a peculiar sense of the terms. Immersion, when performed for religious purification, does not cease to be immersion.

We admit that βαπτω has a secondary sense *to color*, as well as the primary sense to dip; but both these senses are found in classic, as well as sacred literature. The case, therefore, furnishes no analogy which can give countenance to the supposition, that *to purify* is a secondary sense, in which the primary sense of βαπτίζω is lost. No one pretends that this secondary sense is found in classic Greek.

The alleged peculiarity of construction in the New Testament, does not prove that the word has a different meaning in Scripture, from that which prevailed in uninspired writings. As, in English, we say to *dip into*, or to *dip in ;* so, in Greek, βαπτίζω is construed with either εις or εν. Both these prepositions agree perfectly with the sense *to immerse.* Were one of them invariably used in the Scriptures in construction with the verb, the circumstance would furnish no valid argument for a peculiar meaning in the sacred writing. Though εν is commonly used, εις is also found;[1] and the

---

[1] In classic Greek also, both constructions are found. Ex. 45 has εις; Ex. 17 has εν.

example in which it occurs, Mark i. 9, so connects the sacred use of the word with the classical, as to deprive the argument for a peculiar meaning, of the plausibility which an invariable use of one construction might be supposed to give it. The fact that both constructions appear in the inspired writings, supplies additional assurance that the meaning of the verb is not peculiar. We feel that the Greek language is the same, whether we read it on the sacred or the classic page. Dr. Campbell, in his notes on Matt. iii. 11, says:— "*In water—in the Holy Spirit* . . . . . . Vulgate *in aqua* . . . . *in Spiritu Sancto*. Thus also the Syr., and other ancient versions. . . . . I am sorry to observe that the Popish translations from the Vul. have shown greater veneration for the style of that version than the generality of Protestant translations have shown for that of the original. For in this the Latin is not more explicit than the Greek. Yet so inconsistent are the interpreters last mentioned, that none of them have scrupled to render *εν τω Ιορδανη* in the sixth verse, *in Jordan*, though nothing can be plainer, than that if there be any incongruity in the expression *in water*, this *in Jordan* must be equally incongruous. But they have seen that the preposition *in* could not be avoided there without adopting a circumlocution, and saying, *with the water of Jordan*, which would have made their deviation from the text too glaring. The word *βαπτιζειν*, both in sacred authors, and in classical, signifies, *to dip, to plunge, to immerse*, and was rendered by Tertullian, the oldest of the Latin fathers, *tingere*, the term used for dyeing cloth, which was by immersion. It is always construed suitably to this meaning."

Argument 5.—If it were the case that *βαπτιζω* clearly signifies *to dip*, or *immerse all over* in water, when applied to other subjects, it would by no means certainly follow, that it has this signification, when applied to the Christian rite of *baptism*. The word supper in English, and *δειπνον* in Greek, have a very different sense, when applied to the eucharist, from what they have in ordinary cases. Eating a morsel of bread does not constitute a supper, in the ordinary sense; but it is called a supper, in this religious rite. Now, if the word which denotes one Christian rite, has a sense so very different from its usual sense; why may it not be so, with the word which denotes the other Christian rite? Why may it not signify, instead of a complete dipping or washing, the application of water in a small degree?

This argument claims, that words may have a peculiar sense in religious rites. It does not claim this for Greek words only; for it does not object to *supper* as a proper rendering of δειπνον. It claims that these words, both the Greek and the English, have a sense unknown elsewhere, when they are applied to the eucharist. There is, therefore, no necessity in controverting the argument, to transport ourselves to the foreign territory of the Greek language; but we are at liberty to meet it, and try its validity, on English ground. It does not object that *immerse* is an improper rendering of βαπτιζω; but it claims that these words, when applied to a religious rite, may have a meaning which they possess in no other case. We are consequently at liberty, in trying the validity of the argument, to use the word *immerse* as a correct translation of the Greek verb.

The whole argument rests on what is supposed to be a peculiar use of a single word, δειπνον; and it deserves special consideration, that there is but a single instance of this peculiar signification, even with respect to this word. The instances are exceedingly numerous, in which other words are used with reference to religious rites; and even δειπνον is frequently used with reference to the paschal supper. In all these instances it is invariably true, that words when applied to religious rites, have the same signification as in other cases, and are subject to the same rules of interpretation. If δειπνον in 1 Cor. xi. 20, is an exception, it is a solitary exception. It is certainly the part of true criticism, in determining the meaning of βαπτιζω, to follow the general rule rather than the single exception. Besides, we have frequent use of βαπτω with reference to religious rites. The Jewish priests seem never to have thought, that, when Moses enjoined dipping in religious rites, he meant a diminutive dipping, or one that might be performed by sprinkling; and no one has suggested, that these priests mistook the meaning of their lawgiver. Is it not infinitely more probable, that βαπτιζω follows its kindred word βαπτω, in obeying the general rule, than that it follows a very different word in a solitary deviation from all rule and analogy?

If on a single instance we may establish a rule, that words, when applied to a religious rite, may have a meaning which they obtain nowhere else; who will limit the application of this rule, and tell us, how many of the words which apply to religious rites, obtain an extraordinary meaning, or how far their meaning differs from that which they obtain elsewhere? Perhaps the words, which, in the institution of the supper, are rendered *eat* and *drink*, although they have this meaning everywhere else, signify, when applied to a religious rite, nothing more than *to handle* and *to look upon.* Who will determine for us? Has the legislator of the Church committed to any one a lexicon of ritual terms, by which his simple-hearted disciples may find out what he meant? Or has he given to any persons on earth authority to decree what ceremonies they may think proper, by assigning to all the ritual terms of Scripture what sense they please?

That the terms used in reference to religious rites, may sometimes have a figurative rather than the literal meaning, a secondary sense rather than the primary, may be admitted. But this is what happens in all other speaking or writing, and the same rules of criticism are to be applied in this as in other cases. We must prefer the literal and primary signification, if nothing forbids it. We understand the word *is*, in the phrase "This is my body," to signify *represents;* because the literal primary signification would make the sense absurd and false. But this word has the same signification, when not applied to a religious rite, in the phrase, "The field *is* the world." For the same reason, the phrase "As often as ye drink this cup," is to be interpreted according to a common figure of speech, as often as ye drink the liquor contained in this cup. The same literal sense of the terms, and the same rules of figurative interpretation, are found here, as in all other cases.

The premises stated in the argument, cannot, in any view of them, justify the conclusion that baptism may be administered by using a small quantity of water. The proper conclusion would rather be, that we ought to change our mode of administering the eucharist. If we do not literally and fully obey the divine command when we restrict ourselves in this ordinance to a morsel of bread and a few drops of wine, we do wrong so to restrict ourselves; and we ought rather to correct the error than establish it as a precedent.

It deserves to be noticed, further, that βαπτιζω and δειπνον are not applied to the two religious rites in the same manner. One of them is found in the words of Christ's command; the other is not, but is, at most, merely a name which the rite has received.

Our conduct, in obeying the commands of Christ, must be regulated, not by the names which His institutions may receive, but by the words of his commands. Believers are said, in Scripture, to be *buried* with Christ in baptism, at least twice as often as the Eucharist is called a supper. Baptism may, therefore, be called a burial; but no one would infer hence that the body should be left for a long time under the water, as in a real interment. Baptism represents a real burial, in which the body of Christ continued three days in the grave. The eucharist represents the free and abundant communion in which the Lord sups with His people,[1] in which a great supper is spread,[2] and which will be perfected at the marriage supper of the Lamb.[3] Yet Christ did not say, " Go, teach all nations, *burying* them;" nor, " Take a *supper* in remembrance of me." His command in the latter case is, " *Eat* this bread and *drink* this cup;" and he did not institute this ordinance as a supper, but " after supper." Now, if the command is *eat*, *drink*, could this command be obeyed any otherwise than by eating and drinking? Would it suffice merely to apply the bread and cup to the lips? In like manner, when Christ said, " Go, teach all nations, immersing them," can the command be obeyed in any other way than by performing a real immersion? In the eucharist, he commanded to eat bread and drink wine, but not to take a full meal; and we know, from the circumstance that this ordinance was instituted immediately after the disciples had taken a full meal, that a full meal was not intended. The Corinthians, when they converted this ordinance into a full meal, did truly eat and drink, yet they did not fulfil the command more strictly and literally than we do; while, on the other hand, they departed from the example, and manifest intention of Christ, and were censured for so doing by the Apostle Paul.

We have suggested that the eucharist may possibly be called a supper, because of the spiritual feast which it represents. So one of the Jewish feasts was called the Passover, because of what it commemorated. But, after all, it is not certain that the eucharist is, in Scripture, called a supper. The eucharist is several times mentioned in the New Testament, but is never called the Lord's Supper, unless in this instance; and many learned men are of

---

[1] Rev. iii. 20.   [2] Luke xiv. 16.   [3] Rev. xix. 9.

opinion that, what is here called by this name, is not the eucharist itself, but the Love Feast which was anciently celebrated in connection with it. Perhaps it denotes the perversion which the Corinthians made of the eucharist. The phrase is without the definite article in the original text, and might be rendered " a supper of the Lord." Paul does not deny that the Corinthians had made a supper of it, but he denies that it was a supper *of the Lord*—a supper which the Lord had instituted, or which he approved. What proof, then, is there, that the Holy Spirit has ever called the eucharist by the name Lord's Supper? We have no objection to the name in itself considered; but, when so much is made to depend on it, the authority for it needs to be examined. If a universal law of Biblical interpretation, respecting ritual words, is to be established on a single fact, the fact should be well ascertained.

Everywhere throughout the New Testament, the words *baptize* and *baptism* are applied to one of the Christian rites; if the word *supper* is ever applied to the other, it is but in a single instance, and it may be that it is there applied to it as converted by abuse into a full meal. The word *baptize* was used in Christ's command, and directly expresses the act commanded. The word *supper* was not used in the command; and, if it be used as a name of the institution, is not directly descriptive of it. The two cases have no analogy between them to sustain the argument.

Argument 6.—The circumstances attending the baptisms of the New Testament, do not, in any case, prove that they were administered by immersion.

They who urge this argument have alleged that, in the account of Christ's baptism, the phrase "went up straightway out of the water," ought to have been translated, "went up straightway *from* the water."[1] The emendation of the translation leaves us without proof, they say, that he went *into* the water to be baptized. We admit, in this case, the correction of the translation. This clause, we concede, does not prove that Christ was in the water. But we have proof of this, in another verse of the same chapter: "And were baptized of him *in* Jordan."[2] The testimony of Mark to the same point, is very decisive. His record of the transaction

---

[1] Matt. iii. 16. [2] Matt. iii. 6.

may be properly translated thus: "And was immersed by John into the Jordan."[1]

In the account of the eunuch's baptism, the phrases, "they went down into the water," and "they came up out of the water," have been subjected to a similar criticism. It has been alleged that these may be translated with equal propriety, "they went down *to* the water," and "they came up *from* the water." This we deny. The preposition *απο* used in the former case, is not found here, and our translators have, in the present case, rendered the prepositions *εις* and *εκ* according to their usual import. The opponents of immersion do not deny this, or maintain that they *must* be translated otherwise; but a departure from their ordinary signification ought not to be supposed without necessity. That these prepositions signify *into* and *out of*, in the common use of them by Greek authors, might be proved by innumerable citations; but, instead of these, the following extracts from Robinson's Lexicon ought to suffice:—

"Απο is used of such objects as before were *on*, *by*, or *with* another, but are now separated from it (not *in* it, for to this *εκ* corresponds)." "Εκ [is] spoken of such objects as before were *in* another, but are now separated from it."

This decides that our common version gives the true sense of the passage, in the rendering, "they went up *out of* the water." It follows that they must have been *in* the water when the baptism was performed; and that they must have gone down *into* the water for its performance.

It has been argued that, if going down into the water proves immersion, Philip was immersed as well as the eunuch; for they both went down into the water. If we maintained that *going down into the water* signifies going beneath its surface, this argument would be applicable; and it might also be argued against us that the clause which the inspired historian has added, "he baptized him," is superfluous. But we understand the immersion to be denoted by this last phrase; and which of the two persons was immersed, the context clearly shows. But while the phrase, *they went down into the water*, does not express the immersion, it proves it. No other satisfactory reason, for going into the water, can be

---

[1] Mark i. 9.

assigned. But in truth this circumstantial proof is not needed. The phrase, "he baptized him," states expressly what was done. .

In the passage, "John was baptizing in Enon, near to Salim, because there was much water there,"[1] it has been alleged that the proper translation is *many waters;* and it is argued that the waters were many small springs or rivulets, not adapted to the purpose of immersion, but needed for the subsistence and comfort of the crowds that attended John's ministry.

The word rendered *water* properly denotes the element, and not a spring or rivulet. It was used in the plural, as we use the word *ashes* to denote the element, and not separate collections of it. In the phrase " ofttimes it hath cast him into the fire and into the water,"[2] fire is singular, and water is plural in the original text. If the latter word was put in the plural form, to denote the different collections of the element into which the afflicted youth fell at different times, the word fire would, for the same reason, need to be plural. Hence the phrase *many waters* does not signify *many small springs* or *streams.* When Isaiah said, "The nations shall rush like the rushing of many waters;"[3] when David said, "The Lord on high is mightier than the noise of many waters, yea, than the mighty waves of the sea;"[4] and again: "He drew me out of many waters;"[5]— when John said, "His voice was as the sound of many waters;"[6] the supposition that many little springs or rivulets are intended, is inadmissible. The same phrase, *many waters,* is used for the river Euphrates.[7] It follows, therefore, that the proposed change of translation, can be of no avail to lessen the evidence of the passage in favor of immersion. As to the allegation, that the water was needed for the subsistence and comfort of the people; we answer, that this, whether true or not, is not what the historian has stated. "John was baptizing, because there was much water." Water was needed for baptizing; and the connection of the clauses shows that the place was selected with reference to the administration of the rite.

Argument 7.—In several cases the circumstances which attended baptism forbid the belief that it was administered by immersion.

This is a dangerous argument. If the Holy Spirit affirms that

---

[1] John iii. 23.   [2] Mark ix. 22.   [3] Isaiah xvii. 13.
[4] Ps. xciii. 4.   [5] Ps. xviii. 16.   [6] Rev. i. 15.
[7] Jer. li. 13.

persons were baptized, and if *to baptize* signifies *to immerse*, it becomes us to receive his testimony; and, if any difficulty respecting the probability of the fact presents itself to our imagination, we should ascribe it to our ignorance. If an ordinary historian relates what cannot be believed, when understood according to the established laws of language, we do not invent new laws to relieve his veracity; but we pronounce his statement incredible. They who urge this argument, should beware lest they impugn the veracity of the Holy Spirit.

It has been imagined that there was not sufficient water to be obtained in Jerusalem for the immersion of three thousand on the day of Pentecost. Jerusalem was the religious capital of a religious nation, whose forms of worship required frequent ceremonial purifications. These purifications were not performed exclusively by the sprinkling of consecrated water; but in various cases, the defiled person was required to wash his clothes, and bathe himself in water.[1] Provision for such bathing was needed throughout the land. At Cana, an obscure town of Galilee, a poor family unable to supply a sufficient quantity of wine for a wedding feast, had six water pots of stone containing two or three firkins apiece, for the purpose of purifying.[2] Such provision was specially needed at Jerusalem, the centre of their worship. Here their sacrifices were to be offered, and here the whole nation were required to assemble for their appointed feasts; and these they were forbidden to celebrate, if in a state of defilement. In preparation for these feasts, we know from the express testimony of John, that the people went up to Jerusalem "to purify themselves."[3] Some provision, therefore, must have existed, accessible to the people, and sufficient for their use, at these great gatherings. The privilege which was open to the whole multitude out of every nation under heaven at this pentecostal feast, belonged equally to the apostles, and to the three thousand who were baptized; for all these were Jews, fully entitled to enter the temple, and unite in all the public services of the nation. If any of the rulers were inclined to hinder them, they as yet feared the people; for when these baptisms were performed, the administrators and subjects had "favor with all the people."

---

[1] Lev. xiv. 8, 9; xv. 5, 8, 11, 22; xvi. 26, 28.   [2] John ii. 6.
[3] John xi. 55.

If, therefore, any one persist in asking where water was found to immerse so many, we ask in turn where was water found sufficient for the purifying of the assembled nation?

In Jerusalem, as it now is, there are large cisterns of water on the grounds attached to private dwellings; and we may suppose that, when the city was in its ancient prosperity, such reservoirs were far more numerous. It is probable that access to these, as to rooms for keeping the Passover, was often obtained by the assembled worshippers. Of the converts who were baptized on the day of Pentecost, it is likely that many resided in the city; and if the use of private tanks was needed for baptism, their tanks were doubtless at the service of the apostles. There were also public pools, of which Chateaubriand, who visited Palestine about the beginning of the present century, gives the following account:—

"Having descended Mount Zion on the east side, we came, at its foot, to the fountain and pool of Siloe, where Christ restored sight to the blind man. The spring issues from a rock, and runs in a silent stream. The pool, or rather the two pools of the same name, are quite close to the spring. Here you also find a village called Siloan. At the foot of this village is another fountain, denominated in Scripture Rogel. Opposite to this fountain is a third, which receives its name from the blessed Virgin. The Virgin's fountain mingles its stream with that of the fountain of Siloe.

"We have now nothing left of the primitive architecture of the Jews at Jerusalem, except the Pool of Bethesda. This is still to be seen near St. Stephen's Gate, and it bounded the temple on the north. It is a reservoir, one hundred and fifty feet long, and forty wide; the pool is now dry, and half filled up. On the west side may also be seen two arches, which probably led to an aqueduct that carried the water into the interior of the temple."

The dimensions of the Pool of Bethesda, as given by Maundrell, are one hundred and twenty paces long, forty broad, and eight deep. Even the smaller dimensions given by Chateaubriand, indicate a sufficient supply of water in this single pool for the whole pentecostal baptism. A doubt has been recently raised, whether the excavation measured by these travellers, is identical with the ancient Bethesda: and attention has been directed to a neighboring intermittent fountain, the water of which, instead of flowing equably, sometimes rises by a sudden movement, and, after a time, subsides to its former level. This has been thought to agree with John's account of the ancient pool: "For an angel went down at a certain season into the pool, and troubled the water."[1] The hypothesis is liable to strong objections, which our purpose does not require us to present. Nor is it necessary for us to defend the correctness of the tradition, which points to this excavation as the ancient Bethesda. Much water was needed in the city; and, when so many tanks were dug at great labor and expense, it is altogether probable that a cavity, which could hold a large supply of the needed element, was not permitted to remain useless. If it contained water, the pool, by whatever name called, may have been the baptizing place on that memorable day.

But the Pool of Bethesda was not the only reservoir sufficiently capacious for the immersion of three thousand. The facilities for travelling which the present times afford have rendered visits to the old world frequent; and men now living, have greatly increased our knowledge of its geography and antiquities by their investigations. The learned Dr. Robinson has twice explored Palestine, with a special view to biblical illustration; and the result of his researches has been given to the world in a large work abounding with valuable information. The Rev. George W. Samson has also visited the same country within a few years, and has directed particular attention to the question now before us, in a short but excellent work entitled, "The Sufficiency of Water for Baptizing at Jerusalem, and elsewhere in Palestine, as recorded in the New Testament." In this work, the present condition of the pools at Jerusalem, six in number, is described; and the dimensions of five, according to the measurement of Dr. Robinson, are given in feet as follows:—

	Length.	Breadth.	Depth.
Pool of Bethesda	360	130	75
Pool of Siloam	53	18	19
Old or Upper Pool in the Highway of the Fuller's Field	316	{ 200 218 }	18
Pool of Hezekiah	240	140	
Lower Pool of Gihon	595	{ 245 275 }	{ 35 42 }

[1] John v. 4.

The depth of the Pool of Hezekiah varies, its bottom being an inclined plane, and the sides of the Lower Pool of Gihon, which covers more than four acres of ground, are sloping. In these any convenient depth of water for baptizing might be readily obtained. When facilities for immersion were so abundant we can have no plea for inventing a new meaning for the word which the sacred historian has employed in recording the baptisms at Jerusalem. If we were unable to offer any probable conjecture with respect to the supply of water, we ought still to receive the testimony of the Holy Spirit according to the proper import of his words, and to believe his statement to be true; but the investigations which have been made remove all difficulty.

It has been further imagined, that there was not time for the immersion of so many; but this difficulty is not one which ought to impair the credibility of the narrative. Many, if not all of the seventy whom Christ had commissioned, were probably present on the occasion; and the apostles had undoubted authority to command their services in the administration of the rite. With so many agents, the work required but little time. In modern revivals, the number of persons immersed on profession of faith is sometimes large; and, from observing the time required, some have maintained that the apostles themselves could have baptized all the converts on the day of Pentecost. Sprinkling, if performed with the solemnity due to a religious rite, would require not much less time than immersion. We may therefore believe the sacred narrative, without inventing a new meaning for the word baptize.

It has been supposed that the baptism of the Philippian jailer and his household could not have been by immersion; because it took place at night, and in the prison. As to the time; the persecution which had been raised against Paul and Silas, and the relation which the jailer sustained to the government of the city, rendered it more convenient to administer the immersion at night than to postpone it till the next day. As to the place; there is no proof that it was administered in the jail. Paul and Silas had been brought out, and had preached the Word to the jailer, and "to all that were in his house." After the preaching, they must have left the house for the administration of baptism; for it is expressly stated that the jailer afterwards "brought them into his house and set meat before them."[1] Where the rite was performed we are not told. There may have been, as is common in the East, a tank of water in the prison enclosure; and we know, because the inspired historian has so informed us, that there was a river[2] near at hand. There was, therefore, no want of water.

Argument 8.—Jesus said to his disciples, "John truly baptized with water; but ye shall be baptized with the Holy Ghost not many days hence."[3] This promise was fulfilled on the day of Pentecost. The Spirit was then poured out upon them; and since Christ called this baptism, we have proof that pouring is baptism.

The Holy Spirit is not a material agent; and all representations of his operation, drawn from material things, are necessarily imperfect. To immerse in the Spirit, and to pour out the Spirit, are figurative expressions, and the things which they signify are conceived to bear some resemblance to immersion in water, and to the pouring out of water. But the resemblance is in our conception, and not in the things themselves; for between what is spiritual and what is material, there cannot, strictly speaking, be any likeness. Different figures may be employed to represent the same thing, and if the figurative expressions *pour out the Spirit*, and *baptize with the Spirit*, referred to precisely the same thing, it would not follow that the figures by which they represent it are identical. But if the figures are not identical, they can furnish no proof that *to pour* is *to baptize.*

God had promised by the prophet Joel, "I will pour out of my Spirit;"[4] and Christ had promised his disciples, "Ye shall be immersed in the Holy Spirit."[5] Both the promises were fulfilled on the day of Pentecost; but the two promises exhibit the influence of the Spirit then communicated, in different aspects. In one it is viewed as proceeding from God, and is likened to water poured out; in the other it is viewed as affecting all the powers of the apostles, surrounding and filling them, as water surrounds and imbues substances which are immersed in it. The figures, therefore, not only differ from each other, but are employed to represent different things. Hence, they can furnish no proof that *to pour* is *to baptize.*

---

[1] Acts xvi. 34.   [2] Acts xvi. 13.   [3] Acts i. 5.
[4] Acts ii. 17.   [5] Acts i. 5.

5

ARGUMENTS AGAINST LITERAL OBLIGATION.

Argument 1.—Baptism is a mere ceremony, and, in the sight
of God, is of far less importance than moral duties. In instituting it, Christ did not design to bind his followers to the very letter
of his command; but intended that they should be at liberty to
accommodate the mode of their obedience to circumstances which
might arise, provided they accomplished the end which he had in
view. He commanded his disciples to wash the feet of one another.
This command was given at a time when the washing of feet was
a usual act of hospitality; and we now rightly judge, that since
this usage has passed away, we ought to fulfil the command in
some other way. So he commanded to immerse, when immersion
for the purpose of purification was in almost daily use; but to us,
whose ordinary ablutions are partial, another mode of representing purification is better adapted. This has been the judgment
of the pious; and God's abundant blessing on them, shows that
they have his approbation.

Baptism is indeed a ceremony; but it is a ceremony of God's
appointing. In moral duties arising from the relations which we
bear, and founded on reasons which we are able to comprehend,
the duty must vary according to the varying relations, and there
is scope for the exercise of enlightened reason; but positive institutes are founded on the mere will of the lawgiver, and with
respect to them, to obey or disobey is the only question, and the
only variety. A ceremony of positive institution may possibly be
in itself of little moment; but obedience in performing it, is of
great value in God's sight; and disobedience to mere ceremonial
requirements, he has in some cases punished in an exemplary
manner. If he abundantly blesses many who neglect the baptismal command, the fact proves his great goodness, and not their
innocence.

They who, acknowledging a departure from the letter of Christ's
command, satisfy themselves with the belief that they attain all
the ends of baptism, though they be not immersed, assume that
they fully comprehend the subject, and all the ends which the lawgiver had in view. Is not this arrogating too much? It is
certainly safer to believe that Christ is wiser than we are, and to
render implicit obedience to his precepts. If baptism represents
the burial and resurrection of Christ, as well as the washing away
of sin, they do not attain all the ends of baptism who neglect im-

mersion. We have reason to believe that positive institutes were in part given, to test and to promote the spirit of obedience. They who fail to comply strictly with the divine precepts, not only fail to accomplish these ends which infinite wisdom had in view, but counterwork the designs of the lawgiver.

The command to wash one another's feet, is not parallel to that which enjoins baptism. The latter, the advocates of sprinkling acknowledge to be of perpetual obligation, a Christian ceremony of positive institution; but the former they do not so regard. This is not the proper place to enter on the inquiry, whether the washing of feet was designed to be a ceremony of perpetual obligation. In our judgment it was not. If it can be made to appear that we have judged wrong, it will be our duty, not to make our error an argument for disobedience, but to amend our practice, and conform strictly to every divine requirement.

Argument 2.—When Christ instituted the eucharist, he commanded, "this do."[1] Yet no one imagines that we are bound to do all that he did on that occasion. He met in an upper room, and at night; and he reclined while eating. We do not suppose ourselves under obligation to imitate him in these particulars; but only to do so much as is necessary to the moral ends of the institution. By the same rule of interpretation, we are not bound to a literal compliance with the command of baptism.

No reason exists for supposing that the pronoun "this," in the command "this do," refers to the place, the time, or the manner, in which Christ ate the last supper. It evidently refers to the acts of eating bread and drinking wine; and precisely what it does signify, is what we are bound to do; and precisely what the word *baptize* signifies, is what we are bound to do in obeying the command which enjoins baptism. To relieve ourselves from the obligation of strict obedience, on the plea that the moral ends of Christ's institutions may be attained without it, is to legislate for Christ.

Argument 3.—Christ designed his religion to be universal, and adapted to every climate of earth, and every condition and rank among men. Immersion is not suited to cold climates—is frequently impossible to the infirm and sick—is repulsive to the delicate and refined; and the invariable observance of it cannot have

---

[1] Luke xxii. 19.

be:n required by him who said, "My yoke is easy, and my burden is light."

Our simple reply to this argument is, that it is Christ's command. We dare not, by our fallible reasonings from general principles, attempt to determine the will of our divine lawgiver, when we have in our possession his express command on the very subject. Christ knew all the climates of the earth, and all the conditions and ranks among men, and he has adapted his religion to these as far as appeared best to his infinite wisdom. If the infirm and sick cannot obey, there is an end of responsibility in their case. If the delicate and refined will not, they must leave the pleasure of obedience to those, who think it no humiliation to tread where they find the footsteps of their Lord and Master. Though Christ's yoke is easy, it is still a yoke; and pride and false delicacy may refuse to wear it; but love can make it welcome and delightful.

Section III.—SUBJECTS OF BAPTISM.

THOSE ONLY ARE PROPER SUBJECTS OF BAPTISM WHO REPENT OF SIN AND BELIEVE IN CHRIST.

Repentance and faith are associated graces in the hearts of the regenerate, each of them implying the existence of the other. Sometimes one of them is particularly mentioned as a qualification for baptism, and sometimes the other. They manifest themselves by confession of sin; by profession of dependence on Christ, and subjection to his authority; and by holy obedience.

John the Baptist required repentance, with its appropriate fruits, in those whom he admitted to baptism. It has been denied that the rite which he administered was identical with Christian baptism; but, for our present purpose, nothing more is necessary than to satisfy ourselves, that John did not require more spiritual qualifications for his baptism, than were required by Christ and his apostles. If he proclaimed repentance to be necessary because the kingdom of heaven was at hand, it could not be less necessary after the kingdom was established. That John did require repentance, as a qualification for baptism, the following Scriptures testify: "Repent ye, for the kingdom of heaven is at hand . . . . . .

and were baptized of him in Jordan, confessing their sins."[1] "Bring forth, therefore, fruits meet for repentance; and think not to say within yourselves, We have Abraham to our father."[2]

During the personal ministry of Christ, he made and baptized disciples. "There he tarried and baptized."[3] "The Lord knew how the Pharisees had heard that Jesus made and baptized more disciples than John."[4] Those only were baptized by Christ, who were made disciples; and discipleship implies repentance and faith.

The commission which Christ gave to his apostles, connects faith and discipleship with baptism as qualifications for it: "Go, preach the gospel to every creature. He that believeth, and is baptized, shall be saved."[5] "Go, make disciples of all nations, baptizing them."[6]

In executing the commission of Christ, the apostles and their fellow-laborers required repentance and faith as qualifications for baptism. Several passages in the Acts of the Apostles clearly indicate this: "Repent and be baptized, every one of you, in the name of Jesus Christ. . . . . Then they that gladly received the word were baptized."[7] "When they believed Philip preaching the things concerning the kingdom of God, and the name of Jesus Christ, they were baptized, both men and women."[8] "And the eunuch said, See, here is water; what doth hinder me to be baptized? And Philip said, If thou believest with all thine heart, thou mayest."[9] "Can any man forbid water, that these should not be baptized which have received the Holy Ghost as well as we."[10] "Whose heart the Lord opened, that she attended unto the things which were spoken of Paul. And when she was baptized."[11] "He was baptized, he and all his straightway . . . . and rejoiced, believing in God with all his house."[12] . . . "Many of the Corinthians hearing, believed and were baptized."[13]

In the Epistles of the New Testament, baptism is mentioned in such connections as prove that all the baptized were believers in Christ: "Know ye not, that so many of us as were baptized into

[1] Matt. iii. 2, 6.   [2] Matt. iii. 8, 9.   [3] John iii. 22.
[4] John iv. 1.   [5] Mark xvi. 15, 16.   [6] Matt. xxviii. 19.
[7] Acts ii. 38, 41.   [8] Acts viii. 12.   [9] Acts viii. 36, 37.
[10] Acts x. 47.   [11] Acts xvi. 14, 15.   [12] Acts xvi. 33, 34.
[13] Acts xviii. 8.

Jesus Christ were baptized into his death."[1] "Buried with him in baptism, wherein also ye are risen with him through faith."[2] "Ye are all the children of God by faith; for as many of you as have been baptized into Christ have put on Christ."[3] "Baptism doth now save us, ... the answer of a good conscience toward God."[4]

All these quotations from Scripture harmonize perfectly with each other, and incontrovertibly establish the truth, that repentance and faith are necessary qualifications for baptism. This is universally admitted with respect to adult persons; but a special claim is urged in behalf of infants, and the practice of administering the rite to them has prevailed very extensively. The arguments in its defence will be examined in the Chapter on Infant Membership.

SECTION IV.—DESIGN OF BAPTISM.

BAPTISM WAS DESIGNED TO BE THE CEREMONY OF CHRISTIAN PROFESSION.

The religion of Christ was intended for the whole world, and it is made the duty of his followers to propagate it. Men are required not only to receive, but also to hold forth the word of life. The lepers who found abundance of food in the Syrian camp, could not feast on it by themselves while their brethren in the city were famishing; and, if any one thinks that he can enjoy the blessings of religion, and shut up the secret in his own breast, he mistakes the nature of true Christianity. The light kindled within must shine, and the Spirit of love in the heart must put forth efforts to do good.

Profession is, in general, necessary to salvation. With the heart, man believeth unto righteousness; and with the mouth, confession is made unto salvation.[5] Divine goodness may pardon the weakness of some, who, like Joseph of Arimathea, are disciples secretly through fear; but it nevertheless remains a general truth, that profession is necessary. Christ has made the solemn declaration, "Whosoever shall be ashamed of me, and of my words, in this adulterous and sinful generation; of him also shall the Son

---

[1] Rom. vi. 3.   [2] Col. ii. 12.   [3] Gal. iii. 26, 27.
[4] 1 Peter iii. 21.   [5] Rom. x. 10.

of man be ashamed, when he cometh in the glory of his Father with the holy angels."[1]

Profession is the appointed public outset in the way of salvation The apostles exhorted, " Save yourselves from this untoward generation."[2] The world lies in wickedness, and under the curse of God. They who would be saved, should escape from it, as Lot escaped from Sodom. God calls: " Come out from among them, and be ye separate."[3] This call is obeyed, when converted persons separate themselves from the ungodly, and publicly devote themselves to the service of Christ. They then set out in earnest to flee from the wrath to come. The resolution to flee must first be formed in the heart; but the public profession may be regarded, in an important sense, as the first manifest step in the way of escape.

The profession of renouncing the world, and devoting ourselves to Christ, might have been required to be made in mere words addressed to the ears of those who hear; but infinite wisdom has judged it better that it should be made in a formal and significant act, appointed for the specific purpose. That act is baptism. The immersion of the body, as Paul has explained, signifies our burial with Christ; and in emerging from the water, we enter, according to the import of the figure, on a new life. We put off the old man, and put on the new man: " As many of you as have been baptized into Christ, have put on Christ."[4]

The place which baptism holds in the commission, indicates its use. The apostles were sent to make disciples, and to teach them to observe all the Saviour's commands; but an intermediate act is enjoined, the act of baptizing them. In order to make disciples, they were commanded, " Go, preach the gospel to every creature." When the proclamation of the good news attracted the attention of men, and by the divine blessing so affected their hearts, that they became desirous to follow Christ, they were taught to observe his commandments, and first to be baptized. This ceremony was manifestly designed to be the initiation into the prescribed service; and every disciple of Christ who wishes to walk in the ways of the Lord, meets this duty at the entrance of his course.

The design of baptism is further indicated by the clause " bap-

---

[1] Mark viii. 38.   [2] Acts ii. 40.   [3] 2 Cor. vi. 17.
[4] Gal. iii. 27.

tizing them into the name of the Father, and of the Son, and of
the Holy Ghost." The rendering of our version, "*in* the name
of," makes the clause signify that the administrator acts by the
authority of the Trinity; but the more literal rendering "*into*
the name of," makes it signify the new relation into which the act
brings the subject of the rite. He is baptized into a state of professed subjection to the Trinity. It is the public act of initiation into the new service.

The design of baptism proves its importance. The whole tenor
of the gospel forbids the supposition that there is any saving efficacy
in the mere rite: but it is the appointed ceremony of profession;
and profession, we have seen, is, in general, necessary to salvation.
As the divine goodness may pardon disciples who fear to make
public profession, so it may, and we rejoice to believe that it does
pardon those, who do not understand the obligation to make ceremonial profession, or mistake the manner of doing it. But God
ought to be obeyed; and his way is the right way, and the best
way. Paul argues from the baptism of believers, their obligation
to walk in newness of life. The ceremony implies a vow of obedience, a public and solemn consecration to the service of God. The
believing subject can feel the force of the obligation acknowledged
in the act, and Paul appeals to this sense of obligation: "Know
ye not, that so many of us as were baptized into Jesus Christ were
baptized into his death?"[1] Though it is an outward ceremony, it is
important, not only as an act of obedience, but as expressing a
believer's separation from the world, and consecration to God, in a
manner intelligible and significant, and well adapted to impress his
own mind and the minds of beholders.

The faith which is professed in baptism, is faith in Christ. We
confess with our mouths the Lord Jesus Christ, and believe in our
hearts that God has raised him from the dead.[2] If the doctrine
of the resurrection be taken from the Gospel, preaching is vain, and
faith is vain. So, if the symbol of the resurrection be taken from
baptism, its chief significancy is gone, and its adaptedness for the
profession of faith in Christ, is lost. Hence appears the importance of adhering closely to the Saviour's command, "immersing
them."

---

[1] Rom. vi. 3.   [2] Rom. x. 9.

The obligation to make a baptismal profession of faith, binds every disciple of Christ. Some have converted the Eucharist into a ceremony of profession; but this is not the law of Christ. Baptism was designed, and ought to be used, for this purpose. If infant baptism be obligatory, the duty is parental; and if it be a ceremony in which children are dedicated by their parents to the Lord, it is a different institution from that in which faith is professed. He who has been baptized in infancy, is not thereby released from the obligation to make a baptismal profession of faith in Christ. If it be granted, that his parents did their duty in dedicating him to God, he has, nevertheless, a personal duty to perform. The parental act of which he has no consciousness, cannot be to him the answer of a good conscience toward God. Had it left an abiding mark in the flesh, an argument of some plausibility might be urged against the repetition of the ceremony. But the supposed seal of God's covenant is neither in his flesh, nor in his memory, and his conscience has no Scriptural release from the personal obligation of a baptismal profession.

Section V.—CONNECTION OF BAPTISM WITH CHURCH ORDER.

It will be shown hereafter, that in a Church, organized like the primitive churches, none but baptized persons can be admitted to membership. On this account, the present chapter on baptism has been introduced, as a necessary preliminary to the subsequent discussions on church order.

CHAPTER II.

LOCAL CHURCHES.

Section I.—MORAL CHARACTERISTICS.

A Christian Church is an assembly of believers in Christ, organized into a body, according to the Holy Scriptures, for the worship and service of God.

ASSEMBLY.

The word *church*, when it occurs in the English New Testament, is, with one exception, the rendering of the Greek word εκκλησια. The Greek word, however, sometimes appears in the original text, when it could not, with propriety, be translated *church*. No one would render Acts xix. 82, "For the *church* was confused;" or verse 89, "It shall be determined in a lawful *church*;" or verse 41, "He dismissed the *church*." It is hence manifest, that the two words do not precisely correspond to each other in signification.

The meaning of an English word, is ascertained by the usage of the best English authors. By such writers, the word CHURCH is often employed to denote religious societies, consisting of persons who, because of the wide extent of territory which they occupy, never assemble in one place for divine worship. The principles on which these societies are formed, are various; their modes of government differ from each other; and they do not agree in the doctrines which they profess. If we should refuse to call any one of these societies *a church*, the usage of the best English writers might be cited against us; and the usage of such men is the law of the language.

But the disciples of Christ have another law, to which they appeal when they seek direction in forming and organizing churches. This law is contained in the Holy Scriptures. The question then is not, what does the English word *church* mean, or

(74)

to what religious societies may the name be applied; but what is *a church*, according to the teaching of the inspired word.

The Greek word *εκκλησια* denotes *an assembly;* and is not restricted in its application to a religious assembly. But every reader of the New Testament discovers, that the first Christians were formed into religious assemblies, to which epistles were directed; and which acted, and were required to act, as organized bodies. The word is ordinarily used, in the New Testament, to denote these assemblies; and it is only with this use of the term, that we are at present concerned.

The Greek word denotes *an assembly;* and, in this particular, differs from the English word *church*, which is often used to signify *the house* in which men assemble for religious worship. The word "churches," in Acts xix. 37, denotes the temples in which the heathen gods were worshipped; but this is the exception before referred to, in which the Greek word *εκκλησια* does not appear in the original text. This word never denotes *the house* in which the worshippers assemble. The word *συναγωγη* was used, not only for the assembly, but also for the house in which the assembly met; and hence, we read "He hath built us a synagogue."[1] But the word *εκκλησια* differs from it in this particular. The passage of Scripture which most favors the opinion, that the word was applied to a material edifice, is, "Have ye not houses to eat and to drink in? or despise ye the Church of God, and shame them that have not?"[2] Here an antithesis has been supposed, between the private dwellings of the Corinthian Christians, and their house of public worship. But this interpretation weakens the force of the passage. The word "despise," like the word "shame" which follows, has persons for its object; and the injurious treatment which it implies, would be far less criminal, if it affected merely the material edifice in which the church assembled.

The word *εκκλησια*, as used by classic Greek authors, signified *an assembly*. It was used to denote the assembly of the citizens in the democratic towns of Greece, met to decide on matters appertaining to the State. With this use of it, precisely agrees that which is found in Acts xix. 39: "It shall be determined in a lawful assembly." The multitude there convened, were not a lawful

---

[1] Luke vii. 5. [2] 1 Cor. xi. 22.

ecclesia. But we learn from the last verse of the chapter, that the word was not restricted in its use to a lawful ecclesia, for it is applied to the very company congregated on this occasion. " He dismissed the assembly." In the Septuagint, it is the word usually employed to denote the assembly of Hebrew worshippers, called the Congregation of the Lord; but it is also applied to assemblies not organized for religious purposes or business of state.[1] On the whole, therefore, when we meet with the word, we are sure of an assembly, and of nothing else, so far as depends on the word itself.

When we turn to the New Testament, and examine the use of this word in its application to the followers of Christ, we find it for the most part so employed that an assembly is manifestly denoted. " If he shall neglect to hear them, tell it unto the church," " but if he neglect to hear the church," &c.[2] The church in this passage, is an assembly, addressed by the party complaining, and addressing the party offending. Frequently the churches have their place of meeting specified, and are hence called the church at Jerusalem;[3] the church at Antioch;[4] the church at Corinth;[5] the church at Ephesus, &c.,[6] and when mention is made of the Christians in a district of country, so large as to render their habitual and frequent meeting for the worship of God impracticable, the term church is not applied to them in the singular number. Hence, we read, " the churches throughout all Judea, Galilee, and Samaria;"[7] the churches of Galatia;[8] the churches of Macedonia;[9] the churches of Asia.[10] It is clear, from these passages, that the term in the singular number, denoted the separate local assemblies in those districts or countries, and not the whole number of Christians inhabiting a kingdom or province. This is further confirmed by the fact, that the meeting of the Christians in the city of Corinth, is called the meeting of *the whole Church*, if the whole church be come together into one place.[11] If they had been called the church at Corinth, merely as belonging to a class of persons widely scattered through Achaia or the whole world, to

---

[1] Ps. xxvi. 5; Judith vi. 16; xiv. 6.   [2] Matt. xviii. 17.
[3] Acts viii. 1.   [4] Acts xiii. 1.   [5] 1 Cor. i. 2.
[6] Rev. ii. 1.   [7] Acts ix. 31.   [8] Gal. i. 2; 1 Cor. xvi. 1.
[9] 2 Cor. viii. 1.   [10] 1 Cor. xvi. 19.   [11] 1 Cor. xiv. 23.

whom, contemplated in the aggregate, the name church was given; the phrase "the whole church" would necessarily denote the entire aggregate; and it could not be said with truth that the whole church was assembled, when only the Christians in the city of Corinth formed the assembly.

Further proof that the word denoted a particular or local assembly, appears in this, that the churches are mentioned as distinct from one another. "They ordained elders in every church."[1] Also in this, that the churches were compared with each other: "For what is it wherein ye were inferior to other churches?"[2] "No church communicated with me as concerning giving and receiving, but ye only."[3] "As distinct bodies, they sent and received salutations,"[4] and held intercourse by messengers.[5]

By the proof which has been adduced, it is fully established that the word *church*, in such names as The Church of England, The Church of Scotland, The Presbyterian Church, The Episcopal Church, The Methodist Church, does not correspond in signification with the Greek word εκκλησια. These churches never assemble in one place, because their members are dispersed over too large an extent of territory. They are, therefore, not churches in the New Testament sense of the word. It is true that some of these churches have supreme judicatories in which the power of the whole body is supposed to be concentrated; and in these the whole church is conceived to be assembled: thus, the Presbyterian Church has its General Assembly. But whenever the General Assembly of the Presbyterian Church is mentioned, the very title indicates that the Assembly is one thing, and the Church another. The Assembly may be seen in some spacious room, transacting the business of the Church; but no one will affirm that the Church itself is literally there; and no one calls the Church itself an assembly. The people of the United States are conceived to be assembled in Congress; and the people of the several states in their several legislative assemblies; but no one understands this to be literally true, and no one calls the people of the United States or of any single state an assembly. But whenever the word εκκλησια is used, we are sure of an assembly; and the term is not applicable to bodies or societies of men that do not literally assemble.

---

[1] Acts xiv. 23.   [2] 2 Cor. xii. 13.   [3] Phi. iv. 15.
[4] Rom. xvi. 16; 1 Cor. xvi. 19.   [5] 2 Cor. viii. 23.

In defending the Presbyterian form of church government, it has been argued that the term ecclesia is applied in the New Testament to denote all the Christians in a large city, when their number was so great that they could not all assemble for worship in one place. In a large city of the present day, a single denomination of Christians may have many churches assembling at their several places of worship at the same hour. The same division of the worshipping assemblies, is supposed to have existed in ancient times; and yet, it is remarked, we never read in the New Testament of several churches in one city; and it is inferred that the word εκκλησια in the singular number, included in these cases all the separate worshipping assemblies.

Dr. Dick [1] urges the argument just stated, and refers particularly to the church at Jerusalem, and the church at Antioch, as bodies too large for all the members to assemble in one place. It is unfortunate, however, for the argument, that these very churches are expressly declared in the Holy Scriptures to have assembled. Although the disciples in Jerusalem were numbered by thousands, yet, when their number "had multiplied," [2] the apostles gathered the whole multitude together, and directed them to choose out from among themselves seven men to have charge of the distribution to the poor. And when Paul and Barnabas returned to Antioch, after having performed a tour of missionary labor, it is left on record that they gathered the church together, and rehearsed what the Lord had done by them. [3] Against these express declarations of the sacred historian, the conjecture that the number of disciples in these cities was too great to permit them to assemble in one place, is entitled to no consideration.

It is further argued by Dr. Dick, that all the disciples in Jerusalem could not have assembled in one place, because of the persecution to which they were exposed. But an important fact is here overlooked. For a considerable time after the day of Pentecost, the Christians had "favor with all the people." [4] The rulers were opposed to them; but the favor which they had among the people stayed the hand of persecution. While this state of things lasted, they remained one church, one assembly. But when persecution

---

[1] Theology, § 96, 98.   [2] Acts vi. 1, 2.   [3] Acts xiv. 27.
[4] Acts ii. 47.

scattered them, they were compelled to hold their assemblies in several places, and they are no longer regarded as constituting one church; but the historian, with strict regard to accuracy of language, calls them " churches." [1]

If the word εκκλησια in the singular number, could denote several distinct assemblies in a large city, no good reason can be assigned why it might not also denote the assemblies of Christians throughout a province or kingdom. But it is admitted that when applied to these, the word is always used in the plural form. All this exactly accords with what was before stated—that the word always assures us of an assembly.

MEMBERS.

Whether the assembly denoted by the word εκκλησια was religious or political, lawful or unlawful, the word itself does not determine. We must look beyond the word itself, to learn the character of the members who composed the churches of the New Testament; and the purpose for which they were associated.

The character of the persons who composed the New Testament churches, may be readily learned from the epistles addressed to them. They are called " The elect of God;" [2] " Children of God by faith;" [3] "Sanctified in Christ Jesus, called to be saints;" [4] " Saints in Christ Jesus;" [5] " Followers of the Lord;" [6] " Beloved of the Lord." [7] No doubt can exist that these churches were, in the view of the inspired writers who addressed them, composed of persons truly converted to God.

We may learn the same from the Acts of the Apostles. The first church admitted to membership those who repented and gladly received the word; [8] and the Lord added to the church daily such as should be saved. [9] Some have preferred to translate the passage last cited, " The Lord added to the church such as were saved." The former rendering does not so fully determine that the persons added had already undergone a saving change. Neither rendering, however, gives the precise sense of the original, which,

---

[1] Acts ix. 31.   [2] Col. iii. 12.   [3] Gal. iii. 26.
[4] 1 Cor. i. 2.   [5] Phil. i. 1.   [6] 1 Thes. i. 6.
[7] 2 Thes. ii. 13.   [8] Acts ii. 39, 41.   [9] Acts ii. 47.

by the use of the present participle, describes the salvation as neither future nor past, but in present progress. Men who had entered the way of salvation, and were making progress therein, were added to the church in Jerusalem, and all the members of the church were persons of like character, for the multitude were " of one heart."[1] When persecution scattered this first church, its dispersed members formed other churches precisely like the parent church in the character of the members. None were admitted but as believers in Christ.

What has been said must not be understood to imply that none but true believers ever entered the primitive churches. We know from the Acts of the apostles, that Ananias, Sapphira,[2] and Simon the Sorcerer,[3] had a place for a time among the true disciples of Jesus; and we know from the apostolic epistles, that false brethren were brought in unawares into the churches.[4] But we are clearly taught that they were considered intruders, occupying a place that did not properly belong to them, and were ejected when their true character became apparent. Although, even in apostolic times, such men obtained admittance into the churches, they crept in unawares,[5] and, therefore, if we would tread in the footsteps of the apostles, we cannot plead their authority for admitting into the churches any who are not true disciples of Christ.

In our definition of a church, we have called it an assembly of believers in Christ. This definition tells what a church is according to the revealed will of God, and not what it becomes by the criminal negligence of its ministers and members, or the wicked craft of hypocritical men who gain admittance into it. When we study the word of God to ascertain what a church is, we must receive the perfect pattern as presented in the uncorrupted precepts of that word, and not as marred by human error and crime.

ORGANIZATION.

A church is an *organized* assembly. The organization cannot be certainly inferred from the mere name. This is supposed to signify, properly, an assembly legally called together or summoned;

---

[1] Acts iv. 32.   [2] Acts v. 1.   [3] Acts viii. 13.
[4] Gal. ii. 4.   [5] Jude 4.

and the derivation of the word from *εκκαλεω, to call out*, accords with this meaning. A legal summons implies obligation to obey it; and the persons who were under this obligation must be supposed to have been bound, not only to assemble, but also to co-operate with one another in the business for which the assembly was convoked. Although the term was sometimes applied to an assembly not legally convened, or a loose and disorderly assembly, yet it commonly signified an assembly of persons bound to act together as a body for some specified object. This is true of the New Testament churches.

The church at Jerusalem is clearly distinguished, in the sacred narrative, from the loose multitude that heard Peter's sermon on the day of Pentecost. Many of these became "added to the church;" but the church, it is manifest from the record, was a distinct and separate body, and their union and co-operation are plainly exhibited in the sacred history.

A passage in the first epistle to the Corinthians shows that the church at Corinth was a distinct assembly, not including others who might chance to be present in their meeting: "If the whole church be come together into one place, and all speak with tongues, and there come in those that are unlearned or unbelievers."[1] Had the church been a loose or unorganized assembly, these visiters who came in would have formed a part of it. But the distinction between them and the church is marked and clear. Moreover, the phrase, "If the whole church be come together," manifestly implies that there was a definite number of persons who were expected to convene, and who, when convened, constituted the entire body. This would not be true of an unorganized assembly. Let it be further noted, that the word *εκκλησια* is here used to denote the body, not as actually assembled, but as a body of which it was possible for some of the members to be absent when others were present. Sometimes the word was used to denote an actual assembly, as in the passage, "When ye come together in the church"[2]— that is, in the assembly or public meeting: but in the phrase, "If the whole church be come together," the term manifestly applied to the church, not as a body actually assembled, but as organized. Their organization had doubtless a reference to their assembling

---

[1] 1 Cor. xiv. 23.   [2] 1 Cor. xi. 18.

6

for the purpose of carrying the design of their organization into effect; and the name εκκλησια was given to the body because of its actual assembling, or because the members were obliged to assemble by the terms of their organization.

This distinction in the use of the term, as sometimes denoting an organized body, and sometimes an actual assembly, appears also in the Septuagint. The Congregation of the Lord was an ecclesia, whether actually assembled or not; but, in the phrase, "in the day of the assembly," the term εκκλησια is used to denote the actual assembly that stood before Mount Sinai. This is the meaning of the word in 1 Cor. xiv. 34, "Let your women keep silence in the churches"—that is, in the assemblies, or public meetings. It is added: "For it is a shame for a woman to speak in the church." This shame does not attach to her as a member of an organized body, but as being in a public assembly.

The English word *church* always refers to an organized body; but it does not necessarily imply an actual assembly, being very frequently applied to bodies that never actually assemble. On this account, it is not an accurate rendering of εκκλησια, when this term denotes an actual assembly without reference to organization. Dr. Doddridge has very properly rendered Acts vii. 38: "This is he that was in the assembly in the wilderness." If this principle of translation were applied throughout the New Testament, and the word church were admitted only when an organized body is intended, something would be gained in respect of perspicuity.

We have not argued the organization of the primitive churches from the mere use of the Greek name ecclesia. The name was appropriately used to denote an organized assembly; but this was not its exclusive signification. Other considerations which have been adduced, prove that the local churches of the New Testament were, in general, organized bodies; but a doubt exists with respect to the churches or assemblies in private houses, of which four cases are mentioned.[1] In those times, houses had not been erected for the special accommodation of Christian assemblies; and meetings for religious worship were doubtless often held in private houses. That in some cases a regularly organized church may have held its stated meetings in a private house, is by no means

---

[1] Rom. xvi. 5; 1 Cor. xvi. 19; Col. iv. 15; Philem. 2.

Improbable. But we cannot affirm that every Christian assembly to which the word ecclesia was applied, was a regularly organized church. We may admit that the word *assembly* would be a more suitable rendering in these cases of meeting in private houses; and yet the proof is abundant that the churches commonly spoken of in the New Testament were organized assemblies.

INDEPENDENCE.

Each church, as a distinct organization, was independent of every other church. No intimation is anywhere given that the acts of one church were supervised by another church, or by any ecclesiastical judicatory established by a combination of churches. In the direction given by Christ, for settling a difficulty between two members, the aggrieved brother is commanded to report the case to the church, and the action of the church is represented as final. The church at Corinth excommunicated the incestuous person, by its own act and without reference to a higher judicatory. As if to settle the question of church independence, Paul, though possessing apostolic authority, and though he commanded the act to be done, yet required it to be done by the assembled church, as the proper agent for performing the work. Again, when the same individual was to be restored, the action of the church became necessary, and this action completed the deed. In the book of Revelation, distinct messages were sent to the seven churches of Asia. The character and works of each church are distinctly and separately referred to; and the duties prescribed are assigned to each church separately, and that church alone is required to perform them.

The only case in which there is an appearance of appeal to a higher judicatory, is that which is recorded in Acts xv. This was not a case of appeal to a higher judicatory established by a combination of churches, but to the single church at Jerusalem, with the Apostles and Elders; and the decree, when issued, went forth with the authority of the Holy Ghost.

DIVINE RULE.

After we have proved that the primitive churches were organized societies, an important question arises, Whether we are under obligation to regulate the church order of the present time in conformity to ancient usage. Was that usage established by divine authority, and designed to be of perpetual obligation; or was the whole matter of order and government left to human prudence? If the primitive churches consisted wholly of baptized believers, are we now at liberty to receive unbelievers and unbaptized persons? If the primitive churches were independent organizations, are we now at liberty to combine many churches in one organization? If the ancient pastors were all equal in authority, are we now at liberty to establish gradations in the pastoral office, and give one minister authority over others?

It must be admitted, that the Scriptures contain very little in the form of direct precept relating to the order and government of churches. But we have no right to require that everything designed for our instruction in duty, should be made known to us only in the way of direct command. Judicious parents give much instruction to their children by example; and this mode of instruction is often more intelligible and more useful than precept. It was made the duty of the apostles to teach their converts whatsoever Christ had commanded, and to set the churches in order. If, instead of leaving dry precepts to serve for our guidance, they have taught us, by example, how to organize and govern churches, we have no right to reject their instruction, and captiously insist that nothing but positive command shall bind us. Instead of choosing to walk in a way of our own devising, we should take pleasure to walk in the footsteps of those holy men from whom we have received the word of life. The actions of a wise father deserve to be imitated by his children, even when there is no evidence that he intended to instruct them by his example. We revere the apostles, as men inspired with the wisdom which is from above; and respect for the Spirit by which they were led, should induce us to prefer their modes of organization and government to such as our inferior wisdom might suggest.

But the Apostles designed that their modes of procedure should be adopted and continued. Paul commended the church at Corinth, because they had kept the ordinances as he had delivered them. Some things which needed further regulation, he promised to set in order when he came; evidently implying that there was an order which ought to be established. Titus, whom he had instructed, he left in Crete,[1] to ordain elders in every city, and to set in order the things that were wanting. To Timothy, he said: "The things which thou hast heard of me, the same commit thou to faithful men who shall be able to teach others also."[2] As matters of church order formed a part of his own care and action, and a part of what he had committed to Titus, so we must believe that they formed a part of that instruction which he had given to Timothy, to be transmitted by him to other faithful men, and by them to their successors.

The commission which the Lord gave to his apostles, required them to teach the observance of all that he had commanded. Many discourses which he delivered, previous to his crucifixion, are mentioned in the four gospels, without being recorded at length; and he doubtless delivered many others of which no mention is made. In the interviews which he had with the apostles after his resurrection, we are informed that he discoursed with them on the things pertaining to the kingdom of God;[3] and that this subject was so prominently before them, as to induce the inquiry, "Lord, wilt thou at this time again restore the kingdom to Israel?"[4] They were the chosen and commissioned agents for establishing his kingdom, having been appointed by him to "sit upon twelve thrones, judging the twelve tribes of Israel."[5] They were to proceed on the work assigned them, and were now waiting in Jerusalem, until they should be endued with power from on high for its successful prosecution. But what directions he gave them, in the interesting conversations that have not been committed to record, we have no other means of knowing than the precepts and examples which they have left. His parting command and promise were, "Teach them to observe all things whatsoever I have commanded you; and lo! I am with you alway, even unto the end of the world."[6] This plainly implies that commands had been given to them, which were to be observed to the end of time; and that these

---

Titus i. 5.   [2] 2 Tim. ii. 2.   [3] Acts i. 3.
[4] Acts i. 6.   [5] Matt. xix. 28.   [6] Matt. xxviii. 20.

were to be learned from their instructions. The organization and government of the churches, which were to hold forth the word of life, and be the golden candlesticks, among which the glorified Jesus was to walk,[1] were matters intimately pertaining to his kingdom; and it cannot be supposed that he gave no instruction respecting them. Whatever he had commanded on these points, the commission required that they should teach men to observe; and the accompanying promise of his presence till the end of the world, clearly demonstrates that the observance was to be perpetual. We arrive, therefore, at the conclusion that, whatever the apostles taught, whether by precept or example, had the authority, not only of the Holy Spirit by which they were guided into all truth, but also of their Lord who had commissioned them.

It may be objected, that the example of the apostles is clearly not always to be followed; as, for instance, the conduct of Paul in shaving his head at Cenchrea,[2] in purifying himself at Jerusalem,[3] and in having Timothy circumcised.[4] But how do we know that these acts of Paul are not to be imitated? We learn it from the instruction and example of the same great apostle. He has taught us to distinguish between acts of personal obligation and acts performed from regard to the weakness and prejudice of others. He became all things to all men. To the Jews he became a Jew, that he might gain the Jews. He had Timothy circumcised, because of the Jews which dwelt in that quarter: and the other acts which have been cited were performed in the same accommodation to Jewish prejudice. But when it became necessary to defend the rights and privileges of Gentile converts, he boldly asserted their rights, and strenuously opposed the circumcision of Titus.[5] If, with an humble and teachable spirit, we study the instructions as well as the example of the apostles, we shall find it scarcely possible to err in deciding which of their acts were accommodated to particular circumstances, and which of them are proper examples for our imitation. If any doubt should remain in any particular case, it would be highly rash and criminal, on account of it, to throw away the benefit of apostolic example entirely.

When we have made our deductions from the instruction and

---

[1] Rev. i. 20.   [2] Acts xviii. 18.   [3] Acts xxi. 26.
[4] Acts xvi. 3.   [5] Gal. ii. 3.

example of the apostles, we may use them with great profit to interpret the brief directions which the divine Master himself gave. Twice only, so far as the record states, did he use the word church, during all his personal ministry. In one case, he gave a promise of stability and perpetuity: "Upon this rock I will build my church; and the gates of hell shall not prevail against it."[1] From this promise we might infer, even if we had not apostolic instruction on the subject, that the church was to be built of durable materials, of living stones, of real saints. In the other case, the Master gave a precept to his disciples, with reference to personal difficulties that might arise among them: "If thy brother shall trespass against thee, go and tell him his fault between thee and him alone; if he shall hear thee, thou hast gained thy brother. But if he will not hear thee, then take with thee one or two more, that in the mouth of two or three witnesses every word may be established. And if he shall neglect to hear them, tell it to the church; but if he neglect to hear the church, let him be unto thee as an heathen man and a publican."[2] What kind of persons are concerned in the supposed difficulty? They are brethren. The direction was given to the disciples, and the very offender is called "thy brother." The direction was not designed for a case of injury from persecuting Scribes and Pharisees, but for a case of difficulty between Christian brethren. The second step in the process is thus described: "Take with thee one or two more." Who are the persons to be taken? Not persecuting Scribes and Pharisees; not strangers who will have no interest in adjusting the difficulty; but beyond all doubt, they were to be other *brethren*. In the third step it is directed, "Tell it to the ecclesia," the assembly. What assembly? The assembly of Israel, the Congregation of the Lord, collected from all places to keep their feasts at Jerusalem? The assembly of Jewish worshippers met in a synagogue? Jesus did not direct his disciples to refer their matters of grievances to such arbitrators. Evidently the ecclesia consists of the same kind of persons as those concerned in the preceding steps of the process. It is the assembly of the brethren. The constituents are Christian disciples, and none other. It is *the* assembly, and not *an* assembly that might be accidentally convened. The distinctness of the assembly,

---

[1] Matt. xvi. 18.   [2] Matt. xviii. 15, 16, 17.

and to some extent its organization, are here implied. Tell it to the assembly; an assembly actually convened, and capable of being addressed; and not a society scattered through a province or kingdom. "If he will not hear the church." The ecclesia not only hears, but decides; not only decides, but announces its decision. Here organization is clearly implied, and also right of jurisdiction: "Let him be to thee as an heathen man and a publican." This proves the decision to be final, and without appeal to a higher judicatory; otherwise the offended brother would be bound to await the issue of such an appeal. Thus we discover, that this admirable passage contains, in its brief dimensions, an epitome of the doctrine concerning church order and discipline, which was more fully developed afterwards in the instruction and example of the apostles. If the divine authority of their instructions were doubtful, these words of Jesus give them his sanction.

While we find proof that the church order established by the apostles, was designed to be perpetuated to the end of time, we do not find either precept or example for the regulation of every minute particular in the doings of a church. Marriage is a divine institution; and the rules given respecting it are obligatory, though much is left to the judgment and pleasure of the parties. So the regulations prescribed in the word of God for the organization and discipline of churches, are all obligatory, though some things are still left for human prudence to determine.

Objection 1.—A community of goods existed in the church at Jerusalem. This was the first church, and was established under the supervision of all the apostles. If primitive usage were obligatory on all succeeding time, a community of goods would be an indispensable part of church order.

We are informed, concerning the members of the first church, "Neither said any of them that aught of the things which he possessed was his own, but they had all things common."[1] But in this no intimation is given, that any church regulation was established obliging all to give up their private property. The surrender was spontaneous on the part of those who made it. It is not said that the church or the apostles called the possession of each member public property; but the accounting of it public property is

---

[1] Acts iv. 32.

attributed entirely to the owner himself. That each member had a full right to retain his property, is evident from the words of the apostle Peter to Ananias, "While it remained, was it not thine own?"[1] The crime of Ananias and Sapphira, was not that they kept back a part of their possessions, but that they lied about it. The clear recognition of their right to retain possession of the whole, is an explicit declaration from the apostle Peter, that a community of goods had not been established by apostolic authority.

If it could be proved that the apostles established a community of goods in the church at Jerusalem, we should be compelled to class the act with those acts of Paul before noticed, which were the result of peculiar circumstances. In the churches which were afterwards organized, we know that the distinction of rich and poor existed, and that the members were expected to contribute according to what they had. The possession of private property is unquestionably implied; and the apostles, who had the care of all the churches, if they had designed to make a community of goods a permanent arrangement in the churches, would not have permitted a necessary part of church order on a matter of great importance to be wholly neglected.

The circumstances of the church at Jerusalem were peculiar. From that church the gospel was sounded forth through all the world. It was regarded by Paul as having a claim on the carnal things of churches subsequently formed, in return for the spiritual things communicated. The liberality of that church in its contributions to sustain the cause of Christ was extraordinary, because the circumstances were extraordinary; and an extraordinary claim to remuneration for having impoverished themselves in support of the cause was founded on it. Paul commended the liberality of the churches of Macedonia, because "to their power, and beyond their power" they had contributed to the Lord's cause.[2] Jesus commended the liberality of the poor widow who threw all her living into the Lord's treasury. So the liberality of the church at Jerusalem was pleasing to the apostles, and also to the Lord; and the more pleasing, because it was a free-will offering, and not extorted by any church order which the apostles had established.

---

[1] Acts v. 4. [2] 2 Cor. viii. 1, 3.

Objection 2.—The church order which you profess to deduce from the Scriptures, does not agree with that which, according to ecclesiastical history, prevailed in the times that followed the age of the apostles. There is reason, therefore, to suspect that your deductions are erroneous.

In attempting to learn from ecclesiastical history what usages prevailed in the apostolic churches, there is danger of error from two causes: the writers of ecclesiastical history were uninspired men, and therefore fallible; and the churches of the times after the apostles, may have departed from the order first instituted. Neither of these causes of error can mislead us in the course of investigation which we have pursued. The writers on whom we rely were inspired; and the churches concerning which we have inquired, were the first and purest, organized by the apostles under the infallible guidance of the Holy Ghost. Moreover, we have the assurance of inspired authority, that the Scriptures are sufficient to render the man of God perfect, thoroughly furnished unto every good work. If every duty appertaining to church order cannot be learned from the Scriptures, they have not the sufficiency and perfection which Paul ascribed to them. If ecclesiastical history can make any suggestion that will assist us in fairly interpreting the Scriptures, we may thankfully accept its aid. But if it goes beyond the Scriptures, it leaves divine authority behind it; and if it opposes the Scriptures, we must reject it, lest we make void the law of God through our traditions.

But ecclesiastical history says nothing that can lead us to suspect the accuracy of our deductions from Scripture. On the contrary, the nearer we ascend with it to the time of the apostles, the more exact is the agreement which it exhibits between the order of the churches, and that which we have ascertained from the Scriptures to have been established by Christ and his apostles.

The following quotations from Gieseler's Ecclesiastical History, will suffice to show the gradual progress of infringement on the original church order, with respect to the independence of the churches, the equality of the pastors, and the right of the people to elect their church officers. The historian considers it a progress of improvement, rendering the churches "better organized and united;" but we think it a progress towards popery:—

"The influence of the bishops increased naturally with the increasing frequency of synods, at which they represented their churches. Country churches which had grown up around some city, seem with their bishops to have been usually in a certain degree under the authority of the mother-church. With this exception, all the churches were alike independent, though some were especially held in honor on such grounds as their apostolic origin, or the importance of the city in which they were situated."—A. D. 117, 193.[1]

" We have seen that the sphere of individual influence amongst the bishops was gradually enlarging, many churches in the city and its vicinity being united under one bishop, a presbyter or a country bishop presiding over them. But we have now to speak of a new institution, at first found chiefly in the east, which had the effect of uniting the bishops more intimately amongst themselves. This was the Provincial Synod, which had been growing more frequent ever since the end of the second century, and in some provinces was held once or twice a year. * * * By these associations of large ecclesiastical bodies, the whole church became better organized and united."—A. D. 193, 324.[2]

" When once the idea of the Mosaic priesthood had been adopted in the Christian church, the clergy soon began to assume a superiority over the laity. * * * * The old customs, however, were not yet entirely done away. Although the provincial bishops exercised a very decided influence in electing a metropolitan, the church was not excluded from all share in the choice."—A. D. 193, 324.[3]

Objection 3.—God has in other cases unfolded his plans of operation gradually; and it is at least probable, that, in planting the church, the principles of church order were incorporated in the organization seminally, to be developed afterwards in the progress of Christianity. It is, therefore, improper to take for our model, the first embryo of the church.

God has been pleased to unfold the plan of his grace gradually. The first revelation of it in the garden of Eden, was exceedingly obscure; but, like the dawn of day, the light continued to increase, until at length the Sun of righteousness arose, and the full revelation of the gospel was given to mankind. This progress was made by new light from heaven. From time to time were

---

[1] P. 102.   [2] P. 152.   [3] P. 156.

added new revelations from God, through inspired men, whom he commissioned to make known his will. Now, if the principles of church order, inculcated by Christ and his apostles, were left too imperfect for our guidance, the analogy suggests that the additional disclosure which is needed, ought to come down from above. But the objection does not claim, and no one will pretend, who does not claim infallibility for the church, that the progressive change made in church order, was directed by inspired men. What Christ and the apostles planted, could not possibly receive any further improvement, unless God gave the increase; and since we have no proof that the increase was from God, we may fear that men marred the Lord's work, instead of mending it.

In the developments which God makes of his plans of operation, the progress is ever towards perfection : but in the change of church order, to which the objection refers, the progress terminated in the revelation of the Man of Sin. All the steps in the progress tended to this full disclosure. If the wisdom which directed it was from above, we ought to follow its entire guidance. The doctrine of church infallibility must be admitted, and we must take it in all its consequences. The doctrines and practices of the Roman church, however contrary to the word of God, must be taken as developments of the seminal truth which the Bible contains. If we are not willing to go all this length, where shall we stop? Is there a point in the progress of the church, at which it attained its highest perfection, and from which it sunk into the depths of the papal apostasy? If so, how can we ascertain which this point was? If the word of God does not tell us, and if we have no infallible church to tell us, we are left in the dark on this important subject. The only escape from this darkness, is, by flight to the sure word of prophecy, to which we do well to take heed as unto a light that shineth in a dark place.

But were the changes of church order which took place, a development of principles inculcated by Christ and his apostles? If Christ forbade his disciples to call any man master, and constituted them all brethren—is prelacy, or the Roman hierarchy, a development of the principle which he inculcated? If he made final the decision of an ecclesia of the brethren, to which an injured brother might tell his grievance—is the establishment of appellate tribunals a development of his principle? If he established a converted church-membership—is not the admission of unconverted members, a corruption rather than a development of his principle? The progress of the divine development is towards that ultimate state, in which the wicked will be completely and for ever separated from the righteous. His destruction of the old world by a flood, from which righteous Noah was preserved, was a step in this development. After corruption and idolatry had again prevailed, another step was taken, in the call of Abram from his kindred, and the removal of him to a different land in which his descendants were to be a separate nation, maintaining a purer religion. Another separation was made, when John the Baptist preached, "Think not to say within yourselves, we have Abraham to our father;" "The axe is laid unto the root of the trees;" "Whose fan is in his hand," &c. From that time, a converted church-membership was established, which was to be separate from the world, though not removed out of the world. The next step will be, its complete and final separation. Now, after Christ, with his forerunner and apostles, has established a converted church-membership, the admission of unconverted members is a step, not in the direction of God's progressive development, but in a direction backward. Instead of leading to a more perfect state, it leads back to that state which it was a grand aim of John's ministry to alter.

Objection 4.—The mode of church organization and government, which you profess to have deduced from the Scriptures, is not wise, and, therefore, cannot be from God.

The consideration of this objection will be reserved for Chapter X., Section I.

DESIGN.

Every man, as an accountable creature, is bound to worship and serve God; but to render this worship and service apart from all his fellow-creatures, would not accord with his social nature. Many acts of devotion and obedience may be performed more advantageously and more acceptably, by companies of men, than by each man separately. Prayer is acceptable to God, though poured forth from a solitary heart excluded from all the world, and unknown to all the world: but a special promise is recorded in the word of God, for the encouragement of united prayer. Union tends to strengthen our faith, and warm our devotions; and the united petition rises with more acceptance to the ear of him who hears and answers prayer. Churches are companies of men who assemble for united prayer. The first church prayed fervently and effectually, when the number of their names was one hundred and twenty;[1] and they continued in prayer when their number was increased to thousands.[2] When Peter was in prison, prayer was made for him by the church.[3] Praise also is acceptable to God, though offered in secret; but when Paul and Silas sang praises unto God in the prison,[4] their companionship strengthened their hearts, and gave increased sweetness and power to their music. United praise entered largely into the worship of the ancient temple; and the members of Christian churches are enjoined to speak to one another in psalms, and hymns, and spiritual songs, singing and making melody in their hearts to the Lord.[5] The duty and acceptableness of church praise, may be inferred from the words, "In the midst of the church will I sing praise unto Thee."[6] The commemoration of Christ's death in the breaking of bread, is an ordinance committed to the churches. The disciples at Troas, and at Corinth, assembled for this purpose. By the union of Christians, greater efficiency is given to efforts for the spread of the gospel. Hence from the churches sounded out the word of the Lord. Association in public assemblies, gives opportunity for the spiritual instruction, which Christ commanded in the commission given to his ministers; and for the members of the church to promote each other's spiritual interests by mutual exhortation. Accordingly Paul enjoins: "Forsake not the assembling of yourselves together, but exhort one another; and so much the more, as ye see the day approaching."[7] These are among the important purposes, for which it is the will of God that believers in Christ should form themselves into churches.

---

[1] Acts i. 14, 24.   [2] Acts ii. 42; iv. 24.   [3] Acts xii. 5.
[4] Acts xvi. 25.   [5] Eph. v. 19.   [6] Heb. ii. 12.
[7] Heb. x. 25.

SECTION II.—CEREMONIAL QUALIFICATION FOR MEM-
BERSHIP.

BAPTISM IS A PREREQUISITE TO MEMBERSHIP IN A LOCAL CHURCH.

The considerations presented in chapter 1, section 4, determine
the proper position of baptism in the course of Christian obedience.
It stands at the head of the way. In this act, the believer gives
himself to God, before he gives himself to the people of God, to
walk with them in church relation. The duties connected with
church-membership are included among the commands which are
referred to in the commission, and which are to be taught after
baptism. The members of every Christian church must profess
subjection to Christ. They cannot walk together in obedience to
his commands, unless they are agreed on this point. As profession
is necessary to church-membership, so is baptism, which is the
appointed ceremony of profession. Profession is the substance,
and baptism is the form; but Christ's command requires the form
as well as the substance. In reading the Scriptures, it never enters
the mind that any of the church-members in the times of the
apostles were unbaptized. So uniformly was this rite administered
at the beginning of the Christian profession, that no room is left
to doubt its universal observance. The expression, "As many of
you as have been baptized into Christ, have put on Christ,"[1] might
in some other connection suggest that *all* had not been baptized.
But it follows the declaration, "Ye are all the children of God by
faith in Jesus Christ," and is added to prove the proposition; but
it could not prove that *all* were in the relation specified, if the
phrase, "as many as," signified only *some*. The same phrase is
used by Gamaliel, where all are intended: "And all, as many as
obeyed him, were scattered."[2] The same phrase, with the same
meaning, is used in Rom. vi. 3: "So many of us as were baptized
into Christ, were baptized into his death." Paul argues from this,
the obligation of all to walk in newness of life. It follows, therefore, that all the members of the Galatian churches, and of the
church at Rome, were baptized persons; and the same must be
true concerning all the primitive churches. We conclude, therefore, that the authority of Christ in the commission, and the usage

---

[1] Gal. iii. 27.   [2] Acts v. 36.

establisl.ed by the apostles, give baptism a place prior to church-membership.

Many unbaptized persons give proof that they love God, and are therefore born of God, and are children in his spiritual family. If they belong to Christ, it may be asked, why may they not be admitted into his churches? That there are such persons among the unbaptized, we most readily grant; for such persons, and such only, are entitled to baptism. To every such person, an apostle of Christ would say, "And now why tarriest thou? arise, and be baptized." We have not the authority of apostles, but we have the words of Christ and the apostles in our hands; and we owe it to our unbaptized Christian brother, to tell him, by their authority, his proper course of duty.

Objection 1.—Many good men do not understand the words of Christ and the apostles as we do, and consequently do not obey in this particular; yet they give satisfactory evidence, in other ways, that they love God, and conscientiously obey him. Paul says: "Him that is weak in the faith, receive ye;" and he urges, as a reason for receiving him, that "God has received him." Now, if we have satisfactory proof that God has received an unbaptized Christian brother, we are bound to receive him.

We admit the obligation to receive such a brother, but not in any sense that requires an abandonment or neglect of our own duty. We ought not to despise the weak brother. We ought not, by our knowledge, to cause the weak brother to perish. We ought to receive him into our affections, and endeavor to promote his best interests; but if he, through his weakness, disobeys God in any particular, our love for him degenerates into weakness, if it induces us to disobey also. We owe nothing to a weak brother which can render it necessary for us to disobey God. If a weak brother feels himself reproved when we yield our personal obedience to the Lord's command, we are not at liberty to neglect the command, for the sake of keeping the unity of the Spirit in the bond of peace. As I am bound to exercise my affection for a weak brother in such a manner as not to neglect my duty, so is a church. Every church owes its first obligation to Christ, and is bound to regulate its organization and discipline in obedience to Christ's command. If, by strict adherence to the divine rule, we cannot secure the co-operation of a weak brother, we must do our duty, and leave the result to God. Nothing in the law of church organiza-

tion forbids the receiving of a brother into membership, who is
weak in the matter of eating herbs, the case to which Paul refers.
But if a church be required, for the accommodation of a weak
brother, to give up the principles of organization learned from
Christ, and adopt others, she owes it to Christ, and to the weak
brother himself, firmly to refuse.

Objection 2.—If baptism is a prerequisite to church-membership,
societies of unbaptized persons cannot be called churches; and the
doctrine, therefore, unchurches all Pedobaptist denominations.

Church is an English word; and the meaning of it, as such, must
be determined by the usage of standard English writers. Our
inquiry has been, not what this English word means, or how it may
be used. We have sought to know how Christ designed his churches
to be organized. This is a question very different from a strife
about words to no profit. In philological inquiries, we are willing.
to make usage the law of language; and we claim no right, in
speaking or writing English, to annul this law. But our inquiry has
not been philological. We have not been searching English standard writers, to know how to speak; but the Holy Bible, to know
how to act. Even the Greek word ecclesia was applied to assemblies of various kinds; and we are bound to admit the application
of it to an assembly of unbaptized persons, solemnly united in the
worship of God. But we have desired to know how an ecclesia,
such as those to which Paul's epistles were addressed, was organized; and we have investigated the subject as a question of duty,
and not of philology. The result of our investigation is, that every
such ecclesia was composed of baptized persons exclusively.

Section III.—FALSE PROFESSORS.

The disciples of Christ, in obeying their Master's command to
love one another, are liable to mistake the proper objects of the
love enjoined. Men who have not the Christian spirit, frequently
assume the Christian name; and, since none but God can search
the heart, such men frequently obtain admittance among the followers of Christ, and are for a time reckoned true disciples. For
wise reasons, some of which we are able to comprehend, Christ
did not pray that his people should be taken out of the world.
Though the relation which they sustain to the men of the world is

7

often an occasion of painful trial, it gives an opportunity for duties that are profitable to themselves and to mankind, and honorable to God. In like manner, their relation to false professors, gives occasion for the exercise of patience and forbearance, and of careful self-examination.

Local churches possess external organization; and in this organization, human agency is employed. Men unite in it, on the principle of mutual recognition of each other as disciples of Christ. Since God has not endowed the members of a church with the power to search the heart, it is possible for persons, whose hearts have not been sanctified by the Holy Spirit, to obtain admission into a local church. It is not Christ's law that such persons should be received; but they obtain admittance through the fallibility of those to whom the execution of the law has been intrusted.

Since every church on earth has probably one or more false professors in it, and since Christ has not authorized the admission of false professors, it may be questioned whether, strictly speaking, there is a Christian church on earth. But it may be questioned, with equal propriety, whether any individual man should be called a Christian, since no man is fully conformed to the law of Christ. Some, on the other hand, have thought that because no church on earth is perfectly free from false professors, it is folly to aim at a perfect church. But we may, with equal propriety, charge any individual man with folly who is striving after personal perfection. The duty of every individual is, to press toward the mark, for the prize of the high calling of God in Christ Jesus; and the duty of every church, and of every church-member, is, to strive in every lawful way for church perfection. Though full perfection may not be attained, yet approach to it sufficiently rewards our continual effort; and, apart from all respect to reward, we are obliged to this course, by the command of Christ.

It may be objected, that if the Lord had designed the churches to be free from false professors, he would not have committed the management of them to fallible men. We may grant that it was not God's purpose to preserve the churches free from false professors by the exertion of his omnipotence. Had this been his purpose, it would not have failed to be accomplished. But, as in other parts of God's moral government, responsible agents are employed who have laws prescribed, which as free agents they may or may not obey. The fact that the law is not obeyed, disproves neither its perfection nor its obligation.

But the objection may be presented in another form. The failure of a church to keep out false professors, does not necessarily arise from moral delinquency in its members; it may be wholly owing to the unavoidable fallibility of human judgment. Since their failure is not criminal, it is not a violation of divine law; and, therefore, the divine law does not provide for a perfectly pure church.

The objection in this form would be embarrassing, if the church which admits a false professor, were the only party concerned in the transaction. But the false professor himself is a party, and the most responsible party. He does not love Christ; and this want of love not only unfits him for a place in the church, but is criminal. He is certainly in fault; and it too often happens that the members of the church are also in fault. Were they less conformed to the world, the distinction between Christians and men of the world would be more apparent, and fewer cases of mistake in the reception of members would occur. Churches are often criminally careless, both in the reception of members, and in the discipline of them when received. If the piety of churches were very fervent, men of cold hearts could not remain happy among them, and could not continue to have their true character concealed.

The possession of love to Christ is required of every one who seeks admission into a Christian church. The members who admit him are required to demand a credible profession made in obedience to Christ's command. Beyond this they cannot go, and here their responsibility ceases. But in every case in which a false professor is admitted, the law of Christ is violated by one or both of the parties.

CHAPTER III.

THE CHURCH UNIVERSAL.

Section I.—MEMBERSHIP.

THE CHURCH UNIVERSAL IS THE WHOLE COMPANY OF THOSE WHO ARE SAVED BY CHRIST.

Whether the term church is used in the Scriptures to denote the whole body of Christ's disciples, is simply a question of fact. Were we to regard it as an etymological question, we might doubt whether a word, which always assures us of an assembly, could be used to denote a body that has never assembled on earth since the time of the first persecution, which scattered the disciples from Jerusalem. But some reason for such an application of the term may exist; and, if we ascertain the fact that it is so applied, the reason for this peculiar use will afterward become a proper subject of inquiry.

The following are examples in which the word is used with this wide signification: "Gave him to be the head over all things to the church."[1] "Unto him be glory in the church by Christ Jesus throughout all ages, world without end."[2] Let any one attempt to interpret these and similar passages, on the supposition that the term church always denotes a body of Christians assembling at one place—as the church at Rome, at Corinth, or at Ephesus—and he will become fully convinced, that the interpretation is inadmissible. In some of the passages the extension of the term to the whole body of believers, is perfectly apparent. In others, though it is not so apparent that the entire body is intended, yet

---

[1] Eph. i. 22.　　　　　　[2] Eph. iii. 21.

this signification perfectly harmonizes with the use of the term, the context, and scope of the passage.

We shall hereafter investigate the question, whether the term church, in this wide signification, includes those who profess faith in Christ, but are not true Christians. Such false profession has become very common in modern times; but we are inquiring into the use of the term in apostolic times, when fewer motives to false profession operated. Even in those ancient times, some intruded themselves into the brotherhood, who were false brethren, brought in unawares. But the intrusion of such persons was not authorized by the head of the church; and in our effort to ascertain what the church is, we should seek to know what it is as Christ instituted it, rather than what it is as man has misconceived or corrupted it.

After having ascertained the fact that the word is used in the extended sense, the next inquiry which presents itself respects the reason or propriety of this use.

Some have thought that this use of the word is not properly collective, but generic. When we say, gold is heavier than sand, the terms gold and sand are used generically. Were they used collectively to denote all the gold and all the sand in the world, the proposition would not be true; for there is a far greater weight of sand in the world, than of gold. But the comparison is made between the two kinds of matter, without regard to the quantities of them that exist. In the generic use of names to denote the various kinds of unorganized matter, the noun is not preceded by an article: thus—fire, air, earth, and water, as names of elements, are used without an article. So *man* is used generically without an article; and we do not say, *the man*, unless some particular man is meant. When the names of other organized bodies are used generically, the definite article *the* generally precedes them: thus we say, the horse is more tractable than the mule; the cedar is more durable than the oak. So the phrase, the church, is supposed by some to be used generically to denote the kind of organization existing in local churches.

It is an argument in favor of this opinion, that the idea of an assembly is thus fully retained in the signification of the word. Each local church is an assembly.

This generic theory is advocated by Mr. Courtney, a fictitious character in "Theodosia Ernest," a popular work recently published, which maintains, in general, the true doctrine of Scripture on baptism and church organization. The arguments of Mr. Courtney, on the question now before us, are the best that I have met with; we shall, therefore, proceed to examine them.

The question is not, whether the phrase, *the church*, may be grammatically used in a generic sense; but whether the Scriptures do so employ it. This also is simply a question of fact. We must examine the passages in which the word extends its signification beyond a single local church, and endeavor to determine, whether in these cases it is generic or not.

"Upon this Rock I will build my church; and the gates of hell shall not prevail against it." [1]

This is the first text which Mr. Courtney examines in relation to this question. He regards the church which was to be built, as a visible organization; and maintains that no visible organization more extensive than a local church, was instituted by Christ. He hence infers that a local church is the thing here intended; and that the term obtains an extended signification, by being used generically. To this argument, we oppose two objections: 1. There is no proof that the church referred to in the passage, is a visible organization in the sense of Mr. Courtney. The opposing force denoted by the phrase "the gates of hell," is not such an organization; and the text contains no proof that the church differs from it in this particular. 2. The passage does not admit a consistent interpretation, on the supposition that the word "church" is to be taken generically.

It is agreed by all, that this text does not refer to any particular local church—as the church at Jerusalem, at Corinth, or at Rome. The promise of perpetuity was not designed to apply to any one of these churches. One of them may be totally scattered by persecution; another may waste away by gradual decay; and a third may be so overrun by corruption as to become a synagogue of Satan, and no longer a church of Christ. By the universal consent of interpreters, the proper application of this text extends beyond any one local church, and somehow embraces the followers of Christ throughout the world; but how the word church obtains the extended signification, is the question. Most interpreters have

---

[1] Matt. xvi. 18.

supposed that it is used as a collective name for the whole body of Christ's people; but some, with Mr. Courtney, suppose it to be merely a generic use of the term—and our present inquiry is confined to this point: Is the word church, in this passage, a collective or a generic term?

When collective terms are used to denote the subject of any affirmation, what is affirmed may respect the entire body signified by the term, or it may respect the individuals composing that body. On this distinction, a well known rule of grammar is founded: " A noun of multitude, or signifying many, may have a verb or pronoun agreeing with it, either in the singular or plural number, yet not without regard to the import of the word, as conveying unity or plurality of idea." When we say the crowd is large, because the verb is in the singular number, the largeness is predicated of the crowd as a whole; and the meaning is, that there are many persons in it: but when we say the crowd are large, the largeness is predicated of the individuals who compose the crowd; and the meaning is, that it consists of large men. On the same principle the pronouns which refer to collective nouns, may be either singular or plural according to the sense. We may say the crowd is large, but we fear not to meet it; or the crowd are large, but we fear not to meet them. The pronoun *it* refers to the crowd as a whole; and the pronoun *them* to the individuals who compose it.

With regard to generic nouns, our grammars do not give, and the usage of language does not authorize any such rule. In every well constructed sentence in which they are found, the verbs and pronouns which agree with them are always singular; and the things affirmed respecting them always relate to the individuals, and not to the genus or species as a whole. We say "the oak is large," but never " the oak are large;" and the largeness which this sentence predicates of the oak, relates to the dimensions of each single tree, and not to the number of individuals contained in the species.

To illustrate the use of generic terms, appropriate reference is made in Theodosia to the passages in the book of Job, which speak of behemoth, leviathan, and the war horse. All these passages may serve also to exemplify the rule laid down in the preceding paragraph. The verbs and pronouns are all singular; and the things affirmed all relate to the individual animals, and not to their several species considered collectively.

Let us now apply this rule to the interpretation of the text under consideration. On the supposition that church is here a generic term, the rule determines the sense to be, that each individual church is built on the rock, and each individual church has the promise that the gates of hell shall never prevail against it. But this, as Mr. Courtney himself has admitted, cannot be the meaning of the passage.

But is the rule universal? May there not be exceptions, in which the affirmations that refer to generic terms, relate to the species as a whole, and not to the individuals? That there are exceptions, is admitted. A sentence may be so constructed that, if interpreted according to the rule, it makes no sense, or a sense known not to have been intended by the writer: we are, therefore, compelled to account it an exception. Such a sentence Mr. Courtney has given us: "The jury is 'built' upon the 'rock' of the constitution, and the councils of tyrants can never 'prevail against' or overthrow it." This sentence does not conform to the rule. It was constructed for the purpose of furnishing a parallel to the words of Christ: but we may well doubt whether Mr. Courtney himself would ever write such a sentence in the ordinary course of composition. Besides, it does not appear that the sentence expresses what is required by its supposed parallelism to the words of Christ. The promise of perpetuity to the church had not failed, when corruption overspread all the earth, except in the valleys of Piedmont, or the mountains of Wales. But if tyranny had banished the mode of trial by jury from all the earth except in a single obscure court, would any writer say, The jury is built, &c., and the councils of tyrants have not prevailed against it? Any one who should speak or write thus, would depart from all the usual forms of language.

Another difficulty still remains, arising from the use of the pronoun my: "I will build my church." Although the phrase, *the horse*, may be used generically, the phrase, *my horse*, is never so used; and the presence of the pronoun is very unfavorable to the interpreting of "*my* church" as generic. Mr. C. thinks that the juries in the dominions of Queen Victoria, acting by her authority, may be generically called her jury: but if her Majesty, in an address to Parliament, should say, "My jury is built on the rock of the constitution, and the councils of tyrants can never prevail against it," we may well doubt whether her language would be understood.

In the interpretation of Scripture, unusual forms of expression are never to be supposed without necessity; and the most natural interpretation, that interpretation which most nearly conforms to the usus loquendi, is always to be preferred. The difficulties which attend the interpretation of the text under consideration, when the phrase, my church, is taken generically, vanish when it is understood to be a collective term, including the whole body of Christ's people in every age and country.

The rule which has been given respecting generic nouns might be illustrated by innumerable examples. It is said of leviathan : "The arrow cannot make him flee."[1] The intrepidity here . attributed to him, is attributed to each individual animal of the species. It belongs to the whole species, yet not to the whole as an aggregate body, but to every individual. We may say, "The hyena is ferocious; and no human skill has ever tamed him." The ferocity here attributed to the hyena belongs to each individual of the species; and the taming of any one hyena would falsify the assertion. On the same principle, the declaration of Christ, The gates of hell shall never prevail against it, cannot be true, if the pronoun "it" refer to church as a generic noun; for not only one, but many, very many, individuals of the genus have been prevailed against.

Scarcely any rule of language is without exception. Men consult convenience in speaking or writing; and, when they have no fear of being misunderstood, they allow themselves much liberty in the use of words and forms of speech. If any one choose to try his skill in inventing sentences which will not conform to the rule that we have stated, he may succeed; but he will find, on careful examination, that there is some peculiarity which allows the departure from rule. Mr. C. has very properly regarded the generic noun as "representative." One individual is contemplated and spoken of, as representing every individual of the genus. If a noun, generic in its form, is so used as not to retain the "representative" character, but to denote the entire genus directly, and without

---

[1] Job xli. 28.

representation, it becomes in fact a collective noun. It is possible to construct sentences of this kind, which will be apparent exceptions to the rule; and if the text under consideration be an exception of this kind, the word church, instead of being generic or representative, is collective. If the term "church" signifies a local church, considered as a representative of all local churches, the promise that the gates of hell shall never prevail against it, must belong to every local church. But this is not true; and, therefore, the generic interpretation of the passage is inadmissible.

"Because I persecuted the church of God."[1] "Beyond measure I persecuted the church of God, and wasted it."[2] "Concerning zeal persecuting the church."[3]

These passages cannot be relied on for proof, that the signification of the word church ever extends beyond the limits of a local assembly. During the time of Saul's persecution, the only church in existence, so far as we have information in the sacred history, was the church of Jerusalem. Of this church he made havoc, and to this church the three texts above quoted may be understood to refer. But when it has been ascertained from other Scriptures, that, in some manner, the word obtains a more extended signification, the possibility is suggested that it may have a wider signification in these texts. Paul does not say that he persecuted the church which was at Jerusalem. Although this was the only church in existence at the time of his persecution, many others had been planted before he wrote these words. Had his mind, in speaking of his persecutions, been fixed on the church at Jerusalem as a local assembly, it would have been natural to distinguish it from the numerous other local churches that had afterwards originated. When Paul wrote, the church at Jerusalem was no longer *the* church, but only one of the churches. It is, therefore, probable that he used the phrase, the church, in its wide signification; and the question again comes up, How does it obtain this extended signification? Is it as a collective or as a generic term?

When Christ met Saul on his way to Damascus, he said to him, "Why persecutest thou me? I am Jesus whom thou persecutest." The meaning of this language may be learned from the words

---

[1] 1 Cor. xv. 9. [2] Gal. i. 13. [3] Phil. iii. 6.

which, we are informed, he will use on the last day, "Inasmuch as ye have done it unto one of the least of these my brethren, ye have done it unto me."[1] His charge was brought against Saul, because he persecuted his followers, the members of his mystical body. This persecution is explained elsewhere: "Many of the saints did I shut up in prison. And when they were put to death, I gave my voice against them. And I punished them oft in every synagogue, and compelled them to blaspheme; and being exceedingly mad against them, I persecuted them even to strange cities."[2] The saints were the objects of Saul's persecution, and not an institution of Christ called the church. It was not the institution that he put into prison, condemned to death, and compelled to blaspheme, but "men and women;" were the objects of his hatred and fury. He did not persecute the institution, either as the individual institution in Jerusalem, or as a genus, of which this individual institution served as a specimen and representative. But he persecuted the saints; and the term church denotes the saints in no other way than as a collective noun. As a generic term, the word church could not denote the object of the persecution.

As in the former case, so in this, Mr. C. constructs a sentence which he considers parallel to the words of Paul. "I am a cotton planter, and yet I am not worthy to be called a cotton planter, because, some twenty years ago, I was bitterly opposed to Whitney and the cotton-gin." Here the name cotton-gin is clearly generic. The object of dislike is the machine or organ, and not the wood and iron which composed it. Just so, if the persecution of Saul was directed against the church generically understood, it was against the church as an organization, and not against the men and women who were members of it. But the exceeding madness of Saul was against the persons, not against their ecclesiastical organization.

In the sentence, "I persecuted the church and wasted it," there is a peculiarity which deserves to be noticed. As the object of persecution, the term church conveys plurality of idea; for the persecution fell on the individual members, and not on the body as a unit: but as the object of the wasting, unity of idea is presented; for it was the body, and not each individual member, that was laid waste. This two-fold use precisely accords with what is

---

[1] Matt. xxv. 40.   [2] Acts xxvi. 10, 11.

known concerning collective nouns, and recognised in the rule of grammar before cited; but it ill accords with the usage respecting generic nouns. A cotton planter might hate and oppose the cotton-gin as a genus; but how he could lay it waste generically or representatively is not clear. No good writer would say, *he destroyed the snake and the tree in the island,* using the terms snake and tree generically; but, to express the meaning in language which usage approves, he would say, " he destroyed the snakes and the trees in the island." Other sentences may be constructed in which the uncouthness of such generic use of nouns may be less apparent, but it is never in accordance with prevalent usage. Common sense, which Mr. Courtney very highly and very justly commends, seeks to interpret language according to common usage; and it will naturally and readily understand Paul to mean that he wasted the church by persecuting its members; and, therefore, conceived of the church as a collection of men, and used the name by which he designated it as a collective, and not as a generic noun.

The distinction between an organization, and the individuals composing it, is very strongly drawn by Mr. C. when he inveighs against various ecclesiastical organizations of the present day, and charges them with being rebels against Christ; but, at the same time, explains, that he does not make this charge against the individual members. If common sense will keep this distinction steadily in view, when interpreting the texts under consideration, it will clearly perceive, that the object of Paul's hatred and persecution was not the organization, but the men and women, whom he regarded as worthy of death; not because of the organization, but because of their being Christians.

" To the intent that now unto the principalities and powers in heavenly places, might be known by the church the manifold wisdom of God." [1]

" Unto him be glory in the church by Christ Jesus throughout all ages, world without end. Amen." [2]

Mr. Courtney thinks the term church used generically in both these passages. According to his custom, he constructs sentences which he regards as parallel. The first is: " In order that unto kings and princes, in their palaces and on their thrones, might be

---

[1] Eph. iii. 10.　　　　[2] Eph. iii. 21.

made known through the engine [steam-engine] the manifold skill of the inventor." As the skill of the mechanic is exhibited in the construction of the steam-engine, so the wisdom of God is exhibited to the admiration of angels in the institution of the church; that is, of local churches as a genus. This he understands to be the import of the first passage.

Paul's mind, when he penned this chapter, was filled with grand subjects—the unsearchable riches of Christ, the love of Christ which passeth knowledge, and the manifold wisdom of God. In the beginning of the epistle, he had spoken of the great scheme of salvation, in which God "has abounded toward us in all wisdom and prudence." This wonderful scheme, in which Christ is exhibited as the wisdom of God, and into which the angels, those bright intelligences that have long contemplated the wisdom of God in creation and providence, desire to look, that they may learn the higher wisdom displayed in redemption; this wonderful scheme, in all its glorious provisions, was still before the mind of Paul when he wrote the third chapter of the epistle. The whole context proves this. It was the wisdom of God in the redemption and salvation of the universal church, that, in his view, engaged the attention of angels. How does the sublimity of the thought vanish, in Mr. Courtney's interpretation of the passage! It represents the angels as learning the manifold wisdom of God, from the institution of local churches, and their adaptedness to the purposes for which they were designed. These bright spirits leave their celestial abodes, and come down to contemplate a local church of the right order, and admire the manifold wisdom of God in the contrivance of such a machinery; and its superiority to the ecclesiastical organizations of human contrivance. Lest my reader may suspect that I misrepresent Mr. Courtney's interpretation of the text, I will quote his words:—

" The idea in the first of these two passages is, that the angels of God, who are elsewhere called principalities and powers, might look at this wonderful contrivance of Jesus Christ for the execution of his laws, and the promotion of the comfort and piety of his people, and see in it evidences of the wisdom of God. It was a divine contrivance, and characterized by infinite wisdom. *Nothing else could possibly have done so well.* Men have not believed this. *Men* have all the time been tinkering at God's plan and trying to mend it. *Men* have set it aside, and substituted others in its place; but to the angels it appears the very perfection of wisdom. And it was one object of God in having the church established, that his wisdom might, through it, be known to those heavenly powers and principalities. But now, what was this plan? What was this church? It was, as we have seen, a local assembly, in which each member was the equal of every other, and by whom, in the name of Christ, and by authority from him, his ordinances were to be administered, and his laws enforced."

The sentence constructed as a parallel to the other text, is as follows: "Let the poetry of Shakspeare be honored in the theatre by managers and actors, even to the end of time." We make no objection to this sentence, but its parallelism to the text fails in an important particular. Paul did not say, "Be glory in the church to the end of time." Local churches, like theatres, exist only in the present world; and when the end of time arrives, they will cease to exist. It is therefore impossible that this text should refer to local churches, either as a genus, or as individuals; for it speaks of glory in the church, world without end.

Several passages in the New Testament speak of the church as identical with THE BODY OF CHRIST. It, therefore, becomes important in our present inquiry, to investigate the meaning of this last phrase. Mr. Courtney commences this investigation, by citing Romans xii. 4, 5: "As we have many members in one body, and all members have not the same office, so we being many, are one body in Christ, and every one members one of another."

From this passage, we learn that the body of Christ is not a conglomeration of all the local churches. They who hold this opinion, may defend it from the arguments of Mr. Courtney, as best they can. The members of Christ's body are individual Christians, and not churches: but the question remains, whether it includes all Christians, or only some of them. Mr. C. thinks it perfectly clear that, in this passage, it signifies only the saints who were members of the church at Rome, to whom this epistle was addressed; and he quotes, as decisive on this point, the words, "I say to every man that is among you,"[1] putting the pronoun "you" in small capitals. But this is not the only pronoun which might be

---

[1] V. 3.

so distinguished in the passage. Paul says, "WE, being many, are one body in Christ,"[1] including himself among the members of Christ's body, to which the saints at Rome belonged. But Paul was not a member of the local church at Rome. When he wrote this epistle, he had never seen that church; but expected to see them for the first time, when he should make his contemplated journey into Spain.[2] It is hence clear, that the body of Christ included more than the members of that local church. The same may be inferred from ver. 13, "distributing to the necessities of saints." The kind affections, which Paul enjoined on them to exercise, were not to be confined to the saints at Rome, as if they only were members of this body; but all saints were to be accounted co-members with them, and entitled to their sympathies. This appears also in the words, "given to hospitality." Rome was the centre of the Roman empire, the great city of the world, to which men flocked from all nations; and the hospitality here enjoined, must be understood to have for its objects, not the members of that local church only, but all the disciples of Christ who might visit the metropolis.

Mr. Courtney's exposition of the phrase "the body of Christ," is liable to a serious and fatal objection. It converts the beautiful figure which the Holy Spirit employs to represent the union between Christ and his people, into a monster, having one head and many bodies. Every local church is considered a body of Christ; and he is therefore the head of as many bodies, as there are local churches in the world. In Paul's view, Christ's body is one, and not many, though consisting of many members. "We, being many, are one body." His doctrine contemplates one God, one Lord, one Spirit, one faith, one hope, one baptism, and also one body;[3] but the doctrine of Mr. C. destroys the last of these seven unities, and makes it, not one, but thousands.

The doctrine of Mr. C. cannot be relieved from this objection, by the consideration that the churches, though many, are generically one. The members of the church at Rome, were members of a particular, and not of a generic church. A generic church cannot have actual existence, any more than a generic horse, which is neither black, white, bay, nor speckled; but exists only as a mental conception. Mr. C. objects strongly to the opinion, that

---

[1] V. 5.   [2] Rom. xv. 24.   [3] Eph. iv. 4—6.

the term church denotes the church universal, because, he alleges, that this universal body exists only in the imagination; but this misapplied objection falls with crushing weight on his own ideal church generic.

"Now ye are the body of Christ, and members in particular." [1] As the other body of Christ means, according to Mr. C., the church at Rome, this body of Christ means the church at Corinth. The same difficulty as before, recurs here. Paul considered himself a member of the church here intended: "By one Spirit are WE all baptized into one body." [2] And it appears, [3] that he was not the only apostle whose membership was in this church : "God hath set some in the church; first, apostles." Peter had a party in this church, who said, "We are of Cephas;" [4] but no one has hence inferred, that Peter's church-membership was at Corinth—and there is as little proof that Paul and Apollos, though made heads of factions there, had membership in that particular locality. Paul does indeed say to the Corinthians, "Ye are the body of Christ;" but he says also, "By one Spirit are WE all baptized into one body." Paul contemplated the saints at Corinth, as members with himself and all the apostles, of that one body in which the one Spirit operated; and by whose operation, all, whether Jews or Gentiles, are brought into one body. So it is said in another place, "He hath broken down the middle wall of partition between us [Jews and Gentiles], to make in himself of twain one new man, and that he might reconcile both unto God in one body." [5] This one body, this one new man, was not the local church at Corinth, or any other local church, or the church generic; but the universal church, the body of which Christ is the head, and all his people are members.

"And gave him to be head over all things to the church, which is his body, the fulness of him that filleth all in all." [6] This passage declares the church, and the body of Christ, to be identical; and what is affirmed, by no means agrees with the supposition that the body intended, is a local church, the church at Ephesus. Christ was not made head over all things, for the special benefit of this church; and this church was not the fulness of him

---

[1] 1 Cor. xii. 27. [2] V. 13. [3] V. 28.
[4] 1 Cor. l. 12. [5] Eph. ii. 14, 16. [6] Eph. i. 22, 23.

that filleth all in all. Nor can this passage refer to the church
generic. The nouns in apposition, "body and fulness," forbid this
interpretation. The word body is generic in the phrase "the body
without the Spirit is dead," and the generic use of it in this case,
is apparent to common sense; but common sense cannot comprehend how the body of Christ can be generic. His literal body
was not a genus; and to suppose his mystic body to be a genus,
perplexes common sense, and obscures plain Scripture. The word
"fulness" is abstract; and to take it generically, requires a gene-
ralization of abstractions which confounds common sense. Besides,
if "the church" signifies the church at Ephesus, or any other local
church, as a representative of the genus, it follows that each particular church, however small, is the fulness of him that filleth all
in all. This notion, therefore, multiplies not only the body of
Christ, but also the divine fulnesses, to an extent equal to the
number of local churches; but the context leads to the true interpretation of the passage — an interpretation simple, clear, and free
from all obscurity. The grand scheme of redemption and salvation by Christ, filled the expanded mind of Paul. The gathering
together of all things in Christ, the riches of the glory of his inheritance in the saints, and the admission of the Gentiles to be fol-
low-citizens with the saints, and of the household of God, are
subjects which engaged his thoughts, and burst forth from his full
soul, in the sublime language in which he here writes. And who
are the saints that constitute Christ's inheritance, among whom
the Ephesians had been admitted as fellow-citizens? Unquestionably not the church at Ephesus. They can be no other than the
whole redeemed people of Christ, the whole household of faith.
Jews and Gentiles were united under the gospel; constituted one
fold, under Christ, the one shepherd; one body, of which he is
the head; one family, gathered together in him; one house, over
which he, the Son, presides. This body was not a local church.
The epistle to the Hebrews was not addressed to a local church;
and Paul says of all the Hebrew Christians, "Whose house are we,
if we hold fast the confidence, and the rejoicing of the hope firm
unto the end."[1] Amongst these Hebrew Christians, believing
Gentiles had been received into the same family as members of the

---

[1] Heb. iii. 6.

same household. To this united family, the entire household, the whole context alludes; and any interpretation which turns the thought from this great body, to a local church, is wholly unsuited to the subject of the apostle's discourse.

In commenting on the last verse of the third chapter, we argued that the church there referred to cannot be local, either particular or generic, because it is to endure world without end. The same argument applies to the interpretation of the phrase, the body of Christ. If it signifies a local church, or the genus of local churches, it is not immortal and indivisible. If the church at Rome was the body of Christ referred to in Rom. xii., that body saw corruption. Every local church, and the genus of local churches, will cease to exist; and the mystical body of Christ, according to this interpretation, will cease to exist, having yielded to dissolution. The promise that the Lord would not suffer his Holy One to see corruption, was fulfilled in respect of his flesh; much more may we expect it to be fulfilled, in respect of his spiritual body.

In the context, Paul refers to the church under other figures: "a building;" "the whole building;" "a holy temple." These figures do not present to our view an edifice, or genus of edifices, temporary as local churches; but a structure that, with the foundation on which it is built, will endure for ever. It is no objection to this view, that the indefinite article is used in the phrases, "a holy temple," "a habitation of God." Mr. C. notices this last phrase, and seems to infer from it that God has many such habitations. But the inference is unauthorized. He who says that God is *an* infinite being, does not authorize the inference that there are many infinite beings.

The fourth chapter of the epistle abounds with the same subject, and exhibits it clearly and impressively. Paul exhorts the Ephesians to keep the unity of the Spirit. This one Spirit was not confined to the local church at Ephesus; but actuated the saints everywhere. He adds: "For there is one body, and one Spirit; even as ye are called in one hope of your calling."[1] The oneness of the body, like that of the Spirit which vitalized and actuated it, was not confined to this local church, but included all who were called with "the one calling." The church at Ephesus does not

---

[1] V. 4.

appear to have included any of the apostles among its members; but the one body of which Paul speaks had apostles in it, with other ministers, who were designed by the head of the church for the perfecting of the saints, the edifying *of the body* of Christ. All the saints are included in this body; and the design was, that "all should come in the unity of the faith, unto a perfect man, unto the measure of the stature of the fulness of Christ." Christ's body is to be perfect and complete; and all the ministry, appointed and given by the ascended Saviour, was designed to effect this: but all the labor of these is not expended on any one local church. The conception of one head with many bodies never entered Paul's mind; but, in his view, as the head is one, so the whole body is one.

In the fifth chapter, we meet again with the same subject: "The husband is the head of the wife, even as Christ is the head of the church; and he is the Saviour of the body."[1] Here the church is again presented to view as the one body, of which Christ is the one head and Saviour; and there is no intimation that the church is more than one. Everything which follows in the chapter respecting the church, agrees with its unity: "Husbands, love your wives, even as Christ also loved the church, and gave himself for it; that he might sanctify and cleanse it with the washing of water by the word; that he might present it to himself a glorious church, not having spot, or wrinkle, or any such thing. * * * * * No man ever yet hated his own flesh; but nourisheth and cherisheth it, even as the Lord the church: for we are members of his body, of his flesh, and of his bones. For this cause shall a man leave his father and mother, and shall be joined unto his wife, and they two shall be one flesh. This is a great mystery: but I speak concerning Christ and the church."[2]

Mr. Courtney thinks he finds a key to the interpretation of all this in the words first quoted: "the husband is the head of the wife."[3] As the wife here referred to is not any one wife in particular, but is to be understood generically, so, he thinks, the church is to be understood generically throughout the passage. But at verse 28, the generic form of speech is dropped, with respect to the wife, and the plural substituted: "so ought men to love their

---

[1] V. 23.   [2] Eph. v. 25—32.   [3] V. 23.

wives as their own bodies." Yet the plural *churches* is nowhere found in the passage. When the husband is singular, the wife is singular; and when husbands are spoken of in the plural, wives also are mentioned in the plural. This accords with what is said elsewhere: "Let every man have his own wife, and let every woman have her own husband."[1] When one of these correlative terms is used generically, the other is also used generically. When Christ and the church are named together, Christ is not generic, and yet the church is supposed to be. Christ, as the husband of the church, is one; but the church, as the wife of Christ, is, according to the interpretation, not one, but a genus—a whole family of wives! This polygamy, introduced into the interpretation of Paul's words, is wholly discountenanced by the scope of the discourse, and particularly by the clause, "and present it to himself a glorious church"—one glorious church, and not a family of churches.

But Mr. C.'s interpretation represents the object of Christ's conjugal love as the institution. Though the churches are many, the institution is but one; and in this view, the notion of polygamy is excluded. But the institution, apart from the churches instituted, is a mere abstraction: and is the bride of Christ a mere abstraction? Is it an abstraction that Christ loved and gave himself for, that he might sanctify and cleanse it with the washing of water by the word? It was not an abstraction that he designed to perfect and present to himself. He did not expend his love and sufferings to perfect the ecclesiastical institution. Nor was it his design to perfect the instituted churches, and present them to himself as a glorious family of churches. The object to be presented is *a* church. The bride, the Lamb's wife, is but one. Another consideration effectually excludes Mr. C.'s interpretation of this passage. The presentation of Christ's bride to him is reserved for the future world, when the marriage supper of the Lamb will be celebrated. But then, according to Mr. C.'s interpretation, Christ will have no bride; for local churches, as individuals and as a genus, will not then exist.

"And fill up that which is behind of the afflictions of Christ in my flesh for his body's sake, which is the church."[2]

This passage agrees with Eph. i. 22, 23, in declaring that the

---

[1] 1 Cor. vii. 2.   [2] Col. i. 24.

church and the body of Christ are identical. What was said on the other text, is applicable to this.

"I will declare thy name unto my brethren, in the midst of the church will I sing praise unto thee."[1]

"But ye are come unto mount Sion, and unto the city of the living God, the heavenly Jerusalem, and to an innumerable company of angels, to the general assembly and church of the first-born, which are written in heaven, and to God the Judge of all, and to the spirits of just men made perfect, and to Jesus the mediator of the new covenant."[2]

These two passages present much difficulty to the advocates of the generic theory. The first of them contains two parallel clauses, in which "my brethren" and "the church" are corresponding phrases, and signify the same persons. The brethren of Christ are the "many sons" whom he, as the captain of their salvation, is conducting to glory.[3] He declares God's name to the brethren, and in the midst of the church, the assembly of these brethren, he celebrates the praise of God. This is the church universal; for he says, concerning them, in presenting them to the Father, "Behold, I and the children which God hath given me."[4] This cannot be consistently interpreted of a local church, either single or generic.

The other text describes the same company, not on their way to glory, but already arrived in the heavenly city. To them all, as the brethren of Christ, and sharers of the glory which the Father had given him, and joint heirs with him of the inheritance, belong all the dignity and rights of first-born sons. Their names are enrolled as citizens of the New Jerusalem. Believers on earth are citizens of the same city: "The Jerusalem which is above is free, which is the mother of us all."[5] Our citizenship is above. We are made "fellow-citizens with the saints, and of the household of God."[6] Paul says, concerning the saints yet on earth: "Ye are come to the church of the first-born." All make one household, one church. Some having already arrived, and others on the way. The river Jordan separated two and a half tribes of ancient Israel, on the one side, from the remaining tribes who were on the other

---

[1] Heb. ii. 12. [2] Heb. xii. 22—24. [3] V. 10.
[4] V. 13. [5] Gal. iv. 26. [6] Eph. ii. 19.

side; but they constituted one nation, and they united as one, in their festal assemblies, in the earthly Jerusalem. So death separates the saints below from the saints above; but they are one—one company, one church; and the heavenly Jerusalem is the place of their joyful meeting in one glorious and happy assembly. This is the church in which there will be glory to God by Jesus Christ, throughout all ages, world without end.[1]

The text last considered shows clearly the propriety of applying the term ecclesia to the entire body of the saints. Though they do not meet in one assembly on earth, they belong to the assembly above, and are on their way to join it. They have been called out of the world, with the heavenly calling which is the summons to meet in the assembly. In obedience to this summons, they quit the world, count themselves no more of it, and are on their march to the city of which they claim to be citizens, and to the company with which they are to be eternally united. As the church at Corinth were an ecclesia, considered as bound to assemble in one place, though not actually assembled; so believers in Christ, considered as bound for heaven and on their way thither, are one ecclesia with the saints who have already arrived at the place of final meeting.

Some have thought that the extended sense of the word is metaphorical; like body, flock, fold, house, temple, applied to the same subject. They suppose it to mean the whole body of Christ's disciples, not literally assembled, but bearing a relation to each other, similar to that which the members of a local church bear to each other. But, on the general principle of interpretation, the literal meaning is to be preferred whenever the subject admits it. The other terms cannot be taken literally; but a literal assembly of Christ's disciples is not only possible, but is expected by all of them, and is in part the hope of their calling. Besides, if we have not mistaken the sense of the passage last considered, this literal assembly is presented to view in it, and the relation which the saints on earth bear to the church above. To this may be added, that the term church is used as explanatory of the metaphorical phrase the body of Christ, a use to which it would be less adapted if the terms are alike figurative. But the question concerning the reason

---

[1] Eph. iii. 21.

of applying the term to denote the universal church, is wholly distinct from the question whether a universal church exists. The first question may remain undecided, without affecting in the least the doctrine concerning the existence and nature of the universal church.

In the first use of the term ecclesia that occurs in the New Testament,[1] it denotes the church universal. No local church at that time existed; and it is, therefore, improbable that the application of the term to the universal church, should be a metaphor derived from its local signification. When the first church at Jerusalem was formed, it included, for a considerable time, all the disciples of Christ, and was the universal church, as far as it was practicable for that body to be assembled on earth. The distinction of local churches never existed until the church at Jerusalem was scattered: it is, therefore, improbable that the name of the universal body was derived from that of the particular associations subsequently formed. Even the term, as contained in Christ's directions,[2] was first applicable to the one church at Jerusalem, and was not applicable to the separate local churches until the first church had become dispersed.

The most remarkable use of ecclesia as a classical word, is its application to the democratic assemblies of the Grecian cities. It is not to be supposed that the name given to those assemblies, implied in itself the powers of the assemblies or the qualifications to membership in them. It would be useless, therefore, to look to the mere word for information respecting the qualifications of church members, or the nature and design of ecclesiastical organizations. It denoted, in the political use of it, the assembly of all those who had the full rights of citizenship; and the place of assembling was in the city to which they belonged. These particulars agree well with the application of the term to the church universal, which includes all the citizens of the heavenly Jerusalem, whose place of meeting is in the glorious city.

In the Septuagint, the word is applied to the body called in the Hebrew Scriptures the Congregation of the Lord. This use of it corresponds better with the Christian use in application to the universal church, than to local churches. The Hebrew ecclesia

---

[1] Matt xvi. 18. [2] Matt. xviii. 17.

was the assembly of all in the whole nation, who could lawfully unite in the worship of Jehovah according to the forms prescribed in the ceremonial law. The place of this general meeting was in the city Jerusalem. In this city the first Christian ecclesia assembled. It consisted of Jews, who were attached to their holy city, their temple, and the forms of worship to which they had been accustomed. At first they had no conception that gentiles were to be admitted to equal privileges in the Christian dispensation; and they probably expected that Jerusalem was to be the great centre of Christian worship, as it had been for the people of Israel; but persecution soon taught them their mistake. Driven from the city of their affections, and scattered abroad through the earth, they learned to look to another city in which they were to unite in the worship of God, beyond the reach of persecution. They regarded themselves as strangers and pilgrims in the earth, travelling to the city prepared for them by God. As the Israelites, members of the Congregation of the Lord, had been accustomed to travel from all parts of the land which they inhabited, to appear before the Lord in Jerusalem, and to keep their sacred feasts in his presence; so the spiritual Israel are on their pilgrimage to the heavenly Jerusalem, to unite in the great congregation, and enjoy the bliss which God has prepared for them. The pious Hebrews, when journeying to their holy city, longed to appear before God in the great congregation; and often directed their prayers towards his holy temple. In this distant worship, little companies of them would naturally unite in the exercise of like affections, and for mutual encouragement and benefit. So the Christian pilgrims to the heavenly Jerusalem unite in temporary associations, for the worship of God and their spiritual good. Such are the local churches in which they unite on earth.

Although the term church occurs much more frequently in the New Testament in its application to local churches, than to the church universal; yet it is apparent on the face of the sacred pages, that membership in this was far more important than in those. Little is anywhere said of membership in a local church; but the common recognition of Christians is as members of the church universal, the great brotherhood: "Of this way,"[1] "the

---

[1] Acts xi. 2.

sect everywhere spoken against,"[1] "having their names in the book of life."[2] Phebe is mentioned as "a servant of the church at Cenchrea," but she is also recognised as "our sister,"[3] and this relation to the great fraternity, the universal family, has everywhere the chief prominence.

Thus far we have had no occasion for the distinction which theologians have made between the church visible and the church invisible. We have supposed all who profess Christ to be true believers. In apostolic times, the exceptions were comparatively few; and, moreover, in those days, true believers did not delay to receive baptism, the appointed ordinance of profession. In this state of things, there was no practical necessity for the distinction referred to; and the apostle addressed the professors of religion who composed the churches, as true saints, members of the universal ecclesia, citizens of the heavenly Jerusalem, heirs of the incorruptible inheritance.

In this state of things which we have contemplated, the church universal includes all the local churches; but yet it does not include them as organizations. We have before noticed, that the members of the universal church are individual Christians, and not local churches. Moreover, all the local churches taken together do not make up the church universal; for it includes the saints in heaven as well as those on earth. Besides, there may be saints on earth, as the Ethiopian eunuch, who belong to the family of saints, and have not yet been received into any local church.

Section II.—VISIBILITY.

THE MEMBERS OF THE UNIVERSAL CHURCH ARE KNOWN BY THEIR PROFESSION OF CHRIST AND THEIR OBEDIENCE TO HIS COMMANDS.

The religion of Christ was not designed for concealment. From its very nature, it cannot be hid. It inclines every one who possesses it, to do good to all mankind, and to make known the gospel by which all mankind are to be blessed. At every point of contact with human society, Christian benevolence will exhibit itself.

---

[1] Acts xxviii. 22.   [2] Phil. iv. 3.   [3] Rom. xvi 1.

Christ's followers are described as lights in the world.[1] They are a candle which is lighted, not to be put under a bushel, but that it may give light to all who are in the house.[2] They are a city on a hill, which cannot be hid.[3] They are commanded, "Let your light so shine before men, that they may see your good works, and glorify your Father which is in heaven."[4] Their obedience to this command has distinguished them in all ages, and made them visible to the world.

The disciples of Christ are bound to profess their attachment to him before the world. This obligation is taught in such passages as the following: "If thou shalt confess with thy mouth the Lord Jesus, and shalt believe in thine heart that God hath raised him from the dead, thou shalt be saved."[5] "Whosoever shall confess me before men, him will I confess also before my Father which is in heaven."[6]

But something more than mere profession is necessary to distinguish the true followers of Christ. Many say Lord, Lord, who do not the things which he has commanded. To such persons, however loudly they may profess his name, he will say, "Depart from me, ye that work iniquity."[7] He recognises those only as his followers who are obedient to his precepts; and he has taught us to recognise them in the same manner: "By their fruits ye shall know them."[8] "Ye are my friends, if ye do whatsoever I command you."[9] A life of holy obedience to Christ is readily distinguishable from the common course of this world; and where it is exhibited, men cannot fail to see it.

The visibility of the church consists in the visibility of its members. Our Divine Master came, "a light into the world;" and all his followers are lights; some of them burning and shining lights, and others stars of less magnitude. But, as the constellations of heaven have no other light to render them visible than that which the several stars emit, so it is with the church. All its light is the light of its members, and all its visibility depends on their lustre.

Writers on theology have distinguished between the church visible, and the church invisible; but a church in this world to be

---

[1] Phil. ii. 15.   [2] Matt. v. 15.   [3] Matt. v. 14.
[4] Matt. v. 16.   [5] Rom. x. 9.   [6] Matt. x. 32.
[7] Matt. vii. 21, 23.   [8] Matt. vii. 20.   [9] John xv. 14.

invisible must consist, not of children of light, but of those whose light is darkness. Were we to use these designations according to their proper import, we might call the saints in heaven the invisible church, because they are removed beyond the reach of human sight; and the saints on earth, the visible church, because they still remain on earth to enlighten this dark world. But the saints above and the saints below, make only one communion, one church; and theologians, when they mean to distinguish these two parts of the one whole from each other, are accustomed to call them the church militant and the church triumphant. By the church invisible, they mean all true Christians; and by the church visible, all those who profess the true religion. The invisible consists wholly of those who are sons of light; and the visible includes sons of light and sons of darkness in one community. We have seen that Christ does not recognise mere professors as his disciples, and that he has taught us not so to recognise them. A universal church, therefore, which consists of all who profess the true religion, is a body which Christ does not own. To be visible saints, a holy life must be superadded to a profession of the true religion; and they who do not exhibit the light of a holy life, whatever their professions may be, have no scriptural claim to be considered members of Christ's church.

Membership in a local church, is not always coincident with membership in the church universal. This appears on the one hand, in the fact that the pure light of a holy life may sometimes be so successfully counterfeited, as to deceive mankind. Paul has taught us, that Satan may transform himself into an angel of light; and that it is no marvel, if his ministers do the same.[1] John says, "They went out, that they might be made manifest that they were not all of us;"[2] and we hence infer, that they were not manifest before. But this passage teaches us, that their profession of religion, and their successful imitation of the Christian life, were not enough. It was still true, "they were not of us." Simon, the sorcerer, was thought for a time to be a convert; but when his true character was disclosed, Peter decided, "Thou hast neither part nor lot in this matter, for thy heart is not right in the sight of God."[3] If mere profession rendered him a member of the uni-

---

[1] 2 Cor. xi. 14, 15. [2] 1 John ii. 19. [3] Acts viii 21.

versal church, his membership in it was not affected by the discovery that his heart was not right, so long as his profession was not renounced. If membership in the local church at Samaria rendered him a member of the universal church, the local church had not disowned him. When Paul would have the incestuous person at Corinth excommunicated from that local church, he did not pronounce the sentence of excommunication by his apostolic authority; but left it with the church to perform the act.[1] So Peter did not use his apostolic authority, to exclude the sorcerer from the church at Samaria; but pronounced on his relation to the whole community of the saints. It is hence apparent that membership in a local church may be superadded to profession in those who have no part in the matter. They of whom John says, "They were not of us," were for a time members of some local church; and so are many to whom the Saviour will say in the last day, "I never knew you."

On the other hand, men sometimes judge too unfavorably. The church at Jerusalem was unwilling, for a time, to receive the converted Saul as a true disciple; but the Lord Jesus had received him, and given him the place of an apostle in his universal church.

Notwithstanding the errors which human judgment may commit in individual cases, it still remains true, that the light of piety is visible. Time often corrects these errors. The sorcerer, and John's false professors, were made manifest; and the conversion of Saul to the faith which he once destroyed, became universally admitted. Doubtless there are cases which will not be understood till the last judgment; but it nevertheless remains a general truth: "By their fruits ye shall know them." Because some cases are doubtful, and some may be mistaken, it does not follow that sin and holiness are undistinguishable, or that the world and the church are undistinguishable.

The epithet "*invisible*," applied to the true church of Christ, is not only incorrect, but it has led into mistake. Men have spoken of this church as a mere mental conception; and they have asked, whether Saul persecuted an invisible church. They seek a church possessing more visibility than proceeds from Christian profession and a life of piety; and they find it, as they think, in some form

---

[1] 1 Cor. v. 4, 5.

of organization, which they deem necessary to constitute the church. Such an organized body, they call the visible church. But Saul did not inquire, whether those whom he persecuted, as professed followers of Christ, and devotedly attached to his cause and doctrine, were also members of some external organization. He persecuted them as Christian men and women. But the existence of such men and women, like the persecutions which they suffered, was something more than a mere mental conception. Organization is not necessary to visibility; much less is any particular species of it. Rocks and mountains are as visible as plants and animals.

Section III.—UNITY.

THE UNITY OF THE UNIVERSAL CHURCH IS SPIRITUAL.

Material bodies are formed by an aggregation of particles which have an attraction for each other. In like manner, living beings are brought together into bodies, or societies, by various attractions which subsist among them. Bees, birds, and various species of animals, exhibit the social propensity; and it operates in man, as a part of his natural constitution. Together with this innate tendency to seek society, the interests and necessities of men bind them together in various forms of association. In these cases, the principles of association are natural; and a new nature, or a new heart, is not indispensably requisite. But the church is a society, in which this qualification is indispensable. Its members are bound to one another by an attraction which is unfelt by men of the world: "If ye were of the world, the world would love his own; but because ye are not of the world, but I have chosen you out of the world, therefore the world hateth you."[1]

The distinctive principle which separates Christians from the world, and binds them together, is produced in them by the regenerating influence of the Holy Spirit. "The fruit of the Spirit is love." "Beloved, let us love one another; for love is of God."[2] "Every one that loveth is born of God."[3] "We know that we have passed from death unto life, because we love the

---

[1] John xv. 19.   [2] Gal. v. 22.   [3] 1 John iv. 7.

brethren."[1] The same spiritual influence that sheds abroad the love of God in the heart, produces love to all who bear the image of God: "He who loveth God, loveth his brother also."[2] Brotherly love was especially enjoined on the followers of Christ, by their divine Master: "A new commandment I give unto you, that ye love one another."[3] All who feel the love of Christ constraining them, are drawn by its influence to love those whom he loved, and gave himself for. Not only is brotherly love enjoined, but it flows spontaneously from the new heart: "But as touching brotherly love, ye need not that I write unto you; for ye yourselves are taught of God to love one another."[4]

Love, which is sometimes called charity in our translation of the Bible, is declared to be "the bond of perfectness."[5] It binds all the people of God together, and makes them one. It is the essential principle of that sympathy, so beautifully described in 1 Cor. xii., as subsisting between the various members of Christ's body. It is this that cements the living stones of the spiritual temple, which as it groweth together, maketh increase of the body unto the edifying of itself in love. This was the principle of union in the first church at Jerusalem, of which it is recorded: "The multitude of them that believed, were of one heart, and one soul."[6] Persecution drove the members of this church from one another; but it could not sever the tie that bound them together, and made them one. The love of the brethren was never confined to a local church. After Paul had said to the church of the Thessalonians, "Concerning brotherly love, ye have no need that I write unto you," he adds, "and indeed ye do it towards all the brethren which are in all Macedonia."[7] Their love extended beyond the boundaries of their church, into all the region round about. Wherever a child of God, a disciple of Jesus, was found, this love embraced him as one of the spiritual brotherhood. "Every one that loveth him that begat, loveth him also that is begotten of him."[8]

The bond of perfectness which unites the people of God on earth, makes them one with the church in heaven, who are made perfect

---

[1] 1 John iii. 14.   [2] 1 John iv. 21   [3] John xiii. 34.
[4] 1 Thes. iv. 9.   [5] Col. iii. 14.   [6] Acts iv. 32.
[7] 1 Thes. iv. 10.   [8] 1 John v. 1.

in love. This grace is not destroyed by death, nor does death deprive it of its cementing power. Faith and hope may cease, and the unity of faith and the unity of hope belong more properly to the church on earth; but love never faileth, and the unity of love binds and will for ever bind all the redeemed together, as it binds them all to Christ.

The attraction of love, which draws all the people of God to heaven, causes them, while on their way thither, to unite with each other, as they have opportunity, in the worship and service of God. Even without a divine command not to forsake the assembling of themselves together, grace within would incline them to form such societies. It is said of the first Christians, on the memorable day of Pentecost, "They were all with one accord in one place."[1] And when their number was greatly increased by the ministry of the word, it is said, "All that believed were together."[2] The word "together" is a translation of the same Greek phrase that is rendered in the first verse "in one place." The new converts were of one heart and one soul with the original one hundred and twenty; and formed with these one society accustomed to meet for the worship of God. The unity of this assembly was disturbed by persecution; but the tendency to assemble was not destroyed. The disciples were scattered from Jerusalem; and we immediately after read of the churches in Judea, Galilee, and Samaria. The same principle of unity pervaded the whole body; and by it, from the necessity of the case, local churches were multiplied.

The brotherly love which characterizes and unites the followers of Christ, has not for its object all who profess the true religion. Christ did not enjoin such exercise of it; but instructed his disciples to beware of wolves in sheep's clothing. These dangerous intruders into the fold were to appear as professors of the true religion; otherwise, it could not be said that they wore the clothing of sheep. Paul, in his last interview with the elders of the Ephesian church, gave a similar warning: "I know this, that after my departing shall grievous wolves enter in among you, not sparing the flock. Also of your own selves shall men arise, speaking perverse things, to draw away disciples after them."[3] He elsewhere speaks of false brethren, brought in unawares. If these false brethren had not

---

[1] Acts ii. 1.   [2] Acts ii. 44.   [3] Acts xx. 29, 30.

professed the true religion, they could not have found entrance, even for a short time. Such agents of mischief are not the proper objects of brotherly love. Even the beloved disciple, whose heart was so full of love, and who urged the duty of brotherly love with the utmost earnestness, commanded to try the spirits;[1] and directed, concerning such mischievous professors, not to receive them, nor bid them God speed.[2]

Again, all who profess the true religion do not exercise the brotherly love of true Christians. The wolves in sheep's clothing were enemies of the flock. Among others who had not their deadly designs, it was still true, even in the apostolic times, that iniquity abounded, and the love of many waxed cold.[3] In later times, the pages of what is called church history give accounts that contrast painfully with the beautiful exhibitions of brotherly love found in the Holy Scripture. Those who, according to their profession, ought to have laid down their lives for the brethren, have, in multitudes of instances, persecuted them unto death; and, while professing the true religion, have shed the blood of the saints.

From what has been said, it follows clearly that the church, the body of Christ, does not consist of all who profess the true religion. To constitute membership therein, the profession must proceed from love in the heart; in which case it will be manifested externally by obedience to his commandments. Only so far as this evidence of true discipleship appears, are we required, or even authorized, to exercise brotherly love.

Section IV.—ORGANIZATION.

THE CHURCH UNIVERSAL HAS NO EXTERNAL ORGANIZATION.

Organization has respect to action, and is an arrangement and adaptation of parts fitting them to act together to a common end. A society is said to be organized when its members are brought into such connection and relation, that they can act together as one body. A family is a society in which persons are connected with each other in the relations of husband and wife, parent and child. They act towards each other in these relations for the common

---

[1] 1 John iv. 1.   [2] 2 John 10.   [3] Matt. xxiv. 12.

good of the family, and each family stands as a distinct whole in the community. The tie of affection which unites the members of the family, is an internal bond of union; but superadded to this, there is an external organization which makes them one family, even though the internal tie of affection were severed. A nation is a society organized for the purpose of civil government, and the common good of the whole. The members may all love their laws, institutions, and governors; and patriotism, an internal bond of union, may make them one. But an external organization is superadded which would constitute them one nation, even if patriotism failed. A local church is an assembly of believers organized for the worship and service of God. Internal piety is a bond of union; but while piety and brotherly love would bind them equally to saints of other churches, they have an external organization which brings them into special relation to each other, and constitutes them one church.

Believers in Christ may be regarded as composing one family. God is their Father, and all they brethren; but the relationship is spiritual. Believers in Christ compose a nation, a holy nation, over which Christ is the king. They obey his laws, and strive to gain conquests in his cause, but they fight not with carnal weapons; and the bond of their union to each other and to their king is spiritual. The members of a local church may be known by the record of their names in the church book; but the church of the first born are written in heaven, and no record on earth determines their membership. It may be known by their fruits of righteousness, but these are the fruit of the Spirit which dwells and operates in each member, and by immersion in which they are formed into one body.

In the preceding section, the unity of the church universal was proved to be spiritual. Unity may exist in material bodies without organization. A pebble is one, though its parts are not organically united; but in living bodies the parts are organically united, and the organism is necessary to their vitality. The church is called the body of Christ: and the members operate on each other and co-operate with each other like the members of the human body; but the organism is spiritual. The qualification of every member to occupy his proper place and perform his proper duties, is ascribed to the Holy Spirit, who divides to every man severally

9

as he will; and who operates in and through all. Christ is the head of this body, and every member is organically united to the head: but "he that is joined to the Lord is one spirit;" and, therefore, the organization is spiritual.

Theological writers have maintained the existence of what they call the Visible Church Catholic, consisting of all who profess the true religion. They regard this as distinct from the body of true saints, which they designate the Invisible Church. The propriety of this designation we have denied, on the ground that true religion is visible in its effects. But the question as to the propriety of the names used to designate these bodies, is altogether different from the question whether these bodies actually exist. We have maintained the existence of what theological writers have called the Invisible Church, consisting of all who are spiritually united to Christ. Is there another body consisting of all who profess the true religion?

The possibility of uniting all who profess the true religion in one mental conception, and of designating them by a collective name, cannot be disputed. In this way we conceive and speak of the vegetable kingdom, the animal kingdom, &c. If it were impossible to unite all who profess the true religion in one mental conception, the doctrine that a visible church Catholic exists would be an absurdity; but this no one will assert. The existence of such a body in our mental conception is one thing, and the existence of it in fact is another. All who profess the true religion do not form one body by mere juxtaposition, as a number of men gathered together form one assembly; but they are scattered abroad everywhere over the face of the earth. The simple fact that they are alike in professing the same religion is sufficient for the purpose of mental classification; but to constitute them really one body, some species of organization is necessary. Do they compose an organized body?

The Holy Scriptures contain no proof that the followers of Christ, after the dispersion of the church at Jerusalem, ever acted together as one externally organized society. Previous to their dispersion, they were of one heart and one soul, and they were one by juxtaposition as a congregated assembly, and they united as one body in the outward services of public worship, and in such church action as the election of deacons. After their dispersion, they continued to be of one heart and one soul; and they continued to act under the influence of one Spirit to one common end. Their spiritual union and their spiritual organization continued; but their external union and external organization ceased. They no longer constituted one assembly, and they never acted together as one society. They constituted separate local churches which acted independently in their distinct organizations, but never formally united in counsel or in action as one body.

The only fact in sacred history which at all favors the opinion that the churches acted in general council, is recorded in the 15th chapter of Acts. The church at Antioch sent messengers to the church at Jerusalem to consult on a point of duty. After consultation, the church at Jerusalem, with the apostles and elders, sent forth a decree which the disciples of Christ everywhere were required to observe. There is not the slightest intimation that delegates went from the other churches, which were now numerous, and scattered through different countries. The whole church met in the council: not the entire body of those in every place who professed the true religion, but the church at Jerusalem. To this church the messengers from Antioch were sent, and before this church they laid the question. When the decision was made, it was announced, not as the decision of the universal church assembled in general council by its delegates, but as the decision of the church at Jerusalem with the apostles and elders. The decision of this church would have been entitled to respect, as the oldest and best informed of all the churches, and especially in the present case, in which the disturbers of the church at Antioch had claimed the authority of established usage in this, the mother church. But the decree of the assembled body was sent forth with an authority above that of any single church or council of churches: "It seemed good to the HOLY GHOST, and to us."[1] The inspired apostles were present in this consultation, and their decision went forth with divine authority: "Whatsoever ye shall bind on earth shall be bound in heaven."[2] No ecclesiastical council can justly claim this synod at Jerusalem as a precedent for its action, unless it can also claim to act by inspiration, and send forth its decrees with the authority of the Holy Ghost.

---

[1] Acts xv. 28.   [2] Matt. xviii. 18.

No ecclesiastical organization of modern times can, with any show of propriety, claim to be the Visible Church Catholic. No one of them includes all who profess the true religion. Some of them may claim to be THE CHURCH; but most of them have more modest pretensions, and claim to be only branches of the church. Each branch, however, has its own organization, and all the branches do not unite in one organized whole. Were there a combination of all the separate ecclesiastical organizations into one body, and were this body to act as an organized whole, it would possess no authority from the Holy Scriptures; but no such combination does in fact exist. The state of the Christian world falsifies the doctrine.

The bishop of Rome and his adherents, claim to be the Catholic or universal church. They are united by external organization, for the organization itself points out the head, the subordinate officers, and the members of the body. These hold their several positions, whatever may be their moral or spiritual qualifications. The organization is a strong one, as the history of its acts demonstrates; and this history, stained with blood, equally demonstrates that the body is not energized by the spirit of peace and love. This external organization needed an external head, and the bishop of the imperial city became the acknowledged vicar of Jesus Christ. Sitting in the temple of God, and showing himself that he is God, he claims a headship which belongs exclusively to the Lord Jesus Christ. This assumption of power is founded on the doctrine of the visible church Catholic. Destroy the foundation, and nothing remains for the superstructure to stand on. We have, therefore, good reason to regard the doctrine with suspicion, and to examine carefully its claims on our faith.

It will be instructive to notice how naturally the papal usurpation arose out of this doctrine. On the supposition that Christ instituted a universal church of external organization, the declarations and promises which have respect to his spiritual church, would naturally be applied to this external body. It would appear incredible that he should leave this body to degeneracy and corruption, after having promised to be with it always to the end of the world, and that the gates of hell should never prevail against it; and after having constituted and declared it the pillar and ground of the truth. If external organization connects the universal church with the church of apostolic times, it will be difficult, if not impossible, to set aside the pretensions of the Romanists. We may argue that they have lost the doctrine and the spirit of the apostles; but if the church is a body of external organization, the continuity of the organization must determine the true church. If its failure to preserve the truth and spirit of the primitive times has unchurched it; then these last attributes are the distinguishing characteristics of the true church, rather than external organization. Here, then, is the grand controversy between Christ and Antichrist. Jesus Christ has not two universal churches. He is not the head of two bodies, the husband of two wives. His true church is a spiritually organized body, and spiritually joined to him its only head. The body claiming to be the church on the ground of external organization is a substitute, and its head is a substitute for Christ. They first take the place of the true church and its true head, and afterwards oppose and persecute. They who see and deplore the mischief which the papal usurpation has wrought, should learn the secret of its power. The substitution of ecclesiastical organization for spiritual religion has wrought all the evil. Let the pernicious effects teach us to guard against the cause which produced them.

The doctrine of the visible church catholic, is much favored by the use of the epithet *visible*. Things are predicated of the true church which cannot be true of an invisible body. Saul persecuted the church, and this he could not have done if the church had been invisible. We fully admit the visibility of the church, but we distinguish between visibility and organization. Herod persecuted the infants of Bethlehem; but it does not follow that those babes composed an organized society. The rage of the persecuting Saul was directed against the saints, and not against their ecclesiastical organization. To have disbanded their external organization, would not have disarmed his rage. This they might have retained, if they had blasphemed the name of Jesus and renounced his doctrine. The truth and spirit of Christianity are hateful to the world; and without external organization, have been sufficiently visible to awaken the opposition and rage of persecutors.

An argument for an externally organized universal church, is derived from 1 Cor. xii. 28: "God hath set some in the church; first, apostles; secondarily, prophets; thirdly, teachers; after that miracles; then gifts of healings, helps, governments, diversities of tongues." The universal church is here meant, and the offices enumerated imply that the body to which they belong is organized; but the organization is not external. The church which includes all who profess the true religion, contains bad members, and bad officers, as well as good ones. Even in the primitive times, there were, among those who professed the true religion, false apostles and false prophets; pastors who devoured the flock; teachers who brought in damnable heresies; and governments that lorded it over God's heritage, and loved to have the pre-eminence. Considering the church as an externally organized society, these men were as truly officers in it as the most self-denying of its ministers. In the Roman church, the pontiff holds the supreme place, whatever may be his moral character. The priests hold the sacraments, and dispense their mysterious benefits, however unclean may be their hands. If a similar organization existed in apostolic times, the false apostles and other ungodly officers were truly members of the church. Now, did God "set" such men in the church? Did he set them there "for the perfecting of the saints, for the work of the ministry, for the edifying of the body of Christ?" Such men were not the ministers of God, but ministers of Satan, transforming themselves into ministers of righteousness; and the church which excludes them from its boundaries must have those boundaries determined, not by external organization, but by genuine piety. With this view, the whole context of the passage agrees. The qualifications for the officers enumerated are mentioned in the first verses of the chapter, and attributed to the Holy Spirit, dividing, not according to the vote of the church, but according to his own will. The members are brought into the body by immersion in the Spirit; and the sympathy which pervades the body is spiritual. It is no objection to this view, that some of the offices enumerated have respect to local churches, which are confessedly bodies of external organization. The man who labors in the pastorship or government of a local church, if called of God to his office, is a member of the true universal church, and qualified for his office by the Spirit that pervades and animates that body, and is required to labor with reference to the good of the whole. The local church to which he belongs, if organized according to the mind of Christ, consists of real saints; and he labors to introduce no others into their fellowship. He officiates to them as members of Christ's body, and does not bound his aims by the local organization. So Paul taught the elders of Ephesus to consider themselves laboring for the whole redeemed church: "Take heed therefore unto yourselves, and to all the flock, over the which the Holy Ghost hath made you overseers, to feed the church of God, which he hath purchased with his own blood."[1] So Peter taught the elders whom he addressed: "Feed the flock of God which is among you. * * * * Neither as being lords over God's heritage."[2] Every faithful pastor shares in the universal pastoral commission given to Peter: "Feed my sheep—feed my lambs." Though laboring for a part of the flock, he labors for the good of the whole. He who, in his official labors, limits his view to the local organization with which he is connected, and which is temporary in its duration, degrades his office; and so far yields to the antichristian spirit which substitutes external organization for spiritual religion, and a visible for an invisible head.

The opinion has been held, almost as a theological axiom, that baptism is the door into the church. It is not the door into the spiritual universal church; for men enter this by regeneration, and are, therefore, members of it before they are fit subjects for baptism. It is not the door into a local church; for, though it is a prerequisite to membership, men may be baptized, and remain unconnected with any local church. But those who hold that there is a visible church catholic, commonly maintain that it receives and includes all the baptized. They differ among themselves respecting the extent and boundaries of the church, because they differ as to what constitutes valid baptism. Since Baptists admit nothing to be valid baptism but immersion on profession of faith, those of them who hold the doctrine of a visible church catholic, make this church substantially identical with the Baptist denomination. This Baptist modification of the doctrine was its earliest form. While immersion was the universal practice of the churches, and infant baptism had not yet prevailed; before sprinkling was substituted for baptism, and babes for believers; the notion obtained, that the kingdom is the visible church catholic, and that men are

---

[1] Acts xx. 28.   [2] 1 Peter v. 1, 3.

born into it by water. In this notion, Pedobaptism and Popery originated.

Much mischief to the cause of truth has resulted from a misinterpretation of the words of Christ just referred to: "Except a man be born of water and of the Spirit, he cannot enter into the kingdom of God."[1] Not a word is said in this text about baptism and not a word in the whole discourse, of which this verse is a part, leads to the supposition that baptism was intended. But it is not necessary for our present purpose to enter into a discussion of this question. If we admit that the phrase "born of water" intends baptism, it is clear that this alone does not introduce into the kingdom; for it is also an indispensable condition, that a man be born of the Spirit. We have, therefore, the boundaries of the church so narrowed, that it includes none but those who have been both regenerated and baptized.

Persons who have been both regenerated and baptized, are the baptized part of the true universal church; but they do not of themselves constitute a church. They are not the generic church of Mr. Courtney. Each local church is liable to contain false professors; and, therefore, the genus of local churches does not consist of regenerated persons exclusively. They are not the visible church catholic of theologians. This body consists of all who profess the true religion; and, therefore, includes false professors as well as true Christians. Besides, these regenerated and baptized persons do not, in the sense of theological writers, compose a *visible* church. Their regeneration is a spiritual qualification, and is not determined by outward ceremony or external organization. This baptized part of the true spiritual church is as invisible, in the technical sense of the term, as the entire body called the invisible church. No man can say with infallible certainty of any one, though baptized, that he is born of the Spirit. These regenerated and baptized persons do not compose the universal church of the Holy Scriptures; and the church that Christ loved and gave himself for, includes many who, like the penitent thief on the cross, never received baptism. They will form a part in the general ecclesia of the heavenly city; and God will be glorified in them by Jesus Christ, throughout all ages, world without end. This

---

[1] John iii. 5.

universal church is not limited to the baptized; and in no proper sense does the baptized part of it constitute an ecclesia. The true universal church includes the *whole* company of those who are saved by Christ; and their spiritual organization is not dependent on outward ceremony.

SECTION V.—PROGRESS AND DURATION.

THE CHURCH UNIVERSAL IS IN PROGRESS OF CONSTRUCTION, AND WILL BE COMPLETED AT THE END OF THE WORLD, AFTER WHICH IT WILL ENDURE FOR EVER.

The words of the Saviour, "On this rock will I build my church," prove that the building was not then completed. In another place, speaking of the church under the figure of a fold: "Other sheep I have, which are not of this fold: them also I must bring, and they shall hear my voice; and there shall be one fold, and one shepherd."[1] The calling of the gentiles, and the introduction of them into the privileges of the gospel, are here intended. By the ministry of the word accompanied with the influence of the Holy Spirit, great multitudes were converted in the days of the apostles. These converts are described by Peter as lively or living stones, built on Christ the living stone disallowed of men, but chosen of God and precious.[2] Paul uses the same figure; and both of these inspired writers speak of the edifice as a *growing* temple.[3] The work is still in progress; and innumerable multitudes are yet to be gathered, who are to complete the glorious structure. On the last day, when all the redeemed shall have been brought in, Jesus will present them to the Father: "Behold, I and the children which God hath given me."[4] This will be the church completed in number, sanctified and glorified, a glorious church, without spot, wrinkle, or any such thing. The church will remain throughout eternity: "Unto him be glory in the church by Christ Jesus throughout all ages, world without end."[5]

Some difficulty exists in determining the date at which the church of Christ may be properly said to have commenced. The

---

[1] John x. 16.   [2] 1 Peter ii. 4, 5.   [3] Eph. ii. 21.
[4] Heb. ii. 13.   [5] Eph. iii. 21.

same difficulty exists respecting the beginning of the gospel, and of Christ's mediatorial reign. Mark dates the beginning of the gospel of Jesus Christ from the ministry of John the Baptist;[1] but Paul says that the gospel was before preached unto Abraham.[2] The reign of Christ is dated from the time of his exaltation at the right hand of the Father; yet saints were saved by his mediation, and he was David's Lord, under the former dispensation. So Christ said, " on this rock will I build my church," as if the work was still future; and yet the edifice is said to be built on the foundation of the prophets, as well as of the apostles.[3] The Scriptures represent a gathering of all things under Christ, both in heaven and on earth,[4] at the time of his exaltation in human nature to supreme dominion. The Old Testament saints who had been saved by the efficacy of his blood before it was shed, and who had desired to understand what the Holy Ghost signified when it testified to their prophets concerning the sufferings of Christ, and the glory which should follow, were waiting in heaven for the unfolding of this mystery. Moses and Elias evinced their interest in this theme, when, during their brief interview with the Saviour on the mount of transfiguration, they discoursed of the decease which he was to accomplish at Jerusalem.[5] The angels had desired to look into this mystery, but the fulness of time for its disclosure did not arrive until the man Christ Jesus entered the heavenly court, and was crowned with glory and honor. Then the angels gathered around and worshipped the Son. Then the saints drew near, and adored him as their Lord and Saviour. The proclamation was made throughout the courts of glory, and every inhabitant of heaven rendered willing homage to the Mediator. The Holy Spirit brought the proclamation down to Jerusalem on the day of Pentecost, that it might go thence through all the earth. They who gladly received it, were received into his royal favor, made citizens of the heavenly Jerusalem, and members of the great ecclesia.

In the words of Christ before cited, the church is represented as a building. The beginning of an edifice may be dated back to the first movement in preparing the materials. In this view the

---

[1] Mark i. 1, 2.   [2] Gal. iii. 8.   [3] Eph. ii. 20.
[4] Eph. i. 10.   [5] Luke ix. 31.

church was begun, when Abel, Enoch, Noah, and Abraham first exercised faith. But in another view, the building was commenced when the materials were brought together in their proper relation to Jesus Christ. To the Old Testament saints, until gathered under Christ with the saints of the present dispensation, Paul attributes a sort of incompleteness, which may be not unaptly compared to the condition of building materials not yet put together : " These all, having obtained a good report through faith, received not the promise : God having provided some better thing for us, that they without us should not be made perfect." [1]

Section VI.—RELATION TO CHRIST'S KINGDOM.

The doctrine of the Scriptures concerning the kingdom of Christ, has been investigated in the Manual of Theology, pp. 221–229. The result of the investigation, so far as our present subject is concerned, may be briefly stated as follows :—

The kingdom of Christ is the kingly authority with which he, as mediator, is invested, and which he exercises over all things, for the glory of God and the good of his church. The peculiarities of this divine reign are, that it is exercised in human nature, and that it grants favor to rebels. An incomplete administration of it commenced, immediately after the fall of man ; but the full development was not made till the man Christ Jesus was crowned with glory and honor, and seated at the Father's right hand. The subjects of his reign are divided into two classes ; the obedient, and the disobedient. To the obedient, all the blessings of his reign are promised ; and the disobedient, he will ultimately gather out of his kingdom, and banish to everlasting misery. The obedient subjects of his reign, are the same persons that compose the church universal, which has been defined " the whole company of those who are saved by Christ." For the benefit of this church, his kingly authority over all things is exercised.

As theological writers have maintained that there is a visible church catholic, distinct from the spiritual universal church of the Scriptures ; so some of them have maintained that there is a visible kingdom of Christ, a society of external organization, into which

---

[1] Heb. xi. 39, 40.

men enter by baptism. But the kingdom of Christ is not a society of men, bound together by external organization, like a family, a nation, or a local church. This view of it is not authorized by the Holy Scriptures.

The kingdom of Christ is properly the kingly authority with which he is invested; and the phrase is used, by metonymy, to denote the subjects of his reign, and especially the obedient subjects on whom the blessings of his reign are conferred. But the tie which binds these obedient subjects to their king, and his reign, is internal. "Every one that is of the truth, heareth my voice."[1] These men constitute a holy nation, a nation bringing forth the fruits of the kingdom; but they are not made a nation by external organization.

Jesus said, "My kingdom is not of this world."[2] We are not to understand this declaration to imply, that his reign had nothing to do with the men and things of this world. The other sentence just quoted, which was spoken in connection with this declaration, "Every one who is of the truth, heareth my voice," claimed the men who receive and love the truth as the subjects of his kingly authority. Having all power in heaven and earth committed to him, he rules in the army of heaven, and among the inhabitants of the earth. Hence every relation among men, and all the duties arising from it, come under his authority. The family, the nation, and the local church, are all institutions in his kingdom, or under his reign; and the external organization of these institutions should be regulated according to the will of the sovereign king; but the kingdom itself exists, independent of all external organization.

Some passages of Scripture have been supposed to favor the opinion, that the kingdom of Christ is a society of external organization, including good men and bad. The kingdom of heaven is compared to a net cast into the sea, which brought good fish and bad to the shore;[3] to a sower, who sowed seed that fell in bad ground as well as in good;[4] to a field, which contained tares as well as wheat.[5] These parables are designed to illustrate important truths connected with the reign of Christ. The *gospel* of the kingdom was

---

[1] John xviii. 37.　　　[2] John xviii. 36.　　　[3] Matt. xiii. 47—50.
[4] Matt. xiii. 3—8.　　　[5] Matt. xiii. 24—30.

to be preached to every creature; and the commission to preach it, was accompanied with the declaration, "He that believeth, and is baptized, shall be saved; but he that believeth not, shall be damned."[1] However variously men may be affected by the word preached, and however difficult it may be to distinguish their true character, and separate the bad from the good in the present life. the separation will be made in the last day, and none will be a mitted to enjoy the blessings of the reign but obedient subjects To suppose an organized religious society, including good men and bad, to be intended by the net which enclosed good fish and bad, or the field containing tares and wheat, is to overstrain and mis-apply the parables. The Saviour does not so explain them. The field is the world, and not an organized *society* in the world. The command was given that the tares and wheat should be per-mitted to grow together until the harvest, which is the end of the world. Then the King will sit in judgment on the whole world, and not on a particular society in it; and will separate the good from the bad, whom he has permitted to remain together in his kingdom. Then he will remove out of his kingdom all that offends; and will say concerning his enemies, in the midst of whom he now reigns, "Those mine enemies, which would not that I should reign over them, bring hither, and slay them before me."[2] Yet it is the will of the King that bad men and good should be permitted to remain together *in the world*; but instead of commanding that they should be permitted to grow together in religious association with each other, he commands his followers, "Come out from among them, and be ye separate."[3] Moreover, though the tares and the wheat grow together in the field, the tares are called the children of the wicked one; and the good seed, the children of the kingdom. The kingdom does not embrace the good and bad alike, as sustaining the same relation to it; but a society embraces all its members, irrespective of their moral character.

Families, nations, and local churches, are societies of external organization; and they are organized for the present world. At the end of the world, all these organizations will cease. The king-dom of Christ is not of this world; but at the end of the world, when earthly organizations shall have passed away, he will gather

---

[1] Mark xvi. 16. [2] Luke xix. 27. [3] 2 Cor. vi. 17.

the wicked out of his kingdom; and the kingdom itself, freed from all rebellious subjects, will continue for ever. Then shall the righteous, who alone are the children of the kingdom, shine as the sun, in the kingdom of their Father.

Section VII.—RELATION TO LOCAL CHURCHES.

If none but true believers were admitted into the churches, there would be an exact agreement between the character of the membership in the local churches, and in the church universal. And if all believers professed their faith without delay according to the law of Christ, and united with the local churches, the aggregate membership of the local churches, and that of the universal church, so far as it exists on earth, would be identical. Nothing but disobedience to the law of Christ gives occasion to distinguish between the church universal, and the great body of professing Christians united in the several local churches; and in a pure state of Christianity, the distinction might be overlooked. When the church universal was spoken of in the times of the apostles, the thoughts of men were naturally directed to the great body of professing Christians; and for all the ordinary purposes of speaking and writing, the distinction between this aggregate of professors and the true body of Christ was unnecessary. So when we speak of a wheat-field, we disregard the fact that tares may be here and there intermixed with the wheat. The name does not signify this intermixture, but is applied as if nothing but wheat were in the enclosure. In like manner, the name church was used in some cases for the aggregate of Christian professors, although in its strict signification, false professors are not included.

The fact that the same name ecclesia that is applied to local churches, is also applied to the church universal, is liable to mislead into the opinion that the membership must be strictly homogeneous; and, therefore, the universal church must include false professors as well as the local churches. So the name *brass*, denotes the same mixture of metals, whether it is applied to a large mass or a small one. The cases, however, are not analogous. The name brass denotes the metal without respect to its quantity, and is as applicable to a particle as to a mass. But the name ecclesia does not denote the material of which a church is composed, and is not applicable to a single member. It signifies the quantity rather than the quality. There may be an ecclesia of wicked men as well as of righteous. It applies to a local church, because the members of it actually assemble; and it applies to the church universal, because the members of it will actually assemble in the presence, and for the everlasting worship of God. The mere fact that the same name is applied, gives no ground for the conclusion that the membership in the two cases is strictly homogeneous. In the epistles to the local churches, the members are addressed as saints and faithful men in Christ. This was their character according to their profession, and what they ought to be according to the law of Christ. False professors who might chance to be among them, were not of them. When excluded, they were not deprived of rights which had belonged to them. Hence, the churches were addressed as if composed entirely of true Christians.

Though unconverted persons are not entitled to membership according to the law of Christ, they nevertheless obtain admittance into local churches through human fallibility. Membership in the church universal is determined by God himself. When Paul described the Hebrew saints as come "to the church of the first born," he described them as come also "to God, the judge of all." The infallible judge determines membership in the great ecclesia; but fallible men admit to membership in the local churches. Hence, a corrupt element finds entrance into local churches, and because of it they are not strictly homogeneous with the universal spiritual church. This want of homogeneousness existed in some degree, even in the purest age of Christianity; but it became much more manifest when corruption overspread the churches, and the evils attending it are now painfully felt by the lovers of Zion.

CHAPTER IV.

INFANT MEMBERSHIP.

WE have ascertained that believers in Christ are the only persons who have a Scriptural right to membership in the Christian churches. But this right has been claimed for infants; and the number, talents, and piety of those who make the claim, entitle the arguments by which they defend it, to a careful and thorough examination.

SECTION I.—DIRECT ARGUMENTS FOR INFANT MEMBERSHIP.

Argument 1.—In epistles written to church-members, Paul addresses children; and, at the same time, exhorts the parents to bring them up in the nurture and admonition of the Lord. It is clear, therefore, that young children were among the church-members to whom these epistles were written. If such children were in these churches, it cannot be doubted that they were in all the churches, and that they were admitted in infancy.

Because children were addressed in an epistle directed to a church, it does not necessarily follow that they were members of the church. As parents were required to bring up their children in the nurture and admonition of the Lord, the same epistle that enjoined this duty on the parents, might appropriately contain a direct command from the Lord, requiring the children to obey their parents. In performing the duty enjoined on them, the parents would naturally and properly take their children with them to the public worship of the church, where the apostolic epistles would be read in their hearing. The fact, therefore, that an apostolic command was addressed to them, proves nothing more than that the apostle expected it to reach them, and claimed the right of commanding them in the name of the Lord.

But the probability is, that the children whom Paul addressed were members of the church. The command, " Obey your parents *in the Lord,*"[1] is so expressed, as apparently to imply that the obligation was to be felt and acknowledged by them, because of their relation to the Lord. The children to whom Paul addressed this command must have possessed intelligence to apprehend its meaning, and piety to feel the force of the motive presented in these words, " For this is well pleasing unto the Lord."[2] Timothy, from a child, had known the Holy Scriptures. Intelligent piety has, in all ages, been found in children who have not yet reached maturity; and such children have a Scriptural right to church-membership.

The argument that the children were so young as to need the care and discipline of their parents to bring them up in the nurture and admonition of the Lord, does not prove that they were destitute of personal piety. Adult church-members need instruction and discipline adapted to their circumstances; and the instruction and discipline of wise and pious parents are of inestimable advantage to their pious children.

The argument contains a fallacy which deserves to be noticed, in the assumption, that the children who were commanded to obey, and the children who were to be brought up in the nurture and admonition of the Lord, were the same. Masters were commanded how to treat their servants, and servants were commanded to obey their masters; but it would be wrong to infer that no masters were so commanded but those who had pious servants, or that no servants were so commanded but those who had pious masters. On the contrary, those servants who had believing masters are distinguished from those whose masters were unbelievers; and yet the latter class were commanded to obey, as well as the former. The relation of master and servant existed, in some cases, when both of the parties were members of the church; and, in other cases, when one party was in the church and the other party out of the church. No proof exists, that the relation of parent and child may not have been divided in the same manner. Parents were not commanded to bring up their children in the nurture and admonition of the Lord because the children were church-members; and

---

[1] Eph. vi. 1.   [2] Col. iii. 20.

10

children were not commanded to obey their parents because the parents were church-members. The supposition, therefore, that the children in the two cases were the same, is an assumption without proof.

The inference that, if there were children in the primitive churches, they were admitted in infancy, and not because of personal piety, is illegitimate. It cannot be made to appear that they were destitute of personal piety; and, as this was the established condition of church-membership in all other cases, the fair inference is that their membership in the church stood on the common ground.

Argument 2.—The King of Zion has expressly declared, in Matt. xix. 14, that the privileges of his kingdom belong to infants; and, among these privileges, that of church-membership must be included. Children are to be received in the name of Christ, or because they belong to Christ;[1] and this must imply that they are members of his church.

In interpreting and applying the phrase, "Of such is the kingdom of heaven," an important question must be decided; whether the word "such" denotes literal children, or persons of child-like disposition. As the clause stands in our common version, it seems to import that the kingdom consists of such persons exclusively. Now, no one imagines that the kingdom is a community consisting of literal infants only; and, therefore, this rendering, if retained, greatly favors the other interpretation, according to which the whole community are properly described as persons of child-like disposition. The disciples of Christ are humble, confiding, teachable, and free from malice and ambition; and these qualities characterize all who have a part in the kingdom.

But the advocates of infant church-membership have proposed another rendering of the clause. They remark that it corresponds, in grammatical construction, with the clause in Matt. v. 3: "Theirs is the kingdom of heaven;" but, since the word "such" has no genitive in English corresponding to the genitive "theirs," the sense must be expressed thus: "To such belongs the kingdom of heaven." After a careful consideration, I am inclined to think that this rendering gives the true sense of the passage. It makes it analogous to the clause in Matt. v. 3; while the other rendering

---

[1] Mark ix. 37.

is, I think, without any analogy in the New Testament. The kingdom does not consist wholly of its subjects; but it has also its king, its laws, its privileges, and its enjoyments. We have Scripture analogy for saying, that the subjects receive the kingdom, enter into the kingdom, inherit the kingdom, and have part in the kingdom; but none for saying that they compose or constitute the kingdom. Hence the rendering, "To such the kingdom belongs," is recommended to our adoption, as the best interpretation of the Saviour's words. So much having been granted to the advocates of infant church-membership, we proceed to inquire into the true sense of the passage.

In the parallel passage, "theirs is the kingdom of heaven," the persons intended are "the poor in spirit;" and these include all the loyal subjects of the kingdom. If the parallelism between the passages is complete, the word "such" must, in like manner, include all the loyal subjects of the Redeemer's reign, and cannot therefore signify literal children. But if we take the word "such," to signify *a part* only of those to whom the kingdom belongs, we shall still be compelled to consider the declaration as importing that the kingdom belongs to *all* such. Nothing in the words, nothing in the context, nothing in the nature of the subject, leads to the supposition that the kingdom belongs to some infants, and not to others. But the most consistent advocates of infant church-membership, do not admit all infants indiscriminately. If the word "such" was intended to signify any qualifications for membership, peculiar to these children, and not found in all children, no clue whatever has been left us, in the whole context, for ascertaining what these peculiar qualifications were. If Jesus had designed to instruct his apostles how to discriminate between the children to be admitted, and all other children, it is unaccountable that he should have given his instruction with so much obscurity and indefiniteness.

The words demand an interpretation, which will make the term "such" include all who have a right to the kingdom, and no others; and this is precisely the interpretation to which the context leads. Immediately after uttering the words, Jesus explained them: "Whosoever shall not receive the kingdom of God as a little child, he shall not enter therein."[1] To be a little child, and

---

[1] Mark x. 15; Luke xviii. 17.

to act as a little child, are different things; and the latter, not the former, is what the Saviour intended. His explanation shows this clearly; and that the explanation was made, we are expressly informed by Mark and Luke. Matthew has omitted it; but he has recorded, in the preceding chapter, a discourse of Christ on the same subject, giving the same instruction fully and clearly: "At the same time came the disciples unto Jesus, saying, Who is the greatest in the kingdom of heaven? And Jesus called a little child unto him, and set him in the midst of them, and said, Verily I say unto you, except ye be converted and become as little children, ye shall not enter into the kingdom of heaven. And whoso shall receive one such little child in my name, receiveth me. But whoso shall offend one of these little ones which believe in me, it were better for him that a millstone were hanged about his neck, and that he were drowned in the depth of the sea."[1] Here, a child is made the representative of him who was to be greatest in the kingdom; and the phrase, "one such child," denotes one who possesses a child-like disposition. Jesus was accustomed to call his disciples "little children;"[2] and he here calls them, "these little ones which believe in me." In this discourse, no room was left for doubt as to the import of the phrase, "one such child," and this discourse had prepared the minds of the disciples to understand his meaning, when he afterwards said, "To such the kingdom belongs," even if no explanation had followed; but when he added an explanation, reiterating the very teaching which he had before given, no doubt ought to remain, that the same kind of qualification for his kingdom was intended—not literal childhood, but a child-like disposition.

A further demand for this interpretation is found in the nature of Christ's kingdom. Those who suppose literal children to be intended, assume that the kingdom is the visible church catholic; and they understand that membership in this body is here affirmed to belong to infants. Our inquiries in the last chapter have brought us to the conclusion, that Christ's kingdom is not identical

---

[1] Matt. xviii. 6.

[2] John xiii. 33. In the original text a different word is here employed, which seems to have been more appropriate for the expression of endearment. Its literal meaning agrees with that of the other term, and is properly given by our translators in the words "little children."

with the visible church catholic of theological writers; and that such a body as this does not in fact exist. In Christ's kingdom, there are two classes of subjects; the loyal, and the disobedient. To the former class exclusively, the kingdom belongs, according to the uniform teaching of the Scriptures; and the passage under consideration corresponds precisely with this teaching, if persons of child-like disposition be intended. But if the kingdom belongs to literal infants, who are such by natural birth, it must be a different kingdom from that of which Jesus discoursed to Nicodemus, when he said, "Except a man be born again, he cannot see the kingdom of God."

Some persons understand the clause under consideration to import that the kingdom of glory belongs to little children; and they argue that if they have a right to the church in heaven, they ought not to be shut out from the church on earth. But infants have not an unconditional right to the kingdom of glory. If they die in infancy, they are made fit for that kingdom and received into it; but if they remain in this world till they grow up, they cannot obtain that kingdom without repentance and faith. Since the right of children to the kingdom of glory depends on the condition, either that they die in infancy or that they become penitent believers, no inference can be legitimately drawn from it that they have a present and unconditional right to membership in the church on earth. Children are not taken to heaven without being made fit for it; but churches on earth are organized for the worship and service of God, and infants are not fitted for these duties. Even the privileges of the church on earth they are confessedly unfit for. A right to baptism is claimed for them, but a right to communion at the Lord's table is not; yet without this right, it cannot be said that the church or kingdom belongs to them. If by any mode of inference from the passage the right of infants to the church on earth can be established, it must include a right to communion at the Lord's table.

It has been objected to our interpretation of this passage, that the word "such," properly denotes the kind or quality of the thing to which it is applied, and not the resemblance which something else bears to it. In proof of this, such passages as the following have been cited: "Because they suffered such things."[1]

---

[1] Luke xiii. 2.

"With many such parables spake he unto them."[1] In the first example, *such things* means *these very things;* and in the second, *such parables* means *these parables and others like them.* In like manner it is argued, *such children* must mean either *these very children* or *these children and others like them.* Hence, it is alleged that an interpretation which excludes the children present from the import of the word "such," is inadmissible.

It is true that the word *such* denotes the kind or quality of the thing to which it is applied; but just so far as it does this, it denotes also the resemblance which another thing bears to it, if that other thing is of the same kind or possesses the same quality. It denotes the kind or quality of the thing, and not the thing itself. In this particular, it differs from *this* or *these.* If the first of the above examples had read "because they suffered *these things,*" the identical sufferings would have been signified, and not their kind or quality. Hence, *such* does not mean *these.* So in the other examples "such parables" does not mean *these and other parables,* for it denotes the kind and quality of the parables, and this the phrase *these and other* would not do. The fact that "such things" in the first example, denoted the identical sufferings which had just been mentioned, is not determined by the meaning of the word *such,* but by the connection in which it is used. Any other sufferings of like kind would suit the meaning of the word equally as well. So any parables of like kind equally suit the meaning of the phrase "such parables." The fact that the sufferings and parables previously mentioned are denoted by the word *such,* or included in its meaning, is accidental. *Such* does not mean *these,* and does not include *these* in its meaning, unless by accident. However frequent this accidental use of the term may be, its essential meaning refers to kind or quality, and not to particular things. When it is said, "They which commit such things, are worthy of death;"[2] the particular things that had been mentioned are not necessarily intended or included; but any things of like kind are denoted. In the words of Paul, "I would to God, that not only thou, but also all that hear me this day, were both almost, and altogether, such as I am, except these bonds."[3] The word such neither intends nor includes "I," but merely denotes likeness;

<hr>

[1] Mark iv. 33.   [2] Rom. i. 32.   [3] Acts xxvi. 29.

and that likeness is confined to spiritual endowments and privileges, and does not extend to the body or the external condition. So the word such in the case before us, does not intend or include the children present, but denotes a likeness to them; and that likeness does not respect the body or outward condition, but those mental qualities which made them fit representatives of converted men.

If we were unable to distinguish between the essential meaning of the word *such* and its accidental use, we might still be preserved from an erroneous conclusion in the present case by a due regard to Matt. xviii. 5. In this verse the same word is used by the same speaker with reference to the same subject, and in like circumstances, a little child being present as the children were present in the other case. Yet in this case, the word such does not intend or include the child present, but denotes those qualities in which that child was made a representative of converted persons. The verse preceding proves this: and the words which follow the use of the term *such* in the other case, prove the same. The analogy is complete, with the single exception that the explanation follows in one case, and precedes in the other. But it follows immediately as if uttered by the same breath, for it was spoken before Jesus laid hands on the children. If any importance can be attached to the order of time in which the explanation was given, it should be remembered that the whole of the discourse in the 18th chapter preceded the transaction recorded in the 19th, and prepared the minds of the disciples for understanding it. When all these facts are considered, we need not be staggered, though numerous examples be adduced in which *such* may appear to have a different meaning. True criticism will regard the analogy of the cases rather than their number; and if the word has different meanings, will prefer that which is supported by an analogy so remarkable and complete. But the truth is, criticism has no choice to make between different meanings of the word, for in every case the meaning of the word is the same.

If the criticism which we have set aside were just, it would fail to justify the conclusion that has been drawn from it. In the passage recorded in Luke ix. 47, 48, the word *such* is not used: "Jesus, perceiving the thought of their heart, took a child, and set him by him, and said unto them, Whosoever shall receive this child in my name, receiveth me; and whosoever shall receive me, receiveth him that sent me: for he that is least among you all, the same shall be great." Here the expression is, "this child;" but the meaning is not to be taken literally. The whole transaction was symbolical. The disciples had desired the highest place in their Master's kingdom. It was their ambition to sit on his right hand and on his left. But Jesus set the little child *by him*, and constituted that child his prime minister and representative: "Whoso shall receive," &c. All this was symbolical; and was designed to teach the disciples what they must be, to obtain the honor which they coveted. If criticism could convert the word *such* into *these*, and the clause, "of such is the kingdom," into *theirs is the kingdom;* there would be sufficient reason, even then, to regard the children as only symbols or representatives of converted or humble and child-like persons.

It has been further objected, that the clause, "for of such is the kingdom of heaven," could not, according to our interpretation, contain a reason for admitting into Christ's presence the children that were brought to him. We cheerfully grant, that the connection of this clause with what precedes would be quite obvious, if it could be shown to declare the right of infants to church-membership; and if it could also be shown that these infants were brought to Christ to be initiated into his church. This last has been supposed by some, but without any proof from the sacred narrative. The purpose for which they were brought to Jesus is thus expressed: "that he should put his hands on them, and pray;"[1] "that he should touch them."[2] If initiation into the church was the design, it is unaccountable that all the inspired writers should have failed to mention it, and that they should have described the act as performed with a different design. If it was usual for infants to be admitted to church-membership, the apostles must have known it; and their opposition, in the present case, is unaccountable. Moreover, if these infants were brought to be initiated into the church, and if Jesus declared their right to the privileges of his church, it cannot be supposed that they were sent away without the benefit desired. But were they initiated? If so, by what rite? Baptism has been considered the rite of initiation; but there is no evidence that these children were baptized. When Jesus made disciples,

---

[1] Matt. xix. 13.   [2] Mark x. 13; Luke xviii. 15.

they were baptized, not by himself, but by his disciples. There is no evidence that he put these children into the hands of the disciples, with a command to baptize them; but, on the contrary, he took them into his own arms, not to baptize, but to bless them.

On a careful examination of the passage, we discover that the conjunction "for" connects the clause which follows with the command, "forbid them not." This command was addressed to the disciples; and the reason which follows may be supposed to have been introduced for their sake, rather than for the sake of the children. He was displeased with his disciples, and designed to rebuke them. Now, to understand his rebuke, we must view it in connection with the fault of which the disciples had been guilty. They expected their Master to set up a temporal kingdom; and all his teachings to the contrary, and even his crucifixion at last, did not convince them that his kingdom is not of this world. They were ambitious to have the highest place in his kingdom; and this sinful ambition remained, till they ate the last passover with him. He had recently set a little child before them, and used it as a representative of the chief favorite in his kingdom. This discourse they had not understood. Like other discourses designed to explain the nature of the kingdom, and of the qualifications for it, the instruction which it contained was not properly received until after Christ's departure, when the Holy Spirit brought it to their remembrance. Ambition and worldly policy blinded their minds. How they understood the Saviour's discourse, we cannot certainly determine; but they seem, like the advocates of infant church-membership, to have understood the word *such* to refer to age, and not to moral qualities. Hence, the words, "Whoso receiveth one such child," placed little children before their minds as rivals for the highest place of dignity in the kingdom. Whether they feared that Christ would postpone the setting up of his kingdom until these young rivals should be of age, or whether they apprehended that he would, among the miraculous works which he performed, endow them supernaturally, even in infancy, for holding office in his kingdom, we have no means of ascertaining. But, whatever may have been their notions, they seem to have conceived a jealousy of these young rivals. The ministers of Eastern monarchs guarded the way of access to their sovereign. This right of guarding the way of approach to their Master, the disciples assumed on this occasion. Jesus, who never denied access to any that sought favor at his hands, was displeased with their conduct and the worldly ambition which instigated it. To them, and for their benefit, he said what may be thus paraphrased : " Suffer the children to come unto me, and forbid them not. Do not, by this usurpation of power, think to exclude these dreaded rivals from my presence and favor; for to such as these the privileges and honors of my kingdom belong, rather than to those who, like you, are actuated by worldly ambition. Instead of driving these children away, imitate their spirit; for whosoever shall not receive the kingdom as a little child, shall not enter therein."

Whether we have succeeded or not in discovering the true connection of the clause with what precedes, the clause itself does not affirm the right of infants to church-membership. The proofs which have been adduced on this point are clear and decisive.

What has been said, sufficiently explains Mark ix. 27, the other passage quoted in the argument. We admit that to receive one of such children in the name of Christ, is to receive him because he belongs to Christ; but the passage does not teach that literal infants are members of Christ's church. We have proved that the Saviour employed the phrase, *such children*, to denote persons of child-like disposition. Hence, the doctrine of infant church-membership cannot be inferred from the passage.

Some Congregationalists have held that children are members of the church universal, but not of local churches. This distinction may perhaps account for their admission to baptism, and exclusion from the Lord's supper; but it accounts in such a way as to show clearly, that the privileges of the kingdom do not belong to them. No one maintains that unregenerate infants are members of the spiritual church. If they are members of a universal church, it must be the visible church catholic. Now, if such a body exists, it never meets or acts; and the privileges of membership in it, to those who are denied membership in local churches—what are they? To the local churches belong the regular worship of God, a stated ministry, the benefits of discipline and mutual exhortation, and the communion of the Lord's table. The baptized children grow up, without the membership which entitles to these privileges. How, then, can it be said that the kingdom belongs to them?

Argument 3.—Paul declares, that the children of certain members of the Corinthian church were holy.[1] The word *holy*, or *saints*, was used by him to denote church-members, that is, persons consecrated to God. We have, therefore, ground for the conclusion, that these children were members of the church.

The passage referred to, reads as follows: "For the unbelieving husband is sanctified by the wife, and the unbelieving wife is sanctified by the husband: else were your children unclean; but now are they holy." This passage, if the holiness of which it speaks signifies church-membership, will prove too much. The word "sanctified," which is applied to the unbelieving husband and unbelieving wife, means *made holy*. These unbelievers, therefore, were also holy; and must, according to the interpretation, have been members of the church. The text is a process of reasoning; and the laws of reasoning require, that the term "holy" in the conclusion, should be used in the same sense as in the premises. If *holiness* implies church-membership, when predicated of the children, it must imply the same when predicated of the unbelieving husband and wife. But no one imagines that those unbelievers were members of the church; and, therefore, the holiness affirmed of the children, is not church-membership.

If it be asked, what holiness could be predicated of these children, or of the unbelieving husband and wife, which did not include church-membership—the answer is at hand. The Jews accounted gentiles unclean, and thought it unlawful to enter their houses, to keep company or eat with them, or to touch them. The Jewish Christians retained this opinion, as is manifest from Gal. ii. 12. According to this opinion, they with whom familiar intercourse was lawful, were considered holy; and all others were unclean. The question had arisen among the Corinthians, probably from the influence of Judaizing teachers, whether familiar intercourse with unbelievers is lawful.

In the fifth chapter of the epistle, Paul discusses this question, and decides that association in church-membership with such persons, was unlawful; but that ordinary intercourse with them must be admitted, or Christians "must needs go out of the world." As the principle which he opposed had produced a doubt among the

---

[1] 1 Cor. vii. 14.

Corinthians, whether it was lawful for Christians to live in familiar intercourse with unbelieving husbands or wives, Paul considers this case in the seventh chapter. He decides that, if this principle may disturb the domestic relations, it will separate parent and child, as well as husband and wife. If familiar intercourse with the unconverted is unlawful in one case, it is unlawful in the other also. This is the argument of the apostle; and it is precisely adapted to meet the difficulty. But this argument presupposes, that the children, like the unbelieving husband and wife, were not members of the church. The text, therefore, furnishes decisive proof, that infant church-membership was unknown in the time of the apostles.[1]

Argument 4.—The writers of the New Testament used words in the sense in which they were accustomed to read them in the Scriptures of the Old Testament. The Greek word Christ, corresponded to the Hebrew word Messiah; and both words denoted the same person. The Greek word *ecclesia*, was not a newly-invented term; but it was the word by which the LXX. had rendered the Hebrew *cahal*, of the Old Testament, and must therefore be understood to denote the same thing, the Congregation of the Lord. Hence the church was not a new organization. It was the Hebrew congregation, continued under the new dispensation; and, as children were included with their parents, in the former dispensation, the right of membership cannot now be denied to them. The identity of the church under both dispensations is further apparent in the fact, that the names Zion and Jerusalem, derived from the places where the Old Testament worshippers assembled, are given to the church of the New Testament.

It is true that the Hebrew word Messiah, and the corresponding Greek word Christ, denoted the same person; but it cannot be hence inferred as a universal truth, that identity, either of person or things, always attends identity or correspondence of name. The Hebrew name Joshua is applied in Scripture to different persons;[2] and the corresponding Greek name Jesus, is applied to persons different from these, and different from one another.[3] The English words assembly, convention, association, &c., are in common use as names of organized bodies; but the character of the organiza-

---

[1] For a more extended examination of 1 Cor. vii. 14, see a tract entitled "A Decisive Argument against Infant Baptism," published by the Southern Baptist Publication Society.

[2] Ex. xxiv. 13; Zech. iii. 1.   [3] Matt. i. 21; Col. iv. 11.

tion cannot be inferred from the name. The name Assembly sometimes signifies the legislative body of a state, and sometimes an ecclesiastical judicatory. With this name the Hebrew and Greek words for congregation and church very nearly correspond in signification; but were the correspondence perfect, it could not be inferred that organized societies denoted by them must be identical.

But the correspondence between the designations of the church and of the Hebrew congregation is not perfect. Two Hebrew words, קהל and עדה, were used to denote the Hebrew congregation, and neither of these is invariably rendered by the Greek word εκκλησια. In the sixth verse of Exodus 12, the chapter in which the Hebrew congregation first appears on the sacred page, both Hebrew words occur, and one of them the LXX have rendered πληθος, and the other συναγωγη. In Numbers xvi. 3, both words occur, and both are rendered συναγωγη. If any one should argue from hence, that whenever the New Testament writers use the words πληθος, and συναγωγη, they must mean the Hebrew congregation, he would err egregiously. The argument which would be so fallacious when applied to these words, cannot be valid when applied to εκκλησια.

The single words which we have noticed, are, when used to designate the bodies to which they are applied, often accompanied with adjuncts. The Hebrew congregation was called the Congregation of the Lord or Jehovah, and the Congregation of Israel. It was a congregation instituted for the worship of Jehovah as the God of the Hebrew nation. The church is called the church of God, and the church of Christ. These full designations of the two bodies are by no means coincident; but we have proof that the two bodies are not identical, which is far more to be relied on than a want of coincidence in their names.

When the New Testament church is first introduced in the sacred writings, Jesus calls it not the cahal or ecclesia of Israel, but my ecclesia. He moreover speaks of it as yet to be constructed: "On this rock will I build my ecclesia." It cannot be that he intended the cahal of Israel which was instituted in the time of Moses, and its organization completed in the most minute particulars. The next occurrence of the word ecclesia in the New Testament is still more remarkable: "Tell it to the ecclesia. If he will not hear the ecclesia, let him be, &c." Can it be true that the New Testament writer who recorded these words, understood the word ecclesia in the sense in which he had been accustomed to read it in the Scriptures of the Old Testament, as referring to the Hebrew cahal? Can it be that Jesus meant it to be so understood? Did he mean that his followers should refer their matters of grievance to the great congregation of Jewish worshippers, their enemies and persecutors, and be governed by their decision? Incredible! The next mention of the New Testament ecclesia is equally decisive: "The Lord added to the ecclesia such as should be saved." The time was the feast of Pentecost, when the worshippers of the Hebrew cahal were assembled at Jerusalem. From this assembly the converts to the new religion were made; and when made, they were added to the ecclesia. No proof more decisive can be desired; that the ecclesia to which they were added, was not the cahal to which they had previously belonged.

The argument from the name may be retorted with effect. When Jesus said, "Tell it to the church;" the Christian churches in which discipline was to be exercised had not yet been organized. The master of the family was still present to manage the affairs of the household by his direct authority; but he gave the command to be observed after his departure, as a perpetual rule of discipline. The unguarded manner in which he speaks of the ecclesia, furnishes proof of no inconsiderable force, that the word which he employed, was not at the time in familiar use as a name for the congregation of Jewish worshippers. Had it been, this application of the word would have been natural to the disciples, and some accompanying explanations would have been needed to guard them from mistake. When intending that which did not yet exist, of which they had no personal knowledge, and which never had existed, he would not, without explanation, have employed a term to denote it, with which they were familiar as the name of something that had long existed and was well known to them. The conclusion to which this argument tends, is strongly corroborated by the fact, that although the word ecclesia occurs in the New Testament more than a hundred times, it never, with but one exception, denotes the people of Israel; and in this single exception, "He that was in the ecclesia in the wilderness,"[1] it does not

---

[1] Acts vii. 38.

denote the people of Israel as an enduring organization, but refers to a particular time in their history, when they were assembled at Sinai to receive the law, and for this reason it should have been translated *assembly*. As an enduring body, they are called the house of Israel, the commonwealth of Israel, the people, the nation; but the ecclesia they are never called.

The passage, "In the midst of the ecclesia I will sing praise unto thee,"[1] is quoted from the Old Testament, where the word cahal is used, and where there is an allusion to the Hebrew congregation; but as used by Paul, the ecclesia intended consists of the "many sons" brought to glory, who are mentioned in the context. The same ecclesia is afterwards spoken of, "The church of the first born," with an apparent allusion to the assembly of Old Testament worshippers. This allusion may be readily accounted for by the fact, that the worship of the Old Testament dispensation was "a shadow of good things to come." Zion and Jerusalem were types of heaven, the future meeting place of the saints; and the congregation of Israel assembled for the worship of God, typified that future assembly in which the redeemed of the Lord shall come from the east, the west, the north, and the south, and shall sit down with Abraham, Isaac, and Jacob, in the kingdom of Heaven. This fully accounts for the use which the prophets have made of the names Zion and Jerusalem, in predicting the glory of the church.

The Hebrew cahal was an actual assembly. Three times in the year the tribes were required to meet for public worship in the place where the Lord would put his name.[2] This obligation continued as long as the ordinances of their worship were obligatory; and ceased when the handwriting of them was nailed to the cross of Christ. An intimation that the obligation to meet at Jerusalem was to cease, is given in the words of Christ to the women of Samaria: "The hour cometh, when ye shall neither in this mountain, nor yet at Jerusalem, worship the Father."[3] When men were no longer required to meet in Jerusalem, the cahal of Israel was dissolved.

The distinction between the church and the Hebrew congre-

---

[1] Heb. ii. 12. [2] Deut. xii. 5. [3] John iv. 21.

gation, may be further elucidated by an attentive consideration of the design with which the congregation was instituted.

Although, in the divine purpose, a sufficient sacrifice for sin had been provided from eternity, yet it did not seem good to Infinite Wisdom that it should be immediately offered, when sin first entered into the world. Four thousand years of ignorance and crime, God winked at, or overlooked as unworthy of his regard, or unfit for his purpose; and fixed his eyes on that period denominated "the fulness of time," when it would best display the divine perfections, for the Redeemer to atone for transgression; and repentance and remission of sins to be preached in his name, among all nations. As, in the exercises of an individual Christian, the discovery of salvation in Christ is withheld, until an anxiety is excited in his breast that makes the discovery welcome; so in the history of the world, the Messiah makes not his appearance, until mankind have felt the necessity of such a deliverer; then he comes, the desire of all nations. It pleased God that a full experiment should be made of man's power and skill to find a remedy for his moral disease, before God's remedy for the healing of the nations should be revealed and applied. "After that, in the wisdom of God, the world by wisdom knew not God, it pleased God, by the foolishness of preaching, to save them that believe."

The experiment which, in the wisdom of God, opened the way for the Redeemer's entrance into the world, was of a two-fold nature; or, rather, there were two distinct experiments, demonstrating distinct truths. When the bolder enemies of God and religion make their appeal from the volume of inspiration to the volume of nature, and assert the sufficiency of the latter to enlighten and direct them in the search after God; we can refer to actual experiment, to ascertain how far fallen man, without the oracles of God, can advance toward the knowledge of the Divine character. With the light of nature, the bright beams of science, and the keen eye of natural genius, the wisest men of antiquity still *felt* in the dark, after the unknown God.[1]

When those who profess to receive the truth, deny the doctrine of grace, and maintain that man has sufficient native virtue, if properly cultivated, to render him acceptable to God; that there are

---

[1] Acts xvii. 27.

influences of the Word or Spirit common to all men, which are sufficient, without any additional special influence, to bring him to know and enjoy the Most High; we have in the wisdom of God, another completed experiment, which decides against this doctrine, with as much certainty as is anywhere to be found within the limits of experimental philosophy. In the sacred record is the history of a people, who had the advantage over every other people much every way. They were not left to read the volume of nature only; but to them were committed the oracles of God. They were not left with unmeaning forms, and unauthorized rites of religion; but they had ordinances of divine service, instituted on the authority of God. "To them pertained the adoption, and the glory, and the covenants, and the giving of the law, and the service of God, and the promises." Nor were they without instructors in religion; but holy men were raised up among them, who spake as they were moved by the Holy Ghost. Neither were they without motives to obedience; but a covenant was made with them, containing every threat which might deter—every promise that might allure. The experiment was made fairly and completely. Jehovah himself said, "What could have been done more to my vineyard, that I have not done?" And what was the result? It was clearly demonstrated that man is totally depraved; that the best institutions, instructions, and motives, with all common influences of the Spirit, whatever such there may be, are altogether insufficient to restore his fallen nature; and that a direct special influence upon his heart, by the effectual working of Divine power, is indispensably necessary, in order to make him delight in the law of God, and render acceptable obedience to its holy requirements. See Heb. viii. 8, 9, 10.

That society of persons which was the subject of the last-mentioned experiment, is frequently denominated *the Congregation of the Lord.* It appears to have been the only divinely instituted society, organized for religious worship, that ever existed before the coming of Christ. That God designed by the Mosaic dispensation, of which this congregation was the subject, to give a clear demonstration of man's depravity, may be inferred from the end which has actually been accomplished, and from such declarations of Scripture as the following: "The law was added because of transgression until the seed should come. The law entered that

11

the offence might abound." Since unto God all his works from the beginning are known, he well knew the imperfections of the Mosaic covenant, even from the time of its institution, and what would be the result of the experiment. He found fault with it long before its abrogation; and so prepared it at first, that it typified and foretold a better covenant that should succeed it, established upon better promises.

The first account that the Scriptures give of the Congregation of the Lord, we find in the twelfth chapter of Exodus. When a new order of things was introduced; when the year received a new beginning, and became, as it has been called, the ecclesiastical year; when God *took his people by the hand*, to lead them out of the land of Egypt;[1] when that code of laws for the regulation of religious worship, which the apostle means by the first covenant throughout his epistle to the Hebrews, began to be promulgated; and the Passover, as one of the ordinances of divine service pertaining to the first covenant, was instituted; then, first, are the Israelites recognised as a worshipping congregation. Before this, the word of the Lord had come to individuals, and individuals had performed religious rites; but now, the word is sent to a whole congregation, and that congregation, by divine appointment, perform a rite of divine worship simultaneously. Before this, the Israelites had indeed been distinguished from the rest of mankind; but not by the characteristics of a worshipping society. That there were persons among them who worshipped God in sincerity and truth, will not be disputed. But where were their public altars? Where was their sanctuary? Where were their public ministers of religion? Where were their appointed sacrifices? Where their statute book, the laws of their worship, the rules of their society, &c.? A worshipping society, without forms, and rites, and rules of worship, God never constituted.

The seed of Abraham were destined to be the subjects of special dispensations, throughout all their generations. This appears no less in their history since the Christian era, and before their deliverance from Egyptian bondage, than in the intermediate time. But, during all this intermediate time, they were the subjects of that peculiar, experimental, preparatory dispensation, which we

---

[1] Heb. viii. 9.

have been considering. They were constituted, and continued to be, the Lord's peculiar cahal, his only worshipping congregation.[1] But while the ordinances of their worship were wisely contrived to be types and prophecies of Christ, at the same time that they afforded to the world that experiment, which appears to have been so important a part of their design; in like manner, an instructive intimation of the future exclusion of the Jews from gospel privileges, and of the admission of the gentiles, appears to have been given, in the character of the members who composed this sacred congregation. The great body of its constituents were the descendants of Abraham; but provision was made in its charter, that Israelites in some cases should be excluded, and that gentiles might be admitted.[2] Nothing like this can be found in the covenant made with Abraham and his seed, as recorded in the 17th chapter of Genesis. This covenant received into its arms every circumcised son of Jacob (in whom the seed was ultimately called), without any exception; and thrust from its embrace every Gentile, without any distinction. It was, indeed, one of its stipulations that every Israelite should have all the males of his house circumcised; but there is no intimation that they were all thereby incorporated among the covenant seed, or that they had more right to the territory granted in the covenant, than had Ishmael, or the sons of Keturah. Jacob's servants were circumcised; but they did not become heads of tribes in Israel, as they would have been, had circumcision endowed them with the privileges of the covenant seed.

When the end for which any society was instituted has been accomplished, it is natural to expect its dissolution. The experiment for which the Congregation of the Lord had been organized, was completely made, when the Redeemer appeared, in the end of the world, "to take away sin by the sacrifice of himself." The first covenant, established upon conditional promises, was proved, upon due trial, to be faulty, weak, and unprofitable; and the necessity of a better covenant, whose better promises should be all yea and amen in Christ Jesus, was clearly demonstrated: "He taketh away the first, that he may establish the second." When "There was a disannulling of the commandment going before," in which was contained the charter of the Congregation of the Lord, the

---

[1] 1 Chr. xxviii. 8; Mic. ii. 5.   [2] Deut. xxiii. 1—8; Exod. xii. 43—47.

society was dissolved. Deprived of the character of a worshipping congregation, it lost its existence. The wall that had enclosed it from the rest of mankind, was broken down, when its ordinances were nailed to the cross of Christ.[1]

We have not insisted on the obvious difference between the church and the Hebrew congregation, as to the character of the members composing them. The congregation consisted mainly of Israelites; and these were admitted without regard to moral character, if circumcised, and free from ceremonial defilement and bodily defect. Gentiles were admitted, on conforming to the law of circumcision; but a Moabite, or Ammonite, could not be admitted until the tenth generation; and the most pious Israelite was prohibited, if he was ceremonially defiled, or the subject of a particular bodily defect.[2] In Christ Jesus, circumcision availeth nothing, but a new creature. Moabites and Ammonites are not excluded; but, in every nation, he that feareth God, and worketh righteousness, is accepted with him.[3] Ceremonial defilement and bodily defects constitute no obstacle to the fellowship of the saints. If the institution were the same, such radical changes in the membership could not well consist with the continued membership of infants. But the Mosaic institution has been abolished: "For there is verily a disannulling of the commandment going before, for the weakness and unprofitableness thereof."[4] "For if that first covenant had been faultless, then should no place have been sought for the second."[5] "He taketh away the first, that he may establish the second."[6]

Some advocates of infant church-membership, admit the temporary nature of the Mosaic institution; but maintain that there ran through it, and was contained in it, a spiritual and unchangeable covenant, which had been made with Abraham, and which is now in force. To this covenant, our attention will next be directed.

Argument 5.—The Lord promised Abraham, that in him all nations of the earth should be blessed; and entered into a covenant with him, constituting him the father of many nations, and engaging to be the God of him and his seed. Believers in all nations where the gospel is preached, are accounted the children of Abraham;

---

[1] Eph. ii. 14, 15.　　[2] Deut. xxiii. 1—3.　　[3] Acts x. 35.
[4] Heb. vii. 18.　　[5] Heb. viii. 7.　　[6] Heb. x. 9.

and admitted into this covenant, and become members of God's church. In this covenant, children have always been included with their parents; and their right to its privileges was recognised by Peter, on the day of Pentecost, in these words: "The promise is to you and your children." That believing gentiles were received into the same covenant which belonged to national Israel, is taught by these words of Christ: "The kingdom of God shall be taken from you, and given to a nation bringing forth the fruits thereof."[1] And still more clearly by Paul, under the figure of the good olive-tree, of which the people of Israel were the natural branches; but into which believing gentiles were grafted, so as to partake of the root and fatness of the olive-tree. In this way, the blessing of Abraham comes on the gentiles; and the covenant which secures the blessing, embraces their children with them.

In order to estimate the force of this argument, it will be necessary to review some events in the life of Abraham.

The first event that claims our attention, is thus recorded:—

"Now the Lord had said unto Abram, Get thee out of thy country, and from thy kindred, and from thy father's house, unto a land that I will show thee: and I will make of thee a great nation, and I will bless thee, and make thy name great; and thou shalt be a blessing; and I will bless them that bless thee, and curse him that curseth thee; and in thee shall all the families of the earth be blessed."[2] In this narrative, all is to be taken literally. The command was meant, and understood, and obeyed, according to the literal import of the words. The promise has thus far been fulfilled in its literal sense, and is still in progress of literal accomplishment. Abraham was personally blessed with eminent piety, and extraordinary tokens of the Divine favor. Though an humble man, dwelling in a tent, and not distinguished as a conqueror, statesman, or philosopher, he is one of the most renowned of all whose names have been transmitted to our times. The nation of Israel, descended from him, was great in number, and strength, and great in its influence on the world. To this nation, under God, mankind are indebted for the Bible, the gospel; and, above all, the Saviour of the world, who was, according to the flesh, of the seed of Abraham. This nation has given to the world the knowledge of the true God; which knowledge is ultimately to overspread the earth, and bless all nations. In this manner the

---

[1] Matt. xxi. 43.   [2] Gen. xii. 3.

promise made to Abraham, that in him all the families of the earth should be blessed, will be fulfilled. This promise was repeated to the patriarch, after the birth of his son Isaac, in these words: "And in thy seed shall all the nations of the earth be blessed."[1] The source of blessing to mankind was originally in the person of Abraham, but was now transferred to the person of the son that had been born of him : and hence the language of the promise was changed, "In *thy seed*," &c. The same promise was afterwards repeated to Isaac,[2] and to Jacob.[3] This promise is frequently referred to in the Scriptures, and is called the covenant which God made with the fathers[4]—the word covenant being used according to its latitude of meaning, to denote a firm and stable promise ; and it is once called, the gospel preached unto Abraham.[5] No doubt can exist, that this important and distinguished promise included spiritual blessings ; but the language is not spiritual in the sense in which this epithet is sometimes used, to mark what is not literal. Every word of this "gospel to Abraham," is as literal as the gospel declaration of Paul: "Believe on the Lord Jesus Christ, and thou shalt be saved."

The second event which we shall notice, is stated thus :—

"And he brought him forth abroad, and said, Look now toward heaven, and tell the stars, if thou be able to number them ; and he said unto him, So shall thy seed be. And he believed in the Lord ; and he counted it to him for righteousness."[6]

Here, again, all is to be understood in the literal sense. The posterity promised to the patriarch, were literal descendants, persons born out of his bowels.[7] The great blessing of justification, bestowed on this eminent believer, is spiritual in its nature ; but the language in which it is described, is as simple and literal as that which is used in the New Testament, to denote the same blessing: "By him, all that believe are justified from all things."

The third event which claims our consideration, gave existence to the covenant of circumcision. The record of this important transaction is found in the 17th chapter of Genesis :—

"And when Abram was ninety years old and nine, the Lord

---

[1] Gen. xxii. 18.　　[2] Gen. xxvi. 4.　　[3] Gen. xxviii. 14.
[4] Acts iii. 25.　　[5] Gal. iii. 8.　　[6] Gen. xv. 5, 6.
[7] V. 4.

appeared to Abram, and said unto him: I am the Almighty God; walk before me, and be thou perfect. And I will make my covenant between me and thee, and will multiply thee exceedingly. And Abram fell on his face, and God talked with him, saying, As for me, behold my covenant is with thee."

Thus far all is to be taken as literally as any other historical record.

"And thou shalt be a father of many nations."

This has been supposed by some, to be more than was true of Abraham, in the literal sense; but they err. From Jacob, the grandson of Abraham, was descended the nation of Israel—the great nation intended in the promise, "I will make of thee a great nation." From Esau, another grandson, sprang the Edomites, a great and powerful nation. From Ishmael, the son of Abraham by Hagar, twelve nations were descended.[1] These several nations were less great and powerful than the Israelites, or Edomites; but, nevertheless, each of them was called a nation, according to the use of the word in those times. Besides Isaac and Ishmael, Abraham had six sons by Keturah.[2] If these were as prolific as the other two, the whole number of nations descended from Abraham was fifty-six. No reason, therefore, exists for abandoning the literal sense of the clause. We have no right to insist on such a sense for the word "nation," as will correspond with its use in modern history. What it meant, when the covenant was made, is what it means in this clause; and in this sense, the promise has been literally fulfilled.

"Neither shall thy name any more be called Abram, but thy name shall be Abraham."

This change of name has been thought to imply that there is something mystical in the covenant. The change was doubtless significant; but the supposition that it had any signification which militates against the literal construction of the covenant, is wholly unfounded. The posterity of the patriarch, including the many inspired prophets whom God raised up among them, the first preachers of the gospel, and the writers of the New Testament, were accustomed to use this new name Abraham to signify their literal ancestor.

---

[1] Gen. xxv. 16.　　　　[2] V. 1—3.

"For a father of many nations have I made thee. And I will make thee exceeding fruitful; and I will make nations of thee, and kings shall come out of thee."

The first of these clauses explains the change in the patriarch's name. It was not in some mystical sense that God made him exceedingly fruitful; and, therefore, the phrase, "I have made thee a father of nations," does not need a mystical interpretation. God "made Abraham fruitful," not by some mystical appointment, but by literally multiplying his seed; and in this literal sense he made him the father of many nations. The promise, "and kings shall come out of thee," was literally fulfilled; and this clause, a mystical interpretation of which no one has ventured to insist on, binds down the covenant to the literal construction.

"And I will establish my covenant between me and thee, and thy seed after thee in their generations, for an everlasting covenant."

All this is to be understood according to the meaning which common usage assigned to the words. A difficulty would attend the interpretation, if the term "everlasting" always denoted unlimited duration; but this was not its only signification. The grant of the land of Canaan afterwards made in the covenant, could not extend beyond the duration of the present world; and, if the covenant was to continue in force to the end of time, or even till that state of things should cease, for which the covenant was designed to provide, the epithet "everlasting" was properly applied to it. In various passages of Scripture the word is used in this sense.

"To be a God unto thee, and to thy seed after thee."

These words were not designed to be a promise of spiritual grace, or eternal life, to all the descendants of Abraham. A new covenant predicted by the prophet Jeremiah, contained the stipulation: "I will be their God; and they shall be my people."[1] This promise secured spiritual grace; but it would not have been a new covenant if the same grant had been made in the covenant with Abraham. As contained in this covenant, the promise engaged a special divine care over Abraham and his descendants; and particularly over the nation of Israel, the seed to whom the grant of

---

[1] Jer. xxxi. 33.

Canaan was made in this covenant. In this sense, the promise was literally fulfilled. He separated them from all other nations, and acknowledged them to be his people: "You only have I known of all the families of the earth."[1] His providence over them, and his revelations to them, were all peculiar. In all his dealings with them, he acted in the relation of a God. He rewarded as a God, and punished as a God. He made himself known to them as a God, while other nations were permitted to remain in ignorance of him; and as a God, while he granted to this nation means of grace and salvation unknown to the rest of the world, he used the nation as the channel for conveying spiritual blessings to all the nations of the earth.

"And I will give unto thee, and to thy seed after thee, the land wherein thou art a stranger, all the land of Canaan for an everlasting possession."

All this was meant literally, and was literally fulfilled. The import of the word "everlasting," has been explained in the remarks on the phrase "everlasting covenant." Whether the word everlasting, either in application to the covenant or to the possession of Canaan, was limited to the dispensation that preceded the time of Christ, or extended into the present dispensation, and still stretches forward into future time, will be a subject of future inquiry. But whatever may be true on this question, the use of the word militates nothing against the literal construction of the covenant.

"And I will be their God."

This promise, as has already been explained, was literally fulfilled.

"And God said unto Abraham, thou shalt keep my covenant therefore, thou and thy seed after thee in their generations. This is my covenant, which ye shall keep, between me and you, and thy seed after thee; every man child among you shall be circumcised. And ye shall circumcise the flesh of your foreskin; and it shall be a token of the covenant betwixt me and you. And he that is eight days old shall be circumcised among you; every man child in your generations, he that is born in the house or bought with money of any stranger, which is not of thy seed. He that is born

---

[1] Amos iii. 2.

in thy house, and he that is bought with thy money, must needs be circumcised; and my covenant shall be in your flesh for an everlasting covenant. And the uncircumcised man child whose flesh of his foreskin is not circumcised, that soul shall be cut off from his people; he hath broken my covenant."

The precept enjoining circumcision was intended to be understood literally, and it was understood and obeyed literally. An important, very important part of God's design in making this covenant, was to distinguish and separate the descendants of Abraham from the rest of mankind; and this design would have been frustrated if this part of the covenant had not been taken literally. The whole history of the Hebrew nation, and almost every page of the New Testament, testify in favor of the literal construction.

"And God said unto Abraham, as for Sarai, thy wife, thou shalt not call her name Sarai, but Sarah shall her name be. And I will bless her, and give thee a son also of her: yea, I will bless her, and she shall be a mother of nations; kings of people shall be of her."

The new name Sarah, like the new name Abraham, was significant; but neither of them signified anything contrary to the literal construction of the covenant. Abraham was the father of many nations, because he had sons by other wives; but his only son by Sarah was Isaac, the father of Jacob and Esau; and the only nations descended from Sarah, were the Israelites and the Edomites. It was promised that Sarah should be a mother of "nations," not of "many nations;" and this adaptation of the language to what became literally true, proves that the covenant was made in the literal sense of the words. In the literal sense kings came out of Sarah; the kings of Edom, and the long line of kings in Israel and Judah.

Our examination of the covenant has proved conclusively, that it was designed to be understood literally; but a question arises whether it does not admit another and more spiritual sense.

The precepts which enjoined the ceremonies of worship to be observed by the Hebrew congregation, were all designed to be understood and obeyed literally. Literal bulls and goats were to be sacrificed; literal fire was to be used, and all the directions given were to be observed in their literal import. But the various ceremonies of this worship were shadows of things to come; and a large part of the epistle to the Hebrews is employed in explaining their spiritual signification. Persons and events of the Old Testament which appear in their proper connection as subjects of literal history, are in the New Testament made to represent spiritual things, and spiritual instruction is drawn from them. The history of Hagar, as given in the book of Genesis, is literally true; but Paul calls it an allegory, and uses it to represent spiritual things. In the same manner the covenant of circumcision is made a source of spiritual instruction. The chief particulars in the covenant which are made representatives of spiritual things, are three:

1. The literal descendants of Abraham are made to represent believers, who are called his children in a different sense of the word. The metaphorical use of the terms which denote the paternal and filial relations, is frequent in the Scriptures. One who appears at the head of a class of persons as a father appears at the head of his family or tribe, is called the father of that class; and the individuals composing the class, are called his children. Thus, " Jabal was the father of such as dwell in tents, and of such as have cattle: and Jubal was the father of all such as handle the harp and organ." [1] These persons called fathers, were inventors of arts; and the class of persons who practise these arts are regarded as their children. So those who practise the piety of which Abraham was an illustrious example, and walk in the footsteps of his faith, are called his children. In this tropical sense of the term, Jesus said to the wicked Jews, " If ye were Abraham's children, ye would do the works of Abraham." [2] Since the men whom Jesus addressed were children of Abraham in the literal sense, the distinction between the literal and the metaphorical sense is plainly marked; and the latter sense is made to depend on imitation of Abraham in the works for which he was eminent. Paul has distinguished between the literal Jew and the metaphorical Jew; [3] between the children according to the flesh, and the children of promise. [4] The latter, he says, " are counted for the seed;" that is, they are accounted the seed of Abraham when the covenant is viewed as an allegory.

---

[1] Gen. iv. 20, 21.   [2] John viii. 39.   [3] Rom. ii. 29.
[4] Rom. ix. 8.

2. Circumcision is made to represent regeneration, the spiritual change by which men become new creatures. Hence it is said, "In Christ Jesus neither circumcision availeth any thing, nor uncircumcision; but a new creature."[1] A tropical use of the word circumcise to denote a moral change, is found in the Old Testament: "The Lord thy God will circumcise thine heart, and the heart of thy seed, to love the Lord thy God with all thine heart, and with all thy soul, that thou mayest live."[2] Paul distinguishes between the literal and the spiritual circumcision; thus, "Neither is that circumcision which is outward in the flesh. . . . . Circumcision is that of the heart, in the spirit, and not in the letter."[3] This circumcision of the heart is in another passage called the "circumcision of Christ."[4] While the literal circumcision which marked the literal seed of Abraham avails nothing in Christ Jesus, the spiritual circumcision marks those who belong to Christ, and who are, in the spiritual sense, the seed of Abraham. "If ye be Christ's, then are ye Abraham's seed, and heirs according to the promise."[5]

3. Canaan, the land promised to Abraham and his literal seed, is made to represent heaven, the future inheritance of those who have like faith with the patriarch. Abraham at the command of God left his native country, and sojourned in the land of Canaan; but though the land was his by promise, he never obtained possession of it. Paul makes a spiritual use of this fact: "Confessed that they were strangers and pilgrims on the earth. But now they desire a better country, that is, an heavenly."[6] The literal Canaan was present to the sight of the patriarch, as a desirable possession secured by covenant to him and his seed; but the eye of his faith was directed to a better country, of which this was but a type. His spiritual seed are like him in faith, and their faith directs its eye to the same heavenly inheritance.

The allegorical interpretation of the covenant is beautifully harmonious in all its parts. Abraham, the most illustrious example of faith found in the Old Testament, appears at the head of a class of persons who are like him in faith; and he is hence called the father of the faithful. As he was marked by the circumcision

---

[1] Gal. vi. 15.   [2] Deut. xxx. 6.   [3] Rom. ii. 28, 29.
[4] Col. ii. 11.   [5] Gal. iii. 29.   [6] Heb. xi. 13, 16.

of the heart, and distinguished thereby from the rest of mankind, so are they. As he looked beyond the earthly possession granted to him, and sought a heavenly inheritance, so do they.

The spiritual truths which the covenant represents in its allegorical use, were not brought into existence by the covenant, and are not dependent on it. They are above it, as the things which the Mosaic ceremonies typified are superior to the ceremonies; or as a substance is superior to its shadow, and independent of it. In the third chapter of Galatians, Paul teaches that believers are the children of Abraham, and are blessed with him; and he dates back their connection with him to a time that preceded the covenant of circumcision. He says, that "the law was four hundred and thirty years after." Now, reckoning back four hundred and thirty years from the giving of the law, we arrive at the time when Abraham received the first promise. This preceded the covenant of circumcision by twenty-four years. This promise, first made with reference to Abraham himself, and afterwards renewed with reference to his seed, is the covenant to which this passage evidently refers. Hence, believers hold their connection with Abraham receiving the great gospel promise, and not with Abraham receiving the covenant of circumcision; with Abraham as first distinguished by the circumcision of the heart, and not with Abraham as afterwards distinguished by the circumcision of the flesh. Precisely the same view is presented in the fourth chapter of Romans, in which it is taught that believers are connected, not with the circumcised, but with the uncircumcised Abraham, in obtaining the blessing of justification.

The judaizing Christians taught, "Except ye be circumcised and keep the law, ye cannot be saved." This was the current doctrine of the Jews. They gloried in the covenant of circumcision, and their connection with the circumcised Abraham; and for the purpose of securing a title to the earthly Canaan, literal descent from Abraham, and the circumcision that is outward in the flesh, were sufficient. But Paul opposed the doctrine of the judaizing teachers, and opened a different view of the Holy Spirit's teachings in the Old Testament. He taught that to secure the spiritual blessings which Abraham enjoyed, we must seek them in the way in which Abraham obtained them. He did not obtain the favor of God by circumcision and keeping the law; but enjoyed this blessing four hundred and thirty years before the law, and while he was yet uncircumcised. He received the blessing by faith; and every one who would be blessed with him, must seek it in this way. These arguments of Paul, in which he deduced the true doctrine of the gospel from the Scriptures of the Old Testament, were powerful in opposition to the judaizing theory.

The covenant of circumcision in its literal sense, included in the covenant seed none but the literal descendants of Abraham. The patriarch and his sons were commanded to circumcise all the males of the household, including the servants born in the house, and those bought with money; but these servants did not thereby become incorporated with the covenant seed. None of the servants in the families of Abraham, Isaac, and Jacob, had this privilege conferred on them; and it cannot be supposed that the servants of their descendants were more highly favored than the servants of the patriarchs themselves. On the contrary, those servants, though circumcised, are expressly said in the covenant itself, to be " not of thy seed." When the Congregation of the Lord was instituted, provision was made for gentiles to be admitted to the privileges of its worship on conforming to the law of circumcision; but they were nevertheless strangers within the gate, and not a part of the covenant seed, or entitled to a part in the land of Canaan. Genealogical records were kept distinguishing the seed proper from the proselytes of the gate; and hence Paul was able to call himself " a Hebrew of the Hebrews;" that is, a Hebrew by original extraction.

As the covenant of circumcision in its literal sense, admitted none into the covenant seed but literal descendants of Abraham; so in the allegorical sense, none are included in the spiritual seed but true believers. This is clear from many passages of Scripture:—" So then they which be of faith are blessed with faithful Abraham.[1] . . . . If ye be Christ's, then are ye Abraham's seed, and heirs according to the promise."[2] The following passage is perfectly decisive on this subject, and shows conclusively that genuine faith is intended, and not the mere profession of it: " Therefore it is of faith, that it might be by grace; to the end the promise might be sure to all the seed."[3]

---

[1] Gal. iii. 9.　　　　[2] V. 29.　　　　[3] Rom. iv. 16.

One among the promises made to Abraham was, " I will make of thee a great nation." In the covenant of circumcision, it was promised that he should be the father of many nations; and the nation of Israel was contemplated as one of these. The covenant in its literal sense, instituted no ecclesia or worshipping congregation. A cahal for the worship of God, was instituted by Moses; and laws and ceremonies for that worship were instituted with it. The covenant then made with Israel had ordinances of divine service and a worldly sanctuary; but he who looks for these in the covenant of circumcision will look in vain. It contains no sanctuary, no ordinances of divine worship, no priesthood, no assembly. We have shown that the cahal instituted by Moses has been dissolved; and, if the covenant of circumcision still survives, it exists as it did before the days of Moses—a national covenant, made with the literal descendants of Abraham, admitting no others to be incorporated with the covenant seed, and making no provision for the public worship of God. Surely, the Christian church is not founded on this covenant.

Since the covenant of circumcision instituted no ecclesia, and cannot admit gentile infants among the covenant seed, the doctrine of infant church-membership cannot be affected by the question, whether the covenant has been abrogated, or is now in force: and, for any purpose of our present inquiry, we are under no obligation to decide this question. Since this covenant existed before that which was made by Moses, the abrogation of the latter may have left the former just as it had previously been. In it, the land of Canaan was given for an everlasting possession; and the covenant is styled " an everlasting covenant." We may hence infer, that the covenant will continue in force as long as the Israelites shall possess the land of Canaan. If the general expectation be well founded, that they will return to their land and repossess it, the covenant must be still in force. The facts that, since the abrogation of the Mosaic covenant, they have been called the people of God;[1] that they have the promise of being restored again to his favor;[2] and are declared not to be cast off, because the gifts and calling of God are without repentance;[3] confirm this view. To all this we may add the remarkable fact, that, when the apostles

---

[1] Rom. xi. 1 2.   [2] V. 23—30.   [3] V. 29.

declared converts from among the gentiles to be under no obligation to be circumcised, they did not release Jews from this obligation. For a gentile to be circumcised, is an admission that the Congregation of the Lord is still in being, and the Mosaic law still in force; and for any one, whether Jew or gentile, to be circumcised as a means of salvation, is to set aside Christ and render him unprofitable. But can any one prove that it is inconsistent with the gospel for a Jew to retain circumcision, as a token of his connection with Abraham, and his interest in that remarkable people, through whom he still expects God to display the riches of his grace in the most wonderful manner?

Is the covenant of circumcision in force, in its allegorical sense? This question is about as unmeaning as if it were asked, whether a portrait exists in the person of him whom it resembles. The portrait and the man exist independently of each other. The man may die, and leave the portrait; or the portrait may be destroyed, while the man lives. If the covenant of circumcision is in force at all, it is in force in that only sense in which it is a covenant— namely, the literal. No one would say that the ceremonial law is now in force, because the spiritual truths which the ceremonies prefigured abide for ever. Whether the covenant is abrogated, or is now in force, the spiritual instruction derived from it is the everlasting gospel.

While the covenant, literally construed, gives no sanction to infant church-membership, the spiritual use which is made of it in the Scriptures incidentally decides that all the members of the primitive churches were believers. Paul says to the Galatians: "Now *we*, brethren, as Isaac was, are the children of promise." . . . . . "*Ye* are all the children of God by faith in Jesus Christ. If *ye* be Christ's, then are ye Abraham's seed." These texts prove that the members of the Galatian churches were all accounted the children of Abraham, in the spiritual sense—that is, were true believers—and what was true of those churches, must have been true of all other churches instituted by the apostles.

A portrait is not more distinct from the man whom it resembles, nor a shadow more distinct from the substance which casts it, than is the covenant of circumcision from the spiritual truth which it represents, in the allegorical interpretation of it. We ought never to confound things so distinct; but this is done by the doctrine of infant church-membership. It follows the literal sense, from Abraham down to the introduction of the gospel, and accounts the literal seed, during this period, to be the church: it then follows the spiritual sense, and introduces gentile believers among the covenant seed: it then returns to the law of literal descent, and follows this for one generation, and then abandons it. By this unaccountable mixture of interpretations, the immediate literal descendants of those who are, or ought to be, according to their profession, the spiritual seed of Abraham, are supposed to be brought within the covenant, and incorporated with the covenant seed: but, alas! they are a seed which inherit neither the literal nor the spiritual promises made to the patriarch. They do not inherit the literal promises, because they are gentiles; nor the spiritual promises, because these are secured only to believers.

It remains that we examine the other texts of Scripture, which the argument that we are considering, cites in its support.

"For the promise is unto you, and to your children, and to all that are afar off, even as many as the Lord our God shall call."[1]

The word which is here rendered "children," denotes posterity, immediate or remote, without respect to age. The same word is used in the sentence, "Children shall rise up against their parents, and shall cause them to be put to death;"[2] and in the phrase, "children of the flesh,"[3] when used to denote all the natural posterity of Abraham. The promise here referred to appears, from the words which immediately precede, to be the promise of the Holy Spirit; but, whether it be this, or the promise made to Abraham as the argument supposes, it must be understood to include spiritual blessings. Three classes of persons are mentioned, to whom the promise is given; the Israelites of that generation, their posterity, and the gentiles: "you, your children, and all that are afar off." To neither of these classes is the promise given without condition or limitation. When it is said, "Repent, for the promise is to you," the receiving of the promise is evidently suspended on the condition of repentance. The same condition applies equally to the other two classes. This is fully established by the limiting clause, "even as many as the Lord our God shall call." The promise is not absolute to all who are externally called by the

[1] Acts ii. 39.   [2] Matt. x. 21.   [3] Rom. ix. 8.
12

gospel, but to those only who are effectually called to repentance. This limitation applies equally to all the three classes. Though the word "children" may sometimes be used with exclusive application to infants, there is no reason to suppose that such use of it is made here, but the whole posterity are intended; and it cannot be that spiritual blessings were promised to all those, without condition or limitation. The mention of the posterity, in this case, was peculiarly appropriate. Peter had charged them with the crime of crucifying the Lord Jesus. When this crime was committed, in calling on Pilate to crucify him, they had said: "His blood be on us, and on our children." This fact rendered the information suitable and welcome, that the same means of salvation that were granted to them, would be granted to their posterity.

"The kingdom of God shall be taken from you, and given to a nation bringing forth the fruits thereof."[1]

The name of a type is sometimes applied to the thing typified. Regeneration is called circumcision; but, to show that literal circumcision is not intended, it is called the circumcision of the heart, or the circumcision of Christ. Heaven is called a country, in allusion to the country promised to Abraham, which typified it; but, for the sake of distinction, the epithets "better" and "heavenly" are applied: "a better country, that is, a heavenly." The nation of Israel, marked by the literal circumcision, and heirs of the earthly Canaan, typified those who are circumcised in heart, and are heirs of the heavenly country. These last are on this account called a nation; but, to distinguish them from the nation which typified them, they are called "a nation bringing forth the fruits" of the kingdom; that is, the fruits of holy obedience to God as their king. Peter calls them "a chosen generation, a royal priesthood, a holy nation, a peculiar people." They are not a nation, in the literal sense of the term, as the nation of Israel was. Earthly nations included infants, but this spiritual nation consists of those who bring forth the fruits of the kingdom; and who, according to Peter, "show forth the praises of him who hath called them out of darkness into his marvellous light." These things cannot be predicated of infants. It follows, therefore, that, in this transfer of the kingdom, infants are not its recipients.

---

[1] Matt. xxi. 43.

The precise sense in which the kingdom is said to be taken from the nation of Israel, it is not necessary, for our present purpose, to determine. The government of that nation has been called a theocracy. God was their king; and various benefits resulted to them from being under his reign. To these benefits the text may refer; and the sense may be, that the peculiar privilege of having God to reign over them, should no longer distinguish them from other nations of the earth; but this privilege would henceforth be confined to a spiritual people, to be selected out of all nations. But, as the phrase, "kingdom of God," was commonly used by Christ to denote the new kingdom which he was establishing, the reference may be exclusively to this. He was born "King of the Jews," and was crucified with this title. He was sent, as he himself declared, not to the gentiles, but to the lost sheep of the house of Israel. The first proclamation of his reign was made to this people; and the beginning and first benefits of his reign were confined to them. Their rejection of his reign was made the occasion of its extension to the gentiles: "It was necessary that the word of God should first have been spoken to you: but seeing ye put it from you, and judge yourselves unworthy of everlasting life, lo, we turn to the gentiles."[1] The blessings of the Messiah's reign were expected by the nation to be theirs, and the first offer and bestowment of them accorded with this expectation: but the peculiar privilege was taken from them when they rejected their king; and it is now enjoyed by those who obey him in every nation. These, and these only, bring forth the fruits of the kingdom; and, however the transfer to them may be understood, it cannot prove the church-membership of infants.

The last Scripture cited in the argument has been much relied on, as proof that the Christian church is a continuation of an organized society which existed in the Old Testament dispensation. Under the figure of the good olive-tree, Paul is supposed to teach that the church sprang from Abraham, and that it has continued to the present time.

In the passage which contains this figurative representation, the following things may be observed:—

1. The olive-tree underwent an important change when many of

---

[1] Acts xiii. 46.

the natural branches were broken off. The reason for their separation is expressly given: "Because of unbelief, they were broken off." Since the unbelieving branches were taken away by this act, none were left but believing branches. These are the remnant before spoken of; "the remnant according to the election of grace:" the seed intended when it is said, "Except the Lord of Sabaoth had left us a seed, we had been as Sodoma, and been made like unto Gomorrha."[1]

2. A second change took place when branches were engrafted from the wild olive-tree. The character of these branches is made known by the words with which Paul addresses them: "Thou standest by faith." We are hence assured that these also were believing branches. This accords with what is elsewhere taught: "That the blessing of Abraham might come on the gentiles through faith."

3. Another important change is still expected when the natural branches which were broken off shall be "graffed in again." The condition on which it will be done is expressly stated: "They also shall be graffed in again, if they abide not in unbelief." They are recognised as natural branches, and the olive-tree is called "their own;" but neither of these facts will suffice to effect their restoration. If they come in again, they must come as believing branches.

These three comprehend all the changes which the olive-tree is said to undergo; and as a consequence of these, none but believing branches have a present, or can have a future connection with the tree. The design for which this figurative illustration was introduced, and the explanations which accompany it, clearly show that the natural branches were designed to represent the natural seed of Abraham; and the changes which the tree undergoes, are precisely such as substituted the spiritual seed for the natural, the children by faith for the children according to the flesh. The whole scope of the apostle's teaching in connection with the passage, if attentively considered, leaves no reasonable doubt that this was the design of the figure.

Types, parables, and allegories, are founded on similitude; but when spiritual things are likened to natural, the likeness is neces-

---

[1] Rom. ix. 29.

sarily imperfect. He who seeks to extend the likeness beyond its proper limit, is in danger of mistake. In the present case it would be unprofitable, and perhaps worse than unprofitable, to inquire what may be signified by the trunk of the tree, its leaves, and the various other parts of which botanists could tell us. In the sketch which the apostle's pencil has drawn, imperfect indeed, but sufficient for all his purpose, we see nothing of the tree but its branches, its root, and its fatness, unless its fruit may be referred to in v. 16. The chief question before the apostle's mind, related to the branches; and what these signify he has sufficiently informed us. What the root and fatness of the olive-tree signify, we are left to learn from the connection of the passage; and from this we may infer that Abraham, and the promises made to him, are intended.

Some have supposed that Christ is the root of the olive-tree; and that the figure corresponds with that of the vine in the 15th chapter of John. The strongest argument in favor of this opinion, is furnished by the words, "Thou bearest not the root, but the root thee." Since Christ is the only name by which we must be saved, the believing soul is borne or supported by him, and not by Abraham. But such support as this, is not intended by the word "bearest" in this passage. The word is used with evident allusion to the figure, and signifies only what the figure signifies by the dependance of the branches on the root. The natural descendants of Abraham, who are the natural branches of the olive-tree, do not depend on their illustrious progenitor as the believing soul depends on Christ; and, therefore, such dependence is not implied in this passage. Paul, though he was the minister of the uncircumcision, was careful to teach the gentiles their indebtedness to the Jews. He urged the obligation of contributing to relieve the poor saints at Jerusalem by this consideration: "Their debtors they are. For if the gentiles have been made partakers of their spiritual things, their duty is also to minister unto them in carnal."[1] So in the present case, he urges on the gentiles, "Boast not against the natural branches; for if thou boast, thou bearest not the root, but the root thee." The religion which blesses the gentiles was obtained from the Jews. Jesus Christ was a Jew. The Old Testa-

---

[1] Rom. xv. 27.

ment was a Jewish book; and the New Testament is the gospel written by Jews. In the comprehensive words of Christ, "Salvation is of the Jews." The promise to Abraham, "In thee shall all the families of the earth be blessed," contemplated the Hebrew nation to whom the oracles of God were committed, and from whom, according to the flesh, Christ came, as yet in the loins of the patriarch. In this view, Abraham is presented in the figure as the root of the olive-tree; and the spiritual blessings are its fatness of which gentile believers partake.

An objection presents itself, that in the substitution of the spiritual for the natural seed, such a change is supposed as destroys the identity of the olive-tree, and the more so, because the fatness of which the two kinds of branches partake, cannot be the same. To this objection it is a sufficient reply, that figures cannot be expected to hold good in everything. But another reply may be given. The nourishment which proceeds from the root of a tree to its various parts, is assimilated to each according to its nature, and becomes woody fibre, bark, leaf, or fruit. Even the fruit may vary, though deriving nourishment from the same root; for that which is produced by a grafted branch will differ from that produced by a natural branch. All this is found in a natural tree; and yet the change of its branches by grafting, and the variety of nourishment which the root yields, do not affect the identity of the tree in a general view of it. It can, therefore, be no objection to Paul's figure, that it represents natural and spiritual branches as connected with the same root and deriving benefits of different kinds from it. This mode of meeting the objection is proposed merely to show that it has not a solid foundation to sustain it; but we cannot suppose that Paul, in sketching out this figure, had reference to abstruse principles of vegetable physiology. He informs us that the distinction represented by the two classes of branches existed in the days of Elijah, when God informed the prophet that he had reserved to himself seven thousand men who had not bowed the knee to the image of Baal. "Even so," he adds, "there is at this time a remnant according to the election of grace." Besides the natural branches who were bowing to Baal, there then existed a remnant who were faithful and enjoyed spiritual blessings. All these together, the advocates of infant church-membership tell us, composed the visible church of that

day, and were branches of the same olive-tree; and the same constitution of things, uniting natural and spiritual branches on the
same trunk, they suppose continues to the present time.   Accord
ing to the view which we have taken, the great Husbandman has
broken off the natural branches, and but one species of branches
now remains.   It follows, therefore, that the objection, whatever
may be its force, is applicable rather to the opinion which we
oppose, than to that which we defend.

The question whether the passage teaches the church-membership of infants, may be approached aside from the objection which
we have been considering, and from all perplexing inquiry as to
what the root and fatness of the olive-tree signify.   It relates
wholly to the branches of the tree; and with respect to these, we
have the unerring Spirit to guide our interpretation.   His express
teaching determines, that the branches now connected with the
olive-tree, are all believing.   Here a landmark is fixed, which must
not be removed. , If we leave the plain teaching of the Spirit, and
follow the guidance of our own fancy, until we become involved
in error, it must be our own fault.

Infant membership is argued from the identity of the olive-tree;
but, unfortunately for the argument, the changes which the apostle
has described, infringe on the identity of the tree, exactly in the
wrong place.   All these changes respect the branches, and are
made on one principle—the substitution of faith for natural descent; as the bond of connection between the branches and the
root.   Infant membership depends on natural descent; and the
one principle on which all the changes are made, by taking away
natural descent, leaves infant membership to hang on nothing.

Section II.—ARGUMENTS FOR INFANT BAPTISM.

The arguments which were considered in the last section, aim
directly to establish the right of infants to church-membership.
Other arguments, tending indirectly to establish the same point,
have immediate respect to the docrine of infant baptism.

The Holy Scriptures contain no precept or example for infant
baptism; and the qualifications which they uniformly describe, as
necessary to baptism, infants do not possess.   With these facts
before us, we are compelled to reject infants from the ordinance,

unless a special claim in their behalf can be well established. We shall now proceed to consider the chief arguments which have been used, in support of their claim.

Argument 1.—Repentance and faith are as much required by the Scriptures, in order to salvation, as in order to baptism; but as infants may be saved without them, so they may be baptized without them. From the nature of the case, these qualifications are required of adults only. The commission does indeed place *believing* before *baptizing*, but it equally places it before *being saved;* and it even declares, in express terms, "He that believeth not shall be damned." If, therefore, we may infer from it, that infants ought not to be baptized, we may, with as much certainty, infer that they cannot be saved.

This argument has no force, to establish infant baptism. Because infants may be saved without repentance and faith, it does not follow that they are entitled to every privilege which may be claimed for them. The utmost extent to which the argument can go, is to weaken the force of the opposing argument; and this it does in appearance only. How are we to reconcile the declaration, "He that believeth not shall be damned," with the doctrine of infant salvation? The answer is obvious. When Christ commissioned his disciples to preach the gospel to every creature, he meant every creature capable of hearing and understanding it. "He that believeth not," means—he that, having heard the gospel, rejects it. In this obvious meaning of the phrase, it affirms nothing contrary to infant salvation. Adopting the same mode of exposition, in the preceding clause, it signifies—he that hears the gospel, believes it, and is baptized, shall be saved. The commission does not say, whether infants will be saved, or whether they ought to be baptized; for the simple reason, that it has no reference to them. The argument before us, drives us to this exposition of the commission; but what does infant baptism gain by it? We learn from it, that, in the great commission which Christ gave to his apostles, by which baptism was established as a permanent institution to be observed among all nations to the end of time, he had no reference to infants.

Argument 2.—Though the Scriptures contain no positive precept for infant baptism, the same is true with respect to female communion, and the Christian Sabbath. The Lord's Supper is a positive institute; and yet we admit females to partake of it, without a positive precept. The change from the seventh day of the week to the first, in the observance of the Sabbath, has no express command for it in the Scriptures, and is, in part, a repeal of the fourth commandment; yet we admit it on satisfactory inference, supported by the practice of the early churches. In like manner the observance of infant baptism may be vindicated, though not prescribed by positive precept.

We do not exclude all reasoning with respect to positive institutes. No one on earth can point to a positive precept in the Scriptures, requiring him in particular to be baptized. Paul was directly commanded to be baptized; and so were those whom Peter addressed, on the day of Pentecost, and in the house of Cornelius. From these facts, we think it lawful to infer, that persons of like character, and in like circumstances, ought now to be baptized. The commission did not directly command any one to be baptized: but it commanded the apostles to baptize; and from the obligation to baptize laid on one party, we infer the obligation of another party to be baptized; and we infer the perpetuity of the obligation, from the fact that the commission was manifestly designed to be perpetual. Such inferences we hold to be legitimate and necessary; but we maintain, that positive institutes originating in the will of the lawgiver, cannot be determined by mere reasoning from general principles. The obligation to baptize believers, can be referred to express divine command; and if an obligation to baptize infants exists, it cannot be made out by any process of reasoning from the parental and filial relations or general principles of morals; but must be referred, in like manner, to some divine command. We ask for this command. Whatever reasoning may be necessary, to unfold the command, and show that infant baptism is contained in it, we consent to undertake; but we must know that it is the will of Christ, before we can observe it as an institution of his religion.

The necessity for divine command is rendered the more urgent, because infant baptism interferes with the divine institution of believers' baptism, and would, if universally practised, banish it from the earth. God commands a believer to be baptized;—is he released from the obligation by the fact that his parents had him baptized in infancy? Is he now chargeable with the sin of anabaptism, if he obeys the divine command? For proof of all this, some divine authority for infant baptism is needed, as clear and certain as that by which believers' baptism is established.

For female communion, we have divine authority in the command of Christ, "this do," "drink ye all of it." The Scriptures interpret this command. Women were among the disciples mentioned in the first chapter of Acts, verse 8,—and all these, with the three thousand who were added, continued in the breaking of bread.[1] In the same number were included the widows, who were neglected in the daily ministration. Women were in the church at Corinth, when the whole church assembled to celebrate the Lord's supper.[2] In the command, "Let a man examine himself, and so let him eat,"[3] the word rendered man, signifies a human being, of either sex. It is evident, from these facts, that female communion is practised on divine authority; and it, moreover, sets aside no other divine command. If such authority for infant baptism can be produced, we ought to practise it: but even then we might question the propriety of its superseding believers' baptism.

But it is alleged, that the Christian sabbath does supersede the observance of the seventh day prescribed in the decalogue; and therefore, presents a case analogous to the one before us. Is it then true, that our inferences can in any case set aside the express commands of God? We think not. The decalogue requires the observance of the seventh day, regularly returning after six days of labor; and not the seventh day of the week. As thus interpreted, the Christian practice literally conforms to it. If the seventh day in the commandment means the seventh day of the week, it is our duty to obey strictly; and if we can learn, by legitimate inference, that the first day of the week ought to be observed, our course of duty is plain—we ought to observe both days: so, if infant baptism can be made out by legitimate inference, instead of permitting it to supersede believers' baptism, we ought to observe both. We open our minds, therefore, to the inferential reasoning by which infant baptism is to be sustained.

Argument 3.—Christ's commission is, "Teach or make disciples of all nations, baptizing them." Children form a part of all nations; and the commission, therefore, contains authority for baptizing them.

The word "nations" in the original, is of the neuter gender, and the word "them" is masculine. It has been concluded, hence,

---

[1] Acts ii. 42.   [2] 1 Cor. xi. 5—20.   [3] V. 28.

that the pronoun stands properly, for the masculine noun "disciples" understood. But, without the aid of this criticism, the connection of the clauses shows that this is the true meaning. The sense is the same as in the passage, "Jesus made and baptized disciples." If the commission authorizes to baptize every one in the nation, adult unbelievers must be included, contrary to what all admit.

Argument 4.—The commission requires to baptize disciples. A disciple is one engaged to receive instruction from a teacher. In secular matters, parents select teachers for their children, and make engagements for their instruction. In religion, they are under the highest obligation to place them in the school of Christ, that they may be brought up in the nurture and admonition of the Lord. The commission requires, that these young disciples should receive the mark of discipleship. The propriety of considering them disciples, may be proved by the passage, "Why tempt ye God, to put a yoke on the neck of the disciples, which neither our fathers nor we were able to bear?"[1] The yoke of circumcision is here referred to. And every one knows that this fell chiefly on infants. The import of the word used in the commission, and its applicability to infants may be proved by a passage in Justin Martyr, who wrote near the middle of the second century. Among those who were members of the church, he says, "there were many of both sexes, some sixty, and some seventy years old, who were made disciples to Christ from their infancy." The word he uses is εμαθητευθησαν, the same word that is used in the commission. It is evident, therefore, that Justin understood the command of Christ to make disciples and baptize, as applicable to little children. And he wrote only about one hundred years after Matthew, who records that command. This testimony is important, as showing the early prevalence of infant baptism, since these persons must have received the mark of discipleship within a few years after Matthew wrote. But it is cited here, to show the sense of the Greek word which Christ employed in the commission.

In secular concerns, it is possible, though not usual, for parents to engage their children, from early infancy, to some teacher, by whom they may be afterwards instructed; but the *usus loquendi* will scarcely allow us to call them his disciples, until they begin to learn from him.

In the Scriptures, we read of John's disciples, the disciples of the Pharisees, the disciples of Jesus; and such is the current use of the term, that, in these several applications of it, the idea of

---

[1] Acts xv. 10.

infancy is never suggested. We read, "The number of the disciples was multiplied in Jerusalem." * * * "And the apostles called the multitude of the disciples to them, and said, ' Wherefore, brethren, look ye out.' * * 'And the saying pleased the whole multitude: and they chose," &c.[1] If the infants of all the believers in Jerusalem were disciples, they must have been included in the multitude here mentioned; but the things stated in the narrative forbid the supposition. Another passage in the same chapter shows that to be a disciple, and to have faith, are descriptive of the same person: "The number of the disciples multipled in Jerusalem greatly; and a great company of the priests were obedient to the faith."[2] The same is proved by another passage in a subsequent chapter: "Finding certain disciples, he said unto them, Have ye received the Holy Ghost since ye believed ?"[3] But we have still clearer proof on this subject ;—Christ himself expressly declared the qualifications necessary to constitute a disciple: "If any man come to me, and hate not his father, and mother, and wife, and children, and brethren, and sisters, yea, and his own life also, he cannot be my disciple. And whosoever doth not bear his cross, and come after me, cannot be my disciple."[4] Against such declarations of the divine Master, the inference from a merely possible use of the term in secular concerns, can be of no avail.

But the argument alleges that we have Scripture example for the application of the term to infants. In the case referred to, Judaizing teachers had taught, "Except ye be circumcised, and keep the law, ye cannot be saved." The yoke which they imposed on the gentile converts was not circumcision merely, but the whole burden of the legal ceremonies. Circumcision was not, in itself, the intolerable yoke referred to, "which neither our fathers nor we were able to bear." These were circumcised in infancy, and did not afterwards account circumcision a grievous burden. But the burdensome law received from Moses is manifestly the thing intended; and the burden did not fall on infants. The passage therefore contains no proof that infants were intended by the word disciples.

The words of Justin Martyr, απο παιδων, are incorrectly translated *from infancy.* The name *Pedobaptist*, which is given to those

---

[1] Acts vi. 1—5.   [2] V. 7.   [3] Acts xix. 1, 2.
[4] Luke xiv. 26, 27.

who practise infant baptism, and which is derived in part from the Greek word παις, seems to countenance this rendering: but, in truth, παις does not signify *an infant.* It is used, in either the masculine or feminine gender, for one who has not reached maturity; and is applied to the young man who fell from the loft while Paul was preaching;[1] and is used by Justin, in another place, for the boys or young men who were the objects of unnatural lust.[2] A diminutive, παιδιον, formed from this word, is frequently used for infants; but even the diminutive is applied to a person twelve years of age.[3] In classic usage, the primitive word is rendered applicable to infants by a word added—νηπιος παις—*an infant boy.*[4] If the word itself denoted infancy, this addition would not be necessary. Once in the second chapter of Matthew it is applied to infants; but it is remarkable that the diminutive, παιδιον, is used nine times, in the same chapter, for infants. Why did the inspired writer adopt another word in this one case? We have the explanation in the note of Dr. Campbell on the passage: " The historian seems purposely to have changed the term παιδιον, which is used for *child,* no less than nine times in this chapter; as that word being neuter, and admitting only the neuter article, was not fit for marking the distinction of sexes; and to have adopted a term, which he nowhere else employs for infants, though frequently for men servants, and once for youths or boys." This application of παις to infants may be illustrated by a familiar usage in our own language. The words *boy* and *girl* do not signify an infant; and yet we ask whether an infant is a boy or a girl, if we wish to know its sex. Justin had no need to distinguish the sex of the persons whom he referred to, for he says, " There are among us persons of both sexes." Had Justin designed to say that these persons had been made disciples in infancy, the Greek language had words to express the idea; but what he did say amounts to nothing more than that these persons, now sixty or seventy years of age, had become disciples of Christ before they had arrived at maturity. This was the pedo-

---

[1] Acts xx. 12.

[2] Γυναικας εμοιχευσαν, και παιδας διεφθειραν. Justin's Works, London Edition, A. D. 1722, p. 10.

[3] Mark v. 39, 40, 42.   [4] Parkhurst's Lexicon, under the word νηπιος.

baptism which existed in the days of Justin; and to such pedobaptism there can be no objection.

Argument 5.—The commission may be rendered, " Go proselyte
all nations, baptizing them." Christ was a Jew, and addressed
these words to Jews. The Jews had been accustomed to make
proselytes to their religion from among the gentiles. When these
proselytes were received, they were circumcised and baptized,
together with their children. Had Christ commissioned his apostles to proselyte the nations to Judaism, circumcising and baptizing
them, they must have understood that children were to be circumcised and baptized with their parents. Being accustomed to this
mode of receiving proselytes, they would naturally conclude that
their Master intended them to adopt it in executing his command.

The proposed translation, " Go proselyte all nations," is not
correct; for a proselyte and a disciple are not the same thing.
If for the sentence, " Thou art his disciple, but we are Moses'
disciples," we substitute, " Thou art his proselyte, but we are
Moses' proselytes," every one will perceive that an important
change is made in the meaning. A proselyte to Judaism abandoned his former religion; but when John and Jesus made disciples, these disciples did not cease to be Jews. Paul claimed to be
a Jew,[1] and even a Pharisee,[2] after his conversion. The fishermen
of Galilee were indeed Jews, but they knew little, in all probability, of those efforts in which some of their nation compassed sea
and land to make one proselyte; and they could not have understood their Lord to refer to those efforts in the commission under
which they were to act. Some of them had been disciples of John;
and all of them had been associated with Christ in making and
baptizing disciples from among the Jews. Had they witnessed the
admission of a proselyte from heathenism to Judaism, they knew
well that the ceremonies which he underwent did not make him a
disciple of Christ. They could not, therefore, understand the
Saviour to refer to this process. The making and baptizing of
disciples was a process to which they were accustomed, and by it
they would naturally interpret the commission. Even if their
Jewish prejudices had led to the supposed interpretation, it would
have been unauthorized. These prejudices caused them to misinterpret the commission in another particular; and, in consequence,

---

[1] Acts xxi. 39   [2] Acts xxiii. 6.

they did not, for some time, preach the gospel to the uncircumcised gentiles. It was their duty, in interpreting the commission, to look more to the Saviour's words, and less to their Jewish prejudices: and the same obligation rests on us, and deserves the attention of those who urge the argument which we are considering.

The question whether the custom of baptizing proselytes to Judaism existed as early as the time of Christ, has engaged the attention of learned men, who have been divided respecting it. Prof. Stuart has given the subject an extended investigation, and finds no evidence that the custom existed before the destruction of Jerusalem.

Argument 6.—Infants were admitted to church-membership by circumcision, the initiatory rite under the former dispensation; and baptism now takes its place, being the same seal in a new form; and therefore ought to be administered to infants.

The arguments for the church-membership of infants were considered at large in the preceding section of this chapter. In this discussion, it was shown, that the church is not identical with the great nation descended from Abraham, and distinguished by the mark of circumcision. Since baptism was designed for those only who are spiritually qualified for membership in the church, no valid argument for the application of it to infants can be drawn from the fact, that the infant descendants of Abraham were marked by circumcision, as entitled to membership in the commonwealth of Israel.

If baptism is merely a new form of the same seal, the subjects to whom it is to be applied remaining the same, it ought still to be applied to infants on the eighth day. This day was fixed by express divine command. No authority inferior to that which made the covenant, can abrogate or change this precept. Moreover, the seal, as anciently administered, was not confined to descendants of the first generation; and baptism, if it is the same seal under another form, ought to be extended in its application to all the descendants of those who are admitted within the covenant.

It is an argument against the identity of baptism and circumcision, that baptism was administered to those who had previously received the seal in the other form, according to the command of God. They who were baptized under the ministry of John and of Jesus, were children of the covenant, and had been previously marked with the proper seal according to divine command in the covenant. Why was the seal necessary in another form? For some time after the ascension of Christ, the gospel was preached to the circumcised only; and no others were baptized. These persons were addressed as children of the covenant; and had the seal of the covenant in their flesh, affixed when that form of the seal was not only valid, but obligatory. Why was the repetition of the seal in another form necessary?

The command to circumcise, was positive; and every one who did not receive this token of the covenant in his flesh, was to be cut off from among God's people. If the church is founded on the covenant of circumcision, it becomes a deeply interesting inquiry, whether any but circumcised persons can be members. The theory is, that baptism takes the place of circumcision; but how can this theory annul the express command of God? We need authority for changing the form of the seal, as great, and as express, as that by which the original form was instituted; but we look for it in vain in the Holy Scriptures. Instead of finding an express precept for changing the form, or an express declaration that it has been changed, we find decisive proof, that the inspired apostles did not understand baptism to be a new form of the old seal. They discussed the question, whether gentile converts ought to be circumcised, and they decided in the negative; but they did not so decide, on the ground that baptism had taken the place of circumcision, and rendered the continued use of the old form unnecessary. This, according to the pedobaptist theory, was the true ground of their decision, being the true and only sufficient reason for laying aside the old form of the seal. That the apostles did not assign this reason, is decisive proof that they were strangers to the theory. With this evidence before us, how can we hold ourselves bound by the Abrahamic covenant, and expect the blessings which it is understood to promise, if we refuse its only divinely authorized seal?

In describing the completeness of Christians, Paul states, in one verse, that they are "circumcised with the circumcision that is made without hands;" and in the next, that they are "buried with Christ in baptism."[1] From the connexion in which these things

---

[1] Col. ii. 12.

are mentioned, some have argued that baptism takes the place of circumcision: but the passage does not justify the inference. Literal circumcision is not the duty of gentile believers; and is therefore no part of Christian completeness. Literal baptism is a duty of all Christians; and is therefore necessary to their completeness. The adjuncts with which circumcision is mentioned in the passage, shows regeneration to be intended. This, in the order of Christ's appointment, precedes baptism; and in this order Paul mentions both as distinct parts of Christian completeness. Nothing in the passage justifies the confounding of baptism with circumcision. Whatever analogy there may be between the two rites, their identity is not taught in these verses.

Argument 7.—Without insisting on a strict substitution of baptism for circumcision, it may be assumed as unquestionable, that a striking analogy exists between the two rites. Both are initiatory, both are religious, both are outward signs of inward grace, and seals of the righteousness of faith. The parental relation is one of exceeding importance. God has distinguished it greatly in his Word, and uses it, in his providence, as a chief means of perpetuating his church in the world. This relation is the same in all ages, and the essential principles of religion are the same. As, therefore, the relation was marked by a religious rite in the former dispensation, the immutable principles of the divine government make it proper that it should be marked by a religious rite now. Whatever may be said of the Abrahamic covenant as a whole, the stipulation which it contains, that the Lord would be a God to him and his seed, includes spiritual blessings, and is substantially the covenant which God now makes with every believer. As the parent and the child were admitted into the covenant by the same religious rite formerly, so they ought to be admitted by the same religious rite now. In this sense, baptism takes the place of circumcision; and ought, therefore, to be administered to infants.

. This argument is objectionable, on the ground that it rests the proof of a positive institute, on reasonings from general principles. If immutable principles require the parental relation to be marked with a religious rite, why was it not so marked from the beginning of the world? And why, when it became marked, was the relation to male descendants only, affected by the immutable principle? In the family of Abraham, the relation of the patriarch to all his descendants, remote as well as immediate, was marked by the rite then instituted: and if immutable principles require the relation to be marked by a religious rite now, it ought to be applied to remote descendants.

The promise to Abraham, to be a God to him and his seed, is contained in the covenant of circumcision, and is to be understood according to the tenor of that covenant. It extended to remote descendants, contemplated them as a nation, and brought the nation into a peculiar relation to God. It did not absolutely engage the spiritual blessing of justification which had been previously bestowed on the believing patriarch personally. The covenant now made with believers is personal, and secures personal spiritual blessings. "This is the covenant that I will make with the house of Israel : after those days, saith the Lord, I will put my laws into their minds, and write them in their hearts ; and I will be to them a God, and they shall be to me a people." [1] The promise of this covenant is absolute, and secures the putting of the law in the heart. This, the promise in the Abrahamic covenant did not secure ; and, on this account, the covenant established on better promises, is called a new covenant. So different is its nature, from the national covenant made with Abraham, that, if it were right to infer positive institutes from general principles, we could not, with propriety, draw the inference which infant baptism requires.

The agreement between baptism and circumcision, as *initiatory* rites, is urged to no avail, if the bodies into which they initiate are differently constituted. They may both be called religious rites, because religion has to do with whatever God commands ; but we need God's command, to instruct us in the proper use of these rites. They have also been called *sealing* rites : but in what sense they seal, is involved in obscurity. Abraham received the sign of circumcision,—a seal of the righteousness of the faith which he had, yet being uncircumised. His *receiving* of circumcision seems to imply more than merely his being circumcised. It signifies that circumcision began with him. This fact was viewed by Paul as a proof that he was already in the favor of God ; and the apostle regards it as a confirmation or seal of what had been previously said. " Abraham believed in the Lord, and he counted it to him for righteousness." [2] Paul does not say that circumcision was a seal to all to whom it was administered. The case of Abraham, and the faith

---

[1] Heb. viii. 10.   [2] Gen. xv. 6.

of Abraham, are all that his argument had in view, in the use of the word seal.

Baptism is nowhere in the Scriptures called a seal. Believers are said to be sealed by the Holy Spirit; and the validity of this seal God will ever acknowledge; but many receive baptism who are not sealed by the Holy Spirit unto the day of redemption.[1] We need to understand in what sense, and by what authority, the two rites are called sealing, and what engagements they, as seals, confirm, before we can argue, that because one of them was applied to infants, the other must, in like manner, be applied to infants. When we view the nature and design of the two rites in the light of the Holy Scriptures, we discover that circumcision was intended for the literal descendants of Ábraham, but that literal descent from Abraham, without faith, gave no title to baptism. Whatever agreement may be traced between the two ceremonies in other respects, their difference in this particular destroys the analogy, at the very point where alone it can be of use to the cause of infant baptism.

The argument proves too much. We have seen that it extends the application of the religious rite to remote descendants. Besides this, it applies it, not to infant children only, but to children of whatever age, provided they belong to the household. Moreover, it requires that the relation of master and servant be marked in the same way. This also is an important relation, which God has used in extending his church; for servants have often been converted by being brought into pious families. The precept given to Abraham, extended to the whole household; and was given in very explicit language. The argument requires that every believer should put himself in the place of the patriarch, and consider himself bound by this command. At this point, the subject may be viewed advantageously in connection with the following argument.

Argument 8.—The three households of Lydia, the jailer, and Stephanas, are said in Scripture to have been baptized. It is improbable that there were three entire households without any infants in them. The manner in which the facts are recorded, especially in the case of Lydia's household, indicates that it was the prevailing custom to baptize the household, when the head of it became a believer. No intimation is given, that the members

---

[1] Eph. iv. 30.

of the household were all believers, and admitted to baptism on their personal faiths; but their baptism followed, of course, on the admission of Lydia herself into the church. Were such a statement published, in the journal of any modern missionary, every one would understand the missionary to be a pedobaptist. No one expects to read an account of household baptisms, in a history of Baptist missions.

Mention is made in the New Testament, of several households, which appear to have consisted entirely of Christian believers.[1] Such instances are not uncommon in modern times, even among Baptists: and, in times of religious revivals, whole households are not unfrequently baptized on profession of faith. The probability of such occurrences in the slow progress of modern missions in a heathen nation, is far less; and it would be unfair to estimate from a history of missions, the probability that whole households were converted at once, under the ministry of the apostles. A modern missionary sometimes labors for years, and scarcely reports a single convert; but, in primitive times, three thousand were converted in one day, and the Holy Spirit fell on the whole congregation assembled in the house of Cornelius. In this state of things, it is not surprising that three households should have been converted and baptized. We are told that the nobleman of Capernaum "believed, and his whole house;"[2] that Crispus "believed with all his house;"[3] and that Cornelius "feared God with all his house." Here are three households, which consisted entirely of pious persons; and the probability that these three had infants in them, must be as great as in the case of the three households that were baptized. Besides, in the accounts given of these last households, circumstances are mentioned which strongly indicate the absence of children. 1. In the case of the jailer's household, "they spake unto him the word of the Lord, and to all that were in his house;"[5] "he rejoiced, believing in God with all his house."[6] Who would expect to read such statements as these in the journal of a pedobaptist missionary, who, on receiving a convert from heathenism, baptized him with his infant children? 2. In the case of the household of Stephanas we are informed, "that they *addicted*

---

[1] 2 Tim. iv. 19; Acts x. 2; Acts xvi. 34; 1 Cor. xvi. 15, 19; John iv. 53.
[2] John iv. 53.   [3] Acts xviii. 8.   [4] Acts x. 2.
[5] Acts xvi. 32.   [6] V. 34.

themselves to the ministry of the saints."[1] It has been said that this was some years after their baptism, when the infants might have grown up. But, in most families, while some infants grow, other infants are added; and in replying to an argument dependant on probability, we are at liberty to assume, that the probability of finding infants in the house of Stephanas was as great at one time as at the other. We may also notice, that the baptism of this household is not mentioned in connection with the baptism of the head. Paul baptized the household of Stephanas;[2] but who baptized Stephanas himself, we are not informed. So far as appears, the two baptisms were performed at different times, and were independent of each other. 3. In the case of Lydia's household we have the following facts: Lydia was "a seller of purple of the city of Thyatira."[3] No mention is made of husband or children. She had a house at Philippi, which she called "my house;" and the business in which she was engaged, appears to have been under her own management. When Paul and Silas were released from prison, it is said, "they entered into the house of Lydia; and when they had seen the brethren, they comforted them, and departed."[4] The connection of the clauses in this verse, renders it probable, that the brethren here mentioned, belonged to the house of Lydia, and were the persons baptized with her. This probability ought to be admitted, in an argument founded on probability; and it is at least as great, as that Lydia, the apparently single proprietor and manager of her own house and business, should have had infant children. So far as to the argument about probability.

The second part of the argument is, that the narrative states the baptism of the household as following, of course, on the faith and baptism of the head. But this, as we have seen, is not the case, with respect to the household of Stephanas and the jailer. All the weight of the argument rests on the single case of Lydia; and it is merely an argument from the silence of Scripture. We are not expressly informed that Lydia's household were believers; but the silence on this point does not prove that they were not. It is stated, in another place, that "Crispus, the chief ruler of the synagogue,

---

[1] 1 Cor. xvi. 15.   [2] 1 Cor. i. 16.   [3] Acts xvi. 14.
[4] V. 40.

believed, with all his house." No mention is made of their baptism: but the silence of Scripture on this point, does not prove that they were not baptized. Faith and baptism are everywhere throughout the narrative so connected with each other, that the mention of both, in every instance, was unnecessary. The faith of the household is not mentioned in the case of Lydia; neither is it mentioned in Paul's address to the jailer:—"Believe on the Lord Jesus Christ, and thou shalt be saved, and thy house." [1] . Here the promise of salvation is made to the household, without an express requirement of faith from them,—the command, "believe," being in the singular number. We know, from the whole tenor of Scripture, that the jailer's household were not saved on his faith; and we have the same reason for knowing that Lydia's household were not baptized on her faith.

If any one should maintain that, when households are said to *believe* and to *fear God*, infants may have been overlooked in the statement, because known to be incapable of religious affections, we admit the possibility of what is supposed, and we maintain, in turn, that the same may have been true with respect to baptism. In all the sacred volume, and in all the usage of primitive times, faith was a qualification for baptism; and it may be that, in the mention of household baptism, no account was taken of infants, because it was universally known that they were never baptized. Our cause admits this hypothesis; but is not dependent on it.

A distinction ought to be made, between household baptism and infant baptism. The preceding argument, if it proves either, proves household baptism; and the same is true of the argument now before us. Children of various ages, even to adult years, and servants, are included in the proper import of the word household. It was so, when the covenant of circumcision was made with Abraham; for his son Ishmael, and his servants, were circumcised. It is so in the Acts of the Apostles: for in the household of Cornelius, "two household servants" are mentioned.

It deserves to be carefully noticed, that almost every argument for infant church-membership and infant baptism, tends to prove, so far as it proves either, not the church-membership and baptism of infants, but of whole households. The covenant of circumcision

---

[1] V. 31.

required the rite to be administered to the whole household. Under the Mosaic covenant, when a stranger was admitted, he was required to be circumcised with all his household; and the same law was applied to him, in the keeping of the passover, as to those born in the land. When proselyte baptism was practised, it was applied to all the household. No example of infant baptism can be found in the Bible; but the three examples which have been relied on to prove it, are all examples of household baptism. Now, according to a hypothesis stated in the last paragraph, it may be that the infants of a household may be overlooked, when something is affirmed of the household, which is incompatible with infancy; but it can never be supposed, that the term household signifies infants only, to the exclusion of older members. If household baptism has been proved, who will practise it? The admission of ungodly youths and servants to baptism and church privileges, when the father and master becomes converted, is so contrary to the spirit and tenor of the gospel, that no one ventures to advocate it. Yet this is the point to which almost every argument tends, which has been advanced in support of infant baptism. These arguments are numerous: and if each one could bring a ray of light, however feeble, we might expect the combined illumination to render the subject visible; but we have traced the direction of the rays, and find that their concentrated force, whatever may be its illuminating power, falls elsewhere, and leaves infant baptism still in the dark.

Argument 9.—Learned men have searched the writings of the Christian fathers, and have found evidence as abundant, and specific, and certain, as history affords of almost any fact, that infant baptism universally prevailed from the days of the apostles, through four centuries. This ought to satisfy us, that the practice originated in the apostolic churches.

Other learned men have examined the same writings, and have arrived at the conclusion, that infant baptism was wholly unknown, until about the close of the second century;—that it originated in Africa, and in the third century became prevalent there, but did not supplant the primitive baptism in the Oriental churches, until the fifth century.

Amidst this conflict of opinions, derived from the same source, it is a happy privilege which we enjoy, to leave the muddy streams of tradition, and drink at the pure fountain of revelation. The aim of the present work is, to ascertain what the Scriptures teach on the subject of church order; and it does not accord with the design, to enter into an investigation of questions appertaining to ecclesiastical history; but I will state, very briefly, what appear to me, so far as I have been able to investigate the subject, the chief facts to be gleaned from the early fathers, relative to the origin of infant baptism.

No trace of infant baptism can be found, previous to the time of Justin Martyr. The passage of his writings, which is quoted on page 174, has been regarded as the first clear testimony on the subject; but we have shown that this, when properly interpreted, means nothing more than that some persons, then sixty or seventy years of age, had been made disciples of Christ before they were fully grown. In another part of Justin's writings, he purposely gives an account of the usages which existed among Christians, respecting baptism; and, in doing this, he describes the baptism of believers, without any intimation that infants were concerned in the rite. Had infant baptism been the universal practice, his purpose would have required a description of it.

The primitive practice required each candidate for baptism to profess his faith personally. But a custom arose, of permitting the profession to be made by proxy: the candidate being present, and signifying his assent. This custom made it easy for very young persons to be admitted to the rite, and the opinion, which had now become prevalent, that baptism possessed a saving efficacy, produced a tendency to extend the application of it to children. Tertullian, who wrote about A. D. 200, opposed this tendency; and insisted that, instead of granting baptism on the candidate's asking for it, and making profession through his sponsors, the baptism should be deferred until he had become instructed respecting its nature and design. Thus far, it does not appear that the rite was ever administered to children incapable of asking for it; but Cyprian, A. D. 250, interpreted the cries of new-born babes to be an asking for the grace which baptism was supposed to confer. The propriety of giving it to infants was now extensively admitted, but the practice was not universal.

The late Neander, who is esteemed the greatest of ecclesiastical historians, says: "Baptism was administered at first only to adults, as men were accustomed to conceive baptism and faith as strictly connected." "Immediately after Irenæus, in the last years of the second century, Tertullian appears as a zealous opponent of infant baptism: a proof that the practice had not as yet come to be regarded as an apostolical institution; for, otherwise, he would hardly have ventured to express himself so strongly against it."[1] "For these reasons, Tertullian declared against infant baptism; which at that time was *certainly not a generally prevailing practice;* was not yet regarded as an apostolical institution. On the contrary, as the assertions of Tertullian render in the highest degree probable, *it had just begun to spread;* and was therefore regarded by many *as an innovation.*"[2]

Jacobi, a learned friend of Neander, says: "Infant baptism was established neither by Christ nor the apostles." "Many circumstances conspired early to introduce the practice of infant baptism."[3]

Mosheim, in his account of the Second Century, says: "The sacrament of *baptism* was administered publicly twice every year, at the festivals of Easter and Pentecost, or Whitsuntide, either by the *bishop*, or the *presbyters*, in consequence of his authorization and appointment. The persons that were to be baptized, after that they had repeated the creed, confessed and renounced their sins, and particularly the *devil* and his pompous allurements, were immersed under water, and received into Christ's kingdom by a solemn invocation of Father, Son, and Holy Ghost, according to the express command of our Blessed Lord. After baptism, they received the *sign of the cross*, were *anointed*, and, by *prayers* and imposition of hands, were solemnly commended to the mercy of God, and dedicated to his service; in consequence of which they received *milk* and *honey*, which concluded the ceremony. The reasons of this particular ritual coincide with what we have said in general concerning the origin and causes of the multiplied ceremonies that crept from time to time into the church.

"Adult persons were prepared for baptism by abstinence, prayer, and other pious exercises. It was to answer for them that spon-

---

[1] History of Christian Religion and Church, pp. 311, 312 (Torrey's Translation.

[2] Spirit of Tertullian, p. 207. Quoted from Christian Review, Vol. xvi. pp. 517, 520.

[3] Kitto's Cyclopedia; Art. Baptism.

sors or godfathers were first instituted, though they were afterwards admitted also in the baptism of infants."

The use of sponsors is retained in the Episcopal Church. The
officiating minister addresses the child as if he were an intelligent
candidate; and the sponsors give what is regarded as the answer of
the child. In these forms, we may see the remains of primitive
usage, the lifeless corpse of the ancient baptism, which was once
animated with piety, and profession strictly personal.

CHAPTER V.

COMMUNION.

Section I.—PERPETUITY OF THE LORD'S SUPPER.

THE RITE USUALLY CALLED THE LORD'S SUPPER WAS INSTITUTED BY CHRIST, TO BE OBSERVED IN HIS CHURCHES TILL THE END OF THE WORLD.

On the night which preceded the Saviour's crucifixion, he ate the passover with his disciples. At the close of the meal, the ceremony called the Lord's Supper was instituted. The account of the institution is thus given by Matthew: "As they were eating, Jesus took bread, and blessed it, and brake it, and gave it to the disciples, and said, Take, eat; this is my body. And he took the cup, and gave thanks, and gave it to them, saying, Drink ye all of it: for this is my blood of the new testament, which is shed for many for the remission of sins. But I say unto you, I will not drink henceforth of this fruit of the vine, until that day when I drink it new with you in my Father's kingdom."[1] Mark's account is in nearly the same words.[2] Luke's narrative differs in several particulars. He mentions a previous cup, which seems to have concluded the proper paschal supper. At the distribution of the bread, he adds these words, omitted by the other evangelists: "This do in remembrance of me." In the giving of the second cup, he states explicitly that it was "after supper;" and, by this expression, distinguishes it from the preceding cup, which was a part of the supper.[3] In the eleventh chapter of the first epistle to the Corinthians, Paul gives an account of the institution, agreeing substantially with the accounts given by the evangelists. At the

---

[1] Matt. xxvi. 26—29.   [2] Mark xiv. 22—24.   [3] Luke xxii. 17—20.

distribution of the bread, he adds the words: "This is my body, which is broken for you: this do in remembrance of me." And, at the giving of the cup, he adds: "This cup is the new testament in my blood: this do ye, as oft as ye drink it, in remembrance of me." To all this he subjoins, "As often as ye eat this bread and drink this cup, ye do show the Lord's death till he come. Wherefore whosoever shall eat this bread, and drink this cup of the Lord unworthily, shall be guilty of the body and blood of the Lord. But let a man examine himself, and so let him eat of this bread and drink of this cup. For he that eateth and drinketh unworthily, eateth and drinketh damnation to himself, not discerning the Lord's body."

From these several accounts taken in connection, we learn that after Jesus had concluded the last passover with his disciples, he used the bread and cup for a purpose unknown in that supper; and commanded the disciples to use them in the same manner, in remembrance of him. The time during which this memorial of Christ was designed to be kept, we might infer from the words of the evangelist. Jesus directed the minds of the disciples from the feast which he then kept with them to a future feast, to be enjoyed together in the Father's kingdom. During the interval this new institution was to be observed as a memorial of the past, and a pledge of the future. But Paul has drawn the inference for us, "As often as ye eat this bread, and drink this cup, ye do show the Lord's death till he come." The time for the observance is here definitely marked out as extending to Christ's second coming. Baptism was instituted to be observed "till the end of the world," and the supper has the same limit prescribed for its duration.

The institution of the supper described by Paul, he states that he had received from the Lord Jesus, and had delivered to the Corinthian church. These facts show that Christ designed his apostle to inculcate the observance; and that the apostle was not negligent in this particular. He praised the church for keeping the ordinances as he had delivered them; but censured an abuse which had arisen among them in celebrating the supper. He does not, because of this abuse, dissuade from the further observance of it, but he labors to correct the abuse; and he renews the command, "Let a man examine himself, and so let him eat." The proof thus furnished is abundant and decisive, that the observance was designed to be established and perpetuated in the churches.

We have further proof in the Acts of the Apostles. The church at Jerusalem continued steadfastly in the apostles' doctrine and fellowship, and in breaking of bread, and in prayers;[1] and the disciples at Troas assembled on the first day of the week *to break bread.*[2]

The Scriptural designation of the rite in the passages just cited, is *the breaking of bread.* The name *Eucharist* is often given to it, derived from the Greek word *ευχαριστεω*, and referring to the thanksgiving which preceded the distribution of the elements. This name is not used in the Scriptures. Some remarks have been made in another place (pp. 57, 58) respecting the name *Lord's Supper.* It is not clear that we have Scripture authority for using this name to designate the rite. But, considering the rite as a memorial of our Lord's last supper with his disciples, the name is significant—like the name *passover* applied to the rite which kept in memory the fact, that the destroying angel *passed over* the habitations of the Israelites. The name may also refer to the spiritual feast which believers enjoy with their Lord, who graciously *sups* with them. The name *Trinity*, and the name *person*, applied to the three-fold distinction in the Trinity, are used without Scripture authority, merely as convenient terms; and the names *Eucharist* and *Lord's Supper*, may be used in the same way, but we must always be careful to found no article of faith on any use of terms for which we cannot produce divine authority.

The Quakers object to the perpetuity of the supper, as they do to that of baptism. Their chief objections, we shall proceed to consider.

Objection 1.—The bread and the cup belonged to the passover; and the evangelists state, that it was while eating this feast that the bread and cup were used, which constitute the supposed new institution. The breaking of bread is frequently mentioned as customary in ordinary meals. We ought, therefore, to consider it as a common occurrence at table, and to interpret the words of Christ as a command that in all our eating and drinking we should remember him, according to what is said elsewhere, "Whether ye eat or drink, or whatsoever ye do, do all to the glory of God."[3]

---

[1] Acts ii. 42.   [2] Acts xx. 7.   [3] 1 Cor. x. 31.

The simplicity of the rite, is no valid objection against it; but rather a recommendation. Bread and the cup were in common use; but they were not, on this account, less adapted to the purpose for which Christ employed them. Water is a common element, and *immersion* in it was common among the Jews; but these facts did not render immersion in water less fit for a Christian ordinance. The rites are new, not because new elements are used, but because they are used for a new purpose. The whole of the paschal services commemorated the deliverance from Egypt. The new institution was designed to commemorate a different deliverance, by the broken body and shed blood of Christ. No one will maintain, that the breaking of bread in ordinary meals, was designed for this purpose. So distinctly marked was this new purpose, that Paul says, "He that eateth and drinketh unworthily, is guilty of the body and blood of the Lord." If he did it, "not discerning the Lord's body," he overlooked the great design of the institution, and was guilty. This fault the objection commits, in confounding the bread and wine of the eucharist with ordinary food.

Objection 2.—The Acts of the Apostles mention only two instances in which the breaking of bread was observed by the disciples; and both of these manifestly refer to ordinary meals. The church at Jerusalem continued in the breaking of bread; and this is explained in the words, "Breaking bread from house to house, did eat their meat with gladness, and singleness of heart."[1] The disciples at Troas met to break bread; and what is hereby meant, may be learned from what is afterwards said: "When he therefore was come up again, and had broken bread, and eaten, and talked a long while, even till break of day, so he departed."[2] This is clearly an ordinary meal, preparatory to Paul's departure. We see, therefore, that the Acts of the Apostles record no instance of the eucharistic observance; and the silence cannot be accounted for, if the observance had been customary.

No doubt exists that the phrase, *breaking of bread*, sometimes describes what occurred at ordinary meals. Jesus manifested himself to the two disciples at Emmaus, in the breaking of bread, when they had sat down to an ordinary meal; and Paul broke bread to those who were with him in the ship, to terminate their long fast. In the second chapter of Acts, the phrase occurs twice. In the first instance, the connection shows that the eucharistic

---

[1] Acts ii. 46. [2] Acts xx. 11.

observance is intended. "They continued in the apostles' doctrine, and fellowship, and breaking bread, and prayers." In the second instance, the connection shows that ordinary meals are intended. The repetition, instead of proving the same thing to be intended in both instances, proves rather the contrary. Distinct facts are described.

Did the disciples at Troas meet for an ordinary meal? Was this the meeting which the sacred historian so particularly mentions? The character of primitive Christianity forbids the supposition. These disciples were accustomed to meet for the worship of God; and the important design of their assembling together could not have been forgotten or overlooked on this occasion, when they had the presence of Paul. It was appropriate to mention the eucharist, as a part of public worship, in speaking of the purpose for which they assembled; but to describe them as having assembled for an ordinary meal, is inconsistent with their character, and inconsistent with the occasion. If, as is most probable, the breaking of bread next morning, at the break of day, was an ordinary meal preparatory to Paul's departure, it was a different breaking of bread from that which had brought the disciples together on the preceding day.

These are the only two cases in which the observance of the Lord's supper is mentioned in the Acts; but they are sufficient to prove the existence of the observance. The church at Jerusalem continued steadfastly in the breaking of bread. It could have been no commendation of them, that they continued steadfastly in eating ordinary meals; but their steadfast continuance in the divine institution, is historical proof that it was observed by the first church as a part of their public worship. This fact explains what is said about the disciples at Troas, and the two statements make the historical evidence, in this book, as satisfactory as is necessary. The observance of the rite by the church at Corinth, makes the historical proof complete.

Objection 3.—The Jewish worship consisted of meats, and drinks, and divers baptisms, and carnal ordinances; but these are not adapted to the spiritual worship of the Christian dispensation. Paul teaches that "the kingdom of God is not meat and drink; but righteousness, peace, and joy in the Holy Ghost."[1] The Lord's

---

[1] Rom. xiv. 17.

supper comes under the denomination of meats and drinks, and is therefore not appropriate to the new economy. Paul expressly commands, "Let no man judge you in meat or in drink;"[1] and urges believers to leave those things which perish in the using, and set their affections above.

This objection substantially agrees with Objection 5 to the perpetuity of baptism; and what is there said in reply, is applicable here. The meats and drinks of the former dispensation were shadows of good things to come; but the body is of Christ. So Paul teaches, in connection with the text last quoted in the objection; and, in this way, he explains what meat and drink he refers to. The Jewish ceremonies were typical of Christ to come; but the Lord's supper is a memorial of Christ already come. It is, therefore, not included in the meat and drink intended by the apostle. The passover was included in these abrogated meats and drinks; which ceased to be obligatory after Christ, our passover, was sacrificed for us. At the very time when he was about to put an end to this old ceremony, he instituted the Lord's supper; and it is, therefore, incredible that he meant this to expire with the other. Paul says, "Let no man judge you in meat or in drink." The abrogated ceremonies are now without divine authority; and, therefore, he calls *these meats and drinks* the commandments of men. But the bread and wine of the supper, are commandments of the Lord; and therefore Paul says, with reference to these: "Let a man examine himself, and so let him eat."

The numerous and burdensome rites of the Old Testament would not be adapted to the more spiritual dispensation which we are under; but it does not follow that the two simple ceremonies, baptism and the Lord's supper, are incompatible with it. We are yet in the flesh, and need the use of such memorials. In the proper use of them, believers have found them greatly profitable, and well adapted to promote spirituality. Besides the benefit which they yield to the individual believer, these two ceremonies stand, like two monuments, reared up in the time of Christ, and testifying to the world concerning Christ and his doctrine. Their use, as evidences of Christianity and its cardinal doctrines, the Trinity and the atonement, is incalculably great, and displays the wisdom which instituted them.

---

[1] Col. ii. 16.

In addition to the direct arguments which have been adduced, some allusions are found in the New Testament, showing, in an interesting manner, that baptism and the Lord's supper were contemplated as parts of Christianity. In the next chapter to that in which Paul corrects the Corinthian abuse of the supper, he says, " By one Spirit are we all baptized into one body, and have all been made to drink into one Spirit."[1] The allusion to both the ordinances, is manifest. In another part of the same epistle, he speaks of baptism unto Moses, and of their eating and drinking in the wilderness, in a manner which shows an allusion to the two Christian rites.[2]

Objection 4.—At the same supper in which Christ is supposed to have instituted the eucharist, he washed his disciples' feet, and commanded them to wash one another's feet. The command is equally as positive, as that which enjoined the use of bread and wine; yet Christians are generally agreed, that the command does not require to be obeyed literally. The thing signified by the outward form is what demands regard; and the same rule of interpretation ought to be applied to the eucharist.

The command ought, in both cases, to be obeyed strictly, according to the design of Christ. If Christians generally fail to render strict obedience to Christ's command respecting the washing of feet, we ought to begin a reform, and not make one neglect a precedent and argument for another. In the next chapter we shall inquire into the obligation to wash one another's feet. In this, we have ascertained, that Christ designed a literal use of bread and wine, and, this point being ascertained, our duty is determined; whatever doubt and obscurity may remain respecting any other subject.

Section II.—DESIGN.

The Lord's Supper was designed to be a memorial of Christ, a representation that the communicant receives spiritual nourishment from him, and a token of fellowship among the communicants.

The rite is commemorative. The passover served for a memorial of deliverance from Egypt; and, year after year, as the pious

---

[1] 1 Cor. xii. 13.   [2] 1 Cor. x. 2, 3, 4.

14

Israelites partook of it, they were reminded of that marvellous deliverance, and were required to tell of it to their children. The passover was instituted on the night of that deliverance. The Lord's supper was instituted on the night when Jesus was betrayed to be crucified; and serves for a memorial of his sufferings and death. When we remember him, we are to remember his agonies, his body broken, and his blood shed. In preaching the gospel, Paul determined to know nothing but Jesus Christ, and him crucified. So, in the eucharist, Christ is presented to view; not as transfigured on Mount Tabor, or as glorified at his Father's right hand, but as suffering and dying. We delight to keep in memory the honors which they whom we love have received; but Jesus calls us to remember the humiliation which he endured. To the lowest point of his humiliation, the supper directs our thoughts.

The simple ceremony is admirably contrived to serve more than a single purpose. While it shows forth the Lord's death, it represents at the same time the spiritual benefit which the believer derives from it. He eats the bread, and drinks the wine, in token of receiving his spiritual sustenance from Christ crucified. The rite preaches the doctrine that Christ died for our sins, and that we live by his death. He said, "Except ye eat the flesh of the Son of Man, and drink his blood, ye have no life in you."[1] These remarkable words teach the necessity of his atoning sacrifice, and of faith in that sacrifice. Without these, salvation and eternal life are impossible. When Christ said, "My flesh is meat indeed, and my blood is drink indeed,"[2] he did not refer to his flesh and blood, literally understood. He calls himself the living bread which came down from heaven.[3] This cannot be affirmed of his literal flesh. To have eaten this literally, would not have secured everlasting life; and equally inefficacious is the Romanist ceremony, in which they absurdly imagine that they eat the real body of Christ. His body is present in the eucharist in no other sense than that in which we can "*discern*" it. When he said, "This is my body," the plain meaning is, "This represents my body." So we point to a picture, and say, "This is Christ on the cross." The eucharist is a picture, so to speak, in which the bread represents the body of Christ suffering for our sins. Faith discerns what the

---

[1] John vi. 53.   [2] John vi. 55.   [3] John vi. 51.

picture represents. It discerns the Lord's body in the commemorative representation of it, and derives spiritual nourishment from the atoning sacrifice made by his broken body and shed blood.

A third purpose which this ceremony serves, and to which it is wisely adapted, is, to signify the fellowship of the communicants with one another. This is taught in the words of Paul: "The bread which we break, is it not the communion of the body of Christ? For we, being many, are one bread, and one body: for we are all partakers of that one bread."[1] A communion or joint participation in the benefits of Christ's death, is signified by the joint partaking of the outward elements. "What communion," says he, "hath light with darkness; and what concord hath Christ with Belial?" "Ye cannot be partakers of the Lord's table, and of the table of devils."[2] In these words of Paul, to sit at the same table, and drink of the same cup, are regarded as indications of communion and concord. Believers meet around the table of the Lord, in one faith on the same atonement, in one hope of the same inheritance, and with one heart filled with love to the same Lord.

A notion has prevailed extensively, that a spiritual efficacy attends the outward performance of the rite, if duly administered. Some mysterious influence is supposed to accompany the bread and wine, and render them means of grace to the recipient. But, as the gospel, though it is the power of God unto salvation, does not profit unless mixed with faith in those who hear it; much less can mere ceremonies profit without faith. In baptism, we rise with Christ through the faith of the operation of God; and in the supper, we cannot partake of Christ, and receive him as our spiritual nourishment, but by faith: "That Christ may dwell in your hearts by faith."[3] The contrary opinion makes these sacraments as they have been called, saving ordinances, and substitutes outward ceremony for vital piety.

---

[1] 1 Cor. x. 16, 17.   [2] 1 Cor. x. 21.   [3] Eph. iii. 17.

Section III.—COMMUNICANTS.

THE LORD'S SUPPER WAS DESIGNED TO BE CELEBRATED BY EACH CHURCH IN PUBLIC ASSEMBLY.

Intelligence is necessary in order to the proper receiving of the supper. When infant baptism arose, infant communion arose with it. The superstitious notion that the sacraments possessed a sort of magical efficacy, prevailed extensively; and parental affection desired for the children the grace of the supper, as well as that of baptism. The argument was as good for the one as for the other; and infant communion had as much authority from the apostles as infant baptism. But the practice of infant communion is now generally laid aside. It is generally conceded, that infants are incapable of receiving the rite according to its design. They cannot remember Christ, or discern the Lord's body; and they cannot perform the self-examination which is required previous to the communion. If the rite conveyed a magical influence, infants might receive it; but correct views have so far prevailed, as to restrict this ordinance to persons of intelligence.

Faith is also a requisite to the receiving of the supper. If mere intelligence were a sufficient qualification, men who partake of the table of devils, might partake also of the Lord's table. Paul decides that this cannot be, and therefore that none can properly partake of the Lord's table but those who have renounced the devil, and devoted themselves to the Lord. The outward ceremony cannot, of itself, yield profit to those who receive it. They cannot please God in it, without faith; and without faith they cannot derive spiritual nourishment from the body and blood of Christ.

The rite was designed to be social. Of the three purposes which it serves, as enumerated in the last section, the third requires that it be celebrated by a company. It could not serve as a token of fellowship between the disciples of Christ, if it were performed in solitude. To perpetuate a social rite, society is necessary; and the disciples of Christ, by his authority, organize the societies, called churches. As these are the only divinely instituted Christian societies, we might judge beforehand, that the supper would be committed to these, for its observance and perpetuation. This we find to be true. Paul says to the church at Corinth, "I praise you that ye keep the ordinances as I delivered them to you." "I have received of the Lord that which also I delivered unto you."[1] He then proceeds to mention the institution of the supper, and speaks of it as observed by the whole church assembled. Of some other matters, he says, in this connection, "We have no such custom, neither the churches of God;"[2] but everything in his account of the Lord's supper, accords with its being a church rite; and with this, all that is recorded of its observance at Jerusalem and Troas, perfectly harmonizes. The administration of the rite to a dying individual, as is practised by some, has no sanction in the Word of God.

The rite should be celebrated by the church, in public assembly. It is said, "As often as ye eat this bread, and drink this cup, ye do show the Lord's death till he come."[3] To show his death, requires that it be done in public. It should be held forth to the view of the irreligious, who may be willing to attend in the public assembly. In another part of the same epistle, Paul speaks of the effect produced on unbelievers who came into the public assembly of the church.[4] As it is right to hold forth the word of life to them, so it is right to show the Lord's death before them, in the divinely appointed manner.

By the Jews it was held unlawful to eat with the uncircumcised. Paul has taught us, that familiar intercourse with unconverted persons, is not unlawful to Christians; but he says, "If any man, that is called a brother, be a fornicator, or covetous, or an idolater, or a railer, or a drunkard, or an extortioner, with such a one, no not to eat."[5] In this prohibition, eating at the Lord's table with such a wicked person, if not specially intended, is certainly included. Though such an one may have been called a brother, it was wrong for the church to retain him in fellowship, and continue to eat with him, in the peculiar manner by which fellowship was indicated. In the words of Christ, every such wicked person was to be accounted as an heathen man and a publican.

In primitive times, the members of different local churches associated with each other, as members of the great fraternity. Paul was doubtless welcomed at the Lord's table, by the disciples at

---

[1] 1 Cor. xi. 2, 23. [2] V. 16. [3] 1 Cor. xi. 26.
[4] 1 Cor. xiv. 24, 25. [5] 1 Cor. v. 11.

Troas. This transient communion is now practised. The Lord's supper is properly a church ordinance; but an individual, duly qualified to be admitted to membership in a church, may be admitted for the time as a member, and received to transient communion, without any departure from the design of the institution.

SECTION 4.—OPEN COMMUNION.

We have seen that the Lord's supper has been committed to the local churches for observance and perpetuation; and that local churches, if organized according to the Scriptures, contain none but baptized persons. It follows hence, that baptism is a pre-requisite to communion at the Lord's table. The position which baptism holds in the commission, determines its priority to the other commanded observances therein referred to, among which church communion must be included. This is the doctrine which has been held on the subject by Christians generally, in all ages; and it is now held by the great mass of Pedobaptists. With them we have no controversy as to the principle by which approach to the Lord's table should be regulated. We differ from them in practice, because we account nothing Christian baptism, but immersion on profession of faith, and we, therefore, exclude very many whom they admit. But there are Baptists, who reject the principle that baptism is a prerequisite to communion, and maintain that nothing ought to be a condition of communion, which is not a condition of salvation. They hold that all pious persons, baptized or unbaptized, have a right to the Lord's supper. Their practice is called open or mixed communion, and the arguments in defence of it will now claim our attention.

Argument 1.—The Lord's supper, when instituted by Christ, was given to persons who had never received Christian baptism, and therefore baptism cannot be a prerequisite.

The first supper was administered to the apostles. Some of these had been baptized by John; and, since the disciples made by Jesus in his personal ministry, were also baptized, we are warranted to conclude, that all the apostles had been baptized. If it be denied that John's baptism, and the baptism administered under the immediate direction of Christ during his personal ministry, were Christian baptism, we call for proof. Until the distinction is established, the argument has no foundation.

But there is another way in which the argument may be met. We have every certainty, which the nature of the case admits, that the apostles were not baptized after the institution of the Lord's supper. From this time to the ensuing Pentecost, when they entered fully on the work assigned them, their history is so given as to exclude all probability that they were baptized in this interval; and, if they were qualified to enter fully on their work, without another baptism, another baptism was unnecessary; and was therefore never afterwards received. Mr. Hall, the ablest advocate of open communion, says: "My deliberate opinion is, that, in the Christian sense of the term, they were not baptized at all." [1] When Paul was made an apostle, before he entered on his work he was commanded to be baptized. From some cause, the other apostles were not under this obligation. We account for the difference, by the supposition, that they had already received what was substantially the same as the baptism administered to Paul. But, if we are mistaken on this point, it is still true that the eleven apostles were not under obligation to receive any other baptism; and their case, therefore, differed radically from that of persons who are under obligation to be baptized, and are living in neglect of this duty. The latter may be required, and ought to be required, to profess Christ according to his commandment, before they are admitted to church-membership and communion; but the eleven apostles, from some cause, whatever it may have been, were under no such obligation. The cases are not parallel; and, therefore, the argument fails.

Argument 2.—The argument for strict communion, from the position of baptism in the commission, proves too much. If it proves that we ought not to teach the unbaptized to commune at the Lord's table, it proves also that we ought not to teach them the moral precepts of Christ included in the words, "all things whatsoever I have commanded you."

The apostles were commanded to preach the gospel to every creature. In executing their commission, it became their duty to instruct the ignorant and them that were out of the way. They adapted their instructions to every man's character and circum-

---

[1] Hall's Works, Vol. i., p. 303.

stances To the impenitent, they said: "Repent, and be baptized." To the unbaptized disciple, they said: "Why tarriest thou? Arise, and be baptized." The baptized disciple they taught, according to the requirement in the commission, to observe all things whatsoever Christ had commanded. The impenitent were not to be taught to observe *all* things which Christ had commanded. The advocates of open communion deny that they have a right either to baptism, or the Lord's supper; but why? The same moral precepts which are to be taught to the baptized disciple, may be taught to the impenitent. We may, therefore, retort, that if they exclude the impenitent from baptism and the Lord's supper, their mode of reasoning will prove too much, and will equally exclude them from instruction in the moral precepts of Christ. If it be just to argue from the order prescribed in the commission, that baptism belongs to those *only* who have been made disciples; that order equally proves, that the baptized only ought to be taught to observe *all* things that Christ had commanded. Some things that Christ commanded might be taught to the unbaptized, and to the impenitent; but the full observance of *all* Christ's commands, was to be enjoined on the baptized disciples. Had the commission read, "Make disciples of all nations, and teach them to observe all things whatsoever I have commanded you," baptism and the supper would have been included together among the things commanded, and no inference could have been drawn from the commission as to the proper order in which they should be observed. But the separation of baptism from all the other things which Christ had commanded, gives it a peculiar relation to the other things enjoined in the commission; and the order in which it is introduced cannot but signify the proper order for our obedience.

Argument 3.—The fact that, in the primitive times, none but baptized persons were admitted to the Lord's table, is not a rule to us, whose circumstances are widely different. Then, no converted person mistook his obligation to be baptized. Had he refused baptism, the refusal would have proved him not to be a disciple; and now nothing ought to exclude from communion, but that which disproves discipleship.

The argument admits that, if all understood their duty, baptism would always precede the communion, as it did in apostolic times. How far it is our duty to tolerate disobedience to Christ's commands, and produce a church order unknown in the days of the apostles, in accommodation to error or weakness of faith, is an inquiry which will come up hereafter.

Argument 4.—The supper commemorates the death of Christ: baptism represents his burial and resurrection. The order of the things signified is the reverse of that in which they are observed. Hence, the order of observance ought not to be considered necessary.

Baptism represents the burial of Christ, but not to the exclusion of his death: "Know ye not, that as many of us as were baptized into Christ, were baptized into his death? Therefore, we are buried with him by baptism into death." The supper represents the death of Christ; but not to the exclusion of his burial and resurrection. Without the resurrection, the sacrifice would have been unaccepted, and the memorial of it useless. Moreover, the supper directs the thoughts to the second coming of Christ, and therefore supposes his resurrection. The same great facts of Christianity are represented by both rites, though in aspects somewhat different; and, therefore, no valid argument can be drawn, from their objective signification, to determine the proper order of their observance.

But while both rites direct our faith to the accepted sacrifice of Christ, they do not signify our relation to it in the same manner. Baptism represents a believer's dying to sin, and rising to walk in newness of life. It signifies the change by which he becomes a new creature. The supper represents the believer's continued feeding on Christ; and therefore presupposes the change which is denoted by baptism. It follows, that the subjective signification of the rites, so far as any valid argument can be drawn from it, determines the priority of baptism.

If there were anything in the objective signification of the rite furnishing ground for an argument in favor of its preceding baptism, it would tend to establish that precedence as universally necessary, rather than occasionally justifiable.

Argument 5.—Communion at the Lord's table is a token of brotherly love. To refuse it to any true disciple of Christ, is contrary to the spirit of brotherly love, and to the command of Christ which enjoined it.

Christ has commanded us to love every true disciple; but not to give to every one this particular token of love. Neither the law nor the spirit of brotherly love, can require us to treat our brethren otherwise than he has enjoined. We give them the love, and withhold from them the token, in obedience to the same authority, and in the exercise of the same fraternal spirit. If a right participation of the communion were the appointed means of salvation, and if baptism were necessary in order to this right participation, it would be the highest manifestation of brotherly love, to maintain firmly the practice of strict communion. Our firmness might correct an error in our brethren, which, in the case supposed, would, if persisted in, be ruinous to their eternal interests. A false tenderness might incline us not to disturb their misplaced confidence; but true Christian love would direct to a contrary course. Now, we are bound to perform every duty with the same careful regard to the divine will, as if salvation depended on it; and the true spirit of Christian love will incline us to guard our brethren against what is sinful, as well as against what is ruinous. Hence, the argument from brotherly love utterly fails to justify the practice of mixed communion, if that practice can be shown to be contrary to the mind of Christ.

Further, the argument from this topic must be inconclusive, until it be proved that brotherly love cannot subsist without a joint participation of the Lord's supper. But there are surely many modes of testifying and cherishing the warmest affection toward erring brethren, without participating in their errors. We may be ready, in obedience to Christ, to lay down our lives for our brethren—though we may choose to die, rather than, in false tenderness to them, violate the least of his commandments.

Argument 6.—A particular church differs from the church universal, only as a part differs from the whole; and, since Pedobaptist Christians are parts of the true church, they ought to be admitted to membership and communion in the particular churches.

That particular churches differ from the church universal, only as a part differs from the whole, is assumed by Mr. Hall, in his defence of mixed communion. This assumption, made without proof, is the fundamental error of his scheme. It begs the question. We call the atmosphere of a place, that part of the whole atmosphere which chances to be at the place; and if a local church is, in like manner, that part of the universal church which chances to be at the place, the question about communion is virtually decided. We cannot argue that the communion of a church shall be denied to any who have the full right of membership.

We have seen elsewhere, that the universal church is not the aggregate of the local churches, and is not strictly homogeneous with them. Hence the assumption which is fundamental to mixed communion, is erroneous.

Argument 7.—To exclude a Pedobaptist brother from communion, is substantially to inflict on him the punishment of excommunication, the punishment inflicted on atrocious offenders. Such is not the proper treatment of a fellow disciple, whose error of judgment the Lord graciously pardons.

When an advocate of open communion excludes from the Lord's table an amiable neighbor, who does not give evidence of conversion, the exclusion is not regarded as a punishment. Neither ought our exclusion of the unbaptized; much less is it right to speak of it as the punishment inflicted on atrocious offenders. The churches have no scale of penalties adjusted to different grades of crime. When they excommunicate, they withdraw their fellowship, and this may be done for wrongs of very different magnitude. There is no necessity to class the error of pedobaptism with the most atrocious of these wrongs. The church which excludes a Pedobaptist from the Lord's table, does not design to inflict a punishment on him, but merely to do its own duty, as a body to which the Lord has intrusted one of his ordinances. The simple aim is, to regulate the observance according to the will of the Lord.

Argument 8.—To reject from communion a Pedobaptist brother whom God receives, is to violate the law of toleration laid down in Romans xiv. 1–3.

The application of this rule to the question of receiving unbaptized persons to church-membership, has been considered, p. 96. The result of the examination was unfavorable to the admission of such persons; and the reasons which exclude them from church-membership, exclude them from church communion. Regarding the Lord's supper as an ordinance committed to the local churches, to be observed by them as such, the question, who are entitled to the privilege of communion, is decided by a simple principle. None are to be admitted but those who can be admitted to the membership of the church.

The argument does not claim that persons do right in communing while unbaptized, but it pleads for a toleration of their error. Since this is the plea which open communion Baptists chiefly rely on, it deserves a full examination.

It is a difficult attainment in religion, to preserve one's purity untarnished, while mingling with the men of the world, and exercising towards them all that benevolence and forbearance which the gospel enjoins. Our duty to mankind requires that we should not retire from the world, nor cherish a morose and misanthropic temper. In avoiding the error on this hand, there is danger of falling into the opposite one, and becoming too much conformed to the world. Vice is apt to appear less hateful in those whom we greatly love; and even the frequent sight of it, if we are not on our guard, will make its deformity less in our view. Hence arises a great need of much watchfulness and prayer, in those who practise that pure and undefiled religion, which requires them, on the one hand, to visit the fatherless and the widows in their affliction, and to go about doing good to all men; and, on the other hand, to keep themselves unspotted from the world.

There is a still severer trial of Christian principle. We meet it in our intercourse with Christian brethren, who love our Lord Jesus Christ, and in general obey his commandments; but walk disorderly in some matters which are deemed of minor importance. If these brethren are supposed by us, to have more spiritual knowledge than ourselves, there is much danger, lest, through the confiding nature of Christian love, and the readiness to esteem others better than ourselves, we be betrayed into their errors. Had their violations of duty been greater, a suspicion of their piety might have been awakened, and we might have been put on our guard. The man of God, who prophesied against the altar at Bethel, could not be induced, by the wicked king of Israel, to eat bread, or drink water, in the place; yet the old prophet, who came to him in the name of the Lord, found it easy to prevail. Had even he proposed some deed in itself highly criminal, the truth of his pretended message from God would have been suspected. But to eat bread and to drink water were things in themselves lawful; and the man of God too readily yielded to the old prophet, as his superior in the knowledge of the divine will, and ate and drank in violation of God's prohibition.

If we ought to guard against being led into error by our intercourse with good men, when no wrong is suspected, much more ought we, when the existence of wrong is known. But toleration implies wrong; and, if mixed communion be defended on the plea of toleration, the very defence admits that there is wrong somewhere. It becomes us, therefore, to take good heed, lest we be implicated in the wrong. The very names, toleration, forbearance, are commended to us by our sense of God's forbearance and long-suffering toward us; and the motives for their exercise are irresistible when their object is a brother in Christ. Towards such an one, how can we be otherwise than tolerant and forbearing? Shall we persecute him? God forbid. We would rather lay down our lives for him. Shall we indulge in any bitterness, or uncharitableness towards him? We will love him with pure heart fervently. Shall we, in any manner, prevent him from worshipping and serving God according to the dictates of his conscience? The very thought be far from us. Even if he err, to his own Master he standeth or falleth. We, too, are fallible and erring; and we will fervently pray that the grace which pardons our faults may pardon his also. What more do toleration and forbearance require?

When a church receives an unbaptized person, something more is done than merely to tolerate his error. There are two parties concerned. The acts of entering the church and partaking of its communion are his, and for them he is responsible. The church also acts when it admits him to membership, and authorizes his participation of the communion. The church, as an organized body, with power to receive and exclude members according to rules which Christ has laid down, is responsible for the exercise of this power.

Each individual disciple of Christ is bound, for himself, to obey perfectly the will of his Master. Whatever tolerance he may exercise towards the errors of others, he should tolerate none in himself. Though he may see but a single fault in his brother, he ought, while imitating all that brother's excellencies, carefully to avoid this fault. He may not neglect the tithing of mint, though he should find an example of such neglect accompanied with a perfect obedience of every moral precept.

In like manner each church is bound, for itself, to conform, in all its order, to the divine will. How much soever it may respect neighboring churches, which may have made high attainments in every spiritual excellence, it must not imitate them, if they neglect or corrupt any of Christ's ordinances. No argument is needed to render this clear.

The members of a church, who understand the law of Christ, are bound to observe it strictly, whatever may be the ignorance and errors of others. For them to admit unbaptized persons to membership, is to subvert a known law of Christ. Though there be unbaptized persons surpassing in every spiritual excellence, and though the candidate for admission excel them all, yet the single question for the church is, shall its order be established according to the will of God, or shall it not.

It may be asked, whether the persons whom we admit to membership and communion are not, in many cases, guilty of omitting duties more important than baptism. It may be so: and if a church sanctions these criminal neglects, it partakes in the guilt of them. Shall it, to escape the charge of the greater guilt, voluntarily assume that which is less? If Christ has given a law for the organization of churches, we have no right to substitute another, because it would be, in our judgment, more accordant with the proper estimate of moral actions. If the members of the universal church had been left to congregate into small societies, according to their spiritual instincts, if I may use the expression, and not according to a revealed law, these societies might be left to determine, by moral excellence merely, who ought to be admitted. But since it has seemed good to the Christian lawgiver, to prescribe rules for church organization, these rules should be observed. Each church should aim, in its church order, to exhibit a model of perfection to the world, though its several members may be conscious of imperfections in themselves. They should aim, as individuals, to come up to the full measure of their individual responsibility, and strive, each one, to exhibit a model of perfect obedience. If the organization and discipline of the church are not perfect, yet each member should aim to be perfect. If each member is not perfect, this lessens not the obligation to render the organization and discipline of the church perfect.

But may not each individual be left to his own conscience, and his own responsibility? He may be, and ought to be, so far as it can be done without implicating the consciences and responsibili-

ties of others. If each were left wholly to himself, the discipline
of the church would be nothing, and the power to exercise it would
be attended with no responsibility. But the church is under an
obligation, which cannot be transferred, to regulate its organization
and discipline according to the word of God, which enjoins, on the
one hand, to be tolerant and forbearing towards weak and erring
brethren; and on the other hand, to, keep the ordinances of God
as they were delivered.

The argument for toleration is founded on the words, "Him that
is weak in the faith, receive ye. * * * For God hath received
him." It is a full reply to this argument, that God's receiving of
the weak in faith furnishes the *rule*, as well as the reason, for our
receiving of them. That God receives a man in one sense, can be
no reason that we should receive him in a sense widely different.
God receives an unbaptized weak believer as a member of his spiritual church, and we ought to receive him in like manner. We ought
to regard him as a brother in Christ, and a fellow heir of the same
inheritance. His interests should be near to our hearts, and we
should welcome him to all that spiritual communion which belongs
to the members of Christ's body. So, when God has received a
baptized weak believer to local church-membership, we are bound
to receive him in like manner, and allow him to sit with us at the
table of the Lord; a privilege which, through the imperfection of
church discipline, the vilest hypocrite may obtain. Unless we keep
in view this important distinction, in applying this rule for toleration, it will indeed admit the unbaptized weak believer to ceremonial communion, but it will, with equal certainty, admit the hypocrite to that communion which is spiritual.

Argument 9.—The advocates of close communion are accustomed to invite Pedobaptist ministers to preach in their pulpits.
To hold this pulpit communion with them, and at the same time to
deny them a place at the Lord's table, is a manifest inconsistency.

If we admit the conclusion of this argument, it does not prove
close communion to be wrong. Some Baptists admit the validity
of the argument; and avoid the charge of inconsistency by refusing to invite Pedobaptist ministers into their pulpits. Their
views will be examined hereafter, Chapter X., section 5, and we
shall then attempt to show that what has been called pulpit com

munion, may be vindicated in perfect consistency with the principles on which strict communion at the Lord's table is maintained.

Argument 10.—The communion table is the Lord's; and to exclude from it any of the Lord's people, the children of his family, is an offence against the whole Christian community.

There is a table which the Lord has spread, and to which every child of his family has an, unquestionable right. It is a table richly furnished with spiritual food, a feast of fat things, full of marrow, of wine on the lees well refined. This table the Lord has spread for all his children, and he invites them all to come: "Eat, O friends; drink, yea drink abundantly, Q beloved." Any one who should forbid their approach would offend against the community of God's children. The guests at this table have spiritual communion with one another; a species of communion which belongs of right to every member of the church universal.

There is another table which the Lord has commanded his people to spread in each local church. It is not, like the other, covered with spiritual good things, but with simple bread and wine. It is not, like the other, designed for the whole family of the Lord, but for the particular body, the local church, by whom, in obedience to divine command, it has been spread. Though human hands have set out the food, yet the table is the Lord's, because it is designed for his service, and prepared at his command; and the will of the Lord must determine who ought to partake. He knows best the purpose for which he commanded it; and, whatever may be the feelings of the guests, they have no right to invite to his table any whom the Lord has not invited.

We are aware that the practice of strict communion is considered offensive by a large part of the Christian community. We lament this fact; and if the arguments which have been adduced in defence of our practice, have failed to produce a conviction of its propriety, we would still crave from our brethren the forbearance and toleration for which they plead in behalf of the weak in faith. We conscientiously believe that we are doing the Lord's will; and we would gladly invite every child of God to unite in our simple ceremonial observance, if we had the divine approbation. But we believe that the purpose for which the observance was instituted, and the divine will by which it ought to be regulated, require the restrictions under which we act.

Does not the offence taken at our course indicate that the offended party estimate ceremonial communion too highly? To the rich feast of spiritual good which the Lord has spread, we rejoice to welcome every child of God; and we gladly accept an humble seat with them at the bountiful board. When with open hearts and hands we give this welcome, why will they be offended, if we do not also give them a crumb of our ceremonial bread, and a drop of our ceremonial wine? If the elements possessed some sacramental efficacy, there would be an apparent reason for their complaint; but regarding them as a token of union in a church organization to which our brethren object, and into which they are unwilling to enter, the ground and consistency of their complaint do not appear.

When Pedobaptists complain of our strict communion, we would remind them that they hold the principle in common with us, and practise on it in their own way. If they have aught to object, let it be at that in which we differ from them, and not at that in which we agree. The contrary course is not likely to produce unity of opinion, or to promote that harmony of Christian feeling which ought to subsist among the followers of our Lord.

When Baptists object to strict communion, we would propose the inquiry, Whether they do not attach undue importance to the eucharist, in comparison with baptism. Mr. Hall calls the eucharist a principal spiritual function.[1] In this view of it, he complains that the privilege of partaking in it should be denied to any. Is it more spiritual than baptism? If not, why should baptism be trodden under foot, to open the way of access to the eucharist? When both ceremonies were supposed to possess a saving efficacy, the proper order of their observance was still maintained; much more should it be maintained, if both are mere ceremonies. If baptism were a mere ceremony, and the eucharist a principal spiritual function, the arguments for open communion would have a force which they do not now possess: but our brethren will not defend this position.

---

[1] Vol. i. p. 322.

CHAPTER VI.

WASHING OF FEET.

WHEN JESUS REQUIRED HIS DISCIPLES TO WASH ONE ANOTHER'S
FEET, HE DESIGNED, NOT TO INSTITUTE A RELIGIOUS CEREMONY, BUT
TO ENFORCE A WHOLE CLASS OF MORAL DUTIES.

The requirement on the subject is contained in the following
words: "If I then, your Lord and Master, have washed your feet,
ye also ought to wash one another's feet."[1]

Every word of Jesus Christ is important, and every command
which he has left as a rule of our conduct ought to be punctiliously
obeyed. The words quoted above may be regarded as a part of
his dying instructions to his apostles. Every circumstance connected with the time and manner of their being uttered, tends to
invest them with interest. No one deserves the name of his disciple, who could knowingly neglect a duty recommended by such
unparalleled love and condescension.

What, then, was the Saviour's meaning? "If ye know these
things," says he,[2] "happy are ye if ye do them." We must know,
in order to do; and if we mistake his design, how honest soever
our intention may be, we shall not have fulfilled his command. If,
on this memorable night, when he partook of the last passover with
his disciples, and when he instituted the breaking of bread as the
memorial of "Christ, our Passover, sacrificed for us," he designed
to institute the washing of feet as another religious rite, till his
second coming, together with baptism and the breaking of bread;
then, this institution should be observed with punctilious carefulness;
and no plea should be admitted from the neglect of it, to justify

---

[1] John xiii. 14.　　　　　[2] V. 17.

the neglect of any other divine command. But, if it was the Saviour's design, not to institute a religious ceremony for the observance of his disciples, but to enjoin on them a whole class of moral duties of the very highest importance, it would be a lamentable mistake, if we should substitute for these duties a mere external rite which he never meant to institute.

To ascertain the Saviour's design, let the following things be attentively considered :—

1. The particular duty enjoined is *moral*, as distinguished from those which are *positive*.

Baptism and the Lord's supper are positive institutes, because the obligation to observe them could not be inferred from any utility or apparent fitness in the things themselves. On the contrary, the washing of feet was not a mere ceremony, but a necessary act of hospitality which had been in use since the days of Abraham ;[1] and it is accordingly reckoned by the Apostle Paul, in connexion with other moral duties of like kind, as the proper foundation of a reputation for good works. "Well reported of for good works, if she have lodged strangers, if she have washed the saints' feet, if she have relieved the afflicted, if she have diligently followed every good work."[2] It is the utility of the act which gives it a place among the "good" works here enumerated. In those days, when travelling was so generally performed on foot, and when the feet were shod with mere sandals ; to wash the feet of the wayworn stranger was not a mere ceremony, but one of those "good works which are profitable unto men," and to be maintained "for necessary uses."[3]

2. The example of the Saviour recommends the act on the ground of its *utility*.

When Peter wished his hands and his head to be washed, "Jesus saith unto him, He that is washed needeth not, save to wash his feet." The two words here rendered *wash*, are different in the original : the former, denoting a washing of the whole body ; and the latter, which is the word used elsewhere throughout the narrative, a partial washing, as of the hands or feet. The sense is—he that has been bathed, needs only to wash his feet, which may have

---

[1] Gen. xviii. 4; xix. 2. [2] 1 Tim. v. 10. [3] Titus iii. 8, 14.

been defiled in walking from the bath.[1] The apostles had bathed themselves before sitting down to the paschal supper, and therefore did not need any washing except of the feet. On this *need*, small as it may appear, the Saviour placed the fitness and propriety of the act which he performed. He was willing to set an example of performing the least possible act of real kindness; but he would not extend that act a whit beyond the line of necessity and utility. Beyond this line, it was no longer an act of kindness. But Jesus performed it as a good work for a necessary use; and since he therein gave to his apostles an example that they should do to each other as he had done to them,[2] it is manifest that he designed to enforce on them mutual service of practical utility.

3. It was not a *single* duty which the Saviour intended to enjoin:

This is apparent from verse 17: "If ye know *these things*, happy are ye if ye do *them*." Duties were manifestly intended beyond the single act of washing of feet. Of these duties this act was a mere specimen by which they might know the rest; and knowing, practise them.

A proof that the washing performed by our Saviour was a part and specimen of a whole class of duties, may also be derived from verse 8: "Peter saith unto him, Thou shalt never wash my feet. Jesus answered him, If I wash thee not, thou hast no part with me." The true import of this answer seems to be this: "*If I may not wash thy feet*, (so the word here used implies), *I may not, on the same ground, render to thee any of the great benefits resulting from my humiliation, in which I came not to be ministered unto, but to minister, and to give my life a ransom for many. If I may not perform to thee acts of condescending kindness, thou hast no part with me.* As in this declaration, the washing of Peter's feet

---

[1] Some interpreters take the first word to mean, not a bathing of the whole body, but a washing of the hands and face, which the disciples are supposed to have performed before taking their places at supper. "He who washeth his face and hands is considered sufficiently clean, and needs no other washing unless this mark of civility, that his feet be washed by a servant. This civility I exhibit to you, thus acting the part of a servant." This interpretation, though less satisfactory, because less conformed to the ordinary signification of the terms employed, will, nevertheless, serve equally well for sustaining the argument above presented.

[2] John xiii. 15.

was made by the Saviour a specimen and representative of all his acts of condescending kindness; so the washing of feet, enjoined upon Peter and his fellow-apostles, was intended to include all the acts of condescending kindness which they could perform towards their brethren. "A new commandment I give unto you, That ye love one another: as I have loved you, that ye also love one another: by this shall all men know that ye are my disciples, if ye have love one to another."[1]

4. It is an argument of weight against regarding the washing of feet as a religious ceremony instituted in the church, that it does not, like baptism and the Lord's supper, *typify* Christ.

The Lord's supper, in a lively figure, shows forth the death of Christ; and baptism, his burial and resurrection. These standing ordinances of the Christian church lead the mind directly to the great Author of our salvation, and to the atoning sacrifice by which that salvation had been effected. These ordinances teach us the grand doctrine of redemption, in a language which infinite wisdom has invented for the purpose. To this great doctrine these witnesses bear their testimony, in a voice, long and loud, through all the revolutions of centuries, and above all the tumults of heresy. What does the washing of feet teach us of Christ, or of redemption by Him? Does it lead the believer away from himself, and all his own works of righteousness, to the atoning sacrifice or the justifying righteousness on which he must rely for salvation? It might serve, as a religious rite, to remind those of a duty to be performed, whose faith rests upon such duty for righteousness; but of him who is the end of the law for righteousness to every one that believeth, of his suffering and death as the means of our salvation, it tells nothing.

5. The washing of feet was not practised as a religious rite by the primitive Christians.

That baptism and the Lord's supper were so practised we have the clearest evidence, both from the Scriptures and the writings of the Christian fathers; but not so with regard to the washing of feet. It is not necessary to pursue this subject beyond the clear light of Scripture, into the comparatively dark field of investigation which ecclesiastical history presents, as the testimony which

---

[1] V. 34, 35.

this less satisfactory source of evidence affords, though entirely consistent with the testimony of Scripture, is not needed, either for elucidation or confirmation. On opening the inspired history of the church, we read, at the very beginning, "They that gladly received his word were *baptized :* and they continued steadfastly in the apostles' doctrine, and fellowship, and in breaking of bread, and in prayers." Baptism is frequently mentioned in the subsequent history, and in the 20th chap. 7th verse express mention is made that "the disciples came together to break bread." But not a chapter, not a verse, in all the Acts of the Apostles, contains an intimation that any church, or any company of disciples, ever assembled to celebrate the washing of feet. In the Epistle to the Romans,[1] a reference is made to baptism, and an explanation given of its import. The first chapter of the next epistle (the first to the Corinthians), contains an account of several baptisms; and the 11th chapter a very particular account of the institution of the supper, and of abuses in its observance, which had already crept into the church of Corinth. But in these epistles, and in all those which follow, no allusion whatever is found to the washing of feet, as a rite observed by the churches.

There is, indeed, one passage, and only one, in which the washing of feet is mentioned; and this passage, 1 Tim. v. 10, furnishes decisive proof that it was not practised as a church ordinance, as were baptism and the Lord's supper. To demonstrate this, we have but to substitute, in the passage, the mention of these acknowledged ordinances, and the incongruity of such a connexion will immediately appear: "Well reported of for good works; if she have brought up children, if she have lodged strangers, if she have been baptized, or received the Lord's supper, if she have relieved the afflicted, if she have diligently followed every good work." As it must be supposed of every widow in the church that she had been baptized, and had received the Lord's supper; no "if," with respect to these ordinances, could be admitted, and no one widow could, on account of her having observed them, be more entitled to honor than any other. The same would have been true concerning the washing of feet, if this also had been a religious rite in common use in the churches; and it would have been a manifest absurdity to state the fact of any church member hav-

---

[1] Chap. vi.

ing performed the rite, as a reason for regarding him or her as specially entitled to reputation for good works, or to honor from the church.

There is, therefore, not only a total want of proof that such a religious rite was anciently observed, but there is (what few cases in controversy furnish) a proof of the negative, which is as clear and satisfactory as any such proof can be expected to be.

These considerations show clearly that it was the Saviour's design to enforce a whole class of moral duties, and not to institute a religious ceremony; and that he was so understood by his apostles. He who washes the feet of a saint, when those feet do not need washing, is as if he gave a cup of cold water to a disciple who is not thirsty. He may indeed make a show of voluntary humility, but he does not fulfil the command of Christ, nor imitate his example. He ought to remember that Christ declined to wash the hands and head of Peter; not because there would have been less show of humility in so doing, but because those parts did not need washing. He, therefore, who washes the feet of a saint when these feet do not need washing, instead of obeying or imitating Christ, does that which Christ refused to do. And he who washes the feet of a saint merely as a religious rite, without considering or caring whether the act which he performs is necessary and useful, is just as far as the other from obeying or imitating the Redeemer.

If, after a careful consideration of the subject, we have satisfactorily ascertained that our Saviour designed his disciples should perform towards each other every needful act of condescending kindness, even the smallest and the most servile, let us be ready with promptness and pleasure to fulfil his will. If we know these things, happy are we if we do them. If we have the spirit of Christ, we shall be ready, when need requires, to lay down our lives for our brethren, or give them a cup of cold water, or wash their feet, or render them any other comfort. In so far as by any of these means we seek to promote the happiness of a disciple of Christ, our good deeds will be remembered; and the great Judge, in the last day, omitting all mention of our most labored religious-ceremonies, will bring that act of kindness to mind, and will say, "Inasmuch as ye did it to one of the least of these my brethren, ye did it unto me."

CHAPTER VII.

PUBLIC WORSHIP.

SECTION I.—TIME.

THE FIRST DAY OF THE WEEK IS THE CHRISTIAN SABBATH, AND IS SPECIALLY APPROPRIATE FOR THE PUBLIC WORSHIP OF GOD.

The computation of time by weeks, appears to have prevailed at a very early period. It may be traced back to the time of Laban, who said to Jacob: "Fulfil her week."[1] A less visible trace of it may be seen in the account given of Noah, who waited "seven days:" and afterwards "another seven days,"[2] in his attempts to discover whether the deluge had subsided. The hebdomadal division of time existed very early in the gentile world; and no account of its origin is so probable, as that it was received from Noah, the father of the new world. No evidence appears, that Noah received it as a new institution from God; or that it originated with him. The statement of Scripture is, "God rested on the seventh day: wherefore God blessed the seventh day, and sanctified it."[3] This is the origin of the institution. When the decalogue was promulgated from Sinai, it did not speak of the sabbath as an institution before unknown. The command, "Remember the sabbath day,"[4] implies a knowledge of its existence; and this is confirmed by the previous historical fact, that the fall of manna had ceased on the sabbath day.

Since the sabbath originated at the creation, and was known before the giving of the law to the Israelites, it cannot be one of the abrogated Jewish ceremonies. The sabbath was made for man; and not exclusively for the Hebrews. The reason for it is

---

[1] Gen. xxi. 27.   [2] Gen. viii. 10, 12.   [3] Gen. ii. 2, 3.
[4] Ex. xx. 8.   (232)

taken from God's rest on the seventh day, after six days' work in creating the world; and not from anything that pertained specially to the nation of Israel. The institution is adapted to the nature of man, as a religious being, and the relation which he sustains to his Creator.

The decalogue was given as a law to the Israelites. Its preface shows this: "I am the Lord thy God, which have brought thee out of the land of Eygpt." It is further proved by the promise annexed to the fifth commandment: "That thy days may be long in the land which the Lord thy God giveth thee." But, though given to the Israelites, it was given to them as men. The ceremonial law was given to them, as the Congregation of the Lord; and the judicial law was given to them as the Nation of Israel. But the decalogue was adapted to the relations which they bore to God and one another, as men. The same relations are in human society everywhere; and therefore the same obligations bind everywhere. This part of the Mosaic code possesses universal and perpetual obligation; and this part, God specially distinguished from all the rest. He pronounced it audibly from Sinai, and twice engraved it in stone, in token of its perpetuity. In writing to gentiles at Rome, and at Ephesus, Paul refers to the decalogue, as a law which they were bound to obey;[1] and has thus decided that it was not peculiar to the Jews, or confined to the abrogated covenant. The ministration of the law in the letter, he distinguishes from the ministration of the Spirit, and declares it to be done away when the veil is taken away from the heart;[2] but the change then wrought does not consist in making a new law, but in transferring the writing from the tables of stone, to the fleshly tables of the heart.

Among the precepts of the decalogue, we find the command: "Remember the sabbath day." As the whole decalogue binds us, so does this commandment. No man has a right to separate it from the rest, and claim exemption from its obligation. Christians, therefore, must observe the sabbath; and, as a day which God has hallowed, it is specially appropriate for the public worship of God.

Some Baptists, in a conscientious regard to the divine com-

---

[1] Rom. xiii. 8—10; Eph. vi. 2. [2] 2 Cor. iii. 6—12.

mands, observe the same day for their sabbath that the Jews observe, and are thence called Seventh Day Baptists. But they mistake, as we conceive, the true import of the precept. They interpret it, as if it had been expressed "The seventh day *of the week* is the sabbath," and as if the Jewish division of the week were recognised and fixed; whereas the language is, "Six days shalt thou labor, and do all thy work; but the seventh day is the sabbath of the Lord thy God." The seventh day, is that which follows six days of labor; and the words of the precept express no more. From the nature of the case, the regular return of the sabbath, at equally distant intervals of time, must be expected to follow. We may have light thrown on the true meaning of the language employed, by comparing it with that which enjoined the observance of the sabbatical year. The comparison may be advantageously made for this purpose, by examining a passage in which the sabbatical day and the sabbatical year are both enjoined.[1] "Six years thou shalt sow thy land, and shalt gather in the fruits thereof; but the seventh year thou shalt let it rest, and lie still." "Six days thou shalt do thy work, and on the seventh day thou shalt rest." As the seventh year is not determined by a natural division of time into weeks of years; so the seventh day is not determined by a natural division of time into weeks of days. No one thinks of the seventh year otherwise than as the year which follows six years of regular toil in the cultivation of the earth, and as regularly returning at equal intervals. The precise similarity of the command enjoining the observance of the seventh day sabbath, proves that the same method of interpretation must be applied to it. If an obligation exists to observe Saturday, or Sunday, rather than any other day of the week, it cannot be found in this precept of the decalogue, and must be made out in some other way.

The decalogue, in its admirable adaptedness to the relations in human society, displays the wisdom of its Author. We may see this wisdom in the adaptedness of the fourth commandment to universal observance. Since the rotundity of the earth has been demonstrated, it has become apparent, that a precept requiring the observance of the seventh day of the week, could not be

---

[1] Exodus xxiii. 10, 12.

obeyed universally, unless some meridian were established by divine authority for the universal computation of time. A few years ago it was stated in some of our missionary intelligence, that a practical question of duty in the observance of the sabbath had arisen between some missionaries, who had met at their field of labor on the other side of the globe, having sailed to it by different routes, some by the eastern and others by the western. On comparing their computation, their sabbaths differed; and what was Saturday to one party was Sunday to the other. If the seventh day *of the week* had been commanded, these missionaries could not have obeyed without becoming sabbath-breakers to each other; and if no higher wisdom than that of Moses, who was ignorant of the earth's true form, had dictated the decalogue, its admirable adaptedness to the condition and circumstances of men, in every age and country, and under every meridian, would not have been secured.

Another objection to the interpretation which supposes the seventh day of the week to be prescribed, may be seen in the fact that it makes Scripture dependent on tradition. Had the observance of the new moon, or of the full moon, been commanded, the means of ascertaining the time intended would have been within the reach of every one; but had the Scripture commanded to observe the seventh day of the week, who could know the day required? No banner is hung out in the sky, to distinguish it from the other days of the week. The revolution and boundaries of the week are not determined, like the revolution of the seasons, by any natural phenomena. The precept, once engraven in stone, and now indelibly recorded in God's book, would stand before us, binding each individual conscience to obedience; and yet the precept itself would give no clue by which to ascertain its true meaning. How could each individual know that he did not mistake the time, and profane the very day that God had hallowed? He has no other means of knowledge than tradition. The right sabbath may have been handed down without mistake, from the time of the creation, or from the time of Moses; but what proof have we? None but tradition. God has wisely decided to make known his will to men by Scripture, rather than by tradition; but what is the advantage, if the meaning of Scripture must be determined by tradition?

Another argument for our interpretation of the precept, may be drawn, from the word employed in the New Testament, to denote a week. It is the same word that is rendered sabbath, appearing sometimes in the singular form, sometimes in the plural. Take, for an example, the phrase "the first day of the week,"[1] which, literally rendered, is, "the first day of the sabbath or sabbaths." This may be explained, the first day according to the computation of the sabbath or sabbaths. But, however explained, it indicates that the sabbath determined the week, and not the week the sabbath.

According to the view which we have taken of the fourth commandment, Christians obey it, as literally as the Jews. The latter derive their series of weeks by tradition from the time of Moses; we derive ours by tradition from the time of Christ. We see with pleasure, the beginning of our series, in the brief accounts of Scripture, where the day on which Christians met for worship, is specified. On the first day of the week our Lord rose from the dead. This day was filled with the tidings and proofs of his resurrection, and with the admiration and joy of the disciples, and was closed with a meeting of the disciples, in which Jesus appeared in person. In his account of this meeting, the evangelist is careful to repeat that it was on *the first day of the week.*[2]

Another week rolled around, and a meeting of the disciples was held, in which Jesus was again present. A Jewish sabbath had intervened; and if it had been the Lord's design to perpetuate this sabbath, as the day of public worship for his disciples, why did he allow it to pass, and reserve the second joyful interview with his assembled people, to the ensuing day? The evangelist's statement is, "After eight days again his disciples were within, and Thomas with them; then came Jesus, the doors being shut, and stood in the midst."[3] When the chief priests applied to Pilate to have the sepulchre guarded, they said, "that deceiver said, while he was yet alive, after three days will I rise again. Command, therefore, that the sepulchre be made sure until the third day."[4] Here the phrase "after three days," is equivalent to "until the third day." If the phrase, "after eight days," in the above quotation from John, be

---

[1] John xx. 1.   [2] John xx. 19.   [3] John xx. 26.
[4] Matt. xxvii. 63, 64.

interpreted in the same manner, it will bring Christ's second interview with his disciples just one week after the first, and therefore
on the first day of the week. The feast of Pentecost occurred
according to the law,[1] on the day following the Jewish sabbath.
It was therefore on the first day of the week, that the Holy Spirit
was poured out, and three thousand converted under the preaching
of Peter.

The disciples at Troas met together to break bread;[2] and the
inspired historian is careful to tell us, that it was on " the first day
of the week." In writing to the Corinthians, Paul directed them,
in making their religious contribution for the poor saints at Jerusalem, " On the first day of the week, let every one of you lay by
him in store, as God hath prospered him."[3] In describing the
wonderful revelation which he received on the isle of Patmos, John
says, " I was in the Spirit on the Lord's day."[4] By this phrase, he
seems to designate the day on which our Lord arose, and which had
been consecrated to his worship.

As the Mosaic revelation displays divine wisdom, in its mode of
exhibiting the fourth commandment; so does the Christian revelation, in its mode of recommending the first day of the week to our
observance. The old covenant, with its priesthood, and forms of
worship, had passed away, and there was a fitness in instituting a
new form of worship to be introduced, and it was fit that the resurrection of our Lord should begin the new computation, and be commemorated by it. But while the first day of the week is expressly
mentioned, had the observance of it been expressly commanded,
the same difficulties would have originated, that would have attended
the observance of the seventh day of the week. It would have
rendered the Christian Scriptures dependent on tradition for their
interpretation, and the Christian sabbath impossible to be observed
throughout the world, in strict obedience to the requirement. As
the matter has been left, the decalogue is transmitted to us, requiring the consecration of one day in seven; and the New Testament
teaches us, that no times are holy in themselves; and that the
regard which the Jews demanded, for the day on which they kept
their weekly sabbath, and for their other holy days, so far from

---

[1] Lev. xxiii. 16.   [2] Acts xx. 7.   [3] 1 Cor. xvi. 2.
[4] Rev. i. 10.

being obligatory on Christians, is inconsistent with the nature of the Christian economy.[1] The proportion and the succession of time, as prescribed in the fourth commandment, are obligatory; but no particular periods of duration have in themselves special sanctity. We are bound by the example of the apostles, to observe the first day of the week as the Christian sabbath; but not in such a sense as to fetter the conscience with insuperable difficulty, in such a case as that of the missionaries before mentioned.

The worship, adapted to the day, requires to be social; and each individual Christian may unite with his brethren, in the worship of God, on the day set apart for it, with the full conviction that, in so doing, he is honoring the Author of Christianity, and strictly obeying the decalogue.

see also 16 Chap. of Exodus. where the change from the [Paradisaical] Sabbath to the Jewish is made

SECTION II.—MODE.

PUBLIC WORSHIP SHOULD INCLUDE PRAYERS, SONGS OF PRAISE, AND THE READING AND EXPOUNDING OF GOD'S WORD.

Prayer is a natural duty of man, confined to no particular condition of life, or dispensation of religion. It may be performed in private, in the family, in companies accidentally brought together, or designedly convened for the purpose; and in public assemblies for divine worship, it ought always to make a part of the service.

In public prayer, one of the worshippers leads the service, speaking audibly, as Solomon did at the dedication of the temple, and the rest unite in heart in the devotions and supplications. The leading part in the service may be performed by the ministers of the word. The first Christians continued steadfastly in the apostles' doctrine, fellowship, breaking of bread, and prayers. All these, including the prayers, were directed by the apostles; and, when the apostles were relieved from ministering to tables, it was that they might give themselves to the word of God and to prayer. Private prayer cannot be exclusively intended here; for the obligation to this belonged equally to the deacons elected, and to all the members of the church. But, though the ministers of the word may, in general, most advantageously lead in public prayer,

---

[1] Col. ii. 16; Gal. iv. 10, 11; Rom. xiv. 5, 6.

other male members of the church may do it with propriety and benefit. "I will that men pray everywhere."[1] The word rendered "men," properly denotes persons of the male sex, and is distinguished from "the women" mentioned in the next verse. The intimation plainly made, is, that females are not expected to lead in public prayer. This accords with the words of Paul: "It is a shame for women to speak in the church," or public assembly. But there is great propriety in the separate meeting of females for prayer, and much benefit results to themselves and the cause of God.

The Saviour gave a form of prayer to his disciples, for a help and general directory; but it is manifest that the disciples never understood that they were restricted to this form, either in private or in public. Prescribed forms of prayer are objectionable, because they restrain the emotions of the heart, discourage dependence on the Holy Spirit, tend to produce formality, and are not adapted to all circumstances and occasions.

Praise may be mingled with the petitions and thanksgivings offered in prayer; and is then, like these, expressed in prose, and with the ordinary voice. But poetry and music are specially appropriate in the expression of praise. They were used in early times, and formed an important part of the temple worship. In the New Testament, we find frequent use of singing; and it is expressly commanded in several passages.[2] The phrase "admonishing one another in psalms," &c., being addressed to a church, sufficiently indicates that singing was designed to be a part of the church's public worship.

The book of Psalms was composed for the temple worship. It serves as a help and general directory in this part of the public service; but there is no proof that our praises ought to be expressed in no words but those found in this book. We have no book of prayers in the Bible; and we learn from this that a book of prayers is not needed in our public worship; but we have a book of Psalms, because, in a service in which many are to speak together, they cannot speak the same things without previous preparation. We learn hence the lawfulness of using hymn-books; and experience has proved their great utility.

---

[1] 1 Tim. ii. 8.   [2] Col. iii. 16; Eph. v. 19; James v. 13.

Instrumental music formed a part of the temple worship; but it is nowhere commanded in the New Testament; and it is less adapted to the more spiritual service of the present dispensation.

In public worship, we not only address God in prayer and praise, but we honor him by reverent attention to his word, in which he speaks to us. The reading of the Scriptures formed an important part of the synagogue service, and was sanctioned by the Saviour, when, in the synagogue at Nazareth, he read from the prophet Isaiah. In Paul's direction to Timothy, "Give attendance to reading, to exhortation, and to doctrine,"[1] as the exhortation and doctrine or teaching were to be parts of the public service to be performed for the benefit of others, there is no reason to suppose that the reading which is commanded was to be exclusively private. The public reading of God's word appears to be at least included. In the days of Ezra, when the Scriptures were read, the sense was shown to the people.[2] When Christ read in the synagogue at Nazareth, on closing the book, he expounded and applied the passage which had been read. The direction to Timothy required that exhorting and teaching should be added to reading. God is honored when his word is so expounded to the people, that they not only hear the sound with the ear, but receive the meaning of it in their understandings, and feel its power in their hearts. God has graciously provided men who are able so to expound and exhort; and every church ought to seek the help of such gifts.

---

[1] 1 Tim. iv. 13.   [2] Neh. viii. 8.

CHAPTER VIII.

THE MINISTRY.

Section I.—MINISTRY OF THE WORD.

The Ministers of Christ are a separate class of persons, distinguished by a special divine call to preach the word.

A DISTINCT CLASS.

The ministers of Christ are, like ordinary Christians, separate from the world. They are partakers of the heavenly calling, by which men are brought out of the world, and made the servants of Christ. In all his epistles to the churches, Paul claims to be a fellow-saint with them, a member of the same spiritual family, and an heir of the same heavenly inheritance. Throughout the Scriptures, the ministers of Christ are spoken of as persons who love Christ, and are from the heart devoting themselves to his service. They must therefore be of the number who are "called to be saints."

The ministers of Christ are also separate from ordinary Christians. They are one with ordinary Christians, as being called in one hope of their calling; but, besides the call to repentance and faith, which they have received in common with their brethren, they have been called to special service in the Lord's cause. It is clear, from the Holy Scriptures, that there were, among the first Christians, persons to whom the work of the ministry was specially intrusted. Paul says, concerning these, God "hath given to us the ministry of reconciliation."[1] "Giving no offence, that the ministry be not blamed."[2] "Who hath made us able ministers of

---

[1] 2 Cor. v. 18.   [2] 2 Cor. vi. 3.

the new testament."[1]   He speaks of himself, as counted faithful,
and put "into the ministry;"[2] and of the special·grace given to
him, that he should preach among the gentiles the unsearchable
riches of Christ.[3]   The bestowment by the Holy Spirit of special
qualifications for special service in the Lord's cause, is plainly
taught in 1 Cor. xii., and Eph. iv.   The inquiry, "Are all apostles? are all prophets?"[4] &c., shows that the offices designated did
not belong to the whole body of the saints.

The separation of the ministry from the mass of ordinary Christians, is not like the separation of Christians from the world.   In
the latter case, they cease to be of the world, and become strangers
and pilgrims in the earth.   But men who enter the ministry, do
not cease to be saints.   Saul and Barnabas were separated unto
the work to which the Holy Ghost had called them; but this separation did not take from them a place among the saints and faithful in Christ Jesus.   John speaks, concerning the whole company
of the saints: "We are of God; and the whole world lieth in
wickedness."[5]   Here is a strong line of division, like that which
separates land and water.   But the ministry appears, among the
people of God, like the mountains on a continent, forming a part of
it, and closely united with surrounding lands.   Eminent spiritual
gifts distinguish the ministers; but the same spirit that actuates
them, pervades the whole body of Christ.   All the disciples of
Christ are bound, according to their ability, to advance the cause
of their Master, and labor for the illumination and salvation of
men: and the diversity of talent among the ordinary disciples,
may be compared to the diversity of hill and valley in the ordinary
face of the country.   But ministers are distinguished, by their
superior qualifications for service, from the ordinary mass of Christians, like mountains rising above the common undulations of the
surrounding landscape.

The special qualifications which the Holy Spirit bestows, bind
him on whom they are bestowed to use them in the service of
Christ.   They are given to fit him for this service, and they constitute a divine call for him to engage in it.   They are not given

---

[1] 2 Cor. iii. 6.   [2] 1 Tim. i. 12.   [3] Eph. iii. 8.
[4] 1 Cor. xii. 29.   [5] 1 John v. 19.

to confer a privilege merely, but they are a solemn call to duty—a call demanding the service of the whole life.

The apostles, when called by Christ, immediately left their secular employments, and gave themselves ever afterwards to the service of their Lord. Paul, when called, conferred not with flesh and blood. The work of the ministry did not cease, when these holy men left the earth; but other persons have been fitted to carry it on, by the same Spirit that qualified them for the peculiar service. He bestows his gifts "for the perfecting of the saints, for the work of the ministry, for the edifying of the body of Christ, till we all come in the unity of the faith, and of the knowledge of the Son of God, unto a perfect man, unto the measure of the stature of the fullness of Christ."[1]

The ministers of Christ are not a separate class of men in such a sense as to constitute them an organized society. They are fellow-laborers in the Lord's service, but have no power over one another; and have no authority from Christ to combine themselves into an ecclesiastical judicatory to exercise power in any manner. They are all on a level as brethren; are the servants of Christ, and the servants of the churches.

THEIR WORK.

The special service for which the ministry is designed is the preaching of the word. The obligation to spread the knowledge of Christ is shared, to some extent, by all Christians. The effectual call of the Holy Spirit, by which any man is brought to repentance and faith, imposes on him an obligation to show forth the praises of him who hath called him out of darkness into his marvellous light; to let his light shine before men, that they, seeing his good works, may glorify his Father in heaven; and to hold forth the word of life. Every Christian is bound to do what he can for the conversion of others, and for spreading the knowledge of the truth. But special gifts are conferred on some, accompanied with special obligations. These constitute a special call to the ministry of the word.

During the Saviour's personal ministry he made many disciples:

---

[1] Eph. iv. 12, 13.

but he did not intrust to them equally and indiscriminately the work of spreading the knowledge of his religion. He sent forth seventy with a special commission to preach the kingdom of God. He chose the apostles to be his immediate attendants and special witnesses, and gave them a commission—" Go preach the gospel to every creature. * * * Go make disciples, teaching them," &c. Preaching and teaching were prominent and important parts of the service required of them. When Paul was made an apostle, the commission to him, as explained by himself, was to preach the gospel: " Christ sent me, not to baptize, but to preach the gospel." The obligation which he felt to perform this service was beyond that imposed on ordinary Christians, and was exceedingly pressing: " Necessity is laid upon me; yea, wo is unto me if I preach not the gospel."[1] With him, to preach the gospel was not to utter a proclamation in a brief sentence; but at Troas he preached to a late hour of the night. In his ministry teaching was conjoined with preaching, and included in it: " Whereunto I am ordained a preacher and an apostle, a teacher of the Gentiles in faith and verity."[2]

The obligation of particular men to give themselves to the ministry of the word was intended to be a perpetual arrangement, and not confined to the ministers appointed by Christ in person. Timothy was specially appointed to this service, and was commanded, " Preach the word; be instant in season, out of season; reprove, rebuke, and exhort, with all long suffering and doctrine."[3] " Make full proof of thy ministry."[4] " Neglect not the gift that is in thee."[5] A special gift and a special obligation are here clearly recognised, and the duty to be performed is clearly preaching, in the comprehensive sense in which teaching is included. Paul had committed the gospel to Timothy; nor was the succession to cease in him. " The things which thou hast heard of me, the same commit thou to faithful men, who shall be able to teach others also."[6] Special ability and special obligation to preach and teach were to be perpetuated in men, separated to the service from the body of Christ's disciples.

---

[1] 1 Cor. ix. 16. [2] 1 Tim. ii. 7. [3] 2 Tim. iv. 2.
[4] 2 Tim. iv. 5. [5] 1 Tim. iv. 14. [6] 2 Tim. ii. 2.

THEIR CALL.

The ministers of the word receive a special call from God, directing them to the service. The Jewish priests were a separate class of people, distinguished from the rest of the nation by natural descent from Aaron. The Congregation of the Lord was perpetuated by natural descent; and if the Christian church had been a continuation of it, we might expect its ministry to be perpetuated in the same way. But the members of the church are separated from the rest of the world by a divine call; and it is suitable that the ministers of the church should be distinguished in the same manner; accordingly, their designation to office is ascribed to God. "God hath set some in the church, first apostles," &c., and the qualifications for the work are the special gift of the Spirit.[1]

The Holy Spirit calls to the ministry of the word none but true Christians, members of Christ's spiritual body. The apostles were chosen to be the personal attendants of the Saviour, and special witnesses of his daily life and ministry. Though he knew, from the beginning, the hypocrisy and treachery of Judas Iscariot, he chose to have a traitor among his witnesses. The blameless character of the Redeemer extorted, even from this man, the testimony, "I have sinned, in that I have betrayed the innocent blood." This testimony is of great value to Christianity. Had Christ been an impostor, had there been a scheme to deceive the people, Judas must have known it. His testimony, confirmed by his return of the money with which he had been bribed, and by his suicide, banishes every suspicion dishonorable to the Saviour. It was therefore wisely ordered that Judas should be among the apostles. But he was not among them when the last commission was given, under which we now act. When the Holy Spirit calls men to the ministry, he bestows on them qualifications for the work—qualifications both of head and heart. The qualifications of the heart include a sincere desire to glorify God, and save souls; a desire never felt by the unregenerate. Hence, the Holy Spirit never makes unregenerate ministers. When such men enter the sacred office, they, in the language of Paul, are "ministers of Satan."

---

[1] 1 Cor. xii. 11.

As true ministers are members of Christ's spiritual body, so their ministry is intended for its benefit:—" for the perfecting of the saints, for the work of the ministry, for the edifying of the body of Christ." Their office pertains to the spiritual, universal church, of which they are all members. The ministry of some of them may have a relation also to local churches, placed under their special charge; but they serve in these for the good of the whole body of Christ.

In Ephesians iv. 11, Paul enumerates the officers whom God set in the church: "Some apostles, some prophets, some evangelists," &c. Of these the first three are not confined to local churches, but are ministers of the church universal. This is apparent, from the words of Paul: "Who now rejoice in my sufferings for you, and fill up that which is behind of the afflictions of Christ, in my flesh, for his body's sake, which is the church, whereof I am made a minister."[1]

The apostles were, according to the import of the name, persons *sent forth*. The term is applied specially to those whom Christ sent forth in person, and who are called the apostles *of Christ*. Paul claimed to be an apostle in this sense: "Am I not an apostle? Have I not seen Jesus Christ our Lord?"[2] And again: "Paul, an apostle, not of men, neither by man, but by Jesus Christ."[3] Paul numbered himself among the witnesses of Christ's resurrection, and the apostles were chosen to be witnesses of this fact. Peter, when he proposed the election of one to take the place of Judas, stated the qualifications necessary for an apostle in this manner: "Wherefore of these men which have companied with us all the time that the Lord Jesus went in and out among us, beginning from the baptism of John, unto that same day that he was taken up from us, must one be ordained to be a witness with us of his resurrection."[4] These qualifications cannot now be found in any man living, and therefore the apostolic office has necessarily ceased.

The name apostle is applied, in another sense, to Barnabas,[5] the companion of Paul. These two ministers had been *sent forth* by the Holy Ghost, from Antioch, to a special work. Barnabas is probably called an apostle, with reference to this fact; and, in this

---

[1] Col. i. 24, 25.   [2] 1 Cor. ix. 1.   [3] Gal. i. 1.
[4] Acts i. 21, 22.   [5] Acts xiv. 14.

sense, the term corresponds in signification to our modern name, *missionary.* Paul and Barnabas had been sent forth as missionaries, on a tour of missionary service.

Prophets were persons divinely inspired to make revelation from God, consisting sometimes in the foretelling of future events. This office was needed, before the volume of divine revelation was completed. The absence of the prophetic gift in modern times, demonstrates that the Holy Spirit, who imparts every needful gift, accounts further revelation unnecessary. The absence of the gift proves the sufficiency of the Scriptures, and the cessation of the prophetic office.

Evangelists were persons employed in the spread of the gospel. They appear to have labored in connection with the apostles, to extend the religion of Christ and plant new churches. They did not need miraculous endowments for their work; and therefore their office continues to the present time. Every minister of the word, when he labors, not for the special benefit of a local church, but for the spread of the gospel, is doing the work of an evangelist.[1] Timothy was required to do this, though remaining at Ephesus, and laboring for the interest of that particular church.

A knowledge of gospel truth, an aptness to teach, and a heart moved by the desire to glorify God in the salvation of souls, are the evidences of a divine call to the work of the ministry. All these qualifications may exist, in a measure, in ordinary Christians; and a proportionate obligation accompanies them, to use them in the Redeemer's service. No church, no minister of the gospel, can, under a proper influence, forbid the exercise of these gifts, where they exist. Moses repelled the suggestion to forbid some who prophesied; and said, "Would God that all the Lord's people were prophets."[2] An active, prudent employment of the gifts possessed by ordinary Christians, would promote incalculably the interests of religion; and the restriction of all labor for the spread of the gospel, and the promotion of piety, to a select few, is greatly detrimental to the cause of Christ.

But it is still true, that there are some whose gifts for public usefulness rise high above the rest; and, in bestowing superior qualifications, the Holy Spirit, who divides to every man severally as

---

[1] 2 Tim. iv. 5.   [2] Num. xi. 29.

he will, has indicated his will that the possessor of the qualifications should use them for the work of the ministry, for the edifying of the body of Christ.

The Holy Spirit works harmoniously in all the parts of his operation. He diffuses one sympathy through all the body of Christ, so that the eye cannot say to the hand, I have no need of thee. When qualifications for service are imparted by the Spirit to one member, other members, under the influence of the same Spirit, welcome its service. Hence, every man who believes alone, that he is called of God to the ministry, has reason to apprehend that he is under delusion. If he finds that those who give proof that they honor God and love the souls of men, do not discover his ministerial qualifications, he has reason to suspect that they do not exist. The Head of the church has graciously provided, that in the ordinary course of things, men are able to obtain counsel in this matter, and are not compelled to act on their individual responsibility. If, in some extraordinary case, he calls some men to stand alone, as Elijah did, in defence of the truth, this gives no just plea to others to isolate themselves, and act on their own responsibility, when circumstances do not demand it. Elijah's proof of a divine call to the prophetical office consisted wholly in his possession of the prophetical spirit; but Elisha had the additional proof, that he had been anointed to the office by Elijah. Such proof, in ordinary cases, the Holy Spirit has provided for the ministers of the word; and the use of it is necessary to the success of the ministry and the order of the churches.

When any one is introduced into the ministry, the highest responsibility, next to that which he himself sustains, devolves on the ministers with whom he is to associate as a fellow-laborer. On the ministers a peculiar responsibility rests, to pray that laborers may be sent into the harvest; and also to seek out and encourage gifts for the work, and thus continue the succession of laborers. It was made the special duty of Timothy, to look out faithful men, able to teach others, that he might commit the ministry of the word to them. It was to the ministers of the church at Antioch, that the Holy Ghost said, "Separate me Saul and Barnabas for the work whereunto I have called them;"[1] and the

----

[1] Acts xiii. 2.

public designation of them to the work, appears to have been made by these ministers, doubtless with the concurrence of the church. In this method of procedure, there is an obvious fitness. It was fit that Elisha should be anointed to the prophetical office by a prophet. Men whom the Spirit has filled with a burning desire to preach the gospel, and has qualified for the service, are the most suitable persons to look out aids in the service, and judge of their fitness. Hence the obligation was laid on Timothy, already a minister. Hence the duty imposed on Titus: "For this cause left I thee in Crete, that thou shouldst ordain elders in every city." Hence the instructions respecting the qualifications necessary for office, are given in the epistles to these ministers, rather than in those to the churches.

The propriety of ministerial concurrence, in public designation to the ministerial office, appears from the nature of the case apart from apostolic example. But we have apostolic example to assist our reasoning. Saul and Barnabas were solemnly set apart by their brethren in the ministry, with fasting, prayer, and imposition of hands. In this case, he who was not a whit behind the chief of the apostles, bent before those who had no pretensions to apostolic authority, that he might receive the imposition of hands. What a sanction did his act give to the solemn ceremony, and to the established church order, of which it was a part! If such solemn services are appropriate in public designation to a particular service in the ministry, much more are they appropriate when any one enters the ministry itself. We learn from other Scriptures that such services were performed. Paul mentions the appointment of Timothy to the ministerial office in these words: "Neglect not the gift that is in thee, which was given thee by prophecy, with the laying on of the hands of the presbytery."[1]

It has been a question whether the concurrence of a single minister is sufficient in ordination. We have no explicit instruction on this point. From the instruction to Titus, it appears that he alone was authorized to ordain elders in every city. Yet Paul, though a minister of superior authority, did not ordain Timothy alone. He was the chief agent in the work; and says, "By the putting on of my hands;"[2] but yet he chose not to act alone, and

---

[1] 1 Tim. iv. 14.   [2] 2 Tim. i. 6.

therefore he says in another place, "By the laying on of the hands of the presbytery." The concurrence of a presbytery might not be possible in every city of Crete, where the churches had been recently planted; but where it was possible, even Paul with his apostolic authority chose not to act without it. We have, therefore, apostolic example confirming our reasoning on the subject, that where a presbytery can be obtained, its concurrence ought to be procured. The minister, who, from the direction given to Titus, takes it upon himself alone to ordain to the sacred office, assumes a power which Paul himself did not assume.

The institution of local churches has divine authority, and ought to be respected by every disciple of Christ. It is the duty of every one to become a member of some local church, and walk with the other members in love and Christian obedience. Brethren so connected are bound to exhort one another to diligence in the duties for which they are severally qualified. The obligation of a member to labor in the ministry may be recognised by his church, and the church does not go out of its proper sphere when it exhorts to this duty. Paul directed the church at Colosse, " Say to Archippus, take heed to the ministry which thou hast received in the Lord, that thou fulfil it."[1] He did not send the message to Archippus as from himself, but instructed the church to perform this duty. Such exhortation to a minister is therefore proper to be given by a church; and it follows, that a church is not without responsibility as to the question whether its gifted members are using their gifts as they ought. This responsibility makes the church a party in ministerial ordination. We have no express declaration that the church at Antioch concurred in the setting apart of Saul and Barnabas; but it may be inferred, not only from the tenor of the narrative, but especially from the fact that these missionaries, on their return, reported their doings to the whole church.

All the parties concerned in ordination ought to seek the guidance of the Holy Spirit, and act under his influence. The highest responsibility rests on him who is entering the sacred office. He should act under a deep sense of his responsibility, and with a persuasion, the result of prayerful, heart-searching examination, that he is moved by the Holy Ghost. The presbytery have the next

---

[1] Col. iv. 17.

degree of responsibility. They should be persuaded that the Holy Spirit has called the candidate to the ministry; and be prepared, under this conviction, the result of due examination, to receive him as a fellow-laborer with them in the Lord's service. The lowest degree of responsibility rests on the church; but even this is solemn and important. The same Spirit dwells in the ministry and in the churches; and every member is concerned in whatever concerns the spiritual body of Christ. A hearty concurrence of the church is necessary in the ordination; and, without it, a presbytery should never act. When a candidate has the threefold testimony, of his own conscience, of the presbytery, and of the church, he may proceed to labor in the ministry, with an assurance that he is "sent forth by the Holy Ghost."

Every step in the process of ordination recognises the principle that a divine call is necessary to a proper entrance on the ministerial office. The candidate, the presbytery, the church, all admit it, and act on it. This principle is of great importance to the preservation of a spiritual and efficient ministry; and it cannot be neglected, without immense evil to the cause of pure religion. When a father chooses the ministry as a profession for his son, or when the son chooses it for himself, as he would choose any other profession, the authority of God is contemned, and the holy office profaned. If a church should think that they need a minister, and should conclude to appoint one without regard to a divine call; and if a presbytery should aid them in accomplishing their purpose; the church and presbytery together may make a minister; but he will be, if not a minister of Satan, at the best only a minister of men, and not a minister of Christ.

The divine call is not only indispensable, but it is also complete in itself. The presbytery do not assemble to complete it, but to signify their concurrence in the persuasion that it exists. The earliest and the least hurtful form which the pernicious doctrine of baptismal regeneration assumed, regarded baptism as the completion of regeneration. It did not make regeneration consist wholly in the outward ceremony; but it regarded no one, whatever the Holy Sprit may have effected within him, as fully regenerated, until he had gone through the outward ceremony. A similar mistake has been made respecting the Holy Spirit's call to the ministry. The call is supposed to be incomplete, until the outward ceremony of ordination has been performed. In both cases a distinction should be made, between what the Spirit does, and what it is the duty of him to do on whom the Spirit operates. The Spirit regenerates; and it is the duty of the regenerated man to be baptized. The Spirit calls to the ministry; and it is the duty of the man so called, to enter on the work of the ministry through all the forms which are prescribed in the word of God. Why the Holy Spirit permits one whom he has regenerated to err so far as to neglect baptism; and why he permits one whom he has called to the ministry to err so far as to neglect both baptism and regular ordination; I as little understand, as I understand why God permitted sin to enter the world. The proof of all these facts is irrefragable; and I am compelled to admit their existence, and believe that God will overrule them for his glory.

OBJECTIONS.

Objection 1.—The doctrine of a special divine call to the ministry, savors of fanaticism. Such a call was suitable to the day of miracles, but now the grace of God, like his providence, operates by ordinary means. The Spirit resides in the church and ministry; and what they do, the Spirit does. To expect any other call of the Holy Spirit is fanatical.

Had the objection simply maintained that the Holy Spirit uses means, in calling men to the ministry, the proposition would have been admitted. He uses the word as a means, in his call of men to repentance and faith; and he uses the same word in calling men to the work of the ministry. But the objection marks out another channel in which the spiritual influence is supposed to flow, namely, the church and the ministry; but how can the necessary qualifications for the ministry be derived through this channel? If the grace of God now operates by the use of ordinary means, we know that the word is the ordinary means which the Holy Spirit employs in illumination and sanctification; and the conclusion is rational, and not fanatical, that the superior illumination and sanctification necessary for the work of the ministry, are the effect of the same means more successfully employed, or more abundantly blessed. The laying on of apostolic hands could confer spiritual gifts in the day of miracles; but ordaining hands have now no gifts to confer.

It is the objection which carries us back to the day of miracles, and expects effects from causes inadequate to produce them. A ministry made by outward ordination, without a divine call, is a curse to the world.

Objection 2.—If a divine call is indispensable to constitute a minister of Christ, since the call is invisible, we can never know who are true ministers.

The supposed invisibility of religion is presented in various forms of objection. It makes the church invisible, and the ministry invisible. But in what sense is religion invisible? The power of gravity is invisible, but we see its effects everywhere; and we feel it binding us to the earth. The influence of the Spirit is invisible, but its effects are seen and felt as certainly as the effects of gravity. The Spirit's call to the ministry is unseen; but the effects of it have been displayed in the successful conflict which the ministry has waged with the powers of darkness, and in the victories which it has achieved. The history of the world testifies that a divine power has wrought in the ministry of the word; and, wherever the gospel has been faithfully preached, every one has had an opportunity to observe such effects as demonstrate that the ministry of the word is the ministry of the Spirit. Why, then, need we, to render the ministry visible, suppose it to consist in outward form? There is a proper form for the ministry to assume, but the form may be without the power; and the mere form does not constitute a minister of Christ. May we not be deceived in this matter? We may. Ministers of Satan have appeared as ministers of righteousness; and compliance with external forms is a method by which they recommend themselves. We are commanded to try the spirits; and this cannot be done by a mere examination of ordination credentials. An obligation to discriminate otherwise than by ordination certificate, devolves on every church in the choice of its pastor; and on every pastor in inviting a minister to preach to the people of his charge.

Objection 3.—If ordination does not make a minister of Christ, and does not prove a man to be a minister of Christ, it may be dispensed with as useless.

This does not follow. Though it may not accomplish either of these purposes, it may, nevertheless, be of great utility; and if we were wholly unable to see any utility in it, yet, as the will of

God, we ought to observe it. Men may be Christians without baptism; and may profess Christ without baptism; but it does not follow, that baptism is useless. The Head of the church has, in his wisdom, made it the appointed ceremony for the Christian profession, and so he has made ordination the appointed ceremony for a regular entrance into the ministerial office. As every converted man ought to profess Christ by baptism, so every one who has been called of God to the ministry, ought to enter on the work by ordination. The proof of the obligation in the latter case, is not so clear from the Holy Scriptures, as in the former, but it is sufficiently clear to guide our practice.

SECTION II.—ADMINISTRATION OF BAPTISM.

The apostles were commissioned to preach, to baptize, and to teach. If the office held by ordinary ministers were identical with that held by the apostles, there would be no difficulty in deciding, that it includes the administration of baptism. But the apostolic office has ceased, and the work assigned to the apostles has devolved on inferior officers. The apostles could not, in person, preach, baptize, and teach, in every country of the world, and in every age till the end of time; but the commission made it their duty to provide for the full performance of this work; and their apostolic authority, guided by the infallible direction of the Holy Spirit, enabled them to make all necessary arrangements for carrying it into effect. Now, we cannot determine, from the commission itself, whether to preach, to baptize, and to teach, would be assigned, as distinct duties, to three distinct classes of officers; or whether they would be committed, without separation, to one class. For information on this point, we are left to inquire into the instructions given by the apostles by precept and example.

Some have argued, that, because preaching is a more important work than baptizing, the authority to preach necessarily includes authority to baptize. The greater, say they, must include the less. But this mode of argument is fallacious. The whole includes its parts, but the greater does not always include the less. A high dignitary of the realm may be guilty of usurpation, if he assumes the functions of an humble official. So, though preaching is a higher office than baptizing, it does not necessarily include it.

We learn that the Holy Spirit has called men to preach the gospel, by the qualifications which he has conferred; but we can have no proof of this sort, that the Holy Spirit has called any one to the work of baptizing. Spiritual qualifications are not required; and, if we have no other means of knowing, it may remain doubtful, whether the work may not be done by any one whom the candidate may select.

Among those who have held that baptism possesses a saving efficacy, it has often been a matter of pressing importance, to obtain the administration of it, in case of sickness, when a priest was not at hand. It has been held, that, in case of necessity, the rite may be administered by laymen, and even by women. Some persons who are free from such superstitious reliance on the outward ceremony, have held that any one who makes a disciple, may baptize him. According to this interpretation of the commission, it would be proper for a mother, whose instructions have been blessed to the conversion of her son, to be the administrator of his baptism. But this interpretation is inadmissible. If some of the work to which the apostles were specially appointed, may, to some extent, be performed by other persons, it does not follow, that these persons are invested in full with the apostolic commission.

The commission specifies duties, for the performance of which the apostles were to provide. One of these was the administration of baptism. They were commanded, not to make disciples and teach them the duty of being baptized; but to make disciples and baptize them. The administration of the rite was to be their care; and, where they could not perform it in their own person, it was made their duty to provide for its performance. This reasoning proves satisfactorily, that the administration was not designed to be left to any one whom the candidate might select; and it is confirmed by the words of Paul: "Christ sent me not to baptize, but to preach the gospel." These words imply, that Christ had sent some persons to baptize. The duty was to be performed; and these words, taken in connection with the fact that John the Baptist and the other apostles were commanded to baptize, confirm the deduction that the work was to be done by agents provided.

On the question, whether the administration of baptism is necessarily included in the commission to preach, or necessarily connected with it, the words of Paul just quoted, throw some light.

The word translated "sent," is the verb from which the word *apostle* is derived; and, as used by Paul in this passage, it imports that Christ had not given to Paul an apostolic commission to baptize, but to preach the gospel. On comparing the commission given to him, with that given to the other apostles, the difference in this particular is apparent. This proves that the offices of preaching and baptizing were not inseparable. Had the greater included the less, the authority and obligation to baptize were included in Paul's commission, and he could not have said with literal truth, "Christ sent me not to baptize." To understand the passage to signify nothing more than that baptism was a less important part of the work which Paul was authorized to perform, does not satisfy the literal import of the words, and it is a departure, without necessity, from the literal interpretation, which is fully sustained by a comparison of Paul's commission with that of the other apostles. Moreover, the literal import best agrees with the context, since, according to it, the fact alleged by Paul cut off, from those whom he had baptized, all plea to claim him on that account as an apostle for their party leader. If in baptizing them, he had not acted as an apostle, the fact gave them no pretext to claim him as a party leader in that high character. Had Paul's state of mind permitted him to preach on the next day after Jesus appeared to him, and gave him his commission, he was authorized to preach; but not to administer baptism. Yet he did afterwards baptize Crispus, Gaius, and the household of Stephanas; and he must have obtained authority to do this in some way. In what way? If not by extraordinary commission, it must have been in the ordinary way, in which others received authority to baptize. He received the command to be baptized himself, in the ordinary way, and he honored and obeyed the command. In the same way, he must have received the authority under which he acted, in the administration of baptism.

Although baptizing is not necessarily connected with preaching and teaching; yet the manner in which it is conjoined with them in the commission, appears to indicate that the connection is suitable. No separate class of officers is anywhere provided in the New Testament, for administering the rite, and yet, if we have reasoned correctly, the apostles were under obligation to provide for it. We are led to the conclusion, that this provision was made, in the ordinary method instituted for transmitting the ministerial office. Paul had committed the office to Timothy, in the presence of many witnesses, by the laying on of his hands, and the hands of the presbytery. Timothy was, in like manner, to commit the office to others, and enjoin on them the same duties which Paul had enjoined on him. There was a fitness in the arrangement that this ceremonial induction into office, should add the ceremonial authority to baptize. It cannot be proved to be given, in the internal call of the Spirit. It was not given in the extraordinary commission of Paul. If Paul received it in the ordinary way, whether in his being set apart at Antioch, or in some similar service at some previous time, we have this point established :—the authority to administer baptism is conferred in the ordinary course of the ministerial succession, when an individual, called by the Holy Spirit to the ministry of the word, is publicly set apart to this service. The process of reasoning by which we reach this conclusion, is less clear and direct than that which many other subjects admit; but it is sufficiently clear to determine our practice, in the absence of explicit instruction from the holy oracles. We have, moreover, the satisfaction of knowing that this course of procedure has been generally adopted in the churches which have conformed in their order most nearly to the Scriptures.

Section III.—APOSTOLIC SUCCESSION.

We have seen that baptism ought to be administered by an ordained minister of the word. A question, then, arises before every believer who desires to receive baptism, "how shall he know who is authorized to administer it?" Some have thought, that the candidate may lawfully leave the whole responsibility of deciding this question with the administrator. But, if he knew the administrator not to be authorized, it would be wrong to receive baptism at his hands; and it cannot, therefore, be right, to be indifferent to the question whether he is authorized. Moreover, the conscientious administrator is deeply interested in the question. He ought not to act without divine authority, and deceive the confiding disciples, by giving to them for true Christian baptism, that which is but a human counterfeit. How does he know that he has been duly ordained to perform this work; that they who ordained him

17

were duly ordained; and that the line of connection with those who originally received the commission from Christ, has been unbroken? Is there an obligation, binding on the conscience of every individual who seeks baptism, and still more binding on the conscience of him who administers it, to know that his right to administer has been derived by unbroken succession from the apostles?

There is an intrinsic improbability in the supposition, that the Scripture binds all who receive the gospel, in every country and every age of the world, to perform a specified duty; and yet leaves that duty in the dark, so that no one can know what it is, except by the light of tradition? In a former chapter we applied this consideration to the question, whether the consciences of men are bound by Scripture authority to receive the traditionary succession of the Sabbath, as of like authority with Scripture precepts. The examination then made, discovered that the divine precept is most wisely given, in a manner which secures all the ends of the observance, without binding the individual conscience with a responsibility to which it is unequal, and for which it has not the requisite knowledge. The precept does not bind men to observe the seventh day of an unknowable week; and it does not so bind them to the regular succession, that, if they have lost it by circumnavigating the globe, they can never regain it. If we find nothing in the Scriptures, when properly interpreted, binding our consciences to the tradition of the sabbatical observance, we may, from the analogy, expect to find nothing binding our consciences to the apostolic succession.

An humble disciple of Christ desirous to obey all his Lord's commands, learns his duty from the Holy Scriptures, and sees in them the order established in the primitive churches. He looks around him to discover whether there are churches like the primitive churches, and ministers preaching and baptizing, like the primitive ministers. He finds them. The beginning and the end of the succession appear. The middle of it he sees not; but he knows that the Head of the church has lived during all the intermediate time, and that he is the God of providence, and the giver of the Holy Spirit, by whose influence the chain of succession could be preserved. He feels assured, that, if an unbroken succession is necessary for any purpose which the Head of the church has in view, he has preserved it. With this assurance, he proceeds in what appears to him to be the plain path of duty, the same path in which the ancient saints walked ; and he confidently expects that his obedience will receive his Lord's approbation. Is there anything in the Scriptures which can prove such reasoning fallacious ?

Suppose that at some point in the line the apostolic succession was lost, was it impossible to re-establish the ancient order; or, in other words, was it impossible ever afterwards to obey Christ's commands ? The Holy Spirit qualifies and calls persons to preach the gospel, and teach men to observe whatsoever Christ commanded, and we have seen that this call of the Spirit is complete in itself. In the case supposed, how could persons called by the Holy Spirit teach men to observe Christ's commands, if the observance had become impossible ? Surely, the reasoning which infers the impossibility must be fallacious, or the failure of the succession has never taken place, to disturb the counsels of him who said, " Lo, I am with you alway, even to the end of the world." Now, whether it be that the chain has been throughout unbroken, or that the Head of the church has a method of restoring it, the effect is the same to us. It is ours to do our duty, according to the light which we possess. This mode of settling the question is sufficient for all practical purposes.

As a question of mere theory it may be asked, whether a breach in the succession would render a new revelation necessary. To set aside any command of Scripture would require a new revelation. But to depart from the order which Christ has instituted is one thing, and to return to it after having wandered from it is quite another thing. For the latter we need no new revelation. The wisdom from above, given by the ordinary influence of the Spirit, is sufficient for such an emergency, without a miraculous inspiration. If holy men of God have had the responsibility thrown upon them of returning to the good old path after it had been deserted, they doubtless sought wisdom from above to direct them, and the success of their efforts to regain the lost way, is a sufficient assurance to us that the Lord gave them the necessary wisdom.

But is there any wall built along the wayside to prevent the return of wanderers ? So far as I can see, the whole difficulty is resolvable into the question whether ministers of the word, called to the work by the Holy Spirit, may, in any case, perform the full duties of the office without the regular ceremonial induction into it. According to the view which we have taken, the call of the Spirit is complete in itself; but the same Spirit teaches the called to respect the order instituted for ceremonial induction into office. An obligation to respect this order, when it exists, imposes on them the duty of deferring the exercise of the ceremonial functions until they have been ceremonially inducted; but in the case supposed the church order does not exist, and therefore the obligation to defer does not exist. Their duty is to respect the order when it exists, and to restore it when it does not. The Head of the church designed that the ministers of the word should make disciples, baptize them, and teach them to organize churches, to celebrate the Lord's supper, exercise discipline, and walk in all the commandments and ordinances of the Lord. The ministers of the word are officers of Christ's spiritual church, and derive their qualifications and call from the Holy Spirit. Like other men, they are bound to observe what Christ commanded, and therefore to regard established church order. But if church order has become prostrate, their call by the Holy Spirit requires them to restore it, and not to teach that it must now for ever be neglected.

In the regular course of things, ordination stands at the beginning of the ministry, as baptism stands at the beginning of the Christian life; but there are several important particulars in which the two observances differ.

Baptism is enjoined by express precept, ordination is not. Much of the order instituted by the apostles originated in expediency. The appointment of deacons, recorded in Acts, chapter vi., is manifestly a case of this kind. Expediency has its obligation, as well as positive precept; and a question of expediency, decided by apostolic wisdom, binds us in like circumstances. The community of goods in the first church does not bind us, because our circumstances are different. Ordination is expedient, and the observance of it obligatory in the regular order of things, instituted by the apostles; but it cannot be inferred that it is obligatory in all circumstances. Nothing in Scripture determines the number of the presbytery; and if this may be determined by considerations of expediency, the same expediency may determine that ordination by a presbytery may, in some extraordinary circumstances, be dispensed with.

All the disciples of Christ, in the primitive times, were required to be baptized; but all the ministers of Christ were not ceremonially ordained. We have no proof that the apostles, or the seventy whom Christ sent forth, were thus ordained. No presbytery was convened in their case, but they were ordained or appointed by Christ in person. When he baptized disciples, he put the work into the hands of those who were afterwards to perform it. But his direct call conferred the ministerial office without human ordination. We have in the New Testament a much larger number of unordained than of ordained ministers, if imposition of human hands is necessary to ordination. Saul and Barnabas were so ordained to a missionary service, and Timothy was so ordained to the work of the ministry, but who else?

Jesus honored the institution of baptism by receiving it from a human administrator, but he did not so honor ordination. Among the benefits resulting to ministers from ordination, an important one is, that they go forth into the work with the concurrent testimony of the presbytery and the church, recommending them to all as the ministers of Christ. Jesus was willing to receive the testimony of John, but of John as his baptizer, not as his ordainer. "That he should be made manifest," said John, "therefore am I come baptizing." [1] At the beginning of his ministry, Jesus received baptism from John in the Jordan; and when he had gone up from the water, and was standing on the bank, his august ordination took place. The Holy Spirit, by whom his human nature was qualified for the ministry on which he was entering, descended on him in visible form, and the voice of the Father audibly pronounced, "This is my beloved Son, in whom I am well pleased." [2]

From this comparison, it clearly appears that ordination does not come to us enforced by like obligations to those of baptism. If our doctrine of strict communion be correct, baptism is a prerequisite to membership in the local churches; and, since the administration of baptism properly belongs to the ministers of the word, the local churches are, in this particular, dependent for their existence on the ministry. Local churches cannot originate the minis-

---

[1] John i. 31. [2] Matt. iii. 17.

try on which their own existence is dependent. The ministry originated before the local churches, and might have been perpetuated without them, if the Lord had so willed. The power from which the ministry originates is not that of the churches, but of the Head of the Church; and his call to office is the highest authority. John was sent to preach and baptize, without being baptized or ordained; yet the evidence of his mission was clear, and the people believed it. Paul was commissioned to preach the gospel while he was unbaptized and unordained; and the call was not conditioned on his being afterwards baptized and ordained. The call was complete and unconditional. He was under obligation to be baptized, as all other converted persons are; and he discharged this obligation, as every called minister ought to do; but his call was complete while he was yet unbaptized and unordained.

In the view which we have taken, the Christian ministry is an institution of surpassing importance. It does not grow up from the churches, but comes down from heaven. It is a gift sent down to mankind from the ascended Saviour. After stating that the exalted Redeemer "gave gifts unto men," Paul proceeds to enumerate these gifts in the following words: "He gave some, apostles; and some, prophets; and some, evangelists; and some, pastors and teachers."[1] To these heaven-bestowed ministers, the Spirit, which qualifies them for their work, gives testimony. The churches receive the testimony of the Spirit, and, in their turn, add their testimony; and the ministry and the churches become joint witnesses for God to the world. Whether these two witnesses have lived during all the dark period of papal persecution, I leave for others to inquire; but if they were ever slain, I doubt not that the Spirit of God has reanimated them, and will enable them to continue their testimony to the end of the world.

---

[1] Eph. iv. 8, 11.

SECTION IV.—CHURCH OFFICERS.

BISHOPS.

THE CHURCHES SHOULD CHOOSE, FROM AMONG THE MINISTERS OF THE WORD, BISHOPS OR PASTORS TO TEACH AND RULE THEM.

Numerous passages of Scripture speak of persons who bore rule in the churches. "Obey them that have the rule over you."[1] "The elders that rule well."[2] The term bishop signifies overseer, and implies authority to rule. Among the qualifications necessary for a bishop, one was, that he ruleth well his own house; and the reason assigned is, "If a man know not how to rule his own house, how shall he take care of the church of God?"[3] It is clear, from this passage, that the bishops were invested with an authority bearing some analogy to the authority which the head of a family exercises over his household.

The question has been much discussed, whether the authority of a bishop is restricted to a single local church. Episcopalians maintain that it extends to the churches of a large district called a diocese; and that the Scriptural title for the ruler of a single church, is presbyter or elder. Against this opinion, the following arguments appear conclusive. The single church at Philippi contained more bishops than one.[4] The elders of the church at Ephesus are styled overseers or bishops.[5] Peter addresses elders as persons having the *oversight*[6] of the flock, that is, the authority of overseers or bishops. In Paul's epistle to Titus, after the ordination of elders is mentioned, the qualifications of a bishop[7] are enumerated; and the connection plainly indicates that elder and bishop were titles of the same office.

The bishops were the pastors or shepherds of the flock committed to their charge. The bishops or elders of the church at Ephesus were required to "feed the flock." The elders whom Peter addressed were commanded to "feed the flock;" and their office as shepherds is presented to view as subordinate to that of Christ, "the chief shepherd." Since the churches are to be fed, not with

---

[1] Heb. xiii. 17. [2] 1 Tim. v. 17. [3] 1 Tim. iii. 4, 5.
[4] Phil. i. 1. [5] Acts xx. 28. [6] 1 Peter v. 2.
[7] Titus i. 5, 7.

literal food, but with knowledge and understanding, the office of teaching is included in that of pastor. Hence a bishop was required to be "apt to teach." In enumerating church officers, Paul mentions both pastors and teachers. It appears from this that there were teachers in the primitive churches, who were not invested with pastoral authority. These were ministers of the word, authorized by the commission to teach the observance of all Christ's commands, but not authorized to rule. The ministers of the word are officers of the universal church, but, as such, they have no authority to rule in the local churches. This authority belongs to the pastors or bishops.

The ruling authority of a pastor is peculiar in its kind. Though bearing some analogy to that of a father in his family, or of a governor in civil society, it differs from these. Christ distinguished His rule from that of earthly kings by the absence of coercion: "If my kingdom were of this world, then would my servants fight."[1] So the spiritual rulers under Christ have no coercive power over the persons or property of those under their authority. A well marked distinction between their authority and that which is exercised by civil rulers, is drawn in these words of Christ: "Ye know that the princes of the gentiles exercise dominion over them, and they that are great exercise authority upon them. But it shall not be so among you: but whosoever will be great among you, let him be your minister; and whosoever will be chief among you, let him be your servant."[2] Another peculiarity of their rule is that they cannot govern at their own will. This would be to act as lords over God's heritage. Such power, if exercised by them, is a usurpation, and does not legitimately belong to their office. The only rule which they have a right to apply is that of God's word; and the only obedience which they have a right to exact, is voluntary. The civil ruler is armed with the sword, and coerces obedience. Zion's King has put no carnal weapons into the hands of church rulers, and all coercion is inconsistent with the nature of the authority intrusted to them. No submission to the Lord is acceptable but that which is voluntary; and the same kind of submission which the ancient Christians rendered to the Lord, they rendered to their

---

[1] John xviii. 36.   [2] Matt. xx. 25—27.

spiritual rulers:—"They first gave their own selves unto the Lord and unto us by the will of God."[1]

The surrender of their property was voluntary. Peter's address to Ananias and Sapphira proves that this was true, even in the general surrender which was made by the first church; and it is clear that the contributions afterwards made by the churches, were made not of constraint but willingly. They who claim or indirectly exercise a coercive power over the property of church-members, are taking the oversight for filthy lucre's sake, and have no sanction from the authority of Christ, or the example of his apostles.

Since the obedience of churches cannot be coerced, no one can begin or continue the exercise of spiritual rule over them, but at their will. Hence their bishops must be persons of their own choice. The apostles, though all collected at Jerusalem, and invested with full power from on high to do all that appertained to their office, did not appoint even the inferior officers of the church until after they had been chosen by the whole multitude of the disciples. In this procedure they recognised and established the right of the churches to elect their own officers. Even the appointment of an apostle to take the place of Judas appears to have been made by popular vote: and much more ought that of bishops over the several churches. The Greek word rendered *ordain* in Acts xiii. 48, signifies to stretch out the hand, and is supposed to refer to the mode of popular election by the lifting up of the hand; but, whether this criticism be just or not, the proof that church officers were so elected is sufficient without the aid of this passage.

Because the bishops must labor in word and doctrine, as well as rule, the churches should elect them from the ministers of the word. As they have no right to coerce the churches, so the churches have no right to coerce their acceptance of office. The relation must be voluntarily entered into by both parties. This voluntariness on the part of ministers is necessary to the proper exercise of their office: "Not of constraint, but willingly; not for filthy lucre, but of a ready mind."[2] The minister cannot coerce a support from the church, but God has ordained that they who preach the gospel should live of the gospel.[3] The duty of a church to

---

[1] 2 Cor. viii. 5.   [2] 1 Peter v. 2.   [3] 1 Cor. ix. 14.

support its pastor is clearly taught in the word of God; and without the performance of this duty on their part, they have no right to expect his services; and they, in a manner, put it out of his power to render them.

DEACONS.

DEACONS SHOULD BE CHOSEN BY THE CHURCHES, FROM AMONG THEIR MEMBERS, TO MINISTER IN SECULAR AFFAIRS.

By apostolic direction, the church at Jerusalem chose from among themselves seven men, honest, and of good report, who were appointed to serve tables. This measure originated in the expediency, that the apostles might give themselves to the word of God and prayer. The same expediency requires that pastors should be relieved from secular burdens, and be left to the spiritual service of the church. We know that deacons existed in the church at Philippi;[1] and directions were given to Timothy respecting the qualifications necessary for the deacon's office. These facts authorize the conclusion, that the deacon's office was designed to be perpetual in the churches. The mode of appointment should conform to the example of the first church. The persons should be chosen by popular vote, and invested with office by ministerial ordination.

Some have thought that deacons, as well as bishops, are called elders in the Scripture. We read of bishops and deacons in connection, but never of elders and deacons;—of the ordination of elders,[2] without the mention of deacons, when deacons were needed as well as bishops; and of contributions sent to the elders at Jerusalem,[3] after the deacons had been appointed, who were the proper officers to receive and disburse them. It is argued, moreover, that the distinction which appears to be made, in 1 Tim. v. 17, between preaching and ruling elders, naturally suggests that the ruling elders were the deacons of the primitive churches.

In the Presbyterian church, a distinct class of officers exists, called ruling elders. The only Scripture authority claimed for this office, is the text last referred to. This text, however, does not distinguish between different classes of officers, but between different modes of exercising the same office. The word rendered

[1] Phil. i. 1.   [2] Acts xiv. 23.   [3] Acts xi. 30.

"labor," signifies to labor to exhaustion. Not the elder who merely rules, is accounted worthy of double honor, but the elder who rules well; and the special honor is not due to the elder, as merely invested with the office of ministering in word and doctrine, but as laboring therein—laboring to exhaustion. Thus interpreted, the text furnishes no authority for Presbyterian lay elders; and no argument for supposing that deacons are called elders.

The other arguments to prove that the deacons were included in the eldership of the primitive churches, are not without plausibility, but they are not conclusive; and they are opposed by the facts, that all the elders of the church at Ephesus are called bishops; that all the elders addressed by Peter are said to have the oversight or episcopal office; and that the elders whom Titus was to appoint appear to have been all bishops, inasmuch as the qualifications for the deacon's office are not subjoined to those which are described as necessary for the other office.

Among the qualifications of the deacons' office, it is not required that they should be apt to teach; and they are therefore not appointed to act as public teachers of the word: but other qualifications are mentioned, which indicate, that they are expected to be forward in promoting the spiritual interests of the church. An obligation to do this rests on every member; and deacons are not released from it by their appointment to minister in secular affairs. Instead of becoming immersed in secularity, they are expected, by the proper exercise of their office, to purchase to themselves a good degree, and great boldness in the faith.[1] If deacons were everywhere active in holding up the hands of the pastors, as Aaron and Hur held up the hands of Moses, the prosperity of the churches would be greatly advanced, and the success of the gospel far more abundant.

---

[1] 1 Tim. iii. 13.

CHAPTER IX.

DISCIPLINE.

Section I.—ADMISSION OF MEMBERS.

THE CHURCHES SHOULD ADMIT BAPTIZED BELIEVERS TO MEM-
BERSHIP.

A properly organized church consists of disciples who have professed their faith in Christ by baptism. Hence, such persons
only should be admitted to membership. Unity and brotherly love
require that all should be lovers of Christ; and love ought to be
manifested by obedience: but Christ is not obeyed, if his command, directing the mode of Christian profession, is not obeyed.

Each church for itself has the responsibility of admitting to its
own membership. A single church may exclude from its own fellowship, as in the case of the incestuous member excommunicated
by the church at Corinth; and the power to exclude implies the
power to admit. The pastor has not the power; nor is it possessed
by any ecclesiastical judicatory except the church itself. The
church is bound to exercise the power of admitting to membership,
in subjection to the revealed will of Christ; and is, therefore, prohibited from receiving any who do not possess the requisite qualifications.

In order that the church may judge whether a candidate is
duly qualified for membership, they should hear his profession of
faith. He is bound to let his light shine before all men, to the
glory of God; and it is specially needful that they should see it,
with whom he is to be associated in fellowship as a child of light.
He is bound to be ready always to give an answer to every one
that asketh the reason of the hope that is in him;[1] and especially

---

[1] 1 Pet. iii. 15.

should he be ready to answer, on this point, those who are to receive him into their number, as called in one hope of their calling. He is bound to show forth the praise of him who has called him out of darkness into his marvellous light; and he should rejoice to say, "Come and hear, all ye that fear God, and I will declare what he hath done for my soul."[1]

The churches are not infallible judges, being unable to search the heart; but they owe it to the cause of Christ, and to the candidate himself, to exercise the best judgment of which they are capable. To receive any one on a mere profession of words, without any effort to ascertain whether he understands and feels what he professes, is unfaithfulness to his interests, and the interests of religion. In primitive times, when persecution deterred from profession, and when the Spirit operated in a more visible manner, the danger of mistake was less; but even then, all who professed were not received. John the Baptist rejected some from baptism, who did not bring forth fruits meet for repentance. They who are unfit for baptism, are unfit for church-membership.

To preserve unity in the church, the admission of a member should be by unanimous vote. Harmony and mutual confidence are necessary to the peace and prosperity of a church; and, if these are to be disturbed by the admission of a new member, it is far better, both for him and the church, that his admission should be deferred, until it can be effected without mischief.

Admission to membership belongs to churches; but admission to baptism belongs properly to the ministry. A single minister has the right to receive to baptism, on his own individual responsibility; as is clear from the baptism of the eunuch by Philip, when alone. But when a minister is officiating as pastor of a church, it is expedient that they should unite their counsels in judging of a candidate's qualifications; but the pastor ought to remember, that the responsibility of receiving to baptism is properly his. The superior knowledge which he is supposed to possess, and his office as the shepherd of the flock, and the priority of baptism to church-membership, all combine to render it necessary that he first and chiefly should meet this responsibility, and act upon it in the fear of the Lord.

---

[1] Ps. lxvi. 16.

Section II.—SPIRITUAL IMPROVEMENT.

THE CHURCHES SHOULD LABOR INCESSANTLY, TO PROMOTE BRO-
THERLY LOVE IN THEIR MEMBERS, AND INCREASED DEVOTION TO
THE SERVICE OF GOD.

The spirit of unity pervades Christianity, and tends to bring
the disciples of Christ into association with one another. Under
the influence of this tendency, churches are formed; and in them
an opportunity is given for the display of brotherly love. By the
display, Christ is honored, and the world become convinced that
his religion is divine. For the sake of Christ, therefore, and for
the sake of the world, every church should labor to promote
brotherly love.

The churches are the glory of Christ, not only in the brotherly
love which they exhibit, but in their purity and devotion to the
service of God. They are but small and temporary associations;
yet they may reflect the glory of Christ to the view of an admiring
world, as pure dew-drops reflect the brightness of the sun. So to
honor Christ, should be the constant effort of the churches; and
to effect this, care should be exercised over the spirituality of
every member. The pastor should devote himself, with incessant
toil and prayer, to the spiritual good of his flock; the deacons
should unite their efforts with his for the attainment of the great
end; and the members should watch over one another, exhort one
another, and provoke one another to love and good works.

God has given the Christian ministry for the edification of his
people; and every church ought to avail itself of this divine gift,
and use it to the best advantage. For this purpose, the minister
should be supported by cheerful contributions from the members
of the church, that he may devote himself to the promotion of
their spiritual interests. He should be encouraged in every possible way to diligence and fidelity in his duties. His imperfections
should be treated with tenderness; and if, at any time, he should
become remiss in his work, or turn aside from it to secular pursuits, the church ought, in gentleness and love, to address him
with such language as Paul directed to be used to Archippus.[1]

---

[1] Col. iv. 17.

But such an address cannot be made with good effect by a church which does not sustain its minister, and free him from the necessity of worldly care.

Punctual attendance on the ministrations of the word, is necessary to the spiritual improvement of the church. It is necessary to encourage the heart of the minister. He cannot be expected to preach with earnestness and persevering zeal, if his people manifest no pleasure in listening to the truth which he proclaims. Let him know that they drink in the word with delight, that their souls are refreshed by it, and that it greatly increases their fruitfulness in holiness; with this knowledge, he will be stimulated to go forward in his work with boldness, and to endure all his toils with the sustaining assurance that his labor is not in vain in the Lord.

Regular attendance on the ministrations of the word is necessary, that the hearers may grow in grace and in the knowledge of Christ. Food is not more necessary to the body, than spiritual nourishment is to the soul; and the word is the appointed means of spiritual nourishment. It is the sincere milk, which babes in Christ desire, and by which they are nourished; and it is the strong meat, which they can use profitably who have attained to mature age in the divine life. Nor can spiritual health be expected, if the spiritual nourishment which God has provided, be received at far distant and irregular intervals. A regular return of one day in seven has been wisely appointed by the great Author of our being, who knows our frame, and perfectly understands what is best for the promotion of our highest interests. They who neglect this provision of his benevolence, reject the counsel of God against themselves, and bring spiritual leanness on their souls.

It is not enough to receive the spiritual food, but it ought to be inwardly digested. The truth which is heard on the sabbath, ought to be a subject of meditation through the week; and its influence should bring the actions, the words, the thoughts, even the very imaginations into obedience to the gospel of Christ. Thus the process of spiritual nutrition will be carried on, until the next sabbath brings another supply of the heavenly food. Thus the soul will grow in strength, and attain the stature of spiritual manhood.

Besides the public ministrations of the word, other means of promoting religious knowledge ought to receive the attention and support of the churches. The study of the Bible ought to be encouraged, whether by individuals, by Bible classes, or by Sunday schools. It is a great fault if the work of instructing is entirely given up to the young. Let the heads which have grown gray in the service of the Lord, bow with pleasure to impart instruction to the opening minds of the rising generation, and sow in this promising soil the seed which will produce a rich harvest, when the gray-haired instructor shall have gone to his eternal reward. Let the circulation of good religious books and periodical publications be promoted, and a spirit of religious inquiry be fostered in every proper way. Let men be taught, both by the words and the deeds of those who claim to be Christ's, that religion is the chief concern.

The health of the body requires exercise as well as food; so spiritual action is necessary for the health of the soul. Churches should exhort their members to be diligent in every good work, not only for the benefit of those around them, but also for their own spiritual improvement. In this course of active service, their own souls will become strong in the Lord, and their personal experience will verify the words of Christ, " It is more blessed to give than to receive." The great work which demands the energy of all God's people, is the spread of religion. Every church-member should labor for this by his personal efforts within the sphere of his individual influence, and, by co-operating with others, to extend the blessings of the gospel to every part of the earth. The precise mode of co-operating, the word of God does not prescribe; as it does not prescribe the precise mode in which the church-members shall travel to their place of public worship. But the thing to be done is prescribed; and, if the heart is in the Lord's work, it will employ its energies in devising the best method of accomplishing it, and in laboring to effect the object with prayerful reliance on the divine blessing. The gospel is to be preached to every creature; and he who loves Christ ought to feel a holy pleasure in helping those to execute the will of Christ who are willing, at his command, to bear the word of salvation to the perishing. Union in religious effort, not only promotes the spiritual growth of individual Christians, but it also conduces greatly to the harmony of churches. When coldness in religion prevails, the members of a church are like pieces of metal, which are not only separate from each other, but may be employed to inflict blows on each other; but when spiritual warmth has melted them, they flow together and become one. Feuds and unprofitable controversies cease when men are actively engaged in the service of God, and when they strive to provoke one another to nothing but love and good works.

Prayer meetings are an important means of spiritual improvement. It has been said that the prayer meeting of a church is the thermometer by which its spiritual temperature may be known. When Christians love to meet, that they may pour forth their united supplications to the throne of grace, the Saviour, in fulfilment of his promise, meets with them, and bestows blessings which infinitely transcend all earthly good, and are a beginning of heavenly bliss.

Section III.—EXCOMMUNICATION.

THE RIGHT TO EXCOMMUNICATE BELONGS TO THE CHURCH, WITHOUT ANY APPEAL.

This is clear from the words of Christ: "If he will not hear the church, let him be to thee as an heathen man and a publican." That it is not the province of a minister to excommunicate is clear from the instructions of Paul to the church at Corinth.[1] If ministers had a right to excommunicate, Paul, with his high apostolic authority, would have exercised the right himself, or would have directed to the clerical tribunal by which the right was to be exercised. But he instructed the church to do the work, and, therefore, to the church it properly belonged. The punishment was to be inflicted, not by the officers of the church, but by the whole church assembled together with the power and presence of Christ, and the act performed is called the punishment inflicted by many.[2] Some, because the word rendered "many" in the passage is in the comparative degree, have interpreted it *by the majority;* but whether this be its import or not, it seems to imply that the sentence was passed by popular vote.

The obligation to exclude unworthy persons from church-fellowship, is taught in various passages of Scripture. "Therefore put

---

[1] 1 Cor. v. 4, 5.   [2] 2 Cor. ii. 6.

18

away from among yourselves that wicked person."[1]　"A man that is a heretic, after the first and second admonition, reject."[2]　"Now we command you, brethren, in the name of our Lord Jesus Christ, that ye withdraw yourselves from every brother that walketh disorderly, and not after the tradition which he received of us."[3]　"If any man obey not our word by this epistle, note that man, and have no company with him, that he may be ashamed."[4]　"Now, I beseech you, brethren, mark them which cause divisions and offences, contrary to the doctrine which ye have learned; and avoid them."[5]

In excommunication, regard should be had, not only to the glory of God, but to the good of the offender. This appears from the words of Paul: "For the destruction of the flesh, that the spirit may be saved."[6] The happy result of this excommunication, the only one which is particularly recorded in the history of the New Testament churches, is a strong encouragement to the exercise of faithful discipline. It has been remarked, that when discipline leaves a church, Christ goes with it.

---

[1] 1 Cor. v. 13.　[2] Titus iii. 10.　[3] 2 Thes. iii. 6.
[4] 2 Thes. iii. 14.　[5] Rom. xvi. 17.　[6] 1 Cor. v. 5.

CHAPTER X.

MISCELLANEOUS TOPICS.

Section I.—EXPEDIENCE OF THE SCRIPTURAL CHURCH ORDER.

Our obligation to observe the positive precepts of religion is dependent entirely on the revealed will of the Lawgiver. It does not follow, however, that they are without reason, but only that the reason for them is beyond the discovery of human wisdom. After the divine wisdom has instituted them, we may be able to discover their fitness to accomplish the purpose for which they were designed, and may become sensible that they are necessary to the order and harmony of God's arrangements. In this manner the expedience of obeying positive precepts may sometimes be clearly seen by the intelligent student of God's will; but where we are unable to walk by sight, we ought to walk by faith in the way of God's commandments, and to feel assured, in every instance, that to obey God in all things is always most expedient.

Throughout the preceding discussions, we have endeavored to fix our eyes steadily on the divine precepts, and to strengthen ourselves in the purpose of obeying implicitly, even when no reason for the requirement is discoverable; but now, at the close of our investigations, it will be profitable to take another view of the church order which we have deduced from the Holy Scriptures in respect of its expedience.

A fundamental doctrine, in the system of church order which we have deduced from the Scriptures, is, that genuine piety is necessary to church-membership. If this doctrine had been steadfastly maintained from the times of the apostles, the corruption which overspread the churches would have been prevented, and the papal apostasy would never have occurred. The admission of

(275)

unconverted members opened the door to every evil, and ultimately subjected the churches to the spirit that worketh in the children of disobedience. The reformation by Luther corrected many abuses, but this chief inlet of mischief it did not close. Hence the reformed churches do not exhibit the purity, devotion, and zeal which characterized the churches of primitive times. We need a more thorough reformation. We need to have the axe laid at the root of the trees, and this is done when none are admitted to church-membership but persons truly converted. The doctrine which excludes all others establishes the value and necessity of vital religion, and it is therefore of the utmost importance to the interests of the church, and of the world.

Immense mischief has resulted from the ambition of the clergy. This raised the Roman pontiff to his high seat of power, and his adherents are actuated by the same spirit. To counteract its influence, Christ commanded his disciples, "Be ye not called Rabbi, for one is your Master, even Christ, and all ye are brethren."[1] The doctrine of equality among the ministers of Christ is at war with clerical ambition, and a steadfast maintenance of it would have effectually barred out the Man of Sin, and it would now demolish the Roman hierarchy, and teach haughty prelates the need of Christian humility.

The ambition of the clergy needs a combination of the churches to sustain it. The doctrine that every church is an independent body, and that no combination of the churches is authorized by Christ, opposes their schemes for ecclesiastical preferment. It makes the pastors or bishops equal, and allows no other preference than that which is due to superior piety and usefulness.

The independence of the churches, and the democratic form of church government, appeal strongly to individual responsibility, and have, therefore, a powerful tendency to promote holiness among the lay members. Every man feels that the cause of Christ is in some measure committed to him. The church is not a body intermediate between him and Christ, and charged with the exclusive responsibility of glorifying Christ; but he himself is in part the church, and to him belongs the obligation of honoring his divine Master. This doctrine of individual responsibility unites

---

[1] Matt. xxiii. 8.

with the doctrine of a converted church-membership, to render the churches the glory of Christ.

Enough has been said to direct the view of the thoughtful reader to the excellence of the Scriptural church order. In what remains of this section we shall consider some objections against the doctrine of church independence.

Objection 1.—The independent form of church government does not allow sufficient influence to the ministerial office. Learned divines may be outvoted by ignorant laymen; and pastors, who ought to rule their flocks, may have their peace and reputation destroyed by their churches, without any right of appeal.

The objection supposes some other than moral power to be needful for ministers. A man whose piety and call of God to the ministry are unquestionable; who gives full proof to those among whom he ministers that he seeks their highest good, and who serves a people that esteem him highly for his work sake; has an influence over them which is almost unbounded. He comes to them in the name of God, and they perceive that his instruction and precepts are drawn from the word of God. He addresses them with reference to the eternal world; and they realize that he and they are soon to stand together before God. The authority of God, and the momentous interests of the eternal world, give weight to every word which he utters; the powers of their minds bend under its influence. Such a minister as this has so swayed the hearts of Christian men, that martyrdom has had no terrors for them. They have defied the cruel rage of tyrants; and have faced popular fury undaunted. Is not this influence great enough for any minister to wield? Would the objection substitute for it a part of the tyrant's power which it has overcome? The apostles, on the day of Pentecost, were endued with power from on high; but it was not the power of coercion. God's truth, and a holy life, have rendered the ministry invincible; and the minister who asks for other power, mistakes the nature of his office.

It is alleged, that a learned divine may be outvoted by ignorant laymen; and what then? Do truth and holiness lose their power, by being outvoted? The learned divine may be in the wrong; or he may arrogantly claim a deference to which he is not entitled. In this case, to give him governing power would be a sad remedy for the supposed evil. Perhaps he is in the right, and possesses the meekness and gentleness of Christ. In this case, he will teach us how to answer the objection now before us. He will choose in meekness to instruct those that oppose themselves, rather than prevail over them by authority. It may be that they mean well, but need information. The remedy is, to give them the information needed. This is far better, than to deny them the power of thinking and acting. Possibly they may be evil and designing men. If so, they ought not to be in the church. It is certainly not wise to retain them in the church, and seek to render them harmless by depriving them of influence in the church; especially if we are obliged, at the same time, to make all the good lay members of the church equally powerless.

Among the relations in human society, that of a godly pastor to the flock of his charge, is one of the most prolific in blessings. While he points to heaven in his instructions, and leads them in the way by his example, they listen with reverence, and imitate with the affection of children. It is not enough to say, that his happiness and reputation are safe in their hands. They are a wall of defence around him; and a source of purest and sweetest enjoyment. But the benefits of this relation result from the moral tie that binds the parties. They spring out of brotherly love, which flows spontaneously from renewed hearts, and unites them in the service of their common Lord. Substitute for this the mere tie of official relation, and the garden of the Lord becomes a parched desert. When a pastor seeks defence from his people, by entrenching himself in official authority, or appealing to a higher tribunal, there is a radical evil which needs some other remedy.

We concede that the independent form of church government is not adapted to ungodly pastors, and unconverted church-members. It is suited to those only, who are bound together in brotherly love, and are striving together to glorify God, and advance the cause of truth and righteousness. For such persons Christ instituted it; and all the objections to which it is liable, find their occasion in the depravity of men. Church government was never designed to be a remedy for human depravity. It was designed for men whom the Holy Spirit has sanctified; and the wisdom which would adapt it to men of a different character, is not from above.

Objection 2.—Designing men have it in their power to mislead the people; and the evil which results cannot be prevented, if there is no high tribunal to which demagogues are amenable.

The prevention and cure of this evil are not to be sought in the establishment of a high ecclesiastical court; but in the illumination and sanctification of the people. Wisdom and benevolence unite in recommending, that men's minds be fortified against seducers, by being well instructed in the truth; and the expedient of restraining the seducer by high ecclesiastical authority, does not secure the highest possible good. Besides, we have no assurance that the tribunal will be uncorrupt. The same power that claims to restrain a seducer, may restrain a reformer whom God has raised up to bring men back to the right way. It is far better to oppose error with the truth and the demonstration of the Spirit, than with ecclesiastical authority.

Objection 3.—The independent churches have no bond of union and strength; and no means of preventing division.

Love is the bond of perfectness, which unites true members of Christ. When this golden bond is wanting, a band of iron, forged by ecclesiastical authority, may fasten men to each other; but it will not be in the fellowship of the gospel. A want of fellowship in a church, is a disease preying on the spiritual strength of the body; and it is better that it should be seen and felt, until the proper remedy is applied, than that it should be concealed by an outward covering of ecclesiastical forms. When mere organization supplies the union and strength on which we rely, we shall cease to cultivate the unity of the Spirit, and to trust the power of truth. The objection, therefore, is unfounded. What it accounts a fault, is in reality a high excellence of the church order taught in the Scripture, and demonstrates that it originated in the wisdom of God.

Section II.—FELLOWSHIP BETWEEN CHURCHES.

A happy intercourse might subsist between the churches, if they were all walking in the Spirit, sound in faith, correct in order, and careful in discipline. Such a state of things existed, to a great extent, in apostolic times. Christian men passed from one country to another, and found, in every place, that those who professed the name of Christ were of one heart and one soul.

The members of one local church were, in general, welcomed to the fellowship of every other church.

But the relation between different local churches, is not such as to bind each church to receive the ministers and members of every other church. This obligation was not felt even in the days of the apostles. John commanded, "If there come any unto you, and bring not this doctrine, receive him not into your house; neither bid him God speed."[1] These teachers of false doctrine were probably members of some local church, which, like the church at Pergamos, tolerated error;[2] but their membership did not entitle them to universal respect and confidence. Some have regarded each local church, as acting for the whole body of the faithful; and have inferred that its acts are binding on every other church. But this opinion is inconsistent with the true doctrine of church independence, and with the separate responsibility of individuals and churches. When churches do their duty, the recommendation of a minister or member from one church will, like the recommendation given to Apollos,[3] introduce him to the affections and confidence of other churches; but no recommendation of an unworthy person can bind the consciences of those who know his true character. Free intercourse and mutual confidence between the churches is very desirable, and every one should labor to promote it; but purity of doctrine and practice should never be sacrificed to effect it.

For the promotion of Christian fellowship, every one should require more of himself than of his brother. We may lawfully tolerate in others what we cannot tolerate in ourselves, or cannot approve. Some degree of toleration must be exercised, if imperfect Christians dwell together harmoniously in the fellowship of a local church. Such toleration the local churches are bound to exercise towards each other. Some things in the discipline of one church may not be approved by a neighboring church; but it does not follow, that their kind intercourse with each other must be disturbed. Each must act for itself, and not claim to bind the other. But when a church becomes corrupt in faith or practice, neighboring churches are bound to withdraw their fellowship.

---

[1] 2 John 10.   [2] Rev. ii. 14, 15.   [3] Acts xviii. 27.

Section III.—IMPOSITION OF HANDS.

The laying on of hands is sometimes mentioned in Scripture, when something is intended different from mere form or ceremony. Hands were laid on Queen Athaliah, that she might be put to death.[1] Nehemiah threatened to lay hands on those who violated the sabbath;[2] and in the same sense, it is said when they sought to lay hands on Jesus, they feared the multitude.[3] But imposition of hands is also mentioned as a significant form or ceremony. It was used: 1. To represent the transfer of guilt to the victims which were offered in sacrifice.[4] 2. To represent the transfer of authority, as from Moses to Joshua.[5] 3. As a form of benediction, sometimes accompanied with prayer.[6] 4. To confer the Holy Spirit;[7] and 5. To ordain to the ministerial office.[8]

The practice has prevailed in many churches, for the pastor to lay his hands on those who have been recently baptized, accompanying the act with prayer to God on their behalf. No command of Scripture enjoins this ceremony. Hands were laid on those who had been baptized in the times of the apostles, to impart the Holy Spirit; but this was done by the apostles only; and when Cornelius, and they who were with him, had received the Holy Spirit previous to their baptism, the apostle Peter omitted to lay hands on them afterwards.

In solemn consecration to ministerial service, other hands than those of apostles were sometimes laid on the persons ordained. In the case which occurred at Antioch,[9] the only apostle present was one of the persons on whom hands were laid. It follows that this was not done to impart the gift of the Holy Spirit, which appears to have been conferred by the apostles only. In the ordination of Timothy, other persons besides Paul, who are called "the presbytery," were concerned in the imposition of hands. These facts justify the conclusion, that the imposition of hands by ordinary ministers is, according to primitive usage, a proper ceremony in ordination to the ministerial office.

---

[1] 2 Chron. xxiii. 15. [2] Neh. xiii. 21. [3] Matt. xxi. 46.
[4] Lev. iv. 4; xvi. 21. [5] Num. xxvii. 18—20.
[6] Gen. xlviii. 14; Mark x. 16. [7] Acts xix. 6. [8] Acts xiii. 3.
[9] Acts xiii. 1, 2.

The meaning of the injunction to Timothy, "Lay hands suddenly on no man,"[1] is not perfectly clear. It is not probable that it refers to literal force. As directing the use of a significant form, its most probable reference is to ministerial ordination. So understood, the injunction furnishes strongly corroborative proof, that imposition of hands was the proper ceremony for setting apart to the sacred office.

Section IV.—REBAPTISM.

MAY BE NECESSARY.

A believer who has, at some time, received sprinkling for baptism, is not freed from the obligation to be immersed, in obedience to Christ's command. In this case the immersion cannot, with propriety, be called rebaptism.' But if an individual should be immersed in infancy, according to the usage of the Greek Church, this fact would not release him from the obligation to be re-immersed, on his becoming a believer in Christ. On the cases which have been mentioned, no doubt or diversity of practice exists, among those who adhere strictly to the precepts of Christ.

But other cases occasionally present themselves, the decision of which is attended with difficulty. The most common are the following: 1. Men who were once baptized on profession of faith, and afterwards turned away from Christ, sometimes return with proofs of recent conversion. 2. Men who have been immersed by Pedobaptist ministers, or by unworthy Baptist ministers, sometimes present themselves for rebaptism, or for admission into a church. On these two cases, the question arises, is rebaptism necessary, according to the Holy Scriptures?

WHO MUST DECIDE.

In deciding the question, the first responsibility devolves on the candidate. He is bound to make a baptismal profession of faith, according to the revealed will of Christ; and if he has not properly complied with his duty, the obligation to obey rests on him.

---

[1] 1 Tim. v. 22.

A responsibility is brought on the administrator, to whom the candidate may apply for rebaptism. It is clear from the Scriptures, that, in ordinary cases, baptism was designed to be administered but once; and the administrator, as a servant of Christ, is bound to decide, in the fear of God, whether the case before him justifies a repetition of the rite.

Besides the two parties that have been named, and that have the immediate responsibility in the case, the church to which an individual of doubtful baptism may apply for membership, has the responsibility of judging whether his baptism has fulfilled the divine command. If baptism is a prerequisite to membership, the church is not at liberty to throw the entire responsibility of the question on the candidate or the administrator.

It has sometimes happened, that ministers have differed in their views; and a candidate, whom one minister has refused to rebaptize, has been rebaptized by another. In such cases, no breach of fellowship between the ministers occurs; nor ought it to be allowed. In like manner, a difference of opinion may exist between churches; and one church may admit without rebaptism, when another church would require it. This difference should not disturb the kind intercourse between the churches. But if the individual who has been received without rebaptism, should seek to remove his membership to the church that deems rebaptism necessary, the latter church has authority, as an independent body, to reject him.

Though some difference of opinion on these questions does exist, and ought to be tolerated, yet every one should strive to learn his duty respecting them, by a diligent study of the Holy Scriptures. The directions of the inspired word are clear, so long as men keep in the prescribed way; but when they have wandered from it, no surprise should be felt if the method of return is not so clearly pointed out. Hence it arises that men who interpret the express precepts of Christ alike, may, in applying them to perplexing cases, differ in their judgment. In what follows I shall give my views, with deference to those whose investigations have led them to a different conclusion.

FIRST CASE.

The first case supposes that there was in the previous baptism a mistake respecting the qualifications of the candidate.

Baptism was designed to be the ceremony of Christian profession. If, in the first baptism, the candidate believed himself to be a Christian, and received baptism on a credible profession of faith in Christ, no higher qualification can be obtained for a second baptism. They to whom the administration of the rite has been committed, do not possess the power to search the heart. A credible profession of faith, sincerely made, is all that fallible men can expect; and, since the ordinance has been committed to fallible men, it is duly administered on sincere and credible profession.

Some confirmation of this view may be derived from the case of Simon the sorcerer. Though baptized on profession of faith, it was afterwards discovered that his heart was not right in the sight of God. On making the discovery, Peter did not command him to repent and be baptized, as he commanded the unbaptized on the day of Pentecost: but his address was, " Repent, and pray God, if perhaps the thought of thine heart may be forgiven thee."[1] This address, by containing no command respecting baptism, favors the opinion that rebaptism in this case would not have been required.

SECOND CASE.

The second case supposes that there was in the first baptism a want of due qualification in the administrator.

In the discussion of this question we should guard against improper notions respecting the validity of baptism. The rite has no sacramental efficacy, dependent on its validity, as the possession of an estate depends on the validity of the title. Were it so, it might be a matter of great importance to be able to trace the flow of the mysterious virtue through a continuous line of authorized administrators from the days of the apostles. But the validity of baptism means nothing more than that the duty has been performed. If performed, there is no necessity of repeating it.

The question, then, is whether the candidate has done his duty. The responsibility of deciding this question begins with him; but it does not end with him. The church of which he wishes to become a member, must exercise judgment on the case. If the candidate's satisfaction with his baptism would suffice, persons baptized in

---

[1] Acts viii. 22.

infancy might obtain admission into our churches without other baptism. The church is bound to judge, and to regulate its judgment by the will of God.

From the investigations in the preceding part of this work, we have learned that a candidate has no right to baptize himself, or select his own administrator, without regard to his being duly qualified according to the divine will. The proper administrators are persons called of God to the ministerial office, and introduced into it according to the order established by the apostles. To such persons the candidate was bound to apply; and, if he received the ordinance from any other, it was as if he had selected the administrator at his own will, or had immersed himself.

The possibility that a state of things may have at some time existed, in which a regular administrator could not be obtained, does not militate against the conclusion just drawn. This subject has been considered in Chap. VIII. § 3. Because when church order has been destroyed, something unusual may be done to restore it, we are not, on this account, justified in neglecting the regular order when it does exist. Every church is bound to respect this order, and a candidate who has failed to respect it in a former baptism, may, with a good conscience, proceed anew to obey the Lord's command, in exact conformity to the divine requirement.

In order to the proper performance of baptism, a willing candidate and a willing administrator are necessary, both of whom should render the service in obedience to Christ. By a wise provision the social tendency of Christianity is shown at the very beginning of the Christian profession. The candidate cannot obey alone, but he must seek an administrator to unite with him in the act of obedience, and by this arrangement Christian fellowship begins with Christian profession. But that two may walk together in this act of obedience, it is necessary that they should be agreed. If the administrator and candidate differ widely in their views respecting the nature and design of the ordinance, they cannot have fellowship with each other in the service. Some Pedobaptist ministers will administer immersion reluctantly, believing it to be an ineligible mode of baptism, scarcely consistent with refinement and decency. How can a candidate, who conscientiously believes that there is no other baptism, have fellowship in the service with such an administrator? But this is not all. Pedo-

...rs do not, in general, administer the rite as an em-
...ist's burial and resurrection. This important part of
...n they entirely overlook. If an administrator of the
supper, mistaking the design of the ceremony, should
...k bread and distribute wine in commemoration, not of Christ,
...t of the deliverance from Egyptian bondage under Moses, what
Christian could receive the elements at his hands? So, when an
administrator mistakes the design of baptism, and overlooks its
chief symbolical signification, every enlightened and conscientious
candidate, who understands the nature and design of the ceremony,
may well doubt the propriety of uniting with such a minister in a
service about which they are so little agreed.

The odium which has been attached to anabaptism deters many
from a repetition of the ceremony; but the Scriptures nowhere
brand it with reproach. He who would find an anathema against
it, need not search for it in the Bible. The holy book furnishes
satisfactory proof that when the rite has been once duly performed,
there is no necessity to repeat it; but it furnishes no proof that
God will be displeased, if one who has failed to come up to the full
measure of his duty, should seek another opportunity to obey the
livine command with scrupulous exactness.

Section V.—TREATMENT OF UNBAPTIZED MINISTERS.

In a tract, "An Old Landmark Reset. By Elder J. M. Pen-
dleton, A. M., Union University, Murfreesboro, Tennessee," the
author maintains that Baptists ought not to recognise Pedobaptist
preachers as gospel ministers. This tract has been circulated extensively, and its doctrine is embraced by many. The discussions
on the subject may sometimes have produced temporary evil, but
where the parties have a sincere desire to know the truth, and a
willingness to follow wherever it may lead, the final result must be
good. Parties who agree with each other in their views of Christian doctrine and ordinances, and whose only difference respects
the mode of treating those who are in error, ought not to fall out
with each other on this question. Each one must act in the matter on his own responsibility; and discussions to ascertain the right
mode of acting ought to be conducted in the spirit of kindness,
meekness, and gentleness. Discussions so conducted will tend to

develop truth; and if they do not bring us to the conclusions of the Landmark, may enable us to correct the premises from which those conclusions are drawn.

The question is not one of mere taste, about which persons may innocently differ; but it involves moral obligation. This is implied in the word *ought*. "Baptists *ought* not," &c. Whatever is morally wrong ought to be avoided as offensive to God. If we have sinned in this matter, through ignorance and unbelief, though God may have graciously pardoned our sin, we should not persevere in the wrong. Our attention is now called to the subject as a question of duty, and we are bound to examine it in the fear of God, and so act hereafter as God will approve.

Baptists are not the only persons concerned to know what duty is. If Baptists ought not to recognise Pedobaptist preachers as gospel ministers, can other persons recognise them blamelessly? If the thing is right for others, why not for Baptists? If the act is wrong in itself, no one can perform it without some degree of guilt. For Baptists to practise it may involve peculiar inconsistency, and a higher degree of guilt. But if the act is in itself one which God disapproves, all men should be warned not to commit it.

On searching the Landmark to find why *Baptists* ought not to recognise Pedobaptist preachers as gospel ministers, we soon discover that the reason has no exclusive relation to Baptists. The doctrine is, that Pedobaptist preachers are not gospel ministers; and, if this doctrine is true, other persons are bound to receive it, and act on it, as well as Baptists. Nor does the doctrine refer to a few Pedobaptist ministers only, who may be less worthy of esteem and confidence than the rest; but it refers to all. Not one of them is a gospel minister; and not one of them ought to be recognised as such.

The honor of Christ is deeply concerned in his ministry. If some messengers sent by the churches were called by Paul "the glory of Christ,"[1] the same may be affirmed emphatically of the messengers sent by Christ himself into the world, to preach his gospel to mankind. He has promised to be with them, they speak by his authority, and in his stead. They bear in earthen vessels

---

[1] 2 Cor. viii. 23.

an inestimable treasure which he has committed to them; and with which he designs to enrich the world. For men whom Christ has never sent to claim that they bear this treasure, and are authorized to dispense it; that they have a commission from him to address mankind in his name, and have his presence with them, and his approbation of their labors;—for men whom Christ has not sent to claim all this, is an evil of no small magnitude. Their presumption must be highly offensive to him; and all who recognise them as his ministers must oppose his will in a matter which he has greatly at heart. The question, therefore, is one of tremendous magnitude. Have all those offended Christ who have recognised as his ministers, Whitfield, Edwards, Davies, Payson, and other such men from whom they have supposed that they received the word of Christ, and by whose ministry they have thought that they were brought to know Christ? If Baptists ought not to recognise such men as gospel ministers, no one ought; and the respect which they have received from men as ministers of the gospel, must be offensive to Christ.

We do not affirm that all these consequences are stated in the Landmark. But if the doctrine of the tract has not led the author thus far, will it not legitimately conduct us to these conclusions, if we adopt and consistently maintain it? But we seem to have the author's approbation in making this application of his principles. He says, " If it is not too absurd to suppose such a thing, let it be supposed that there were persons in apostolic times corresponding to modern Pedobaptists. Can any Baptist believe that Paul, beholding the practices of such persons—seeing the sprinkling of infants substituted for the immersion of believers—would have recognised the ministers of such sects as ministers of Christ, acting according to the gospel? Surely not. Paul would have protested against such a caricature of the Christian system. He would have said to such ministers, ' Will ye not cease to pervert the right ways of the Lord?'' '[1]

Conclusions so unfavorable to the entire Pedobaptist ministry are revolting to the minds of multitudes. They see in many of these ministers proofs of humble piety, sincere devotion to the cause of Christ, and deep concern for the salvation of souls. To

---

[1] P. 14.

these manifestations of the proper spirit for the gospel ministry, are added a high degree of Scripture knowledge, and a talent for imparting instruction. When such men are seen devoting their lives to arduous toil for the conversion of souls, and when God appears to crown their labors with abundant success, it is difficult to resist the conviction that they are truly ministers of the gospel, acting with Divine authority and approbation. But the Landmark teaches that these men are not gospel ministers; and its arguments in support of this opinion need a careful examination.

From what premises does the Landmark draw its conclusion? The author informs us in his letter to Dr. Hill. He says, "By a reference to what I have written you will see that Dr. Griffin, a celebrated Pedobaptist, has furnished the premises from which my conclusion is drawn."[1]

He does not profess to have derived them directly from the Scriptures. The tract does not contain a single quotation from the Scriptures, designed to sustain them. Whatever may be the weight of Pedobaptist authority in an argument with Pedobaptists, when Baptists are laboring in the fear of God to ascertain their duty, they ought to seek information from a higher source.

In the quotations made from Dr. Griffin we find the following statements: "Baptism is the initiatory ordinance which introduces us into the visible church; of course, where there is no baptism, there are no visible churches. * * We ought not to commune with those who are not baptized, and, of course, are not church-members, even if we regard them as Christians. * * * I have no right to send the sacred elements out of the church."[2]

These are the premises from which the Landmark draws its conclusion. Is the principle here laid down a doctrine of the Holy Scriptures? If so, we are bound to receive it with every consequence which can be legitimately drawn from it.

In Chapter III. we have investigated the Scripture doctrine concerning the church universal. If we have not mistaken the divine teaching on the subject, every man who is born of the Spirit is a member of this church. Regeneration, not baptism, introduces him into it. The dogma that baptism initiates into the church, and that those who are not baptized are not church-members, even

---

[1] P. 53.　　　　　[2] P. 4.

19

if they are Christians, denies the existence of this spiritual church, and substitutes for it the visible church catholic of theologians. The evils resulting from this unscriptural substitution, have been shown on pp. 132, 133. They are sufficient to deter us from an inconsiderate admission of the dogma from which they proceed.

Dr. Gill called infant baptism "a part and pillar of popery," and we may justly call the dogma of Dr. Griffin a part and pillar of infant baptism. If the true universal church is spiritual, comprising all the regenerate and no others; and if local churches are temporary associations of persons belonging to the universal church, no place is found in either for unregenerate infants. But when baptism is made the door of entrance, instead of regeneration, a way of entrance is opened for infants. Pedobaptism began in the doctrine of baptismal regeneration, and this doctrine, in some form, is necessary to its support. The regenerating power first attributed to baptism; appears to have been understood to be the conferring of the new relation constituting membership in the church. A spiritual church, with a spiritual door of entrance, did not suit the carnal tendency which was rapidly leading men to Romanism. The substitution of the visible church catholic for the spiritual church of Christ, and of baptism for regeneration, led to infant baptism, a corrupt church-membership, and all the evils of popery.

This dogma now efficiently sustains the cause of Pedobaptism. That Dr. Mason considered it a chief pillar of infant baptism, fully appears in his Essays on the Church. Its practical effect is clearly exemplified in the case of the late Dr. Alexander. That excellent man, with two other distinguished Presbyterian ministers of Virginia, became dissatisfied with the proofs of infant baptism on which they had relied. One of them for a time became a Baptist, and the others were strongly inclined to follow him. But all these men settled down at last in the belief of Pedobaptism: and the process of reasoning which satisfied Dr. Alexander's mind, and probably the minds of the rest, is given in his biography. Two considerations kept him back from joining the Baptists. The first was, that the prevalence of infant baptism as early as the fourth and fifth centuries, appeared to him unaccountable on the supposition that no such practice existed in the time of the apostles. The other was his inference that if the Baptists are right, they are the only Christian church on earth, and all other denominations are

out of the visible church.   He had perceived the corrupting tendency of infant baptism : but the dogma of a visible church catholic
with a baptismal boundary, assisted to hold his noble mind fast
fettered in error.   Shall Baptists receive this dogma with all its
consequences ?

How thoroughly this Pedobaptist doctrine enters into the reasonings of the Landmark, appears in such passages as the following :
" Who can be a minister of Christ according to the gospel, without
belonging to the church ?"[1]   " Now, if Pedobaptist preachers do
not belong to the church of Christ, they ought not to be recognised as ministers of Christ."[2]   " Our refusal to commune with
the Pedobaptists grows out of the fact that they are unbaptized,
and out of the church."[3]   In these passages, the Landmark uses
the phrase, " the church," in apparent conformity to the common
doctrine of the visible church catholic; since none are members of
it, but baptized persons.   But another passage in the pamphlet
sets forth a different doctrine : " There is no universal visible
church ; and if the universal invisible church, composed of all the
saved, has what Dr. E. calls ' form,' it is impossible to know what
it is.   We have no idea of ' form' apart from visibility."[4]   According to this, the true and only universal church is " composed of
all the saved."   How can this be reconciled with the preceding
quotations, which represent all unbaptized persons as out of · " the
church ?"   How can it be reconciled with the premises adopted
from Dr. Griffin, that " those who are not baptized are not
church-members, even if we regard them as Christians ?"   A
church composed of " *all* the saved," must contain some unbaptized persons, unless all the unbaptized are unsaved ; and if we
may account any unbaptized persons members of " the church,"
we abandon the premises of the Landmark.   · I do not find evidence, that the pamphlet adopts Mr. Courtney's theory of the
church generic ; but whether it uses the phrase " the church"
generically or collectively, the result is the same.   In some way,
its signification extends beyond the bounds of a single local church ;
and yet it is not the true universal church, " composed of all the
saved."   But " the church" which appears in the premises and
reasonings of the Landmark is, at best, only a Baptist modification
of the visible church catholic, the church that has given Pedobap-

---

[1] P. 12.   [2] P. 13.   [3] P. 16.   [4] P. 42.

tism and Popery to the world.   Many able Baptist writers have
fallen into this Pedobaptist error respecting the church; but the
discussions to which the Landmark has given occasion, will tend,
we may hope, to establish a sounder theology.

The Landmark inquires for the authority on which Pedobaptist preachers act.   "If Pedobaptist societies are not churches of
Christ, whence do their ministers derive their authority to preach?
Is there any scriptural authority to preach which does not come
through a church of Christ?   And if Pedobaptist ministers are
not in Christian churches, have they any right to preach? that is
to say, have they any authority *according to the gospel?*   They
are doubtless authorized by the forms and regulations of their
respective societies.   But do they act under evangelical authority?
It is perfectly evident to the writer, that they do not."[1]   We
answer, that, if the Holy Spirit has qualified men to preach the
gospel, they preach it with divine authority.   The Holy Spirit,
who divides to every man severally as he will, does not give the
necessary qualifications for the gospel ministry, without designing
that they shall be used; and since he only can give these qualifications, we are sure that every man who possesses them, is bound,
by the authority of God, to use them to the end for which they
are bestowed.   We arrive at this conclusion, aside from all reasoning about ceremonies and churches; and the proof brings irresistible conviction.   Here is a landmark of truth, which must not
be deserted, however much we may be perplexed with reasonings
about outward forms.

We have maintained, in Chapter VIII., that ministers of the word,
as such, are officers of the universal church; and that their call to
the ministry by the Holy Spirit, is complete in itself, without the
addition of outward ceremony.   The person called fails to do his
duty, if he neglects the divinely appointed method by which he
should enter on the work to which he is called; and this failure
tends to obscure the evidence of his divine call.   But when, through
the obscurity, evidence of his call presents itself with convincing
force, we act against reason and against Scripture if we reject it.
The seal of divine authority is affixed to that minister who brings
into his work qualifications which God only can bestow.

---

[1] P. 11.

While we maintain that Pedobaptist preachers, who give proof that they have been called to their work by the Holy Spirit, ought to be regarded as gospel ministers, we do not insist that Baptists ought to invite all such to occupy their pulpits. This is a different matter. When the Holy Spirit calls, he makes it the duty of the called to study the Holy Scriptures, and to preach what is there taught. His call does not render ministers infallible, or pledge the divine approbation to whatever they may teach; and it therefore does not bind any one to surrender the right of private judgment, and receive with implicit faith whatever may be preached. Much error is sometimes inculcated by preachers, whose divine call to the ministry we cannot question. Even baptism and ordination, however regular, do not make a minister sound in doctrine, and worthy to occupy any and every pulpit. The responsibility of inviting ministers into the pulpit, ought to be exercised with a conscientious regard to the glory of God, and the interests of souls.

An argument for excluding Pedobaptist preachers from our pulpits is drawn by the Landmark from our close communion:—" It is often said by Pedobaptists that Baptists act inconsistently in inviting their ministers to preach with them, while they fail to bid them welcome at the Lord's table. I acknowledge the inconsistency. It is a flagrant inconsistency. No one ought to deny it."[1]

This Pedobaptist objection is endorsed not only by the Landmark, but also by Baptists who practise open communion. All these maintain that we are inconsistent in admitting ministers into the pulpit, when we deny them a seat at the communion table. But a charge of inconsistency made against us by persons who are in error on the very point, ought not to surprise or disquiet us. Let our procedure, in each case, be regulated by the word of God, and we may be sure that, in the end, we shall be found consistent, even if we cannot at once make our consistency apparent to all. The insidious tendency to substitute ceremony for spirituality meets us everywhere, and lies, I apprehend, at the foundation of this charge. If communion at the Lord's table is "a principal spiritual function," as affirmed by Mr. Hall, and if, as is done in this objection of the Landmark, it may be classed with the preaching of the word, as a thing of like character, the charge of incon-

---

[1] P. 16.

sistency in requiring a ceremonial qualification for one, and not for the other, will have a show of justness. But if the Lord's supper is a ceremony, a ceremonial qualification for it may be necessary, which may not be indispensable to the ministry of the word. And it may be the duty of Baptists, both by theory and practice, to teach their erring brethren the important distinction, too often overlooked, between spiritual service to God and that which is ceremonial.

The lawfulness of inviting Pedobaptist preachers into the pulpit, has been defended on the ground that any Christian has the right to talk of Christ and his great salvation. Our Landmark brethren admit that all have a right to make known the gospel privately, but deny that any have the right to proclaim it publicly, except those who have been regularly inducted into the ministerial office. The distinction between talking of Christ privately and proclaiming his gospel publicly, appears to me to respect obligation rather than right. If a Christian has a right to tell of Christ to a fellow man who sits by his side, or walks in the highway with him, he has the same right to address two in like manner, and, so far as I can see, he has an equal right to address ten, a hundred, or a thousand. The obligation to exercise this right is limited only by his ability to do good, and the opportunity which Providence presents of using such talents as he possesses to the glory of God and the benefit of immortal souls. A divine call to the work of the ministry being always accompanied with qualifications for public usefulness, creates obligation rather than confers right, as wealth creates obligation rather than confers right, to relieve the poor. Now, to defend the lawfulness of inviting a Pedobaptist preacher into the pulpit, it has been deemed sufficient to maintain that the person so invited has a *right* to talk of Christ to perishing men, and recommend his salvation to their acceptance. The argument appears to me to be valid; but I have chosen to take higher ground, and to maintain that many Pedobaptist ministers give convincing proof that the Holy Spirit has called and qualified them to preach the gospel, and that it is therefore not only their right, but their duty, to fulfil the ministry which God has committed to them.

We have supposed that an undoubted divine call of any one to the gospel ministry, would command the respect of all who revere the authority of the Most High; but on this point the Landmark holds the following remarkable language :—"I go farther and say, that if God were, with an audible voice, as loud as heaven's mightiest thunder, to call a Pedobaptist to preach, we would not be justified in departing from the Scriptures, unless we were divinely told the utterances of that voice were intended to supersede the teachings of the New Testament.   Such information would intimate the beginning of a new economy, and I am writing of the present dispensation."[1]

To this we know not what to say.   We have no argument to offer.   If God's voice from heaven cannot prevail, all our arguments must be ineffectual, for we have nothing more forcible to urge than the word of the King Supreme.   For ourselves, were the undoubted voice of God from heaven to fall on our ears, we have nothing to oppose to his authority.   We reverence the Scriptures, but all our reasonings from the Scriptures are as nothing when God speaks.   We claim no right to demand explanations respecting his dispensations as a condition of receiving his word. What if God's voice from heaven ushers in a new economy, we want no higher authority than his mere announcement, even if unaccompanied with any explanation; and we may be well assured that all our reasonings about economies, church order, and similar topics, are erroneous, if they lead us to reject the voice of God speaking from heaven.

But how does a divine call of the unbaptized to preach the gospel, constitute a new economy ?   John the Baptist, who preached by divine authority, at the beginning of the present dispensation, was unbaptized; and, after the dispensation had been established by the exaltation of Christ, and the gift of the Holy Spirit, Saul of Tarsus was called to preach the gospel while unbaptized.   Cases now occur in which persons who undergo examination in order to ordination, refer their convictions of duty with reference to the ministry, to a period anterior to their baptism; and no ordaining presbytery would be justified in denying the possibility of a call by the Holy Spirit, while the subject of it was unbaptized.   He who calls the unbaptized to repentance and faith, has the power and right to call them to the ministry also, if it is his pleasure. God has never bound himself in any manner to require none but

---

[1] P. 48.

baptized persons to preach his word; and we have no right to limit the Holy One of Israel. In our view, the bestowment of ministerial grace and qualifications by the Holy Spirit, indicates the divine will: if not as certainly as it would be indicated by a voice from heaven, yet we cannot resist the conviction which it brings to our minds. When God speaks from heaven, or otherwise clearly indicates his will, we know nothing but reverence and submission.

It has been argued that Baptists ought not to invite Pedobaptist ministers into their pulpits, while they would exclude, both from their communion and their pulpits, a Baptist minister who should inculcate Pedobaptist doctrine. This argument also is a mere appeal to consistency. Such argument ought never to be used when better can be had. If there is any established usage among Baptists with which the invitation of Pedobaptist ministers is inconsistent, the usage may need to be changed. Then the present argument will fall to the ground. But, so far as I know, men who have left the Baptist ministry for the ministry in a Pedobaptist denomination, are, other things being equal, regarded and treated like other Pedobaptist ministers, each case being judged according to its merit. If a false-hearted Baptist minister should retain his connection with a Baptist church, and avail himself of it to disseminate Pedobaptist error, he would deserve to be excluded both from the communion and the pulpit. But if a Baptist minister should become a Pedobaptist, and leave behind him, in the minds of his Baptist brethren, a full conviction that in so doing he acted honestly and conscientiously, I am not aware that he would be viewed less favorably than other Pedobaptist ministers. I remember a case which will illustrate this point. A young Baptist brother, of fervent piety and distinguished talent, was licensed by his church and entered on a course of study to prepare himself for usefulness in the ministry. In prosecuting his studies, his mind came under Pedobaptist influence, and he announced to his church a change of his views, and a desire to connect himself with Pedobaptists. The church separated him from their communion; but the very men who voted this separation, invited him afterwards into their pulpit. They had licensed him because they believed him called of God to the work of the ministry. Their full belief of this remained; and they invited him to preach, not as a Pedobaptist, but as a minister of Christ, whom, as such, they loved. In their view, it was improper for him to remain in a Baptist church·and partake of its communion; but they believed it to be right for him to fulfil the ministry to which he had been divinely called. In their view, the exclusion from the communion, and the admission to the pulpit, were perfectly consistent. If others think differently, they will still admit that there was no principle violated in this case, merely because of his having been once a Baptist. This admission will nullify the present argument, and leave the question to be settled on other grounds.

If we admit a Pedobaptist minister into our pulpits, do we not countenance his errors? We do, if we expect him to inculcate these errors, or if we permit him to inculcate them without correction. But this is equally true with respect to Baptist ministers. The responsibility of inviting generally devolves on the pastor of a church, who is bound to instruct the people of his charge in truth and righteousness, and to guard them, as much as possible, from all error. He is, therefore, under obligation, when he invites others to occupy his pulpit, to exercise prudent caution; and this caution is needed with respect to Baptists as well as Pedobaptists. On various occasions I have invited Pedobaptist ministers to preach, where I have been accustomed to officiate; and, in every case, I have been able to approve the doctrine which they preached. In a single case, it happened, that a minister invited to occupy the pulpit, preached doctrine so erroneous, that I deemed it my duty to correct it in a discourse subsequently delivered; but the preacher of this error was a Baptist. If this experience is of any practical value, I would infer from it, not that the Baptist ministry is less orthodox than the Pedobaptist, but that caution is needed where we least suspect danger; and that the inviting of Pedobaptist ministers does not necessarily introduce unsound preaching. If a pastor invites into his pulpit a Pedobaptist minister, whom he sincerely believes to be called of God to the ministry, and who, he believes, will, in his preaching, know nothing but Christ, and him crucified; that pastor may enjoy a pure conscience towards God, undisturbed by any errors of his Pedobaptist brother which he has never approved.

But it will be said, that, although the pastor does not design his invitation of the Pedobaptist minister to be an approval of his errors, it will be so understood by the minister himself, and by others. This, I think, is a mistake. If the pastor has taken due pains to make the truth known, and has clearly defined his own position, and maintained it with firmness and consistency, there will be little danger that his act, in this case, will be misconstrued. What we have maintained is, that the invitation of a Pedobaptist minister to preach in a Baptist pulpit, is not in itself unlawful; but whether it is expedient in any particular case, must depend on the circumstances of the case. If a Baptist pastor is conscious that he has failed to set forth the truth clearly and fully, the objection which we are considering may justly embarrass him; but the proper mode of escape from it, is, to declare the whole counsel of God habitually and unreservedly.

If we were under no obligation with respect to Pedobaptist ministers, we might, as a safe course, decline to have any connection with them. But our Divine Master has commanded us to love all who are born of God. Many of these men manifest strong love to Christ; and we are bound to love them for Christ's sake. They are laboring zealously and faithfully, to honor Christ, and save the souls of men; and the proof that they are called of God to this work, compels us to admit, that they are fellow-laborers with us in the glorious cause, notwithstanding the irregularity of their entrance into it. Can we turn away from such men; and proclaim to the world, that they are not God's ministers? It is surely not necessary, in discountenancing their irregularities, to discountenance their entire ministry. We may approve all that they do right, and rejoice in it, without approving the wrong. This is the simple mode of solving the whole difficulty; and, if people do not at once understand the solution, let us act upon it, conscientiously, and in the fear of God, till men do understand it. In this way we shall give the most effectual recommendation of the truth.

CONCLUSION.

DUTY OF BAPTISTS.

THE church order which this treatise claims to have adduced from the Holy Scriptures, could not rely for support on human authority. The sect that maintains it, makes no imposing figure on the pages of ecclesiastical history, and does not hold such rank among the Christian denominations, as to recommend its peculiarities to the general acceptance of mankind. When the gospel was first introduced into the world, but few of the wise, the mighty, and the noble, appeared in its defence. God was pleased, with the weak things of the world, to confound the mighty, that no flesh should glory in his presence. The gospel is not a system of human devising; and true faith receives it as the wisdom of God, however weak and contemptible the instruments of its promulgation may appear. The true disciple of Christ ought not to permit the odium of the anabaptist name to deter him from strict obedience to all his Lord's commands.

Although the truth of God does not need human authority, or the patronage of great names, it is nevertheless the Divine pleasure to make it known to the world by human instrumentality; and this instrumentality needs to be adapted to the purpose for which it is employed. If God has commissioned a sect everywhere spoken against, to make known truth which the wise and learned have overlooked, that sect ought to understand the service to which they have been appointed, and ought to fulfil the prescribed duty firmly, faithfully, and in the fear of the Lord. As men designed for a peculiar service, let us, by earnest and constant endeavor, seek to ascertain the will of him to whose supreme authority we yield all our powers, and let us diligently and perseveringly obey that will, whether men revile or praise.

(299)

1. It is our duty to maintain the ordinances of Christ, and the church order which he has instituted, in strict and scrupulous conformity to the Holy Scriptures.

If the investigations of the sacred volume, which have been attempted in this work, have not been unsuccessful, the great body of Christ's professed followers have wandered from the right way. They have established ecclesiastical organizations which are not in accordance with his will; and have corrupted the ceremonies of worship which he instituted.   These errors have the sanction of age, and of men venerable for their wisdom.   To maintain our peculiarities in opposition to such influences has the appearance of bigotry and narrow-mindedness; and, if they are peculiarities which God's word does not require, we ought to relinquish them. But if we have attained to a knowledge of the Divine will, on points where the great mass of our fellow Christians have mistaken it, a duty of solemn responsibility is imposed on us, to hold fast what we have received, and defend the truth specially committed to our charge.

The plea is often urged that there are good men in all the denominations, and that the various forms of religion, being alike consistent with piety, are matters of minor importance, and ought to be left to the preferences of individuals.   If we do not readily admit this plea in its full extent, we are perhaps understood to deny that piety can be found out of our own party, or to claim undue deference to our judgment in religious matters.   But whether men understand us or not, we are bound to obey God in everything.   No command which he has given can be so unimportant that we are at liberty to disobey it at our pleasure.   When the finger of God points out the way, no place is left to us for human preferences.   And when we know the will of God, we are not only bound to obey for ourselves, but also to teach others to obey, so far as they are brought under the influence of our instruction.   We may, without arrogant assumption, declare what we are firmly persuaded to be the will of God; and we must then leave every one to the judgment of him to whom all must give account. The man who can disobey God, because the thing commanded is of minor importance, has not the spirit of obedience in his heart; and the man who, knowing the will of God, forbears to declare it, because the weight of human authority is against him, fears men more than God.

2. It is our duty, while rendering punctilious obedience to all the commands of God, to regard the forms and ceremonies of religion as of far less importance than its moral truths and precepts.

One of the earliest corruptions of Christianity consisted in magnifying the importance of its ceremonies, and ascribing to them a saving efficacy. With this superstitious reverence of outward forms, a tendency was introduced to corrupt these forms, and substitute ceremonies of human invention for the ordinances of God. To restore these ordinances to their original purity, and, at the same time, to understand and teach that outward rites have no saving efficacy, appears to be a service to which God has specially called the Baptists. We are often charged with attaching too much importance to immersion; but the notion that baptism possesses a sacramental efficacy finds no advocates in our ranks. It introduced infant baptism, and prevailed with it; and it still lingers among those by whom infant baptism is practised. Our principles, by restricting baptism to those who are already regenerate, subvert the doctrine of baptismal regeneration, and exhibit the ceremony in its proper relation to experimental religion. To give due prominence to spirituality above all outward ceremony, is an important service to which God has called our denomination.

3. It is our duty to hold and exhibit the entire system of Christian doctrine in all its just proportions.

An important advance is made in the proper exhibition of Christian truth, when ceremony is rendered duly subordinate to spirituality. This gives an opportunity to adjust the parts of the system in their proper harmony. An additional security for the preservation of sound doctrine, is found in the converted church-membership which our principles require. The church universal is the pillar and ground of the truth, because it consists of those who love the truth; and in proportion as local churches are formed of the same materials, they are prepared to stand as bulwarks against heresy. This service Baptist churches have been known to render to the cause of truth. The general agreement of Baptist churches, in doctrine as well as church order, is a fact which gives occasion for devout gratitude to God. Let it be our continued care never to distort the beautiful system of divine truth by magnifying any part of it beyond its just proportion, or suppressing any part of the harmonious whole.

Because we differ from other professors of religion in our faith and practice respecting the externals of religion, we are under a constant temptation to make too much account of these external peculiarities. Against this temptation we should ever struggle. If we magnify ceremony unduly, we abandon our principles, and cease to fulfil the mission to which the Head of the church has assigned us.

4. It is our duty to maintain lives of holy obedience in all things.

Many persons have the form of godliness who are strangers to its power. They render obedience to ceremonial precepts, while they neglect weightier matters of moral obligation. But a punctilious observance of ceremonies has no necessary connexion with remissness in more important duties. In an affectionate family, the children who strive to please their parents, and gratify their wishes in the most trivial concerns, are expected to be most dutiful in things of greatest moment. Such children of our heavenly Father ought Baptists to be. We claim to obey his will more fully in the outward forms of religion than any other people. Consistency requires that we should be more obedient also in matters of highest importance. It is highly offensive to God, if, while we neglect his most important commands, we attempt to please him with mere outward service. His omniscient eye detects the attempted fraud, and his holiness detests it. Even short-sighted men discover the cheat, and contemn our hypocrisy. The reputation of religion suffers by our unfaithfulness, and men, who observe our conduct, become confirmed in unbelief, to their everlasting ruin. Persons who do not profess to obey God in all things, may, with less pernicious effect, neglect his holy precepts; but Baptists ought to be holy in all things. Our profession requires us to be the best people in the world; and it should be our constant effort to walk according to this profession.

5. It is our duty to labor faithfully and perseveringly to bring all men to the knowledge of the truth.

We claim that we execute the commission which Christ gave to his apostles more fully than other Christian denominations. This commission requires us to preach the gospel to every creature; and we ought to be foremost in obeying it. This obligation has been felt by some of our faith and order, and all of us ought to feel it. The English Baptists have the honor of being foremost in the work of modern missions; and the names of Carey, and his fellow-laborers, who were the pioneers in this difficult service, deserve to be had in lasting remembrance. The names of Judson and Rice appear among the foremost in the history of American missions; and the conversion of these men to the Baptist faith may be re-garded as a special call of God on American Baptists to labor for the spread of the gospel throughout the earth. On the Continent of Europe, Oncken and his noble band of associates, are, by their laborious and successful efforts in the Redeemer's cause, but ful-filling the obligations which every Baptist should feel. Voluntary devotion to Christ, and immediate responsibility to him, are con-spicuous in our distinguishing peculiarities; and we ought to be conspicuous among the followers of Christ, by our labors or suffer-ings in his cause.

6. It is our duty to promote the spiritual unity of the universal church, by the exercise of brotherly love to all who bear the image of Christ.

Various schemes have been proposed by the wisdom of men for amalgamating the different Christian denominations. All these originate in the erroneous conception that the unity of the univer-sal church must be found in external organization. To effect the union sought for, compromises are required of the several parties, and the individual conscience must yield to the judgment of the many. All these schemes of amalgamation are inconsistent with the Baptist faith. We seek spiritual unity. We would have every individual to stand on Bible ground, and to take his position there, in the unbiassed exercise of his own judgment and conscience. There we strive to take our position; and there, and there only, we invite our brethren of all denominations to meet us. We yield everything which is not required by the word of God; but in what this word requires, we have no compromise to make. We rejoice to see, in many who do not take our views of divine truth, bright evidence of love to Christ and his cause. We love them for Christ's sake; and we expect to unite with them in his praise through eternal ages. We are one with them in spirit, though we cannot conform to their usages in any particular in which they deviate from the Bible. The more abundantly we love them, the more carefully we strive to walk before them in strict obedience to the commands of our common Lord. And if they sometimes misunderstand our motives, and misjudge our actions, it is our consolation that our divine Master approves; and that they also will approve, when we shall hereafter meet them in his presence.

APPENDIX.

SINCE *to baptize* is *to immerse*, the declaration of Scripture that "John was *baptizing* in Enon," is proof that the place afforded water in sufficient quantity for the purpose of immersion. Additional proof is furnished in the statement of the inspired writer, that John selected this place of baptizing, "because there was much water there." In the remarks made on this subject in p. 60, I did not think it necessary to enter into any inquiry respecting the geographical situation of Enon. This subject has been considered by the Rev. G. W. Samson, in the tract referred to on p. 63, and he arrives at the following conclusion:—"It was at the point upon the Jordan where the great thoroughfare from Western Galilee and Samaria crosses it, that John selected his favorable location for baptizing." "The permanent record of the early Christians, sanctioned by the New Testament writers, and confirmed by all subsequent observations, leaves no doubt that Enon was at a passage of the Jordan." In this part of the river, its course is very winding, its average width forty-five yards, and its average depth four feet.

The tract of Mr. Samson has been published, in connection with several other valuable tracts, in a duodecimo of 194 pages, entitled "Baptismal Tracts for the Times." The reader who desires to understand the baptismal controversy, will find some important topics discussed in this little volume with much ability.

A different situation has been assigned to Enon, in a work which has just issued from the press—"The City of the Great King; or Jerusalem as it was, as it is, and as it is to be." The author of this work, Dr. Barclay, a resident missionary in Jerusalem for three years and a half, thinks he has found the ancient baptizing-place within a few miles of the Holy City. He describes it thus:—"Returning by a circuitous route to the place whence we had started, from the brow of Wady Farah, we descended with some difficulty into that 'valley of delight'—for such is the literal signification of its name—and truly I have seen nothing so delightful in the way of natural scenery, nor inviting in point of resources, &c., in all Palestine. Ascending its bold stream from this point, we passed some half dozen expansions of the stream, constituting the most beautiful natural natatoria I have ever seen; the water, rivalling the atmosphere itself in transparency, of depths varying from a few inches to a fathom and more, shaded on one or both sides by umbrageous fig trees, and sometimes contained in naturally excavated basins of red mottled marble—an occasional variegation of the common limestone of the country. These pools are supplied by some half dozen springs of the purest and coldest water, bursting from rocky crevices at various intervals. Verily, thought I, we have stumbled upon Enon." * * * "Although this *conjecture*—that Ain Farah was Ænon—must be set down to the account of a mere random suggestion of the moment, yet a more intimate acquaintance with the geography of the neighborhood has brought me to an assured conviction that this place is indeed no other than the 'Enon near to Salim, where John was baptizing, because there was much water there.'"

PLACE OF THE EUNUCH'S BAPTISM.

The sacred writer who has recorded the Acts of the Apostles, has informed us that the Eunuch was baptized in "the way that goeth down from Jerusalem unto Gaza, which is desert."[1] The word "desert" seems to have suggested to some minds the idea, that the baptism occurred in an arid region, in which water of sufficient depth for immersion could not be found. Gaza, though once

---

[1] Acts viii. 26.

a populous city with massy gates,[1] was now almost without inhabitants, according to the prediction of the prophets, "Baldness is come upon Gaza:"[2] I will send a fire on the wall of Gaza, which shall devour the palaces thereof."[3] In Scripture language, the name *desert* or *wilderness*, is applied to a thinly inhabited country, even though including cities or towns distant from each other. It was, therefore, applicable to the region in which Gaza was situated, and into which the road of the Eunuch's descent from Jerusalem penetrated.

Dr. Barclay describes a journey which he took from Jerusalem to Gaza. He found the way passing through a fertile country, well supplied with water. He sought for the place of the Eunuch's baptism; but the disquieted condition of the country stopped his prosecution of the search. He says: "We were the more anxious to visit El-Hassy, on account of information received recently from Sheikh of Felluge, and abundantly confirmed at Burrier, that in Wady-el-Hassy about two or three hours distant, at Ras Kussahbeh and at Moyat es-Sid, in the same wady, the stream of water is as broad as our tent (twelve feet), and varies in depth from a span to six or seven feet—occasionally sinking and reappearing. This was, doubtless (Moyat es-Sid), the certain water of which we were in quest; but we were constrained, however reluctantly, to abandon the idea of seeing it."

Mr. Samson's description of the country through which the Eunuch journeyed, agrees with that of Dr. Barclay. Several places are noticed on the way, in which immersion may have been performed. Concerning one of these, he thus writes: "In front of the fortress by us is a fine gushing fountain of sweet water, and broad stone troughs in which we water our horses. This spot has been fixed on by Dr. Robinson as the *Bethsur* mentioned by Eusebius and Jerome as the place where the Eunuch was baptized. The ground in front of the fountain, and of the structure behind it, is so broken up and covered with stones, that it is difficult to determine what was once here. There is now a slightly depressed hollow, with a sandy or gravelly bottom. It is hardly conceivable that, in the days of Herod, the fountain-builder, this most favorable spring should not have been made to supply a pool in this

---

[1] Judges xvi. 1—3.   [2] Jer. xlvii. 5.   [3] Amos i. 7.

land of such structures; and even now water sufficient to supply such a reservoir flows from the troughs, and soaks into the soil; as, according to Jerome's mention, in his day it seems also to have been absorbed. That an ancient 'chariot' road passed this way, the observant traveller will often perceive on his journey. Dr. Robinson twice between Hebron and Jerusalem, notices this; and we have traced even plainer evidences."

IMMERSION IN COLD CLIMATES.

To the objection stated on p. 67, that immersion is not suited to cold climates, I have not attempted a formal reply. It gives me pleasure to present to the reader the following remarks on this subject, which have been written at my special request, by the Rev. Mr. Samson:

The idea that immersion, as an ordinance of Christ's church, is incompatible with his design that his religion should spread to all nations and climates, is alike disproved by Scripture, and by the facts of history in the spread of Christianity.

When Jesus said " Go teach," or make disciples of " all nations," he added, " baptizing them in the name of the Father, and of the Son, and of the Holy Ghost." The word *baptize* in the language in which Christ spoke, as every Greek scholar allows, meant nothing else than immerse. It is impossible to reconcile it with the supreme wisdom of Jesus, that without qualification of language, he commanded this ordinance in this form to be performed among the nations of every clime, if there really were anything in immersion inconsistent with health in any latitude, or with propriety in any age of refinement.

Early in the apostolic history this was tested. The apostle was accustomed to baptism at first in the neighborhood of Jerusalem, among the "common people" that bathed in Jordan, and the pools of the Holy City. He writes a letter to Rome, the centre of refinement and luxury, where some members of "Cæsar's household" had joined the Christian church, in a region *ten degrees* north of Jerusalem, where the cold of winter compelled the self-denying martyr to send as far as Old Troy for a Roman coat he had left there; yet there had not been, either on account of the peculiar refinement and delicacy of the people of Rome, or on account of the rigor of their winter, any change in the mode of baptism, if we may draw an inference from the apostle's words: "Therefore we are buried with him by baptism into death." [1] It ought to be remembered that summer is warm in every climate; that bathing is often practised, as it was in Rome, and as it is in our country, more by people in northern than in southern latitudes; and that the winter of the southern climate, in the latitude of Jerusalem, where the snow thaws almost immediately on its fall, is more trying than in far northern regions, the air being chillier, and the water more icy-cold.

Subsequent history is more convincing than even these facts of the apostolic age in this regard. The Eastern or Greek Church (by the side of which the Western or Roman Church, occupying three or four little countries of Southern Europe, is a speck on the map), embraces every variety of climate and class of people. Beginning with Abyssinia, in the hot regions of Central Africa, extending through Egypt in Northern Africa, it spreads along all Western Asia, takes in half of Europe, and embraces especially all Siberia and Northern Russia; thus comprising the very coldest regions, as well as the hottest, in which man can live. In all these climates, among all these people, baptism is administered by triple immersion. If it be an infant that is brought, despite his struggles and cries, he is three times plunged in the broad baptismal font. In mid April, while the Jordan's waters are yet chilly with the melting snows that cover the top of Hermon and all the Lebanon range (from which that stream flows), every year from 5000 to 6000 persons of every age, sex, climate, and condition in life, go down into the chilling stream, and either bury themselves or are buried by others beneath its waters. At St. Petersburgh a stranger expression still is given, at midwinter, in reply to the objection that climate renders immersion impracticable. The chosen day for immersion is at Christmas, near New Year's; and that through the ice of the Neva. A temporary chapel is erected on the ice, a large hole is cut, and with a round of ceremonies the water is consecrated by the priest; when mothers bring their infants and plunge them, and people of mature age come and dip themselves there. Moreover, at any time in the winter, when proselytes in the most

---

[1] Rom. vi. 4.

northern regions of the Russian possessions are made, they are baptized through the ice. Any one wishing to verify these statements, may consult such a work as William Burder's Religious Ceremonies, published at London, 1841; or he may perhaps be personally an eye-witness.

It is the Western, especially the Roman church, that has departed from the original mode of baptism; and that not from reasons connected with climate. All the Northern portion (not the Southern) of Western Europe, which originally was converted to pure Christianity and denied the authority of the Roman church, which in the age of subsequent corruption departed least from the faith as it is in Jesus, and only nominally became allied to the Roman church, and which was the first to hail and to embrace the call for the reformation,—all the coldest regions of Western Europe received and maintained the longest the rite of immersion. It was the warm latitudes that departed from it.

To verify this, one needs but turn to the Latin chronicles of Alcuin and others of those Judson-like missionaries, who, during the reign of Alfred of England and Charlemagne of France, carried pure Christianity into the heart of Germany, and won all the rude tribes of those lands, from which our ancestry sprung, to Christianity. It impresses the thoughtful mind with gratitude, that the truth as it was in Jesus was preached and embraced by the rude men from whom our strong race has come, as we read Alcuin's letters to Charlemagne, rather commanding than entreating his sovereign to be true to Christ's appointment; charging him not to *force* these people by the sword, which he never could do, to receive Christian baptism; and quoting Jerome's Commentary on Matt. xxviii. 19, 20: " Primum eos doceant, deinde doctas intinquant aquâ," to show that the fathers of the church taught that missionaries " *must first teach their people, and then immerse them in water.*" And in the cold northern Vistula, thousands on thousands, the records of the times tell us, were, in the heat of summer, and in the cold of winter, baptized on sincere personal profession of faith in Christ.

If farther confirmation of this fact be desired, that the people of *cold* countries have preferred immersion, it may be found in the work of " *Wheatly on the Book of Common Prayer of England,*" Bohn's edition, pp. 337—350. Of the fonts now found in the old English churches, he says, "So called, I suppose, because baptism in the beginning of Christianity was performed in springs or fountains. * * In the primitive times we meet with them very large and capacious, not only that they might comport with the general customs of those times, viz.: of persons being immersed or put under water, but also because the stated times of baptism returning so seldom, great numbers were usually baptized at the same time. In the middle of them was always a partition, the one part for men, the other for women; that so by being baptized asunder they might avoid giving offence and scandal." The author here cites the orders of Edward, when the crowd was so great they could not be gathered around the church door; all of which shows that baptism was often administered to adults, that it was by immersion, and that a very large number could be baptized on one occasion in the ordinary font. Again the author says, "Except upon extraordinary occasions, baptism was seldom, or perhaps never, administered for the first four centuries but by immersion or dipping. Nor is aspersion or sprinkling ordinarily used, to this day, in any country that was never subject to the Pope; and among those that submitted to his authority, England was the last place where it was received; though it has never obtained so far as to be enjoined, *dipping* having been always prescribed by the rubric. The Salisbury Missal, printed in 1530 (the last that was in force before the Reformation), expressly requires and orders dipping. And in the first Common Prayer Book of King Edward VI., the priest's general order is to dip it in water." Here we see that it was not on account of climate any change grew up; the people in the extreme north were the last to surrender the original mode; and not even the Pope's authority could compel them to strike out of their Missal the form received in the simplicity of their early reception of Christianity. Farther, we read that from love for the primitive ordinance, "fonts were in times of popery unfitly and surreptitiously placed near the churches." The author states the alleged, and then the real cause why affusion took the place of immersion, as follows:—"Many fond ladies at first, and then by degrees the common people, would persuade the minister that their children were too tender for dipping. But what principally tended to confirm this practice, was that several of our English divines flying to Germany, Switzerland, &c., during the bloody reign of Queen Mary, and returning home when Queen Elizabeth came to the crown, brought back with them a great love and zeal for the customs of those churches beyond sea, where they had been sheltered and received. And consequently having observed that in Geneva and some other places, baptism was ordered to be performed by affusion, they thought they could not do the church of England a greater service, than to introduce a practice dictated by so great an oracle as Calvin. So that in the times of Queen Elizabeth, and during the reigns of King James and King Charles I., there were but very few children dipped in the font." So it appears it was not on the score of health (which down to 1500 years after Christianity had existed in England never had been thought of), but it was *fashion* which led to the change. Of subsequent times, and the folly of the Reformers of Elizabeth's and of James' day, the author adds, " These reformers, it seems, could not recollect that fonts to baptize in had been long used before the times of popery, and that they had nowhere been discontinued from the beginning of Christianity, but in such places where the Pope had gained authority. But our divines at the Restoration, understanding a little better the sense of scripture and antiquity, again restored the order for immersion." Yet though this is still the order of the Book of Common Prayer, the author regrets that it is ineffective. Custom, fashion triumphs, even over a statute of the realm of England.

The struggle of his own mind to be satisfied with the appeal to climate as an argument for sprinkling, speaks out in these two sentences of the author. The present Order of the Prayer Book as to baptism is he says " keeping as close to the primitive rule for baptism as the coldness of our region, and the tenderness wherewith infants are now used, will sometimes admit. Though Sir John Floyer, in a discourse on cold baths, hath shown from the nature of our bodies, from the rules of medicine, from modern experience, and from ancient history, that nothing could tend more to the preservation of a child's health than dipping it in baptism."

THE END.

CPSIA information can be obtained
at www.ICGtesting.com
Printed in the USA
BVHW030906101221
623724BV00001B/1